McGraw-Hill Series in Psychology

CLIFFORD T. MORGAN, *Consulting Editor*

BARKER, KOUNIN, AND WRIGHT · Child Behavior and Development
BARTLEY · Beginning Experimental Psychology
BLUM · Psychoanalytic Theories of Personality
BROWN · Psychology and the Social Order
BROWN · The Psychodynamics of Abnormal Behavior
CATTELL · Personality
CRAFTS, SCHNEIRLA, ROBINSON, AND GILBERT · Recent Experiments in Psychology
DEESE · The Psychology of Learning
DOLLARD AND MILLER · Personality and Psychotherapy
DORCUS AND JONES · Handbook of Employee Selection
FERGUSON · Personality Measurement
GHISELLI AND BROWN · Personnel and Industrial Psychology
GRAY · Psychology Applied to Human Affairs
GRAY · Psychology in Industry
GUILFORD · Fundamental Statistics in Psychology and Education
GUILFORD · Psychometric Methods
HIRSH · The Measurement of Hearing
HURLOCK · Adolescent Development
HURLOCK · Child Development
HURLOCK · Developmental Psychology
JOHNSON · Essentials of Psychology
KARN AND GILMER · Readings in Industrial and Business Psychology
KRECH AND CRUTCHFIELD · Theory and Problems of Social Psychology
LEWIN · A Dynamic Theory of Personality
LEWIN · Principles of Topological Psychology
MAIER · Frustration
MAIER AND SCHNEIRLA · Principles of Animal Psychology
MILLER · Experiments in Social Process
MILLER · Language and Communication
MOORE · Psychology for Business and Industry
MORGAN AND STELLAR · Physiological Psychology
PAGE · Abnormal Psychology
REYMERT · Feelings and Emotions
RICHARDS · Modern Clinical Psychology
SEASHORE · Psychology of Music
SEWARD · Sex and the Social Order
SHAFFER AND LAZARUS · Fundamental Concepts in Clinical Psychology
STAGNER · Psychology of Personality
TOWNSEND · Introduction to Experimental Method
VINACKE · The Psychology of Thinking
WALLIN · Personality Maladjustments and Mental Hygiene
ZUBEK AND SOLBERG · Human Development

John F. Dashiell was Consulting Editor of this series from its inception in 1931 until January 1, 1950.

McGraw-Hill Series in Psychology

Clifford T. Morgan, *Consulting Editor*

PSYCHOMETRIC METHODS

Psychometric Methods

J. P. GUILFORD

Professor of Psychology
University of Southern California

SECOND EDITION

McGRAW-HILL BOOK COMPANY, INC.

NEW YORK TORONTO LONDON

1954

PSYCHOMETRIC METHODS

Library of Congress Catalog Card Number 53-12430

THE MAPLE PRESS COMPANY, YORK, PA.

PREFACE

Eighteen years have elapsed since the publication of the first edition of *Psychometric Methods*. They have been eventful years for psychological measurement. The purpose of the first edition was to encompass within a single volume the various areas of psychological measurement and the statistical procedures attendant to them, as a guide to the graduate student. It was emphasized that experimental and statistical operations are intimately related, a point of view that seems now to be taken for granted. It was also emphasized that there is an essential unity among the different fields of psychological measurement that had grown up somewhat independently. That potential unity is clearer today. Although a single logical system for psychological measurement has not yet been developed, the lines of such a system are taking form.

In this edition an attempt has been made toward further unifying steps in theory and in measurement and statistical operations. The introductory chapter attempts to base all psychological measurement on a general foundation of the logic of measurement. The second chapter lays the logical ground for psychophysical concepts and methods. A third chapter (Chap. 13) is devoted to the logical problems of psychological tests. Still another chapter (Chap. 12) attempts to bring under a minimum number of principles a great many phenomena of human judgment, and in doing so depends very much on Helson's concept of adaptation level.

To make room for the enormous amount of new material and yet to keep the length of this volume within reasonable bounds, it was necessary to eliminate most of the statistical treatments given in the first edition. This was done by depending very much upon the author's *Fundamental Statistics in Psychology and Education*. Even with the statistical eliminations, it has been necessary to be very selective in the incorporation of new material. Some of the readers will look for, and miss, general references to information theory and methods. While the writer recognizes the merits of these new ideas, and that they may well have revolutionary effects upon psychological measurement, he is not prepared at this time to give them an appropriate place in the general treatment of psychological measurement. Let us say, then, that this volume represents the general field of psychological measurement as of about 1950.

As usual, the author is in great debt to others who have contributed in many ways to the preparation of this volume. Three persons, while serving as assistants in the psychometric laboratory, contributed toward the compiling of bibliography and toward the collection and treatment of experimental data for illustrations used in some of the chapters: Dr. Marcella A. Sutton, Dr. Paul C. Davis, and Harvey Dingman. Lisbeth Goldberg has permitted the use of data obtained for her Master's thesis. Eugene A. Bouvier has applied his drafting talents to the preparation of the new abacs. James W. Frick and John R. Hills have checked computations of answers to problems. Other special contributions will be noted at appropriate places. Several of my friends have given generously of their time to the reading of various chapters, including Dr. Harry Helson, Dr. J. W. Holley, Dr. William B. Michael, and Dr. Norman C. Perry. None but the author is responsible for errors that still remain. To my wife, Ruth B. Guilford, I am as usual indebted for faithfully assisting in the preparation of the manuscript.

J. P. Guilford

CONTENTS

CHAPTER 1

PSYCHOLOGICAL MEASUREMENT

The progress and maturity of a science are often judged by the extent to which it has succeeded in the use of mathematics. The "psychometric methods" are procedures for psychological measurement. Measurement means the description of data in terms of numbers and this, in turn, means taking advantage of the many benefits that operations with numbers and mathematical thinking provide.

Mathematics itself is not an empirical science; it gathers no facts through observations of nature. Instead, it is a universal language that any science or technology may use with great power and convenience. Its vocabulary of terms is unlimited and yet defined with rigorous accuracy. Its rules of operation, or its "syntax," are unexcelled for logical precision.

Some of the more obvious consequences of measurement are not difficult to see or to accept. Measurement permits accurate, objective, and communicable descriptions that can be readily manipulated in thinking. The accuracy is as great as the care and the instruments of the observer will permit. Objectivity is one of the major goals of science. According to a convenient, operational definition, "objectivity" means interpersonal agreement. Where many persons reach agreement as to observations and conclusions, the descriptions of nature are more likely to be free from the biases of particular individuals. They form the body of knowledge that is taken to be "true." Furthermore, the descriptions are in a form that can be communicated to others. Science is a social institution. One of its chief values is that observations and conclusions of some individuals can be passed on meaningfully to others. Toward these ends quantitative description, called *measurement*, makes its significant contributions.

In this chapter we will give considerable attention to the philosophy underlying measurement as it applies to psychology. Measurement in the physical sciences has come so naturally that in that connection little thought has had to be given to what measurement really is. There are some physical scientists who maintain that what is called measurement in psychology is not measurement at all. It is true that the term *measurement* is sometimes defined in such a way that it does not apply to most of the operations in psychology commonly known as measurement. Definition of an abstract term such as *measurement* is an arbitrary matter, however, and psychologists will either define it to cover what they are doing under that concept or they will invent a new term for what they are doing with numbers and arithmetical operations. Fortunately, measurement can be defined sufficiently broadly to include the operations known as psychological measurement.

It is true that the difficulties in the way of psychological measurement have been very great. But as Spearman has said, "The path of science is paved with achievements of the allegedly unachievable. And in point of fact, mathematical treatment is perhaps just the region where psychology has made its steadfast and most surprising advances" (23,[1] p. 89). If psychology cannot achieve operations of measurement that fit the pattern set by the physical sciences, it should and does proceed to develop its own measurement techniques peculiarly adapted to solving its own problems. The variety of these techniques is very great, as will be seen in chapters to follow. Psychology is obligated, however, to justify the application of numbers and mathematics in general to its data. This is a problem in logic which we shall face in this chapter, but first we shall take a very brief look at the history of measurement in psychology in order to gain a better perspective for meeting that problem.

Orientation to Mental Measurement

The earlier history of mental measurement shows development along two relatively independent lines. On the one hand there was the psychophysical tradition, the forerunner of the first genuinely experimental psychology. On the other hand there was the mental-test tradition, centering its interest upon individual differences. The former developed out of experimental physiology and the quantitative methods that grew up in connection with the natural sciences. It drew upon the ingenuity of those who had previously used similar quantitative and statistical methods in astronomy and physics. The mental-test tradition, inspired by the evolutionary biology of the nineteenth century and biology's interest in inherited traits, borrowed directly from those mathematicians who had indulged more or less seriously in problems of probability and the then embryonic statistical methods. Both derived much, directly or indirectly, from a common source, the mathematics of probability. We turn, therefore, to a synoptic account of the development of statistical method as related to the psychophysical and the mental-test traditions.

The Origin of Statistical Methods. It can be said that before the year 1600 no mathematical conceptions of probability were recognized. Gamblers had speculated much concerning games of chance when it came time to consider their losses and gains, particularly their losses. They had even attempted to interest mathematicians in their problems, though with small success. Mathematicians were too busy with the newly discovered fields of analytical geometry and the calculus to be bothered with problems of gambling. The seventeenth century, however, saw the beginnings of serious interest in the mathematics of chance. Bernoulli (1654–1705) published the first well-known book to be entirely devoted to the subject. De Moivre (1667–1754) may be credited with the discovery of the normal distribution curve at about 1733. From that time on, interest was aroused among astronomers as well as mathematicians. By 1812, Laplace (1749–1827) had written what is considered the greatest single work on probability. In it he gave proof of the method of least squares (see Chap. 3). It was Gauss (1777–1855) who demonstrated the great practical value of the normal curve,

[1] The number refers to the list of references at the end of the chapter.

showing how it applied to the distribution of measurements and to errors made in scientific observations. It was he who devised the fundamental modes of computation of means, probable errors, and the like. To this day we often see the normal curve referred to as the Gaussian curve.

The application of the normal curve and elementary statistical methods to biological and social data must be attributed first to Quetelet (1796–1874), royal astronomer to the king of Belgium. He became the great promoter of statistical method on the continent of Europe. He encouraged the keeping of records of the weather and of such social phenomena as births, deaths, marriages, diseases, and crimes. He demonstrated the fact that the normal law of distribution applies to various types of anthropometric measurements when unselected populations are used. So impressed was he with the normal distribution of populations that he is said to have suggested that nature aimed at an ideal average man, *l'homme moyen*, but missed the mark and thus created deviations on either side of the average (3, p. 477).

The Mental-test Tradition. The essential link between Quetelet and psychology lies in Sir Francis Galton (1822–1911), who, impressed by the former's work and fired by the ambition to unravel the problems of human heredity, undertook to measure individuals on a large scale. His anthropometric laboratory, which was set up at South Kensington in 1882, was equipped to make a variety of simple sensory and motor tests. Not finding the normal curve and its simpler applications adequate, he invented a number of additional statistical tools, among them (with Karl Pearson's help) the method of correlation, the use of standard scores, the median, and such psychological scaling methods as the order-of-merit and the rating-scale method (13). The remainder of mental-test history is more generally known. On the side of statistics, Karl Pearson and R. A. Fisher head the list of contributors. On the side of test development, the names of Cattell, Binet, Terman, Otis, Thorndike, Spearman, and Thurstone stand out from the crowd.

The Psychophysical Tradition. The groundwork for psychophysics was laid long before Galton appeared on the scene with his simple psychological tests. Intensive differences in sensory experience had been a matter of common knowledge for centuries. The concept of an absolute threshold, or lower limit of sensation, had been suggested by Herbart[1] (1776–1841) many years before Fechner's announcement of a science of psychophysics. Weber (1795–1878) had also previously proposed his concept of the just noticeable difference (*jnd*) and his law that the just noticeable increment in a stimulus is proportional to the stimulus.

Fechner saw in Weber's law the basis for his own famous psychophysical relationship, *i.e.*, the strength of the sensory process is proportional to the logarithm of the stimulus. Once the logarithmic law had occurred to him, Fechner launched a program of research on a truly remarkable scale. He defined psychophysics as "an exact science of the functional relations of dependency between body and mind" (12, p. 8). This conception was suf-

[1] It is interesting to note that Herbart made some very astute applications of mathematical logic to mental processes. He even suggested some rational equations which were intended to express the attracting and repelling forces existing between "ideas."

ficiently broad to include not only the measurement of sensory magnitudes but also the quantification of perception, feeling, action, and attention; in fact, any psychological process that could be correlated with stimuli. Fechner's own pioneer approach was confined largely to the study of sensation, although he did make a number of excursions into the field of aesthetic perception and thus became the founder of experimental aesthetics.

Of chief interest to us here is the fact that, in order to make the necessary measurements for this new "exact" science of psychophysics, Fechner was compelled to adapt known methods or to invent new ones. To him belongs credit for laying the foundations for all the traditional psychophysical methods, the *method of average error*, the *method of minimal changes*, and the *constant method*.

Among the important critics of Fechner's psychophysics, who also made many contributions to theory and to method, were Delboeuf, Wundt, and G. E. Müller. More recent contributors to psychophysical theory and method have been Urban, Culler, and Thurstone. We shall see that Thurstone's *law of comparative judgment* has enlarged considerably the scope of psychophysical operations and the understanding of its problems.[1]

Mental Testing and Experimental Psychology. As we shall see (Chap. 13), the connection between psychophysics and mental tests is a very direct and intimate one. It is a curious fact that although psychophysics was intimately connected with experimental psychology from the first and although the experimental psychologist has used test methods extensively in the laboratory, it has not been the experimental psychologist who has bridged the gap between the two. The reason is that the experimental psychologist has been very slow in realizing that he uses mental tests as measuring instruments. He has associated mental tests with individual differences, failing to recognize that they also measure "occasional differences" in the same individual.

Although many of the measurements made by the experimental psychologist have been in terms of physical variables—physical properties of both stimulus and response, in the familiar centimeter-gram-second system—beginning with Ebbinghaus, in particular, the experimental psychologist's measurements have been largely in terms of test scores. The many experiments on learning, memory, motivation, and thinking usually yield data in terms of numbers of right responses, numbers of errors, numbers of items in a list, numbers of crossings of a barrier, and so on. Although the experimental psychologist has kept abreast of the very latest statistical tests of significance in extracting conclusions from his data, he has been very slow to take advantage of the very thorough mathematical and statistical rationale provided as a basis for mental-test measurement. Measurement in terms of time, distance, or energy scales may be elegant from the standpoint of experimental technique. It is questionable, however, how well those scales represent psychological phenomena. The variable of "habit strength," for example, is a well-accepted psychological variable, however it is named or defined. Different indices of it, even those in physical units, give rise to different shapes

[1] See Chap. 2 for a presentation of the law of comparative judgment.

of learning curves. They cannot all be linearly related to habit strength, for they are not linearly related to one another.

The Psychological Scaling Methods. The psychological scaling methods, including such methods as *pair comparisons*,[1] *ranking method* (*order of merit*), *rating scales*, *equal-appearing intervals*, and their variations, have helped to find a common meeting ground for psychophysics and mental tests. Their chief purpose has been to evaluate stimulus objects on linear scales, such as a scale of affective values, or of belief, or of persuasiveness; quality of handwriting, of drawings, or of compositions; personality traits such as leadership, tactfulness, or sociability; and the like. In these cases there are no physical evaluations of the stimuli, so a complete psychophysical treatment is out of the question. Yet many of the scaling methods had their origin in psychophysics, and of recent years Thurstone in particular has rationalized them on the basis of psychophysical theory.

The usefulness of the scaling methods in educational problems and especially in the systematic, objective mode that they offer for deriving accurate judgments of individuals has endeared them to mental testers. The latter have depended much upon them for criteria against which to check the validity of their tests, and have used them in lieu of tests in the estimation of traits for which there are as yet no established tests. The scaling methods can therefore claim the joint parentage of psychophysics and mental testing. The former contributed their rational and mathematical bases and encouraged their application in experimental psychology, and the latter contributed much empirical information from their use in education and in the problems of individual differences.

General Theory of Measurement

The present consensus seems to be to follow the thinking of Campbell, who defines measurement as the *assignment of numerals to objects or events according to rules* (7). At least, this is a much quoted definition. The writer finds it satisfying except for the term *numerals*. Some writers prefer the term *numbers*. The distinction between the two terms is not always clear. Roughly, numerals are merely symbols. Some say they are merely scratches on paper. They are more than that, of course, for each numeral is a distinct form and not identical with any other. As such, they are often used to label objects or groups, without having much implication of number meaning. For example, we often speak of "group 1," "group 2," and so on, without any good reason except to distinguish the groups. Numerals thus used do imply at least one property of numbers, however, that of uniqueness or identity. This justifies our speaking of numbers in this connection. We shall see later that the use of numbers to identify categories is the lowest form of measurement.

The Nature of Mathematics. The close relation of measurement to mathematics has been implied in earlier paragraphs. We cannot understand the nature of measurement without knowing about the properties of mathematics. Many students take courses in mathematics without realizing what

[1] This method has traditionally been called *paired comparisons*. It is not comparisons that are paired; it is pairs of stimuli.

kind of thing mathematics really is. Teachers of mathematics and writers of textbooks seem often not to appreciate the underlying nature of their subject. Perhaps this is because they have been much too close to their subject. It has taken the philosophers, such as Bertrand Russell, to discover what mathematics really is like. They have come to the conclusion that mathematics is a highly logical language, if not a branch of logic.

Postulates and Theorems. Any branch of mathematics begins with a set of postulates. A postulate is a statement assumed to be true without need of proof of any kind. A postulate states an assumption that we make about some relationship between objects. For example, we may postulate that $a + b = b + a$. This simply says that if we combine two objects, a and b, the order in which the combination occurs makes no difference in the result. We could just as well assume the contrary, that order *does* matter, but then we would draw other conclusions from the second postulate than we would from the first. A postulate is useful because of the conclusions or deductions that we can draw from it and from combinations of it with other postulates. In developing a system from a set of postulates, it is imperative that no two shall be contradictory. There must be internal consistency. For the sake of economy, no two postulates should be duplicative or overlapping, though if they were, they would not invalidate the system. The number of postulates will depend upon the number needed to support the system.

By logical deductions, other statements, called *theorems*, are derived. If the reasoning is logic-tight or consistent with the postulates, the theorems are true because the postulates are true. The kind of truth involved here is of the logical type and not of the empirical type. From postulates to theorems we are entirely within the realm of ideas. There is no point in asking for experimental proof of the deductions. Such a request would be meaningless. The only appeal for proof that is appropriate is entirely within the realm of logic.

Mathematical Models. In other words, neither postulates nor theorems of mathematics report anything about the world in which we live, the world of observation. The ancient idea of the Greeks that the world operates on a mathematical basis is incorrect. *Mathematics is an invention of man, not a discovery.* It is also incorrect to say that the curve of Gaussian, or normal, distribution is a biological curve or that it is a psychological curve. It is neither. It is a mathematical curve, purely and simply. The fact that it can be used to describe obtained distributions of observations in biology and in psychology is coincidental. This does not deny the great convenience, and even the accuracy, of using the normal distribution as a model for describing events in biological and psychological nature. Indeed, this is a good example of *the general function of mathematics—to provide convenient and fruitful models for the description of nature.* Nature is never *exactly* described by any mathematical model. All such descriptions are only approximations, some better and some worse.

Isomorphism. We should not say, then, that nature obeys mathematical laws. If this statement is true, how, then, can we use mathematical models to describe nature? How can we assign numerals or numbers to objects and events? How can we measure that which does not exist in the form of numbers? The answer is that the structure of nature as we know it has properties that are sufficiently parallel with the structure of logical systems in mathematics. There exists between the two what is called an *isomorphism:* an equivalence of form. At some places the equivalence is excellent in detail, while at other places the equivalence is very rough. The *application* of any mathematical system to some aspect of nature *can* be tested empirically. For example, if we apply the normal distribution curve to the description of a given set of measurements, we can test the "goodness of fit" by making a chi-square test. If the chi square is small, we accept the normal-curve model as applicable to these data. If the chi square is so large as to be obtainable with a very small likelihood, we reject the model as being descriptive. If we find the fit acceptable, we can take advantage of the mathematical properties of the normal curve in drawing conclusions about the data and in making predictions dependent upon its properties. We can do so with confidence that our conclusions and predictions will have very small errors. The conclusions and predictions will serve our purposes.

The Nature of Numbers. Since numbers are the very basis of measurement and since the number system is an important part of the general body of mathematics, we should next give attention to the properties of numbers. We shall find that they fit the picture of mathematics that was painted above.

There is no definition of number that covers all kinds of numbers. There is a definition, often attributed to Bertrand Russell, that does well when applied to rational numbers. It is to the effect that a number is a "class of all classes." This is indeed a high-level abstraction. What is meant can best be stated in the form of an illustration. Some classes of objects (it does not matter what the objects are) belong in the same class because they have in common the property of having two objects in them. Two fish, two men, two pencils, two ideas, all belong to a class for one reason. The common element is twoness. All duos, trios, quartettes, etc., form classes merely by reason of identical "numerosities" in them. The experimental operation by which we can determine whether two classes belong in the same class is to pair off members in the two classes one to one to see whether they come out even. If they do, they have identical numerosity and can have the same number assigned to them. If either has one or more members not matchable with one in the other, they do not have the same numerosity and should not have the same number assigned to them. The sequence in the number system of integers is established by finding classes that have just one left over as we compare each class with the one above it in the system.

This discussion may have seemed trivial to some readers, but the subject is of great importance for those who want secure logical foundations. It is one of the curious features of the history of human thought that it takes great minds to reach what may seem to be very simple ideas.

Development of the Number System. The number system, or more accurately, number systems, have undergone an interesting course of development. From the beginning with the system of natural numbers to the present-day system of complex numbers there has been an increasing realization of new properties of numbers and an expansion of operations that can be applied to them.

The *natural system* of numbers includes all the positive integers. It was undoubtedly devised to meet the needs for the operation of counting discrete objects. For this purpose one needs only the positive integers. It was discovered that with this system the operations of addition and multiplication could be applied. Either operation resulted in a number that is also a positive integer; in other words, the result was within the system. The operation of subtraction, however, was limited in its application within this system. It would work except when one attempted to subtract a number from itself or from a smaller number. For such instances there were no numbers in the system. This limitation called for the extension of the system to include zero and negative numbers: two very important new concepts. The operation of division was even more limited. It worked so long as the two numbers involved were in simple ratio, that is, one was an exact multiple of the other. To take care of other cases, fractional numbers were invented.

The number system that includes positive, negative, and fractional numbers is called the *rational system.* In this system any number can be expressed as the ratio of two whole numbers in the system. All of the four fundamental operations can be performed except division by zero. The rational system provides about all that is needed for all types of measurements.

The treatment of metric data, however, often requires some mathematical operations not possible in the rational system. For example, the square roots of many numbers cannot be expressed as rational numbers. The square root of 2 goes beyond the rational number system. The concept of irrational numbers had to be invented to take care of such results. For practical purposes the square root of any number can be approximated by giving a rounded number that *is* in the rational system. This serves most of the purposes of computation with which we are concerned in practice.

Application of Numbers to Measurement. According to the principle of isomorphism, which was mentioned before, we may legitimately use numbers in measurement (attach them to objects or events) when and in so far as the properties of numbers are paralleled by properties of the objects or events to which we apply them. This calls for a closer examination of the properties of numbers and their interrelationships.

Some Properties of Numbers Used in Measurement. Roughly speaking (we will have much more exact specifications later) the properties of numbers that are most important for measurement are three: *identity*, *rank order*, and *additivity*. Numbers, except for cases of equality, can be placed in an incontrovertible order along a linear scale. By "additivity" is meant the fact that the operation of addition gives results that are internally consistent. This will be explained more fully later. At the moment it is more important to see what the concept of additivity implies. What it implies is that all four of the fundamental operations can be applied, for subtraction, multiplication, and division can all be conceived as special cases of addition. Where addition can be applied in the use of rational numbers so can the other three operations. Subtraction is addition of two numbers one of which has a negative sign. Multiplication is a process of successive additions of the same number. Division, conversely, is a process of successive subtractions, which, by virtue of a statement just made about subtraction, is a matter of successive additions of negative numbers. Thus the requirement of additivity covers all the fundamental numerical operations.

When are the properties of order and additivity present in phenomena of nature? Unless one or both are present, the assignment of numbers in a particular domain of observation will do us little good. The numbers so assigned will have little meaning, and consequently there is little we can do with them that is of much utility or significance. What do we need to do and what can we do in terms of experimental operations to prove to our satisfaction that these two number properties do apply in a given domain? We might just assume that they apply, from a rough knowledge of the domain, but we should not be very secure unless we have some information that supports the assumption. Some who have thought about the problem insist that we be able to demonstrate the parallels to numerical properties in the phenomena measured, by actual experimental operations.

Experimental Demonstrations of Order. How can the properties of order and additivity be demonstrated? An example of demonstration of order is easy to find. In geology a scale of order for hardness of minerals is demonstrated in terms of the operation of scratching. A mineral that will scratch a second mineral is harder than the second. An order for hardness is thus established. In animal psychology, a hen that habitually pecks a second hen when they are in competition for the same food is said to be more dominant. By the pecking test a pecking (or dominance) order can be established. By direct observation, tones are ordered for pitch on the basis of judgments "higher than"; reds are ordered for saturation on the basis of judgments "redder than"; and pictures are ordered for degree of pleasure on the basis of judgments of "more pleasant than." We will not be concerned here with the phenomenon of occasional reversals of order apparent for neighboring pairs of objects. Such reversals are usually regarded as "errors of observation" or "errors of measurement" and are not allowed to invalidate the general principle of order or operation of measurement. It is sometimes necessary, however, to prove by correlation methods or otherwise that there is at least *some* consistency among the ranks. This is the problem of reliability (see Chap. 13).

Experimental Demonstration of Additivity. The property of additivity is rarely experimentally demonstrable, even in the physical sciences. Let us see how it can be done. An example from the property of physical length is probably the most obvious one. First, let us see how properties of order are demonstrated in this domain. If we take two linear objects (rigid wires, sticks, or boards) and lay them side by side with one end of one object even with the corresponding end of the other, we can tell from a comparison of the other ends whether they are equal in length or whether one is longer than the other, and if so which one it is. Note that the decision about order is made on the basis of a visual observation. If the ordering of physical lengths is possible on the basis of a human judgment, so is the ordering of the perceptual and feeling properties referred to above: pitch, redness, and pleasure. All rest on an observer's reaction.

In the case of the lines, we can demonstrate addition in a way that cannot be duplicated for pitch, redness, or pleasure. We can place the lines end to end, producing a total length. If we have a calibrated scale of distance, we can prove that the combination $a + b$ equals a predicted length c that is verified by the scale number of c. No such experimental heaping of psychological properties is possible. If we are to demonstrate the operation of addition of psychological properties, it will have to be done in some other way.

Other demonstrations of empirical addition in physics are in the field of weights and the field of electric resistances. Weights can be heaped on scales. Resistances can be placed "end to end" in an obvious fashion. But beyond these simple examples, even in physics an empirical operation of addition is difficult or impossible at present to achieve. On the ordinary temperature scales, there is no operation for the summation of two temperature levels. Even in the realm of length or distance there are very serious limitations to the proof of addition by experimental operations. No one has ever placed light-years end to end, nor has anyone demonstrated the addition of atomic distances. There can even be some doubt whether linear distances of astronomical proportions (and perhaps of atomic proportions) have a genuine continuity with those in the range of common experience. In all the sciences, then, the assumption of applicability of number properties rests on very limited empirical proof. Each science must be permitted to supply its own kind of empirical evidence for measurability. We shall find that psychology has its own unique ways for obtaining evidence that its phenomena partake of the requisite properties that justify measurement.

Measurement with Limited Number Properties. Another important point is that phenomena need not satisfy *all* the properties of number, including additivity, in order for us to make useful measurements. For many purposes the property of order is sufficient. When the requirement of additivity is not satisfied, however, the numbers we assign are limited in meaning, and not all the numerical operations can be applied to them. As we shall see, measurements, as they are now obtained, may have different degrees of completeness. They are meaningful and useful to the extent that they are complete. It is important that we recognize their incompleteness, however, and that we do not attempt to place any more meaning upon them than they will bear.

The common centile scale used in psychology is a good example of limited measurement. A centile is a rank among 100 rank positions. A centile of P_{80} indicates the 80th position from the bottom of the range. The difference $P_{80} - P_{60}$ means that there are 20 per cent of the cases between these two limits. In that sense we have made a meaningful subtraction. The difference $P_{60} - P_{40}$ has a similar interpretation. The two differences may be regarded as being equal from this point of view. From a different point of view, however, they are not equal. If we are thinking of a scale of ability, where we want differences to mean changes in amount of ability, the difference $P_{80} - P_{60}$ is greater than the difference $P_{60} - P_{40}$. The latter difference is in the middle of the range of ability. The same number of individuals (20 per cent) cover a wider range of ability away from the center ($P_{80} - P_{60}$) where cases thin out.

Some Postulates Basic to Measurement. Before we go into a discussion of the four general levels of measurement that are now commonly distinguished, it will be helpful to specify rigorously the properties of numbers that must be satisfied. The nine postulates given here are essentially those proposed by Campbell and repeated after him with variations (9, 15, 18, 26). The first three postulates have to do with identities. The next two postulates have to do with the establishment of order. The last four have to do with additivity.

1. Either $a = b$ or $a \neq b$
2. If $a = b$, then $b = a$
3. If $a = b$ and $b = c$, then $a = c$
4. If $a > b$, then $b \ngtr a$
5. If $a > b$ and $b > c$, then $a > c$
6. If $a = p$ and $b > 0$, then $a + b > p$
7. $a + b = b + a$
8. If $a = p$ and $b = q$, then $a + b = p + q$
9. $(a + b) + c = a + (b + c)$

A few comments may help to make these postulates more meaningful. The first postulate establishes the identity of a number. Numbers are identical or they are different. The second postulate states that the relation of equality is *symmetrical.* A statement of equality can be reversed and still be true. The third postulate expresses in equation form the familiar dictum: "Things equal to the same thing are equal to one another." Postulate 4 points out that the relation > is *asymmetrical.* We cannot reverse either the statement $a > b$ or the statement $a < b$, interchanging a and b, and end with a true statement. Postulate 5 is a *transitive* statement. An example of an intransitive set of relationships in experience would be to find that team A defeated team B and team B defeated team C, but C defeated A. The ranking was circular rather than linear. Other irregularities may destroy the transitivity in a set of objects. Postulate 6 indicates the possibility of summation. It also implies the fact that the addition of zero leaves a number invariant. Postulate 7 means that the order in which things are added makes no difference in the result. Postulate 8 means that identical objects may be substituted for one another in addition. Finally, postulate 9 means that the order of combinations or associations makes no difference in addition.

Four General Levels of Measurement. It is common to distinguish four levels of measurement, which have been most clearly delineated by Stevens (25, 26). From lower to higher levels we have *nominal*, *ordinal*, *interval*, and *ratio* measurement scales. These scales are distinguished in terms of several criteria. In accordance with our definition of measurement—assignment of numerals to objects and events according to rules—the rules for the way in which numerals are assigned constitute the essential criteria defining the scales. The higher-level scales require more restrictive rules; more of the basic postulates apply. There are also differences in how much can be done in the way of mathematical and statistical operations with numbers applied at the different levels of measurement. The higher the level of scale, the more we can do with the numbers we obtain in measurement. The rules and the permissible operations will now be considered for each level.

Nominal Scales. In nominal-scale measurement we merely use a number[1] as a label for a class or category.[2] The members of a class are regarded as being equal or equivalent in some respect. We refer to them collectively as "group 1," "group 2," and so on. The numbers could be interchanged and our purposes would be served just as well. The only rules for assigning numbers are that all members of any class shall have the same number and that no two classes shall be assigned the same number.

Of the basic postulates, the first three pertaining to equality apply. Equality of two objects in some respect is the basis for putting them in the same category. This fact calls for some comment on the term *equality.* The basic postulates imply that equality means identity. The operation of judging two objects as equal only approximates this ideal condition. Sometimes objects are placed in the same category because they are indistinguishable by the prevailing methods of observation. At other times there are observable differences, and yet these differences may be tolerated in order to avoid having too many categories. The fineness of discrimination, then, depends upon our observational powers as well as upon our demands for accuracy or our tolerance of inaccuracy. For practical purposes of classification we sometimes accept, and even prefer, categories of relatively wide latitudes.[3]

It is interesting to find that classification is logically the lowest form of measurement. When the classes can be ordered on a linear scale, which is the case in quantitative classification, we have taken one step up the ladder toward complete measurement. Even in the measurement of the highest type the principle of classification still applies.

Even with classification in qualitative categories a few statistical operations can be utilized. We can count the number of cases in each category and we thus obtain *frequencies*. We may be interested in knowing which is the most populous or popular class. This class is the *mode* of the distribution of classes. The modal class is useful in making categorical predictions.[4] If we have the same objects classified in two ways, on the basis of two aspects or principles of classification, we can determine the interdependence of those two aspects by computing a *coefficient of contingency*. Frequencies, modes, and coefficients of contingency are the statistics that may be utilized with categorical data. We shall find that they also apply in higher forms of measurement.

Ordinal Scales. In measurements on an ordinal scale, the numbers assigned utilize the property of rank order. The logical basis for rank order is to be found in postulates 4 and 5 above. If a and b are not equal, they

[1] The term *number* is used in this discussion because the numerals used, even in this rudimentary manner, have some number meaning involved, namely, that of identity.

[2] This is perhaps a surprising use of the term *scale*. In the numerical and mathematical context, a scale has serial and graduated properties. One dictionary definition of "scale" refers to it as "that which determines alternatives," however, which seems to fit this use of the term. The serial and graduated properties come into the higher levels of measurement.

[3] For a discussion of the procedures for classifying data, see Guilford (14, pp. 14–17).

[4] See Guilford (14, p. 365).

may differ in some direction that is shared by other pairs of objects. The direction is usually in terms of some one aspect of objects—height, warmth, loudness, or verbal ability.

Sometimes the basis of classification into categories is a composite of two or more variables. For example, we may attempt to rank individuals for "socioeconomic level," where there are two or more indices of the variable, such as income, education, and occupation. Two individuals might be in one rank order for income and in the opposite rank order for education. As long as we stay within either variable, postulate 4 will not be violated. We cannot satisfy this postulate with respect to the composite variable, however, unless we adopt relative weights for the indices making up the composite in such a way that the composite establishes one ranking and only one.

Rankings on composite variables are very common in psychology. Most psychological variables with which we operate are composites of latent, or basic, or primary variables. We force what is essentially a multidimensional quantity onto a linear scale. Sometimes the weighting is explicit, as in the use of multiple regression equations, but often it is implicit, as in the use of ratings made by human observers. In the latter instance, the weighting is intuitively accomplished and there is no way of knowing what the weights are or whether they are uniformly applied, unless we resort to the operations of *multidimensional scaling* or *factor analysis*.[1]

The operation of rank ordering may be regarded as classification in quantitative categories. The distinction between categories is based on some quality or property of the objects ranked. Complete discrimination would mean placing only one object in each category, as in the *method of rank order*. Each category then has a frequency of 1. But in a more general sense, ties may well be tolerated in order not to force discriminations beyond the limits of observational precision. We then have frequencies greater than 1 in some or all categories. A method that fits this description best is known as the *method of successive categories*. There is no implication here that any ranked categories are necessarily equally spaced on a scale, that the intervals between categories are equal. Equal-interval scales come under the next higher level of measurement.

The statistics that are permissible at the level of nominal-scale measurement also apply to measurements on ordinal scales—frequencies, modes, and contingency-correlation coefficients. The principle of order makes possible the use of additional statistics, including *medians*, *centiles*, and *rank-order coefficients of correlation*. A median divides combined frequencies into two equal quantities above and below the median point. The number to attach to a median obtained from rank-order numbers is itself merely indicative of rank position within the range of rank numbers used. The median may coincide with one of the rank numbers used or it may lie midway between two neighboring rank numbers. Finer discriminations in reporting medians of ranks are unjustified.[2] Centiles are also rank numbers, the median of any collection of centile ranks being itself a rank position in one hundred.

[1] See Chap. 10 for a discussion of multidimensional scaling and Chap. 16 for a description of factor analysis.

[2] A median of rank numbers may apply to three different situations. If we have the

Some writers hesitate very much to say that the rank-order coefficient of correlation is appropriately applied to ordinal-scale values.[1] This hesitation seems unwarranted. Spearman's rank-order coefficient ρ, for example, presupposes a complete ranking, using consecutive numbers, with any ties being properly evaluated within the series. The formula for computing ρ is a product-moment formula. Its formula rests on the assumption of equal distances *between the rank numbers* (that is why complete distribution of the objects and consecutive integers are used). As such, the rank numbers *are* equally spaced. This does *not* carry any implication that on an ideal scale of equal units the successive objects are equally spaced. The obtained coefficient tells us directly only about the agreement between the two sets of rank numbers. When we estimate a Pearson product-moment r from a ρ coefficient, we are merely predicting what such an r coefficient would be if instead of knowing the ranks of the objects we had their evaluations on two equal-unit scales and applied the Pearson formula.

The application of the Pearson product-moment correlation formula to centile-rank values under usual circumstances probably gives a fair estimate of correlation. Using centile values that apply very well to a sample in both the X and Y variables correlated, we should find the computed r differing from an r that would be found from correlation of interval-scale values to about the same extent as the rank-order ρ differs from r.

Interval Scales. Interval scales are also called *equal-unit* scales. The important property over and above those in lower types of scales is that numerically equal distances stand for empirically equal distances in some aspect of objects. Concerning observed quantities we can say, for example, that two objects having assigned numbers of 5 and 10 are as far apart on the scale as two other objects having assigned numbers of 15 and 20. We can also say that the distance from A to B plus the distance from B to C equals the distance from A to C. In equation form these last two statements may be stated: $R - Q = T - S$ and $AB + BC = AC$. There are experimental operations by which such statements may be checked.

Although we can talk about the addition of intervals, this does not mean that we have achieved the important property of additivity in the absolute sense. The addition of amounts on the scale has little meaning. The reason is that the zero point is placed in some arbitrary position. The quantity of the property defining the scale to which zero is assigned is probably not the lower limit at which the property vanishes. Take any two numbers on an

---

first n consecutive integers assigned to n objects, the median is the middle rank if n is an odd number and a mid-value for two ranks if n is even. If there are frequencies greater than 1 in the categories, and if there is a frequency greater than 1 in the category containing the median, interpolation within the interval is meaningless. Interpolation rests on the assumption that there is continuity within the category, that the category width is known, and that cases within the category are evenly distributed. None of these assumptions is well supported. The most useful application of the median to rank numbers is when the same object has been ranked a number of times in a list of the same objects with the same categories. Here, too, interpolation is precluded. The median should be reported as a category number or as a number midway between two neighboring category numbers.

[1] See in particular Stevens (25, 26).

interval scale, such as 7 and 11. The first is 7 units from the arbitrary zero and the second is 11 units from zero. Add the two and we obtain 18 units, which would imply that we have a quantity 18 units from zero. But suppose that the arbitrary zero happened to be 5 units above the genuine zero point. The two values should have been 12 and 16, if we wanted their actual distances from the absolute and meaningful zero. Add 12 and 16 and we get 28, not 18. Thus the sum varies as the position of zero varies on the scale.

Examples of interval scales include the ordinary temperature scale, either Fahrenheit or centigrade. Calendar time is an interval scale, an arbitrary zero having been set by convention. Any interval of time is a measure from a selected starting moment just as the altitude of a mountain is a distance taken from another selected starting point (sea level). These are both actually distances or differences on interval scales, but they may be treated as absolute amounts. In other words, in general, *distances* on interval scales have the property of additivity and may be treated as we do measurements on the highest-level scale, the *ratio scale*, to be discussed next.

We have yet to consider what statistical operations may be applied to interval-scale measurements. In this we refer to the scale numbers, not to the differences between them. Almost all the common statistical procedures may be applied to interval-scale values—the important ones such as the *mean*, *standard deviation*, *Pearson product-moment r*, and other statistics that depend upon these values. The only common statistic that may not be applied, and it is not very often used, is the *coefficient of variation*. This statistic is based upon the ratio of the standard deviation to the mean of distribution. The formula is $CV = 100\sigma_x/M_x$. The reason is that the ratio of σ_x to M_x depends upon where the arbitrary zero is located. The standard deviation is a fixed *distance* on the measurement scale; it will be the same no matter where the zero point is placed. But the mean will vary with any shift of the zero point. Add a constant to all the measurements and the mean will be larger by that same constant. If we shift the zero point downward, M_x will rise in value and CV will fall. If we shift the zero point upward, M_x will fall and CV will rise.

As we come to each measurement method in the chapters to follow, we shall consider what type of psychological scale is achieved in each instance. Here it can be said that there are many who believe that most psychological scales that are treated as if they are interval scales are actually of the ordinal type. Yet psychologists rarely hesitate to apply the statistics that call for an interval scale, as if they believed they had interval-scale measurements. There is usually little or no awareness of the assumption that an interval scale is involved. The assumption is one of the many hidden ones that frequent psychological investigations. Here and there psychologists recognize the assumption and attempt to do something to see that it is justified.

There are many approaches to the achieving of equal units. Various observational techniques, transformation methods, and scaling procedures are available for approaching the equality of units. Even without these devices, however, experimental data often approach the condition of equal units sufficiently well that there is tolerable error in applying the various statistics that call for them. This is one of those occasions for making use of approximations, even gross ones, in order that one may extract the most information from his data. This is often justified on the basis of evidence of the internal consistency of the findings and the validity of the outcomes. This does not excuse the investigator, however, from being on the alert for intolerable approximations and for results and conclusions that are essentially a function of his faulty application of statistics.

Ratio Scales. Ratio scales have absolute zeros, where zero stands for neither more nor less than none of the property represented by the scale. All the postulates mentioned previously apply. It is possible to equate meaningfully ratios of numbers on the scale. For example, the ratio 12/8 is equal to the ratio 3/2, and both stand for the same relation between two real quantities. In fact, all the fundamental number operations are possible and meaningful and all the statistical operations, including the *coefficient of variation*, may be utilized. It may not be possible to demonstrate additivity experimentally with the empirical quantities to which the ratio-scale numbers are applied. This is not essential. There are certain observational operations which may defensibly be used as evidence that a ratio scale exists. For example, in the *method of fractionation* (see Chap. 9) an observer is asked to find pairs of stimuli that have a simple ratio like 1 to 2. If the operation is successful, and this can be checked by examining the measurements for internal consistency, a ratio scale is achieved. Stevens' *sone scale* (24) and his *mel scale* (27) are of this type. There are other scales that have been intended to satisfy the requirements of the equal-ratio principle.[1]

Measures of numerousness (obtained by the counting of objects) are ratio-scale measurements. There is a genuine zero (no objects), and we may speak meaningfully of ratios of frequencies. The statistics f and N, which appear so universally in our computations, have the property of additivity and may ordinarily be given the complete treatment in numerical operations. This statement is qualified by saying "ordinarily," because there are certain uses of frequencies which take them out of the ratio-scale category. For example, when a score on a test is the number of items correctly answered, we obtain the number by counting. If we stay within the sphere of "number of items correct," we have ratio values. But such a number is given a new function or use when it is taken to indicate the position of an individual on a scale of ability or some other trait. The truth is that we are talking about two scales here, not one. When we transfer to the ability scale, frequency values such as these lose their ratio properties. Zero correct answers may mean definitely more than zero ability; 50 items correct probably does not mean twice as much ability as 25 items correct. We may not even have equal units and probably rarely do have exactly equal units. There is evidence, however, that such scores approach interval measurements when tests are long and items are well distributed for difficulty.[2]

Transformation and Invariance of Scale Values. It is interesting and significant to ask under what conditions we can transform obtained scale numbers into other numbers by various operations and yet maintain the same descriptive accuracy. Simple examples of transformation are changes

[1] See Chap. 9.

[2] See Culler (10).

of unit or of zero point. When the descriptive accuracy remains the same under such transformations, we say that we have "invariance." Invariance is important because it means dependability. It also means the possibility of generalizing conclusions.

With nominal-scale measurements, there is the broadest possible latitude in making transformations. Since one number is as good as any other for describing a class, any kind of substitution leaves the structure of the scale (the classes and the contents of the classes) the same. The equality of cases within classes and the distinctions between classes are not violated in any way.

With ordinal-scale measurements, any transformation that will still preserve rank order will leave the scale inviolate. We may multiply all numbers by a constant or add a constant to every one and the obtained numbers retain the same rank order as before. We could even square every number, take its (positive) square root, or find its logarithm. The resulting numbers would still be in correct order. All these changes are called *monotonic* transformations because the functional relationship between the original rank numbers and the transformed values is a continually increasing or decreasing one. There are no maxima or minima in the function relating the two.

In the case of interval-scale measurements, the kind of transformation permitted must be not only monotonic but also linear. Functions involving roots, powers, and logarithms are, of course, nonlinear. The linear transformation, expressed by the equation $y = a + bx$, results in a change of unit and of zero point. We both multiply by a constant and add a constant. Either operation is applied separately when a or b is zero. The transformed values are also on an interval scale. Equality of units and intervals is maintained, but the position of the zero point is still arbitrary.

For ratio-scale measurements, there is only one kind of transformation that will leave the scale numbers properly describing the data also on a ratio scale. That transformation is multiplication by a constant. The equation is of the form $y = bx$, where b is the constant multiplier, and it may be greater or less than unity, but may not equal zero.

Scales of Index Numbers. Psychologists and others often deal with numbers that are known as index values. They are not like most measurements. One familiar example is the *IQ* and another is the coefficient of correlation. The division of mental age by chronological age, both being in terms of year units or month units, gives us a number that is not on the year scale. The occurrence of the common time unit in numerator and denominator cancels out the original scale unit. The result is a pure ratio number. This does not justify the assumption that the *IQ* scale is in the ratio-scale level or even that it has equal units. Without further proof it is best regarded as an ordinal scale. If the population distribution of *IQ*'s is Gaussian and if an obtained distribution in a large, random sample is normal, we would have evidence that we have an interval scale. Not being able to establish the fact that the population distribution is normal, we cannot depend completely upon this line of proof. To say that the sample distribution establishes the form of the population begs the question. What is ordinarily done is boldly to assume that the population distribution is normal; then if an obtained representative-sample distribution is normal, we feel some confidence in the equality of units of whatever scale is being applied.

The coefficient of correlation is another index number. Again, numerator and denominator values are in terms of the original measurement units, which cancel out. The Pearson-*r* scale has a meaningful zero point but lacks equality of units. If we square *r* to obtain the coefficient of determination, we have an index of the proportion of total variance in either variable accounted for by variance in the other. In theories of reliability and factor analysis it is usually assumed that proportions of variance are on a ratio scale. Thus, while *r* is essentially on an ordinal scale, r^2 is on a ratio scale.

For other index numbers it will be necessary to examine the properties of each one in order to draw a conclusion as to what kind of measurement scale it represents. Operations with it and interpretations of it depend upon such a conclusion. If an index by nature belongs on a lower type of scale, a transformation of some kind may qualify it for a higher type of scale, as in the case of the coefficient of correlation.

References

1. Bartlett, R. J. Measurement in psychology. *Rep. Brit. Ass. Advance. Sci.*, 1939, 1–20.
2. Bell, E. T. *The Development of Mathematics.* 2d ed. New York: McGraw-Hill, 1945.
3. Boring, E. G. *A History of Experimental Psychology.* 2d ed. New York: Appleton-Century-Crofts, 1950.
4. ———. The logic of the normal law of error in mental measurement. *Amer. J. Psychol.*, 1920, **31**, 1–33.
5. Bridgman, P. W. *The Logic of Modern Physics.* New York: Macmillan, 1928.
6. Campbell, N. R. Symposium: Measurement and its importance for philosophy. *Aristotelian Soc. Suppl.*, Vol. 17, 1938.
7. ——— *et al.* Final report. *Advancement of Sci.*, 1940, No. 2, 331–349.
8. Carnap, R. Foundations of logic and mathematics, *International Encyclopedia of Unified Sciences*, Vol. 1, No. 3, 1939.
9. Comrey, A. L. An operational approach to some problems in psychological measurement. *Psychol. Rev.*, 1950, **57**, 217–228.
10. Culler, E. Studies in psychometric theory. *J. exp. Psychol.*, 1926, **9**, 271–279.
11. Dantzig, T. *Number: The Language of Science.* New York: Macmillan, 1939.
12. Fechner, G. T. *Elemente der Psychophysik* (reprint). Leipzig: Breitkopf und Härtel, 1889.
13. Galton, F. *Memories of My Life.* London: Methuen, 1908.
14. Guilford, J. P. *Fundamental Statistics in Psychology and Education.* 2d ed. New York: McGraw-Hill, 1950.
15. Helson, H. *Theoretical Foundations of Psychology.* New York: Van Nostrand, 1951, Chap. 11.
16. Hogben, L. *Mathematics for the Millions.* New York: Norton, 1940.
17. Müller, G. E. *Zur Grundlegung der Psychophysik.* Berlin: Grieben, 1878.
18. Reese, T. W. The application of the theory of physical measurement to the measurement of psychological magnitudes, with three experimental examples. *Psychol. Monogr.*, 1943, **55**, No. 251.
19. Russell, B. *Introduction to Mathematical Philosophy.* 2d ed. New York: Macmillan, 1920.
20. ———. *The Principles of Mathematics.* New York: Norton, 1937.

21. SCATES, D. E. How science measures. *J. exp. Educ.*, 1937, **5**, 296–312.
22. SMITH, B. O. *Logical Aspects of Educational Measurement.* New York: Columbia University Press, 1938.
23. SPEARMAN, C. *Psychology Down the Ages.* New York: Macmillan, 1937.
24. STEVENS, S. S. A scale for the measurement of a psychological magnitude: loudness. *Psychol. Rev.*, 1936, **43**, 405–416.
25. ———. On the theory of scales of measurement. *Science*, 1946, **103**, 670–680.
26. ———. *Handbook of Experimental Psychology.* New York: Wiley, 1951.
27. ——— and VOLKMANN, J. The relation of pitch to frequency: a revised scale. *Amer. J. Psychol.*, 1940, **53**, 329–353.
28. TITCHENER, E. B. *Experimental Psychology.* Vol. II, Pt. II. New York: Macmillan, 1905.
29. WALKER, H. M. *Studies in the History of Statistical Method.* Baltimore: Williams & Wilkins, 1929.
30. WEITZENHOFFER, A. M. Mathematical structures and psychological measurements. *Psychometrika*, 1951, **16**, 387–406.
31. WEYL, H. *Philosophy of Mathematics and Natural Science.* Princeton, N.J.: Princeton University Press, 1949.

CHAPTER 2

PSYCHOPHYSICAL THEORY

The early chapters in this volume will deal with the psychophysical methods. Preparatory for that subject it is important that we have clearly in mind certain fundamental ideas concerning psychophysics.[1]

From the time of Fechner, psychophysics has been regarded as the science that investigates the quantitative relationships between physical events and corresponding psychological events. In more familiar terms, this means quantitative relationships between stimuli and responses. In a very broad sense, then, much of psychology is psychophysics, for the understanding of behavior involves the knowledge of how responses depend upon stimuli. We shall see more of this broad view of psychophysics later. We shall be concerned first with the more restricted, traditional view of psychophysics. We shall then see how more recent thinking has broadened the logical base of the subject. We shall also see what recent developments have meant with respect to the traditional psychophysical laws of Weber and Fechner and how Thurstone's *law of comparative judgment* has extended very greatly the possibilities of psychological measurement.

Classical Psychophysics

The classical psychophysics of Fechner, G. E. Müller, and Wundt was concerned primarily with the determination of sensory thresholds, or limens. Fechner's original interest was in the philosophical question of the relation between body and mind, between the physical and the psychical aspects of the world. He saw in his logarithmic law describing the relationship between stimulus and sensation a principle of cosmic importance. His energies and his ingenuities were bent toward the testing of the universality of his law. To the experimental psychologists who followed Fechner the new psychophysical methods provided the experimental procedures whereby sensory phenomena in general could be investigated. They continued to use those methods primarily for the purpose of determining sensory limens. The methods are so used today, not only by psychologists who specialize in sensory problems but also by engineers who constantly face problems of illumination, sound phenomena, and sometimes of taste and smell.[2]

[1] Students whose backgrounds in mathematics are weak may do well to read large parts of Chap. 3 before proceeding far in this chapter.

[2] It is also interesting to note that biologists who study the tolerance of organisms to drugs, with interest in what doses are lethal, employ methods that are essentially psychophysical. Also, those who investigate problems of explosives in connection with military ordnance deal with limens for the detonation of explosives, by methods that are clearly analogous to psychophysical procedures.

conditions. It may be a matter of matching two lines for length, one appearing on the right and one on the left, or one above the other. The spatial separation of the two lines may be little or relatively great. It may be a matter of two weights lifted in succession, the second to be equated to the first, with varying time interval between them. It may be a matter of matching distances between two compass points applied to the forehead and two points applied to the forearm. In each case one of the stimuli, in one position or at one moment of time, is taken to be the "standard" and an observer somehow (according to which psychophysical method is employed) in a series of trials selects stimuli he calls "equal" to the standard. If S_j is the standard, S_k is varied and the observer (O) selects various values of S_k to match S_j. The central tendency of the judgments (S_k values selected) is taken as the *point of subjective equality*, or *PSE*. This is another important landmark in classical psychophysics, though it has had much less attention than limens. It is often computed as a by-product when limens are the center of interest.

Classical Psychophysics Is an Incomplete Psychophysics. Thus far, we have seen that classical psychophysics did not attempt to state scale values for responses on the R continuum. All measurements are made on the stimulus scale, corresponding to certain landmarks on the R continuum (absolute limens) or to unitary distances (difference limens) on the same continuum. The landmarks are statistically derived at points of equal likelihood of two different judgments. The *DL* is also established in terms of a distance at which there is equal likelihood of two different judgments. In a sense this does not give us a complete psychophysics, for we have no basis for relating measurements on R to measurements on S. Before we can do this, we need to evaluate different R's and see how they depend upon their corresponding S's.

In this sense, Weber's law is not a psychophysical law. It relates two physical measurements—ΔS with S. Only the fact that ΔS stands for a presumably constant psychological increment measured on the stimulus scale provides anything psychophysical about it. The Fechner law, which states that R increases as the logarithm of the stimulus, is a psychophysical law. It implies measured values on the response scale and this means that we must make such measurements in order to subject the Fechner law to experimental checking. We have just seen one reason why it is inappropriate to speak of "the Weber-Fechner law" as if it were one law. Later we shall see in what sense they are related and we shall see that under certain conditions the one law may apply and the other not apply to the same data.

Modern Psychophysical Theory

During the past 25 years psychologists have taken more seriously the possibility of constructing mathematical models for the description of mental phenomena. This has been true also in the field of psychophysics and we now have a much better rational basis for psychophysical methods and for psychological measurement in general. Not all of this rationalizing will be mentioned here, but enough of it to furnish us with a logical foundation on which to build a system of operations. Much of it can be credited to an outstanding article by Thurstone in 1927, in which he developed the third important psychophysical law—the *law of comparative judgment* (25). We shall give some attention to this law later in the chapter, but first consider some more basic ideas.

A General Behavior Equation. Graham has well expressed explicitly what experimental psychologists with a quantitative bent have assumed for a long time (7). This is to the effect that any response of an organism is a function of many contributing determiners. Among the determiners of a response are various properties of the stimulus, various internal conditions of the organism, and various previous stimulations of the organism. In terms of a very general equation Graham states that

$$R = f(a,b,c,d, \ldots, n, \ldots, t, \ldots, x,y,z) \tag{2.3}$$

where R = response, or some measured aspect of it
a, b, c, d = aspects of the stimulus
n = number of times the stimulus has been applied to the organism
t = time
x, y, z = internal conditions of set, motivation, etc.

In the typical psychophysical experiment, we are interested in R as a function of the stimulus properties a, b, c, d, etc. We assume that by experimental controls we have kept constant all the determiners n to z and also all except one of the stimulus properties. The equation is limited to the form

$$R = F(a) \tag{2.4}$$

Studies involving the effect of n upon R we place in the category of learning. Those involving the relation of R to t are in the category of forgetting and fatigue. Finally, those relating R to x, y, and z are in the area of motivation or emotion.

These last-named types of functional relationships are outside the realm of psychophysics proper, but along with psychophysical functions like that described by equation (2.4), they help to complete the general picture of quantitative psychology. Even equation (2.3) does not complete the picture, however. There are also problems in which we can state one response as a function of another, as when we describe the affective value (degree of preference) for a stimulus as a function of some psychological variable also related to the stimulus. For example, preferences for colors are related to the variables of hue, brightness, and chroma, which are psychological variables. Such relationships come under another category which the writer has called *psychodynamics* (9). There is also the very large realm of individual differences which makes up another important aspect of psychological measurement.

The Response Matrix. To return to the more specific psychophysical problem, let us select one of the stimulus properties, a, b, or c, etc., in equation (2.3), which varies along a physical continuum S. Let various quantities be designated by the symbols $S_1, S_2, S_3, \ldots, S_j, \ldots, S_n$, where there are n stimuli selected for study. Let these stimuli be administered in turn to the same organism on different occasions designated by $O_1, O_2, O_3, \ldots, O_h, \ldots, O_q$, where there are q occasions. For each stimulus applied on each occasion there will result a quantity of response designated by R_{hj} in general terms. That is, R_{hj} is the response arising on occasion O_h from stimulus S_j. We can express the responses for all combinations of occasions and stimuli by means of a matrix, as in Table 2.1. The occasions are represented by rows and the stimuli by columns. The double subscripts stand for occasions and stimuli, in that order.

TABLE 2.1. A RESPONSE MATRIX SHOWING RESPONSES FOR VARIOUS STIMULI ADMINISTERED ON VARIOUS OCCASIONS TO THE SAME INDIVIDUAL

$R_o =$ (rows: Occasions; columns: Stimuli)

	S_1	S_2	S_3	. . .	S_j	. . .	S_h
O_1	R_{11}	R_{12}	R_{13}	. . .	R_{1j}	. . .	R_{1n}
O_2	R_{21}	R_{22}	R_{23}	. . .	R_{2j}	. . .	R_{2n}
O_3	R_{31}	R_{32}	R_{33}	. . .	R_{3j}	. . .	R_{3n}
.	. . .	. . .	. . .	. . .	. . .	. . .	. . .
O_h	R_{h1}	R_{h2}	R_{h3}	. . .	R_{hj}	. . .	R_{hn}
.	. . .	. . .	. . .	. . .	. . .	. . .	. . .
O_q	R_{q1}	R_{q2}	R_{q3}	. . .	R_{qj}	. . .	R_{qn}

A similar matrix was presented by Mosier, except that he assumed a population of individuals instead of a population of occasions (19). His type of matrix is given in Table 2.2. It is a better basis for psychological-test theory than for psychophysical theory, but if we substitute individuals for occasions, it can be used to serve both purposes. The occasion matrix and the individual matrix can be combined to form a solid figure in which each solid cell represents a particular stimulus given to a particular individual at a particular time. In psychophysics we are usually concerned with variations of responses for constant individuals over a range of occasions, though in some instances we are interested in variations in responses over individuals on a single occasion. In this instance we have what is called "group psychophysics."

TABLE 2.2. A RESPONSE MATRIX SHOWING RESPONSES FOR VARIOUS STIMULI ADMINISTERED TO VARIOUS INDIVIDUALS ON A SINGLE OCCASION

$R_i =$ (rows: Individuals; columns: Stimuli)

	S_1	S_2	S_3	. . .	S_j	. . .	S_n
I_1	R_{11}	R_{12}	R_{13}	. . .	R_{1j}	. . .	R_{1n}
I_2	R_{21}	R_{22}	R_{23}	. . .	R_{2j}	. . .	R_{2n}
I_3	R_{31}	R_{32}	R_{33}	. . .	R_{3j}	. . .	R_{3n}
.	. . .	. . .	. . .	. . .	. . .	. . .	. . .
I_i	R_{i1}	R_{i2}	R_{i3}	. . .	R_{ij}	. . .	R_{in}
.	. . .	. . .	. . .	. . .	. . .	. . .	. . .
I_N	R_{N1}	R_{N2}	R_{N3}	. . .	R_{Nj}	. . .	R_{Nn}

The Discriminal Process and Discriminal Dispersion. It is a well-recognized fact that the same stimulus S_j will not always elicit from the same organism the same response on different occasions. In fact, the quantity of response is a notably variable phenomenon. The variability in R is, however, restricted to a relatively narrow range on the R continuum. The fact of variability can be expressed in terms of a simple equation

$$R_{hj} = R_j + e_{hj} \tag{2.5}$$

where R_{hj} = response to stimulus S_j on occasion O_h
R_j = "true" response to stimulus S_j
e_{hj} = an error or deviation of R_{hj} from the true response R_j

Let us assume that the deviations e_{hj} vary at random and that they are unrelated to one another and to R_j. Assume, also, that $\Sigma e_{hi} = 0$.

Figure 2.3 illustrates three dispersions of such errors. For stimuli S_a, S_b, and S_c there are "true" responses R_a, R_b, and R_c, respectively. A true response, like a true score in a mental test, is the response this individual should give to a certain stimulus if there were no disturbing forces at the moment. Operationally, it can be defined as the central tendency of all responses the individual would give to the stimulus on a very large number of occasions. Thurstone refers to each response occurring at any moment as a *discriminal process* (25). He refers to the true response as the modal *discriminal response*—modal because it is the most often elicited by this stimulus.

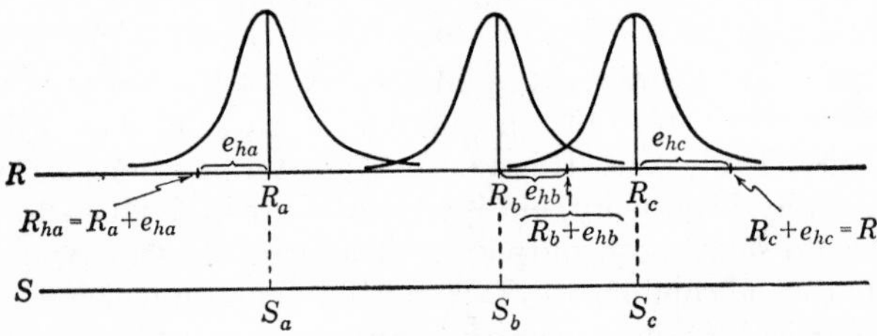

FIG. 2.3. Three discriminal dispersions on the R scale corresponding to three stimuli S_a, S_b, and S_c. Three typical errors e_{ha}, e_{hb}, and e_{hc} are shown for one occasion O_h.

Figure 2.3 shows that each discriminal process is symbolized by $R_j + e_{hj}$. Each distribution of the discriminal processes for a given stimulus is called a *discriminal dispersion*, following Thurstone's terminology. The degree of dispersion is measured by the standard deviation or by any other common measure of variability.

Questions immediately arise concerning the shape of these discriminal dispersions and whether the dispersions are equal on the response scale. The simplest and most plausible assumption is that the dispersions are normal, though there may be notable departures from normality. The direct evidence of normality is best seen in distributions of stimuli that an observer matches to a standard. Ask him to draw 50 lines to match a standard line and the distribution of his reproductions is likely to be close to normal. It is true that his reproductions are measured on the S scale and not on the R scale. If R is related to S according to Fechner's logarithmic function, and if the distribution of reproductions is normal on the S scale, the corresponding distribution of R's should be at least slightly skewed on the R scale. If R is normally distributed, the distribution of S should be skewed. Over a short range of values of S, however, the corresponding values of R are for practical purposes in linear relationship, where discrimination is very fine, as it is in the case of lengths of lines.

There is so much evidence of this sort (from reproductions of stimuli) that we feel some confidence in assuming normality for the discriminal dispersions in general. There are several indirect experimental signs of lack of normality, as we shall find later. In practice, it is not necessary to assume that the dispersions are normal. Neither is it necessary to assume that the dispersions are equal, as they appear to be in Fig. 2.3. Things are much simpler, however, if we can assume both normality and equality of discriminal dispersions.

The Judgment Continuum. Thus far we have assumed a response continuum for R without necessarily relating it to any externally observable aspects of behavior. In a sensory response it might be variations in loudness of sounds, brightness of lights, or degrees of a salty sensation. No experimenter (E) can obtain direct evidence as to quantities of R of this kind, nor can O exhibit those quantities for inspection. The evidence that E has of quantity is in the form of a judgment of some kind, and this is usually a verbal or other symbolic response. In other words, the data on which psychological measurements in psychophysics are based are in the form of judgments. It is from these judgments that E must derive evidence of quantity of R. It is therefore important, for logical clarity, that we bring into the picture a third continuum which will be known as the *judgment continuum*. Continuum J parallels continuum R and, through this relationship, is also related to continuum S. Psychophysical theory has heretofore ignored this logical step. The response continuum in psychophysics is thus to be treated as an intervening variable. A judgment, of course, is a response and the judgment continuum is another response continuum. It is an overt one, whereas the R continuum is an inferred one.

It has been common practice in psychophysics to assume, implicitly, a linear regression relating J to R, with perfect correlation. We shall find much evidence in Chap. 12, and elsewhere, to the effect that the regression is not always linear and the correlation is not always perfect. It may be that under certain conditions of good experimental controls, favorable attitude of O, and a stabilized learning status, J is perfectly, linearly related to R. The facts reported in Chap. 12, however, show that we have much to learn concerning the way in which the language mechanism becomes related to quantities on an R continuum.

Figure 2.4 illustrates the introduction of the judgment continuum. Let the S continuum represent increasing quantity from left to right. The R continuum and the J continuum maintain the same order. Let the stimulus quantity S_l indicate the position of a limen of some kind or a point of subjective equality. Corresponding to S_l there is on the R continuum a quantity R_l, a modal discriminal process for S_l. Assuming a perfect correlation between R and J, there is a corresponding point on the J continuum called L_a. As is common in the determination of a limen, two categories of judgment are utilized. O reports the presence or absence of a certain experience. In this illustration, he reports "present" when R exceeds R_l and "absent" when R is lower than R_l.

Let us consider a particular superthreshold stimulus S_m. Its discriminal dispersion is shown on the R scale. This dispersion is broad enough that some of the responses will lie below R_l, but most will lie above it. The proportion of the judgments J_1 is represented by the area under the curve to the right of R_l and the proportions of judgments J_0 is represented by the area to the left of R_l. By assuming that the distribution is normal, we can express the distance of R_m from R_l on the R scale in terms of a deviate or standard-measure value z_m which we can find from a table of the unit normal distribution (Table C).

Consider another stimulus S_j, shown in part (*b*) of Fig. 2.4. The proportion of judgments J_1 for S_j will be less than .50, since it is a subliminal stimulus. Stimulus S_l, which is the liminal one, will, of course, yield 50 per cent judgments J_1 and 50 per cent J_0. Although in practice no single stimulus may be found to yield exactly 50 per cent of either category of judgment, by interpolation between other stimuli we can always estimate what such a

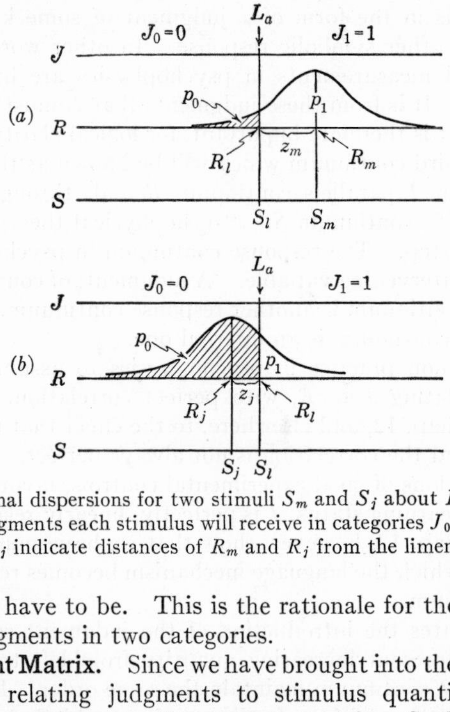

FIG. 2.4. Discriminal dispersions for two stimuli S_m and S_j about R_m and R_j, showing the proportions of judgments each stimulus will receive in categories J_0 and J_1. The standard measures z_m and z_j indicate distances of R_m and R_j from the limen R_l.

stimulus would have to be. This is the rationale for the determination of a limen from judgments in two categories.

The Judgment Matrix. Since we have brought into the picture a judgment continuum, in relating judgments to stimulus quantities, we can write another matrix, passing over the response matrix. Such a matrix is shown in Table 2.3. It represents the data from which we compute various summary statistics in psychophysics. You will find that few psychophysical methods result in a complete judgment matrix, for the sake of economizing on research time. It is not essential to obtain a complete matrix in order to determine limens and other results.

To make the use of a judgment matrix more concrete, let us assume that we have applied 10 different stimuli to the same O on 10 occasions. The occasions are usually successive series of trials. Operationally, an occasion cannot be a single instant of time. It can only mean a limited time interval. The spacing of occasions with lapsing time intervals between them is also a relative matter. For the sake of uniform experimental conditions, one series (occasion) is usually end to end with another, except for rest pauses or other kinds of delays.

In the judgment matrix of Table 2.4, the stimuli were in equal physical steps with intervals of two units. The judgments were in two categories and they were recorded as 1 or 0. These numbers may be taken for practical purposes as actual measurements on a two-step scale. The data in matrix J are fictitious but quite representative to illustrate some general principles of determining a limen.

TABLE 2.3. JUDGMENT MATRIX, SHOWING DIFFERENT JUDGMENTS GIVEN IN RESPONSE TO DIFFERENT STIMULI ON DIFFERENT OCCASIONS

$J_O =$ (rows: Occasions; columns: Stimuli)

	S_1	S_2	S_3	. . .	S_j	. . .	S_n
O_1	J_{11}	J_{12}	J_{13}	. . .	J_{1j}	. . .	J_{1n}
O_2	J_{21}	J_{22}	J_{23}	. . .	J_{2j}	. . .	J_{2n}
O_3	J_{31}	J_{32}	J_{33}	. . .	J_{3j}	. . .	J_{3n}
.	.	.	.	. . .	.	. . .	.
O_h	J_{h1}	J_{h2}	J_{h3}	. . .	J_{hj}	. . .	J_{hn}
.	.	.	.	. . .	.	. . .	.
O_q	J_{q1}	J_{q2}	J_{q3}	. . .	J_{qj}	. . .	J_{qn}

General Principles of Determining a Limen. In determining what stimulus value would give judgments $J = 1$ with a probability of .5, two general approaches may be taken. In the first of these, which will be encountered in the *method of minimal changes* (see Chap. 5), an estimate is made of the limen from the data for each occasion. In Table 2.4 these are called S'_1 and they are given in the last column. For occasions 2, 5, 6, and 8, the location of a stimulus value clearly dividing the two kinds of judgments is obvious in each case. The zeros and ones are segregated on either side of a division point. Taking as the value of the division point the value midway between the two limiting stimuli, S'_1 for series 2, 5, 6, and 8 may be given as 11, 13, 13, and 9. In other series there are reversals. Here we make a rough approximation to a midpoint by noting the numbers of zeros and ones and artificially segregating them to the left and right, respectively. In series 1, with 5 zeros and 5 ones, the division point comes at 11. In series 3, with 4 zeros and 6 ones, the division point is taken as 9. An obvious defect of this procedure is that no attention is paid to the *extent* of the overlap, only to the number of overlapping judgments. Having 10 estimates of the limen in the last column of Table 2.4, the mean of the 10 is taken as the best estimate of the limen. This mean is 10.8.

Another general principle of determining the limen works with the columns. First, the judgments in each column are summed. This gives the frequency with which each stimulus yielded the judgment of 1. Dividing each frequency by q, the number of occasions, gives the mean of the column and at the same time the proportion of judgments of 1 in each column. These are also the probabilities of judgment 1 for the various stimuli. We want to know the stimulus value that would have a probability of .5 for a judgment of 1. No one stimulus gives this probability. Looking for probabilities nearest to .5 we find that stimuli 10 and 12 have probabilities of .4 and .6, respectively. Interpolating, we find that a stimulus of 11.0 should have a probability of .5, and therefore 11.0 is an estimate of the limen. This is close to the 10.8 found by the other method.

Table 2.4. Matrix of Judgments Obtained in a Hypothetical Experiment Designed to Illustrate Some General Principles of the Determination of a Limen

	Stimulus values										
	2	4	6	8	10	12	14	16	18	20	S'_1
Occasions 1	0	0	1	0	0	1	0	1	1	1	11
2	0	0	0	0	0	1	1	1	1	1	11
3	1	0	0	0	1	1	1	1	0	1	9
4	0	0	1	0	0	1	0	1	1	1	11
5	0	0	0	0	0	0	1	1	1	1	13
6	0	0	0	0	0	0	1	1	1	1	13
7	0	1	0	1	1	0	0	0	1	1	11
8	0	0	0	0	1	1	1	1	1	1	9
9	0	0	0	1	0	1	1	1	1	1	9
10	0	0	0	0	1	0	1	1	1	1	11
$\Sigma J_s = f_1$	1	1	2	2	4	6	7	9	9	10	$108 = \Sigma S'_1$
$\Sigma J_s/q = p_1$	.1	.1	.2	.2	.4	.6	.7	.9	.9	1.0	$10.8 = Ms'_1$
z_r	−1.28	−1.28	−0.84	−0.84	−0.25	+0.25	+0.52	+1.28	+1.28	....	$= S_1$

If we want to utilize more than the two proportions, .4 and .6, either of which might be seriously in error and thus throw off the estimate of the limen, we can resort to another principle which utilizes practically all the

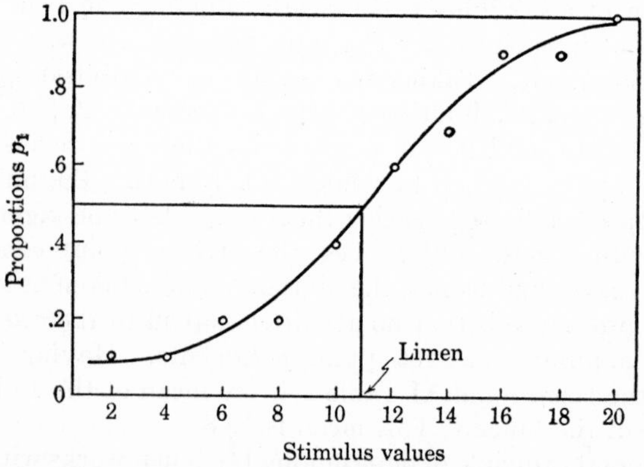

Fig. 2.5. The relation of the proportions of responses J_1 to stimulus values, with a smoothed (freehand) curve drawn through the points. The limen or limit is at approximately 11.

data. Draw a diagram showing proportions on the ordinate and stimulus values on the abscissa, as in Fig. 2.5. Plot the points from the pairs of S_j and p_1 in Table 2.4. The trend is usually an S-shaped curve. Draw a smoothed curve through the points, and note where it crosses the level at

$p = .50$. The corresponding S value is the limen. The result agrees fairly closely with the two estimates previously obtained.

Still another type of solution is to find for each value of p the corresponding z value in the table for the unit normal distribution. These are given in the last row of Table 2.4. These z values are plotted against corresponding S values in Fig. 2.6. The z values obtained from this process are the same kind of measurement as illustrated in Fig. 2.4. In using the z values as recommended, we have assumed that the discriminal dispersions are normal and that their standard deviations are equal. The former assumption is necessary to justify the use of the normal-curve tables. The second is necessary in order to place all z values on the same linear scale. The chief advantage of the transformation from p to z is that, on the assumption that the

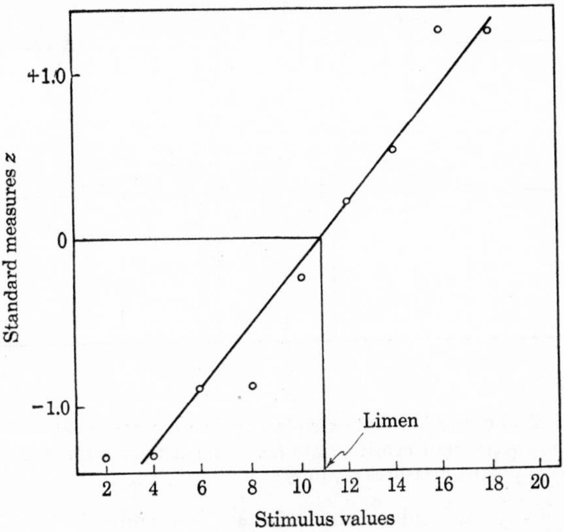

FIG. 2.6. The relation of standard measures, derived from proportions of judgments J_1, to stimulus values. A straight line has been drawn by inspection, showing a limen at about 11.

relation of p to S is that of the cumulative normal distribution or normal ogive, the regression of z on S will be a straight line. Reference to Fig. 2.6 will show that the relationship is linear, which is indirect indication that the assumptions have been sound. It is easier to fit a straight line to points than to fit a complex curve. The estimation of the limen by this principle, although it involves an additional assumption, seems justified.

The last three principles are applied in determining limens in the *method of constant stimuli*. In Chap. 6 we shall see these principles applied with variations. Here we are only concerned with a general preview of the operations involved in computing a limen as related directly to underlying psychophysical theory.

Judgments in Successive Categories. Thus far we have considered only the case of two alternative judgments. The judgment scale in this case is a dichotomy. The judgment scale may be divided into three or more categories. In order to serve a useful purpose in measurement, the categories must be ordered. They need not represent equal distances on the R scale. We may ask O to sort a number of weights by lifting and placing them in three categories, heavy, medium, and light. Finer gradations could be utilized by breaking up the heavy and light into two or more categories each.

Figure 2.7 illustrates a situation with five categories, J_1 to J_5. With five categories there are four division points, or limits, L_a to L_d, as shown in Fig. 2.7. Stimulus S_9 has a discriminal dispersion that spreads through all five of these categories. Its modal discriminal process is at R_9, the mean of the distribution on R. If we may assume a normal distribution of the deviations from R_9, by knowing the proportion of the judgments below each category limit we can express the distance of each category limit from R_9 in terms of a z value. The distance of limit L_a from R_9 is given by z_{9a}; that for

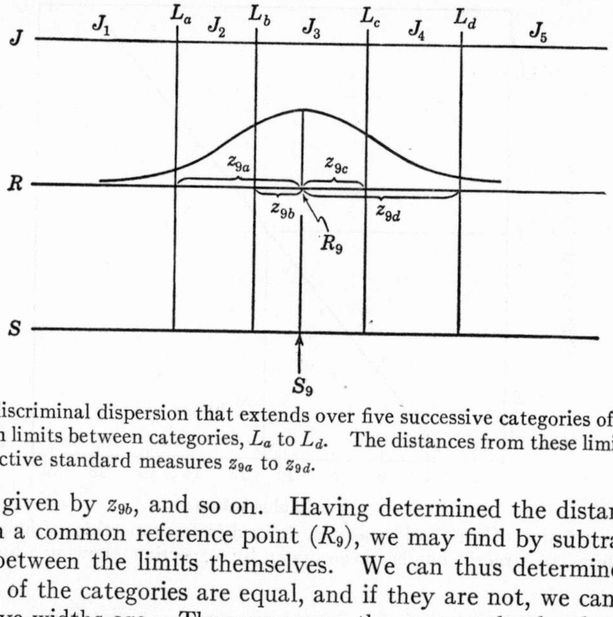

FIG. 2.7. A discriminal dispersion that extends over five successive categories of judgments, J_1 to J_5, with limits between categories, L_a to L_d. The distances from these limits are given by the respective standard measures z_{9a} to z_{9d}.

limit L_b is given by z_{9b}, and so on. Having determined the distances of all limits from a common reference point (R_9), we may find by subtraction the distances between the limits themselves. We can thus determine whether the widths of the categories are equal, and if they are not, we can see what their relative widths are. Thus we are on the way to the development of a purely psychological scale of equal units. The unit might be arbitrarily chosen as one standard deviation or any fraction of a standard deviation. With the use of other stimuli higher or lower on S than S_9, we can verify the scaling obtained from the use of S_9 and also extend its range. It is not necessary to assume that the discriminal dispersions are all equal. We can determine when they are not and make necessary corrections to achieve internal consistency among the data. We also have ways of checking up on the assumption of normal distributions (see Chap. 10).

The method of psychological scaling implied by the principle just described comes under the general category of *absolute scaling*. Besides stating the positions of the limits between categories as distances from means of observations of stimuli, we can turn the limits and mean R's around, and, using the scale derived from the limits as the frame of reference, we can state values for the R's. It is the R corresponding to each stimulus that we wish to evaluate or measure. The procedure is not circular in any undesirable sense nor is it a matter of lifting one's self by one's boot straps. The absolute-scaling principle can be applied to data obtained by various experimental methods.

Psychophysical Laws

Before we return to the Weber and Fechner laws it is important for us to get acquainted with Thurstone's *law of comparative judgment.* It not only opens up new principles of psychological scaling but incidentally throws light on the older psychophysical laws.

Comparative Judgments. We first need to understand the theory behind the comparative judgment. In making a comparative judgment we are usually offered two stimuli, let us say S_a and S_b, and are asked to make

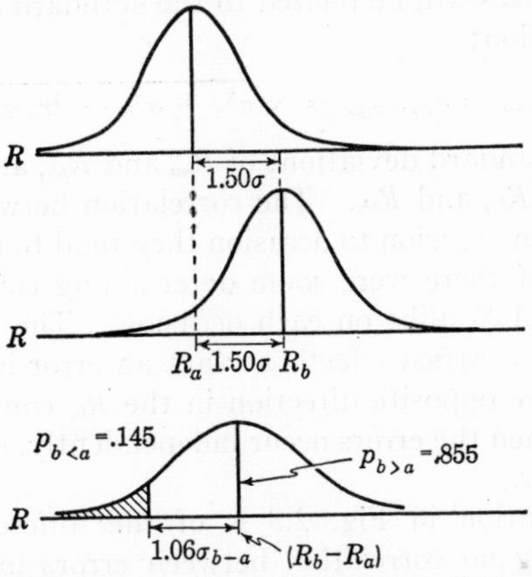

Fig. 2.8. Two discriminal dispersions, about R_a and R_b, and the dispersion of differences about the mean $R_b - R_a$.

one of two reports; either S_a is greater than S_b or S_a is less than S_b. When two stimuli are close together so that their discriminal dispersions overlap, there is some confusion of the two. Part of the time one of the two judgments is given and part of the time the other. The overlapping of the dispersions is, of course, due to the chance combinations of errors e_{hj}. At any one moment (occasion O_h) e_{ha} may be positive and e_{hb} may be negative to the extent that R_{ha} is greater than R_{hb}. At another moment, O_m, e_{ma} may be negative and e_{mb} may be positive to the extent that R_{ma} is less than R_{mb}.

Figure 2.8 illustrates these events in terms of discriminal dispersions. We have the dispersion of R_{ha} for stimulus S_a about the mean R_a and the dispersion of R_{hb} for stimulus S_b about the mean R_b, both on the same R scale. They are shown on two separated scales here merely for the sake of clarity. Here the two discriminal dispersions happen to be equal, so that $\sigma_a = \sigma_b$. The mean R_b is $1.50\sigma_a$ distant from the mean R_a and the mean R_a is $1.50\sigma_b$ distant from the mean R_b. Since $\sigma_a = \sigma_b$, it does not matter which one we use for the unit of the R scale. With σ as the unit we may say that R_b and R_a are 1.50 units apart, or $R_b - R_a = 1.50$.

The scaling problem is to discover what this distance is and what other distances exist between R_a and R_b and other R values on the same R scale. This can be done from the information about the proportion of the time the individual judges R_b to be greater than R_a and the proportions of the time he judges R_a and R_b to be greater than other stimuli.

The Distribution of Differences. The distance $R_b - R_a$ is a difference between two quantities. As the response to S_a varies up and down the R scale, the response to S_b also varies up and down the same scale. At the moment of comparison of the two stimuli, in general terms at occasion O_h, there will be a difference $R_{hb} - R_{ha}$, which varies from occasion to occasion. This is due to the combination of pairs of errors e_{hj}. If the discriminal dispersion for R_{hb} and that for R_{ha} are normal, the distribution of the differences $R_{hb} - R_{ha}$ will also be normal. We shall assume normality of distribution of R_{ha} and R_{hb} and of their differences. The standard deviation of the dispersion of differences will be related to the standard deviations of R_{ha} and R_{hb} in the usual fashion:

$$\sigma_{b-a} = \sigma_{R_{hb}-R_{ha}} = \sqrt{\sigma^2{}_a + \sigma^2{}_b - 2r_{ab}\sigma_a\sigma_b} \tag{2.6}$$

where σ_a and σ_b = standard deviations of R_{ha} and R_{hb}, and r_{ab} = coefficient of correlation between R_{ha} and R_{hb}. The correlation between responses would be positive when from occasion to occasion they tend to rise and fall together. This could happen if there were some determining condition affecting the impressions of S_a and S_b alike on each occasion. The correlation would be negative if there are contrast effects, so that an error in R_{aj} is compensated for by an error in the opposite direction in the R_{bj} compared with it. The correlation is zero when the errors occur independently, one having no strings attached to the other.

The third distribution in Fig. 2.8 is of the differences in momentary responses. Assuming no correlation between errors in the two responses, the standard deviation of this distribution should equal $\sqrt{2}$, when

$$\sigma_a = \sigma_b = 1.0$$

The standard deviation of the difference is therefore $1.414\sigma_a$ or $1.414\sigma_b$. If the difference $R_b - R_a$ is equal to $1.50\sigma_a$ or $1.50\sigma_b$, how many of the larger units σ_{b-a} does it equal? Dividing 1.50 by 1.414, we obtain 1.06, which tells us that the two responses are $1.06\sigma_{b-a}$ units apart on the scale of differences. The distribution of differences is shown with its mean of $R_b - R_a$. A difference of zero is shown at a distance of $1.06\sigma_{b-a}$ from the mean. The larger unshaded area lying above zero represents the judgments $S_b > S_a$ and smaller shaded portion the judgments $S_b < S_a$. From the normal-curve tables we find that the clear area must include .855 of the total and the shaded portion .145 of the total. These are the proportions of the two kinds of judgments where only the two categories are allowed. It is assumed that when $R_{hb} - R_{ha}$ is positive a judgment of $S_b > S_a$ is bound to occur and that when $R_{hb} - R_{ha}$ is negative a judgment of $S_b < S_a$ is bound to occur. If R_{hb} should happen to equal R_{ha}, the judgments will be divided in the same proportions as $p_{b>a}$ and $p_{b<a}$.

In experimental practice we do not know the size of the scale separation either in terms of σ_{b-a} as the unit or in terms of σ_a or σ_b. The experimental data consist of the proportions of judgments in which each stimulus is judged greater or less than another. It is from such data that we proceed to scaling, and the work is in reverse order to the steps given above. This will be explained in detail in Chap. 7 on pair comparisons. Here it is sufficient to see the possibilities for deriving scale separations from a knowledge of proportions of comparative judgments.

The Law of Comparative Judgment. Thurstone's law of comparative judgment is stated in the following form

$$R_b - R_a = z_{ba} \sqrt{\sigma^2_a + \sigma^2_b - 2r_{ab}\sigma_a\sigma_b} \qquad (2.7)$$

where z_{ba} = the normal deviate, or standard-measure distance corresponding to $p_{b>a}$, and where other terms are as defined in preceding paragraphs.

The effect of the radical expression is to state the unit in which the measurement is made. This is important because the unit may change with every pair of stimuli compared. Until we demonstrate that the radical term is uniform for all pairs of stimuli, it should be explicitly stated in the equation. As the equation stands, it states that a given response separation on the R scale is a function (1) of z_{ba} (which can be derived directly from the experimental proportion $p_{b>a}$), (2) of the dispersions of the two stimuli σ_a and σ_b, and (3) of r_{ab}.

Obviously there are three unknowns (z_{ba} being known from the experimental data) when we attempt to put equation (2.7) into use: σ_a, σ_b, and r_{ab}. In order to achieve a more workable formula, Thurstone makes several additional assumptions, eliminating some of the unknowns. If we assume that all the intercorrelations are zero, the last term under the radical drops out, thus eliminating one unknown. Having made this assumption, we have several ways of estimating the relative values of the σ's for different stimuli which can be used in the equation to solve for $R_b - R_a$ or any other separation. If we assume that the discriminal dispersions are all equal and that all r's are equal, the standard deviations of the differences become equal for all pairs. We could then substitute the value of 1 or 10 or any number we chose for the radical term in equation (2.7), and there is left only one value z_{ba} which is derivable from the experimentally obtained proportions.

There have been no direct experimental checks made of the validity of the law of comparative judgment. The necessary experimental conditions, giving data from which we could compute σ_a, σ_b, and r_{ab} as well as z_{ba}, should not be difficult to achieve. For the most part, we have had to be satisfied with indirect evidence of the kind that will be pointed out in Chap. 7.

Fechner's Law. Fechner's law is usually stated

$$R = C \log S \qquad (2.8)$$

where S is measured in multiples of the absolute-threshold stimulus. The reason for using S_0 as the unit will soon become apparent. Figure 2.9 shows this relationship graphically. From the selected stimulus values and their corresponding response values, it is clearly shown that as R increases in equal steps, S increases in ratio steps. The ratios $S_2/S_1 = S_3/S_2 = S_4/S_3$, etc., correspond to equal increments in R.

The Derivation of Fechner's Law from Weber's Law. Starting with the equation for Weber's law, $\Delta S/S = K$, where ΔS is a small stimulus increment, Fechner assumed that all corresponding small increments in R are psychologically equal. Let ΔS decrease in size and ΔR decrease correspondingly with it. Let these decreasing values be called δS and δR, respectively, and assume with Fechner that

$$\delta R = c\frac{\delta S}{S} = K$$

where c is the constant of proportionality between δR and $\delta S/S$. This equation is known as Fechner's *fundamental formula*. The student may recognize it as a differential equation. Since all the R increments are equal, δR may be used as the unit of the sensory scale and any R value is the sum of all the δR units from zero up to that particular R value. To summate all the

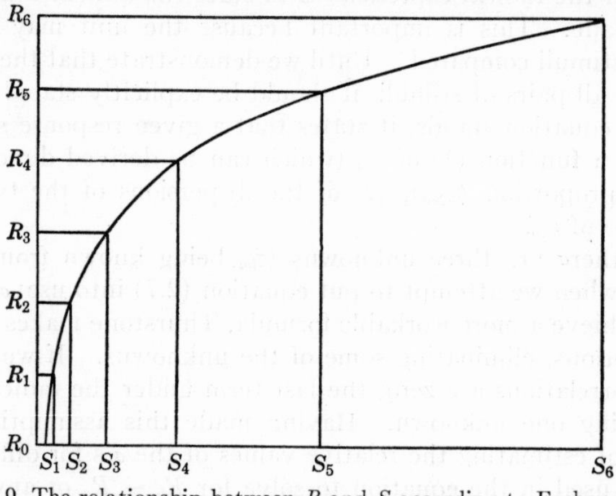

FIG. 2.9. The relationship between R and S according to Fechner's law.

δR values means to integrate the above equation. The result of the integration is

$$R = c \log_e S + A \tag{2.9}$$

where A = the constant of integration and e = the base of natural logarithms.[1]

In order to find the value of A in terms of S values, we may make the following substitutions: Let S_0 be the value of S when $R = 0$, S_0 being the absolute threshold. Substituting these values ($R = 0$ and $S = S_0$) in equation (2.9),

$$0 = c \log_e S_0 + A$$

from which, by transposing,

$$A = -c \log_e S_0 \tag{2.10}$$

The complete formula, substituting (2.10) in (2.9), then becomes

$$R = c \log_e S - c \log_e S_0 = c(\log_e S - \log_e S_0)$$

or

$$R = c \log_e \frac{S}{S_0} \tag{2.11}$$

[1] Logarithms, natural or otherwise, are explained in Chap. 3.

The ratio of S to S_0 is what calls for measuring each stimulus in terms of S_0 as the S unit when applying Fechner's law.

In order to use common logarithms instead of the natural logarithms, we need to change the symbol c to some other, for example C, where C is a multiple of c. Equation (2.11) thus transformed reads

$$R = C \log \frac{S}{S_0} \tag{2.12}$$

Since we do not always know the value of S_0, when we make experimental tests of Fechner's law, we can write the equation in the form

$$R = C \log S + a \tag{2.13}$$

where the constant $a = -C \log S_0$. Knowing C and a from a least-square fit of the linear function relating R to $\log S$, we can compute $\log S_0$ and consequently estimate S_0, the absolute limen.

The experimental verification of Fechner's law depends upon scaling a series of stimuli for psychological values R, then fitting the data relating R to $\log S$ by the method of least squares (see Chap. 3). The test of goodness of fit will indicate whether the law fits the data sufficiently closely. A rough or preliminary test is to plot R against $\log S$. This test can be made on semilog paper without finding $\log S$ for each stimulus. By inspection we can usually tell whether the regression is linear.

Discrepancies between the Weber and Fechner Laws. Although Fechner derived his law, as we have seen, from Weber's law, the two do not always apply together, as Thurstone has shown (25, p. 382). For one thing, note that the experimental test of each law is conducted by different operations. For Weber's law, we need to determine whether small changes in S that are psychologically equal by some criterion, such as being equally often noticed, are equal percentagewise; in other words whether the ratio $\Delta S/S$ is constant. The test of Fechner's law is made with supraliminal differences and with psychologically scaled values derived differently than ΔS.

Only when the discriminal dispersions of different stimuli along the S scale are equal will the two laws be related as Fechner assumed them to be. Fechner's law is not affected by the sizes of the dispersions, whereas Weber's law is. In testing Fechner's law, we are concerned only with the central tendencies of the discriminal processes for stimuli. It is they we relate to S. In testing Weber's law, the size of ΔS is directly dependent upon the spread of the discriminal processes. If the dispersions for stimuli are not equal, the ΔR intervals that yield equal proportions of judgments are not equal. Thus, when dispersions on R are not equal, we cannot say that "equally often noticed differences are equal, unless always or never noticed," which is a well-known generalization known as the Fullerton-Cattell principle (6). When the Fullerton-Cattell principle applies, Weber's and Fechner's laws will be found verified together or not verified together. It is improper to speak of the Weber-Fechner law except when the Fullerton-Cattell principle holds.

Some Alternatives to the Weber and Fechner Laws. Since the Weber and Fechner laws have been found to have limited applications, it is necessary to improve the situation in one way or another. Fechner's logarithmic law, or some other relationship in which R is a negatively accelerated function of S, seems to express the R-S relationship fairly well. At least there is a common practice of expressing stimulus values on a log S scale. The decibel scale for sound intensities is a logarithmic transformation that serves very well in spite of the fact that Fechner's law does not apply exactly, as Stevens has shown (22, 24). Occasionally the logarithmic relationship is demonstrated in new and unexpected ways. For example, Luckiesh and Moss (17) have shown that within certain limits both nervous tension during reading, as measured by finger pressure, and change in rate of involuntary blinking diminish in linear relationship to log S.

There have been three general approaches to meet the fact that these traditional psychophysical laws do not apply in the particular instance. One reaction is to attempt to explain why they do not apply, taking into account certain disturbing influences unique to the situation. A second reaction has been an attempt to find general substitute laws with wider ranges of application. A third reaction has been to forgo the idea of universally applicable laws and to seek some special mathematical relation that describes the particular case.

Some Reasons Why the Laws Do Not Apply. We have already encountered Thurstone's suggestion that the Weber law may not apply because discriminal dispersions for stimuli vary. There is also the possible influence of the correlation term in the law of comparative judgment on the sizes of measured DL's.

Bartlett attributes the increase in $\Delta S/S$ as we approach the extreme values of S to the fact that away from the middle range of S values with which we have had most experience there are increasing constant errors which inflate ΔS (1). Whether this is a matter of systematic distortions in R, as related to S, or in J, as related to R, is not clear. Householder and Young believe that Weber's law will hold if a proper transformation is applied to the S values (13). Since the departures of $\Delta S/S$ from a constant are systematically related to S, this suggestion should be effective, but the type of transformation would probably have to be cut to fit each situation. Fechner thought that the breakdown of Weber's law at the lower stimulus levels is due to the fact that the stimulus is added to already prevailing stimulation. In lifting weights, for example, the arm must be lifted. In visual stimulation there is a base of ideoretinal stimulation. Other suggestions have pointed out changes in the functioning of sensory mechanisms as stimulus levels change, for example, the shift from rod to cone vision at some lower level of stimulation.

Some Substitute General Psychophysical Laws. Fullerton and Cattell (6) found that the relation of ΔS to S could be expressed by the equation

$$\Delta S = M\sqrt{S} \tag{2.14}$$

where M = a constant, better than by the Weber law. The operation by which they obtained a measure of ΔS was different from that usually employed. They asked O to reproduce a given standard stimulus N times; then they computed the probable error of the distribution of reproductions. This measures the size of average dispersion on the S scale, which parallels a similar measure of dispersion of the discriminal processes on the R scale If Weber's law is satisfied, the ratio of the probable error to the mean of the distribution should be a constant. Taking the probable error as the measure of errors of observation, the Fullerton-Cattell square-root law states that the average error of observation increases in proportion to the square root of the stimulus.

Fullerton and Cattell and others have found that most data lie somewhere between their square-root function and Weber's linear function. Woodworth believed that the answer to this was to be found in the correlation between errors of observation (27). If we may regard larger stimulus quantities as being made up of sums of smaller stimulus quantities, we can also think of the errors of observation in the components as summing to produce the errors in observing the total. If the correlations between errors for the components are perfect and positive, Weber's law is satisfied. If the correlations between errors are zero, the Fullerton-Cattell law is satisfied. With positive correlations between .0 and +1.0, the data will fall somewhere between the two functions.

The writer has elsewhere found reasons to doubt the validity of Woodworth's law (8) and has proposed in its place an nth-power law. Note that the Fullerton-Cattell law may be written

$$\Delta S = MS^{1/2}$$

This gives S a power or exponent of $\frac{1}{2}$. In the Weber equation the power of S is 1.0. To take care of data between these two functions let the power of S vary as needed to fit the data. We then have the general equation

$$\Delta S = kS^n \tag{2.15}$$

where n may be expected to vary between .5 and 1.0, but could possibly go outside that range. This type of equation, in which n is computed from the data, has been shown to fit data from judgments of lengths of lines and sound intensities (8, 14) and from judgments of muscular tension (5).

If equation (2.15) is integrated, we arrive at a form of law parallel to Fechner's, expressed by the equation

$$R = JS^{1-n} + B \tag{2.16}$$

where n is the same constant as in (2.15). We shall see that this type of equation applies very well to lifted-weight data used for illustrations in Chap. 9.

Spiegelman and Reiner (21) take a cue from the concept of "steady states" in the field of biology and come out with a complicated equation that takes into account the fact that the ratio $\Delta S/S$ is a function of the stimulus, not a constant.

Some Special Substitutes for Weber's Law. Although the nth-power law has a much improved chance of fitting data over wide ranges, there are still some limitations at the extremes of the S scale and some situations in which it will not fit well even in the moderate ranges. A few special laws have been proposed from time to time by investigators to describe data in certain situations. Among these may be mentioned the law of Macdonald and Robertson (18), which seemed to fit data from both sound and tactual stimuli, and the laws of Hecht (11) and of Cobb (3), who were dealing with visual problems.

REFERENCES

1. BARTLETT, R. J. Measurement in psychology. *Advancement of Sci.*, 1939, 1–20.
2. BORING, E. G. The logic of the normal law of error in mental measurement. *Amer. J. Psychol.*, 1920, **31,** 1–33.
3. COBB, F. W. Weber's law and the Fechnerian muddle. *Psychol. Rev.*, 1932, **39,** 533–551.
4. FECHNER, G. T. *Elemente der Psychophysik* (reprint). Leipzig: Breitkopf und Härtel, 1889.
5. FITTS, P. M. *Psychological Research on Equipment Design. Army Air Forces Aviation Psychology Program Research Reports*, No. 19. Washington, D.C.: Government Printing Office, 1947.
6. FULLERTON, G. S., and CATTELL, J. MCK. On the perception of small differences. *Publ. Univ. Penn., Phil. Series,* No. 2, 1892.
7. GRAHAM, C. H. Behavior, perception and the psychophysical methods. *Psychol. Rev.*, 1950, **57,** 108–118.
8. GUILFORD, J. P. A generalized psychophysical law. *Psychol. Rev.*, 1932, **39,** 73–85.
9. ———. A study in psychodynamics. *Psychometrika*, 1939, **4,** 1–23.
10. GULLIKSEN, H. Paired comparisons and the logic of measurement. *Psychol. Rev.*, 1946, **53,** 199–213.
11. HECHT, S. A theory of visual intensity discrimination. *J. gen. Physiol.*, 1935, **18,** 767–789.
12. HELSON, H. (ed.). *Theoretical Foundations of Psychology.* New York: Van Nostrand, 1951.
13. HOUSEHOLDER, A. S., and YOUNG, G. Weber laws, the Weber law, and psychophysical analysis. *Psychometrika*, 1940, **5,** 183–193.
14. HOVLAND, C. I. A note on Guilford's generalized psychophysical law. *Psychol. Rev.*, 1938, **45,** 430–434.
15. KLEMM, O. *A History of Psychology* (trans.). New York: Scribner, 1914.
16. LICKLIDER, J. C. R., in Stevens, S. S. *Handbook of Experimental Psychology.* New York: Wiley, 1951.
17. LUCKIESH, M., and MOSS, F. K. A restricted extension of Fechner's law from sensation to behavior. *Psychol. Rev.*, 1942, **49,** 135–141.
18. MACDONALD, P. A., and ROBERTSON, E. M. The psychophysical law. *Phil. Mag.*, 1930, **10,** 1063–1073.
19. MOSIER, C. I. Psychophysics and mental test theory: Fundamental postulates and elementary theorems. *Psychol. Rev.*, 1940, **47,** 355–366.
20. ———. Psychophysics and mental test theory: The constant process. *Psychol. Rev.*, 1941, **48,** 235–249.
21. SPIEGELMAN, S., and REINER, J. M. A note on steady states and the Weber-Fechner law. *Psychometrika*, 1945, **10,** 27–35.
22. STEVENS, S. S. A scale for the measurement of a psychological magnitude: loudness. *Psychol. Rev.*, 1936, **43,** 405–416.
23. ———. *Handbook of Experimental Psychology.* New York: Wiley, 1951.
24. ——— and VOLKMANN, J. The relation of pitch to frequency: a revised scale. *Amer. J. Psychol.*, 1940, **53,** 329–353.
25. THURSTONE, L. L. Psychophysical analysis. *Amer. J. Psychol.*, 1927, **38,** 368–389.
26. ———. A law of comparative judgment. *Psychol. Rev.*, 1927, **34,** 273–286.
27. WOODWORTH, R. S. Professor Cattell's psychophysical contributions. *Arch. Psychol.*, N.Y. 1914, **4,** No. 30, 60–74.
28. ———. *Experimental Psychology.* New York: Holt, 1938.

CHAPTER 3

A MATHEMATICAL INTRODUCTION

The Psychologist's Need for Mathematics. The psychology student today is well aware that the training of a psychologist almost always includes one or more courses on applied statistics. The need of the research psychologist for at least a moderate mastery of the ordinary statistical operations is well recognized. It is unfortunate that there is not a similar recognition of the need for a fair background of mathematical training. As psychology, or any social science, becomes more mature, it grows more quantitative. Mathematical models are more commonly applied and mathematical operations enter more into the daily routine.

Speaking in 1949 in a symposium on the subject of quantitative training for research in social sciences, Gulliksen (8) expressed what would seem to be a realistic goal. He clearly had the research psychologist in mind when he mentioned the kind of training needed. The basic mathematical training, he said, should include courses on the differential and integral calculus, differential equations, and elementary matrix theory.

Unfortunately, numerous students still come to advanced courses in psychology without much of this mathematical background; in fact, some have had only algebra which they have largely forgotten. It is for this reason that the present chapter has been included, with the hope that it will not long be needed. It does contain some material, such as that on curve fitting, however, that is not often treated in the mathematics courses mentioned.

Mathematical Background Needed for this Volume. This chapter does not attempt to make up for all deficiencies in mathematical training. It treats only those aspects that come into use somewhere in the other chapters. It attempts to renew the student's acquaintance with mathematical functions, both linear and nonlinear, and with exponents and logarithms. It demonstrates processes of curve fitting, with both linear and curvilinear functions and methods of testing for goodness of fit. It discusses the elements of probability and touches upon the subject of distribution functions. Some introductory material on matrix theory and on some operations in matrix algebra has been postponed to the chapter on factor analysis where it is needed. This volume presupposes one or two courses in elementary statistics and avoids reintroduction to basic statistical ideas. It does introduce many new applications of statistics at various places where needed.

Mathematical Functions

The Meaning of a Mathematical Function. Like most of the sciences, psychology is perpetually seeking to find laws that state in a simple way the manner in which one variable depends upon another. For example, how does memory ability of the individual depend upon age? In the general law of retention, how does the percentage retained depend upon the time elapsed since practice ceased? In the well-known Weber law, how does the just noticeable increment of a stimulus depend upon the magnitude of that stimulus? As we alter the exposure time of a color stimulus, how will the duration of the negative afterimage vary? How does the ability in any mental test vary with increasing age of those tested?

In all these examples one variable depends upon another. As one variable increases or decreases, there is a corresponding change in the other. One of them we call the *independent variable* and the other the *dependent variable*. In the last example, age is the independent variable. Choose any age you wish, and if the mathematical relationship between age and the score in a mental test is known, you can predict the most probable score. The score, in other words, depends upon the age that you arbitrarily choose. We could, of course, turn the variables around and predict the age of an individual from his test score. In this case we have made the test score the independent variable and age the dependent variable.

Ordinarily we assign the symbol Y to the dependent variable and the symbol X to the independent variable. For example, we say that the circumference of a circle is a function of its diameter. If we call the circumference Y and the diameter X, we can set up the equation $Y = 3.1416X$. No matter what value we assign to X, we can find a corresponding value for Y by using this equation. And if we were to locate for every pair of values of X and Y a point on coordinate paper, the series of points would lie in a straight line. We would say that the function is linear in form.

Linear Functions. It is important for the student to grasp the meaning of functions, whether they appear in the form of an equation or whether they appear plotted in graphic form. With a little practice and close observation one can learn to picture to oneself a graphic representation of a function when the equation is given, or to guess the type of equation when the graph alone is given.

In Fig. 3.1 a number of linear equations are plotted. Line A, for example, represents the equation $Y = .5X$. From the equation it can readily be seen that when X equals zero, Y also equals zero. The line therefore passes through the *origin*. When X equals 1, Y equals .5; when X equals 2, Y equals 1; and so on. For every gain of one unit in X there is a gain of only a half unit in Y. The coefficient of X, namely, .5, determines the slope of the line. This coefficient tells us how rapidly Y is increasing as compared with X. In this equation Y is gaining only half as fast as X.

The slope of a line that passes through the origin can be found, roughly, from the coordinate system in which it is plotted, by using the following procedure: Select any point far out along the line, such as the point m in Fig. 3.1, line A. Note both the X value and the Y value of that point. The slope of the line is equal to the Y value of this point divided by its X value, or $6/12$, which is .5. To come back to the equation for this line, $Y = .5X$; if we divide both sides of the equation by X, the result is $Y/X = .5$. Thus it can be seen that any Y value divided by its corresponding X value gives the slope of the line. This is true only when the line passes through the origin.

Now notice line D with its equation $Y = 2X$. In this function Y is increasing two times as rapidly as X. The slope of the line is 2, which can be verified by taking a point such as n where $Y/X = {}^{10}\!/_5 = 2$. The steeper the line, the greater the slope. The slope of lines that slant upward to the right, *i.e.*, have positive slope, may vary all the way from zero, when the line is horizontal, or parallel with the X axis, to plus infinity when the line is perpendicular to the X axis. Similarly, lines that slant downward to the right may vary in slope from zero through negative values to minus infinity.

Now notice line E with its equation $Y = -.5X$. Here the slope of the line is negative. As X gains, Y loses, and vice versa. As in line A, Y changes

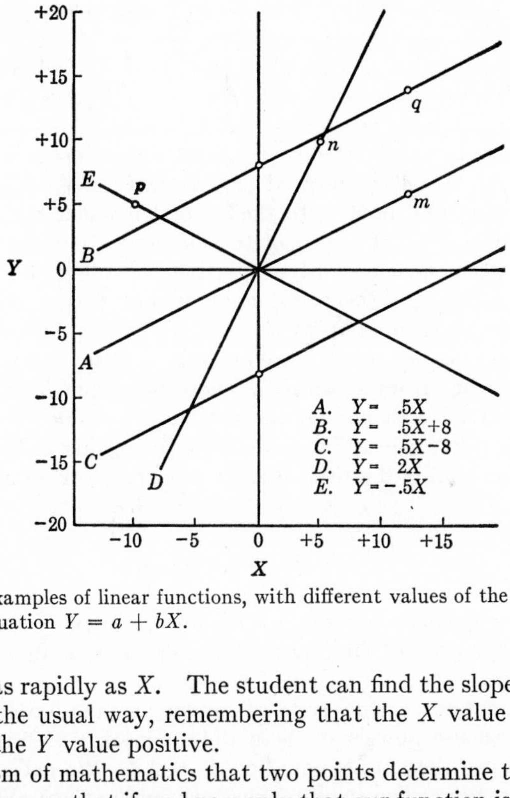

FIG. 3.1. Some examples of linear functions, with different values of the constants a and b in the general equation $Y = a + bX$.

only one-half as rapidly as X. The student can find the slope by making use of point p in the usual way, remembering that the X value of this point is negative and the Y value positive.

It is an axiom of mathematics that two points determine the position of a line. It can be seen that if we knew only that our function is linear and that it passes through the two points (0,0) and (12,6), we have the complete function plotted by drawing a straight line through those two points. Let us suppose, to take a simple example, that we knew that the scores in a certain mental test increased with age in the form of a straight line. We know also that the average six-year-old makes a score of 3 and that the average fourteen-year-old makes a score of 7. Knowing only these three facts, the nature of the function and the two necessary points for drawing the line, we are ready to predict the most probable score for any age between six and fourteen. This is one of the great conveniences of a mathematical function. It enables us to interpolate or to predict a host of additional values from the measurement of only a few.

The student should note that the statement about prediction applied only to the ages between six and fourteen. To predict beyond those limits is always a risky procedure unless one knows beforehand that the same mathematical function applies beyond those values. It should also be noticed that it is the *most probable score* that is predicted. This qualification is necessary because, in psychology especially, no two variables are so perfectly measured or so perfectly isolated that we can expect exact predictions. There is always a margin of error in our predictions owing to the imperfect correlation of the two variables concerned.

To return to Fig. 3.1, let us notice line B. The equation is

$$Y = .5X + 8$$

The slope of this line is .5, and it is obviously parallel to line A, which has the same slope. The only reason that it is so much higher in the plane than line A is that there is +8 in the equation. This additional constant is known as the *Y intercept*. It will be noticed that line B intercepts the Y axis at the value $Y = 8$. We may now state the general formula for a straight line: $Y = a + bX$, where b is the slope of the line and a is the Y intercept. It will be seen that the equation for line C in Fig. 3.1 follows that rule. Whenever a line passes through the origin, a equals zero; thus it is simply omitted entirely, as in the equation $Y = .5X$.

A slight change will now have to be made in the rule given above for reading the slope of a line from a diagram. Point q on line B in Fig. 3.1 has an X value of 12 and a Y value of 14, and yet the slope is not $^{14}\!/_{12}$. The slope is no longer Y/X, but $(Y - a)/X$. For the proof of this, consider the general equation, $Y = a + bX$. Transposing, we have $bX = Y - a$. Dividing by X, we have

$$b = \frac{Y - a}{X}$$

which gives us the general formula for finding the slope of a line. The constant a can always be read directly from the figure by finding where the line crosses the Y axis.

Nonlinear Functions. One type of nonlinear function illustrates what happens when we use powers of X in the equation. In Fig. 3.2 note the result when we use the simple equation $Y = X^2$. We get a *parabola* with two curved branches. The two branches are symmetrical about the Y axis, the one being a mirror reflection of the other. The reason is simple. It does not matter whether X is positive or negative; X^2 is always positive. If X is either plus or minus 2, Y is 4; if X is plus or minus 3, Y is 9, and so on. Curve B with the equation $Y = X^2 + 5$ is a duplicate of curve A, except that all points are raised by the constant amount 5. As in the linear equations, the constant here is the Y intercept. The slope of these curves can be altered by changing the coefficient of X^2. In equations A and B, the coefficient of X^2 was really 1, although this needed no mention in writing the equation. When the coefficient of X^2 is .2, as in curve C, the slope of the two branches is considerably reduced. By making the coefficient of X^2 smaller and smaller, we could make a whole family of parabolas, each one flatter than the one before.

Curve *D* shows what happens when the coefficient of X^2 is made negative and when the *Y* intercept is also negative. The slope is of the same degree of flatness as for curve *C*, but the branches extend in the downward direction, just the reverse of curve *C*.

The sample equations given for parabolas are actually special cases. The general equation of the second degree (no power higher than 2) is of the form $Y = a + bX + cX^2$. In the illustrative equations given, coefficient *b* has been zero. Its effect when not zero is merely to modify the shape of the branches of the curve. There are also equations of this type with higher powers included. Parabolas have not found much use as yet in psychological research.

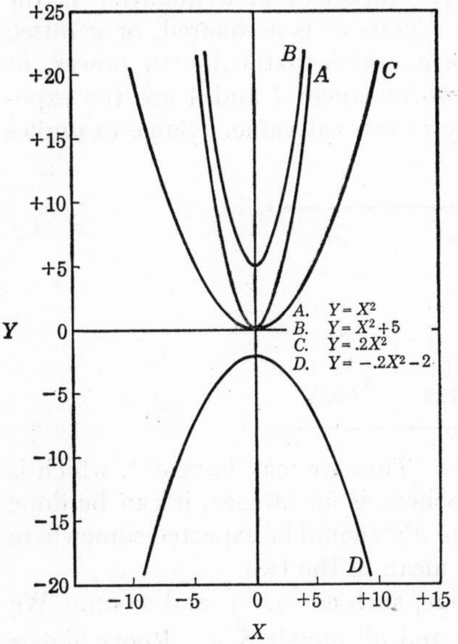

FIG. 3.2. Graphic illustrations of parabolas.

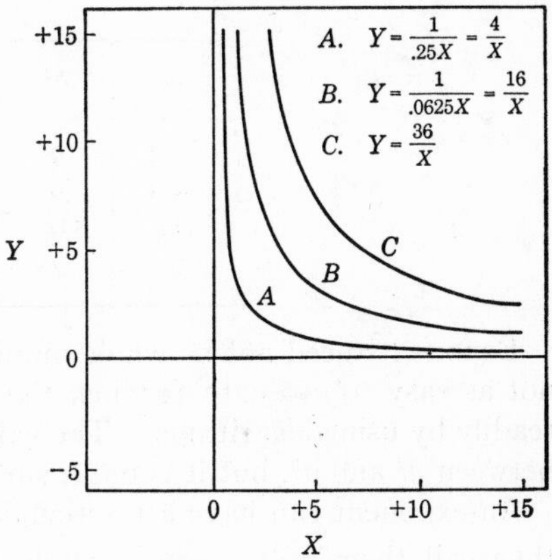

FIG. 3.3. Examples of simple hyperbolas.

Another common nonlinear function is the *hyperbola*. This has an equation of the general type

$$Y = \frac{1}{a + bX}$$

In this equation, if *b* is positive, *Y* is inversely related to *X*, and if *b* is negative, *Y* is directly related to *X*. This can be more easily seen if we take reciprocals of both sides of the equation and it reads $1/Y = a + bX$. Now we see that it is the reciprocal of *Y* that has a linear relationship to *X*.

Figure 3.3 shows some examples of simple hyperbolas in all of which $a = 0$ and in which *b* varies. In this simple form it can be seen that since $Y = 1/bX$, multiplying both sides of the equation by *X* we obtain $XY = 1/b$. In other words, the product *XY* is a constant, and that constant is the reciprocal of *b*.

Examination of the plots in Fig. 3.3 shows that the two branches of the curve approach the *X* and *Y* axes as *asymptotes* (limits to which they tend to become eventually parallel). It will be noticed that as b becomes smaller the whole curve comes closer to the axes. Actually, there are three other hyperbolas corresponding to these shown. These are for *negative* values of X. When X is negative, with b positive, Y also takes on negative values. As parameter a takes on nonzero values, it modifies the symmetry of the curve and establishes other X and Y values (other than zero) to which the branches become asymptotic.

Before going into other types of nonlinear functions we need to do some reviewing of the subjects of exponents and logarithms. Logarithmic and exponential functions are much more commonly used in quantitative psychology than the simple parabola and hyperbola just mentioned.

Some Operations with Exponents. An exponent of a quantity is the power to which that quantity is raised. Thus a^2 is a squared, or a raised to the power 2, or $a \times a$. Thus a^4 is a raised to the fourth power, or $a \times a \times a \times a$, and so on. In these two instances 2 and 4 are the exponents of a, where a can have almost any numerical value. Some examples are given in the following table:

a	a^2	a^3	a^4
3	9	27	81
−3	9	−27	81
⅓	⅑	1/27	1/81
.5	.25	.125	.0625

Exponents need not be whole numbers. Thus we may have $a^{2.5}$, which is not as easy to evaluate as when the exponent is an integer; it can be done readily by using logarithms. The value of $a^{2.5}$ should be expected somewhere between a^2 and a^3, but it is not a simple mean of the two.

An exponent can have a fractional value, such as ½, ¼, and so on. We then call them roots, for $a^{1/2}$ equals $\sqrt{a}$ and $a^{1/4}$ equals $\sqrt[4]{a}$. Roots higher than 3 or 4 are best evaluated by using logarithms.

An exponent can have a negative value. Thus we may have a^{-3} and a^{-5}. These are equivalent to saying $1/a^3$ and $1/a^5$. This operation works in reverse, for a^3 and a^5 may be written as $1/a^{-3}$ and $1/a^{-5}$. We usually get exponents into positive values by using reciprocals when it is necessary to evaluate quantities.

An exponent may be zero. By convention it is agreed that any number to the power zero equals unity. Thus $a^0 = 10^0 = 1.0$. This can be readily proved by taking the following steps:

$$1 = \frac{a^n}{a^n} = a^{n-n} = a^0$$

This proof will be clearer after reading the next paragraph.

Arithmetical Operations with Exponents. We very commonly apply the fundamental operations of addition, subtraction, multiplication, and division to exponents. The principal rules are as follows:

1. Addition: $(x^m)(x^n) = x^{m+n}$
   Thus $(2^3)(2^4) = 2^7$
   $(2^{-2})(2^5) = 2^3$
   $(4^{.5})(4^{2.5}) = 4^3$
2. Subtraction: $\frac{x^m}{x^n} = x^{(m-n)}$
   Thus $\frac{2^6}{2^4} = 2^2$
   $\frac{2^3}{2^{-2}} = 2^5$
   $\frac{2^{2.5}}{2^{.5}} = 2^2$
3. Multiplication: $(x^m)^n = x^{mn}$
   Thus $(2^3)^2 = 2^6$
   $(2^{-2})^3 = 2^{-6}$
   $(2^{1.5})^3 = 2^{4.5}$
4. Division: $\sqrt[n]{x^m} = x^{\frac{m}{n}}$
   Thus $\sqrt[2]{2^4} = 2^2$
   $\sqrt[3]{2^5} = 2^{5/3}$

Besides these fundamental operations, there are one or two others that should be mentioned because of their utility. They have to do with combining operations. A product of two quantities each with the same exponent can be written either as $(xy)^m$ or as $x^m y^m$. The one implies multiplication first and then raising to power m, and the other implies raising to power m first and then multiplying. The same choice of order may be made in combining the operations of division and taking powers, for example, $(x/y)^m = x^m/y^m$. Since roots are essentially powers, the same choices may be made with respect to roots. Thus $\sqrt{x} \times \sqrt{y} = \sqrt{xy}$, and $\sqrt{x}/\sqrt{y} = \sqrt{x/y}$.

Logarithms. It is possible to express one number as another number raised to the appropriate power. Thus the number 8 can be expressed as 2^3, or 2 raised to the power 3. It is easy to see this when the one number is an integral power of the other. Remembering that we may have fractional exponents, the way is opened for us to express any rational number as any other number raised to the power given by an appropriate exponent. Because of certain very useful operations that exponents make possible to us, it is convenient for many purposes to transform numbers into certain common values (bases) raised to appropriate exponents. The "common" bases adopted by convention because of certain useful properties have been the number 2, the quantity known as e, which has the approximate value of 2.71828, and the number 10. These three have become the base numbers for three systems of logarithms. The base 10 is used in the *common* system of logarithms. The base e is used in the *natural*, or *Napierian*, system. The common system is used most in practice.[1] The Napierian system has properties that make it more useful in mathematical equations.

A logarithm is an exponent. The logarithm of Y to the base 10 is the

[1] We often see the base designated, as in the expressions $\log_2 15$, $\log_e 15$, and $\log_{10} 15$. Without a specified base, *e.g.*, log 15, we understand that the base is 10.

exponent of 10 needed to make 10^X equal Y. In other words,

$$\text{If } Y = 10^X,\ X = \log Y$$

Here the logarithm of Y is X. We also say that Y is the antilog of X. This goes in reverse; from the exponent X, of 10, to the number that equals 10^X.

Let us take a few simple examples of logarithms where the numbers are multiples of 10 and therefore the exponents of 10 (logarithms) are integers (see Table 3.1). Several principles can be seen in this short table. First, we have the numbers, Y, forming a geometric progression. Each number is 10 times the number immediately below it. A geometric series is formed when there is a constant *ratio* between successive numbers; the ratio need not be 10. The list of corresponding logarithms composes an arithmetic series. Each logarithm is one unit greater than the one below it. Thus, an arithmetic mean of logarithms corresponds to a geometric mean of their corresponding numbers (antilogs). The geometric mean of 10 and 1,000 is equal to $\sqrt{10 \times 1{,}000} = \sqrt{10{,}000} = 100$. The arithmetic mean of the logarithms of 10 and 1,000 (those logarithms being 1 and 3) is 2. The antilog of 2 is 100, which checks with the geometric mean.

A second thing to notice is that the logarithms are given not as integers but have four decimal places. This is because most numbers are not simple multiples of 10 and hence their logarithms are rounded decimal fractions. The logarithm of 5, for example, is 0.6990 to four decimal places. We should have expected it to be between 0.0000 and 1.0000. For the great majority

TABLE 3.1. SOME SIMPLE EXAMPLES OF NUMBERS AND THEIR LOGARITHMS

The number Y	Equivalent value in terms of 10^X	Logarithm X
1,000	10^3	3.0000
100	10^2	2.0000
10	10^1	1.0000
1	10^0	0.0000
.1	10^{-1}	$\bar{1}.0000$
.01	10^{-2}	$\bar{2}.0000$
.001	10^{-3}	$\bar{3}.0000$

of numbers the last four digits will not be zeros. Some tables of logarithms, as Table *K* in the Appendix, provide four decimal places and some provide five or more. Four-place tables do for most practical purposes.

The logarithm of 50 is 1.6990; that for 500 is 2.6990; that for 5000 is 3.6990, and so on. Notice that for the same basic or nonzero part of the number, namely 5, in this case, the four digits to the right of the decimal point in the logarithm are identical. The part of the logarithm to the right of the decimal point is known as the *mantissa*. It is the only part of the logarithm that you will find in the tables. The part to the left of the decimal point is called the *characteristic*. It never appears in the tables but must be determined on the basis of the number itself. The way in which this is done is clearest in Table 3.1. When the exponent of 10 is positive, the number being 1.0 or greater, the characteristic is one less than the number of digits that the number has to the left of the decimal point. When the number is less than 1.0, the characteristic is negative and is one more than the number of zeros between the decimal point and the first nonzero digit. Reference to Table 3.1 will bear out both of these rules. Even when the characteristic is negative, the mantissa depends entirely on what digits are in the number and is a positive value. The logarithm of .5 is $\bar{1}.6990$; that for .05 is $\bar{2}.6990$; and that for .005 is $\bar{3}.6990$. In this form the characteristic is negative and the mantissa is positive. We must treat them as two separate numbers. That is why the negative sign is placed above the characteristic and not in front of it. When we want to use such a logarithm as a single number by way of adding, etc., we have to make some adjustments that will be explained. First, we shall see what numerical operations may be performed with logarithms.

Numerical Operations with Logarithms. The operations with logarithms are similar to those with exponents in general mentioned above. The main difference is that we transform numbers to exponents of 10 first, perform the operations, and then transform back to antilogs. The operations can be described in a few simple equations.

$$\log ab = \log a + \log b$$

$$\log \frac{a}{b} = \log a - \log b$$

$$\log a^n = n \log a$$

$$\log \sqrt[n]{a} = \frac{\log a}{n}$$

We might generalize these operations by saying that corresponding to the multiplication and division of numbers we add and subtract their logarithms. Corresponding to the assigning of a power (or root) to a number we have the multiplying (dividing) of the logarithm by that power (root). Numbers can be multiplied by finding their logarithms and adding them and then finding the antilog of the sum. The simplified value of 2^{15} can be found by multiplying the log of 2 by 15 and then finding the antilog. The fifth root of 15 could be found by dividing its log by 5 and then determining the antilog of the result. The only limitation is in having a table of logarithms sufficiently refined to evaluate antilogs to enough significant digits.

Negative Logarithms. We now come back to the question of how to operate with logarithms parts or all of which are negative. This happens when we find logarithms of very small numbers or when in subtracting logarithms we end up with a negative value. The chief trouble arises because logarithmic tables include only positive mantissas.

If we want to find the fourth power of .5, we multiply its logarithm by 4. The logarithm from the tables is $\bar{1}.6990$, part of which is negative and part positive. Before multiplying this logarithm by something, or dividing it by something, it is best to reduce it to a single number with one algebraic sign. Summing the two parts, we obtain $-.3010$. Multiplying this by 4, we obtain -1.2040. Before we can find the antilog of this, we have to remember that the mantissa of it is negative; we must convert to an appropriate positive mantissa. We can do this by adding 1 to the mantissa and subtracting a like amount from the characteristic. Add 1.0000 to $-.2040$ and we have $+.7960$. Subtract 1 from the characteristic and we have $-1 - 1 = -2$. The new form of the logarithm reads: $\bar{2}.7960$. The antilog of this is .0625, which is the fourth power of .5.

In adding and subtracting negative logarithms, another type of solution is commonly used. Suppose we want to find the product of $.005 \times 150$ by means of logarithms. log .005 is $\bar{3}.6990$ and log 150 is 2.1761. Before summing a logarithm like $\bar{3}.6990$, we add 10 to the characteristic and take it away from the whole logarithm and then perform the addition thus:

$$\begin{array}{l} 7.6990 - 10 \\ 2.1761 \\ \hline 9.8751 - 10 \end{array}$$

After performing the addition (the same procedure would apply to a subtraction), we reverse the operation with 10, adding 10 to the entire logarithm and deducting it from the characteristic. We thus obtain $\bar{1}.8751$, the antilog of which is .750.

Some Logarithmic and Exponential Functions. We are now ready to consider a few typical logarithmic and exponential functions. Logarithmic functions involve logarithms of either X or Y, or both. In exponential functions, X appears as an exponent or as part of an exponent. We shall consider four general types in these two areas.

Y as a Function of log X. The first type has a general equation of the form

$$Y = a + b \log X \tag{3.1}$$

If we let $a = 0$, we have the class of equations into which Fechner's law falls. If we let $b = 1.0$, we have the simple relationship between a number and its logarithm with which we have been dealing in the preceding section. Figure 3.4 I shows three examples of functions coming under this general type. There we have let $a = 0$, but b is in turn 4, 2, and 1. The only effect of the coefficient b is, in effect, to magnify the vertical scale and thus increase the apparent curvature. All such curves are asymptotic to the Y axis and when $a = 0$ they pass through the point (1,0), since $\log 1 = 0$. The effect of the coefficient a is merely to raise and lower one of these curves as a whole.

Generalized Parabolas and Hyperbolas. The second type has the general equation of the form

$$Y = a + bX^n \tag{3.2}$$

Here Y is a function of X to some power n. When n is equal to 1.0, this equation reduces to linear form, for X to the power 1.0 is X. When n is greater than 0, the function is parabolic. In demonstrating the parabola in Fig. 3.2, the power of X was 2. Now it can be seen that this is a very special case. The exponent can be any value we choose. Two curves in Fig. 3.4 II are clearly parabolic, with n equal to 1.5 and 0.5, respectively.[1] We have only the positive branches, of course. When n is greater than 1.0,

[1] For simple examples here it is assumed that $a = 0$. The effect of a is simply to raise and lower entire curves.

the branches are symmetrical about the Y axis. When n is less than 1.0, they are symmetrical about the X axis. With n negative, we have a hyperbola, as in Fig. 3.4 II. The reason for this is that when the exponent is negative the effect is to give us a reciprocal of X, $1/X$, where X has the same exponent with positive sign. When Y and X have a reciprocal relationship, the function is hyperbolic.

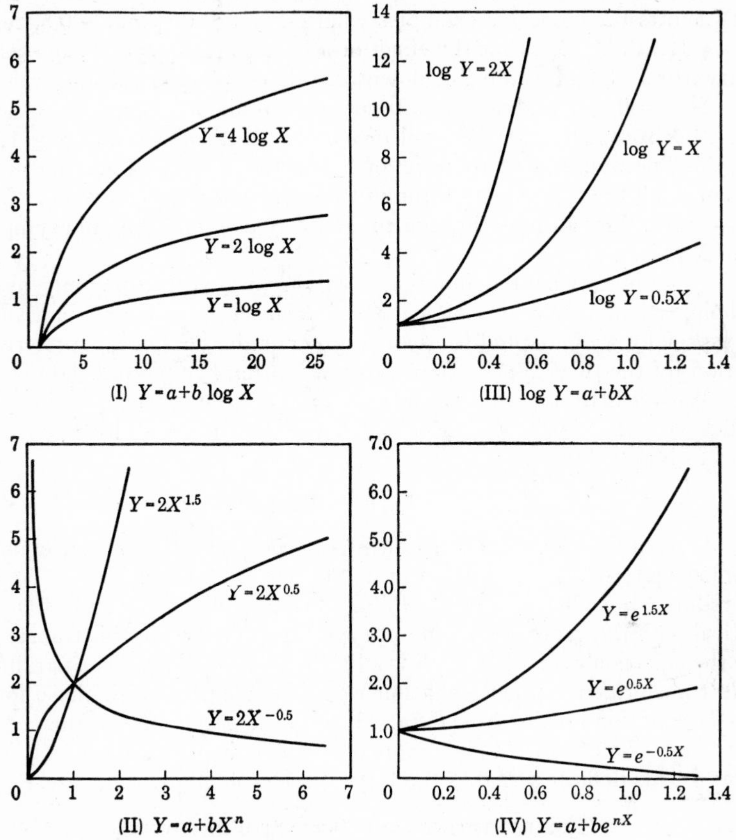

FIG. 3.4. Some logarithmic and exponential functions.

When log Y is a Function of X. The third type of equation is of the form

$$\log Y = a + bX \tag{3.3}$$

Figure 3.4 III shows three examples of this curve, with the coefficient $a = 0$ in all cases and b equal to 2, 1, and 0.5 in the three equations. All these curves (when $a = 0$) pass through the point (0,1).

Y Is an Exponential Function of X. The fourth type looks very different from the others, but, as we shall see, it bears some resemblances to the third type. The general form of equation is

$$Y = a + be^{nX} \tag{3.4}$$

where a and b are the usual kind of parameters, e is the base of the Napierian system of logarithms, and n is a coefficient in the exponent of e. In order to simplify the equation for illustrative purposes, let us assume that $a = 0$. Its only function is, as usual, to determine the vertical position of the entire curve in the coordinate system. To simplify the equation still further, let $b = 1.0$. The general effect of b, as in other functions that we have seen, is to control the slope of the curve. We have left, then, $Y = e^{nX}$. Figure 3.4 IV shows three specific examples where n is 1.5, 0.5, and -0.5, respectively. It will be seen that the effect of n is to control general slope as well as curvature. Slope upward or downward depends upon the algebraic sign of n. If $n = 0$, the exponent of e becomes zero and e^{nX} equals 1, so that we have a horizontal line at the level of $a + b$. With $a = 0$ and $b = 1.0$, as here, this line would be at the level of 1.0 on the Y axis. Regardless of the value of n, all the curves pass through the point $(0,b)$ in Fig. 3.4 IV. When a is not zero, they all pass through the point $(0,a + b)$. All are asymptotic to the X axis.

This type of exponential function involving e is very commonly used in psychological investigations of learning, retention, recall, and motivation. It is especially well adapted to theorizing. For this reason it is preferred to equations of the third type. Both types will often fit the same data equally well. With a little transformation we can bring the fourth type in a form parallel with the third. Using equation (3.4) with $a = 0$, by taking logarithms of both sides we have

$$\log Y = \log b + n(\log e)X$$

It can be seen that $\log b$ is a constant, like coefficient a in a linear equation, and $n \log e$ is a constant multiplier of X, like b in a linear equation. We have thus reduced the equation of type IV (for the case in which $a = 0$) to a form identical with the general equation of type III. That is, in this transformed state the equation reads that $\log Y$ is a linear function of X. The parameters of the transformed type-IV equation would be identical with those for the type-III equation for the same data. It is to the parameters of the untransformed equation of type IV, however, that one looks for meaning in terms of theory. This definitely makes the latter preferable in ordinary use.

Curve Fitting and Transformations

Rational and Empirical Equations. Given a set of measurements in variable Y that have been taken in conjunction with corresponding measurements in variable X, we often want to relate the two in a mathematical way. A very common example would be measures of performance Y taken after different amounts of practice time X. We may have some theory which leads us to expect that proficiency in a task increases in a certain fashion as practice increases and that this relationship can be expressed in terms of a mathematical equation of a certain type. Such an equation is known as a *rational equation*, since it was developed by deduction from known or assumed facts. Having derived the type of equation logically, we set up the kind of experiment that should be expected to yield data conforming to such a function. In order to decide whether the predicted function is satisfied by the data, we need some procedure for determining how well the data fit that function. The work of Hull and his associates on learning is one of the most outstanding examples of the use of rational equations in experimental psychology. The work of Thurstone, Gulliksen, and others illustrates the application of the same kind of approach to the investigation of test performance.

Sometimes, and this is more likely to be the case, the investigator either does not have sufficient basis to rationalize his problem in advance or he does not take the trouble to do so. After he has obtained his data, he asks what type of mathematical equation will describe them best. Some rationalizing may enter into his determining the choice of function, but it is after the fact and with knowledge of how his data look. He may find a type of equation to which his data conform very well without having much idea of why they do so. We say that he has found an *empirical equation*, which is good for descriptive purposes but which has no theoretical implications. It enables him to make predictions of Y from X, or vice versa, within the limits of the range of his data. It may serve as a starting point for later rationalization and theorizing concerning the nature of the relationship between Y and X.

Transformations. A third use of equations is to effect transformations of data. Certain measurements obtained under a set of conditions are not made on a scale of equal units or the unit and the zero point are not what we would like them to be. The unit may be one that we know or strongly suspect to be systematically changing in size as X changes. This shows up in terms of a skewed distribution in a situation that we have reason to believe to be normally distributed. The lack of normality of distribution also makes impossible the usual statistical tests of significance. For these various reasons we want to apply a certain equation to the obtained measurements to effect the desired correction. If the measurements were made on an interval scale but we want to change either the unit or the zero point, we may apply a linear transformation. If there is skewing in otherwise regular data and we want to normalize the distribution, we may apply some nonlinear transformation equation.

In this section we shall be concerned with fitting data to mathematical functions and with methods of transforming data into the terms of another measuring scale. The two procedures have much in common and are therefore treated in proximity.

Determining the Type of Relationship. Before we can find out whether our data fit a mathematical function we have to decide what function to use. If we have a rational equation, the kind of curve is decided in advance. If we are seeking an empirical equation, we depend upon inspection of the data and upon some trial and error.

As an illustrative problem, let us take a set of data that is shown in Table 3.2. In the experiment from which these data came, a single observer O was asked to reproduce horizontal straight lines of various standard lengths. These standards varied from 20 mm. by steps of 10 mm. through 350 mm. Sixty experiments were performed, in each of which O made fifty reproductions of a standard line, as in the method of average error (see Chap. 4). The object of the experiments was to determine the kind of relationship between the length of the line observed and the average of the variable errors of observation. The measure of the average variable error of observation was the probable error of the distribution of reproductions. We therefore have 60 pairs of measures—60 standard lengths of line and 60 corresponding probable errors. The former may be regarded as X, the independent variable, and the latter as Y, the dependent variable. Let us symbolize the former by S, for stimulus, or standard, and the latter by s, for ΔS, treating the probable error as one operational approach to the determination of a difference limen. We therefore have a basis for making a test of Weber's law as it applies to the relation of the average variable error to its corresponding stimulus quantity.

TABLE 3.2. DATA GIVING THE RELATION BETWEEN LENGTHS OF LINES REPRODUCED AND THE PROBABLE ERRORS OF THE DISTRIBUTIONS OF REPRODUCTIONS, IN MILLIMETERS

Length of line	*PE* of distribution	Length of line	*PE* of distribution	Length of line	*PE* of distribution	Length of line	*PE* of distribution
20	1.5	40	2.5	350	12.4	320	11.5
40	3.0	80	5.1	260	10.4	270	10.5
210	9.0	240	9.6	100	5.4	150	7.6
180	8.4	200	9.5	130	7.2	140	7.6
330	12.2	340	10.1	150	8.0	100	5.5
300	11.2	350	11.4	150	8.2	120	6.4
190	8.7	210	9.5	90	5.1	120	7.6
200	11.9	250	12.3	60	5.2	80	4.4
300	11.9	280	11.4	90	6.6	110	6.1
290	11.2	310	12.9	270	11.6	300	11.1
200	10.5	250	9.3	220	8.8	250	10.1
160	9.0	170	8.4	30	2.7	60	4.1
50	4.4	330	11.6	30	2.4	50	3.9
100	6.8	70	4.9	230	9.5	240	9.8
150	7.0	180	7.3	300	10.8	350	11.1

Plotting the Correlation Diagram. It is certainly not obvious from Table 3.2 what kind of relationship exists between s and S, except for a general tendency for s to increase as S increases. In order to get a much clearer picture of this relationship, we plot a correlation diagram as in Fig. 3.5.

From Fig. 3.5 it is even more obvious that s is an increasing function of S. From Weber's law, we should expect a linear relationship with an equation of the type $s = KS$. This means a line through the origin would represent all the points well enough. Such a line in Fig. 3.5 would seem to be unsatisfactory. There is a possibility, however, that a straight line not passing through the origin would describe the relationship. Before we assume that the relationship is linear, we should examine the trend of the points more carefully. This we can do by means of some averaging.

Discovering Trends by the Use of Averages. In our illustrative problem the same stimulus was used in more than one set of observations. We can get a somewhat clearer notion of the trend of the curve if for every S value we compute an average of the corresponding s values. In Fig. 3.5 the solid line that zigzags its way upward is based upon these averages. The graphic relationship shown by this line is not without its inversions; it does not rise continuously. Owing to the extremely small samples of s at each S level, there is much sampling error in these means. We can improve upon this approach by doing some grouping of S values. This has been done in Table 3.3. The S values have been grouped in ranges of 50 mm., resulting in frequencies of from 7 to 10 s values in each class. The grouping need not be in terms of equal intervals. It is often more important to effect frequencies as large as possible in all intervals, and hence approximately equal frequencies.

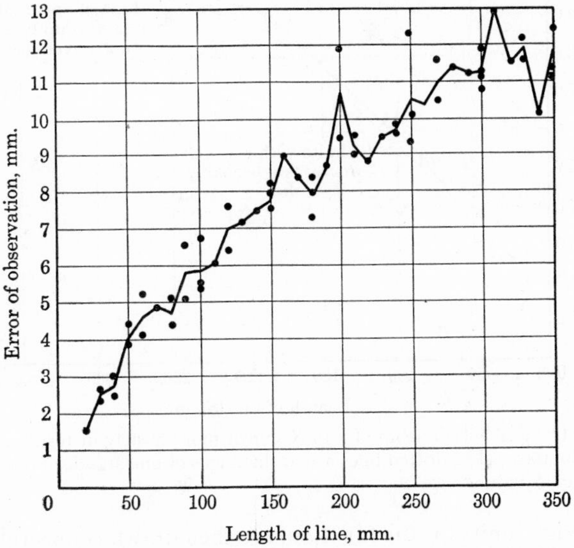

FIG. 3.5. Correlation diagram showing the relation between the length of line reproduced and the PE of the distribution of reproductions.

Instead of using the midpoint of S values to stand for the value of each interval, it is better to obtain the mean S for that interval. We now have, in Table 3.3, seven pairs of values, each pair including a mean S and a mean s. The relationship of these two series is shown in Fig. 3.6.

In order to take into account the reliability of observations in each interval, standard errors of the means (σ_M) of s values are employed. These are given in the last column of Table 3.3 and are represented by the short vertical lines through the plotted points in Fig. 3.6. Each vertical line extends from $+1\sigma_M$ to $-1\sigma_M$. Thus we see graphically the range within which such means would be expected to fluctuate in sampling.

We have treated each mean S for an interval as a fixed value. The standard lengths of lines were chosen for the experiment and, as such, they have no sampling error. Each set of standard lines in an interval may be regarded as a population whose mean is exact. There are many experimental situations, however, in which the obtained values of X have sampling fluctuations.

An example would be where X is a measure of performance as well as Y. When X is subject to sampling fluctuations as well as Y, a good policy is to find estimates of σ_M for the means on X and to represent them as horizontal bars in the figure. Around each point one then draws a rectangle whose width and height are determined by the *two* bars. The dotted lines, which

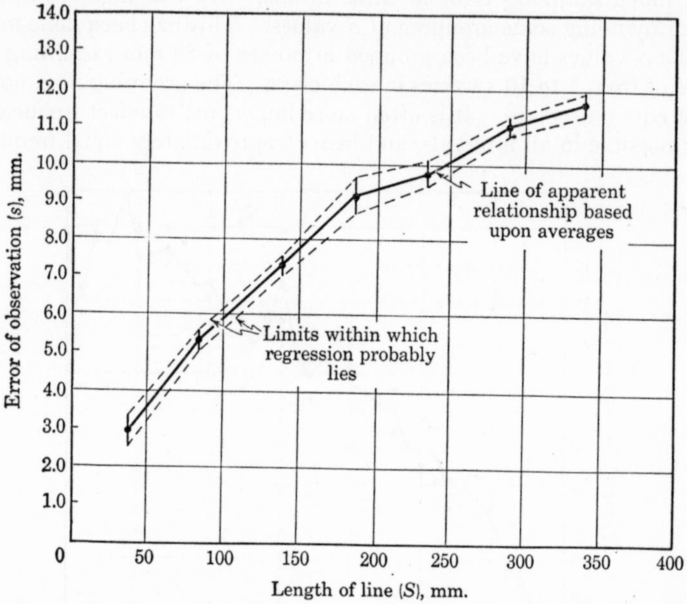

FIG. 3.6. The trend of relationship of s to S shown more clearly in terms of seven pairs of average coordinates. The dotted lines are at distances of one standard error of the mean s at each average S value.

represent rough limits for the function, are then drawn connecting the corners of the rectangles.

Since the true means for intervals, as in Fig. 3.6, are unknown, of course, and the dotted lines are spaced with reference to the *observed* means, the

TABLE 3.3. RELATION BETWEEN THE MEAN LENGTH OF LINE REPRODUCED AND THE MEAN *PE* OF THE DISTRIBUTION OF REPRODUCTIONS, WITH STANDARD ERRORS OF THE MEANS OF *PE*'s

Length of lines (class limits)	N_c	Mean length	Mean *PE*	σ_M for mean *PE*
10– 59	7	37.1	2.91	0.38
60–109	10	83.0	5.31	0.26
110–159	9	135.6	7.29	0.23
160–209	8	185.0	9.21	0.51
210–259	9	233.3	9.77	0.33
260–309	9	285.6	11.12	0.18
310–359	8	335.0	11.65	0.30

dotted lines can only be suggestive as to the position of the "true" function. They serve somewhat as limits of confidence, however, as we use deviations of any standard errors of means.

The general trend of relationship as shown by Fig. 3.6 seems to be nonlinear. It would not be possible, at least, to draw a single straight line all within the limits of the dotted lines. There is some possibility that the true function lies outside those limits at some points, but the probability of this is rather small. We will tolerate the idea of a linear relationship for the sake of an illustration and in the next paragraphs proceed to find the best-fitting straight line. It is usually possible to find a best-fitting straight

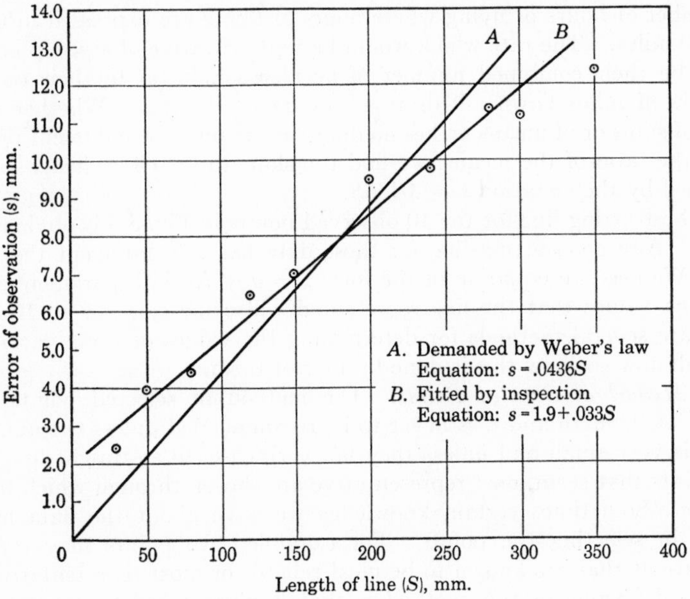

FIG. 3.7. A plot of the 10 selected points whose coordinates are given in Table 3.5, showing the line that would be called for by Weber's law (A) and a line adjusted by inspection to the data (B).

line to any data so long as they have some distribution on both X and Y. In this situation we may use a straight line as a way to describe the relationship of s to S, as a first approximation. We shall find how much error this entails, and then fit the same data to a nonlinear function and see whether the latter shows any apparent improvement in terms of prediction and errors of prediction.

Fitting Data to a Straight Line. In order to have a simpler illustration, let us select from Table 3.2 somewhat at random a set of 10 pairs of measurements, seeking to cover the whole range with some degree of evenness. The results of such a sampling may be seen in the first two columns of Table 3.5. These observations are plotted in Fig. 3.7.

If Weber's law held exactly for these data, line A should represent the 10 points very well. Obviously it does not, but there is some need for us to see how a line like A is located. It must, of course, pass through the origin. Its slope, which is K in the equation $s = KS$, is determined by the data. From this equation we see that the slope is s/S. We have the possibility of making 10 estimates of s/S from our 10 pairs of measurements. It might seem reasonable to compute the 10 ratios, each of which is an estimate of the slope, and then compute a mean of the slopes. A better procedure is to find the means of s and of S and let the slope of the line equal M_s/M_S. A slope is a rate, and an average rate is most reasonably indicated by the ratio of means or of sums. Take accident rates, for example. If we know that each of several military aircraft of a certain type has a certain number of accidents per 100,000 miles of flying, its accident rate is the ratio of number of accidents to number of hours of flying where hours of flying are expressed in units of 100,000 miles. The rate which would be representative of a group of planes would be their combined number of accidents in ratio to their combined numbers of miles flown. This implies a ratio of sums. Whether we use ratios of sums or of means makes no difference in our line-judgment problem. Using the ratio of the means, we find the slope to be .0436; hence line A is described by the equation $s = .0436S$.

The best-fitting line for the 10 observed points in Fig. 3.7 is obviously not line A. Any good-fitting line for these data has a Y intercept that is not zero. We need an equation of the form $s = a + bS$ with parameters a and b of such values that the line represented will come close to all 10 points. There are several methods for determining the values of these parameters. We shall now see how this is done by four of them.

The Method of Selected Points. The method of selected points is the crudest of them all and it is never to be recommended unless the number of points is very small and unless they fall very close to a straight line. Any two points that seem most representative are chosen through which to draw the line. Sometimes certain knowledge we have about the data may be helpful in selecting the points. For example, two points may represent observations that are known to be most reliable or most representative.

The chief value of this method is that it gives a quick, computational method of estimating parameter b. Let the two points be (Y_2,X_2) and (Y_1,X_1), the first-mentioned pair of coordinates being greater than the second pair; then b is equal to $(Y_2 - Y_1)/(X_2 - X_1)$. The Y intercept a can be readily seen from the graph. Having obtained a, a check on the value of b is to use the ratio $b = (Y - a)/X$, where Y and X are any pair of corresponding values chosen on the line at some distance from the origin, other than those already used to locate the line.

The Graphic Method. By what is ordinarily called the graphic method, we attempt to adjust a line to all the points in such a way that it seems to come as near as possible to all of them. A good aid to use is in the form of a thin, dark thread or a clear, plastic rule with a line running the long way. Placing thread or line upon the points, move it up and down and change its slope until its position seems satisfactory. Usually, many points will deviate from the line no matter where it is placed. It is the vertical or Y deviations about which we are usually concerned. In its final position the line should be adjusted so that approximately the same number of points are above the line as below it; furthermore, the sum of the positive vertical discrepancies should equal approximately the sum of the negative ones. If the means of X and Y are known, another, and more useful, aid is to put the line through the point whose coordinates are (M_x, M_y). This establishes the general level of the line. There remains only the determination of its slope. The reason for putting the line through this point is that the best-fitting line by the method of least squares always goes through M_x and M_y.

When a satisfactory adjustment has been reached, mark two distant points along the thread or line, and draw the regression line. The parameters can be found as described in connection with the method of selected points.

The graphic method can be used to advantage only when the points are fairly close to the line and deviate from it in a somewhat regular fashion. Two investigators would be expected to differ slightly on the location of their regression lines. The same investigator might obtain slightly different results on different occasions. Nevertheless, the parameters found by this method are often very close to those obtained by the most accurate method—that of least squares. There are even occasions when an investigator might prefer his graphic solution to a least-square solution, since he knows something about the data that demands a certain position for the regression line, a position that the least-square solution would not achieve.

A graphic solution is seen in line B of Fig. 3.7. The closeness of the points to a single line is barely sufficient to make possible a good graphic solution. Being able to put the line through the point representing the means of S and s was a great help. The estimated parameters that describe this line are $a = 1.9$ and $b = .033$. The equation reads $s = 1.9 + .033S$. We shall see later how well this solution agrees with that found by the least-square solution and how large, relatively, the errors of prediction are.

The Method of Averages. The method of averages is an algebraic one from which we derive computed values for parameters a and b. As a simple way of approaching the method, let us assume that each pair of X and Y values furnishes us with information that helps in evaluating the parameters. We can substitute in the general equation $Y = a + bX$ any pair of observed values for X and Y. For example, using the first pair of values in Table 3.5, we may say that $2.4 = a + 30b$. Using the second pair, we have $3.9 = a + 50b$. The parameters a and b are the unknowns for which we are looking. Elementary algebra teaches that if we have two equations and two unknowns that we want to evaluate, we have sufficient information to find those values. The two equations just given could be solved simultaneously and values for a and b would be found that satisfied both equations. We could continue thus with every possible pair of equations. But we would obtain a different pair of values for a and b with every pair of equations. What we want is some kind of averaging that will give us single values for a and b. We want just two equations that represent all the data.

We achieve this by pooling the data into two groups, the one group composed of data involving the lowest values of X and the other involving the highest values of X. If the number of pairs of X and Y, which is N, is even, the division into two groups should ordinarily be even, with $N/2$ equations in each group. Sometimes, certain irregularities of the data may reasonably lead to an uneven division of the data. The 10 equations for the line-length data are given grouped in Table 3.4.

We next find the sums and the means of these two groups of equations. The means provide us with the two equations that we want.[1] We proceed to solve them simultaneously:

TABLE 3.4. EQUATIONS FOR THE SOLUTION OF PARAMETERS a AND b BY THE METHOD OF AVERAGES

	Group I	Group II
	$2.4 = a + 30b$	$9.5 = a + 200b$
	$3.9 = a + 50b$	$9.8 = a + 240b$
	$4.4 = a + 80b$	$11.4 = a + 280b$
	$6.4 = a + 120b$	$11.2 = a + 300b$
	$7.0 = a + 150b$	$12.4 = a + 350b$
Σ	$24.1 = 5a + 430b$	$54.3 = 5a + 1370b$
M	$4.82 = a + 86b$	$10.86 = a + 274b$

$$
\begin{array}{ll}
(A) & 10.86 = a + 274b \\
(B) & 4.82 = a + 86b \\
(A) - (B) & 6.04 = 188b
\end{array}
$$

Subtract equation (B) from equation (A), which eliminates one unknown. From this subtraction we find that

$$188b = 6.04$$

and therefore

$$b = .0321$$

Having determined the value for b, we substitute it in either of the two equations, for example, in equation (B)

$$4.82 = a + (86)(.0321)$$
$$4.82 = a + 2.76$$

from which

$$a = 4.82 - 2.76 = 2.06$$

The equation describing the regression line by the method of averages reads:

$$s = 2.06 + .0321S$$

Although other groupings of the data could be used, the one recommended is probably best as a general rule. If we grouped odd-numbered equations versus even-numbered ones, we would run the risk that the difference between the two averaged equations that are solved simultaneously would be very small and lacking in as many significant digits as we could have by other groupings.

It should also be pointed out that different groupings would yield slightly different estimates of a and b. Suppose we had grouped the first four equations and the last six. We would have found the two equations (based on sums)

$$
\begin{array}{ll}
(A') & 61.3 = 6a + 1{,}520b \\
(B') & 17.1 = 4a + 280b
\end{array}
$$

[1] One could also solve the equations based on sums rather than means.

In order to make variable a vanish by subtraction, we must make its coefficient identical in the two equations. This is done by multiplying A' by 4 and multiplying B' by 6. Then we have

$$
\begin{array}{lrl}
(4A') & 245.2 = & 24a + 6{,}080b \\
(6B') & 102.6 = & 24a + 1{,}680b \\
\hline
(4A') - (6B') & 142.6 = & 4{,}400b
\end{array}
$$

from which $b = .0309$ and $a = 2.01$. From this we gain some idea of the amount of risk of obtaining different estimates of a and b, depending upon how we form the two groups. The results should be very similar for different groupings, and not far from those found by other methods. For a really unique solution, the method of least squares is recommended.

The Method of Least Squares. The method of least squares gets its name from the *principle of least squares.* Before we can understand the principle of least squares, we need the concept of *residual.* A residual is a discrepancy between an obtained Y value and the Y value we would predict from its corresponding X on the basis of the equation we are using.[1] The predicted Y is often denoted as Y'. Actually, our regression equation reads $Y' = a + bX$. The discrepancy $Y - Y'$ is the deviation of an observed Y value from its corresponding predicted value. The line of best fit according to the principle of least squares is *that line from which the sum of the squares of the residuals is a minimum.* The principle of least squares also applies to an arithmetic mean. An arithmetic mean is that value in a distribution such that the sum of squares of deviations is a minimum. The line of best fit is in a sense a moving arithmetic mean of the Y values as we vary X.

In the preceding method, the method of averages, we grouped the N possible equations into two pools and found their means in order to solve for a and b. In the method of least squares we are able to reach the same goal by keeping the data in one pool and by dealing with sums and means of all the equations taken together.

But we have two unknowns, and there must be as many equations as there are unknowns. Grouping the data in one pool gives us only one equation. Whence comes the other? This cannot be fully explained to the nonmathematical student, since a bit of differential calculus is involved. Let it suffice here to say that the other *normal equation* (for that is the technical term applied to the two equations we need) is obtained in the following manner: Every equation (such as those appearing in Table 3.4) that comes from a single pair of Y and X values is multiplied through by the value of X in that equation. For example, the first equation in Table 3.4, which reads $2.4 = a + 30b$, would then become $72 = 30a + 900b$, X being equal to 30 in this equation. The second equation would read $195 = 50a + 2{,}500b$; the third would be $352 = 80a + 6{,}400b$; and so on. From the sums of these equations we derive the other normal equation. In general terms, the two normal equations are[2]

[1] The equation for a line describing a relationship of Y to X in observed data is often called a *regression equation* and the line is called a *regression line.* For a discussion of regression, see Guilford (7, pp. 397–404).

[2] For a proof of these equations, see Guilford (7, p. 583).

$$(A) \qquad \Sigma Y = Na + (\Sigma X)b$$
$$(B) \qquad \Sigma XY = (\Sigma X)a = (\Sigma X^2)b \qquad (3.5)$$

In finding all the known values in the two normal equations, it is not necessary to write out all the equations as they appear in Table 3.4; that would be a waste of paper and ink. It is convenient to prepare a work sheet similar to Table 3.5, with columns for the following items: X, Y, X^2, Y^2, and XY. The item of Y^2 is included, not because it is needed in finding the parameters, but because it will be necessary to know ΣY^2 if we want to compute the standard deviation of the Y distribution or the coefficient of correlation, as

Table 3.5. Least-square Solution for a Linear Fit for the Relationship between Length of Line and the *PE* of Reproductions

(S) X	(s) Y	X'	X'^2	$X'Y$	Y^2	(S') Y'	$(Y - Y')$ δ	δ^2	Y'^2
30	2.4	3	9	7.2	5.76	3.16	−0.76	.5776	9.99
50	3.9	5	25	19.5	15.21	3.78	+0.12	.0144	14.29
80	4.4	8	64	35.2	19.36	4.72	−0.32	.1024	22.28
120	6.4	12	144	76.8	40.96	5.97	+0.43	.1849	35.64
150	7.0	15	225	105.0	49.00	6.90	+0.10	.0100	47.61
200	9.5	20	400	190.0	90.25	8.46	+1.04	1.0816	71.57
240	9.8	24	576	235.2	96.04	9.71	+0.09	.0081	94.28
280	11.4	28	784	319.2	129.96	10.96	+0.44	.1936	120.12
300	11.2	30	900	336.0	125.44	11.58	−0.38	.1444	134.10
350	12.4	35	1,225	434.0	153.76	13.14	−0.74	.5476	172.66
Σ 1,800	78.4	180	4,352	1,758.1	725.74	78.38	−0.02	2.8646	722.54
M 180.0	7.84	18.0	435.2	175.81	72.574	7.838	−0.002	0.28646	72.254
σ 105.5	3.33	10.55				3.29	0.535		

we often do. The other headings will be explained later. It will be noted that in the third column we have reduced the numerical size of the X values by dropping the zero. This is for the purpose of keeping the numerical values small in the process of squaring and in finding the *cross products* (XY values). This is a process of "coding," which is legitimate and useful. We need only make the proper adjustments in the final answers.

Table 3.5 illustrates the least-square procedure. The sums of the columns are the important values. From them we can set up the two normal equations:

$$78.4 = 10a + 180b$$
$$1{,}758.1 = 180a + 4{,}352b$$

The solution of these equations has been reduced to a routine formula in the following manner. Let us start from the generalized equations (A) and (B) which are given in formula (3.5). In order to solve for b, the coefficients of a must be made identical. Equation (A) must be multiplied through by the constant ΣX and equation (B) by the constant N. The result is

$$(A') \qquad (\Sigma X)(\Sigma Y) = N(\Sigma X)a + (\Sigma X)(\Sigma X)b$$
$$(B') \qquad N(\Sigma XY) = N(\Sigma X)a + N(\Sigma X^2)b$$

Finding the difference, $(B') - (A')$,

$$N(\Sigma XY) - (\Sigma X)(\Sigma Y) = N(\Sigma X^2)b - (\Sigma X)^2 b$$

Transposing and collecting terms,

$$[N(\Sigma X^2) - (\Sigma X)^2]b = N(\Sigma XY) - (\Sigma X)(\Sigma Y)$$

and hence

$$b = \frac{N(\Sigma XY) - (\Sigma X)(\Sigma Y)}{N(\Sigma X^2) - (\Sigma X)^2} \tag{3.6a}$$

Dividing throughout by N gives the alternative formula,

$$b = \frac{\Sigma(XY) - N(M_x)(M_y)}{\Sigma(X^2) - N(M_x)^2} \tag{3.6b}$$

Parameter a is found by the general formula

$$a = M_y - (M_x)b \tag{3.7}$$

In our illustrative problem, by formula (3.6*a*),

$$b' = \frac{(10)(1{,}758.1) - (180)(78.4)}{(10)(4{,}352) - (180)^2}$$
$$= \frac{17{,}581 - 14{,}112.0}{43{,}520 - 32{,}400} = \frac{3{,}469}{11{,}120} = .3120$$

Note that b' is the coefficient of X in terms of the *coded* values X', where $X' = X/10$. We must now adjust b' so that it will apply to X, which means dividing it by 10. Consequently, $b = .0312$. Next we find parameter a by use of formula (3.7).

$$a = 7.84 - (180)(.0312) = 2.224$$

The equation of the best-fitting line found by the method of least squares is therefore $s = 2.22 + .0312S$. Describing the data with this line, we may say that for every millimeter increase in S there is .0312 mm. increase in the probable error of reproductions by a particular observer. We can also say that the error of observation as measured by the probable error increases 3.12 per cent as rapidly as the length of line observed.

Alternative Formulas. We can also compute parameter a directly from the sums in Table 3.5 by the formula suggested by Blankenship (2):

$$a = \frac{(\Sigma X^2)(\Sigma Y) - (\Sigma X)(\Sigma XY)}{N\Sigma X^2 - (\Sigma X)^2} \tag{3.8}$$

After applying formula (3.8) we can compute parameter b by the equation

$$b = \frac{\Sigma Y - Na}{\Sigma X} \tag{3.9}$$

It might be well to estimate a and b by both these equations and the others for the purpose of checking.

Testing Goodness of Fit. By means of the equation that has just been obtained we may next predict Y for any chosen value of X. How accurate will such predictions be? There are several ways in which this question can be answered, directly and indirectly. The most direct indicator is the *standard error of estimate*, which is designated as σ_{yx}. Like all standard errors this statistic tells us the limits within which two-thirds of the Y values lie. In this case it indicates the amount of dispersion expected about the predictions made from given values of X. This is strictly true under two conditions: (1) there is homoscedasticity, that is, the dispersions of Y values about the predicted value Y' are homogeneous for all values of X and (2) the distributions are normal. In practice, these conditions must be approached within the limits of sampling errors. Other common indicators of goodness of fit are the coefficient of correlation between Y and X and other statistics derived from it.

The Standard Error of Estimate. The standard error of estimate can be computed directly from the residuals or indirectly from the coefficient of correlation. It is, in fact, the standard deviation of the residuals or discrepancies between Y' and Y. By this approach we need to know the Y' values corresponding to all observed values of X. Applying our regression equation to the X values in the first column of Table 3.5, we have the Y' values in the seventh column. They are computed to at least one more digit than the values of Y. Next we find the discrepancies, we square them, and find their standard deviation, which is σ_{yx}. We find that it is .535 mm. We can say that if the conditions specified above prevail, two-thirds of the observed Y values are within .535 mm. of the predicted Y values, or within approximately a half millimeter.

Figure 3.8 has been drawn to show the limits that are prescribed by a σ_{yx} equal to .535. The dotted lines are drawn at a vertical distance of .535 mm. from the regression line. We see that 7 of the 10 points are within the limits of $\pm 1\sigma_{yx}$ from the regression line, which is as we would expect; but because we suspect actual curvature in the relationship, it is likely that some of the vertical distributions about the Y' values are skewed. We should not have been surprised, therefore, if the two-thirds interpretation did not hold. The very small sample is also an unfavorable condition for satisfying the interpretation.

We might note in passing that the sum of the Y' values is 78.38, or only .02 from the sum of the Y values. The two sums should be identical except for rounding errors. This serves as a check of the computations of Y'. It is also of interest to compute the standard deviation of the Y' values, which has been done in Table 3.5. This standard deviation $\sigma_{y'}$ equals 3.29. This is smaller than σ_y, as it should be. There will be further discussion of the relation of the two later.

It should also be noted that the algebraic sum of the residuals, which is +0.02, is very close to zero, as one might expect. This serves as another check at this point, though not a completely dependable one in all situations.

The Coefficient of Correlation as an Indicator of Goodness of Fit. Because of its general familiarity to investigators in psychology, the Pearson product-moment coefficient of correlation has some appeal as an index of goodness of fit of observations to a line fitted by least squares. The coefficient of correlation is very closely related to other statistics involved in the least-square solution and can be easily computed from them or from the sums used in the normal equations. Using this information, the common formula for computing r is

$$r = \frac{N\Sigma XY - (\Sigma X)(\Sigma Y)}{\sqrt{[N\Sigma X^2 - (\Sigma X)^2][N\Sigma Y^2 - (\Sigma Y)^2]}} \tag{3.10}$$

Applying this formula to the line-length data, we find that $r_{yx} = .987$. The subscript in r_{yx} is simply to remind us that we are dealing with the regression

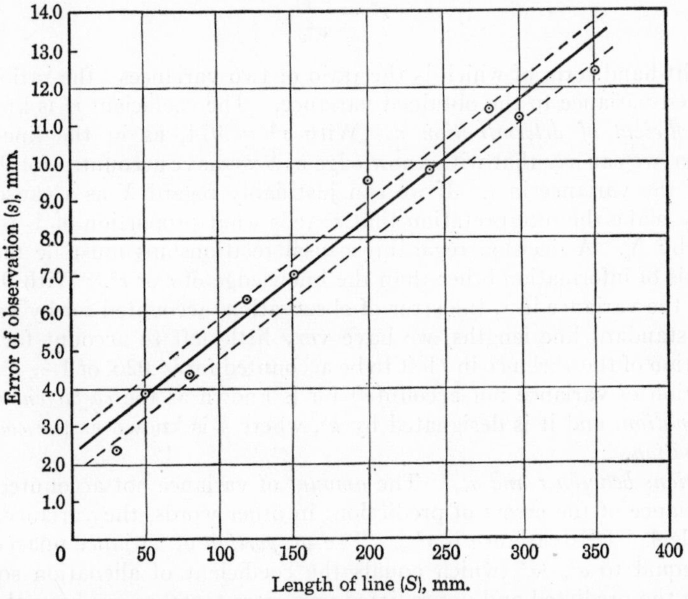

FIG. 3.8. The line fitted by the least-squares method to the 10 observations represented in Table 3.5. Dotted lines are at distances of one standard error of estimate from the regression line.

of Y on X. When the function fitted is linear, $r_{yx} = r_{xy}$; but when the function is curvilinear, the two coefficients probably differ.

When we possess as much information as we have in Table 3.5, including a value for σ_y and for $\sigma_{y'}$, the Pearson r can be computed by the simple ratio of the two in the formula

$$r = \frac{\sigma_{y'}}{\sigma_y} \tag{3.11}$$

From the illustrative data, using four significant digits, r is equal to

$$\frac{3.290}{3.333} = .987$$

as by the previous solution. The last formula is interesting because it gives an interpretation of r not often seen. This interpretation is that r is the ratio of the predicted variation in Y to the obtained or total variation in Y. If the correlation were $+1.0$, $\sigma_{y'}$ would equal σ_y. In other words, the predicted variation is then as great as the obtained. Another way of saying it is that when the correlation is perfect the predictions account for all the variation in the observed values. When the correlation is zero, $\sigma_{y'}$ has to be zero, which means that regardless of the size of X our predictions would all be the same, namely, M_y. The regression line would then be horizontal at the level of the mean of Y.

The Coefficient of Determination. If we square both sides of equation (3.11), we have

$$r^2 = \frac{\sigma^2_{y'}}{\sigma^2_y} \tag{3.12}$$

the right-hand term of which is the ratio of two variances—the ratio of the predicted variance to the obtained variance. The coefficient r^2 is known as the *coefficient of determination d.* With $r^2 = .974$, as in the line-length problem, we can say that with knowledge of S we have accounted for 97.4 per cent of the variance in s. If we can justifiably regard X as a cause of Y, we may make the interpretation that r^2 tells what proportion of Y is determined by X. A decision regarding causal relationships must be made on the basis of information other than the knowledge of r or r^2. With 97.4 per cent of the variance in s, the error of observation, accounted for by variance in the standard line lengths, we have very little left to account for. The proportion of the variance in s left to be accounted for is .026, or $1 - r^2$. The proportion of variance not accounted for is known as the *coefficient of nondetermination,* and it is designated by k^2, where k is known as the *coefficient of alienation.*

Relations between r and σ_{yx}. The *amount* of variance not accounted for is the variance of the errors of prediction; in other words, the variance in the residuals δ. This variance is σ^2_{yx}. The *proportion* of variance unaccounted for is equal to σ^2_{yx}/σ^2_y which equals the coefficient of alienation squared. Putting the predicted and unpredicted variances together, we have the total variance σ^2_y. From all this we may state several relationships,

$$\sigma^2_{y'} + \sigma^2_{yx} = \sigma^2_y$$

Dividing through by σ^2_y, we have

$$\frac{\sigma^2_{y'}}{\sigma^2_y} + \frac{\sigma^2_{yx}}{\sigma^2_y} = \frac{\sigma^2_y}{\sigma^2_y} = 1.0 \tag{3.13}$$

Substituting r^2 and k^2 for the first two terms, we have

$$r^2 + k^2 = 1.0$$

Substituting r^2 only, for the first term of (3.13),

$$r^2 + \frac{\sigma^2_{yx}}{\sigma^2_y} = 1.0$$

Transposing,

$$\frac{\sigma^2_{yx}}{\sigma^2_y} = 1 - r^2$$

Multiplying through by σ^2_y,

$$\sigma^2_{yx} = \sigma^2_y(1 - r^2)$$

Taking square roots of both sides,

$$\sigma_{yx} = \sigma_y \sqrt{1 - r^2} \tag{3.14}$$

which is the common textbook formula for computing the standard error of estimate from knowledge of σ_y and r. Some space has been given to its derivation here because it may help to establish better the ideas connecting the several variances and r. Applying formula (3.14) to the data of the line-length problem,

$$\sigma_{yx} = 3.333 \sqrt{1 - .987^2} = .535$$

as it was found to be directly from the residuals.

Estimates of Population Values for r and σ_{yx}. The values for r and σ_{yx} pertaining to the line-length problem and the formulas from which they were computed all have reference to the particular sample involved. Only when we restrict ourselves to the particular sample will the computed values have the internal consistency that has been pointed out.

As usual, in a statistical solution, we want to generalize beyond the sample to the larger universe or population from which the sample was drawn. We want to estimate population parameters that stand for the situation in the entire population so that more general conclusions can be drawn. If our sample has been randomly drawn from the population, we may do so. When we make such population estimates, we will find that the coefficient of correlation shrinks somewhat and the size of the standard error of estimate enlarges. Making such estimates is sometimes referred to as "correction for bias" and also as "correction for number." The biasing is due to the smallness of sample; the smaller the sample, the greater the correction.

The "corrected" coefficient of correlation (squared) is given by the equation

$$_cr^2 = 1 - (1 - r^2)\left(\frac{N - 1}{N - m}\right) \tag{3.15}$$

where $N - m$ = the number of degrees of freedom and m = the number of parameters.

For the line-length problem,

$$_cr^2 = 1 - (1 - .987^2)(9/8) = 1 - (.025831)(1.125) = .970940$$
$$_cr = .985$$

With r so close to 1.00, the correction is very small, even with a sample as small as 10.

The corrected standard error of estimate (squared) is given by the formula

$$_c\sigma^2_{yx} = \sigma^2_{yx}\left(\frac{N}{N - m}\right) \tag{3.16}$$

where the symbols are as defined before. For the line-length problem,[1]

$$_c\sigma^2_{yx} = (.286225)(1.25) = .357781$$

from which $_c\sigma_{yx} = .598$.

Comparison of Results from the Linear Solutions. Before leaving this section on fitting data to a straight line it will be of some interest to compare the linear equations obtained by different methods. From the principle of least squares we should expect that the sum of squares of the residuals would be smallest for the least-square solution. Since the standard error of estimate comes directly from these sums of squares, that statistic should also be smallest for the least-square solution. The coefficient of correlation should be largest for the same solution. The summary of these statistics for the three methods, as shown in Table 3.6, bears out this expectation. Of the other two

TABLE 3.6. A SUMMARY COMPARISON OF THE RESULTS OF THREE METHODS FOR FITTING THE LINE-LENGTH DATA TO A STRAIGHT LINE

Method	Sum of squares of residuals	Standard error of estimate	Coefficient of correlation
Least squares	2.8646	.535	.9870
Averages	2.9640	.544	.9866
Graphic	3.2268	.568	.9854

methods, the method of averages seems to have given better results, as we might expect.

Fitting a Nonlinear Function by the Method of Least Squares. The fitting of a straight line to the line-length data seemed to give excellent results statistically, but from the appearance of the plot we have serious doubts that the regression is truly linear. A linear fit that would satisfy Weber's law should also pass through the origin. The line of best fit definitely does not. Logically, any function used to describe these data should pass through the origin, because the variability for observations of a line of zero length (no line at all) should be zero. To find a good-fitting function that does pass through the origin, we must look to other than linear ones. One possibility that comes to mind is the *n*th-power law, which was mentioned in Chap. 2. According to this law, we should fit the data to a function of the type $s = KS^n$. This falls in type II of Fig. 3.4.

[1] For the limited "population" of 60 paired observations from which this sample of 10 was drawn, the corrected r and σ_{yx} were .942 and 1.02, respectively. The reason for such a large discrepancy between sample and estimated population values is that the sample was not entirely random. There was the restriction that the X values must cover the range rather evenly.

Determining the Choice of Function. If we have no logical reasons of these kinds to help us in the choice of function, a good practical approach, involving some trial and error, is to see what types of curves our plot resembles. In Fig. 3.4 there are two types that have some resemblance to the plots in Figs. 3.5 and 3.6. They are of types I and II. The next step is to reduce equations of those general types to linear form relating Y to $f(X)$. In the first type, Y has a linear relationship to $\log X$. In the second type, $\log Y$ has a linear relationship to $\log X$. We therefore transform s and S into their corresponding logarithms and make two plots, one with s against $\log S$ and the other with $\log s$ against $\log S$. This has been done in Fig. 3.9. A much more convenient procedure for making this test of linearity is to use logarithmic graph paper. This obviates the necessity for finding logarithms of X and Y, at this stage and perhaps only for this purpose.

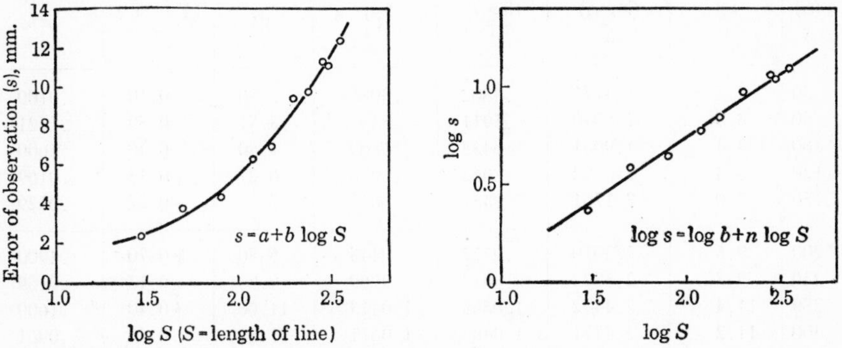

FIG. 3.9. Plots of line-length data transformed into logarithmic scales for S alone and for both s and S.

It is obvious from examination of the plots in Fig. 3.9 that the regression is linear for the log-log plot and not for the other. We therefore choose to fit the data to a function of the form $Y = bX^n$.

The Least-square Solution of Parameters. Having a linear relationship between $\log s$ and $\log S$, we can proceed as if fitting data to a straight line. It is the sum of squares of errors in $\log s$ that will be minimized. The statistical work is demonstrated in Table 3.7, which is parallel with the work in Table 3.5. We let the symbols $\bar{Y}$ and $\bar{X}$ stand for $\log s$ and $\log S$, respectively. The parameters we obtain, a' and b', will stand for the constants $\log b$ and n in the linear equation $\log s = \log b + n \log S$. From the usual normal equations we find that

$$b' = \frac{188.819 - 181.208}{473.059 - 461.567} = \frac{7.611}{11.492} = .6623$$

and $$a' = .8434 - (.6623)(2.1484) = -.5795$$

The equation, in logarithmic form, is

$$\log s = -.5795 + .6623 \log S$$

We want the equation in final form to be of the type $s = KS^n$. We began by taking logarithms of both sides of this equation. We now need to reverse the process and take antilogs of both sides of the obtained equation. The result of this operation is

$$s = .263S^{.6623}$$

Interpreted, this equation says that for certain *proportional* increases in S there are corresponding *proportional* increases in s. The value .6623 tells how rapidly the one proportional increase is advancing as compared with the other. The proportional increase in s is 66.23 per cent as rapid as the proportional increase in S.

TABLE 3.7. LEAST-SQUARE FIT OF THE DATA ON REPRODUCTIONS OF LINES TO A FUNCTION OF THE TYPE $\log Y = a + b \log X$

(S) X	(s) Y	(log S) $\bar{X}$	(log s) $\bar{Y}$	$\bar{Y}'$	Y'	$(\bar{Y} - \bar{Y}')$ δ	δ^2
30	2.4	1.4771	.3802	.3988	2.50	−0.10	.0100
50	3.9	1.6990	.5911	.5457	3.51	+0.39	.1521
80	4.4	1.9031	.6435	.6809	4.80	−0.40	.1600
120	6.4	2.0792	.8062	.7976	6.27	+0.13	.0169
150	7.0	2.1761	.8451	.8617	7.27	−0.27	.0729
200	9.5	2.3010	.9777	.9445	8.80	+0.70	.4900
240	9.8	2.3802	.9912	.9969	9.93	−0.13	.0169
280	11.4	2.4472	1.0569	1.0413	11.00	+0.40	.1600
300	11.2	2.4771	1.0492	1.0611	11.51	−0.31	.0961
350	12.4	2.5441	1.0934	1.1055	12.75	−0.35	.1225
Σ	78.4	21.4841	8.4345	8.4340	78.34	+0.06	1.2974
M	7.84	2.1484	.8434				
σ	3.333					0.360	

$\Sigma\bar{X}^2 = 47.3059$ $\Sigma\overline{XY} = 18.8819$ $\Sigma\bar{Y}^2 = 7.6240$

The Index of Correlation. As in the case of linear equations, the closeness of fit of the observed points to the assumed function may be estimated by means of the standard error of estimate or by means of a measure of correlation. Although the product-moment coefficient of correlation was designed for linear relationships, it can be applied to curvilinear relationships that can be reduced to linear form, provided, of course, that the usual assumptions are satisfied with respect to that linear form. The correlation as applied to a curvilinear relationship is not between Y and X but between Y and $f(X)$ or between $f(Y)$ and $f(X)$. Such a correlation coefficient is known as an *index of correlation*, which is expressed by the symbol ρ_{yx}.

In the illustrative problem, the linear relationship exists between Y and X^n, or between log Y and log X. The degree of correlation can be estimated by correlating log Y with log X. Using the cross products $\overline{XY}$ from Table 3.7 and formula (3.10),[1]

[1] With numerator and denominator squared as a convenience in machine computation.

$$p^2_{yx} = \frac{57.9273}{(11.492)(5.099)} = .9886$$
$$p_{yx} = .994$$

In correcting the index of correlation for the number of observations and the number of variables, formula (3.15) is used, with m here equal to 3. It takes at least three points to determine the position of a curve. Here m is 3 because there are three parameters in the equation. There appear to be only two, but $a = 0$. That is, the origin is one of the points determining the curve. The corrected p_{yx} is

$$_cp^2_{yx} = 1 - (1 - .9886)(9/7) = .9853$$
$$_cp_{yx} = .993$$

The correlation p_{yx} in this problem is barely higher than the linear correlation r_{yx} (.994 as compared with .987). This would indicate that there has been very little improvement in fitting the curve as compared with the straight line. The comparison is better made ordinarily in terms of corrected coefficients of correlation (.993 as compared with .985), which makes no difference here. When r is so close to 1.00 as these are, however, a very small difference may be significant. There are chi-square and F tests for such differences in curve fitting which would require more space than can be afforded to describe them here.[1] Without any such tests of statistical significance, it is rather clear on other grounds that the curved regression is much to be preferred in this problem.

The Index of Determination. As in connection with fitting data to the linear function, we may square the index of correlation to find what is called an *index of determination.* This is interpreted similarly to a coefficient of determination. Since $p^2_{yx} = .989$, we can say that 98.9 per cent of the variance in Y is accounted for by variance in $f(X)$. This figure is based on the uncorrected p_{yx} and as such applies only within the sample. For an inference about such a conclusion applying to the universe of such data, we need the square of $_cp_{yx}$, which is .985. The difference is trivial here.

The Standard Error of Estimate for Nonlinear Functions. The standard error of estimate also applies when the fit is to a nonlinear function. It may be estimated either directly from the residuals or from the coefficient of correlation. For example, applying the two formulas for this standard error, which is symbolized as $\sigma_{y \cdot f(X)}$, we obtain

$$\sigma_{y \cdot f(X)} = \sigma_y \sqrt{1 - p^2_{yx}} = 3.333 \sqrt{1 - .988036} = .364$$

and

$$\sigma_{y \cdot f(X)} = \sqrt{\frac{\Sigma \delta^2}{N}} = \sqrt{\frac{1.2974}{10}} = .360$$

The difference is accounted for by the fact that we are dealing with errors in Y rather than in $f(Y)$. If we were to estimate the standard error of estimate in log Y rather than in Y, the two approaches should give identical results.

[1] See Deming (3, 4) or Lewis (10) for a description of these tests.

Of the two results, in terms of errors in Y, the one found directly from the residuals is the more realistic.

The corrected standard errors of estimate by application of formula (3.16) are .435 and .430, respectively. In Fig. 3.10 are shown two dotted lines at about .4 mm. above and below the regression curve of best fit by this solution. Only two points fall outside the limits of those lines.

Fitting Other Nonlinear Functions. As in the problem just illustrated, most nonlinear equations that are chosen to fit particular data must be transformed into linear form before the method of least squares can be applied. This frequently requires the use of logarithms, as in the problem above, and it also

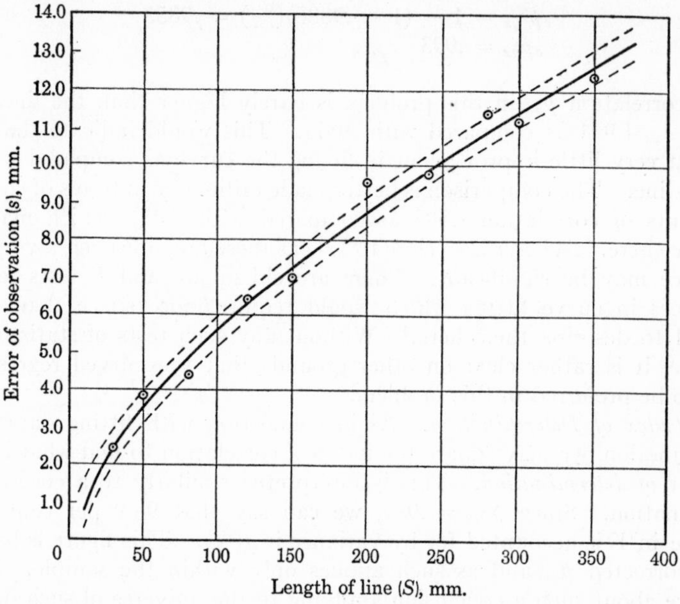

FIG. 3.10. The curve of best fit to the line-length data, the equation being of the type $X = KX^n$. Dotted lines are at one standard error of estimate from the regression curve.

involves the determination of more than two parameters. A hyperbola of the form $Y = 1/(a + bX)$ can be made linear by taking reciprocals of both sides, giving $1/Y = a + bX$. An equation of the type $Y = a + b/X$ becomes linear if transformed into $Y = a + b(1/X)$. An equation of the form $Y = be^{nX}$ can be made linear in the form $\log Y = \log b + n(\log e)X$. The term $\log e$ can be evaluated by the fact that $e = 2.718$ and the logarithm of 2.718 to the base 10 is .4343. When the parameter a in this and some other equations is not zero, there is a problem of estimating a before proceeding. For methods of making such estimates and for further details on curve fitting, the student is referred to Lewis (10). Huntington (9) offers many suggestions for converting equations to linear form.

The Problem of Weighting Observations. The fitting of data to a function by the method of least squares rests on the assumption of homoscedasticity (homogeneity of variances). When we fit data to a nonlinear function, this assumption is likely to be violated, especially if we had homogeneity before we transformed the data into linear form. Correction for unequal variances can be made by introducing weights. As we shall see in Chap. 6, weighting often makes little difference in the results, but the student should be aware of the problem.[1]

Linear Transformations. A linear transformation is effected by means of a linear equation. The regression equation that describes a line we have fitted to data is one example. This transformation may give us a result that satisfies certain purposes or objectives, such as minimizing errors of prediction. But there are other reasons for wanting to make a linear transformation. One of these is to bring about a change of unit of measurement or a change of zero point, or both. Such a transformation is executed in going from centigrade to Fahrenheit temperature scales.

Although a linear equation is used for both this purpose and for making predictions in psychological data, the two situations differ in that a different coefficient of correlation is assumed. In converting from one scale to another it is assumed that the correlation is +1.0. Although correlations of variables in psychology are rarely or never +1.0, there are times when we want to assume r to be +1.0 in making a lineart ransformation. One example would be when we have numerical ratings made of the same objects by two or more raters. We find that each rater has his own peculiar mean rating and his own peculiar dispersion. Many of the differences between ratings of the same object by different raters are due to such personal idiosyncracies. The mean and distribution of the values of the objects are the same no matter who rates them. In order to give each rater's ratings a numerical comparability to those of another, we need to effect linear transformations.

Another example would be the derivation of two or more sets of psychological scale values for the same objects along the same continuum. The values from the different sources are numerically not equivalent due to different scaling operations. For greater comparability we want to give the ratings in terms of a scale of the same unit and same zero point. We may assume that this has been achieved when they have the same mean and the same standard deviation.

How to Achieve a Desired Mean and Standard Deviation. The problem is a more general one, for it amounts to deriving a linear equation to apply to a set of measurements so that they achieve a desired mean and standard deviation. As an example, let us take the two sets of measurements X_1 and X_2 in Table 3.8. Let us assume that these are measurements of the same objects along the same continuum. The means are 16.3 and 1.45, respectively. Their units and zero points are not equivalent, as a plot of the two in a coordinate frame would show. The measurements X_1 seem to have a more convenient range and they are whole numbers. Suppose it were also known that the values X_1 are ratio-scale values with a meaningful zero point, while the X_2 values are not but do have equal units. Any lack of perfect correlation is due to the unreliability of measurement on either scale.

Let us transform the values X_2 so that they will have the same mean and

[1] For discussions of the weighting problem, see Deming (4) or Mueller (11).

standard deviation as the values X_1. Let us effect a change in standard deviation first. The two standard deviations are 7.82 and .356, respectively. We have a statistical principle to the effect that multiplying a set of values by a constant C will increase their standard deviation by the same ratio.[1] For example, doubling all values will double their standard deviation. To bring the standard deviation σ_2 up to the level of 7.82, we must multiply all the X_2 values by the ratio of the two standard deviations, σ_1/σ_2. This ratio is 21.966.

TABLE 3.8. ILLUSTRATIONS OF LINEAR TRANSFORMATIONS OF DATA

X_1	X_2	X''_{12}	X'_{12}	X_{12}	X'_{n2}	X_{n2}
30	2.1	46.1	30.5	30	8.7	9
25	1.8	39.5+	23.9	24	7.0	7
22	1.5	33.0	17.4	17	5.3	5
19	1.6	35.2	19.6	20	5.8	6
17	1.4	30.8	15.2	15	4.7	5
15	1.7	37.3	21.7	22	6.4	6
14	1.1	24.2	8.6	9	3.0	3
11	1.4	30.8	15.2	15	4.7	5
8	.9	19.8	4.2	4	1.9	2
2	1.0	22.0	6.4	6	2.5−	2
Σ 163	14.5	318.7	162.7	162	50.1	50
M 16.3	1.45	31.87	16.27	16.2	5.0	5.0
σ 7.82	.356	7.79	7.79	7.79	2.00	2.09

Multiplying all X_2 values by 21.966, we obtain the transformed X_1 values, called X''_{12}, in column 3 of Table 3.8. Their mean is 31.87, which should be 21.966 times M_2, which equals 31.85. This demonstrates another principle to the effect that multiplying a set of values by a constant C will increase their mean by the same ratio. The standard deviation of X''_{12} is equal to 7.79, which is within rounding error of σ_1, which is 7.82.

We have now achieved the desired standard deviation, but we have a mean for the transformed X_2 values that is much too large. We have a third statistical principle to the effect that adding a constant to each value in a set increases the mean by the same constant. Here we need a decrease; therefore we find the amount to be deducted from the X''_{12} values by computing the difference $M''_{12} - M_1$, which equals 15.57. Deducting this from each X''_{12} value, we have the numbers X'_{12} in column 4 of Table 3.8. The mean of these X'_{12} values is 16.27, and the standard deviation is 7.79. A fourth principle is to the effect that adding a constant to all values in a set leaves the standard deviation unaltered. In the fifth column of Table 3.8 we have the transformed values rounded to whole numbers. The mean and standard deviation are still within rounding errors of those for X_1.

[1] For proof of this and the following principles, see Guilford (7, pp. 577–579).

Relation of the Transformation Equation to Linear Regression. Combining the operations of changing X_2 to a distribution with new mean and new standard deviation, we have actually used the linear equation

$$X'_{12} = -15.57 + 21.966X_2.$$

It is of interest to see what the least-square linear equation would have been like. The regression equation by the least-square solution would have been $X'_1 = -11.38 + 19.22X_2$. This equation is written as if we were predicting the most probable X_1 from knowledge of X_2 for each object.

Let us consider what the mean and standard deviation of the X'_1 values would be. In applying the regression equation, we have effected two changes in X_2. We have multiplied by 19.22 and then added -11.38. The mean of X'_1 can be found by applying these operations to M_2. When we do this, we find that $M_{1'} = 16.30$. The standard deviation of the X'_1 values will be affected only by the multiplier in the equation, 19.22. The standard deviation .356 multiplied by 19.22 gives us 6.84. Thus the effect of the least-square equation is to give us a mean that is equal to that of X_1 but a standard deviation that is lower. This should be expected from the regression effect, which is due to imperfect correlation. From previous sections the student should recognize $\sigma_{1'}$ as the standard deviation of predicted values, like $\sigma_{y'}$. Its ratio to σ_1 should give an estimate of the coefficient of correlation. The ratio 6.84/7.82 equals .875, as an estimate of r_{12}. If we know the correlation between Y and X, we can estimate the value of $\sigma_{y'}$ by the product $r\sigma_y$. In the *transformation* equation we assume an r of 1.0, so that the standard deviation of the transformed values is fully equal to that of the dependent variable.

In statistics textbooks we find that a common formula for the regression coefficient b is

$$b_{yx} = r_{yx}\frac{\sigma_y}{\sigma_x} \tag{3.17}$$

For the linear transformation equation, we assume $r = 1$, so that the multiplying coefficient becomes σ_y/σ_x. A common formula for the complete regression equation is

$$Y' = r_{yx}\frac{\sigma_y}{\sigma_x}(X - M_x) + M_y \tag{3.18}$$

If we let $r = 1$, and if we substitute subscripts n and o for y and x, respectively, where n stands for "new" or transformed values and o stands for "old" or untransformed values, we have the formula

$$X_n = \frac{\sigma_n}{\sigma_o}(X_o - M_o) + M_n \tag{3.19}$$

Suppose we want to transform the X_2 values in Table 3.8 into others that have a mean of 5.0 and a standard deviation of 2.0. These statistics are M_n and σ_n, respectively. The equation would be

$$
\begin{aligned}
X_n &= \frac{2.0}{.356}(X_o - 1.45) + 5.0 \\
&= 5.618(X_o - 1.45) + 5.0 \\
&= 5.618X_o - 8.15 + 5.0 \\
&= 5.618X_o - 3.15
\end{aligned}
$$

Applying this transformation to the X_2 values in Table 3.8, we obtain the X'_{n2} values in the sixth column. The mean and standard deviation are as desired. Rounding the new values, we have in the last column integers whose distribution remains almost exactly the same with respect to mean and standard deviation. It should be added that a linear transformation leaves a distribution with the same shape as before; skewness and kurtosis are not altered.

Probability and Distribution Functions

Examples of Probability. Everyone knows that when a coin is tossed the theoretical chances of its landing with head or tail up are "fifty-fifty." This means that, granting a perfectly balanced coin and an unbiased throw, the chances are even for getting a head or a tail. Stated in more mathematical terms, we say that the probability of getting heads is 1/2, or .50, and the probability of getting tails is also 1/2, or .50.

In throwing a single die the probability of getting a one-spot is 1/6, or .167. Likewise, the probability of getting a two-spot, or any other specified number of spots not greater than six, is also .167.

As another example, let us suppose that an urn contains 80 balls differing only in color. Of the 80 balls, 8 are white, 24 are black, and 48 are red. They are thoroughly mixed. You reach in and draw out one ball. The probability of drawing a white ball is 8/80, or .10; the probability of drawing a black ball is 24/80, or .30; and of drawing a red ball is 48/80, or .60.

A Definition of Probability. Suppose that in the urn problem we are interested in only one of the three possibilities, for example that of getting a white ball. We can ask the question, what is the probability of *not* getting a white ball? If the probability of getting a white ball is .10, the probability of *not* getting a white ball is 1.00 − .10 or .90. An event will happen or it will not, if it is as discrete a thing as drawing a white ball. The probability of an event occurring we call p, and the probability of its not occurring we call q. The total probability of events in any situation is 1.00, and $p + q$, as defined, always equals 1.00. We are now ready for a formal definition of probability, which may be stated as follows: *If an event can happen in a certain number of distinguishable ways, and if some of the ways be regarded as favorable, then the ratio of the number of favorable ways to the total number of ways is called the probability of the event occurring favorably, provided the total number of ways of occurrence are independent and equally likely.*

In the urn problem the total number of ways is 80. The drawing of each ball is as likely as that of any other ball, due to the thorough mixing and the drawing at random. Each can be drawn independently of the others; there is no connection between them. The "favored" way of occurrence is that kind specified or chosen to be of interest at the moment. "Favoring" in this context does not mean biased drawing. If we "favor" the red-ball event, the total number of favored ways of occurrence is 48.

A Priori versus Empirical Probability. Everything that has been said concerning probability thus far is about purely theoretical situations. The "coins," "dice," and "balls" are merely ideal instruments of thought. The probabilities stated concerning events with these instruments are a priori. They are stated entirely on the basis of defined properties of the objects and situations. They apply before the event. Actual tossings of coin and dice and drawings of balls will turn out with ratios that only approach the a priori probabilities as the number of trials becomes very large. Obtained ratios stand for *empirical* probabilities of events. They pertain to samples, whereas a priori probabilities pertain to hypothetical or ideal populations. Tests of statistical significance have essentially to do with determining whether empirical probabilities are within reasonable limits of a priori probabilities.

The Probability of Alternative Events. The probability of tossing a head is .5; the probability of tossing a tail is .5. The probability of tossing a head *or* a tail is .5 + .5, or 1.00. In this particular case the two probabilities completely exhaust the total possibilities. In tossing a die the probability of coming up with a two or a three is $1/6 + 1/6$, or $1/3$. The probability of coming up with a number greater than 3 is $1/2$, or $1/6 + 1/6 + 1/6$, for the three numbers 4, 5, and 6. In the urn problem, with 8 white, 24 black, and 48 red balls, the probability of drawing a white *or* a black is $8/80 + 24/80$, or $32/80$. The probability of drawing a white or a red one is $8/80 + 48/80$, or $56/80$. The probability of drawing a white or a black or a red one is $8/80 + 24/80 + 48/80$, which equals 1.00. We are certain to get one of the three colors. A probability of 1.0 means certainty. The important principle of this discussion is that *to obtain the probability of two or more alternative events we sum the probabilities of the separate events.*

The Probability of a Repeated Event. Let us take as an example an urn with 50 white and 50 black balls. What is the probability that in two successive drawings you would get two white balls? We shall assume that, after the first ball was drawn, it was put back and the balls were stirred up again so as to restore the original probability. The probability of drawing a white ball the first time is $1/2$, and the probability of drawing one the second time is also $1/2$. Recall the definition of probability—the number of favored ways (*WW*) divided by the total number of ways. There are two ways in which the drawing can happen in the first trial, that is, *W* or *B*. For each one of these ways there are two ways in which the second drawing can occur. The total number of ways is four, specifically, *WW*, *WB*, *BW*, and *BB*. The probability we are looking for is $1/4$, or .25. What is the probability of drawing three white balls in three successive draws? There is only one favored way, namely *WWW*. The total number of ways is eight; therefore p is $1/8$, or .125. The probability of four white balls in four successive drawings is $1/16$, or .0625. It should be clear by now that, *in order to find the probability of a repeated or combined event*, we multiply the probabilities of the single events. The probability of two successive white balls is $1/2 \times 1/2$, or $1/4$; that of three successive white balls is $1/2 \times 1/2 \times 1/2$, or $1/8$, and so on.

The same reasoning holds for the repeated tossing of a single coin, or the simultaneous tossing of two or more coins. The probability of three heads in three successive throws is 1/8. Now for a new type of question. In tossing two coins simultaneously, what is the probability of getting *one head and one tail?* Here there are *two* favorable ways. We could have HT or TH. The total number of ways is four, the other two, unfavored ways, being HH and TT. The probability is 1/2. In tossing three coins the probability of getting two heads and one tail is 3/8. In tossing four coins the probability of getting two heads and two tails is 6/16.

In all these cases it will be noted that the denominator of the fraction, the total number of ways, is 2^n, where n is the number of coins. It will be noted

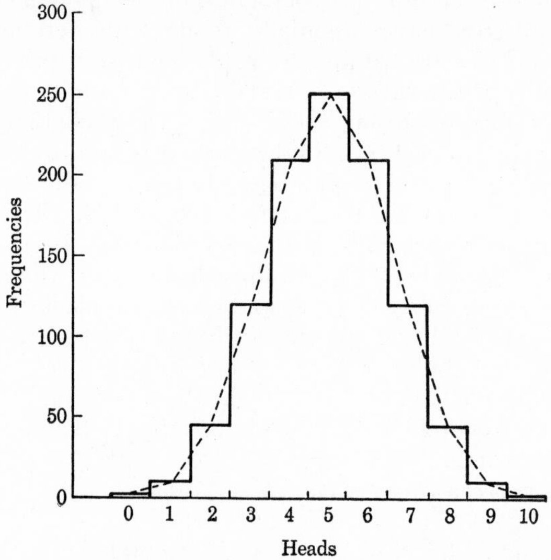

FIG. 3.11. Distribution of expected frequencies of various numbers of heads in 1,024 throws of 10 coins.

also that when the case of two heads is called for, the numerator depends upon the number of combinations of two heads that can be found among three or four coins. Three coins or objects taken two at a time give three combinations. Four coins taken two at a time give six combinations. One could write out all the single possibilities, for example, the three coins could give HHT, HTH, or THH. The four coins could give $HHTT$, $HTHT$, $HTTH$, $THHT$, $THTH$, or $TTHH$. There is a general formula by which the number of combinations of n objects taken r at a time can be readily calculated. It reads

$$_nC_r = \frac{n!}{r!(n-r)!} \tag{3.20}$$

The formula reads: The number of combinations of n objects taken r at a time equals n *factorial* divided by r factorial times $(n - r)$ factorial. The expression n factorial when expanded reads as follows: $n(n - 1)(n - 2)(n - 3) \cdots (n - n + 1)$, and the other factorials are expanded likewise. Solving the last example given, that of four coins taken two at a time,

$$ {}_nC_r = \frac{4 \times 3 \times 2 \times 1}{(2 \times 1)(2 \times 1)} = 6 $$

Assume now that we have 10 coins that are tossed together. What are the probabilities of getting the various numbers of heads and tails? The total number of ways in which 10 coins could fall is $(2)^{10}$, or 1,024. The value 1,024 will be the denominator of every fraction expressing a probability. The numerators are to be found by using formula (3.20). Table 3.9 gives the results, and Fig. 3.11 expresses the distribution of probabilities graphically.

TABLE 3.9. THE PROBABILITIES OF GETTING EACH NUMBER OF HEADS AND TAILS IN TOSSING 10 COINS

Heads	Tails	Favored ways, frequencies (f)	Probabilities (p)		q ($q = 1 - p$)
			Fractions	Decimal numbers	
0	10	1	1/1024	.00098	.99902
1	9	10	10/1024	.00977	.99023
2	8	45	45/1024	.04395	.95605
3	7	120	120/1024	.11719	.88281
4	6	210	210/1024	.20498	.79502
5	5	252	252/1024	.24609	.75391
6	4	210	210/1024	.20498	.79502
7	3	120	120/1024	.11719	.88281
8	2	45	45/1024	.04395	.95605
9	1	10	10/1024	.00977	.99023
10	0	1	1/1024	.00098	.99902
	Σ	1024	1024/1024	.99983	

The Binomial Expansion. The probabilities of the various numbers of heads in tossing a group of coins are given by the terms of the *binomial expansion.* Every student probably remembers that $(p + q)^2$ is equal to $p^2 + 2pq + q^2$. The coefficients of the three terms of this expansion are 1, 2, and 1, respectively. If we substitute for p and q the probabilities of our problem, we have $(1/2 + 1/2)^2$, which gives $1/4 + 2/4 + 1/4$, when expanded. These are the three probabilities of getting 0 heads, 1 head, and 2 heads, respectively, when tossing two coins. With three coins the expansion is of $(1/2 + 1/2)^3$, which equals $1/8 + 3/8 + 3/8 + 1/8$, giving the probabilities of 0 heads, 1 head, 2 heads, and 3 heads, respectively. The general formula is

$$ (p + q)^n = p^n + n\,p^{n-1}q + \frac{n(n-1)}{1 \times 2}\,p^{n-2}q^2 + \frac{n(n-1)(n-2)}{1 \times 2 \times 3}\,p^{n-3}q^3 + \frac{n(n-1)(n-2)(n-3)}{1 \times 2 \times 3 \times 4}\,p^{n-4}q^4 + \cdots + q^n $$

Students who are familiar with the terms of the binomial expansion may prefer to use them in working out the probabilities in tossing coins.

The Normal or Gaussian Function. The normal distribution curve is a mathematical function for which we can write a mathematical equation. It is beyond the scope of this book to show how that equation has been derived, but the student can readily believe that it has been derived from the binomial expansion that was just mentioned. The histogram in Fig. 3.11 was drawn from the theoretical distribution of the frequencies of various numbers of heads when 10 coins are tossed. The heights of the different columns, as was said before, were found from the binomial expansion of $(1/2 + 1/2)^{10}$. We have as the result a binomial distribution.

Now suppose we double the number of coins, letting the total width of the curve remain the same, with the new columns just half as wide. Suppose we keep on increasing the number of coins without limit. The rectangles then approach lines in width and their tops merge into a smooth curve without steps. We have at last the smooth normal distribution curve. We may think of the smooth normal distribution curve therefore as representing the frequencies of different numbers of heads when an infinite number of coins have been tossed.

The general formula for the normal distribution curve is usually given as follows:

$$Y = \frac{N}{\sigma\sqrt{2\pi}} e^{-\frac{x^2}{2\sigma^2}} \tag{3.21}$$

where N = number of measurements
π = pi, or 3.1416
σ = standard deviation of the distribution
e = base of Napierian system of logarithms and has fixed value of approximately 2.718
x = a deviation $(X - M)$

Let us see what equation (3.21) means. The first terms, N, σ, and the square root of 2π, are constant for any given distribution. They have nothing important to do with the general shape of the curve. The symbol e is also a constant value, namely, 2.718. The independent variable x appears in the exponent of e. Y changes according to that exponent, and the value of the exponent changes according to the value of x. Let us assign a few values to x and then see what happens to Y. If x is equal to zero, the whole exponent becomes zero. We know that any number to the power zero is equal to 1. Thus e to the power zero equals 1. We know from this fact that the expression $e^{-\frac{x^2}{2\sigma^2}}$ will never be greater than 1 and that, when x departs from zero, either plus or minus, this expression becomes smaller. The curve will be symmetrical about the Y axis because of the x^2 in equation.

It will be noticed that instead of capital X we have small x in these equations. X stands for the original measurements made on the experimental scale. In applying the Gaussian equation to any particular set of data, we must make two changes. We must change the unit of measurement and we must shift the origin. The origin is shifted to the mean of the distribution; the mean then becomes zero. All measurements are then expressed as deviations x, where $x = X - M$.

The other required change is effected by making the standard deviation of the distribution the unit of measurement. Any measurement that is expressed in terms of sigma units from the origin is called a *standard measure* or *standard score* or *deviate*. The general formula for transforming a raw measurement into a standard measure is

$$z = \frac{X - M}{\sigma} = \frac{x}{\sigma} \tag{3.22}$$

It will be noted that the expression for the standard measure squared appears in the exponent of equation (3.21). The exponent is $(1/2)(x^2/\sigma^2)$. It could also be written as $z^2/2$.

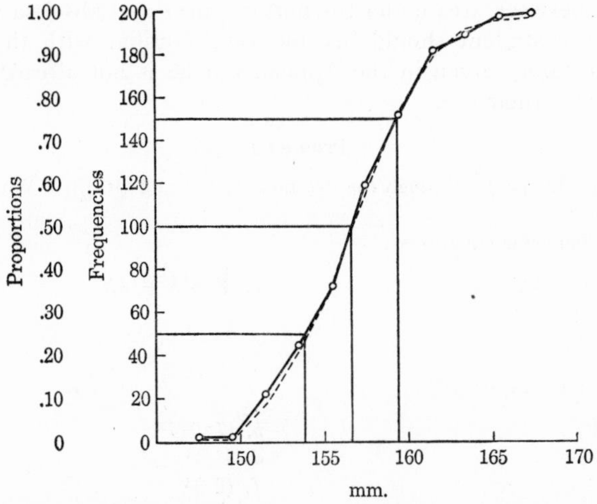

FIG. 3.12. Cumulative frequency distributions. Actual frequencies are indicated by the solid lines and expected frequencies by the dotted lines.

The Cumulative Normal Distribution. The student is probably already familiar with cumulative frequency distributions. A cumulative frequency corresponding to a class interval in a distribution is the sum of the number of cases in that interval plus all those below that interval. If we think of a normal distribution as being made up of a very large number of extremely narrow class intervals and also think of the frequencies in those intervals being cumulated, the cumulative values give us a continuously rising function of x. The total result is an S-shaped curve known as the *ogive* (see Fig. 3.12).

The ogive curve is mathematically known as the integral of the normal distribution curve. Its general mathematical formula is written

$$p = \int_{-\infty}^{x} \frac{1}{\sigma\sqrt{2\pi}} e^{-\frac{x^2}{2\sigma^2}}\, dx \tag{3.23}$$

where x = a deviation from the mean, as usual, and p = the proportion of the area below any assigned value of x.

The integral sign is an elongated letter S and stands for sum. The limits on the abscissa that bound the area are given at the top and bottom of the integral sign. The expression dx is merely a sign of differentiation and need not concern the nonmathematical student. The formula may be interpreted as follows: The proportion p of the area under the curve between the limits of minus infinity to a given x value is equal to the sum of all the areas between those two limits. The values of p corresponding to a given x can be obtained directly from tables of the normal probability integral, or they can be obtained less directly from Table B in the Appendix.

There are several types of distribution curves and functions other than the Gaussian, which has been discussed here. Space is not taken to describe the other types because only the normal curve encounters utilization in the chapters to follow. Much use is made, especially, of the cumulative curve and of the relations between area under the normal curve and abscissa values. For this reason the student should become very familiar with the use of the normal-curve tables given in the Appendix if he is not already sufficiently acquainted with their use.

Problems

1. A straight line passes through the two points (2,6) and (10,18). What is the equation for this line?

2. Plot the following equations:

   a. $Y = 5 - .4X$ *b.* $Y = 5 + .3X$

   c. $Y = \frac{1}{.3X}$

3. Simplify these expressions:

   a. $(3^2)(3^4)$ *b.* $(7^{-1})(7^5)$

   c. $(5^{1.1})(5^{1.7})$ *d.* $4^7/4^5$

   e. $6^{-3}/6^2$ *f.* $(2^{.5})^4$

   g. $\sqrt[4]{3^2}$

4. Find the logarithms (to the base 10) of:

   a. 516 *b.* 51.6

   c. 5.16 *d.* .516

   e. .0516

5. By using logarithms find:

   a. $24^{2.5}$ *b.* $\sqrt[5]{24}$

   c. $\sqrt[3]{.024}$ *d.* (2.4)(.015)

6. Data 3*A* includes 10 pairs of observations selected from Table 3.2. Perform the following operations:

   a. Fit a straight line to these 10 points by the four methods described in this chapter.

   b. Compute the statistics r, r^2, σ_{yx}, and correct for number.

   c. Plot all pertinent figures.

DATA 3*A*. TEN PAIRS OF OBSERVATIONS OF LINE LENGTH (S) AND CORRESPONDING PROBABLE ERROR OF REPRODUCTIONS (s)

S	20	40	70	100	130	170	210	250	290	340
s	1.5	2.5	4.9	5.5	7.2	8.4	9.0	10.1	11.2	10.1

7. Fit the same data to what seems to be the most appropriate curvilinear function, derive the equation, and compute the essential statistics. Plot diagrams.

8. Transform the X_2 values in Table 3.8 into other values that have a mean of 50.0 and SD of 10.0. Compute M and σ of the new values as a check.

9. In tossing two dice, what is the probability of throwing two 3's? A 2 and a 3? Either a pair of 3's or a pair of 5's? A sum of 7 spots? A sum of 11 spots?

10. What is the probability that a coin will turn up 5 heads in succession? 6 tails in succession?

11. In throwing 6 coins, what are the probabilities of obtaining: 0 heads? 1 head? 2 heads? 3 heads? 4 heads? 5 heads? 6 heads?

Answers

1. $Y = 3 + 1.5X$.
3. (*a*) 3^6; (*b*) 7^4; (*c*) $5^{2.8}$; (*d*) 4^2; (*e*) 6^{-5}; (*f*) 2^2; (*g*) $3^{0.5}$.
4. (*a*) 2.7126; (*b*) 1.7126; (*c*) 0.7126; (*d*) $\bar{1}.7126$; (*e*) $\bar{2}.7126$.
5. (*a*) 2822; (*b*) 1.888; (*c*) .2885; (*d*) .036.
6. Equation:

$$s = 2.36 + .0289S \qquad r = .943;\ r^2 = .889;\ \sigma_{yx} = 1.052$$
$$_cr = .936;\ {}_cr^2 = .876;\ {}_c\sigma_{yx} = 1.176$$

7. Equation:

$$\log s = .713 \log S - .703 \qquad p = .984;\ p^2 = .968;\ \sigma_{yf(x)} = .563$$
$$s = .198S^{.713} \qquad {}_cp = .979;\ {}_cp^2 = .959;\ {}_c\sigma_{yf(x)} = .673$$

9. 1/36; 1/18; 1/18; 1/6; 1/18.
10. 1/32; 1/64.
11. 1/64; 6/64; 15/64; 20/64; 15/64; 6/64; 1/64.

References

1. Baker, G. A. An application of linear regression analysis to biometric data. *Poultry Sci.*, 1949, **28,** 293–297.
2. Blankenship, A. B. Regression and standard error calculation from the normal equations. *J. exp. Educ.*, 1937, **5,** 294–295.
3. Deming, W. E. The chi-test and curve fitting. *J. Amer. statist. Ass.*, 1934, **29,** 372–382.
4. ———. *Statistical Adjustment of Data.* New York: Wiley, 1943.
5. Ezekiel, M. *Methods of Correlation Analysis*, 2d ed. New York: Wiley, 1941.
6. Feller, W. *An Introduction to Probability Theory and Its Applications.* New York: Wiley, 1950.
7. Guilford, J. P. *Fundamental Statistics in Psychology and Education*, 2d ed. New York: McGraw-Hill, 1950.
8. Gulliksen, H. Quantitative training for research in social sciences. *Research Bulletin.* Princeton, N.J.: Educational Testing Service, 1950.
9. Huntington, E. V. Curve-fitting by the method of least squares and the method of moments, in Rietz, *Handbook of Mathematical Statistics.* Boston: Houghton Mifflin, 1924.
10. Lewis, D. *Quantitative Methods in Psychology.* Iowa City, Iowa: D. Lewis, 1948.
11. Mueller, C. G. Numerical transformations in the analysis of experimental data. *Psychol. Bull.*, 1949, **46,** 198–223.

CHAPTER 4

THE METHOD OF AVERAGE ERROR

The method of average error is one of the oldest and most fundamental of the psychophysical methods. The aim of the method is to determine equal (equivalent) stimuli by active adjustment on the part of the observer *O*. *O* is provided with a standard stimulus S_s. He is also provided with a stimulus S_v which is obviously different from S_s, being of greater or less quantity than S_s in some defined respect. *O* adjusts S_v until it seems to him to be equivalent to S_s in that respect. His adjustment is his judgment of S_s, represented on the *S* scale. A number of such judgments are obtained from *O* and their central tendency (almost always an arithmetic mean) is taken as the *S* value that is equivalent to S_s under the experimental conditions prevailing.

The method sometimes goes by other names. Because *O* is attempting to reproduce a given stimulus, it is often called the *method of reproduction*. Its unique feature, among psychophysical methods, is that *O* actively controls a comparison stimulus. This suggests the name *method of adjustment* (13, p. 395). In terms of what the investigator is attempting to achieve, it might be called the *method of equivalent stimuli*. Adjustment by *O* is used for other purposes than equating stimuli, and there are other procedures for equating stimuli than by having *O* adjust one of them. There is no good, short term descriptive of a method in which *O* equates stimuli by active adjustment. We shall therefore follow tradition which calls it the method of average error, in spite of the fact that this refers to the process for treating results rather than the process of obtaining judgments.

Origin of the Method. According to Titchener (11, II, p. 160) the method is a "free gift to psychophysics from the exact sciences of physics and astronomy." K. A. Steinheil published a paper in 1837 in which he described a method of equating variable lighted surfaces to the brightness of certain stars. A similar method of measuring the brightness of stars was employed by P. A. E. Laugier.

Fechner introduced the method into psychophysics, describing his use of it in his *Elemente* with visual and tactual measurements. In his revision of the *Elemente* in 1882 he gave the details of his procedure, which are worth quoting (4, p. 105).

> A certain distance, *e.g.*, between compass points or parallel threads, is presented. This I call the normal distance. I am to make another distance, the error distance, as nearly equal to this as it can be made by eye. First of all, starting from an error distance that is too large or too small, I adjust it roughly, in an irresponsible sort of way, to apparent equality with the normal. Then I consider whether or not it really corresponds to sensible equality, and I shift the boundary of the error distance, thread or compass point, to and fro—until I seem, with a definitive adjustment, to have touched equality as closely as I may.

This is essentially as the procedure stands today, although certain alterations have been suggested. G. E. Müller, for example, would have *O* adjust the variable stimulus back and forth in the region of equality, attempting to find the total range of settings that can be taken as equal. Having found this range, *O* then tries to find the midpoint of that range. Others have found such a task very difficult to follow. Still others have not permitted *O* to shift the variable setting back and forth in order to satisfy himself that the two are equal. Moving S_v toward the point of equality from one direction, *O* may not change direction, but must take pains to stop just when he has reached the point of equality. This procedure has been used by Kellogg (7) and others.

A Typical Experimental Design

The psychophysical methods provided fairly good experimental designs before the modern statistics of R. A. Fisher came on the scene. Each method implies a design of its own or a kind of design that can be adapted to meet

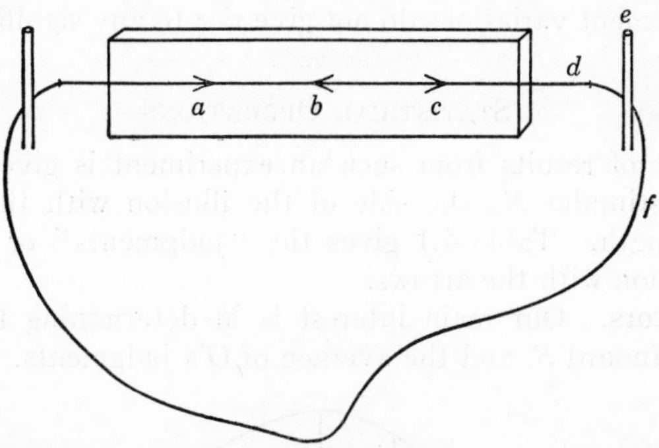

Fig. 4.1. A simple apparatus for an experiment on the extent of the Müller-Lyer illusion. The observer moves arrow *c*, which is attached to the central line *d*, by pulling string *f*.

special requirements. Some of these designs lend themselves very readily to treatment by analysis-of-variance procedures, as we shall see. We should take advantage of that powerful and convenient type of statistical procedure when it is called for. Good experimental designing is likely to make such procedures the natural ones for determining the effects of variations of conditions. Designing principles that have arisen from the use of analysis of variance undoubtedly offer some improvements over the classical psychophysical designs.

An Experiment on the Müller-Lyer Illusion. The problem with which the method of average error will be illustrated has to do with the measurement of the amount of distortion of line lengths in the well-known Müller-Lyer illusion. The standard stimulus is a horizontal line with "feathers" added and the variable stimulus is a horizontal line with arrowheads (hereafter referred to as arrows) added. The experimental apparatus is illustrated in Fig. 4.1. The apparatus is crude but will serve to illustrate the method.

In half of the observations S_v should be on *O*'s left and in the other half on his right. These two space arrangements are denoted as *L* and *R*, respectively. In half of each of these sets, R and L, the trials should start with S_v obviously too great so that the movement of the terminal arrow is inward. In the other half S_v is set obviously too small so that the movement is outward. The latter distinction gives rise to two conditions denoted by I and O, respectively. There are consequently four combinations of conditions: RO, RI, LO, and LI. Let us suppose that a total of 80 settings is made by O. In sets of 10 observations of a kind, complete counterbalancing of the space (R and L) and movement (O and I) conditions can be achieved by following the sequence: RO, LI, LO, RI, LI, RO, RI, LO. Within each set of 10 the experimenter should randomize the settings among large, medium, and small starting lengths for S_v.

The reason for the systematic variation in space and movement conditions is that we want any conclusions regarding the extent of the illusion to be somewhat general. We do not want them restricted to one space arrangement and one movement arrangement, if we can help it. Whether or not we can thus generalize the conclusion will depend upon the finding that these space and movement variations do not give rise to any significant differences in means.

Statistical Operations

A typical set of results from such an experiment is given in Table 4.1. The standard stimulus S_s, the side of the illusion with the feathers, was 140 mm. in length. Table 4.1 gives the "judgments" or settings of the side of the illusion with the arrows.

Constant Errors. Our main interest is in determining the discrepancy between the standard S_s and the average of O's judgments. This measures

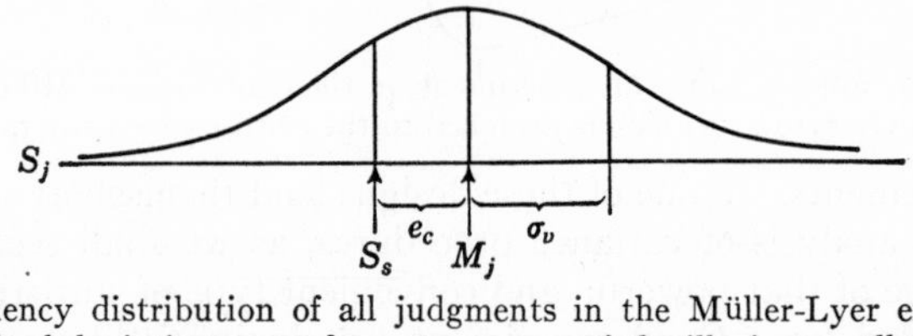

Fig. 4.2. Frequency distribution of all judgments in the Müller-Lyer experiment, with mean M_j, standard deviation σ_v, and constant error of the illusion e_c, all measured on the judgment scale S_j.

the extent of the illusion. It is the main constant error in the experiment. A constant error is produced by a uniform condition or set of conditions and it represents a deviation in a fixed direction and of a given extent. It is obvious from an inspection of Table 4.1 that the constant error of the illusion is a positive deviation. The mean of the judgments M_j is greater than S_s, and the difference $M_j - S_s$ is positive. There has been a general overestimation of the line with the feathers and a general underestimation of the line with the arrows, as we should expect. If we call this constant error e_c, we define it as follows:

$$e_c = M_j - S_s \tag{4.1}$$

The relations of S_s, M_j, and e_c are shown graphically in Fig. 4.2. The line S_j stands for the judgment scale, on which both S_s and M_j are measured.

TABLE 4.1. EIGHTY OBSERVATIONS (REPRODUCTIONS) OF A LINE IN THE MÜLLER-LYER ILLUSION. THE STANDARD STIMULUS (WITH THE FEATHERS) WAS 140.0 MM. IN LENGTH. THE VARIABLE STIMULUS WAS THE LINE WITH THE ARROWS. TWO CONDITIONS WERE VARIED: VARIABLE ON THE RIGHT (*R*) AND ON THE LEFT (*L*); VARIABLE TERMINUS MOVED OUTWARD (*O*) AND INWARD (*I*)

Movement condition	Space Condition: *R*		*L*	
O	156	156	160	157
	163	159	156	166
	157	150	163	161
	158	159	164	154
	148	160	161	159
	159	156	156	160
	150	157	155	162
	159	159	153	163
	155	164	159	156
	156	155	158	155
I	159	160	160	156
	159	160	155	149
	156	156	160	160
	149	157	164	153
	158	156	161	161
	160	158	158	165
	150	152	164	161
	157	157	153	153
	161	148	158	159
	160	153	156	158

There are two other constant errors that are of incidental interest here—in the difference between the means for the *R* and *L* observations and in the difference between the means for the *O* and *I* observations. In *some* experiments the differences might well be of much more interest, for example, if there were some prior hypotheses concerning the effects of space and movement variations. Here we are concerned about these differences only if they are so large that we do not feel justified in combining all four sets of data in order to compute one M_j which consequently represents a broader set of conditions. In designing the experiment, it was hoped that these differences would be statistically insignificant. In this event, it could be assumed that all four sets of judgments arose by random sampling from the same universe or population of observations. If either of the differences is statistically significant, we should have to assume at least two populations of observations and to report two e_c values. If both are statistically significant, we should have four constant errors of the illusion, each holding for a single combination of space-and-movement conditions. We next examine the four sets of data to see whether they are sufficiently homogeneous to justify the conclusion that they came from the same population and hence can be justifiably treated as such. We shall be quite liberal about combining data and not reject the null hypothesis unless differences are significant beyond the .01 point.

Testing the Data for Homogeneity. We could compare the means M_r and M_l by means of a t test on the one hand, combining the O and I data in doing so, and compare means M_o and M_i on the other hand, combining the R and L data in doing so. But this would assume homogeneity in the one direction while testing for homogeneity in the other. The more efficient and more defensible procedure is analysis of variance, with a two-way classification.[1]

The computation of means and sums of squares for sets, rows, and columns is carried out in Table 4.2. To reduce computational labor, the data of Table 4.1 were coded by deducting the constant 145 from each value. This will lower the means by the constant 145 but will have no effect on the variances. We begin the analysis with a table of k columns and r rows, with n observations in each set. The columns and rows are composed of sets of 40 observations each, so that $k = 2$, $r = 2$, and $n = 20$.

The Sums of Squares. The total sum of squares is given by the equation

$$\sum x^2_t = \sum X^2_{ij} - \frac{(\Sigma X_{ij})^2}{N} \tag{4.2}$$

where X_{ij} = each single observation (coded). Applying (4.2) to the data in Table 4.2,

$$\sum x^2_t = 13{,}866 - \frac{(1{,}004)^2}{80} = 13{,}866 - 12{,}600.2 = 1{,}265.8$$

The sum of squares from between the four sets is given by the general equation

$$\sum d^2_{rk} = \frac{\Sigma(\Sigma X_{rk})^2}{n} - \frac{(\Sigma X_{ij})^2}{N} \tag{4.3}$$

where ΣX_{rk} stands for the sum of the observations in a set at the intersection of row r and column k. Note that the last term in this equation is the same as the last term in (4.2). This value will appear as the last term in subsequent equations and will be replaced with the symbol C (for correction factor). From the data in Table 4.2,

$$\sum d^2_{rk} = \frac{236^2 + 278^2 + 226^2 + 264^2}{20} - 12{,}600.2$$
$$= 12{,}687.6 - 12{,}600.2 = 87.4$$

[1] See Guilford (6, Chap. 10) for solving this type of problem, or Edwards (3) or Snedecor (10). The subscripts used here will be consistent with those in (6, Chap. 10). The necessary formulas will be repeated here for convenience.

TABLE 4.2. COMPUTATION OF MEANS AND SUMS OF SQUARES FOR CODED VALUES CORRESPONDING TO OBSERVATIONS IN TABLE 4.1

Code: $X = S_j - 145$

Movement condition		Space Condition *R*		Space Condition *L*		ΣX_r	M_r	ΣX^2_r
O		11	11	15	12			
		18	14	11	21			
		12	5	18	16			
		13	14	19	9			
		3	15	16	14			
		14	11	11	15			
		5	12	10	17			
		14	14	8	18			
		10	19	14	11			
		11	10	13	10			
	ΣX	236		278		514		
	M_{rk}	11.8		13.9			12.85	
	ΣX^2		3,090		4,114			7,204
I		14	15	15	11			
		14	15	10	4			
		11	11	15	15			
		4	12	19	8			
		13	11	16	16			
		15	13	13	20			
		5	7	19	16			
		12	12	8	8			
		16	3	13	14			
		15	8	11	13			
	ΣX	226		264		490		
	M_{rk}	11.3		13.2			12.25	
	ΣX^2		2,844		3,818			6,662
	ΣX_k	462		542		1,004		
	M_k	11.55		13.55			12.55	
	ΣX^2_k		5,934		7,932			13,866

The sum of squares from between rows is given by

$$\sum d^2_r = \frac{\Sigma(\Sigma X_r)^2}{nk} - C \tag{4.4}$$

where ΣX_r means the sum of all observations in row r. As indicated above, C is the correction factor $(\Sigma X_{ij})^2/N$. From the data in Table 4.2,

$$\sum d^2_r = \frac{514^2 + 490^2}{40} - 12{,}600.2$$

$$= 12{,}607.4 - 12{,}600.2 = 7.2$$

The sum of squares between columns is given by

$$\sum d^2_k = \frac{\Sigma(\Sigma X_k)^2}{nr} - C \tag{4.5}$$

where ΣX_k is the sum of all observations in column k.

For the present data,

$$\sum d^2_k = \frac{462^2 + 542^2}{40} - 12{,}600.2$$
$$= 12{,}680.2 - 12{,}600.2 = 80.0$$

The sum of squares for interaction is given by

$$\Sigma d^2_{r\times k} = \Sigma d^2_{rk} - \Sigma d^2_r - \Sigma d^2_k \tag{4.6}$$

The three terms at the right are already known, so that

$$\Sigma d^2_{r\times k} = 87.4 - 7.2 - 80.0 = 0.2$$

The sum of squares from within sets is given by

$$\Sigma x^2_s = \Sigma x^2_t - \Sigma d^2_{rk} \tag{4.7}$$

Using values already obtained above,

$$\Sigma x^2_s = 1{,}265.8 - 87.4 = 1{,}178.4$$

Degree of Freedom. The numbers of degrees of freedom to use in estimating each type of variance in this kind of problem are as follows:

Source	Degrees of Freedom
Between rows	$r - 1$
Between columns	$k - 1$
Interaction	$(r - 1)(k - 1)$
Within sets	$N - rk = rk(n - 1)$
Total	$N - 1$

The F Ratios. Using these degrees of freedom and the sums of squares given above, the estimates of variance and the F ratios arising from them are given in Table 4.3. Only one F is at all significant, but it is not significant beyond the .01 point. We therefore do not reject the hypothesis that these

TABLE 4.3. SUMMARY OF ESTIMATED VARIANCES AND F RATIOS FOR THE MÜLLER-LYER PROBLEM

Source	Sum of squares	df	V	F	Significance
Space (S)	80.0	1	80.0	5.16	$.05 > p > .01$
Movement (M)	7.2	1	7.2	0.46	$p > .05$
Interaction ($S \times M$)	0.2	1	0.2	0.01	$p > .05$
Within sets	1,178.4	76	15.51		

data came from the same population. We may combine the data to obtain a single mean and a single estimate of the amount of the illusion.

The Constant Errors of Space and Movement. Although the differences $M_r - M_l$ and $M_o - M_i$ did not prove to be statistically significant here, within the criterion adopted, those differences deserve some discussion. In other experiments they may prove to be significant and their interpretation then is in order.

It should be said, first, that what we call the space error is not equal to the difference $M_r - M_l$, but to half that distance. Denoting the space error by e_s, by formula

$$e_s = \frac{|M_r - M_l|}{2} \tag{4.8}$$

From the means in Table 4.4 we see that the space error is

$$\frac{|156.55 - 158.55|}{2} = 1.00$$

Interpreted, this means that M_r is 1.00 mm. less than M_j and that M_l is 1.00 mm. greater than M_j. The space error is illustrated in Fig. 4.3.

Likewise, the constant error of movement is given by the formula

$$e_m = \frac{|M_o - M_i|}{2} \tag{4.9}$$

Using the means we have obtained, $e_m = |157.85 - 157.25|/2 = 0.30$. When the movements of the end of S_v were outward, the mean error was +0.30, and when they were inward, the mean error was −0.30.[1] A figure similar to Fig. 4.3 could be used to illustrate the error of movement.

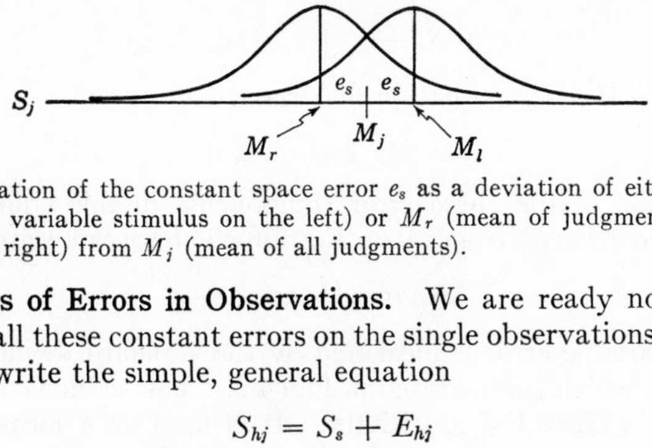

FIG. 4.3. Illustration of the constant space error e_s as a deviation of either M_l (mean of judgments with variable stimulus on the left) or M_r (mean of judgments with variable stimulus on the right) from M_j (mean of all judgments).

An Analysis of Errors in Observations. We are ready now to consider the effects of all these constant errors on the single observations or judgments. We can first write the simple, general equation

$$S_{hj} = S_s + E_{hj} \tag{4.10}$$

where S_{hj} = the judgment (expressed on the stimulus scale) on occasion O_h, and E_{hj} = a total error of observation made at the same moment. This equation is similar to (2.5), except that the latter is in reference to the

[1] Doughty (2) has found that the direction from which O approaches equality does often have a marked effect. This is overcome to a large extent by allowing O to make readjustments after arriving in the proximity of his final judgment.

response scale. Later discussion will relate the whole matter of observations in the method of average error to the psychophysical theory discussed in Chap. 2.

TABLE 4.4. A SUMMARY OF THE MEANS OF JUDGMENTS IN THE MÜLLER-LYER EXPERIMENT FOR DATA FRACTIONATED BY SPACE CONDITIONS AND MOVEMENT CONDITIONS AND FOR THE TOTAL DATA

	Condition				
	Space		Movement		Total
	R	L	O	I	
M	156.55	158.55	157.85	157.25	157.55
σ	3.87	3.83	4.03	4.20	4.13
σ_M	.62	.61	.65	.67	.46

Our interest in E_{hj} is to examine its several components which have been identified and evaluated in the preceding statistical operations. In the present sample it is composed of the main constant error e_c of the illusion, a space component e_s, and a movement component e_m. There is also a residual component e_r. We may express this information by the summative equation

$$E_{hj} = e_c + e_s + e_m + e_r \tag{4.11}$$

In all this discussion of component contributions to total error we assume that the components are mutually independent. We also assume that the sum of errors of each kind (except for e_c) equals zero. With E_{hj} thus broken down into components, we may rewrite (4.10) as follows:

$$S_{hj} = S_s + e_c + e_s + e_m + e_r \tag{4.12}$$

Since $S_s + e_c = M_j$ [from equation (4.1)], we may write

$$S_{hj} = M_j + e_s + e_m + e_r \tag{4.13}$$

The combination of the three error components in this equation may be defined as the *occasional variable error* E_{hv}, for which we can write the equation

$$E_{hv} = e_s + e_m + e_r \tag{4.14}$$

The average variable error is measured by the standard deviation σ_v of the combined data, which is illustrated in Fig. 4.2. This value is often used as a measure of O's differential sensitivity. It is used as a measure of ΔS in testing Weber's law. Other measures of variability, such as the average deviation, the semi-interquartile range Q, and the probable error have also been used for this purpose. If e_s and e_m prove to be statistically significant, however, it would be best to use a measure of e_r as the index of differential sensitivity. This residual component contains both the interaction and the within-sets variations. Should the interaction variance prove to be significant also, the residual source of variance should be broken down further and the within-sets standard deviation used as the measure of a ΔS.

General Evaluation of the Method

In this concluding section of the chapter we shall consider several general and specific aspects of the method. We shall see in what way the method is related to the general psychophysical theory proposed in Chap. 2. We shall consider some of its strong and weak points. We shall also see where it best applies and where its application is in some doubt.

Psychophysical Theory and the Method of Average Error. In the method of average error, O is observing and comparing two stimuli, but he is not making a comparative judgment. In asking O to make comparative judgments, we usually instruct him to *avoid* judgments of equality. In producing equivalent-appearing stimuli, O is giving judgments of equality and avoiding nonequality judgments. These facts furnish the cues to the general description of psychophysical events in the method of average error.

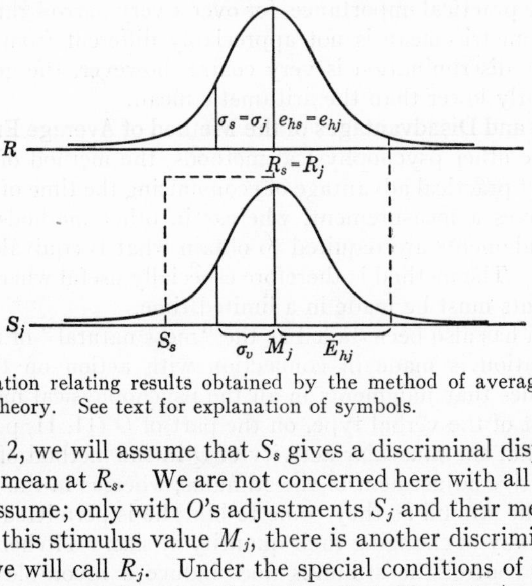

FIG. 4.4. Illustration relating results obtained by the method of average error to basic psychophysical theory. See text for explanation of symbols.

As in Chap. 2, we will assume that S_s gives a discriminal dispersion on the R scale with a mean at R_s. We are not concerned here with all the quantities that S_v may assume; only with O's adjustments S_j and their mean M_j. Corresponding to this stimulus value M_j, there is another discriminal dispersion whose mean we will call R_j. Under the special conditions of stimulation in the experiment, $R_j = R_s$ in spite of the fact that $M_j \neq S_s$ (see Fig. 4.4).

There are also two discriminal dispersions to consider, with σ_s and σ_j, corresponding to R_s and R_j. What relationship exists between them?

If we apply equation (2.5) to this situation, we have two errors of observation involved. We have the relation $R_{hs} = R_s + e_{hs}$, pertaining to the observation of the standard stimulus, and $R_{hj} = R_j + e_{hj}$, pertaining to the adjusted or judgment stimulus. Since O is attempting to make the two stimuli appear equal, and since, as we have concluded before, $R_j = R_s$, if R_{hj} is to equal R_{hs}, the two errors on that occasion must be equal so that $e_{hj} = e_{hs}$. Since the two errors are equal, they are perfectly correlated and $\sigma_j = \sigma_s$. The two discriminal dispersions corresponding to S_s and M_j are shown as identical on the R scale in Fig. 4.4.

From this line of reasoning it follows that the dispersion of S_j, measured by the standard deviation of σ_v of the equated stimuli, is merely a representation on the stimulus scale of a corresponding dispersion of R_{hj} on the psychological scale. And because of the equivalence of errors e_{hs} and e_{hj}, the same conclusion can be stated about the dispersion R_{hs}.[1] The upshot of these conclusions is that the distribution of judgments is a fair picture of the discriminal dispersion for the standard stimulus. In this discussion, however, we have ignored the possible contributions of *O*'s motor adjustments to errors in his judgments. Without excellent controls of the adjustment apparatus, *O*'s motor errors are likely to expand the dispersion of judgments somewhat.

Use of the Geometric Mean. Because the judgments expressed on the *S* scale stand for variations on the *R* scale, it has sometimes been suggested that we compute geometric means of the judgments in finding M_j.[2] This suggestion assumes that Fechner's logarithmic relationship of *R* to *S* applies. An arithmetic mean of log *S* would then be equivalent to averaging *R* values instead of *S* values. The geometric mean of S_j would place the final result back on the *S* scale. The use of a geometric mean in this connection is a matter of little practical importance, for over a very narrow range of stimulus values the geometric mean is not appreciably different from an arithmetic mean. Where discrimination is very coarse, however, the geometric mean would be slightly lower than the arithmetic mean.

Advantages and Disadvantages of the Method of Average Error. As compared with the other psychophysical methods, the method of average error has the distinct practical advantage of economizing the time of both *E* and *O*. Every trial gives a measurement, whereas in other methods several trials and several judgments are required to obtain what is equivalent to a single measurement. The method is therefore especially useful wherever a number of measurements must be made in a limited time.

The method has also been hailed as the "most natural" of methods, since the discrimination is made in connection with action on the part of *O*. Titchener replies that judgments in all the psychophysical methods involve action, at least of the verbal type, on the part of *O* (11, II, p. 147). But it may be said that the muscular activity of *O* in the method of average error involves an active adjustment of the stimulus, whereas in the other methods *O* must take the stimuli as they come to him; he is permitted to do nothing with them by way of changing their quantity or size. Titchener admits that being able to control the stimulus does induce a favorable attitude in *O* (11, II, p. 147) and that it is sometimes baffling in the other methods not to be able to do anything with the stimuli. The active participation of *O*, aside from being able to control the stimulus, may have its beneficial influence. This difference may be noted, for example, in the difference in *O*'s attitude during passive versus active estimations of weights.

Perceptual versus Motor Errors. Müller has criticized the method on the score of the muscular participation. The average measurements, he says, are partly dependent upon the "uncertainty of the hand" (9, p. 80). Under the "uncertainty of the hand" we may include several things. The most obvious, perhaps, is the occasional inability of *O* to stop the moving apparatus exactly at the point of phenomenal equality. This difficulty can be overcome by providing *O* with arrangements consisting of levers, worm gears, or

[1] An exception to this conclusion would be if there is something in the experimental conditions disturbing equivalence of the errors as well as of S_s and M_j.

[2] For a discussion of the computation of a geometric mean, see Guilford (6, p. 81).

screw adjustments with which to manipulate the setting of the stimulus. Another thing that might be included is the feeling of muscular effort. This may act as a distracting influence, on the one hand, vying with visual comparison and therefore making visual comparisons less accurate; on the other hand it may act as an irrelevant criterion, if *O* comes to depend upon it for his judgments of equality or inequality.

Fullerton and Cattell took seriously the distinction between "errors of perception" on the one hand and "errors of movement" on the other. After *O* had made an adjustment of a stimulus, they would ask him to state whether the standard and variable stimuli then appeared to be equal. Anyone who has been a subject in one of these experiments will agree that, often, the moment he ceases his adjustments, he may notice that the two stimuli are not exactly equal. Fullerton and Cattell (5) obtained a great many such judgments, and from the number of right and wrong judgments they were able to compare the margin of error as obtained by *O*'s original settings and the margin of error of his visual observations made following the settings. The former errors were greater on the average than the latter, presumably from the contamination of the judgments with the "uncertainty of the hand" (5, pp. 111*ff*.). Titchener, however, minimizes the importance of these muscular contaminations and states that, if the apparatus is easily and accurately adjustable, one need not be concerned about them (11, II, p. 147).

The Constant Time Error. There is one inherent characteristic of the method of average error which puts certain limitations upon its usefulness. This is the constant time error. When S_s and S_v must be given in succession, they must usually be in the same time order: S_s then S_v. With many kinds of stimulation there is often a negative time error. Under some circumstances the time error becomes positive. In the case of a negative time error, the second of two observed stimuli tends to be overestimated. The reverse is true of a positive time error. With other psychophysical methods, when time errors are statistically insignificant, we can balance them out, much as we did the space and movement errors in the illusion experiment, by reversing the time order of presentation of stimuli. With the method of average error this balancing out of a time error is usually precluded. This may not be a serious matter if the constant time error remains the same under variations of experimental conditions. We could still then compare the main constant errors, the time error not affecting differences among them. Or if we are interested in variable errors, the latter are probably not influenced by the time errors. But many times our conclusions would have to be restricted to the particular time order we are able to use.

Other Uncontrolled Errors. Another time factor that may interfere with the validity of the results is the time taken by *O* to make a setting. This is usually uncontrolled. *O* is permitted within limits to take his own time. He is not permitted to make his settings so swiftly that they are carelessly done, nor is he permitted to dally too long and thus impede the progress of the experiment. Within these limits, will variations in speed of adjustment influence the results? If *O* were permitted to make only one movement, in or out, we should readily expect such an influence to be at work. But when *O* may readjust the stimulus a number of times before ceasing his movements, the speed of his movements probably has little effect. Each *O* will probably adapt himself to a tempo that is suitable to him and to the experimental situation, and E may impose upon him any reasonable limits that he feels are adequate. An exact control of timing of O's adjustments would be out of the question, for it would defeat some of the good points of the method. Fullerton and Cattell believed that a change in the time of the movement did have its effect upon the judgment, but Titchener maintained that such errors as they have pointed out can be attributed to such factors as "timidity, warming up, and anxiety" (11, II, p. 150). These factors can be noticed and reported by O and can be brought under control to some extent.

Some Applications of the Method of Average Error. In general, it can be said that the method applies only in those cases in which O can manipulate the variable stimulus, and then only if the variable stimulus is continuously variable. The method has probably found its most useful application in the study of visual extent as in the classical Galton bar experiment and in the measurement of geometric illusions, as was illustrated in this chapter. It has been used in the study of visual intensities, in matching colored papers to equivalent grays, and in measuring the chromas of colors. It can likewise be used in the study of tonal attributes, pitch, and intensity. It has been adapted to the study of bodily movements, O being asked to reproduce a certain pull on a dynamometer or a certain extent or time of movement of the arm. It can be adapted to certain problems in memory, for example, memory for size and shape of objects after different time intervals. Although it is a convenient method for the investigation of the perception of time, it should be so used with some hesitation. When O tries to reproduce a standard time interval, his own reaction time enters into his response. This would be only a minor source of error when the standard time intervals are relatively large, but it jeopardizes the results when the time intervals are small.

The Measurement of Difference Limens. Fechner suggested that the method of average error could be used to measure the DL, and he has been followed in this belief by many others. Usually it has been the probable error (PE) of a distribution that has been used as a DL. Not all have maintained that the PE is a quantity equivalent to the DL that is found by other methods, but many believe that the PE is at least roughly proportional to the DL and that it measures inversely the sensitivity of O.[1]

As a matter of fact, Weber's law can be verified by the use of any of the measures of dispersion, and the law will be satisfied if

$$\frac{PE}{M} = K$$

$$\frac{\sigma}{M} = K'$$

$$\frac{AD}{M} = K''$$

[1] Urban (12) has maintained that the average deviation of the dispersion is the most appropriate constant to use in this case. He gives proof that under certain conditions the AD is equivalent to one-half the "interval of uncertainty" of his constant process (see Chap. 6) and thus is a comparable index of sensitivity.

Kellogg has attacked the question experimentally (7). With light intensities and sound intensities he used both the method of average error and the method of constant stimulus differences. In 106 cases out of 120 the σ obtained by the former method was smaller than the corresponding σ obtained by the latter method. This means that the two methods give numerically different measurements of differential sensitivity. Both methods would still verify Weber's law, however, if the σ's from both increase in proportion to the magnitude of the average stimulus. But the correlation between the σ's, obtained by the two different methods, was .81 for the light stimuli and only .35 for the sound stimuli (7, p. 59). The discrepancies between the two σ's are so large that one or both may be invalid for the testing of Weber's law. Since the σ's for the method of average error were on the whole more variable from day to day in the same observer, Kellogg concluded that it is an inferior method for testing Weber's law. But it might be mentioned that Kellogg did not follow the letter, and perhaps the spirit, of the method of average error since he permitted *O* to make only one movement of the stimulus in bringing it to the point of equality, not allowing any further adjustments. His method of computing the σ's in the method of constant stimulus differences is also open to question since it involves certain guesses about the ends of the distributions of judgments. In view of these facts, all we can say is that the measure of variability found in the method of average error is roughly proportional to the *DL* as found by other methods and that further work is needed to determine the nature of the relationship between the two.

Problems

1. Test the data in Table 4*A* for homogeneity by making an analysis of variance.

DATA 4*A*. THE FOLLOWING 40 OBSERVATIONS WERE MADE IN AN EXPERIMENT ON THE MÜLLER-LYER ILLUSION SIMILAR TO THAT DESCRIBED IN THIS CHAPTER. THE STANDARD STIMULUS (WITH FEATHERS) WAS A LINE 100 MM. IN LENGTH

Variable left		Variable right	
Movement			
Out	In	Out	In
123	122	116	119
117	122	115	119
120	114	117	116
122	117	112	119
117	117	118	118
113	116	119	120
116	120	120	116
118	120	110	117
119	116	115	113
118	120	114	120

2. Compute the various constant errors, including the main error of the illusion, the space error, and movement error. Also estimate a measure of variable error.

Answers

1. F (for space) = 3.78; F (for movement) = 1.85; F (for interaction) = 1.05; all below the .05 point for significance.

2. M_t = 117.5 mm.; constant error of the illusion, 17.5. Error of movement, 0.55 mm.; space error, 0.85 mm.; standard deviation σ_t = 2.85. M_R = 116.65; M_L = 118.35; M_O = 116.95; M_I = 118.05.

References

1. Brown, W., and Thomson, G. H. *The Essentials of Mental Measurement.* 4th ed. New York: Cambridge University Press, 1940.
2. Doughty, J. M. The effect of psychophysical method and context on pitch and loudness functions. *J. exp. Psychol.*, 1949, **39,** 729–745.
3. Edwards, A. L. *Experimental Design in Psychological Research.* New York: Rinehart, 1950.
4. Fechner, G. T. *Revision der Hauptpunkte der Psychophysik.* Leipzig: Breitkopf und Härtel, 1882.
5. Fullerton, G. S., and Cattell, J. McK. On the perception of small differences. *Publ. Univ. Penn., Phil. Series,* No. 2, 1892.
6. Guilford, J. P. *Fundamental Statistics in Psychology and Education.* 2d ed. New York: McGraw-Hill, 1950.
7. Kellogg, W. N. An experimental comparison of psychophysical methods. *Arch. Psychol. N.Y.*, 1929, **17,** No. 106.
8. Kirschmann, A. Grundzüge der psychologischen Maszmethoden, in Abderhalden, *Handbuch der biologischen Arbeitsmethoden.* Abt. VI, Teil A. Berlin: Urban & Schwarzenberg, 1927.
9. Müller, G. E. *Zur Grundlegung der Psychophysik.* Berlin: Griefen, 1878.
10. Snedecor, G. W. *Statistical Methods.* 4th ed. Ames, Iowa: Collegiate, 1946.
11. Titchener, E. B. *Experimental Psychology,* Vol. II, Pts. I and II. New York: Macmillan, 1905.
12. Urban, F. M. *Die Methode des durchschnitlichen Fehlers. Arch. ges. Psychol.*, 1930, **74,** 141–162.
13. Woodworth, R. S. *Experimental Psychology.* New York: Holt, 1938.

CHAPTER 5

METHOD OF MINIMAL CHANGES

(METHOD OF LIMITS)

Nature of the Method

The Method of Just Noticeable Differences. The method of minimal changes grew out of the *method of just noticeable differences*. This method presupposed that the human observer can recognize a just noticeable difference (*jnd*) when he experiences one. Weber, for example, would set the variable stimulus S_v equal to the standard stimulus S_s and then increase S_v (or decrease it) by small steps until the observer reported that he perceived a *jnd*.

Fechner recommended a change in the method which has been generally adopted. He recommended the approach to the *jnd* not only from the position of physical equality but also from positions of inequality. S_v is decidedly greater than (or less than) S_s; then S_v is made to approach S_s by small steps until *O* reports that the difference is no longer noticeable. This gave rise to the concept of the *just not noticeable difference* (*jnnd*).

But, as would be expected, the *jnd* and the *jnnd* gave two different measurements of the difference limen, the latter being usually somewhat smaller than the former. It was not a long jump to the conclusion that neither is by itself a true measure of the limen, but that the true limen lies between them. This conclusion was best brought out by Müller, who asserted that the difference limen is not an observable psychological quantity as Weber and others had thought. It is rather an ideal, calculated, statistical value to be reached by averaging the *jnd* and *jnnd* (11, p. 63). This statistical conception of the limen, not only of the *DL* but also of limens in general, has become the prevailing one since Müller's time.

Wundt's Method of Minimal Changes. In 1880, Wundt introduced what he called the method *Minimaländerungen* (18, pp. 326*ff*.). The striking thing about the method for him was the serial order in which the stimuli were presented. *O* knows much about the arrangement of the stimuli. He knows whether it is one of increasing differences or of decreasing differences. Wundt seemed to regard this as one of the virtues of the method. *O*'s judgments of successive stimuli are determined somewhat by all his previous judgments in the series. He is able to keep in mind the particular kind of change that is to occur. His attention can be relaxed at first but it increases to a maximum as the limen is approached. This eliminates the necessity for a maximal degree of attention for every stimulation and guarantees a favorable attitude for observation at the critical moment. The method of Wundt has been called the method with complete knowledge. *E* knows where the point of physical equality is, and *O* knows when the series starts with equality and when it starts with a difference in a given direction.

Constant Errors of Habituation and Expectation. Others have been impressed with the constant errors in Wundt's procedure. One is the *error of habituation*. This tendency, if *O* is not on his guard, will induce him to continue to give the same judgment too long in any one series. He may suddenly become aware of the fact that the difference has changed to equality, or vice versa, after the phenomenal change should normally have occurred. The result would be that the point of *jnnd* would be much nearer the point of equality than the point of *jnd*. Of course, since the limen is obtained from the mean of these two points, the error of habituation would be canceled out, assuming that this error is equally strong in both directions.

Wundt's procedure may introduce still another constant error, the *error of expectation*. This factor induces *O* to be too ready for a change in a series; the heightened attention and the strong expectation, as in all cases of suggestion, may force an early change, or *O* may report a change before any has phenomenally occurred because he thinks a change ought already to have occurred. This expectation factor, if stronger than the habituation factor, makes the *jnd* measurement nearer the point of equality than is the *jnnd*. The former *DL*, based on the *jnd*, would therefore be smaller in size than the latter. But the use of both ascending and descending series tends to cancel out this constant error as well as that of habituation. Wundt recognized these errors and maintained that it is better to work with full cognizance of them and to cancel them out as best one can by varying the order of the stimuli than to work with haphazard order of presentation, in which the same constant errors may be present but not so well controlled.

The Stimulus Error. Other errors in the procedure with complete knowledge may be pointed out. One of these is the so-called stimulus error which has been emphasized by Titchener, Boring (1), and others. Since *O* knows when the two stimuli at the beginning of a series are physically equal, he takes his two corresponding phenomenal experiences as also being equal, whereas, if he did not know that the two stimuli are equal, he might take the two experiences as being phenomenally unequal. This may have its influence upon the judgments of the entire series. Again, starting with two stimuli that are physically unequal, he may keep in mind this fact of physical inequality, for example, the fact that S_v is greater than S_s; this phenomenal relationship he maintains until he guesses that it is about time for S_v to equal S_s.

We know from other methods, when the relationship between S_v and S_s is changed haphazardly and in a manner entirely unknown to *O*, that, when S_v is physically greater than S_s, *O*'s judgment may be the reverse, that S_v is less than S_s in a small proportion of the times. His knowledge in Wundt's serial presentation of stimuli prevents such reversals.

Whenever the term is used in this book, a stimulus error will mean merely that certain items of knowledge about the stimulating conditions serve as irrelevant criteria in the formation of *O*'s judgments. Further mentions of stimulus errors will be found from time to time.

The Method with Part Knowledge. A modified procedure, suggested by both Titchener (13, I, pp. 55*ff.*) and Kirschmann (8, p. 414), overcomes to some extent the stimulus error. It has been called the method with part knowledge. Instead of setting S_v equal to S_s, every series is begun with the two stimuli noticeably different. If S_v is set at the beginning so as to appear decidedly greater than S_s, *E* does not end the series when *O* reports "equal," but keeps on until *O* makes the second change in his judgments, namely, the report of "less." The part knowledge consists in the fact that *O* knows in which direction the change in the stimulus difference is tending. This undoubtedly keeps his judgments in line, so that his only report at the first part of a descending series is that S_v is greater than S_s, until he notes a lack of difference. His report tends not to revert back from $S_v = S_s$ to the previous judgment, but to continue until he can say S_v is less than S_s, at which point the series ends.[1] The extent of the part knowledge can be further reduced by altering the starting points of the series so as to produce long, short, and medium series.

We are now ready to illustrate how the method is applied, first in the determination of a stimulus limen S_0 and then in the determination of a difference limen.

The Determination of a Stimulus Limen

The application of the method of minimal changes to the determination of a stimulus limen will be illustrated by means of a crude experiment on the threshold for pitch. The apparatus used was Appunn's lamella, which consists essentially of a steel strip clamped to a rigid support at one end. The free end is plucked to set it in vibration. Frequency of sound waves is varied by changing the length of the vibrating segment of the strip.

Ten ascending series and ten descending series were given to provide the experimental data recorded in Table 5.1. The sequence of the series was ordered in counterbalanced manner, as shown at the top of the table. The small changes were 1 cycle per second (c.p.s.). The starting points for ascending series were varied from 5 through 9 c.p.s. and for the descending series from 21 through 16 c.p.s. A plus sign was recorded when *O* reported a tone and a minus sign when he reported no tone. Each series was stopped as soon as his report was changed from + to − or from − to +. An estimate of the limen is made for each series, taking the midpoint between the two stimulus values where the change occurred. Thus, in the first series, the last report of + was at 13 c.p.s. and the first report of − at 12 c.p.s. The limen is estimated at 12.5.

Computation of the Stimulus Limen. The value to report for S_0 will be an average of the limens obtained from the different series. First, however, we should see whether the limens obtained under the various conditions are homogeneous; whether they could have arisen by random sampling from a single population of measurements. We have both ascending and descending

[1] According to Titchener (13, II, p. 21) it was Kraepelin who in 1891 called the procedure the *method of limits*. This name arose from the fact that the series always ends when *O* reaches a limit at the point of change in his judgments. The name is commonly used at the present time, although it would seem to the writer that it is not so suggestive as minimal changes.

TABLE 5.1. RECORD SHEET FOR THE METHOD OF MINIMAL CHANGES IN FINDING A STIMULUS LIMEN

Series order	*d*	*a*	*d*	*a*	*d*	*a*	*d*	*a*	*d*	*a*	*a*	*d*	*a*	*d*	*a*	*d*	*a*	*d*	*a*	*d*
Stimulus values, c.p.s																				
22																				
21	+								+											+
20	+								+											+
19	+				+				+			+		+						+
18	+		+		+				+			+		+				+		+
17	+		+		+		+		+			+		+				+		+
16	+		+		+		+		+			+		+		+		+		+
15	+		+		+		+		+			+		+		+		+		+
14	+		+		+		+		+	+		+		+		+		+		+
13	+	+	+	+	+		+	+	+	−		+		+		+	+	+		+
12	−	−	+	−	−		+	−	+	−		−	+	+	+	+	−	+	+	+
11		−	−	−		+	−	−	−	−	+		−	+	−	+	−	+	−	−
10		−		−		−		−		−	−		−	−	−	−	−	−	−	
9		−		−		−		−		−	−		−		−		−		−	
8		−				−					−		−		−		−		−	
7						−					−		−						−	
6						−					−								−	
5						−					−								−	
Limens............	12.5	12.5	11.5	12.5	12.5	10.5	11.5	12.5	11.5	13.5	10.5	12.5	11.5	10.5	11.5	10.5	12.5	10.5	11.5	11.5

series. We also have the possibility of learning and fatigue effects. The former phenomenon may have given us decreasing limens as time progressed and the latter may have given us increasing limens. Since these two effects are opposite in direction, they may tend to cancel one another. But one might be stronger than the other. If learning were rapid and if rests were frequent, the learning effects should outweigh the fatigue effects. If learning had become ineffective and if there were insufficient rest pauses, the fatigue effects should predominate.

We will therefore first make a study of homogeneity by analysis of variance in a two-way factorial design. There are two orders and two time blocks, including first half and last half of the observations. The results of the analysis are summarized in Table 5.2, where it is seen that there is only one

TABLE 5.2. SUMMARY OF F RATIOS FOR THE DETERMINATION OF INTERNAL HOMOGENEITY OF THE DATA ON THE STIMULUS LIMEN FOR PITCH

Source of variance	Sum of squares	Degrees of freedom	Estimate of variance	F ratio	Significance
Series order (O)........	0.8	1	0.8	1.14	$p > .05$
Time (T)................	3.2	1	3.2	4.57	$.01 < p < .05$
Interaction ($O \times T$)......	0.0	1	0.0	0.0	$p > .05$
Within sets.............	11.2	16	0.70		
Total..................	15.2	19	0.80		

variation which suggests significance and that is just barely beyond the .05 point. We will therefore accept the hypothesis of homogeneity and treat all the data as one set.

A summary of the means, standard deviations, and standard errors of means is given in Table 5.3 for the data as a whole and also fractionated according to order and according to time. The mean limen is 11.7 c.p.s. with a standard error of .19.

TABLE 5.3. MEANS, STANDARD DEVIATIONS, AND STANDARD ERRORS OF MEANS UNDER DIFFERENT CONDITIONS OF THE PITCH-LIMEN EXPERIMENT*

	All data	Ascending series	Descending series	First 10 series	Last 10 series
M	11.7	11.9	11.5	12.1	11.3
$_c\sigma$	0.84	0.87	0.71	0.75	0.69
σ_M	0.19	0.29	0.24	0.25	0.23
Difference......		0.4		0.8	

* Sheppard's correction applied to the standard deviations.

The Constant Errors. If we want to know about the relative effects of serial order in a case like this, by analogy to the determination of space and movement errors in the preceding chapter, we would examine the difference between the means for ascending and descending series. The difference is 0.4 c.p.s., which is not statistically significant. Such a difference would not indicate the strength of either the error of habituation or of anticipation, but of an excess of the one over the other. Since the mean for the ascending series is higher here, there is in the sample a slight excess in favor of the error of habituation. Here we can well tolerate the conclusion that the order error was due to chance.

As between the factors of learning and fatigue, the balance is in favor of learning, with a gross difference of 0.8 c.p.s. This error is significant just beyond the .05 point. We tolerated this much difference in combining the data, so we should stay by the original choice of confidence level and conclude that there is insufficient reason to believe that there was a genuine excess of learning over fatigue effect.

Determination of a Difference Limen and a Weber Ratio

An Experimental Design for Obtaining a Difference Limen. To illustrate the determination of a difference limen by the method of minimal changes, we will find a *DL* for gray near the middle range of stimuli for gray.

The data appearing in Table 5.4 were obtained from an ordinary color rotator. Against a gray background *O* saw an outer gray disk 20 cm. in diameter superimposed upon which was a gray disk 15 cm. in diameter. The standard disk was composed of 180 degrees of white and 180 degrees of black. In half the observations S_v was on the outside (condition *VO*) and in the other half S_v was on the inside (condition *VI*). Ascending series were started with S_v distinctly darker than S_s, and descending series were started with S_v distinctly lighter than S_s. Each series was continued through a run of equality judgments to the first + or − judgment in ascending or descending series, respectively. The step for the minimal changes was 4 degrees.

The Computation of a *DL*. We will assume that each series of observations represented in Table 5.4 is an occasion and that it gives us an estimate of the *DL*. In each series of judgments there is an upper limit, at the transition from "greater" to "equal" judgments, and there is a lower limit at the transition from the "equal" judgments to the "less" judgments. This range of equality judgments covers a span of two *DL*'s; from the *point of subjective equality* to one *DL* higher and from the same point to one *DL* lower.

It is the simplest procedure to make an estimate of $2DL$ for each occasion. In Table 5.4 you will find the value $2DL_h$ listed for each column. Each value is simply obtained by counting the number of equality judgments in the column. Each stimulus interval covers a range of 4 degrees; therefore we are working in terms of a class-interval unit i. In other words, $i = 4°$. The numerical work will be much simpler in terms of this scale.

Before we compute summarizing statistics for $2DL$, and hence the *DL*, we make the usual test of homogeneity. Treating the data in a two-way design, we can determine the significance of the series-order variation and the space-arrangement variation. The analysis of variance shows all the F ratios to be insignificant. We conclude that so far as the *DL* estimates are concerned, the errors of habituation and anticipation have balanced out and the space arrangement makes no real difference in the size of the *DL*. As a matter of

TABLE 5.4. JUDGMENTS OF DIFFERENCES IN BRIGHTNESS BY THE METHOD OF MINIMAL CHANGES. THE STANDARD STIMULUS WAS A ROTATING DISK WITH 180° WHITE AND 180° BLACK

Order	*VO*						*VI*						*VI*						*VO*						Code for *PSE*
S_v	*d*	*a*	*d*	*a*	*d*	*a*	*a*	*d*	*a*	*d*	*a*	*d*	*d*	*a*	*d*	*a*	*d*	*a*	*a*	*d*	*a*	*d*	*a*	*d*	
216	+									+												+			
212	+									+					+							+			
208	+				+			+		+					+							+		+	
204	+				+			+		+					+					+		+		+	
200	+		+		+			+		+		+	+		+		+			+		+		+	
196	+		+		+			+		+		+	+		+		+			+		+		+	
192	+	+	+		=			+		+		+	+		+	+	+		+	+	+	=		+	10
188	+	=	+		=			=		+	+	+	+	+	+	=	=		=	=	=	=		+	8
184	=	=	=	+	=	+	+	=	+	=	=	=	+	=	=	=	=		=	=	=	=	+	=	6
180	=	=	=	=	=	=	=	−	=	=	=	=	=	−	=	=	=	+	=	=	−	=	=	−	4
176	−	−	−	=	−	=	=		=	=	=	−	=	−	−	=	−	=	=	=	−	=	=		2
172		−		=		−	=		−	−	=		=	−		=		=	−	−	−	−	−		0
168		−		=		−	−		−		−		−	−		−		−	−		−		−		
164		−		−		−	−		−		−			−		−		−	−		−		−		
160		−		−		−	−		−		−			−		−		−	−				−		
156		−		−					−		−			−		−			−				−		
152		−		−					−		−			−		−							−		
148				−							−			−									−		
144				−							−			−									−		
$2DL_h$	2	3	2	4	4	2	3	2	2	3	4	2	3	1	2	5	3	2	4	4	2	5	2	1	
PSE_h	5	6	5	1	7	3	2	7	3	4	3	5	2	6	5	4	6	1	5	5	7	6	3	6	

TABLE 5.5. SUMMARY OF THE COMPUTATION OF THE DIFFERENCE LIMEN FOR GRAY, FOR THE DATA AS A WHOLE AND ALSO FRACTIONATED

	Series order		Space arrangement		All data
	Ascending	Descending	*VO*	*VI*	
M	5.67	5.50	5.83	5.33	5.58
$_c\sigma$	2.21	2.10	2.30	1.97	2.15
σ_M	0.62	0.63	0.70	0.61	0.45

interest, however, we may compute means and other statistics of the data fractionated four ways, as shown in Table 5.5. The mean *DL* for all data combined is also given, with standard deviation and standard error of the mean. All values are in terms of degrees of white.

The computations were carried through with the coded values, from which it was found that the mean M' was 2.792 interval units and the standard deviation ${}_c\sigma'$ (with Sheppard's correction) was 1.075.[1] Since in this case both the mean and standard deviation are distances on the scale, they may be treated as ratio-scale values. The mean and standard deviation of $2DL$ in terms of degrees are found by the products iM' and $i\sigma'$. This operation gives us 11.17 degrees for the mean and 4.31 degrees for the standard deviation. But since we are interested in the DL rather than $2DL$, we divide by 2 and obtain the values found in Table 5.5.[2] The DL under these conditions may be taken as 5.58 degrees. The standard error of the mean is 0.45 degree, which indicates a very small margin of probable departure from the population mean.

Computation of the Point of Subjective Equality. In finding a value for the DL, we have one of the two terms needed in $\Delta S/S$, or the Weber ratio. We need a value for S. One might use for this purpose the value of the standard stimulus S_s. This is sometimes done. But it is better practice to use for S the point of subjective equality (PSE). This is because the limits are distributed symmetrically about the PSE and not about S_s, unless the two happen to coincide. The symmetry just referred to is a result of the fact that the PSE is estimated in each series at the mid-value between the two limits. It is the midpoint or median of the equality judgments. The mean of these midpoints is taken as the PSE for the experiment. We shall proceed to compute the PSE for the data on judgments of grays.

In computing the PSE from the data in Table 5.4, a different coding is used for convenience than was used for computing the DL. The system is given in the last column, where it will be seen that the value 0 is assigned to stimulus 172 and even numbers are assigned to the next few higher stimulus intervals up to 10 at stimulus 192. This range includes all the midpoints of the equality judgments. The reason for using even numbers in the code instead of successive integers is that some midpoints come between stimuli. Use of the latter would result in fractions, which would defeat the purpose of coding. The PSE_h values in the bottom row of Table 5.4 range from 1 to 7 and are all integers. The unit of the code scale is 2 degrees.

An analysis of variance applied to these 24 PSE estimates shows one F ratio, that for the variation in series order, to be significant just beyond the .05 point. This kind of result has not been regarded as sufficient reason to forego the combination of data in one composite. The results for the composite and for the data fractionated in four ways are given in Table 5.6. The results show that the setting of S_v must be 180.92 degrees, on the average, to seem equal to the S_s of 180 degrees. The difference between means from ascending and descending series is 3.17, in favor of the error of expectation. The space error is not significant, but it took more white on the outside than on the inside, in this sample. The standard deviations were computed with Sheppard's correction. The standard error of the mean for the total sample is 0.74.

The PSE as a Geometric Mean. In the treatment of the PSE in this problem we have assumed it to be at the arithmetic mean of the two limiting

[1] See Guilford (6, p. 108). The formula used here was ${}_c\sigma = i\sqrt{\sigma'^2 - .0833}$.

[2] It can be easily shown that the standard deviation of CX equals $C\sigma_x$ (see 6, p. 579).

limens. We assumed the distance between the two average limits to be $2DL$. If Fechner's law applies, the PSE should be a geometric mean of the limits rather than an arithmetic mean. To arrive at such a value, we would need to compute the two mean limits and from them compute a geometric mean. The geometric mean would be equal to $\sqrt{L_u L_l}$, where L_u and L_l are the upper and lower limits, respectively. Since these limits are so near together, however, the geometric mean would be only slightly lower than the PSE as already obtained. When discrimination is rather poor, the difference between the two kinds of means of limits would be appreciable.

TABLE 5.6. SUMMARY OF THE MEANS, STANDARD DEVIATIONS, AND STANDARD ERRORS OF MEANS FOR THE DETERMINATION OF A POINT OF SUBJECTIVE EQUALITY FOR THE JUDGMENT OF GRAYS

	Series order		Space arrangement		All data
	Ascending	Descending	*VO*	*VI*	
M	179.33	182.50	181.83	180.00	180.92
$_c\sigma$	3.73	2.53	3.36	3.51	3.56
σ_M	1.12	0.76	1.01	1.06	0.74
Difference....	3.17		1.83		

Determination of a Weber Ratio. We will next be concerned with the ratio $\Delta S/S$ to find the Weber constant K. We have one measured DL, such as is needed for the numerator, and we have a corresponding measured PSE, such as is needed for the denominator. Ordinarily we could proceed to compute the ratio. Here, owing to the peculiar scale of measurement of S, we shall have to resort to a little scale transformation. The reason is that degrees of white will not indicate the correct amount of light being reflected to the eye of *O*. It would do so if the black reflected zero light, but this is not true.

By means of a photometer we could determine how much light the black does reflect relative to the white. The ratio of the two is all we would need. Then, letting the unit of reflection equal 1 degree of black and knowing the degrees of white and black in the disk at any setting, we could compute the total reflection. It is probably safe to assume a ratio of 25 to 1 for reflection from white and black paper, respectively (8, p. 404). On the basis of this assumption, the reflectance of any setting of the disk is given by the formula

$$S = B + 25W$$

where B = degrees of black and W = degrees of white. Since $B = 360 - W$, with this substitution we have

$$S = 360 - W + 25W = 360 + 24W$$

Applying this equation to the obtained PSE, we find that

$$S = 360 + (24)(180.92) = 4{,}702$$

This value is in photometric units where the unit is 1 degree of black.

We also need to express the *DL* in the same photometric units. We can do this through finding the number of photometric units in a stimulus one *DL* above the *PSE*. The *PSE* plus one *DL* equals 180.92 + 5.58 = 186.50. The latter corresponds to 4,836 photometric units. The difference between this and 4,702 units is 134. The *DL* is therefore 134 photometric units.

The ratio $\Delta S/S$ is therefore equal to 134/4,702, which equals .028. It takes a change of 2.8 per cent to give a difference in brightness at the level of 4,702 units.

Psychophysical Theory and the Method of Minimal Changes. After having the procedure in the method of minimal changes described in some detail, it is easier to see its relation to the theory set forth in Chap. 2. We shall consider this relationship in connection with the illustration in Fig. 5.1. This figure pertains to the finding of a *DL* and a *PSE*. The same reasoning applies to the determination of a stimulus limen.

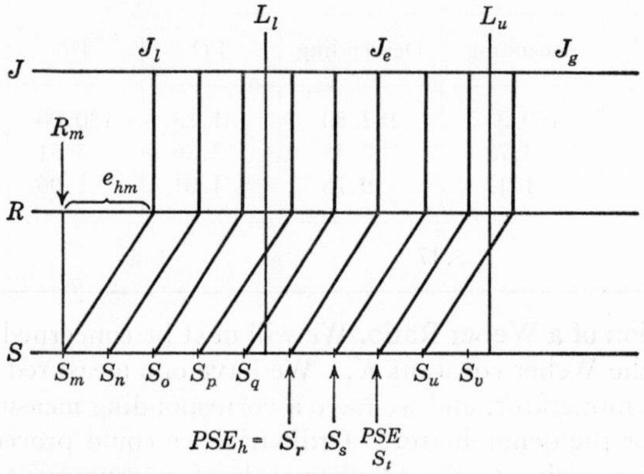

FIG. 5.1. Relationships of events on the scales J, R, and S in an ascending series of variable S_v being compared with a standard S_s. L_l and L_u are the positions of the lower and upper limens dividing three categories of judgments, J_l, J_e, and J_g.

The judgment scale is divided into three categories, J_l, J_e, and J_g, for the "less," "equal," and "greater" judgments, respectively. The illustration shows an ascending series, with S_v beginning at S_m. The typical response for S_m is R_m, consistent with previous theory. At occasion O_h, however, the response is $R_m + e_{hm}$. For the sake of a simple drawing it is assumed that on the same occasion all other responses have a similar error. The errors in R are assumed to be perfectly correlated. It is, indeed, likely that in the serial presentation of S_v the errors are strongly positively correlated. The limens L_l and L_u are the limens of the occasion. As the step-by-step increases in R pass a limen, the judgment changes category. The judgments change in this series from "less" to "equal" as we go from stimulus S_o to S_p. They change from "equal" to "greater" as we pass from S_t to S_u. The *PSE* is shown at the midpoint of the range between L_l and L_u. The *PSE* here just happens to coincide with S_t. In this particular series, PSE_h, the point of subjective equality for occasion O_h, happens to be at S_r.

There is no implication intended in Fig. 5.1 that e_{hj} will necessarily be generally positive in an ascending series, nor should one expect e_{hj} to be negative in a descending series. The degree of intercorrelation of the errors e_{hj} is unknown and certainly should not be expected to be as near +1.0 as the illustration shows. The fact that *O* does not reverse his judgments is one indication that the correlations among errors are positive. If the correlations are actually zero, there must necessarily be compensating variations in the relations of *J* to *R*. In other words, *O* may not be reporting what he actually experiences but is then shifting connections between *R* values and *J* values. The perfect correlation that has usually been assumed between *J* and *R* would then break down. Whatever the relations of *R* to *S* on the one hand and *R* to *J* on the other, the relations of *J* to *S* must be somewhat as shown in Fig. 5.1.

Uses and Criticisms of the Method

The Measurement of Thresholds. As was said at the beginning of this chapter, the method of minimal changes has been used primarily for the measurement of thresholds. It is generally applicable wherever the stimulus series is variable in equal small steps. It has been used to find intensity thresholds for sounds, odors, tastes, colors, temperature, pain, lights, and tactual sensations, to name only a few types of stimulus limens. The procedures may have to be modified to some extent to meet certain peculiarities of some sense departments. For example, descending series cannot be used with success in measuring taste and smell thresholds owing to the rapid adaptation in the latter case and to the persistence of the stimuli in both. Helson found, in a study of the lowest illumination necessary for perceiving visual form, that the descending series had to be given up, since a knowledge of the form made it difficult for *O* to decide just when the form had vanished (7).

There is hardly a qualitative or quantitative psychological variable that yields a *DL* measurement to which the limiting procedure will not apply. In addition to the *DL*'s for the simpler sensory attributes, one can find with this method *DL*'s for more complex perceptual variables such as areas of rectangles and the like, time intervals, and thresholds for visual movement, although Stratton found (12) that the method had to be rejected in his study of movement.

One should, of course, mention in this connection the measurement of two-point limens, tactual and visual, and difference limens of localization of auditory impressions. The mapping of such things as color zones and blind spots comes under the limiting principle and might be included in the list of applications.

Equivalent Stimuli. There is a derivative of the method which is used in finding equivalent stimuli—the so-called *method of equivalents*. In a broad sense, the method of average error, as described in Chap. 4, is a method of equivalents. The main problem involved is for *O* to adjust one stimulus until it appears equivalent to a standard. It is possible to accomplish the same end by letting *E* do the adjusting and by asking *O* merely to judge when the point of equality has been reached. The adjustment may be made by *E* in small steps, in serial changes, or by a continuous variation of the stimulus. It is nearly always more expeditious for *O* to do the adjusting rather than *E*, and by continuous rather than stepwise changes. But circumstances may require the less expeditious method. For example, suppose we want to find out what distance between two points applied to the forehead is equivalent to a longitudinal distance of 5 cm. on the forearm. *O* cannot manipulate the variable stimulus, nor can it be changed continuously. The method of minimal changes is easily adapted to such a problem. The series are begun on either side of the point of subjective equality and are extended through the range of equality judgments to the first change beyond. The computation of the *PSE* is the final result.

Some Criticisms. Some criticisms of the method have already been mentioned and steps taken to meet them have been explained. The errors of habituation and expectation and of practice and fatigue are minimized by the order and arrangement of the series. The stimulus error is partially, although not fully, eliminated. One should, perhaps, say stimulus errors, for there are many aspects of the stimuli and *O*'s knowledge about them which help to form his judgments. In addition to those already discussed, there is the size of the step between stimuli. Undoubtedly, at least in the measurement of a *DL*, the size of the step influences *O*'s judgments. If *O* has had any previous experience with the method, he comes to expect a certain length of series, or at least to expect a certain approximate spread of the equality judgments. *E* usually chooses the size of the step with this in mind. Having a preconceived notion that Weber's law holds, *E* will use smaller steps in the lower part of the scale and larger steps in the upper part of the scale. It is conceivable that, with a highly experienced *O* and *E*, unless measures are taken to prevent it, Weber's law or any other law could be demonstrated to hold merely by a systematic choice of steps.

It may therefore be a good plan in some cases to vary the size of the step in different series of the same set of observations. For example, if in the experiment for determining the *DL* for brightness the customary steps were 168, 171, 174, 177, 180, 183, 186 degrees, etc., the step might be made larger or smaller in some of the series, or it might begin at other points, as 170, 173, 176, 179, 182, 185, etc. To be systematic, the same alteration should be made in all four arrangements, *a* and *d* series and *VO* and *VI* arrangements.

Limiting DL Not Identical with Other DL's. It is rather doubtful whether the *DL* as found by the method of limits is ever directly equivalent to a *DL* that is obtained with other methods, the method of constant stimuli, for example. Although the concept of a *DL* is the same for both methods, the procedures for obtaining it are different.

It may be said in defense of the method that, even if the limiting *DL* is not identical with other *DL*'s, it may still be a valid test of Weber's law. It is a psychological increment, obtained under certain specified conditions, and it should be proportional to *DL*'s found by other methods.

Too Much Depends on the Terminal Judgments. The limit of a series of observations depends upon where the last change in judgment occurs. Since the series is terminated immediately upon a change in judgment, very much depends upon that terminal judgment. If *O* were given additional stimuli beyond the last one in a series, and if given freedom to do so, he would probably reverse his judgment at times. Stopping him immediately after the change seems to assume that he would not reverse himself. Since chance errors weigh relatively heavily in making single judgments, it would seem that the limen derived from each series is not very reliably evaluated. Even to continue until *O* gave two of the new judgments in succession would increase very much the probability that his change was not due to chance. This standard would, of course, enlarge the size of the *DL*.

The terminal judgment is not entirely independent of other judgments in the series, however. We may *not* say, therefore, that *everything* that a series has to contribute is staked upon the one judgment. The interdependence of judgments is assured by the serial order of presentation. This helps to stabilize all judgments. If *O* were judging the same stimuli in haphazard order in a series, his consistency would suffer considerably. It is perhaps not a very great source of error, therefore, to permit the last judgment in a series to determine a value for that series. In terms of degrees of freedom in computing statistics, we treat each series as the source of one observation. In view of the interdependence of judgments in a series this is as liberal as we should be in counting degrees of freedom.

Variations of the Method

Continuous Variation of the Stimulus. Under some circumstances, instead of altering S_v by small steps, it is convenient to produce in it a continuous change. This type of series may be regarded, theoretically, as one in which the size of the steps is infinitely small. It is a great timesaver whenever it can be used. It can be employed, for example, in measuring certain visual thresholds. It is typically the kind of variation that one uses in mapping the blind spot or the color zones. It is similar to the method of reproduction or the procedure in the method of average error, except that *E* varies the stimulus instead of *O* and the change in S_v is never reversed in the same series or observation.

Haphazard Presentation of Stimuli. In 1891, Kraepelin introduced a procedure that substituted a haphazard order of presentation for the serial order of presentation of the stimuli. His main motive was to eliminate the errors of habituation and of expectation. No single judgment is embedded in a series of judgments, and *O* knows almost nothing about the conditions surrounding each stimulation.

Several objections can be offered against the haphazard presentation of stimuli in the method of minimal changes. From a theoretical standpoint it would seem that the method of minimal changes has been entirely deserted, for the changes from one S_v to the next in a series are large as well as small, in a hit-and-miss order. The notion of approaching a limit from either side also seems to be entirely abandoned except in the computation of the threshold. It will be seen later that the procedure of obtaining data is practically the same as in the method of constant stimuli, the only differences being that more stimuli are used for fewer trials each and that the method of computation of the limen is different. In both respects the haphazard order of presentation in the method of minimal changes seems inferior to the constant method.

The data obtained by this procedure present a complete matrix, with as many rows and columns as there are stimuli and occasions (series) with all cells filled. The principles for computing a limen as described in a general way in Chap. 2 may be applied here, or the data may be treated as if they had been derived from the use of the method of constant stimulus differences (see Chap. 6).

The Up-and-down Method. Studies of the sensitivity of explosives have called for psychophysical methods like that of minimal changes. In fact, a method known as the *staircase method* which has been so employed is essentially the method of minimal changes. An object of selected weight is dropped from a constant height upon a sample of the explosive. In ascending series the starting weight is entirely too small to set off an explosion. The weight is increased, with different samples, until an explosion occurs. In a

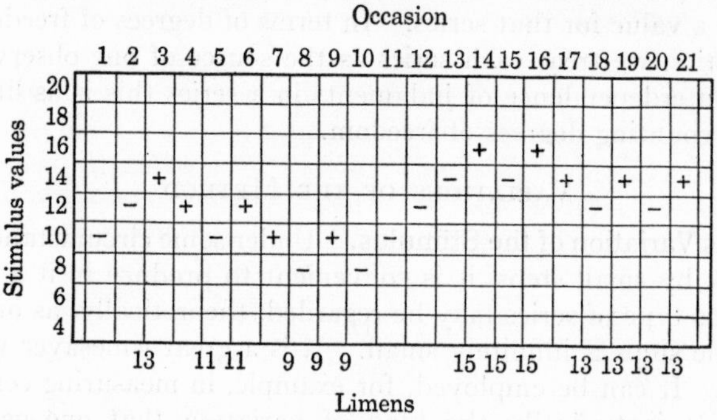

FIG. 5.2. Illustration of judgments obtained by the "up-and-down" method.

descending series the starting weight is sufficiently heavy to touch off an explosion (9).

This method is regarded as too costly, for two reasons. It uses up a relatively large number of samples of material in order to obtain one estimate of the limen (from one series). For this reason some modified procedures have been introduced. In the *up-and-down* method, the direction of minimal change in S each time depends upon whether or not the last stimulus gave an explosion. If it did, the next S will be at the step immediately lower. If it did not, the next S will be at the step immediately higher. The results are something like those illustrated in Fig. 5.2. Every time there is a change in "judgment" it can be assumed that the threshold has been crossed and the best estimate of the threshold at the moment is midway between the two stimuli representing the change. The mean of these estimates may be taken as the limen. Thus a maximum number of observations of the limen is obtained for what is near a minimum number of stimulations.

The method would seem to be a very efficient one. It would be very useful particularly as a preliminary exploration to locate the approximate location of the limen after which a more refined method like that of constant stimuli could be applied. In psychological experimentation single stimulations are much less expensive than in the study of explosives. Another application in which single stimulations are expensive is in the study of the lethal quantities of drugs. A dose of each level in each series requires the use of a different animal. Then those that die are lost to any further use.

The method has had no reported trial in psychophysics. There is a habit of judgment, quite common among human observers, that results in their avoidance of repeating judgments. If that habit were found to apply to the up-and-down method, it would tend to make the human limens appear much more stable than they appear by other methods. It might not give rise to constant errors in the *levels* of thresholds. *O* would, however, readily gain knowledge as to what direction each change of *S* will be.

The Sequential Method. This method was also developed by those working with explosives (9). It also aims at the accurate determination of a limen with an economy of trials. Its specific aim is to find the stimulus that will show a given probability of response. This could be a probability of .50, as usual, but it could also be some selected proportion lower than .50 in order to prevent so many explosions. At any rate, the method begins with the selection of a stimulus of a given quantity and a certain percentage of explosions is hypothesized. By Wald's sequential-analysis statistical procedures we continue with trials of this kind until one of three decisions is reached—the obtained proportion is greater than the hypothesized p, less than the hypothesized p, or E should keep on testing (17). To prevent an indefinitely large number of tests, one may decide in advance to end testing at a certain number of stimulations. If this number is reached before one of the other decisions is reached, it is decided that the limen is at the level at which the tests are being made. If the stimulus proves to be greater than the limen, a lower one is chosen and a new series of tests is begun. There is insufficient space to go into the details here. They may be found discussed in (10).

Problems

1. The data in Table 5*A* were obtained according to methods described in this chapter. Compute the limen and other statistics as described in this chapter.

Data 5*A*. Determination of an Absolute Limen for Pitch by the Method of Minimal Changes

First 10 series		Second 10 series	
Ascending	Descending	Ascending	Descending
16.5	18.5	15.5	15.5
19.5	19.5	15.5	19.5
17.5	18.5	14.5	14.5
14.5	16.5	12.5	15.5
16.5	15.5	15.5	17.5

2. The data in Table 5*B* were obtained according to methods described in this chapter. Compute the *DL*, *PSE*, Weber ratio, and other statistics. Apply the conversion to photometric units that were described in this chapter.

Data 5*B*. Determination of the *DL* for Gray (for a Rotated Disk with 180° White and 180° Black) by the Method of Minimal Changes*

Upper and lower limits (*u* and *l*)								Points of subjective equality			
Variable outside (*VO*)				Variable inside (*VI*)				*VO*		*VI*	
a		*d*		*a*		*d*		*a*	*d*	*a*	*d*
u	*l*	*u*	*l*	*u*	*l*	*u*	*l*				
183	177	181	179	181	177	181	179	180	180	179	180
181	173	187	183	181	177	181	179	177	185	179	180
187	181	189	187	181	179	183	179	184	188	180	181
179	173	183	179	181	177	183	177	179	180	176	181
183	177	187	179	177	175	183	179	176	181	180	183
179	175	181	177	181	179	183	179	180	181	177	179

* The headings *u* and *l* stand for upper and lower limits, respectively. For each series, the quantity 2*DL* is found by the subtraction $u - l$.

Answers

1. $S_o = 16.45$; $_c\sigma = 1.86$; $\sigma_M = 0.43$; $M_a = 15.8$; $M_d = 17.1$; $M_1 = 17.3$; $M_2 = 15.6$.
2. *DL* (in terms of degrees of white) = 2.08; $_c\sigma = 0.93$; $\sigma_M = 0.19$; *DL* (in terms of photometric units) = 49.92; *PSE* (in terms of degrees of white) = 180.25; $\sigma = 2.66$; $\sigma_M = 0.54$; *PSE* (in terms of photometric units) = 4,686; $K = .01065+$.

References

1. Boring, E. G. The stimulus-error. *Amer. J. Psychol.*, 1921, **32,** 449–471.
2. Brown, W., and Thomson, G. H. *The Essentials of Mental Measurement.* 4th ed. New York: Cambridge University Press, 1940.
3. Fechner, G. T. *Elemente der Psychophysik.* Leipzig: Breitkopf und Härtel, 1860.
4. Fernberger, S. W. On the relation of the methods of just perceptible differences and constant stimuli. *Psychol. Monogr.*, 1913, **14,** No. 61.
5. Fullerton, G. S., and Cattell, J. McK. On the perception of small differences. *Publ. Univ. Penn., Phil. Series,* No. 2, 1892.
6. Guilford, J. P. *Fundamental Statistics in Psychology and Education.* 2d ed. New York: McGraw-Hill, 1950.
7. Helson, H., and Fehrer, E. V. The role of form in perception. *Amer. J. Psychol.* 1932, **44,** 79–102.
8. Kirschmann, A. *Grundzüge der psychophysischen Maszmethoden,* in Abderhalden, *Handbuch der biologischen Arbeitsmethoden.* Abt. VI, Teil A. Berlin: Urban & Schwarzenberg, 1927.
9. McCarthy, P. J. A class of methods for estimating reaction to stimuli of varying severity. *J. educ. Psychol.*, 1949, **40,** 143–156.
10. ———. Staircase methods of sensitivity testing. *NAVORD Report,* 65–46, 21 March 1946.
11. Müller, G. E. *Zur Grundlegung der Psychophysik.* Berlin: Griefen, 1878.
12. Stratton, G. M. The method of serial groups. *Psychol. Rev.*, 1902, **9,** 444–447.
13. Titchener, E. B. *Experimental Psychology,* Vol. II, Pts. I and II. New York: Macmillan, 1905.

14. Urban, F. M. *The Application of Statistical Methods to Problems of Psychophysics.* Philadelphia: Psychological Clinic Press, 1908.
15. ———. On the method of just perceptible differences. *Psychol. Rev.*, 1907, **14**, 244–253.
16. ———. Die psychophysischen Maszmethoden als Grundlagen empirischer Messungen. *Arch. ges. Psychol.*, 1909, **15**, 261–355; **16**, 168–227.
17. Wald, A. *Sequential Analysis.* New York: Wiley, 1947.
18. Wundt, W. *Grundzüge der physiologischen Psychologie,* 4 aufl. Leipzig: W. Englemann, 1890.

CHAPTER 6

THE CONSTANT METHODS

The constant methods are generally regarded as the most accurate and the most widely applicable of all the psychophysical methods. They are employed with convenience in the measurement of stimulus limens, differential limens, equal sense distances, and equivalent stimuli, and in the determination of many other psychological constants outside the sphere of psychophysics as well as within its limits. Briefly, the method is conducted as follows.

After preliminary trials E selects a limited number of stimuli, usually four to seven, which are presented to O a large number of times, usually from 50 to 200 times each, in a prearranged order unknown to O. In finding an S_0, each stimulus is presented alone, and O judges either the presence or absence of the desired experience, for example, "two" when studying the two-point threshold. In finding a DL, each stimulus is presented simultaneously with, or in temporal sequence with, a single standard, and O is to report whether the one stimulus is apparently "greater" or "less" than the other; if he is uncertain, he reports "doubtful." The former procedure is known as the *method of constant stimuli* and the latter as the *method of constant stimulus differences.* In either case the limens are computed from the proportions of judgments of different kinds for every stimulus.

The Two-point Tactual Threshold by the Method of Constant Stimuli. As an example of an absolute threshold determined by the method of constant stimuli, let us take the ordinary two-point tactual threshold. Having selected the region of the skin on which the limen is to be determined, E makes some preliminary trials with compass points or an aesthesiometer to determine very roughly the transition zone, within which some judgments are "two" and some are "one." E selects five stimuli such that the middle one is probably close to the limen; the smallest stimulus is likely to give reports of "two" about 5 per cent of the time; and the largest stimulus, to give reports of "two" about 95 per cent of the time. The stimulus intervals are equal. E then applies the stimuli in random (or in some prearranged order not serial) until each stimulus has been applied 100 times. The data from which the limen is to be computed consist of the proportion of the time each stimulus receives the judgment "two." Such data will be seen in Table 6.1. The limen may be computed by several different methods.

Determination of an Absolute Limen[1]

1. The Linear Interpolation Process. The two-point limen, as strictly defined, is that separation of two points that yields 50 per cent judgments of

[1] The general rational basis for finding a limen by the constant method is described in

TABLE 6.1. DATA FOR THE TWO-POINT LIMEN

Stimulus separations (S), mm.	8	9	10	11	12
Proportions of judgments "two" (p).	.01	.05	.29	.66	.93

"two" and 50 per cent judgments of "one." It can readily be seen from the data in Table 6.1 that such a stimulus lies between 10 and 11 mm. The simplest solution is a linear interpolation between the proportions of .29 and .66 to find the limen L which would have given a proportion of .50. We may assume that the two points for $p = .29$ and $p = .66$ are joined by a straight line, as in Fig. 6.1 they appear to be. The interpolation of a median

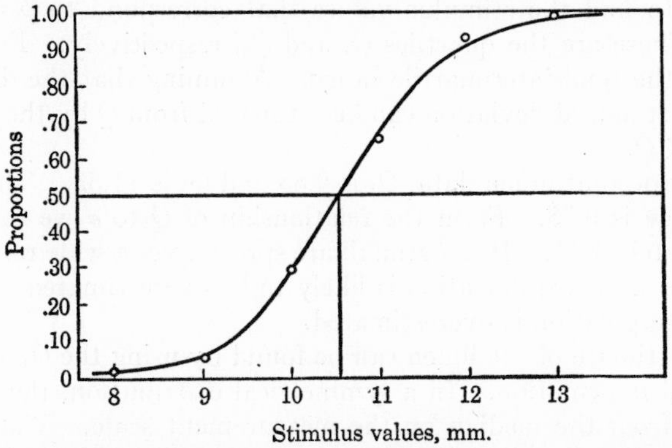

FIG. 6.1. Diagram showing the functional relationship between proportions of judgments "two," in the two-point-limen data, and stimulus values. The points show the obtained relationships. The curve is the best-fitting cumulative normal distribution.

is, of course, no new task for the student. The limen, at $p = .50$, lies .21/.37 of the way in the stimulus interval between 10 and 11 mm., or

$$10 + .57 = 10.57 \text{ mm.}$$

A general formula to fit this particular problem is

$$L = S_l + \frac{(S_h - S_l)(.50 - p_l)}{p_h - p_l} \tag{6.1}$$

where S_h = stimulus immediately higher than the limen
S_l = stimulus immediately lower than the limen
p_h = proportion of "two's" for the stimulus immediately higher than the limen
p_l = proportion of "two's" for the stimulus immediately lower than the limen

Objections to the Linear Interpolation Method. *a.* The linear interpolation method is objectionable because it does not use all the data. In the example above, only two of the five proportions are employed. This is obviously a

Chap. 2. Some of the principles by which such a limen is computed are also described there and may be recognized in the processes to be described in the following pages.

wasteful procedure. To overcome this objection, some investigators recommend that in the experimental procedure we use only two stimuli, which are carefully chosen so as to lie on either side of the limen. In many cases this curtailment of the method is justifiable, as has been shown by Linder (39).

b. The assumption that the curve is a straight line between two points is open to question. In the immediate neighborhood of the limen, however, most psychometric curves of this type are so nearly linear that an insignificant error is made by interpolation.

c. No accurate estimate of dispersion or of reliability can be made. If more than two stimuli have been used and if the extreme proportions are below .25 and above .75, we can make crude estimates of the amount of dispersion and we can improve the estimate of the limen. The procedure is to interpolate to find the stimulus values that correspond to $p = .25$ and to $p = .75$. These are the quartiles Q_1 and Q_3, respectively. From them we can find Q, the semi-interquartile range. Assuming that the distribution is normal, the standard deviation can be estimated from Q by the relationship: $\sigma = 1.483 \times Q$.

For the two-point-limen data, Q_1 is 9.83 and Q_3 is 11.33. The semi-interquartile range is 0.75. From the relationship of Q to σ we can say that σ is approximately 1.11. If few stimuli are spread over a wide range, as in this problem, the standard deviation is likely to be overestimated because the Q found by interpolation is overestimated.

A better estimate of the limen can be found by using the Q_1 and Q_3 values as additional information. In a symmetrical distribution, the quartiles are equidistant from the median on the measurement scale. The distances of Q_1 and Q_3 from the median (10.57) already found are 0.74 and 0.76, respectively, which indicates good symmetry. This fact, combined with the appearance of the plot in Fig. 6.1, is an indication to us that the distribution is very close to normal and thus justifies estimating σ from Q. It also justifies our averaging Q_1, Q_3, and the median to obtain an improved estimate of the limen. This average is 10.58, which does not change the estimate of the limen appreciably. In averaging the three statistics, it is probably best to weigh the median two and each Q one.

This procedure uses four of the observed proportions, which removes most of objection (*a*), that not all the data are used in finding the liminal value. It does not avoid objection (*b*), for in the neighborhood of Q_1 and Q_3 there is much more likely to be nonlinearity than in the neighborhood of the limen. A study of the plot such as in Fig. 6.1 will show why this is so. It also shows why the Q and σ are overestimated. Better estimates of the quartiles and the statistics derived from them can be made by drawing a smoothed S-shaped curve through the trend of the points in such a figure and seeing where the curve crosses the 25 and 75 per cent levels.

2. The Arithmetic Mean of the Uncumulated Distribution. The second procedure must be credited to Spearman (50). The assumption is made that every application of the stimulus locates the limen as above or below the *S* value applied. For example, with the *S* value at 11 mm., if *O* reports "two," the limen is below 11 mm.; with the *S* value at 12, if *O* reports "one," the limen is above 12 mm. To return to our illustrative problem of Table 6.1, at an S value of 8 mm., O reported "two" only once in 100 times. This means that 99 of the limens are above 8 mm. and 1 limen is below that point. With an S value of 9 mm., there are 5 reports of "two." Interpreted in the same manner, 95 of the limens are above 9 mm. and 5 are below. Now if 1 of the limens is below 8 mm. and 5 are below 9 mm., 4 of them must lie between 8 and 9 mm. In the same manner, 24 of them lie between 9 and 10 mm., 37 between 10 and 11 mm., 27 between 11 and 12 mm., and 7 above 12 mm. The cumulative distribution with which we started has thus been transformed into a noncumulative distribution of the more common form.

The greatest difficulty in this procedure, an error that sometimes precludes its use, pertains to the "tail assumptions" that have to be made. We find that one of the limens falls below 8 mm., and it is very reasonable to assume

TABLE 6.2. SOLUTION OF THE TWO-POINT LIMEN BY SPEARMAN'S PROCESS OF COMPUTING AN ARITHMETIC MEAN

S	f	x'	fx'	fx'^2
13–13.9	2	+3	+6	18
12–12.9	5	+2	+10	20
11–11.9	27	+1	+27	27
10–10.9	37	0	0	0
9– 9.9	24	−1	−24	24
8– 8.9	4	−2	−8	16
7– 7.9	1	−3	−3	9
Σ	100		+8	114

$$M = 10.5 + 8/100 = 10.58 \qquad \sigma = \sqrt{114/100} = 1.07$$

$$\sigma_M = 0.10 \qquad {}_c\sigma = 1.02$$

that it lies between 7 and 8 mm. But there are seven limens above 12 mm. Shall we assume that all these lie between 12 and 13 mm.? This is unlikely, but we might assume this for lack of definite information to the contrary.[1] Knowing that the distribution is symmetrical, however, and that the limen comes about midway between 10 and 11 mm., which coincides with the mode (see Table 6.2), we can reasonably divide the seven tail cases into frequencies of 5 and 2, balancing the frequencies of 4 and 1 in the other tail and at the same distance from the median. We shall make this assumption, though we shall find that it does not change results very much.

The results by this procedure compare very well with those obtained by other methods to be described later. We evidently made good tail assump-

[1] According to Thomson (53, p. 75) the simplest tail assumption, that the class interval just beyond the terminal stimulus value at either end of the series contains all the remaining frequencies, may be made when certain conditions are satisfied. First, the proportion of .50 must lie very near the middle stimulus (in the data above this is not true). With five stimuli each judged 100 times, the range of proportions should be as much as from .06 to .94. With seven stimuli judged 100 times each, the range should be .04 to .96. With more than 100 judgments per stimulus, the range should be greater. Thomson describes ways of making tail assumptions other than the simplest when these conditions are not satisfied.

tions. Had we assumed that all seven of the highest limens fell in the interval 12 to 12.9 mm., the (uncorrected) standard deviation would have been 1.02 instead of 1.07. We shall see that these values are very close to those computed by less questionable methods.

Owing to the small number of class intervals, a Sheppard's correction would ordinarily be applied to σ in a problem like this. If we apply this correction to the σ of 1.07, we find that the corrected σ is 1.02. Unless the data extend nearly to proportions of .00 and 1.00 or unless satisfactory tail assumptions have been made, the application of Sheppard's correction here is in some doubt. We might be making even smaller an estimate of dispersion that is already small enough. For example, if we had not divided the tail category, thus extending the range, the corrected standard deviation would have been less than 1.00.

The error in the mean due to faulty tail assumptions is less serious than that in the standard deviation. In the present problem, the difference would be only .02 mm., whether we divided the end frequency or whether we did not. The standard error, as estimated from the (corrected) standard deviation, is .10 mm. The obtained limen is therefore very close to the population value. The error in this statistic due to faulty tail assumptions is fortunately so trivial that it can be ignored.

The Case of Negative Frequencies. If there should happen to be any inversion in the experimental data, which means that the proportions do not increase at every step between stimuli, the corresponding uncumulated frequency is a negative one. Such a frequency should be treated as a negative value in the computation of the limen and standard deviation. You will find such statistics to be in line with those computed by other methods directly from the cumulative frequencies.

3. The Summation Method. Woodworth (63) recommends a process based on the general procedure for computing moments of a distribution. Since the summation method utilizes successive cumulations of the frequencies, the application of the method is natural here where we already have a cumulative distribution to start with. This process, like Spearman's, is best applied when the stimulus range is sufficiently broad to yield terminal proportions of 0 and 1.00. It can be applied when the terminal proportions are so close to those extremes that we may assume that the next ones would have been 0 and 1.00. We will so assume in applying the method to the two-point-limen data, for the sake of an illustration.

There are two equations that give the mean of the distribution and two that give the standard deviation. The mean may be computed by using the equations

$$M = S_1 - .5i - i\Sigma p \qquad (6.2a)$$
$$M = S_0 + .5i + i\Sigma q \qquad (6.2b)$$

where S_1 = stimulus value where p = 1.0 (or is assumed to do so)
S_0 = stimulus value where p = .0 (or is so assumed)
i = size of stimulus interval
p = proportion of judgments in higher judgment category
$q = 1 - p$

The standard deviation may be computed by two other equations:

$$\sigma = i\sqrt{2\Sigma cp - (\Sigma p)^2 - \Sigma p} \quad (6.3a)$$

$$\sigma = i\sqrt{2\Sigma cq - (\Sigma q)^2 - \Sigma q} \quad (6.3b)$$

where i, p, and q are as defined above

cp = proportions p cumulated (from low to high values of p)

cq = a similar cumulation of proportions q.

The application of these formulas to the two-point-limen data is shown in Table 6.3, with the solutions for the means and standard deviations. The results are quite in line with previous estimates of the mean and standard deviation.

TABLE 6.3. SOLUTION OF THE LIMEN AND OTHER STATISTICS BY THE SUMMATION METHOD

S	p	q	cp	cq
12	.93	.07	1.94	.07
11	.66	.34	1.01	.41
10	.29	.71	.35	1.12
9	.05	.95	.06	2.07
8	.01	.99	.01	3.06
Σ	1.94	3.06	3.37	6.73

$S_0 = 7 \qquad S_1 = 13$

$M = 13 - (.5)(1) - (1)(1.94) = 10.56$ $\qquad M = 7 + (.5)(1) + (1)(3.06) = 10.56$

$\sigma = \sqrt{(2)(3.37) - (1.94)^2 - 1.94} = 1.02$ $\qquad \sigma = \sqrt{(2)(6.73) - (3.06)^2 - 3.06} = 1.02$

4. The Normal-interpolation Process. The normal-interpolation process was first suggested by Newhall (45). It is undoubtedly an improvement over the linear-interpolation process mentioned previously. The method assumes that the psychometric function relating p to S is the cumulative normal curve. The essential step is the transformation of the p values into corresponding deviates or standard-measure values z. The relationship of z to S should then be approximately linear.[1] The limen is the S value corresponding to a z of zero, which can be obtained by interpolating between the two stimuli giving z's immediately on either side of zero. Objection (b) to

TABLE 6.4. TRANSFORMATION OF PROPORTIONS INTO CORRESPONDING STANDARD-MEASURE VALUES FOR THE TWO-POINT-LIMEN DATA

S	8	9	10	11	12
p	.01	.05	.29	.66	.93
z	−2.326	−1.645	−0.553	+0.413	+1.476

[1] Strictly speaking, linearity should exist between z and R rather than z and S. This problem is discussed later in the chapter.

the previous linear interpolation method is practically removed. Objection (*c*) is also at least partially met. Objection (*a*) still applies.

Table 6.4 gives the z values corresponding to the original proportions and their stimulus values. Corresponding to an S of 10 is a z of $-.553$. Corresponding to an S of 11 is a z of $+.413$. The limen lies between these two S values. The interpolation is simply done by the formulas

$$L = S_l + \left(\frac{-z_l}{z_h - z_l}\right) i \tag{6.4a}$$

$$L = S_h - \left(\frac{z_h}{z_h - z_i}\right) i \tag{6.4b}$$

where S_l = stimulus value immediately lower than the limen
S_h = stimulus value immediately higher than the limen
z_l = standard measure corresponding to S_l
z_h = standard measure corresponding to S_h
i = interval between stimuli, or $S_h - S_l$

The application of these formulas gives

$$L = 10 + \left[\frac{+.553}{.413 - (-.553)}\right] 1 = 10.57$$

and

$$L = 11 - \left[\frac{.413}{.413 - (-.553)}\right] 1 = 10.57$$

It should be noted that since this is an interpolated value, we have estimated a median of the distribution. If the distribution is normal, of course, and if the fit of the z values to the linear regression on S is very close, the median and mean are practically identical.

The standard deviation of the distribution can also be estimated from the data in Table 6.4. It is simply a matter of interpolating to find the S values corresponding to $z = +1.0$ and $z = -1.0$. The former, by interpolation between S_{11} and S_{12}, is 11.55, and the latter is 9.59. The interval between the two is 2σ, so that half the difference is an estimate of σ. The difference is 1.96, from which σ is estimated to be .98. This is smaller than any estimate yet obtained for these data.

The statistics estimated by this process have the objection that each interpolation is obtained from only two observed frequencies. If either is in error, this will be reflected in the estimates of the mean and of the standard deviation. Figure 6.2 shows the plot of the z values as a function of S. Although the linear trend is obvious and a straight line can be drawn through the points easily by inspection, it will be seen that single points may deviate from the line. The interpolations are made on the dotted lines, and where these depart from the solid line, they yield errors in our estimates. There was apparently no departure in the immediate region of the limen, but there were departures in the regions of $+1\sigma$ and -1σ such as to give the underestimation we found.

5. The Normal Graphic Process. Figure 6.2 suggests another solution to the problem, which avoids the errors just mentioned. Having drawn the straight line as near all the points as we can by inspection, we can use the line as the source of our estimates of the limen and the standard deviation. With the plot made on good graph paper, all we need to do is to note the positions at which $z = -1$, 0, and $+1$ and to see what S values correspond to them. Applying this approach, the limen is estimated at 10.55 mm. and the standard deviation as 1.05. Both of these are in line with previous estimates.

The Use of Normal-probability Graph Paper. The same principle can be applied even more simply to the determination of a limen from constant-method data. The process is also a graphic one, but it does not require the

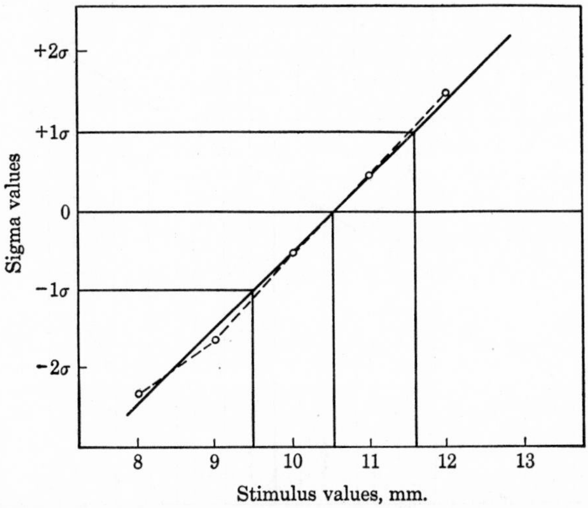

FIG. 6.2. Relationship of the standard-measure (z) values (derived from proportions of judgment "two" in the two-point-limen experiment) to stimulus values. The straight line has been fitted by inspection for a normal-graphic solution for the limen and standard deviation.

transformation of proportions into standard measures. It employs probability graph paper on which the one axis is divided in uneven steps of proportions (or percentages). The steps are spaced according to the normal-distribution function so that when proportions are plotted against stimulus values the regression is linear. The two-point-limen data have been plotted in Fig. 6.3. The use of such a plot to find the limen and standard deviation is essentially the same as in using the plot in Fig. 6.2. The location of the $+1\sigma$ and -1σ positions can be made by using the corresponding percentages of 84.1 and 15.9, respectively. These operations give us an estimate of 10.56 for the limen and 1.03 for the standard deviation.

In both of these graphic solutions, one should give most attention to the points nearest the 50 per cent level and least to those near the extremes. The reason for this will become clear in connection with the use of Müller-Urban weights in the most exact least-square solution.

6. Least-square Solutions with Unweighted Observations. If the distribution of proportions is normal on the stimulus scale, the regression of z on

S is linear, as we saw in connection with the preceding normal graphic process. We can write an equation of the form $z = a + bS$, in which the parameters a and b can be determined by applying the principle of least squares. The parameters then describe a line the deviations from which in the direction of the z variable have been minimized in the sense that the sum of the squares of the z deviations is a minimum. From the parameters a and b we can estimate the parameters of the best-fitting normal distribution, the mean and standard deviation of S. We shall first see how this is done without weighting the experimental observations and later how it is done with weights.

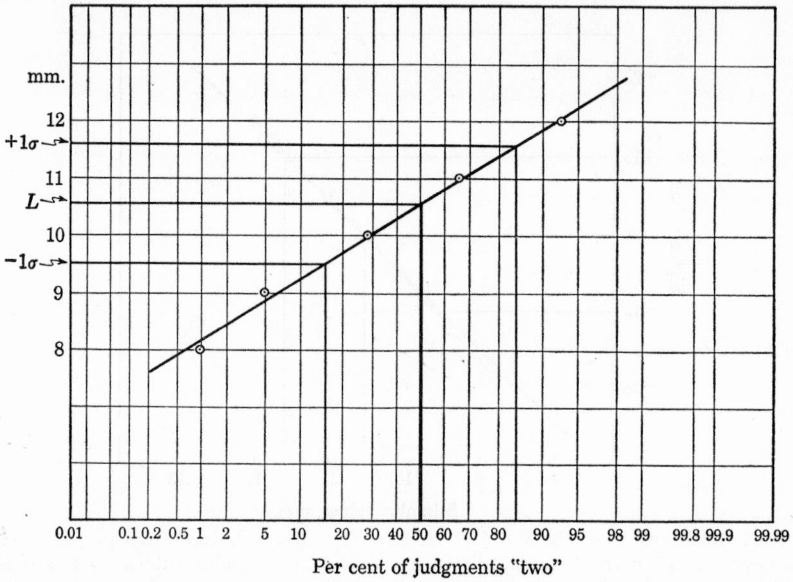

FIG. 6.3. A normal-graphic solution for the two-point limen and the standard deviation based on use of normal-probability paper.

The Phi-gamma Function and the Phi-gamma Hypothesis. The assumption that the normal cumulative distribution describes accurately the relationship of p to S has been known as the *phi-gamma hypothesis*. The psychometric function has been known as the phi-gamma function, or the phi function of gamma. That is to say, $p = \phi(\gamma)$, where γ is a deviation from the mean in terms of a standard measure which bears a close relation to z. Using the more familiar symbols and parameters, the equation for the cumulative normal distribution can be written

$$p = \int_{-\infty}^{z} \frac{1}{\sqrt{2\pi}} e^{-\frac{z^2}{2}} dz \tag{6.5}$$

In the classical psychophysics of Müller and Urban, a parameter γ was used in place of z and a parameter h was used in place of σ. The latter two parameters are related by the equation

$$h^2 = \frac{1}{2\sigma^2} \quad \text{or} \quad h = \frac{1}{\sigma\sqrt{2}}$$

Since h and σ are inversely related, h measures the *precision* or steepness of an ogive curve, whereas σ measures its dispersion or flatness. The constants z and γ are positively related, however, for they both measure deviations from the mean in standard units. Gamma is equal to the product $h\delta$, where δ is a deviation from the mean in stimulus units. Where in general

$$z = (X - M)/\sigma,$$

the corresponding deviate $\gamma = h(S - L)$. The phi-gamma equation reads

$$p = \int_{-\infty}^{\gamma} \frac{1}{\sqrt{\pi}} e^{-\gamma^2}\, d\gamma \tag{6.6}$$

It is clear that we have the choice of utilizing either function (6.5) or (6.6) in fitting experimental data to a normal curve. In what follows we will use the more familiar function involving z and σ rather than the classical one which is rapidly losing favor. If a value for h is wanted for a particular purpose, it may be computed from the relationship to σ given above.

A Solution Based on Uncoded Values. When stimulus values are simple integers or when a calculating machine is available, a very direct solution can be obtained without resort to a guessed mean and a class interval. In this case, it is unnecessary to use z values to more than two decimal places. The equations for estimating the mean and standard deviation are derived from the solution for the parameters in the linear equation $z = a + bS$. By an ordinary least-square solution

$$b = \frac{n\Sigma Sz - (\Sigma S)(\Sigma z)}{n\Sigma S^2 - (\Sigma S)^2} \tag{6.7}$$

where n = the number of pairs of values, S and z. Having computed b, we can find a by the equation

$$a = M_z - bM_s \tag{6.8}$$

By setting $z = 0$ it is easily shown that the mean of the psychometric function (in other words, the limen) is equal to $-a/b$. Since b is the slope of the line relating z to S, we find that a unit change in z (in other words, one standard deviation) is equal to a change of $1/b$ units in S. The standard deviation of the psychometric function is therefore equal to $1/b$.

We have an expression for finding b directly from the experimental data [equation (6.7)]. The reciprocal of this gives us the standard deviation directly from the data. Thus

$$\sigma = \frac{n\Sigma S^2 - (\Sigma S)^2}{n\Sigma Sz - (\Sigma S)(\Sigma z)} \tag{6.9}$$

From the equation given above for a and the equation for relating the limen to a and b, we derive a simple way of finding the limen once the standard deviation is known. The limen is then given by the equation

$$L = M_s - M_z\sigma \tag{6.10}$$

The work is shown in Table 6.5, with the L and σ computed below it using formulas (6.9) and (6.10). The mean of the best-fitting ogive by this method is found to be 10.54 and the standard deviation is 1.034.

TABLE 6.5. A LEAST-SQUARE SOLUTION OF THE LIMEN AND STANDARD DEVIATION WITHOUT WEIGHTS AND WITHOUT CODING

S	p	z	S^2	Sz
12	.93	+1.48	144	+17.76
11	.66	+0.41	121	+ 4.51
10	.29	−0.55	100	− 5.50
9	.05	−1.64	81	−14.76
8	.01	−2.33	64	−18.64
Σ 50	. . .	−2.63	510	−16.63

$$\sigma = \frac{(5)(510) - (50)^2}{(5)(-16.63) - (50)(-2.63)} = 1.034 \qquad M = 10 - (-.526)(1.034) = 10.54$$

A Solution with Coded Values. Table 6.6 illustrates the solution of the limen and its standard deviation by using a guessed mean M' and a class interval i. With an odd number of stimuli, using the middle stimulus value as the guessed mean is much preferred, even though the limen is not nearest to it, because it simplifies very much the computations. The reason is that

TABLE 6.6. A LEAST-SQUARE SOLUTION FOR THE TWO-POINT-LIMEN DATA WITHOUT WEIGHTS BUT WITH CODED VALUES

S	p	s'	z	s'^2	$s'z$
12	.93	+2	+1.48	4	+2.96
11	.66	+1	+0.41	1	+0.41
10	.29	0	−0.55	0	0.00
9	.05	−1	−1.64	1	+1.64
8	.01	−2	−2.33	4	+4.66
Σ			−2.63	10	9.67

$$M = 10 - \left[\frac{(10)(-2.63)}{(5)(9.67)}\right]1 = 10.54 \qquad \sigma = \left(\frac{10}{9.67}\right)1 = 1.034$$

Check: $M = 10 - (-.526)(1.034) = 10.54$.

the sum of the coded stimulus values s' is zero. Compare the formulas for computing the standard deviation (6.9) and (6.12), and you will see how two terms and the constant n drops out because $\Sigma s'$ is zero.

The two formulas for this solution are

$$L = M' - \left[\frac{(\Sigma s'^2)(\Sigma z)}{n\Sigma s'z}\right] i \tag{6.11}$$

$$\sigma = \frac{\Sigma s'^2}{\Sigma s'z} i \tag{6.12}$$

The application of these formulas just below Table 6.6 gives results identical with those from the previous least-square solution. Since we were able to compute L from σ by the previous method, we could also do that here, which would mean skipping the use of formula (6.11) and applying first (6.12) and then (6.10). It is a good idea to use both for checking purposes.

When there is an even number of stimuli, Woodworth (63) suggests placing the value of the guessed mean midway between the two middle stimuli and giving only odd numbers, +1, +3, and +5 above M' and −1, −3, and −5 below M'. The sum of the s' values will be zero so that formulas (6.11) and (6.12) may be applied. The value of i is then one-half the distance between neighboring stimuli.

7. The Least-square Solution Using the Müller-Urban Weights. The most refined statistical process for the method of constant stimuli is the least-square solution using the Müller-Urban weights. There are two reasons for weighting the transformed observations (the z values corresponding to the proportions), one of which was pointed out by Müller and the other by Urban.

The Principles of Müller's and Urban's Weights. Müller urged that the proportions near .50 should be weighted most, and as they differ from .50, they should be weighted less. It is the sum of squares of deviations of the z values from the regression line that we are to minimize. In the relationship of p to z it is clear that large changes in p correspond to small changes in z near the center of the ogive and that small changes in p correspond to large changes in z near the extremes. Errors in observed p values will accordingly be reflected in small errors in z near the middle and in large errors in z at the extremes. To equalize the effects of errors in p upon errors in z, so to speak, the Müller weights were introduced. Müller's weights are proportional to y^2, the squared ordinate in the curve of normal distribution at a given z distance from the mean as derived from the observed proportion of judgments.

Urban pointed out that it is a principle of least squares that observations should be weighted in proportion to their reliabilities. The reliability of a proportion is indicated, inversely, by its standard error squared, sometimes called its *mean-square error*. The standard error of a proportion is given by the familiar formula $\sigma_p = \sqrt{pq/N}$. The mean-square error is pq/N. Since all stimuli are administered the same number of times, N is the same for all proportions in a particular set of data. The weights are therefore proportional to $1/pq$. This ratio varies from 4 to 101, as p varies from .50 to .01 (or .99).

In practice, the Müller weights and the Urban weights are combined by using the product of the two for each proportion. It will be noted that taken separately the two weights vary inversely. The effect of the Müller weight is greater (since its range is very much greater) than the effect of the Urban weights. The range of the combined weights is from 1.000 when $p = .50$ down to .1127 when $p = .01$ or $p = .99$ (see Table H in the Appendix). The products have been divided by a constant to make the maximum weight equal to 1.000.

The Least-square Solution with Weights and Coded Values. The equations for solving for the limen and the standard deviation, using the Müller-Urban weights and coded values for S, are

$$L = M' + \left[\frac{(\Sigma ws')(\Sigma ws'z) - (\Sigma ws'^2)(\Sigma wz)}{(\Sigma w)(\Sigma ws'z) - (\Sigma ws')(\Sigma wz)}\right] i \qquad (6.13)$$

$$\sigma = \left[\frac{(\Sigma w)(\Sigma ws'^2) - (\Sigma ws')^2}{(\Sigma w)(\Sigma ws'z) - (\Sigma ws')(\Sigma wz)}\right] i \qquad (6.14)$$

The worktable for this solution is seen in Table 6.7. The values for z are found from Table C in the Appendix, as usual. The weights and their products with s' and z are given in Table H in the Appendix. Great care should be taken with regard to signs. All z values are negative when p is less than .50. All weights are positive. Algebraic sums are computed for all columns where needed. The work for the two-point limen is shown below Table 6.7.

TABLE 6.7. SOLUTION FOR THE TWO-POINT LIMEN, USING MÜLLER-URBAN WEIGHTS AND CODED DATA

S	s'	p	z	w	ws'	wz	ws'^2	$ws'z$
12	+2	.93	+1.4758	.4351	+.8702	+.6421	1.7403	+1.2842
11	+1	.66	+0.4125	.9398	+.9398	+.3876	0.9398	+0.3876
10	0	.29	−0.5534	.8939	.0000	−.4947	0.0000	0.0000
9	−1	.05	−1.6449	.3519	−.3519	−.5788	0.3519	+0.5788
8	−2	.01	−2.3263	.1127	−.2254	−.2622	0.4508	+0.5243
		Σ	−2.6363	2.7334	+1.2327	−.3060	3.4828	+2.7749

$$M = 10 + \left[\frac{(1.2327)(2.7749) - (3.4828)(-.3060)}{(2.7334)(2.7749) - (1.2327)(-.3060)}\right] 1 = 10.56$$

$$\sigma = \left[\frac{(2.7334)(3.4828) - (1.2327)^2}{(2.7334)(2.7749) - (1.2327)(-.3060)}\right] 1 = 1.005-$$

As the reader will readily see, the solution using the weights is a relatively laborious one, particularly without the aid of a good calculating machine. The reader has also probably noticed that the solutions without weights are so close to those with weights that it is pertinent to raise the question whether weights are worth the trouble. This query is well justified. Actually, few sets of data are so carefully obtained or with a sample of sufficient size to justify the use of weights. If the weights are to be used, it is sufficiently accurate to round them to two significant digits. It is also sufficiently accurate to use z values rounded to two decimal places. If weights are not used, it would be wise to drop any extreme proportion, like .99 or .01, especially if in the plot of z against S the point for such an observation obviously departs from the general linear trend. With the use of weights, such an observation, of course, receives so little weight that its large discrepancy is rendered less potent.

The Regression Problem. The curve-fitting solutions mentioned thus far follow the Müller tradition of minimizing sums of squares of errors in z. In a correlation problem such as this there are two regressions. The traditional solution uses the regression of z on S. Holway (30) and, more recently, Davis (14) have proposed that we use instead the regression of S on z. In this case, we minimize the sums of squares of errors in estimating S from z. The traditional approach recognizes the fact that the stimulus values are selected as fixed quantities and that the experimental errors are in z. The important defense for using the other regression is that we are using the proportions, which stand for positions on an R scale, from which to predict or estimate certain landmarks and distances on the S scale. Putting the problem in the form of a prediction proposition, there is much reason for choosing the regression of S on z. The equations for estimating L and σ, using this regression, are given by Holway (30).

As a matter of practice, which regression do we want? If we use the traditional one, we are asking, "What stimulus value L does it take to give rise to a predicted z equal to zero?" Such a stimulus value should be expected to give rise to a proportion of .50, which seems to satisfy the definition of a limen. Regarding the standard deviation, from the traditional regression of z on S, we are asking, "What amount of change on the S scale does it take to produce a unitary change in z?" If we employ the regression of S on z, with respect to the limen, we are asking, "When we obtain an experimental proportion of .50, consequently a z of 0, what is the most probable stimulus value?" With respect to the standard deviation we are asking, "For a unitary change in z what change should be predicted in S?"

When the regression problem is put in the form of these questions, it seems to the writer that the traditional approach has more advantages. Actually, if the correlation between z and S is close to 1.00, it makes practically no difference which regression is used. When the correlation is +1.0, the two regressions become identical. In the two-point-limen experiment, the solution using Holway's equations without weights gave $L = 10.54$ and $\sigma = 1.029$. These values are to be compared with $L = 10.54$ and $\sigma = 1.034$ by the other least-square solutions without weights. The coefficient of correlation between z and S was found to be .998, which accounts for the excellent agreement from the two regressions.

The Standard Error of a Limen from the Constant Methods. The estimation of a standard error of a limen obtained from the constant method and the various constant processes used in computing the limen has been a very controversial question. It is probably clearest what to do in connection with the Spearman process of computing a mean from the uncumulated distribution. The standard error may then be estimated in the usual manner. The standard deviation computed for the sample (assuming no tail-assumption problems) may be taken as an estimate of the population standard deviation. The value for N is not so clear. We have Nn judgments (where there are n

stimuli each judged N times), but for purposes of computing a mean no single judgment gives us an estimate of the limen. A single judgment merely places the limen somewhere above or below a certain S value. It takes n judgments to narrow the estimate of the limen to one class interval. This is shown by the fact that when we uncumulate the distribution we end up with a distribution of N values in all the intervals combined. It is quite defensible, therefore, to say that the standard error of the mean is given by the customary formula $\sigma_M = \sigma/\sqrt{N - 1}$. The standard error of the mean obtained by the summation process can be estimated by the same formula.

The limens computed by the interpolation processes are best regarded as median values. The standard error of a median is ordinarily estimated by the formula $\sigma_{Mdn} = 1.253\sigma/\sqrt{N}$. Accepting N as the number of judgments per stimulus, we may adapt this general formula to the limen found by the two interpolation processes. All that can be said for it is that it gives a very rough idea of the extent of the sampling errors in the limen. It probably errs on the conservative side, that is, in giving an estimate that is too large. It cannot be used with confidence for deriving t ratios.

In connection with the limens computed on the basis of the phi-gamma assumption and according to the principle of least squares, the Thomson formula (52) has been found to give a result that comes closest to that found in a sampling experiment by Linder (40). Unfortunately, this formula involves a prohibitive amount of computation and therefore is not reported here. Woodworth recommends using the customary formula for the standard error of a mean (63). This possibly gives an overestimation when N is taken as the number of judgments per stimulus. The reason is that the number of degrees of freedom is probably somewhat greater than this under the usual experimental conditions.

Culler has proposed a formula that takes into account the number of stimuli (11). It is a standard error of a median and utilizes the Müller-Urban weights. This formula reads

$$\sigma_L = \frac{1.253\sigma}{\sqrt{N\Sigma wp}} \tag{6.15}$$

The chances are good that the Σwp will be greater than 1.0, so that the denominator will be greater than $\sqrt{N}$. This sum depends upon the number of stimuli (as logically it should) and also upon how near the stimuli come to the limen (in consistency with the principle of the weighting used to determine the position of the limen). This should not necessarily mean for us to use many stimuli and bunch them close to the limen. It is not known whether Culler's formula will function properly under those conditions.

Linder has shown in a sampling experiment that Culler's formula gave better results if put in the form of a standard error of a mean (40). This entails the dropping of the constant 1.253 from the numerator of formula (6.15). With this modification of Culler's formula we have the computation of a standard error of the mean in Table 6.8. Using 1.005 as the estimate of the population standard deviation, we find by Culler's modified formula that the standard error is .089. We may say that with this size of sample and

TABLE 6.8. COMPUTATION OF THE STANDARD ERROR OF THE LIMEN WHEN REGARDED AS A MEAN, BY A MODIFIED CULLER FORMULA

p	w	wp
.93	.4351	.4046
.66	.9398	.6003
.29	.8939	.2592
.05	.3519	.0176
.01	.1127	.0011
		Σ 1.2828

$$\sigma_L = \frac{1.005}{\sqrt{100(1.2828)}} = .089$$

this number of stimuli dispersed as they are, the computed limen is within .1 mm. of the population limen, with odds of 2 to 1.

Testing the Goodness of Fit to the Psychometric Function. It is often of interest and significance to obtain the proportions to be expected from the best-fitting normal curve. This enables us to plot the best-fitting curve if we want to do so. By comparing expected and obtained frequencies we can also look into the question of how well the curve actually fits the experimental data. Although the coefficient of correlation is some indication of the closeness of the observed points to the curve, the coefficients are usually very close to 1.00, and it would take an obviously bad fit, as seen by inspection, to cause much of a drop in correlation. A better test of goodness of fit is that using chi square. We will proceed to find the expected frequencies and to make a chi-square test. The work is summarized in Table 6.9. The

TABLE 6.9. WORKTABLE FOR COMPUTING THE EXPECTED PROPORTIONS FROM THE BEST-FITTING OGIVE AND A CHI-SQUARE TEST OF GOODNESS OF FIT

S	s $(S - L)$	z (s/σ)	p'	p	$p - p'$	$(p - p')^2$	$\frac{1}{p'q'}$	$\frac{(p - p')^2}{p'q'}$
13	+2.44	+2.428	.992					
12	+1.44	+1.433	.924	.93	+.006	.000036	14.26	.000513
11	+0.44	+0.438	.669	.66	−.009	.000081	4.51	.000365
10	−0.56	−0.557	.289	.29	+.001	.000001	4.86	.000005
9	−1.56	−1.552	.060	.05	....	....	.....	(.000174)
8	−2.56	−2.547	.005	.01	....	....	.....	(.000174)
8 and 9	......	....	.0325	.03	−.0025	.00000625	27.95	
								Σ.001231

$$\chi^2 = (100)(.001231) = .1231 \qquad p > .90$$

best-fitting curve for the two-point-limen data is shown in Fig. 6.1. In this procedure we have taken the limen to be 10.56 and the standard deviation to be 1.005.

In order to be able to plot the entire curve, we include an extra stimulus value of 13. The reason is that the end stimulus of 12 mm. gave a proportion of .93, which is somewhat short of the end of the ogive. The steps for deriving in turn the deviations of stimuli from the mean and dividing them by the standard deviation to find z values is well known to the student. From the z values we find from the normal probability tables the expected proportions p'. These were used for plotting the best-fitting curve in Fig. 6.1.

In testing the goodness of fit by means of chi square, the formula for that statistic to fit this particular case is

$$\chi^2 = N \sum \left[\frac{(p - p')^2}{p'q'} \right] \tag{6.16}$$

where N = number of judgments per stimulus
p' = expected proportion
$q' = 1 - p'$

Chi square properly applies only to frequencies. The use of the constant N in the equation steps the result up to the level of frequencies.

The solution of χ^2 is shown in the last columns of Table 6.9. Instead of dividing the squared discrepancies by $p'q'$, it is sometimes convenient to multiply by the reciprocal, $1/p'q'$. Something must usually be done to take care of small frequencies. No expected frequency (which is given by Np' for each stimulus) should be less than 5. In this problem, no p' should be less than .05. We have one such p', for stimulus 8. Lewis and Burke (38) recommend the approach followed in the table. This calls for averaging the two neighboring tail frequencies. These are given for both p' and p in the last row. We carry through to the last ratio, which proved to be .000174, then use it in the rows for both stimuli 8 and 9. Should there be a tail proportion at the other end of the series giving an expected proportion greater than .95, a similar combination would be employed, provided, of course, that N is no greater than 100. This situation would mean an expected frequency less than 5 in the following sense. The chi-square test, if it were completely carried out would involve the proportions of judgments in the other category as well as the ones with which we have been concerned. If the expected frequency for judgments of "two" were 96 ($p' = .96$), the expected frequency for judgments of "one" is 4 ($q' = .04$). Since the discrepancy $p - p'$ is identical with the discrepancy $q - q'$, we treat them both as $p - p'$. The division by $p'q'$ in effect divides each squared discrepancy for a stimulus by its corresponding p' and q'.

The obtained chi square is only .1231. Reference to the chi-square table for the row with 2 degrees of freedom ($n - 3$) will inform us that the obtained value could occur by chance more than 90 times in a hundred. There seems little possibility that such discrepancies as occurred could be due to anything but sampling errors.

Choice of the Processes in Practice. Several different processes have been described for computing a limen from constant-stimulus data. Which one shall be used? A few suggestions can be made, but the research worker will always have to use his own judgment.

1. The linear interpolation method is most appropriately used when:
   a. Only two stimuli near the limen have been employed.

b. The distribution is so lacking in normality that it would not be described very well by an ogive.
c. Only a threshold value is wanted and its standard error is immaterial or need only be roughly approximated.
d. Four stimuli have been used and good estimates are possible of quartiles Q_1 and Q_3 by interpolation, as well as the median.

It should *not* ordinarily be used when:
a. Five or more stimuli have been employed.
b. An accurate limen and its standard error are wanted.
c. Stimuli do not give proportions on both sides of .50. Extrapolation should not be attempted.
d. There are inversions of the first order in the region of the limen.

2. Spearman's arithmetic-mean process and the summation method may be used:
a. When proportions of 0 and 1.0, or values approaching them fairly closely, are obtained.
b. When the number of stimuli is reasonably large; never with less than five stimuli.
c. When a very accurate limen is wanted.
d. When a good estimate of the standard error of the limen is wanted (assuming that a good estimate of the standard deviation can be made).

3. The normal interpolation process will apply:
a. Whenever the linear-interpolation process applies, and with greater accuracy.
b. In some cases when the linear interpolation method does not apply:
(1) Extrapolations can be made (when the distribution is normal).
(2) When five or more stimuli have been employed.

4. The normal graphic processes are of greatest value:
a. When there is insufficient time to make a least-square solution.
b. When greater accuracy is needed than the interpolation methods provide.
c. Only when a straight line can be easily adjusted to the points.

5. The least-square solutions without weights are best used when:
a. Four or more stimuli have been employed.
b. The Spearman or the summation processes cannot be applied.
c. The data give reasonable promise of fitting an ogive. This can be decided usually from inspection of the plotted data, especially on probability paper.
d. An accurate measure of dispersion is wanted.
e. Distributions are reasonably symmetrical about the limen.

6. The least-square solution with the Müller-Urban weights has advantages when:
a. The conditions under 5 above are satisfied.
b. The data are sufficiently refined to justify the extra work.
c. There is a wide range of proportions. (Then one can weight the extreme proportions less than the others.)

DETERMINATION OF A DIFFERENCE LIMEN

A difference limen is found from comparative judgments. In the method of constant stimulus differences, a selected standard S_s near the center of a range is paired off with each of several variable stimuli S_v. Judgments of "greater" or "less" under a two-category instruction, or judgments including a middle category such as "equal" or "doubtful" may be called for.[1] We will begin with the more traditional type of experiment as an illustration,

[1] The term *doubtful* is generally considered best for the middle category for several reasons. Not all nonequal judgments can be reported by *O* as "greater" or "less." Not all responses that can be called neither "greater" nor "less" seem exactly equal.

determining a difference limen for lifted weights, using three categories of judgment.

The standard weight is of 200 grams (g.). The variable weights weigh 185, 190, 195, 200, 205, 210, and 215 g. *O* lifts S_s first and S_v second in half of the observations, and S_v first and S_s second in the other half. He renders a judgment always with respect to the second stimulus, reporting it "greater," "less," or "doubtful" as compared with the first. The sequences of S_v are random or by some prearranged system avoiding serial order.

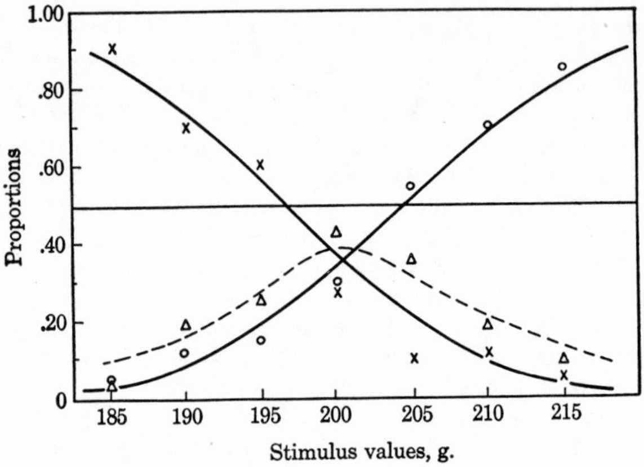

FIG. 6.4. Distributions of proportions of judgments "less," "doubtful," and "greater" from the lifted-weight experiment.

Computation of the Limens. Typical data from a lifted-weight experiment with three categories of judgment are shown in Table 6.10. The number of judgments per stimulus pair was 100. These data are shown graphically in Fig. 6.4. There are several constants to be computed. There are the two medians or means of the cumulative distributions, one of which (for judgments "less") is shown as a descending curve in Fig. 6.4. The latter can be transformed into an ascending curve by deducting the proportions of judgments "less" from 1.0. The two curves are shown as ascending func-

TABLE 6.10. DATA FROM A LIFTED-WEIGHT EXPERIMENT, WITH PROPORTIONS OF EACH TYPE OF JUDGMENT FOR EACH STIMULUS S_v COMPARED WITH S_s, WHERE S_s = 200 G

S_v	"Greater"	"Doubtful"	"Less"
215	.85	.09	.06
210	.70	.18	.12
205	.55	.35	.10
200	.30	.42	.28
195	.15	.25	.60
190	.12	.18	.70
185	.05	.04	.91

tions in Fig. 6.5. There it can be seen how the two functions divide the three categories of judgment into three regions.[1]

The Interval of Uncertainty and the DL. The medians, or means, of the two functions are the upper and lower limens, and are known as L_g and L_l, respectively. The distance between them, $L_g - L_l$, is known as the *interval of uncertainty IU*. One-half this interval is taken as the difference limen *DL*.

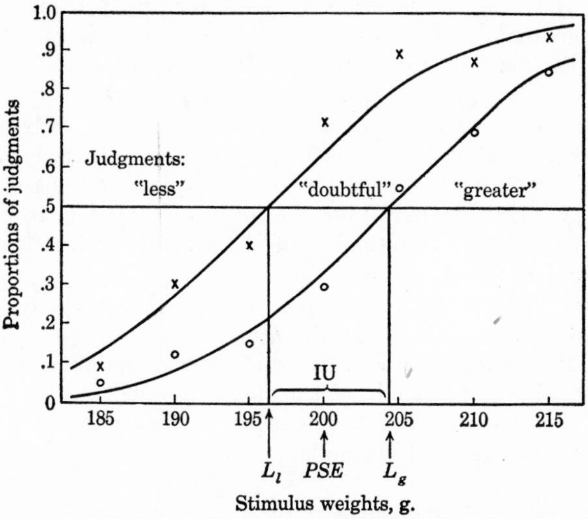

FIG. 6.5. Illustration showing how the two psychometric functions whose medians are at the upper and lower thresholds L_g and L_l for the lifted-weight data divide the area representing the three categories of judgment into three regions and in turn divide the transition zone into three segments.

The processes of computing the two limens L_g and L_l are the same as were applied to the two-point-limen data. There are essentially no new problems here. The results by some of the processes are given in Table 6.11.

TABLE 6.11. A SUMMARY OF LIMENS, STANDARD DEVIATIONS, INTERVALS OF UNCERTAINTY, DIFFERENCE LIMENS, AND POINTS OF SUBJECTIVE EQUALITY FOR THE LIFTED-WEIGHT DATA

Process	L_l	σ_l	σ_{L_l}	L_g	σ_g	σ_{L_g}	*IU*	*DL*	*PSE*
Linear interpolation....	196.56	9.3	....	204.67	9.9	....	8.11	4.05	200.89
Arithmetic mean.......	196.80	9.8	0.98	204.25	10.20	1.02	7.45	3.73	200.83
Normal graphic (probability paper)........	196.2	9.6	....	204.3	10.0	....	8.1	4.05	200.2
Urban process.........	196.18	10.17	0.71	204.33	10.90	0.73	8.15	4.08	200.11

The Point of Subjective Equality and Xi. In order to find a Weber ratio, we need to know the value of the point of subjective equality. This is a constant that we have not yet encountered in connection with the constant method. As usual, it is that stimulus value in the S_v series that is psycho-

[1] When the data are put in this form, it is clear that we have a problem related to the prediction of measurements from categories as described by the author (26, p. 377).

logically equal to S_s for the conditions of the experiment. There are several ways of estimating it, depending upon the process used in computing the limens.

If the linear-interpolation process is used, in which the limens are medians, it would be consistent practice to use the interpolated median of the "doubtful" judgments as the estimate of *PSE*. While these judgments are called "doubtful," they may be taken as "equal," for practical purposes for they mean "not greater" and "not less." If the arithmetic means of the two cumulative distributions are computed, either by Spearman's uncumulative process or by Woodworth's summation process, the most appropriate estimate of the *PSE* is an arithmetic mean of the "doubtful" judgments. With the normal-interpolation process for finding L_g and L_l there is no direct way of determining the *PSE*. If the two standard deviations σ_g and σ_l are approximately equal, we may take the mean of L_g and L_l to represent the *PSE*. If they are not, a method used in connection with the least-square solutions may be applied.

When a least-square solution, with or without the use of weights, is used, the *PSE* is located on the basis of the *principle of equal likelihood*. That is, the *PSE* is that stimulus value at which the probability of a judgment "greater" equals the probability of a judgment "less." This gives a constant that Urban has called *xi*. This principle also applies when we use the normal graphic process. By formula,

$$\xi = L_l + \frac{\sigma_l(L_g - L_l)}{\sigma_g + \sigma_l} = L_l + \frac{\sigma_l(IU)}{\sigma_g + \sigma_l} \tag{6.17}$$

This formula finds the stimulus value at which the best-fitting ascending and descending ogives intersect and also where the two regression lines relating z to S would intersect.

Applying formula (6.17) to our lifted-weight data, using the constants obtained by using weighted observations,

$$\xi = 196.18 + \frac{(10.17)(8.15)}{10.17 + 10.90} = 200.11$$

The Culler Phi Process. Culler and others have severely criticized the use of one-half the interval of uncertainty as the *DL* because the size of it depends too much upon *O*'s attitude. The size is very dependent upon *O*'s willingness or unwillingness to give "doubtful" judgments. The more "doubtful" judgments *O* gives the larger his *IU* and his *DL*. This would be reasonable if a large number of such judgments meant only poor sensitivity. Unfortunately it may mean a number of other things as well.

Suppose that *O* is unwilling to give any "doubtful" judgments at all and guesses either "greater" or "less" when he is in doubt. With no "doubtful" judgments in the data, the two ogives would cross at the .50 level and L_g would equal L_l. The *IU* would be zero and the *DL* would be zero. The situation in Fig. 6.7 is an example of this. This is a limiting case, but it merely highlights the dependence of the *DL* so computed upon the tendency of *O* to report "doubtful" or not to report "doubtful." Doubt may represent a number of different things. It may mean scientific caution, dislike for guessing, a high standard for certainty, or other things. The size of the *DL* may therefore be a measure of personality traits other than the trait of sensitivity.[1]

For these reasons Culler (11) has recommended that we take as the estimate of the difference limen the probable error (*PE*) of the cumulative distribution. This he thought would be a good index of sensitivity regardless of the number of "doubtful" judgments. It would also be a more reliable index of the *DL* in that the standard error of a probable error is much smaller than that of a mean or median with the same size of sample. The standard deviation would also serve an index of differential sensitivity, though it would be a coarser unit, being about 50 per cent larger than the *PE*. Since we have found other processes giving estimates of the standard deviation, from which the *PE* can be computed, there is nothing new in the Culler phi process except his definition of the *DL*. Culler's is called a *phi process* as he, like Müller and Urban before him, assumes the phi-gamma hypothesis and solves for the *DL* by using weighted observations.

Culler's and Urban's DL's Inversely Related. There is a curious inconsistency between the Culler *DL* and the Urban *DL* which leads to the conclusion that the two do not measure the same thing. Figure 6.6 will provide an illustration of this point. When *O*, through high degree of sensitivity or through a negative set toward "doubtful" judgments or for any of a number of reasons, fails to give many judgments in the intermediate category, Urban's *DL*'s are small and Culler's are large. As *O* gives more and more judgments in the equal or doubtful category, the Urban limens spread apart, indicating lowered sensitivity, whereas the steepness of the two ogives increases, indicating according to Culler's method increased discriminatory power or sensitivity. Surely two estimates which vary inversely, or even tend to do so, cannot be taken as equivalent measures of the same thing. The illustrations selected are perhaps overdrawn in order to prove a point. It is conceivable that there are factors which tend to make the *DL*'s of Urban and Culler correlate positively, just as there are obviously factors which tend to make them vary inversely.

A Difference Limen from Two Categories of Judgment. The way out of the dilemma posed by the difficulties of the Urban and Culler *DL*'s seems to be to get rid of the middle category entirely. There are three possibilities for doing this. One procedure would be to permit *O* to give only judgments "greater" or "less," forcing him to guess even when he is really in doubt and would like to avoid guessing. A second procedure would be to allow *O* to give "doubtful" judgments but to divide them between the "greater" and "less" categories before starting computing procedures. The third possibility would be to allow "doubtful" judgments but to ask *O* to repeat such observations at later trials, so that although many trials may be unusable,

[1] It is interesting that Urban has recently pointed out (59) that the product h times IU yields a constant Δ which is a personal characteristic independent of the standard stimulus used. An objective test of personality might be built on the total proportion of "doubtful" judgments. Its meaning would have to be established through intercorrelation studies.

one would end up with the requisite total number of "greater" plus "less" judgments for every stimulus.

There has been a voluminous literature on studies concerning this problem of the "doubtful" judgments.[1] Arguments pro and con and experiments on the problem have been numerous. Experience seems to show, however, that for most purposes two-category data are best and that of the three choices mentioned in the preceding paragraph the third is wisest. If *O* will accept the two-category instruction, well and good. If he wants to avoid a

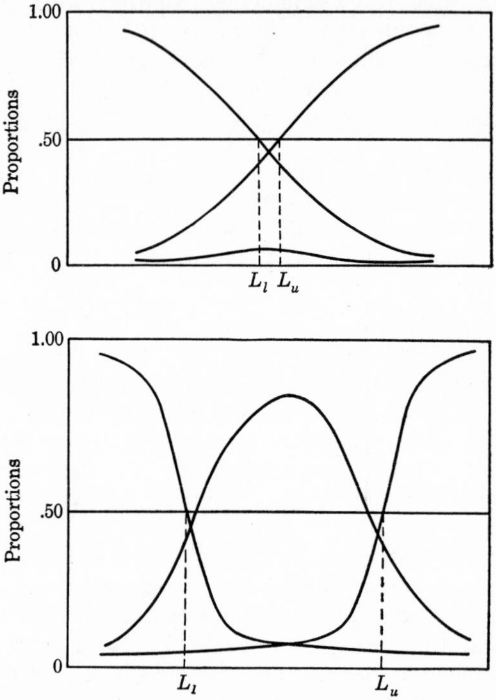

FIG. 6.6. Psychometric curves showing how, when the number of "doubtful" judgments varies, the Urban and Culler difference limens tend to vary inversely. In the upper diagram the Urban *DL* is small and the Culler *DL*'s are relatively large. In the lower diagram the reverse is true.

forced choice, let him report "doubtful." Repeating such trials, as prescribed in the third case, eliminates all except "greater" or "less" judgments from the data and their treatment is then straightforward.

If the second approach is adopted, the problem of how to divide the "doubtful" judgments is something of a problem. Some investigators have divided them equally at each stimulus level between the other two categories. The defense for this is that when *O* says "doubtful" he is equally inclined toward "greater" or "less." Other investigators reject this hypothesis, believing that a "doubtful" judgment means that *O* is inclined toward "greater" or "less" in proportion to the numbers of those two categories of judgments he has already given. The latter hypothesis is supported by

[1] See in particular Boring (7), Fernberger (18), George (23), and Kellogg (34).

experiment. We know from the very thorough work of Warner Brown (8) that when *O* is forced to guess, even with differences as small as .2 g., more right than wrong judgments will be given. Judgments of differences below the limen may differ only quantitatively from those from supraliminal differences.[1]

TABLE 6.12. PROPORTIONS OF JUDGMENTS WITH THOSE IN THE "DOUBTFUL" CATEGORY DISTRIBUTED PROPORTIONATELY BETWEEN THE "GREATER" AND "LESS" CATEGORIES AT EACH STIMULUS VALUE

S_s	185	190	195	200	205	210	215
p_g	.052	.146	.200	.517	.846	.853	.934
p_l	.948	.854	.800	.483	.154	.147	.066

The lifted-weight data of Table 6.10 have been reduced to two-category data by proportional divisions of the "doubtful" judgments at each stimulus level. The results appear in Table 6.12 and are shown graphically in Fig. 6.7. Such data would seem to be relatively free of the disturbing elements that affect the Urban and the Culler limens. The index of sensitivity based

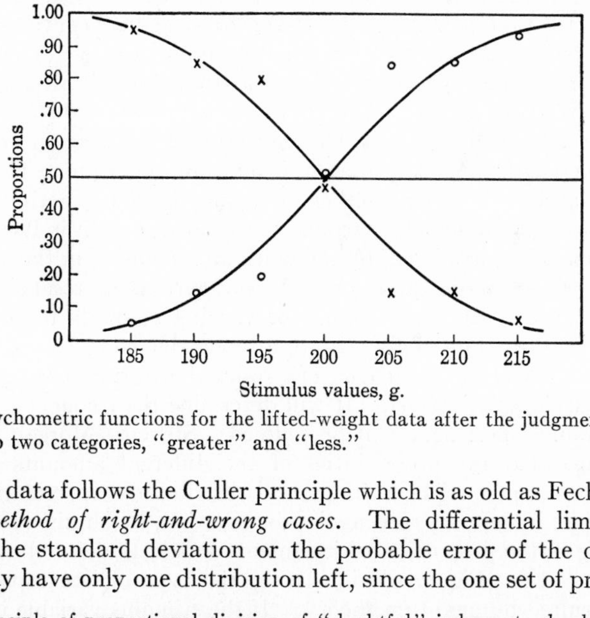

FIG. 6.7. Psychometric functions for the lifted-weight data after the judgments have been reassigned to two categories, "greater" and "less."

upon these data follows the Culler principle which is as old as Fechner and his original *method of right-and-wrong cases*. The differential limen may be taken as the standard deviation or the probable error of the distribution. We actually have only one distribution left, since the one set of proportions is

[1] This principle of proportional division of "doubtful" judgments should not be generalized too far. In public-opinion polling, for example, it is sometimes found that the "don't know" responses when actually followed up may be divided in the opposite direction to proportions in the other two categories. In the South, where admission of Republican beliefs is unpopular, many people with such ideas report "don't know" rather than reveal their ideas. In responses to personality-inventory items the question-mark response is likely to mean that it should have been the less favorable of the two other choices as shown by correlations of these responses with total-score criteria.

a complement of the other. The point of subjective equality is the mean or median of the distribution. Since the processes for estimating these statistics have been described earlier, they will not be given here. A least-square solution, with weighted observations, gave an estimate of 5.97 for the *PE* of the best-fitting ogive, with a point of subjective equality equal to 199.84.

Variations of the Constant Methods

Variations of the constant methods are of different kinds. Some have to do with the procedures for obtaining judgments, while others have to do with the processes for computing limens. Some are essentially parallel or substitute methods, while others are minor variations in the traditional procedures either in obtaining data or in computation of the end values. A psychophysical method that represents a rather close parallel is the *quantal method*. A nonpsychophysical method that rests upon very similar theory but provides a very novel procedure for computing limens is the method of *probit analysis*. A new theory and process for computing limens from constant-stimuli data is the *logistic method*. A broad extension of the constant-method principles is seen in the *method of single stimuli*.

The Quantal Method. It was hypothesized by Stevens, Morgan, and Volkmann (51) that increments on a sensory-response continuum are not essentially continuous but occur in small units or quanta. The knowledge of neural functioning suggests this. It was thought that although the sensory increment corresponds to more than a single neurone discharge, there is nevertheless a discrete change. The detection of a change in making comparative judgments depends upon this unit or quantum. The standard stimulus S_s arouses a given number of quanta of neural activity. It also provides varying amounts of a surplus that is not sufficient in itself to arouse one more quantum but in conjunction with an increment in the stimulus ΔS it may arouse one more quantum. As the surplus or residual excitation varies, it requires a stimulus change of varying amounts to complete the extra quantum and thus to give rise to a reportable change.

The probability of the occurrence of a residual or surplus excitation of each size is of considerable interest. It will determine the frequency with which a given stimulus increment will be noticed. Stevens, Morgan, and Volkmann assume that the probabilities of the different amounts of residual excitation are equal. Their frequency distribution is rectangular, not normal. If we integrate a rectangular distribution, we obtain a straight line. The increase in the proportion of judgments should therefore be linear from $p = 0$ to $p = 1.0$. Figure 6.8 illustrates the type of linear psychometric function required by quantum theory. If the stimulus variable is measured in terms of $\Delta S/S$, increments below one quantum should yield no reports of change. It takes at least one quantum of increment in excitation to yield any psychological change. When the increment in excitation is two quanta or more, a psychological change is certain. This assumes that *O* adopts a two-quanta change as his criterion of a difference. Thus, the smallest $\Delta S/S$ that gives rise to noticed changes all the time is twice that which just begins to give rise to a noticed change. The *DL*, when defined as that stimulus difference that gives a change with a probability of .5, is therefore equivalent to 1.5 quanta, or one quantum is equivalent to two-thirds of a *DL*. With a linear regression the determination of the size of a quantum or of a *DL* is very easy. The points at which the slanting line cuts the 0 and 1.0 probability levels would be determined by fitting a line to points between those limits either graphically or by a least-square solution.

The demonstration of the quanta requires very rigorous experimental controls. It was first shown by Békésy (1) in connection with judgments of sounds. In general, certain requirements must be met. The judgment task must be made as simple for *O* as possible. The observations must be made over a very limited period of time. The sizes of quanta seem to change from time to time, such as from day to day. A warning signal is needed by some *O*s. All *O*s need some practice in the particular kind of observation. The stimulus change must be very abrupt and of short duration. There must not be time for conditions affecting the residual excitation within *O* to change during a single observation.

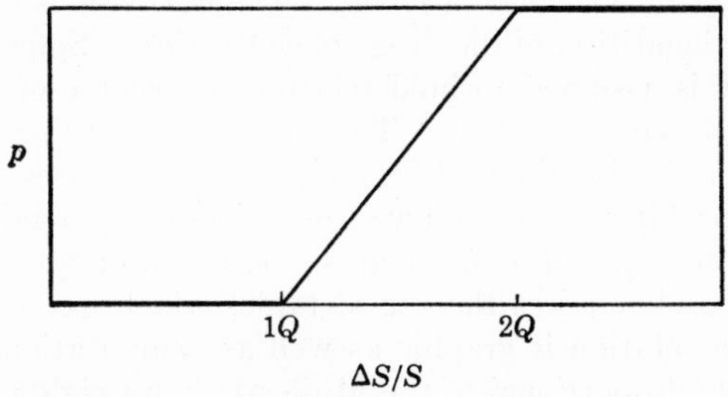

FIG. 6.8. The psychometric function to be expected from application of the quantal method. The proportion of upper-category judgments as a function of a relative change in $S(\Delta S/S)$ is linear.

An example of this type of experiment involved judgments of loudness of tones (51). The standard tone was one of 1,000 c.p.s. given continuously. Increments were given at intervals of 3 sec., each lasting for only .15 sec. *O* was told to begin reporting changes as soon as he felt ready. The same difference was judged 25 times in succession before changing to another difference. The differences were changed in sets in random order.

Others have verified the quantal psychometric function with observations of sounds and have also found under what conditions the function is likely to go in the direction of an ogive. Flynn (21, p. 33) concluded that the ogive function indicates experimental conditions have not been well controlled. Miller and Garner (43) found that some departures toward the ogive were due to the fact that *O* apparently changed his criterion of an observed difference from a one-quantum to a two-quantum, and even to a three-quantum affair. This is likely to happen if the size of difference is changed on every trial. Then *O* is not given an opportunity to establish one criterion and stick to it. Departure toward an ogive is likely to occur if results from different days or from different *O*s are combined.

Jerome (33) found linear functions in judgments of odors as a function of stimulus pressure. But the stimulus value at which the function reached 1.0

was not double the stimulus value at which it left 0. The steepest slope of any linear function was .45 and all the rest tended to have slopes that were multiples of .45. An increment of .45 mg. was therefore taken to be one quantum of stimulation which held for all *O*s.[1]

Probit Analysis. Probit analysis was developed in connection with the study of lethal doses of drugs applied to insects. A lethal dose is defined much the same as a limen. It is the quantity of dose that has a probability of .5 of killing. In an experiment with a drug, selected concentrations are applied to different samples of insects of the same species and the proportion dying at each degree of concentration is taken as the datum. The increase in proportion dying as a function of increasing concentration is obviously S-shaped and fits an ogive very well.

The computation methods which give the method its name were devised by Bliss, Finney, and others (4, 20). The first step is to convert each proportion into a deviate under a normal distribution plus the number 5. The addition of the constant 5 is for the purpose of getting rid of negative numbers. The value $z + 5$ is called a *probit.* The next step is to plot probits as a function of the logarithm of the drug concentration. Something analogous to Fechner's law is assumed to hold relating the degree of biological effect of the drug to its concentration. The method of finding the best-fitting ogive function is radically different from any of the processes described above. The process in probit analysis follows the principle of maximum likelihood rather than the principle of least squares. It is too involved to be reported in limited space and requires the use of tables which we cannot take space to present. The solution is graphic as well as computational. It involves the use of weights proportional to the Müller-Urban weights. The fitting of data to a function is an iterative process which emphasizes the use of "working probits" at the extremes of the regression line relating probits to drug concentration. One of its most attractive features is that it provides confidence limits for a limen computed by the method.

The Logistic Method. Berkson recommends the substitution for the phi-gamma function of an equation known as the *logistic function* (2). This is also known as the autocatalytic curve and as a growth function. The general equation is

$$Q = \frac{1}{1 + e^{\alpha - \beta x}} \tag{6.18}$$

where Q = a "true" logistic rate of mortality (in the context of the lethal-dose problem) and x = quantity of dose in log units. The lethal dose (corresponding to a limen with $p = .5$) is given by the ratio α/β. Berkson claims that the function is easier to fit than is the phi-gamma function and that it gives as good or better fits to data than the ogive (2, p. 364). It is actually very close in appearance to the ogive. Thus far no one seems to have attempted to apply this procedure in psychophysics. It would appear to be promising in that connection.

[1] Blackwell (3) has obtained data that throw doubt upon the validity of judgments obtained under the experimental conditions used to demonstrate quanta.

The Method of Single Stimuli. Some investigators, for example, Wever and Zener (60), instead of calling for comparative judgments of pairs of stimuli when S_s and S_v are given together, ask for judgments of an absolute type and present each S_v alone. The categories of judgment might be "heavy," "medium," and "light." The results look like those obtained from three-category judgments in the method of constant stimulus differences when pairs of stimuli are presented. The results can be treated in the same way, giving an interval of uncertainty, a difference limen, and a point of subjective equality. More than three categories of judgment may be used, such as "very heavy," "heavy," "medium" "light," and "very light." With five categories there are four limens dividing them and the widths of the intervals between them can be determined.

Even larger numbers of categories may be utilized. It is obvious that we are dealing with some kind of a rating method. The method of single stimuli, while developed as an offshoot of the constant method, really belongs, along with rating methods, in the more general class known as *method of successive categories.* The general principles underlying judgments in successive categories were explained briefly in Chap. 2. Scaling from such judgments will be treated in Chap. 10.

The Method of Judgment Time. As early as 1887, Cattell had proposed that a difference could be measured psychologically by the time of the reaction to that difference (62). Henmon (29) took up the suggestion in 1911 and found that this was very roughly true. A right judgment required less time than a wrong one and was less variable. The time also decreased regularly with the degree of assurance as reported by *O.* The motive behind these efforts seems to have been to get a purely objective indicator of observed differences in order to avoid dependence upon the verbally reported judgments of *O.* Kellogg (35) has found that if *O* does not know that his reaction times are being measured, the relationships are all the more significant. He was able to state the general law, "The psychometric time curves for all categories tend to be inversions of the psychometric relative-frequency curves." That is, when *O* is unaware that his reaction time is being recorded, the time is an inverse function of the proportion of right judgments and the relation is roughly ogive in form.

Flynn (21) has found that judgment time decreases as ΔS increases, with a degree of relationship indicated by a correlation of $-.48$. Judgment time correlated $-.52$ with the proportions of correct judgments. Since proportions usually correlate much higher than this with ΔS (Flynn found this correlation to be $+.72$), it appears that verbal judgments are as yet more dependable indicators of sensory response than are judgment times.

The Use of a Variable Standard. Culler has proposed the use of a variable standard stimulus, recommending that every stimulus in the series be compared with every other one. In the determination of a limen there can be computed as many pairs of limens as there are stimuli. He cites the following advantages: (1) A maximum range of differences can be obtained with minimum equipment. (2) It guarantees some very high and some very low proportions. (3) It permits more very small S differences and stimulates *O*'s caution. (4) It eliminates the error of "absolute impression," by which is meant a constant judgment tendency due to the repeated application of the same standard with every pair (11, p. 76). It will be recognized that this proposed variation is none other than the method of pair comparisons, a near relative of the constant method.

Correction of Proportions for Chance. In studying thresholds in the sense of taste (this may apply elsewhere) the stimulus error is especially bothersome. Harrison and Harrison (28) solved this problem by presenting beakers in pairs, one with distilled water and the other with one of several degrees of concentration of the substance to be tasted. *O* is to say which has the substance in it. In the ordinary method of constant stimuli, all stimuli would presumably have concentrations of the substance and this knowledge favors the stimulus error.

In the paired presentations the element of chance success is great. The proportions vary between .50 and 1.00 rather than between .00 and 1.0. The treatment of results must therefore be different. Harrison and Harrison first correct the obtained proportion for chance success by the relation

$$ {}_cp = 2(p - .5) \tag{6.19} $$

where ${}_cp$ is the corrected proportion and p is the obtained one. They use a modified Müller-Urban weight, for the Müller component applies to the corrected proportion (it is the one from which the deviate z would be obtained) and the Urban component applies to the original proportion (since it pertains to the variability of an observed proportion). With these modifications the solution for a limen proceeds as usual.

Group Presentation of Stimuli. As a timesaving device, Shaad and Helson (49) suggest that the same stimulus or stimulus pair need not be changed at every presentation. It is sometimes inconvenient, as in finding the two-point limen, to make a change in the apparatus after every trial. They have found that, either with the two-point-limen technique or the lifted-weight experiment, the repetition of a stimulus from 10 to 25 times in succession makes no significant difference in the results. The best procedure, they concluded, was to warn *O* that the same stimulus might be given in succession, but to vary the number of repetitions in a group.

Using a Geometric Series of Stimuli. Thurstone has pointed out that the phi-gamma hypothesis is in violation of Fechner's law or of any similar psychophysical law. The distribution of observed proportions of judgments should theoretically not be normally distributed if plotted against equal stimulus intervals on the abscissa. We ought, rather, to assume a *phi-log-gamma hypothesis*, using log S on the abscissa instead of S. This would mean the selection of equal *logarithmic* steps between stimuli, as Galton proposed many years ago. When the Weber ratio is relatively large, perhaps 1:3 to 1:10, the error involved in the usual phi-gamma hypothesis is rather serious; when it is relatively small, 1:50 or less, the error is negligible. This notion of Thurstone's (54) has been substantiated by Lufkin (42), who found that the usual ogives are skewed negatively, as we should expect from Fechner's law. After all, however, Lufkin found that the normal ogive fitted the data about as well as any type of skewed curve. The author has found slightly, but only slightly, better correlations between z and log S than between z and S in connection with lifted weights (25).

When the Limen Is Not the Median. At certain times it is reasonable to reject the median of the ogive function as the limen. Brown (9) found in a study of the stimulus limen for taste, for example, that, owing to shifts of attitude from time to time and other uncontrollable central factors, the median was a highly variable quantity. He proposed, instead of the median, to take as the limen that point on the psychometric function where the curve was rising with greatest steepness. This would ordinarily be at the median, but when the curve is skewed, this is not so. Brown actually found that points of steepest rise occur all the way from 5 to 80 per cent, with the majority of them between 42 and 62 per cent. Such limens were more constant from one time to another and under different conditions, such as a change in the range of stimuli.

General Evaluation of the Constant Methods

It is impossible to give an adequate evaluation of the constant methods in a limited space. These widely used methods have been the subject of considerable methodological research which has demonstrated both strengths and weaknesses and has resulted in improvements, many of which have been indicated in preceding pages. Here we shall review some of the high lights in the way of advantages and disadvantages of the methods.

Advantages of the Constant Methods. Undoubtedly one of the appeals of the constant methods is their versatility and broad range of applicability. Other appeals, to some investigators, lie in the accuracy with which limens can be determined and the refinement with respect to the computational processes that are available. The relative simplicity of making judgments is attractive to observers. Although all judging of stimuli in the proximity of limens is difficult, the task usually reduces to an either-or proposition for the observer. These methods also avoid some of the experimental errors found in connection with other methods, the method of minimal changes, for example.

Range of Application of the Constant Methods. There is no type of constant in traditional psychophysics—absolute limen, relative limen, or point of subjective equality—that cannot be determined by this method. It would also be adaptable to the equating of intervals and ratios by direct observation, but it has had almost no use for these purposes. By extension of the judgments to three or more categories, as in the method of single stimuli, the determination of multiple limens and the scaling of intervals and of stimuli becomes possible by this basic approach.

Outside the field of psychophysics, unless psychophysics is defined in a very broad sense, we find applications of the constant-method principles to the determination of psychological constants in terms of stimulus values. Appropriate adaptations have been made to measurement in the areas of attention, memory, associative recall, and mental tests.

Boring and Williams (61) first suggested application of the principle to measurement of the strength of memory impressions for series of materials. It has been recognized that the number of retained-and-recalled members of a list breaks down as a measure of memory when none is recalled and when all are recalled. The establishment of a point of complete mastery has been difficult for this reason. Boring and Williams defined a new standard of recall as that level at which the probability of recall is .5. This is an associative limen. The point of half learning would be much more accurately determined than the point of complete learning. It is approximately midway from the point of apparently no recall and apparently perfect recall. The operational test of recall might be in the form of paired associates, retained members, or anticipation. The proportion of successful recalls as a function of the number of repetitions (or the logarithm of the number of repetitions) would be expected to follow the ogive form. This idea has even broader implications. If the learning curve when memory is measured in terms of proportions of correct responses is an ogive function of learning time or effort, the normal-curve deviates z should give a linear learning function. It is highly possible that z is a better measure of memory than is a proportion or number of responses. It might be wise to make z a more general measure of amount remembered. It might be defended as a measure of memory on a linear psychological scale.

Fernberger (17) first made the suggestion that a span of apprehension be measured as a limen, using the constant method. The proportion of correct responses is usually a clear ogive function of numbers of items exposed. Guilford and Dallenbach (27) suggested the analogous application to the measurement of a memory span. In both cases, the span is statistically defined as that amount of material that is successfully reported with a probability of .5.

In establishing the age levels of his various tests of intelligence, Binet adopted a rough, practical standard. A test that could be passed by from two-thirds to three-fourths of the children of a certain chronological age was placed at that age level. This means that the average child at a given age level can more than pass each test at that level. It might seem, therefore, that the tests for a given age level are calibrated too high for that level. This is not the whole story, however, when several tests are used together at an age level. The amount of intercorrelation of tests must also be considered, as was pointed out by Jaspen (32). Only if the intercorrelations were perfect would the .5 level for each item work. With correlations less than 1.0, something greater than .5 correct responses must be obtained. In the selection of items, intercorrelations were usually unknown or ignored and resort was taken to a "cut-and-fit" procedure which would result in the approximate number of each age level passing from one to six of the tests at that level. In dealing with a single test, however, the principle of the limen still holds. Kreezer and Dallenbach (37), for example, applied it in determining age levels for items on concept mastery. We shall see other applications to test methods in later chapters.

Some Disadvantages of the Constant Methods. The constant methods are by no means free of faults. We have seen that in spite of refined computational processes the determination of standard errors is not fully satisfactory. The methods are certainly not as economical as some others—the method of average error, for example. Many of the difficulties with the constant methods have to do with biases of various kinds in judgments. Many of these are not unique to the constant methods, by any means, but some of them are more conspicuous in connection with it. We shall look into the general subject of biases in judgments in a later chapter, which is entirely devoted to the subject of judgment (Chap. 12). Here we will consider only a few sources of bias of special note in the constant methods.

Biased Judgments in the Constant Methods. When there is a middle category of "doubtful" judgments, we have already seen that general tendencies to favor or to avoid such a category have been very disturbing. We have already seen, also, that the solution is somehow to end the experiment with judgments in only two categories. With this problem solved, though perhaps not to the satisfaction of all, we have remaining two other important sources of bias having to do with the asymmetry of the series of stimuli being judged and with habits of sequences of judgments.

By the "asymmetry" of a series is meant the departure of the standard S_s from the center of the series of variable stimuli S_v. The effect shows up in terms of a constant error, the difference between the *PSE* and S_s. This difference may differ in the two time or space orders for pairs of S_s and S_v, but with an equal number of judgments in each order, with time or space errors canceled out, there is often still a difference. Doughty (15) and others have shown that as the standard S_s is moved up or down in a series the *PSE* tends to shift somewhat. The *PSE* tends toward the mean of the entire series. When the standard is low, the constant error *CE* ($CE = PSE - S_s$) tends to be positive, and when S_s is high in the series, *CE* tends to be negative. When S_s is exactly in the middle, you might expect the *CE* to equal zero. As a matter of fact, even then the *CE* tends to be negative, which indicates that the geometric mean of the series (which is slightly lower than the arithmetic mean) is the apparent level toward which the *PSE* tends to gravitate. If the series were in equal logarithmic units, the *PSE* would tend toward the arithmetic mean of the stimulus values expressed in such units. The principles just stated do not tell the whole story, however, for the general level of the entire series has some bearing upon the *CE*. The whole question of relativity of judgments will be discussed in Chap. 12.

Related to the problem of the effects of asymmetry is the empirical finding that an observer tends to keep his total proportions of "greater" and "less" judgments relatively constant under changing conditions such as the shift of S_s to different positions of the series. It is as if he had a compulsive habit to achieve balance of this kind. Such a habit shows up also in *O*'s sequences of judgments. Which is cause and which is effect cannot be stated with certainty. But it seems to be true, as Preston (46, 47) and others have shown, that *O* tends to avoid repeating the same judgment. Such a habit tends to effect a more even distribution of *G* and *L* judgments. The habit is most effective when judgments are difficult; Preston used zero differences exclusively in his experiment.

Goodfellow has thrown a little more light on the peculiar judging habits of observers (24). In connection with experiments on extrasensory perception he determined how *O*s tend to distribute sequences of two-category judgments (such as "black" and "white," or "heads" and "tails") in a run of five guesses. Besides finding that *O*s tend to avoid repeating judgments in succession, he found that they avoid simple alternations and other systematic patterns. His hypothesis is that the average *O* has had some experience with games of chance and has learned that chance events do not come in regular patterns. Expecting irregularity in sequences of chance events, he performs accordingly.

It is not certain how much such habits apply to the situation of a psychophysical experiment. Such habits come into play most when *O* feels there is little basis for making a judgment and when he senses the chance atmosphere of the situation. The chief operational difficulty is that too many stimulations involve guessing when *O* knows it is a matter of guessing. It would be desirable to arrange the conditions so that when *O* has a sensory difference he knows that he has it, as in the procedure for the quantal method. It is partly a matter of making possible the development of a good criterion of a difference and enabling *O* to use it. It is partly a matter of ensuring that *O* has enough easy judgments to keep him assured that the whole thing is not a gambling proposition.

Problems

1. Estimate the two-point limen for Data 6*A* using several of the methods described in this chapter. Estimate, also, the standard deviation of the distribution, the measure of precision *h*, and the standard error of the limen.

Data 6*A*. In Determining the Two-point Limen by the Constant Method, the Following Proportions of Judgments "Two" Were Obtained, Each Stimulus Being Applied 100 Times

S, mm.	18	22	26	30	34
p ("two")	.05	.23	.55	.72	.91

2. Estimate the upper and lower limens for Data 6*B*, and the standard deviations and standard errors that go with them, using any of the available methods.

Data 6*B*. The Following Data Were Obtained from a Comparison of Lifted Weights, the Standard Being 100 Grams and Each Pair Being Judged 100 Times

S	88	91	94	97	100	103	106
p_g	.01	.03	.10	.29	.52	.66	.82
p_d	.07	.17	.27	.36	.26	.21	.13
p_l	.92	.80	.63	.35	.22	.13	.05

3. Estimate the point of subjective equality, the interval of uncertainty, the difference limen, and the Weber ratio for Data 6*B*.

4. Convert the proportions in Data 6*B* into estimates of proportions that would have been obtained with two-category judgments. Compute a *PSE* for the data in this form, also the standard deviation and probable error.

Answers

1. By the Urban process, with weights, the following results were obtained: $L = 26.21$; $\sigma = 5.63$; $h = .126$; $\sigma_M = 0.41$ (using Culler's formula).

2. $L_u = 100.58$; $L_l = 95.86$; $\sigma_u = 5.37$; $\sigma_l = 5.92$; $\sigma_{M_u} = .37$; $\sigma_{M_l} = .39$ (Culler formula). Solution was by least-square method without the Müller-Urban weights.

3. $PSE = 98.33$ (Urban's xi); $IU = 4.72$; $DL = 2.36$; Weber ratio $= .024$.

4. Converted p_g: .011, .036, .137, .453, .703, .835, and .943. $PSE = 98.41$; $\sigma = 4.47$; $PE = 3.02$. (Computations made by least-square solution without weights or coding.)

References

1. Békésy G. von. Über das Fechner'sche Gesetz und seine Bedeutung für die Theorie der akustischen Beobachtungsfehler und die Theorie des Hörens. *Ann. Physik.*, 1930, **7**, 329–359.
2. Berkson, J. Application of the logistic function to bioassay. *J. Amer. statist. Ass.*, 1944, **39**, 357–365.
3. Blackwell, H. R. The influence of data collection procedures upon psychophysical measurement of two sensory functions. *J. exp. Psychol.*, 1952, **44**, 306–315.
4. Bliss, C. I. The calculation of the dosage-mortality curve. *Ann. appl. Biol.*, 1935, **22**, 134–167.
5. Boring, E. G. Urban's tables and the method of constant stimuli. *Amer. J. Psychol.*, 1917, **28**, 280–293.
6. ———. A chart of the psychometric function. *Amer. J. Psychol.*, 1917, **28**, 465–470.
7. ———. The control of attitude in psychophysical experiments. *Psychol. Rev.*, 1920, **27**, 440–452.
8. Brown, W. The judgment of difference. *Univ. Calif. Publ. Psychol.*, 1910, **1**, No. 1.
9. ———. The judgment of very weak sensory stimuli. *Univ. Calif. Publ. Psychol.*, 1914, **1**, No. 3, 199–268.
10. ——— and Thomson, G. H. *The Essentials of Mental Measurement.* 4th ed. New York: Cambridge University Press, 1940.
11. Culler, E. Studies in psychometric theory. *Psychol. Monogr.*, 1926, **35**, No. 163, 56–137.
12. ———. Studies in psychometric theory, *J. exp. Psychol.*, 1926, **9**, 271–298.
13. ———. Studies in psychometric theory, *J. exp. Psychol.*, 1927, **10**, 463–477.
14. Davis, R. C. The comparison of series of proportions: The problem and a new solution. *Psychol. Bull.*, 1951, **48**, 348–359.
15. Doughty, J. M. The effect of psychophysical method and context on pitch and loudness functions. *J. exp. Psychol.*, 1949, **39**, 729–745.
16. Fernberger, S. W. The effect of the attitude of the subject upon the measure of sensitivity. *Amer. J. Psychol.*, 1914, **25**, 538–543.
17. ———. A preliminary study of the range of visual apprehension. *Amer. J. Psychol.*, 1921, **32**, 121–133.
18. ———. The use of equality judgments in psychophysical procedures. *Psychol. Rev.*, 1930, **37**, 107–112.
19. ———. On absolute and relative judgments in lifted weight experiments. *Amer. J. Psychol.*, 1931, **43**, 560–578.
20. Finney, D. J. *Probit Analysis.* New York: Cambridge University Press, 1947.
21. Flynn, B. M. Pitch discrimination. The form of the psychometric function and simple reaction time to liminal differences. *Arch. Psychol. N.Y.*, 1943, **39**, No. 280.
22. Fullerton, G. S., and Cattell, J. McK. On the perception of small differences. *Publ. Univ. Penn., Phil. Series*, No. 2, 1892.
23. George, S. S. Attitude in relation to the psychophysical judgment. *Amer. J. Psychol.*, 1917, **28**, 1–37.
24. Goodfellow, L. D. The human element in probability. *J. gen. Psychol.*, 1940, **23**, 201–205.
25. Guilford, J. P. Some empirical tests of the method of paired comparisons. *J. gen. Psychol.*, 1931, **5**, 64–76.

26. ———. *Fundamental Statistics in Psychology and Education.* 2d ed. New York: McGraw-Hill, 1950.

27. ——— and Dallenbach, K. M. The determination of memory span by the method of constant stimuli. *Amer. J. Psychol.*, 1925, **36**, 621–628.

28. Harrison, S., and Harrison, M. J. A psychophysical method employing a modification of the Müller-Urban weights. *Psychol. Bull.*, 1951, **48**, 249–256.

29. Henmon, V. A. C. The relation of the time of a judgment to its accuracy. *Psychol. Rev.*, 1911, **18**, 186–201.

30. Holway, A. H. Normal equations and the $\phi(\gamma)$ hypothesis. *Amer. J. Psychol.*, 1935, **47**, 334–337.

31. Irwin, F. Psychophysical measurement methods. *Psychol. Bull.*, 1935, **32**, 140–171.

32. Jaspen, N. A note on the age-placement of Binet tests. *Psychol. Bull.*, 1944, **41**, 41–42.

33. Jerome, E. A. Olfactory thresholds measured in terms of stimulus pressure and volume. *Arch. Psychol. N.Y.*, 1942, **39**, No. 274.

34. Kellogg, W. N. An experimental evaluation of equality judgments in psychophysics. *Arch. Psychol. N.Y.*, 1930, **17**, No. 112.

35. ———. The time of judgment in psychometric measures. *Amer. J. Psychol.*, 1931, **43**, 65–86.

36. Kirschmann, A. *Grundzüge der psychologischen Maszmethoden*, in Abderhalden, *Handbuch der biologischen Arbeitsmethoden.* Abt. VI, Teil A. Berlin: Urban & Schwartzenberg, 1927.

37. Kreezer, G., and Dallenbach, K. M. Learning the relation of opposition. *Amer. J. Psychol.*, 1929, **41**, 432–441.

38. Lewis, D., and Burke, C. J. The use and misuse of chi square. *Psychol. Bull.*, 1949, **46**, 433–489.

39. Linder, F. E. A statistical comparison of psychophysical methods. *Psychol. Monogr.*, 1933, **44**, No. 199, 1–20.

40. ———. The accuracy of the constant methods. *Amer. J. Psychol.*, 1935, **47**, 504–508.

41. Litchfield, J. T., Jr., and Wilcoxon, F. A simplified method of evaluating dose-effect experiments. *J. Pharmacol. exp. Therap.*, 1949, **95**, 99–113.

42. Lufkin, H. M. The best-fitting frequency function for Urban's lifted-weight results. *Amer. J. Psychol.*, 1928, **40**, 75–82.

43. Miller, G. A., and Garner, W. R. Effect of random presentation on the psychometric function: Implications for a quantal theory of discrimination. *Amer. J. Psychol.*, 1944, **57**, 451–467.

44. Müller, G. E. *Die Gesichtpunkte und die Tatsachen der psychophysischen Methodik.* Wiesbaden: Bergmann, 1904.

45. Newhall, S. M. An interpolation procedure for calculating thresholds. *Psychol. Rev.*, 1928, **35**, 46–66.

46. Preston, M. G. Contrast effects and the psychophysical judgments. *Amer. J. Psychol.*, 1936, **48**, 389–402.

47. ———. Contrast effects and the psychometric functions. *Amer. J. Psychol.*, 1936, **48**, 625–631.

48. ———. Psychophysical measurement methods. *Psychol. Bull.*, 1938, **35**, 63–83.

49. Shaad, D. J., and Helson, H. Group presentation in the method of constant stimuli as a time-saving device. *Amer. J. Psychol.*, 1931, **43**, 422–433.

50. Spearman, C. The method of 'right and wrong cases' without Gauss' formulae. *Brit. J. Psychol.*, 1908, **2**, 227–242.

51. Stevens, S. S., Morgan, C. T., and Volkmann, J. Theory of the neural quantum in the discrimination of loudness and pitch. *Amer. J. Psychol.*, 1941, **54**, 315–335.

52. Thomson, G. H. The accuracy of the $\phi(\gamma)$ hypothesis. *Brit. J. Psychol.*, 1914, **7**, 44–45.

53. ———. Fitting of frequency functions to Urban's lifted-weight results. *Amer. J. Psychol.*, 1929, **41,** 70–82.

54. THURSTONE, L. L. The phi-gamma hypothesis. *J. exp. Psychol.*, 1928, **11,** 293–305.

55. TITCHENER, E. T. *Experimental Psychology.* Vol. II, Pts. I and II. New York: Macmillan, 1905.

56. URBAN, F. M. *The Application of Statistical Methods to Problems of Psychophysics.* Philadelphia: Psychological Clinic Press, 1908.

57. ———. Die psychophysischen Maszmethoden als Grundlagen empirischer Messungen. *Arch. ges. Psychol.*, 1909, **15,** 261–355; **16,** 168–227.

58. ———. Die Verallgemeinerung der Konstanzmethode. *Arch. ges. Psychol.*, 1931, **80,** 167–178.

59. ———. The psychometric constant delta. *Amer. J. Psychol.*, 1950, **63,** 100–107.

60. WEVER, E. G., and ZENER, K. E. The method of absolute judgment in psychophysics. *Psychol. Rev.*, 1928, **35,** 466–493.

61. WILLIAMS, H. D. On the calculation of an associative limen. *Amer. J. Psychol.*, 1918, **29,** 219–226.

62. WOODWORTH, R. S. Professor Cattell's psychophysical contributions. *Arch. Psychol. N.Y.*, 1914, **4,** No. 30, 60–74.

63. ———. *Experimental Psychology.* New York: Holt, 1938.

64. WUNDT, W. *Logik.* Vol. II. Stuttgart: Enke, 1895.

CHAPTER 7

THE METHOD OF PAIR COMPARISONS

In the next few chapters, beginning with this one, we deal with a group of methods known as psychological-scaling methods. They differ from the traditional psychophysical methods in that the end results are not values on physical scales but are on psychological scales. With few exceptions, there is no physical scale on which the stimuli can be readily calibrated. Nor is there usually an interest in psychophysical laws, although where the stimuli can be measured physically such laws can be investigated. Where stimuli *are* physically measurable, the measurements are often used merely as labels.

Rationale for the Scaling of Comparative Judgments

In the method of pair comparisons, all stimuli to be evaluated on a psychological scale are typically presented to the observer O in all possible pairs. O judges whether one of the pair is of greater quantity than the other in some defined respect. His judgments are in two categories and guessing is required. The stimuli are of similar nature, such as colors to be judged for pleasantness, samples of handwriting to be judged for excellence, or names of actors to be judged for acting ability. The response of O is ostensibly a comparative judgment.[1] The same O may judge all pairs a large number of times on different occasions, giving an occasion matrix, or many similar Os may judge all pairs only once, giving an individual matrix. In either case, we have as the numerical result the number and proportion of the times each stimulus is judged higher on the scale than every other stimulus. This gives us a proportion matrix P such as is shown in Table 7.1.

Table 7.1. General Design of the Proportion Matrix Showing the Proportion of the Time Each Stimulus at the Top Is Judged Greater than Each One at the Side

		S_a	S_b	S_c	. . .	S_j	. . .	S_n
	S_a	$p_{a>a}$	$p_{b>a}$	$p_{c>a}$	. . .	$p_{j>a}$	. . .	$p_{n>a}$
	S_b	$p_{a>b}$	$p_{b>b}$	$p_{c>b}$	. . .	$p_{j>b}$	. . .	$p_{n>b}$
	S_c	$p_{a>c}$	$p_{b>c}$	$p_{c>c}$	. . .	$p_{j>c}$	. . .	$p_{n>c}$
$P =$	.	. . .	. . .	. . .	. . .	. . .	. . .	. . .
	S_j	$p_{a>j}$	$p_{b>j}$	$p_{c>j}$	. . .	$p_{j>j}$	. . .	$p_{n>j}$
	.	. . .	. . .	. . .	. . .	. . .	. . .	. . .
	S_n	$p_{a>n}$	$p_{b>n}$	$p_{c>n}$	. . .	$p_{j>n}$	. . .	$p_{n>n}$

The scaling problem begins with matrix P. From this information we seek to give each stimulus a single value on a linear scale which we hope will

[1] The judgment may partake of absolute properties to some extent. See later pages for further discussion of this point.

have the properties of an interval scale. At least we can approach this objective. We shall next consider the principles of scaling from such data.

The Law of Comparative Judgment. The key to the scaling operations that start with comparative judgments is to be found in Thurstone's law of comparative judgment. It may be well for the student to review the discussion of that law in Chap. 2. Here we will begin with a statement of the law as in equation (2.7) with changes in subscript notation:

$$R_j - R_k = z_{jk} \sqrt{\sigma^2_j + \sigma^2_k - 2r_{jk}\sigma_j\sigma_k} \qquad (7.1)$$

where R_j and R_k = mean psychological values characteristically attached to stimuli S_j and S_k, respectively

z_{jk} = standard-measure distance or deviate from the mean of a unit normal distribution

σ_j and σ_k = standard deviations of distributions of R_{hj} and R_{hk}, respectively

r_{jk} = coefficient of correlation between R_{hj} and R_{hk}

The radical term is the standard deviation of the differences $R_{hj} - R_{hk}$ and is expressed as a function of the terms under the radical. It is the unit of the scale on which each separation $R_j - R_k$ is expressed.

The size of each separation $R_j - R_k$ can be determined if we know the values on the right-hand side of equation (7.1). We find z_{jk} from a knowledge of the experimental proportion $p_{j>k}$. The remaining parameters are unknown. This lack of information would thwart us if it were not possible to take some arbitrary steps. One of these is to make some assumptions that simplify the equation, eliminating some of the unknowns. The other is to make rough approximations to some of the needed values.

Approximations to the Law of Comparative Judgment. Thurstone has distinguished five "Cases" with respect to applications of the law of comparative judgment:

Case I. The use of the law in its complete form, as stated in equation (7.1), applying to repeated judgments of a single *O*. This is the ideal case for which the law was first conceived. It would require our obtaining experimental values for the unknown parameters.

Case II. Application of the law in group situations, in which many *O*s give single judgments of pairs. This requires the same kind of complete data as in Case I.

Case III. Assume that $r_{jk} = 0$; that there is no correlation between responses to any pair of stimuli. This assumption is especially defensible when the stimuli are not identifiable. In more general terms, there is less likelihood of interaction of stimuli if they vary clearly in only one aspect.

With the intercorrelation of stimuli being zero, the last term in equation (7.1) drops out, and we have an abbreviated law in the form

$$R_j - R_k = z_{jk} \sqrt{\sigma^2_j + \sigma^2_k} \qquad (7.2)$$

Since there are ways of estimating the relative values of σ_j and σ_k and since z_{jk} is known from the experimental data, the equation becomes solvable.

Case IV. Assume that the discriminal dispersions are approximately equal. The law then reduces to the form

$$R_j - R_k = .707 z_{jk}(\sigma_j + \sigma_k) \tag{7.3}$$

as Thurstone has shown (17). Discriminal dispersions will be equal when stimuli are equally easy to place on a scale. One sample of handwriting or a drawing or an English composition might be more difficult to judge than another because of contaminating features or because of a multiplicity of criteria. More objective stimuli such as lifted weights or visually perceived lines, in which the few relevant properties can be more easily isolated, should be expected to have nearly equal dispersions. There is more likelihood of unequal dispersions among group judgments than within a single individual's judgments.

Since the standard deviations must be estimated in applying Case IV as well as in applying Case III, and since there is little more work involved in Case III, there is good reason to prefer the latter because of its greater accuracy.

Case V. One additional assumption is made for the simplest solution of all, the assumption that the discriminal dispersions are all equal. Letting $\sigma_j = \sigma_k$, and letting σ_j stand for both, the law reduces to

$$R_j - R_k = z_{jk}\sigma_j \sqrt{2} \tag{7.4}$$

Letting σ_j become the unit of the scale, and therefore equal to unity,

$$R_j - R_k = z_{jk} \sqrt{2} \tag{7.5}$$

Letting the unit of the scale become $\sigma_j \sqrt{2}$, the law reduces to

$$R_j - R_k = z_{jk} \tag{7.6}$$

Case V*a*. Mosteller (11) has recently demonstrated that we need not go so far as to assume that the correlations between momentary responses are zero in connection with Case V. It is only necessary to assume that the correlations are equal. Then the unit of the separation becomes $\sigma_j \sqrt{2(1 - r)}$ and equation (7.6) applies, with this unit in place of $\sigma_j \sqrt{2}$. Letting $r = 0$ in the Mosteller unit reduces it to the same value as the unit in (7.5). Since the unit is an arbitrary matter, its size need not be known in terms of the actual values of σ_j and r.

The risk involved in making the assumptions of Case V or of Case III or Case IV is minimized by the fact that after we have scaled a set of stimuli on the basis of those assumptions we can check up on the results to see whether they are internally consistent. The test of internal consistency involves an attempt to reproduce the original proportion matrix from the scale values obtained for the stimuli. A chi-square test is available to determine the goodness of fit of expected to obtained proportions. If the results are internally consistent, we may say that we have found nothing contradictory to the assumptions we made. The test of internal consistency will be described later.

Relation to the Method of Constant Stimulus Differences. It is easy to point out close parallels between scaling in the method of pair comparisons and the constant processes that were described in Chap. 6. The technique of obtaining judgments in pair comparisons is equivalent to Culler's proposal of the constant method with a variable standard. Comparing each stimulus with every other one is equivalent to making each stimulus in turn the standard.

If the phi-gamma hypothesis can be applied to comparative judgments in the constant method, there is no reason why it cannot be likewise applied to pair-comparison judgments, with one or two modifications. In the constant method, the phi-gamma function is commonly assumed to describe the regression of proportions of judgments on corresponding *stimulus* values. According to the logic of the law of comparative judgment, the proportions of judgments "greater" should bear the ogival relationship, strictly speaking, to the values of the stimuli on the psychological scale, not those on the physical scale. This led Thurstone to propose his "phi-log-gamma" hypothesis as a substitute for the phi-gamma hypothesis, assuming the applicability of Fechner's law. In a more general sense, we may state a *phi-R hypothesis*, where the R is a psychological scale value. This follows from the law of comparative judgment and will be valid whether Fechner's law applies or not.

TABLE 7.2. PROPORTION MATRIX FOR SEVEN LIFTED WEIGHTS THAT WERE JUDGED BY PAIR COMPARISONS. ONE OBSERVER JUDGED EACH PAIR IN BOTH TIME ORDERS A TOTAL OF 200 TIMES

Stimulus	185	190	195	200	205	210	215
185	.48	.65	.78	.92	.93	.95	.99
190	.35	.50	.69	.80	.85	.97	.94
195	.22	.31	.48	.63	.72	.89	.91
200	.08	.20	.37	.52	.67	.78	.86
205	.07	.15	.28	.33	.54	.64	.74
210	.05	.03	.11	.22	.36	.46	.62
215	.01	.06	.09	.14	.26	.38	.56

In Table 7.2 we have a matrix of proportions obtained from pair comparisons of seven lifted weights, each pair having been judged 200 times by a single *O*. Each row of the matrix represents judgments against a single standard which varies from row to row. Applying the phi-R hypothesis (we need not know the R values for the stimuli in order to do this), our first step is to transform each proportion into a corresponding deviate value z_{jk}. This gives us a Z matrix of the form shown in general terms in Table 7.3. It can be seen that each row of Z gives us one basis for estimating the linear psychological distances between neighboring stimuli. Seven rows give us seven sets of such estimates. Means of the seven estimates should give us more accurate values than those derived from any single row. Assuming a constant unit for z_{jk} throughout, as in Case V or V*a*, we may proceed to compute the averages, from which we obtain the scale values R_j. This procedure will be illustrated later with other data. Application of the same procedure to the lifted-weight data gave the following R values for the seven stimuli in increasing order of magnitude (4): -1.151, -0.775, -0.324, $+0.048$, $+0.376$,

+0.782, and +1.057. With these values representing the stimuli on the R scale, the proportions given in Table 7.2 were plotted in Fig. 7.1. For each "standard" stimulus in turn there is a portion of an ogive which crosses the .50 level at an abscissa value very close to the scale value for that particular stimulus.

TABLE 7.3. GENERAL DESIGN OF THE DEVIATE MATRIX SHOWING THE DIFFERENCE BETWEEN THE SCALE POSITION OF EACH STIMULUS AT THE TOP OF THE COLUMN AND THE STIMULUS AT THE LEFT

$Z =$

	S_a	S_b	S_c	. . .	S_j	. . .	S_n
S_a	z_{aa}	z_{ba}	z_{ca}	. . .	z_{ja}	. . .	z_{na}
S_b	z_{ab}	z_{bb}	z_{cb}	. . .	z_{jb}	. . .	z_{nb}
S_c	z_{ac}	z_{bc}	z_{cc}	. . .	z_{jc}	. . .	z_{nc}
.	.	.	.	. . .	.	. . .	.
S_j	z_{aj}	z_{bj}	z_{cj}	. . .	z_{jj}	. . .	z_{nj}
.	.	.	.	. . .	.	. . .	.
S_n	z_{an}	z_{bn}	z_{cn}	. . .	z_{jn}	. . .	z_{nn}

With proportions transformed into z values, another diagram was plotted (Fig. 7.2) showing regressions of z on R. The regressions are definitely linear, which supports the hypothesis of normal distributions. Lines have been drawn by inspection. Each line crosses the level $z = 0$ at a scale position almost identical with the R value for that standard stimulus. The slopes

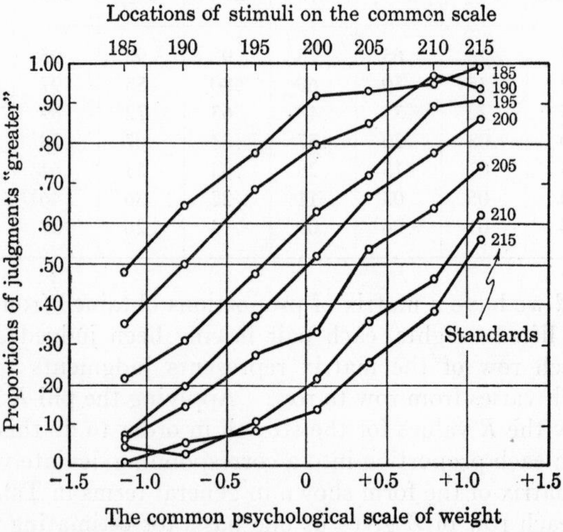

FIG. 7.1. Psychometric functions, with proportions of judgments "greater" as a function of psychological scale values of stimulus weights. Each of seven weights was used in turn as a "standard" stimulus in a pair-comparison experiment.

of the regression lines are approximately the same, with slight exceptions in the lines for standards 200 and 205. Since the slope of the regression line for z is inversely proportional to the standard deviation of the corresponding ogive, we can see that the standard deviation for standard 200 is smaller than the average and that for standard 205 is slightly larger than the average.

Such standard deviations are not simply the measures of dispersion of stimuli on the psychological continuum, but they are related to those dispersions, as can be seen from the equation for the law of comparative judgment, Case III.

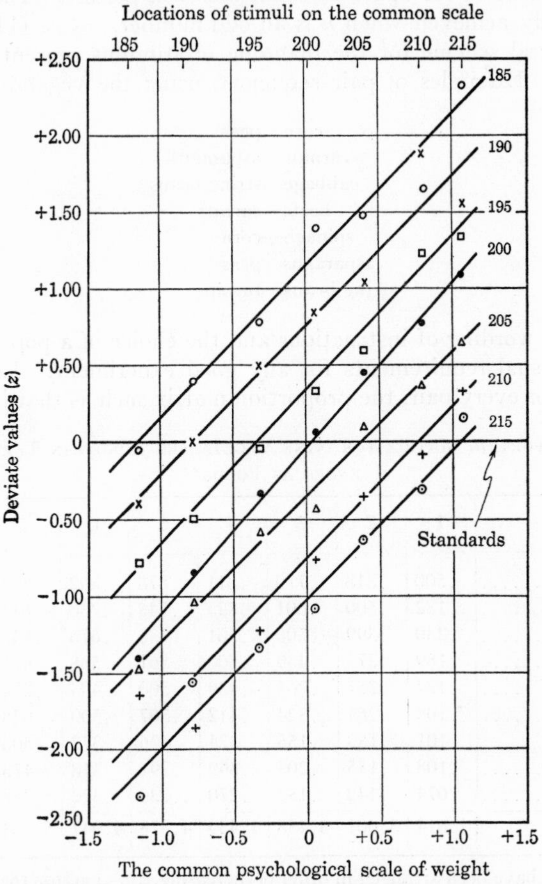

FIG. 7.2. Linear functions corresponding to the psychometric functions in Fig. 7.1, after transformation of each observed proportion to a normal-curve deviate z.

ESSENTIALS OF A PAIR-COMPARISON EXPERIMENT

The method of pair comparisons in both its experimental and statistical aspects will be illustrated by a simple experiment in preferences for vegetables. First, nine vegetables that are commonly served with meals were selected. A fairly large range of popularity is desirable, but one in which the most preferred is not selected 100 per cent of the time over the least preferred is desirable for illustrative purposes. The reason for this will become clear later.

The nine vegetables were combined in all possible pairs. The number of pairs for n stimuli is $n(n-1)/2$. With $n = 9$, there are 36 pairs. The sequence of pairs should be in a prearranged scheme, observing several objectives. Every vegetable appears equally often on the right and on the left, to control the space error. The vegetable's position on right and left should be alternated. No vegetable is given in two successive pairs; in fact the spacing should be as far apart as conditions will permit. These objectives are more easily achieved when n is an odd number. Ross (14, 15) has presented a general scheme for the planning of stimulus presentations in pair comparisons. Examples of pair sequences using the vegetables would be:

corn—peas
turnips—asparagus
cabbage—string beans
beets—carrots
spinach—corn
asparagus—peas
string beans—turnips

The careful wording of instructions and the choice of a population should observe the usual requirements for any good experiment. From the tally of responses for every pair, the proportion matrix such as that in Table 7.2 is

TABLE 7.4. PROPORTION MATRIX FOR NINE VEGETABLES JUDGED IN TERMS OF PREFERENCES AS FOODS*

Vegetable	1	2	3	4	5	6	7	8	9
1. Turnips	.500	.818	.770	.811	.878	.892	.899	.892	.926
2. Cabbage	.182	.500	.601	.723	.743	.736	.811	.845	.858
3. Beets	.230	.399	.500	.561	.736	.676	.845	.797	.818
4. Asparagus	.189	.277	.439	.500	.561	.588	.676	.601	.730
5. Carrots	.122	.257	.264	.439	.500	.493	.574	.709	.764
6. Spinach	.108	.264	.324	.412	.507	.500	.628	.682	.628
7. String beans	.101	.189	.155	.324	.426	.372	.500	.527	.642
8. Peas	.108	.155	.203	.399	.291	.318	.473	.500	.628
9. Corn	.074	.142	.182	.270	.236	.372	.358	.372	.500
$\Sigma p_{j>k}$	1.614	3.001	3.438	4.439	4.878	4.947	5.764	5.925	6.494

* Food stimuli have been arranged in order of increasing $\Sigma p_{j>k}$ across the columns.

prepared. It is desirable to arrange the stimuli in increasing order of rank of the final scale values. This order can be learned by summing columns of matrix P. Remember to rearrange rows as well as columns. The final result should be like that in Table 7.4, where the vegetables have been rearranged and renumbered.

COMPUTATION OF SCALE VALUES

In scaling the vegetable-preferences data, we shall first assume Case V, or Case V*a*; the procedure is exactly the same. We shall then make a test of internal consistency to see whether on the basis of the obtained scale values the original proportion matrix P could have occurred by random sampling. We shall find that the chi square is significant; therefore we shall then apply Case III and repeat the scaling. The chi-square test following

Case III will show that we may accept the assumptions of Case III and be satisfied with the scale values found by that approach.

Scaling under the Assumptions of Case V. Starting with the proportion matrix in Table 7.4, we next use the normal-curve tables to derive the corresponding matrix Z in Table 7.5. When p is greater than .50, z_{jk} receives a positive algebraic sign; when p is less than .50, it receives a negative sign. The upper-right portion of the matrix is numerically identical with the lower-left portion except for algebraic sign. Any z_{jk} represents an estimate of the distance $R_j - R_k$, where the latter are the as yet unknown scale positions of stimuli S_j and S_k. In every case, S_j is the stimulus designated at the top of the column and S_k is the stimulus designated at the left of the row. Thus, $R_1 - R_2$ is estimated to be $-.908$, whereas $R_2 - R_1$ is estimated to be $+.908$.

Averaging Scale Separations. While .908 is one estimate of the distance from stimulus S_2 to stimulus S_1, as reflected on the R scale, we can also derive other estimates from Table 7.5. This value, .908, is directly obtained from a single proportion representing direct comparisons of S_2 and S_1. These two stimuli were also compared with all other stimuli, and their relative preferences when paired with other stimuli should be useful as additional information. We can obtain another estimate of the separation $R_2 - R_1$ from each of the other stimuli S_3 to S_9, inclusive. We have seven equations for doing this from these seven stimuli:

$$\begin{aligned} R_2 - R_1 &= (R_2 - R_3) - (R_1 - R_3) = -.256 - (-.739) \\ R_2 - R_1 &= (R_2 - R_4) - (R_1 - R_4) = -.592 - (-.882) \\ &\cdots\cdots\cdots\cdots\cdots\cdots \\ &\cdots\cdots\cdots\cdots\cdots\cdots \\ R_2 - R_1 &= (R_2 - R_9) - (R_1 - R_9) = -1.071 - (-1.447) \end{aligned} \tag{7.7}$$

To complete the list of equations, we should add two more at the top of this list:

$$\begin{aligned} R_2 - R_1 &= (R_2 - R_1) - (R_1 - R_1) = .908 - .000 \\ R_2 - R_1 &= (R_2 - R_2) - (R_1 - R_2) = .000 - (-.908) \end{aligned}$$

With these equations included at the head of the list, inspection of the two columns of numerical values at the right shows that they are identical with the first two columns of Table 7.5. Since the difference between the means is equal to the mean of the differences, we can arrive at the same end result by summing the columns first and then finding the two means. We can do this for all columns, and since the differences between neighboring pairs of stimuli are mean estimates of their appropriate separations, the means themselves will serve as scale values.

The sums of the columns of Z are shown in Table 7.5. A good check of these computations is to sum the sums. The result should equal zero, which it does. The means $M_{z_{jk}}$ should also sum to zero, which they do within rounding error. The means may be taken as scale values for the nine vegetables, whose mean is arbitrarily (as a by-product of the procedure) the zero point of the scale. If one wishes to be rid of negative signs, one can give the value zero to the lowest stimulus in the list, which requires us to add to each mean a positive number equal to the absolute value of the mean of the lowest

TABLE 7.5. SCALE-SEPARATIONS MATRIX Z FOR THE NINE VEGETABLES JUDGED IN TERMS OF PREFERENCES AS FOODS, ASSUMING CASE V

Vegetable	1	2	3	4	5	6	7	8	9	Σ
1. Turnips	.000	.908	.739	.882	1.165	1.237	1.276	1.237	1.447	8.891
2. Cabbage	− .908	.000	.256	.592	.653	.631	.882	1.015	1.071	4.192
3. Beets	− .739	− .256	.000	.154	.631	.456	1.015	.831	.908	3.000
4. Asparagus	− .882	− .592	− .154	.000	.154	.222	.456	.256	.613	.073
5. Carrots	−1.165	− .653	− .631	− .154	.000	− .018	.187	.550	.719	−1.165
6. Spinach	−1.237	− .631	− .456	− .222	.018	.000	.327	.473	.327	−1.401
7. String beans	−1.276	− .882	−1.015	− .456	− .187	− .327	.000	.068	.364	−3.711
8. Peas	−1.237	−1.015	− .831	− .256	− .550	− .473	− .068	.000	.327	−4.103
9. Corn	−1.447	−1.071	− .908	− .613	− .719	− .327	− .364	− .327	.000	−5.776
Σz_{jk}	−8.891	−4.192	−3.000	− .073	1.165	1.401	3.711	4.103	5.776	.000✓
$M_{z_{jk}}$	− .988	− .465	− .333	− .008	+ .129	+ .156	+ .412	+ .456	+ .642	+0.001✓
R_j	.000	.523	.655	.980	1.117	1.144	1.400	1.444	1.630	8.893✓
R_c*	−0.7	1.4	1.9	3.3	3.8	4.0	5.0	5.2	5.9	29.8✓

* $R_c = 4.107M_z + 3.31 = 4.107R_j - 0.75$.

stimulus. Adding .988 to all means, we have the new R_j values in the next-to-the-last row in Table 7.5. The sum of R_j should equal n times the constant added, or $.988n$. A method for locating a psychologically meaningful zero point will be described later in the chapter. The row of values R_c will be explained in that connection.

The unit of the scale of R_j is equal to $\sigma_j \sqrt{2}$, as we saw from equation (7.4), under the assumptions of Case V, or it is $\sigma_j \sqrt{2(1 - r)}$, under the assumptions of Case V*a*. If the discriminal dispersions are not all equal and consequently the unit of z_{jk} varies from pair to pair, the unit for the means is an average of them all.

Mosteller has shown (11) that this process of averaging z_{jk} values in the columns is essentially a least-square solution. He has also shown that if most of the stimuli have equal discriminal dispersions, such stimuli will be properly scaled even though other stimuli have differing dispersions (12). The scaling of the latter stimuli will be in error. If there are several sets of stimuli, each with homogeneous dispersions within sets but differing in dispersion between sets, the scaling within sets will be correct but there will be inconsistency of scaling between sets.

Scaling When There Are Extreme Proportions. When proportions are very extreme, the scaling derived from them is somewhat risky. It is common practice not to use z_{jk} values more extreme than $+2.0$ or -2.0, which arise from proportions of about .977 and .023, respectively. Omitting such extreme values sometimes leaves vacancies in the Z matrix. Then the simple averaging procedure described above cannot be applied. The best procedure then is to solve all the equations (7.7), finding as many estimates of each separation between neighboring stimuli as the data will permit and averaging the differences. Having the average differences, one can assign the value zero, or any other arbitrary value, to the lowest stimulus and find other scale values by cumulating the differences.

The Test of Internal Consistency; Case V. Given the scale values for the vegetables found in Table 7.5, what proportion of judgments should we have expected for each pair? Do these proportions agree sufficiently well with those experimentally obtained? If our assumptions have been correct, the agreement should be so close that the discrepancies can be attributed to sampling errors. We could find the expected proportions, taking steps in reverse to those we took in scaling. We could compare each expected proportion with its corresponding obtained proportion and make a t test for significance of the departure of the obtained from the expected. This would mean $n(n - 1)/2$ t tests. Mosteller has recently proposed a way of making a single chi-square test for the entire matrix of proportions (13). We will use his test here.

The first step is to set up a matrix Z' containing the expected scale separations; expected, that is, in view of the obtained scale positions of the stimuli. Using the scale values R_j shown in Table 7.5, and by making all possible subtractions of pairs, we arrive at the matrix Z' shown in Table 7.6. We are concerned only with half the table (ignoring the diagonal cells for which we have no actually experimentally obtained values) since the two halves are identical. From the expected scale separations we find the corresponding expected proportions, using the normal-curve tables. These make up matrix P', shown in Table 7.7.

Since many of these proportions are close to 1.00, in a region where sampling distributions of proportions are not normal even for reasonably large samples, the procedure is to transform each proportion to a statistic θ, whose sampling distribution *is* normal. Theta is the angle whose sine is $\sqrt{p}$. The transformations are readily made by use of Table L in the Appendix. The resulting values for the expected proportions are given in Table 7.8. There

TABLE 7.6. EXPECTED SCALE SEPARATIONS z' BETWEEN VEGETABLES, DERIVED FROM SCALE VALUES OBTAINED BY THE ASSUMPTION OF CASE V (MATRIX Z'_5)

	1	2	3	4	5	6	7	8
2	.523							
3	.655	.132						
4	.980	.457	.325					
5	1.117	.594	.462	.137				
6	1.144	.621	.489	.164	.027			
7	1.400	.877	.745	.420	.283	.256		
8	1.444	.921	.789	.464	.327	.300	.044	
9	1.630	1.107	.975	.650	.513	.486	.230	.186

TABLE 7.7. EXPECTED PROPORTIONS p' DERIVED THROUGH z' FROM THE SCALE VALUES OBTAINED FOR THE NINE VEGETABLES UNDER THE ASSUMPTION OF CASE V (MATRIX P'_5)

	1	2	3	4	5	6	7	8
2	.700							
3	.744	.553						
4	.836	.676	.627					
5	.868	.724	.678	.554				
6	.874	.733	.688	.565	.511			
7	.919	.810	.772	.663	.611	.601		
8	.925	.821	.785	.679	.628	.618	.518	
9	.948	.866	.835	.742	.696	.686	.591	.574

TABLE 7.8. EXPECTED PROPORTIONS CONVERTED INTO ANGLES IN TERMS OF DEGREES (θ') BY MEANS OF THE FUNCTION $\theta' = \arcsin \sqrt{p'}$ (MATRIX θ')

	1	2	3	4	5	6	7	8
2	56.79							
3	59.60	48.04						
4	66.11	55.30	52.36					
5	68.70	58.31	55.43	48.10				
6	69.21	58.89	56.04	48.73	45.63			
7	73.46	64.16	61.48	54.51	51.41	50.83		
8	74.11	64.97	62.37	55.49	52.42	51.83	46.03	
9	76.82	68.53	66.03	59.47	56.54	55.92	50.24	49.26

would be a parallel table of θ coefficients corresponding to the obtained proportions of Table 7.4.

The formula for chi square to apply to this situation is

$$\chi^2 = \frac{N}{821} \sum (\theta - \theta')^2 \tag{7.8}$$

where N = the number of judgments per stimulus pair. This calls for the differences between expected and observed θ's and the squares of those differences. For our illustrative problem concerning the nine vegetables, the sum of the squared discrepancies is 300.833, so that

$$\chi^2 = \frac{(148)(300.833)}{821} = 54.23$$

The interpretation of this chi square, as usual, depends upon the number of degrees of freedom. For this situation, Mosteller (13) gives the degrees of freedom by the formula

$$df = \frac{(n - 1)(n - 2)}{2} \tag{7.9}$$

where n = number of stimuli. When n is 9, $df = 28$. Reference to the table of chi square shows that it takes a chi square as large as 48.278 to be significant at the .01 point. We may say that the obtained chi square is significant beyond the .01 point.

The conclusion to be drawn from such a result is somewhat ambiguous. Something is wrong with the application of Case-V assumptions, including the basic assumptions for the law of comparative judgment. According to Mosteller (13), the significant chi square could mean lack of normality, lack of unidimensionality, or unequal standard deviations. Chi square is not very sensitive to lack of normality in this situation. In our particular problem we have some evidence (from the linear regressions of z on R) that the discriminal dispersions are normal. Lack of unidimensionality would affect chi square similarly if other cases were applied. The thing to do at this point is to obtain a solution assuming Case III, to see whether the scaling is notably improved and to see whether the chi square is still significant. If the chi square is significant, we still have two possible reasons. If it is not, we have evidence that inequality of dispersions is one cause of the significant chi square after applying Case V.[1]

Scaling under the Assumptions of Case III. For scaling in a Case-III solution we need to make estimates of the standard deviations for the vegetable stimuli. We can only approximate the relative values of these standard deviations. Burros (2) has recently proposed some convenient formulas for this purpose. They are:

$$\sigma_j \doteq \frac{c}{V_{z_j}} \tag{7.10}$$

[1] It should also be added that the use of chi square assumes independence of the proportions, which, in turn, means zero correlations among the stimuli.

where σ_j = the standard deviation for the dispersion of stimulus S_j, V_{z_j} = variance of deviations of z_{jk} in each column of matrix Z from the mean of the column $M_{z_{jk}}$ (such values are found in Table 7.5), and c is estimated by the formula

$$c \doteq \frac{n}{\sum \frac{1}{V_{z_j}}} \tag{7.11}$$

where n = number of stimuli and V_{z_j} is defined as in equation (7.10).

Table 7.9 gives the main steps in applying Burros's formulas. The variances V_{z_j} were computed from the z_{jk} and M_z values in Table 7.5. The sum of their reciprocals, 37.500, is used in (7.11), giving $c = .2400$. The standard deviations in row 3 of Table 7.9 should sum to n, which they do.

TABLE 7.9. ESTIMATION OF STANDARD DEVIATIONS OF THE RESPONSES TO VEGETABLES ON THE PSYCHOLOGICAL SCALE

	1	2	3	4	5	6	7	8	9	Σ
V_{z_j}	.1670	.3416	.3098	.2082	.3234	.2672	.2662	.2315	.1772	
$1/V_{z_j}$	5.988	2.927	3.228	4.803	3.092	3.742	3.757	4.320	5.643	37.500
σ_j	1.437	.702	.775	1.153	.742	.898	.902	1.037	1.354	9.000✓
σ^2_j	2.065	.493	.601	1.329	.551	.806	.814	1.075	1.833	

This is a check on the computations and it is due to the fact that the method assures a mean σ_j of 1.00. From row 3 we see that the estimates give a rather wide range of dispersions, the largest, which is σ_1, being about twice the size of the smallest, which is σ_2. There seems to be least agreement among the observers as to the scale positions of turnips, corn, and asparagus. There seems to be the greatest agreement as to preferences for cabbage, carrots, and beets. It is not true that there is most agreement on the extreme stimuli. On the contrary, there is a tendency for better agreement in the central region, with one exception. The squared σ_j's, which we use in the Case-III solution, are given in the last row of Table 7.9.

In the solution by Case III, in which it is assumed that

$$R_j - R_k = z_{jk}\sqrt{\sigma^2_j + \sigma^2_k}$$

it is convenient to prepare three worktables in the solution for the separations $R_j - R_k$. These worktables include the values of (1) $\sigma^2_j + \sigma^2_k$; (2) $\sqrt{\sigma^2_j + \sigma^2_k}$; and (3) $z_{jk}\sqrt{\sigma^2_j + \sigma^2_k}$. Not all these worktables will be shown here for the vegetable problem. The third, which we may call matrix Z_3, is shown in Table 7.10.

Table 7.10 is completely parallel with Table 7.5. The treatment from here on is the same as in Case V. We sum the columns of z_{jk} values and check to see that the sum of sums is zero. Next we find the means of the columns, and if the matrix is complete, these can be taken to be the scale values. If we wish to eliminate negative signs, we add the numerical value of the lowest

TABLE 7.10. SCALE SEPARATIONS BETWEEN PAIRS OF VEGETABLES IN THE SOLUTION ASSUMING CASE III (MATRIX Z_3)

	1	2	3	4	5	6	7	8	9	Σ
1	.000	1.452	1.207	1.625	1.884	2.095	2.165	2.192	2.856	15.476
2	−1.452	.000	.268	.799	.667	.719	1.008	1.271	1.633	4.913
3	−1.207	− .268	.000	.214	.677	.541	1.208	1.076	1.416	3.657
4	−1.625	− .799	− .214	.000	.211	.324	.668	.397	1.090	.052
5	−1.884	− .667	− .677	− .211	.000	− .021	.218	.701	1,110	−1.431
6	−2.095	− .719	− .541	− .324	.021	.000	.416	.649	.531	−2.062
7	−2.165	−1.008	−1.208	− .668	− .218	− .416	.000	.093	.592	−4.998
8	−2.192	−1.271	−1.076	− .397	− .701	− .649	− .093	.000	.558	−5.821
9	−2.856	−1.633	−1.416	−1.090	−1.110	− .531	− .592	− .558	.000	−9.786
Σz_{jk}	−15.476	−4.913	−3.657	− .052	1.431	2.062	4.998	5.821	9.786	0.000✓
Mz_{jk}	− 1.720	− .546	− .406	− .006	.159	.229	.555	.647	1.087	−0.001✓
R_j	.000	1.174	1.314	1.714	1.879	1.949	2.275	2.367	2.807	15.479✓
R_c*	− 1.1	1.9	2.3	3.3	3.7	3.9	4.7	5.0	6.1	29.8✓

* $R_c = 2.580M_z + 3.30 = 2.580R_j - 1.13$.

mean, 1.720, to each of the means and the next-to-the-last row in Table 7.10 is the result.

Test of Internal Consistency; Case III. As before, the first step in the test of internal consistency is to estimate the expected scale separations z'_{jk} from the known scale values. These are given by the equation

$$z'_{jk} = \frac{R_j - R_k}{\sqrt{\sigma^2_j + \sigma^2_k}} \tag{7.12}$$

The numerator $R_j - R_k$ comes directly from the interpair differences in the next-to-the-last row of Table 7.10. The denominator comes directly from each corresponding cell of the worktable just preceding Table 7.10 (not shown). From the z'_{jk} values we next find the expected proportions $p'_{j>k}$. These are transformed into angles θ' and are compared with the similarly transformed experimental proportions. The chi square is found by formula (7.8). For the vegetable problem, the sum of squared discrepancies is 182.277, from which chi square is found to be 32.86.

By estimating standard deviations from the data and using them to adjust the data we have lost some additional degrees of freedom. According to Mosteller (13), we lost $n - 1$ degrees of freedom in connection with solution by Case V, since we used $n - 1$ means to solve for the expected separations, one mean being used merely to locate the zero point of the scale. We lose $n - 1$ more degrees of freedom, one for each standard deviation, except that one was used in determining the unit for them. By formula, for the Case-III situation,

$$df = \frac{(n-1)(n-4)}{2} \tag{7.13}$$

With $n = 9$, $df = 20$; and with 20 degrees of freedom we find that the obtained chi square of 32.86 is significant between the .05 and .02 points. Had we adopted a confidence level of .01 in advance, we would not reject the hypothesis that it can well be sampling errors that are producing such discrepancies in proportions as we find. It is probably good practice to adopt the .01 level in this connection. There are apparently situations in which the test is oversensitive and other situations in which it is undersensitive. In going from the Case-V solution to the Case-III solution, it is obvious that the discrepancies in thetas are smaller and the drop in chi square is numerically marked. The relative changes in scale values of the vegetables, however, are very small. The regression of the Case-V scale values on the Case-III scale values is linear with a correlation of .992. The greatest discrepancies are in the two end stimuli, turnips and corn, which were not as far from the other stimuli in the Case-V solution as in the Case-III solution. This is a function of their greater dispersions. With the correlation as high as it is, one could well question whether the extra work under Case III is justified. One could also point to a chi square that is significant beyond the .05 level for Case-III solution and ask whether inclusion of the parameter r_{jk} would not improve the scaling materially over that in both solutions. Without experimental information concerning the correlation terms, however, there is no way of including them in scaling. If there should be significant lack of internal consistency even after inclusion of experimental estimates of all the parameters, the stimuli probably represent more than a one-dimensional system. The general problem of multidimensional scaling is discussed in Chap. 10.

Weighting of the Observations. In connection with the constant methods we found that for refined adjustment of data to the psychometric function the Müller-Urban weights were used. The same weighting problem exists in connection with treatment of data from pair comparisons, and Thurstone has described a procedure for applying the Müller-Urban weights in scaling operations (20). The computations involving the weights are very cumbersome, however, and results with and without weighting are so similar that their use cannot be recommended in general practice.

Variations of the Method

The chief objection to the method of pair comparisons is that it takes too much time and is wearying to the judges. When the number of stimuli becomes relatively large—and any number greater than 15 would be regarded as relatively large for pair comparisons—the task of judging pairs of stimuli becomes long and irksome. Not only is the task long for the judges; it is also very long for the investigator. With 20 stimuli there are 190 pairs, 190 judgments, 190 proportions, and 190 deviates to look up in the tables and to deal with thereafter. There are ways of shortening the tasks of either the judges or the investigator or of both.

Reducing the Number of Pairs of Stimuli. There is nothing sacrosanct about pairing each stimulus with every other one in the series. To do so probably does tend to emphasize the unity of the continuum in question in the minds of the judges. And yet some stimuli in long series are so far apart psychologically that the proportions of judgments approach 1.00; hence the differences are so unreliable as to be useless for the computation of scale values. Therefore, not every stimulus is a good standard with which to compare all the stimuli of the series. It is often a proper procedure to select from all the stimuli a limited number to become the standards for the scale. These should be chosen at approximately equal intervals along the scale and they should be among the least ambiguous of the lot. In a series of seven lifted weights the writer found that the number of standards could be reduced to three or five without serious loss in accuracy of the results (4).

A very practical plan is suggested by Uhrbrock and Richardson (23). A list of the names of 45 supervisors whom they wished to evaluate was broken up into four groups (*A*, *B*, *C*, and *D*) of 10 each and an additional group (*K*) of 5 "key" men. Within each group of 10, each man was compared with every other man. Every man in groups *A*, *B*, *C*, and *D* was compared with every one of the 5 "key" men in group *K*. Thus the number of pairs was reduced from a possible 990 to 390.

McCormick and Bachus (10) have proposed another plan for reducing numbers of judgments in an industrial situation. Having 50 individuals to evaluate they systematically sampled pairings from what would have been a complete matrix. Each individual was compared with from 40 to 7 others instead of the complete 49, in different experimental trials. The results showed that much reduction in number of comparisons could well be tolerated. The amount of reduction an investigator will accept depends upon how much loss in accuracy he is willing to tolerate.

Savings can also be made by taking a cue from Thorndike. Having established the approximate rank order of his samples from the method of equal-appearing intervals—any other rough method will do—he obtained pair comparisons between neighboring pairs of stimuli. This plan might be extended somewhat, pairing every stimulus with a limited number of its neighbors on either side. Since scale separations coming from proportions near .500 should carry the greatest weight in fixing the final scale values, the proportions from relatively close neighbors are what we want. This plan would give us a few reliable differences from which to find a final mean scale separation between neighbors and thus the total scale.

Reducing the Labor of Computation. The author (3) has suggested a means whereby the labor of computing scale values may be very materially reduced even when a complete pairing of the stimuli has been used. The essential part of this process consists in finding the mean of the proportions of judgments for every stimulus as compared with every other one as well as with itself. The scaling is done starting with these proportions. The procedure as applied to the vegetable data is illustrated in Table 7.11. From the mean proportions we find deviates in the unit normal distribution, z_j. Negative signs may be eliminated as usual to find the scale values R_j.

The advantage, from the point of view of economy of effort, is at once apparent. Only n proportions need be dealt with instead of $n(n - 1)/2$. A still greater saving can be made in tallying the judgments. The mean proportions can be found without calculating the $n(n - 1)/2$ single proportions at all. We need merely tally the total number of times any stimulus is chosen in all its comparisons and then apply the formula

$$M_p = \frac{C + .5N}{nN} \tag{7.14}$$

where C = total number of choices given to a stimulus
N = number of judges
n = number of stimuli

The correction $.5N$ in the numerator is for the assumed number of choices the stimulus would have received if it had been compared with itself. This makes clearer the theory underlying the short-cut method proposed here. It is assumed that the standard is a composite of all the stimuli in the series and that M_p is the proportion of the times any given stimulus is chosen in preference to that standard.

Table 7.11. Solution of the Scaling of the Vegetables by the Composite-standard Method

	1	2	3	4	5	6	7	8	9	Σ	M
Σp	1.614	3.001	3.438	4.439	4.878	4.947	5.764	5.925	6.494	40.500	4.500✓
M_p	.179	.333	.382	.493	542	.550	.640	.658	.722	4.500	.500✓
z_j	− .919	− .432	− .300	− .018	.106	.126	.358	.407	.589	−0.083	−0.009
R_j	.000	.487	.619	.901	1.025	1.045	1.277	1.326	1.508	8.188	✓
R_c*	−0.8	1.4	2.0	3.2	3.8	3.9	4.9	5.1	6.0	29.5	3.28✓

* $R_c = 4.487z_j + 3.31 = 4.487R_j - 0.81$.

The assumption of a composite standard is very defensible in the light of Helson's concept of the "adaptation level," (7) which will be discussed at greater length in Chap. 12. Whether we ask O for comparative judgments or for judgments in successive categories, there is a wealth of experimental evidence to show that his verbal responses will be influenced very much by the total range of stimuli to which he is exposed in the experiment. He develops during the experiment a central, standard level as a general frame of reference for all his judgments. The adaptation level can be defined operationally as that level of stimulus that would be judged "medium" or "neutral" by the observer. Thus, in making comparative judgments O's report of "greater" is likely to mean in part that this stimulus is greater than the adaptation level as well as greater than the one with which it is paired. Another way of putting it would be to say that as each stimulus is judged in comparison with the $n - 1$ other stimuli, the net result is that he has judged it in comparison with the average of all the stimuli. The average impression can be taken as a fixed quantity with no variability or as a varying quantity with a small uniform variability for the general run of comparisons, such as we find for averages.

Some evidence for the accuracy of scaling by the composite-standard (*CS*) method can be seen in Fig. 7.3. There we have the plot of the scale values for vegetables by the *CS* method as a regression on scale values found by the Case-III solution. The coefficient of correlation is .993. The procedure assumes Case V and therefore may be expected to give results deviating from a Case-III solution in a manner similar to the deviations of a Case-V solution. Experience has shown a tendency for a regression like that in Fig. 7.3 to be very slightly ogival in form. This affects the extreme stimuli more than others. If the range of scale values of stimuli is very great, this procedure should be used with some hesitation.

Other Scaling Principles and Methods. There have been two other noteworthy contributions to scaling theory and practice in connection with the method of pair comparisons, one by Guttman (6) and one by Lienau (9). The former sets up the objective of achieving scale values for stimuli such that one could reproduce from them the original judgments. Guttman claims that his method is adaptable to the scaling of more complex objects

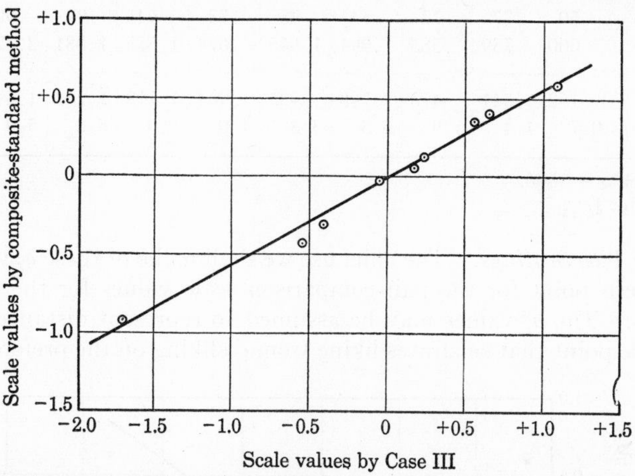

FIG. 7.3. An illustration showing the close agreement between scale values obtained for the nine vegetables by the composite-standard method and scale values obtained by application of Thurstone's Case III of his law of comparative judgment.

and propositions and that it can handle curvilinear relationships. The method provides a least-square solution but with laborious iterative operations that are forbidding.

Locating a Meaningful Zero Point. There is nothing about pair-comparison data in themselves that gives us any basis for locating a psychologically meaningful zero point. We therefore need outside information if one is to be established. There are several kinds of information that might be used. The source of the information we will use here comes from two-category judgments.

Scaling from Dichotomous Judgments. The nine vegetables were presented along with several others, by name, to 100 *O*s similar to those who made the pair-comparison judgments. It would have been better had the same *O*s been involved in making the two kinds of judgments, but these data will suffice for illustrative purposes. Table 7.12 shows the proportion of the judgments that were in the favorable category. The two categories were essentially those of "like" and "dislike." From the proportion of judgments "like" a corresponding deviate z is found in the normal-curve tables. The deviates are called a_j in Table 7.12 to avoid confusion with z in the pair-comparison solutions. This scaling procedure assumes that the discriminal dispersion is normal for each vegetable. If we also assume that the dispersions are equal for all vegetables, we may allocate the nine z values to the same scale whose unit is the standard deviation of a single dispersion.

TABLE 7.12. SCALE VALUES DERIVED FROM ABSOLUTE JUDGMENTS AND A LINEAR TRANSFORMATION OF THE VALUES OBTAINED FROM PAIR COMPARISONS, THE CASE-V SOLUTION

	Vegetable									Σ
	1	2	3	4	5	6	7	8	9	
$p_{s>0}$	.50	.77	.72	.84	.95	.75	.94	.97	.99	
a_j	.000	.739	.583	.994	1.645	.674	1.555	1.881	2.326	
M'_{z5}*	− .182	.341	.473	.798	.935	.962	1.218	1.262	1.448	7.255✓
R_c†	−0.7	1.4	1.9	3.3	3.8	4.0	5.0	5.2	5.9	29.8✓

* $M'_{z5} = M_{z5} + .806$.
† $R_c = 4.107 M'_{z5}$.

Relating Two Scalings. The chief use we shall make of these a_j values is to locate a zero point for the pair-comparison scale values for the same nine vegetables. The a_j values may be assumed to represent distances from an indifference point that separates liking from disliking on the preference scale,

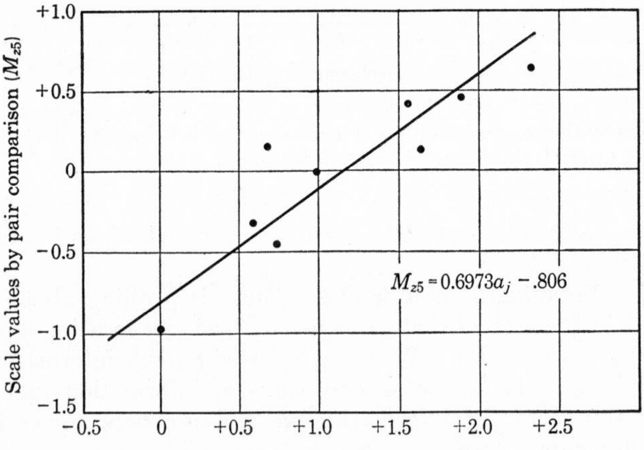

FIG. 7.4. Plot of the linear-transformation function by which a meaningful zero point is determined for the scaling of the nine vegetables from pair comparisons (solution by Case V).

except for sampling errors. We should expect the a_j values to be linearly related and highly correlated with the scale values found by pair comparisons. In Fig. 7.4 nine points are plotted relating the a_j values to the M_z values found by assuming Case V. In this connection we shall call the latter values

M_{z5}. From the relationship of Fig. 7.4 we expect to find what value of M_{z5} corresponds to zero on the a_j scale.

From the fact that the lowest vegetable, turnips, had exactly .50 favorable judgments we might conclude that this same vegetable should be at the zero point on the pair-comparison scale. If this were the case, the R_j values in Table 7.5 are at correct distances from zero. But this would use only the information concerning one stimulus. It would base the location of zero on only one proportion. There might be an unusual error in the a_j for this stimulus. We can use the information provided by all the stimuli by bringing into consideration all the points in Fig. 7.4. The correlation between M_{z5} and a_j is .90, which indicates sufficient covariation in the two to justify the use of all the a_j values, although we would ordinarily like the correlation to be higher.

Let us derive a linear-transformation equation by which we can determine a value of M_{z5} that corresponds to $a_j = 0$.[1] The general procedure for such an operation is described in Chap. 3. The two standard deviations are .487 and .698, for M_{z5} and a_j, respectively. The regression coefficient b_{Ma} is equal to .697 and the coefficient $a = -.806$. The latter is the Y intercept and gives us the value of M_{z5} when $a_j = 0$. Since the scale value M_{z5} for turnips was $-.988$, that vegetable is actually below zero to the extent of $-.182$, when we consider the whole list of a_j values. Adding the constant .806 to all the M_{zj} values in Table 8.5, we have the new values M'_{z5} in the third row of Table 7.12.

Changing a Scale Unit. Let us next consider changing to a smaller unit so that most or all of the scale values will be greater than 1.0. It will also be desirable to have a common scaling for these stimuli as derived by different operations so that they can be more directly compared. Let us choose a scale with a standard deviation of 2.0 for these nine vegetables. The zero point has already been located; therefore all we need is a change of unit, which is achieved by using a constant multiplier. That multiplier must be equal to the ratio 2.0/.487, which is 4.107. Let the new scale values be called R_c (common psychological scale); then $R_c = 4.107M'_{z5}$. These values are given to one decimal place in the last row of Table 7.12. The sum of these values should equal the product $4.107\Sigma M'_{z5}$, which it does.

In the bottom row of Table 7.5 will be found a duplicate set of R_c values arising from the Case-V solution. The operations by which R_c was obtained in Table 7.12 have been combined and generalized to apply directly to $M_{z_{jk}}$ and R_j in Table 7.5. The resulting equations are given below the table. If we combine the two operations in deriving R_c, as in Table 7.12, we have

$$R_c = 4.107M'_{z5} = 4.107(M_{z5} + .806) = 4.107M_{z5} + 3.31$$

This gives the first equation at the bottom of Table 7.5. To obtain the other equation involving R_j, we need to express M'_{z5} in terms of R_j. Because

[1] Preference is given here to a transformation equation over a regression equation that would be found by a least-square solution. When the correlation is very close to 1.0, it makes little difference which is used. Here the zero point would have been $.08z$ units higher had we used a regression equation.

$M'_{z5} = M_{z5} + .806$ and $M_{z5} = R_j - .988$, we have

$$M'_{z5} = R_j - .988 + .806 = R_j - .182$$

Therefore,

$$R_c = 4.107M'_{z5} = 4.107(R_j - .182) = 4.107R_j - 0.75-$$

The check for the sum of the R_c values in Table 7.5 is to find $4.107\Sigma R_j - 0.75-$.

Similar transformations have been made in the scale values found by the Case-III solution in Table 7.10 and for the composite-standard solution in Table 7.11. The three sets of R_c values are very close numerically. Those from the Case-III solution should be regarded as a trifle better than the others. They have been used as the basis for showing the vegetables scaled graphically in Fig. 7.5.

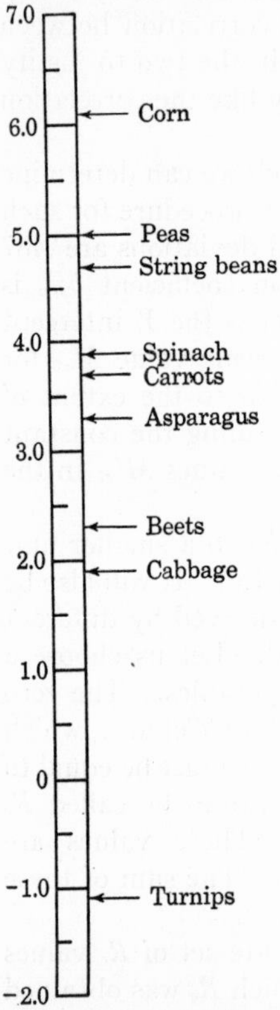

FIG. 7.5. Scale values for the popularity of nine vegetables as determined by pair comparisons (Case-III solution). The zero point is at an estimated place of indifference.

APPLICATIONS OF PAIR COMPARISONS

The range of applicability of the method of pair comparisons is so great that not all the specific uses can be referred to here. In general, it can be applied whenever stimuli can be presented in pairs, either simultaneously or in succession. Its chief use up to the present time has been in the determination of affective values and of aesthetic values; colors, designs, rectangles, musical intervals, names of nationalities, and the like have been the favorite stimuli. Opinions on such questions as prohibition, war, religion, and the like can be treated and evaluated by this method, although the handling of such material in pair comparisons becomes a bit awkward at times. The application to the evaluation of individuals on some trait of personality or character or on their value to a certain employer would seem to have great possibilities. It might replace the less accurate and less valid methods of rating scales, where more exacting practical or experimental work needs to be done. The results might very well serve as the criterion of validity against which to check any of the less accurate or less dependable methods of evaluating stimuli, either persons or things, attributes or opinions, wherever the results of those less reliable methods are held in question.

An Application to Learning Data. Hull (8) and his associates have recently made an interesting application of scaling by pair-comparison principles that is worthy of special recognition. Realizing that ordinary scores of performance in learning—correct responses, errors, latent times, and the like —do not necessarily provide interval-scale measurements of "reaction potential" and hence of "habit strength," they sought to transform such data into a form that would have equal units. In a learning experiment involving a large number of rats, each selected trial was taken as a "stimulus" to be psychologically evaluated. The proportion of the rats that had a shorter latent time in each trial as compared with every other trial was determined and a proportion matrix was set up. Scaling proceeded according to the Case-III solution. Thus latent time was taken merely as a rank-order measurement for the purpose of obtaining "comparative-judgment" proportions. With the scale values thus derived to measure learning on a psychological interval scale, quantitative laws stating achievement as a function of practice could be derived. It would be presumed that such laws would more faithfully describe the nature of learning progress and would be more generally applicable, since they would be more independent of the properties of incidental measuring scales.

One conclusion of these investigators is of much interest in connection with theory of comparative judgments. They found evidence for the belief that the distribution of reaction potentials at any one trial is leptokurtic. The scaling process was repeated assuming leptokurtic distributions with an index of kurtosis of about 4.0 (for normal distributions the index is 3.0). The scale separations found by this method were found to be more consistent internally than those based on the assumption of normality (25). These investigators suggest that in ordinary psychological-scaling use of the pair-comparison method many instances of departure from normality in the direction of leptokurtosis will be found. One indirect sign of this is that in a Z matrix the estimates of the same scale separation as by equations (7.7) will be systematically larger as we go farther from the direct estimates, which are smallest. The longer the series of indirect estimates, the greater the discrepancy becomes.

The author is of the opinion that the effect that these writers have noticed may be due to variations of intercorrelations of responses to stimuli in pairs rather than to departure from normality. In the learning data with which Hull and his associates were dealing, especially, there would undoubtedly be intercorrelations due to individual differences between rats. It is likely that the farther apart the trials, the lower the correlation would be. Such possible correlations were entirely ignored. They could have been computed from the experimental data. Whether there is a similar systematic shift of correlations in judging stimuli is hard to say. There is no very obvious reason which would lead us to expect that the farther apart two stimuli on the scale the lower would be their intercorrelation. This might well be investigated. One interesting finding of Hull and his associates was that the evidence for leptokurtosis was lacking in the lifted-weight data mentioned early in this chapter. They predict that such evidence would be forthcoming if the experiment were repeated with more weights and smaller steps. Another interpretation of this minor finding would be that weights, because of their greater psychological simplicity, should be less intercorrelated psychologically, perhaps not at all, for lack of secondary criteria such as would identify them for the observer. The Case-V scaling for these weights gave results that were highly consistent internally, with a chi square of 21.04, which was significant between the .20 and .10 points. Until there is better evidence, then, we should not let the learning results reported by Hull cast serious doubt on the assumption of normality of distribution of discriminal processes in general. The findings of Hull's group should, however, indicate the importance of paying attention to the correlation term in the law of comparative judgment, with the need for making efforts to estimate that correlation experimentally.

Problems

1. Apply a Case-V solution to Data 7*A*, following the procedures of this chapter.

DATA 7*A*. PROPORTIONS OF THE TIME EACH OF SIX VEGETABLES WAS PREFERRED TO EVERY OTHER BY 237 MALE STUDENTS

Vegetable	1	2	3	4	5	6
1. Turnips	(.500)	.728	.774	.833	.873	.950
2. Cauliflower	.272	(.500)	.588	.624	.751	.914
3. Beets	.226	.412	(.500)	.584	.733	.878
4. Spinach	.167	.376	.416	(.500)	.683	.751
5. Tomatoes	.127	.249	.267	.317	(.500)	.683
6. Corn	.050	.086	.122	.249	.317	(.500)
Σp	1.342	2.351	2.667	3.107	3.857	4.676

2. Convert the scale values into values R_{c1} by making the appropriate linear transformation to achieve a mean of 5.0 and standard deviation of 2.0. Check to see that this has been achieved.
3. Make a statistical test of the internal consistency of the scale values obtained.
4. Whether or not the statistical test in Prob. 3 gave a significant chi square, estimate the standard deviations for the six stimuli on the *R* scale.
5. Compute scale values by use of the composite-standard method. Convert the scale values to a scale common with that derived in Prob. 2, and compare results.

Answers

1. The scale values R_{j1} are 0.000, 0.523, 0.681, 0.909, 1.259, and 1.740.
2. The transformed values are 1.9, 3.8, 4.4, 5.2, 6.5, and 8.2.
3. The chi square is 13.608, which with 10 degrees of freedom is significant just above the 20 per cent point.
4. The standard deviations are 1.20, 0.83, 0.82, 1.05, 1.13, and 0.97.
5. The values R_{j2} are 0.000, 0.485, 0.618, 0.804, 1.125, 1.528. The values R_{c2} are 1.8, 3.9, 4.4, 5.2, 6.5, and 8.2.

REFERENCES

1. ANGOFF, W. H. An empirical approach to a problem of psychophysical scaling. *J. appl. Psychol.*, 1949, **33**, 59–68.
2. BURROS, R. H. The application of the method of paired comparisons to the study of reaction potential. *Psychol. Rev.*, 1951, **58**, 60–66.
3. GUILFORD, J. P. The method of paired comparisons as a psychometric method. *Psychol. Rev.*, 1928, **35**, 494–506.
4. ———. Some empirical tests of the method of paired comparisons. *J. gen. Psychol.*, 1931, **5**, 64–76.
5. GULLIKSEN, H. Paired comparisons and the logic of measurement. *Psychol. Rev.*, 1946, **53**, 199–213.

6. GUTTMAN, L. An approach for quantifying paired comparisons and rank order. *Ann. math. Statist.*, 1946, **17**, 144–163.

7. HELSON, H. Adaptation-level as a frame of reference for prediction of psychophysical data. *Amer. J. Psychol.*, 1947, **60**, 1–29.

8. HULL, C. L., FELSINGER, J. M., GLADSTONE, A. I., and YAMAGUCHI, H. G. A proposed quantification of habit strength. *Psychol. Rev.*, 1947, **54**, 237–254.

9. LIENAU, C. C. Discrete bivariate distribution in certain problems of statistical order. *Amer. J. Hyg.*, 1942, **33**, 65–85.

10. MCCORMICK, E. J., and BACHUS, J. A. Paired comparison ratings. I. The effect on ratings of reductions in the number of pairs. *J. appl. Psychol.*, 1952, **36**, 123–127.

11. MOSTELLER, F. Remarks on the method of paired comparisons: I. The least squares solution assuming equal standard deviations and equal correlations. *Psychometrika*, 1951, **16**, 3–9.

12. ———. Remarks on the method of paired comparisons: II. The effect of an aberrant standard deviation when equal standard deviations and equal correlations are assumed. *Psychometrika*, 1951, **16**, 203–206.

13. ———. Remarks on the method of paired comparisons: III. A test of significance for paired comparisons when equal standard deviations and equal correlations are assumed. *Psychometrika*, 1951, **16**, 207–218.

14. ROSS, R. T. Optimum orders for the presentation of pairs in the method of paired comparisons. *J. educ. Psychol.*, 1934, **25**, 375–382.

15. ———. Optimal orders in the method of paired comparisons. *J. exp. Psychol.*, 1939, **25**, 414–424.

16. THURSTONE, L. L. Psychophysical analysis. *Amer. J. Psychol.*, 1927, **38**, 368–389.

17. ———. A law of comparative judgment. *Psychol. Rev.*, 1927, **34**, 273–286.

18. ———. Equally often noticed differences. *J. educ. Psychol.*, 1927, **18**, 289–293.

19. ———. The method of paired comparisons for social values. *J. abnorm. and soc. Psychol.*, 1927, **21**, 384–400.

20. ———. The measurement of opinion. *J. abnorm. and soc. Psychol.*, 1928, **22**, 415–430.

21. ———. Theory of attitude measurement. *Psychol. Rev.*, 1929, **36**, 222–241.

22. ———. Stimulus dispersions in the method of constant stimuli. *J. exp. Psychol.*, 1932, **15**, 284–297.

23. UHRBROCK, R. S., and RICHARDSON, M. W. Item analysis. *Person. J.*, 1933, **12**, 141–154.

24. WOODWORTH, R. S. Professor Cattell's psychophysical contributions. *Arch. Psychol. N.Y.*, 1914, **4**, No. 30, 60–74.

25. YAMAGUCHI, H. G., HULL, C. L., FELSINGER, J. M., and GLADSTONE, A. I. Characteristics of dispersions based on the pooled momentary reaction potentials $_sE_r$ of a group. *Psychol. Rev.*, 1948, **55**, 216–238.

CHAPTER 8

THE METHOD OF RANK ORDER

The method of rank order has been one of the most popular and one of the most practical of the psychometric methods. Its appeal has consisted largely in the ease with which a relatively large number of stimuli can be judged with reference to one another, and also in its wide range of applicability. It forces observers to make the maximum number of discriminations, as in the method of pair comparison, and thus provides as much discriminatory information as it is possible to obtain from them. Any stimuli that can be manipulated in any manner so that *O* can place them in serial order can be treated with this method, whether they be lifted weights, names of scientists, artistic designs, advertisements, or jokes. Stimuli that have been ranked by a number of observers can be placed in a "pooled" rank order. More than that, scale values that refer to an interval scale can be assigned to the stimuli.

The method bears some superficial resemblance to that of successive categories on the one hand and to that of pair comparisons on the other. It resembles the former in that the stimuli are arranged by *O* along some psychological continuum. It differs in that there is only one stimulus to a category and in the manner of scaling from the judgments. The resemblance to pair comparisons is more fundamental in that each stimulus is in essence compared with every other stimulus. Any stimulus S_j may be said to have been judged greater than all stimuli $S_k, S_l, \ldots, S_n$ that are ranked lower in the list and judged less than those placed higher, $S_i, S_h, \ldots, S_a$. One difference here is that in the rank-order method all the stimuli are present for simultaneous observation, whereas in pair comparisons they usually are not. Another difference is that pair comparisons give opportunity for deviation from a strictly consistent rank order. The method of rank order enforces upon *O* a certain internal consistency, which, in some instances, may be more apparent than real, and which results in some loss of degrees of freedom.

Scale Values from Rank-order Judgments

The Rank-order Frequency Matrix. The typical result from an experiment that utilizes the rank-order method is in the form of a table. Each column represents a stimulus and each row an observer. Each cell represents a rank given to a particular stimulus by a particular observer. This is the usual custom when the number of *O*s is reasonably small. When the number of *O*s is large, however, the table can be condensed considerably by setting up a matrix of the general form seen in Table 8.1, a specific example of which is included in Table 8.2.

In the rank-order frequency matrix each column also stands for a certain stimulus, where stimuli vary from S_a to S_n. There are n stimuli, with S_j denoting the general case. The rows of this matrix represent ranks 1 through n, where a rank of 1 is regarded as standing for the highest quantity. The general case is denoted r_i. In each cell is a frequency with which a certain stimulus is assigned to a specified rank. Thus, f_{3g} indicates the number of times any of the N observers gave a rank of 3 to stimulus S_g. In addition to

TABLE 8.1. MATRIX OF FREQUENCIES WITH WHICH EACH OF n STIMULI IS ASSIGNED TO EACH OF n RANKS

Ranks (r_i)	Stimuli (S_j): S_a	S_b	S_c	. . .	S_j	. . .	S_n
r_1	f_{1a}	f_{1b}	f_{1c}	. . .	f_{1j}	. . .	f_{1n}
r_2	f_{2a}	f_{2b}	f_{2c}	. . .	f_{2j}	. . .	f_{2n}
r_3	f_{3a}	f_{3b}	f_{3c}	. . .	f_{3j}	. . .	f_{3n}
.	.	.	.	. . .	.	. . .	.
r_i	f_{ia}	f_{ib}	f_{ic}	. . .	f_{ij}	. . .	f_{in}
.	.	.	.	. . .	.	. . .	.
r_k	f_{ka}	f_{kb}	f_{kc}	. . .	f_{kj}	. . .	f_{kn}
.	.	.	.	. . .	.	. . .	.
r_n	f_{na}	f_{nb}	f_{nc}	. . .	f_{nj}	. . .	f_{nn}

the general rank r_i, the rank r_k is also explicitly mentioned in Table 8.1 for the reason that in the last part of the chapter we will be interested in the special experimental situation in which only the first k ranks are assigned. In such a situation, the matrix would end with the row for r_k.

Ranks and Rank Values. The popular custom of giving the greatest stimulus a rank of 1 is followed here, but only to the point of recording the data. In order to make the rank numbers used in further treatment of the data correspond to increasing magnitudes of stimuli, let us define a new term *rank value*. The rank values are a series, denoted by R_i, that are in exact reverse order to the ranks r_i. R_i is related to r_i by the simple equation $R_i = n - r_i + 1$. In other words, $R_i + r_i = n + 1$. The first two columns of Table 8.2 show this transformation in a particular problem.

There are several reasons for this double-scale approach. One is the naturalness of the ranks 1, 2, 3, . . . , n for the observer, who thinks in terms of first place, second place, and so on. Another is that n varies from one experiment to another, whereas rank 1 does not. This same circumstance is also reflected in the common way of writing a matrix, such as that in Table 8.1. With the transformation made at the point of starting to work with the tabulated data, the chances for confusion should be minimized.

The Use of Means and Medians of Rank Values. Since rank values are strictly ordinal numbers, there is little numerical meaning to be attached to means of such values. One may legitimately compute medians of rank values, but the results are nothing more than ordinal numbers. Since interpolation is risky within intervals whose widths are of unknown value and are probably unequal, giving such medians to more digits than whole numbers is of questionable value except to break ties for cases whose medians are within the same rank-interval. If one wants to know the complete composite ranking for a set of stimuli judged by a number of observers, with little question about ties, the sums of the rank values for the various stimuli would probably give the best indications. For example, the 15 actors represented in Table 8.2 would come in descending rank order as follows: *C B A O E L I N F G D M H K J*, as based on sums of rank values.[1] This

TABLE 8.2. MATRIX OF FREQUENCIES WITH WHICH EACH OF 15 ACTORS WERE RANKED IN EACH OF 15 POSITIONS BY 100 MALE STUDENTS

r_i	R_i	*A*	*B*	*C*	*D*	*E*	*F*	*G*	*H*	*I*	*J*	*K*	*L*	*M*	*N*	*O*	Σ	*P*	*C*
1	15	9	17	15	8	10	4	4	1	3	1	0	9	2	2	15	100	96.7	9
2	14	7	11	15	8	8	3	6	6	4	2	1	8	1	8	12	100	90.0	8
3	13	18	9	11	8	5	2	3	6	6	3	2	5	5	4	13	100	83.3	7
4	12	11	11	16	4	8	7	2	5	5	1	4	6	8	7	5	100	76.7	6
5	11	9	8	9	6	9	9	6	3	6	4	5	3	7	10	6	100	70.0	6
6	10	6	11	10	4	6	5	13	6	9	2	4	7	4	7	6	100	63.3	6
7	9	9	9	6	6	5	9	7	4	8	5	3	10	7	8	4	100	56.7	5
8	8	6	4	4	5	10	12	6	10	6	2	6	9	9	3	8	100	50.0	5
9	7	11	5	1	3	6	4	10	5	14	3	6	7	11	10	4	100	43.3	5
10	6	5	4	2	3	6	7	6	15	13	4	7	7	7	8	6	100	36.7	4
11	5	1	3	6	6	7	13	10	4	6	9	9	3	12	7	4	100	30.0	4
12	4	1	2	1	9	7	8	5	7	9	15	11	5	8	8	4	100	23.3	4
13	3	6	1	2	5	8	6	9	13	6	9	12	6	7	5	5	100	16.7	3
14	2	1	3	1	6	3	5	7	6	4	16	19	11	6	7	5	100	10.0	2
15	1	0	2	1	19	2	6	6	9	1	24	11	4	6	6	3	100	3.3	1
Σf_{ji}		100	100	100	100	100	100	100	100	100	100	100	100	100	100	100	1,500		
$\Sigma f_{ji}C$		597	621	642	464	544	471	477	442	500	333	368	510	457	486	588	7,500 = $5Nn$✓		
$M_c = R_j$		6.0	6.2	6.4	4.6	5.4	4.7	4.8	4.4	5.0	3.3	3.7	5.1	4.6	4.9	5.9	75.0 = $5n$✓		
R_c*		7.1	7.6	8.1	3.9	5.8	4.1	4.2	3.4	4.8	0.8	1.7	5.0	3.8	4.4	6.9	71.6✓		

* $R_c = 2.357 R_j = 7.01$.

order coincides with that found by the best pair-comparison treatment (Table 8.7).

If there has been a reasonably large number of judges, one probably wants to know scale values for the stimuli on an interval scale. Interval scaling from rank-order judgments can be approached essentially from two directions. One may be called the *normalized-rank* approach and the other may be called the *comparative-judgment* approach. The latter has many resemblances to the scaling from pair comparisons, with some new variations. The two approaches and the processes involved will now be described. The illustrative data represent the ranking of 15 well-known motion-picture actors by a hundred male college students. The instruction was essentially

[1] Not shown in Table 8.2. The actors, in alphabetical order, are William Bendix, Humphrey Bogart, Gary Cooper, Kirk Douglas, Glenn Ford, Clark Gable, John Garfield, Van Heflin, Alan Ladd, Victor Mature, John Payne, Walter Pidgeon, Dick Powell, Randolph Scott, and John Wayne.

of the form "Rank these 15 actors in terms of how well you like their acting." It was first determined that the group of judges knew these 15 actors sufficiently well to feel that they could rank them.

The Normalized-rank Method. When one observer places a set of 10 objects in rank order and as a result the rank values 1 to 10 are assigned to them, we have essentially a rectangular distribution with 10 intervals and a frequency of 1 in each interval. The rank values, as numbers, are equidistant. The objects ranked are probably not equidistant on the continuum in question. If the objects are living things or the products of living things, there is a good possibility that they come from a normally distributed population. Even in a small sample, the distances between neighboring objects

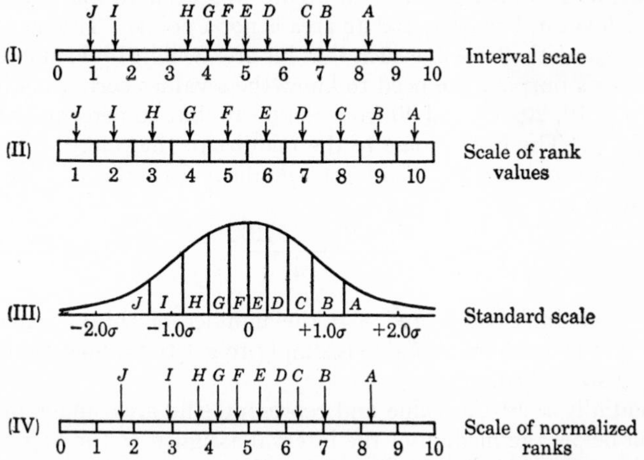

FIG. 8.1. Illustration of what happens in scaling by the normalized-rank method.

are probably smaller as we go toward their central tendency and larger at the extremes.

Figure 8.1 was designed to illustrate the basis for the normalized-rank procedure. On a 10-unit scale at the top are shown 10 of the actors selected from the 15 for illustrative purposes. They are localized at points on the scale according to the best information we have concerning them. Their scale values called R_c were taken from column 4 of Table 8.7. It will be seen that with some irregularities, such as would be expected in a small sample, the actual distribution follows the normal-curve principle of bunching in the center and thinning out toward the extremes.

Let us assume that some particular judge places the 10 actors in this "correct" rank order. We will not be concerned here with the fact that other judges will deviate from this particular order. This is to be expected from the fact of discriminal dispersion. A case of correct ranking will give us a clearer picture for illustrative purposes. The ranking is shown in part II of Fig. 8.1. Each actor occupies as much space as any other on this rank-value scale. The more precise location of each actor is shown in terms of an arrow placed at the midpoint of his rank interval.

In order to give the actors numerical values that are more closely in line with their actual interval-scale positions, let us assume that they are normally distributed. Part III represents this assumption. Each actor is assumed to occupy the same amount of area and the rank order of the actors is preserved. In these two respects the representations in parts II and III are alike. But the areas in part III are shaped by the normal curve. Equal areas do not mean equal intervals on the base line as they do on scale II. They mean increasing intervals as we go out from the mean.

Centile Positions. Since there are 10 objects occupying the total surface under the normal distribution curve here, each one takes up 10 per cent of the area. From the normal-curve tables we can determine the boundaries of the 10 intervals (except for the 2 extreme ones). That is the way in which the vertical lines in part III were located. We want to find a single point value for each actor, however, and an area is not a point. The point for each actor is located on the base line such that his area will be divided in two equal parts. For this purpose, we need to know the z values corresponding not to percentages of 10, 20, 30, and 40 from the mean, but to percentages of 5, 15, 25, 35, and 45. The latter come to the middles of the ranked *areas*. Each is what we call the *centile position* for a stimulus. In terms of a formula, the centile position is

$$P = \frac{(R_i - .5)100}{n} \tag{8.1}$$

where R_i = the rank value and n = the number of things ranked. The deduction of .5 from the rank value is simply to get to the middle of the area for the thing so ranked.

P is essentially a centile value and represents the area under the normal distribution below the median of the interval assigned to the object. From the normal-curve tables we find corresponding z values to represent linear distances from the mean on the base line. Since z values are awkward numbers to use, we make a linear transformation to values of a convenient type. Hull (9) was probably the first to propose for this purpose a scale of 10 units covering a range of 5 standard deviations.

The author has recommended that his common C scale be used in this connection (5, p. 553). The C scale is one of 11 units, with a mean of 5.0 and standard deviation of 2.0. Table M in the Appendix has been developed for convenience in connection with normalized ranks. For different numbers of things ranked, n, corresponding C-scale values are given immediately, which makes unnecessary the computing of centile positions. The C-scale values are given only in terms of whole numbers. In view of the many irregularities in small-sample distributions and the inevitable errors in the normalized-rank values, this is probably as fine a scale as one should use.

Scaling with C Values. Fortunately, if all *O*s rank all n objects, only one set of normalized-rank values need be determined in the solution of any one problem. In Table 8.2, the last two columns, we have the 15 centile positions, P, and the linear scale values, C, corresponding to the 15 rank values, R_i, which are in column (2). We now regard the frequencies in the columns as distributions on the new scale of C values. Assuming that these are interval-scale values, we may now compute means, which are known as response values R_j and are shown in the next-to-the-last row in Table 8.2.

In the process of computing means, we may use two checks. The sum of the sums of the columns (each symbolized by $\Sigma f_{ji}C$) should equal $5Nn$, since there is a total frequency of Nn in the entire matrix and the mean of the 15 C values is 5.0. The mean is 5.0 because the row sums are equal and the distribution of C values about their mean is exactly symmetrical. The sum of the means should equal $5n$ for obvious reasons. The linear transformation performed on R_j to produce the last row of Table 8.2 was to achieve a common scale of values with a mean of 4.78 and standard deviation of 2.0. The reasons for this will be explained later.

To return to the illustration in Fig. 8.1, we find in part IV the result of scaling one observer's ranks. The z values at the centers of the intervals in part III were transformed to a scale whose mean is 5.0 and whose standard deviation is 2.0 and plotted to the nearest tenth of a unit. Except for actors J and I, the normalized-rank values are quite close to the correct scale values in part I. We shall see later how very closely the means of C-scale values in Table 8.2 agree with scale values for the actors obtained by what is probably the best method.

Pair-comparison Treatment of Complete Ranks. Rank-order information can be used to indicate comparative judgments for all pairs of stimuli. If four stimuli, B, D, A, and C, are ranked in the order given, which is of decreasing quantity, we may readily infer six comparative judgments: $B > D$, $B > A$, $B > C$, $D > A$, $D > C$, and $A > C$. From repeated judgments of the same series of stimuli we can determine the proportion of the time each stimulus is judged greater than every other stimulus.

One procedure for deriving such proportions from rank-order data starts with the original ranks assigned. In a matrix in which columns stand for stimuli and rows stand for individual judges, with rank numbers in the cells, one could go down every pair of columns and count the number of times one stimulus of the pair is ranked higher than the other. This would be an exact method of determining proportions. With the data in terms of a frequency matrix, however, such counting is precluded, but we can approximate the proportions by a procedure that will now be explained. With a large N this procedure is more efficient than counting pairs.

Estimation of Proportions of Comparative Judgments. The procedure for estimating the proportions is rationalized in the following manner. We have a series of stimuli:

$$S_a, S_b, S_c, \ldots, S_j, \ldots, S_n$$

as in the matrix of Table 8.1. These stimuli have been assigned the rank values

$$R_1, R_2, R_3, \ldots, R_i, \ldots, R_n$$

by each of N observers. These are in increasing order of magnitude. From such information we want to find the proportion of the time $p_{j>k}$ that stimulus S_j is judged greater than stimulus S_k.

Let f_{ji} = number of times S_j is given rank value R_i

f_{ki} = number of times S_k is given rank value R_i

$f_{k<i}$ = number of times S_k is given rank values less than R_i

Then $f_{ji}f_{k<i}$ = the number of times that S_j when given rank value R_i is judged distinctly greater than S_k.

When S_j and S_k are both given rank value R_i, there are $f_{ji}f_{ki}$ comparisons. To make the simplest assumption, let us say that half of the judgments involved when there are tied rank values are of the type $S_j > S_k$ and half of the type $S_k < S_j$. This adds $\frac{1}{2}(f_{ji}f_{ki})$ to the number of judgments $S_j > S_k$. So far as any one rank value R_i is concerned, then, the total number of judgments $S_j > S_k$ is given by the equation

$$C_{(j>k)i} = f_{ji}f_{k<i} + \tfrac{1}{2}f_{ji}f_{ki} = f_{ji}(f_{k<i} + \tfrac{1}{2}f_{ki}) \tag{8.2}$$

Summing for all rank values, 1 through n,

$$C_{j>k} = \Sigma[f_{ji}(f_{k<i} + \tfrac{1}{2}f_{ki})] \tag{8.3}$$

The total number of comparisons is equal to N^2, where N is the number of times each stimulus is ranked. The reason for this is that for every placement of a certain stimulus there are N placements of the other member of the pair to be considered. Thus, the proportion of the time that S_j is estimated to be judged greater than S_k is given by the equation

$$p_{j>k} = \frac{\Sigma[f_{ji}(f_{k<i} + \tfrac{1}{2}f_{ki})]}{N^2} \tag{8.4}$$

In the application of formula (8.4), it is convenient to prepare a tabulation of the frequencies such that for each rank value R_i and each stimulus S_k we

TABLE 8.3. CUMULATIVE FREQUENCIES BELOW THE MIDPOINTS OF THE RANK VALUES FOR THE RANKED JUDGMENTS OF ACTORS A TO E

R_i	A	B	C	D	E
15	95.5	91.5	92.5	96.0	95.0
14	87.5	77.5	77.5	88.0	86.0
13	75.0	67.5	64.5	80.0	79.5
12	60.5	57.5	51.0	74.0	73.0
11	50.5	48.0	39.5	69.0	64.5
10	43.0	38.5	29.0	64.0	57.0
9	35.5	28.5	21.0	59.0	51.5
8	28.0	22.0	16.0	53.5	44.0
7	19.5	17.5	13.5	49.5	36.0
6	11.5	13.0	12.0	46.5	30.0
5	8.5	9.5	8.0	42.0	23.5
4	7.5	7.0	4.5	34.5	16.5
3	4.0	5.5	3.0	27.5	9.0
2	.5	3.5	1.5	22.0	3.5
1	.0	1.0	.5	9.5	1.0

have the quantity $f_{k<i} + \frac{1}{2}f_{ki}$. Table 8.3 is a partial matrix of such cumulative frequencies for the actor problem. With these values tabulated, one can readily find the sum of products needed for the numerator of (8.4) by multiplying appropriate pairs of values in a column of Table 8.2 and a column of Table 8.3. To illustrate how this is done in detail, we have Table 8.4

where the two proportions for $S_a > S_b$ and $S_b > S_a$ are worked out. The two should be complements, as they prove to be. It is well to compute both as a matter of checking the work. With a good calculating machine it is unnecessary to form tables such as in Table 8.4. The estimation of the proportion $p_{a>b}$ from the first five ranks only, at the very bottom of Table 8.4,

TABLE 8.4. SAMPLE WORKTABLE FOR ESTIMATING A PROPORTION FOR A COMPARATIVE JUDGMENT OF A STIMULUS PAIR IN TERMS OF RANK ORDER, WHEN UTILIZING ALL RANKS AND WHEN UTILIZING ONLY THE FIRST FIVE RANKS

R_i	f_{ai}	$f_{b<i} + \frac{1}{2}f_{bi}$	$f_{ai}(f_{b<i}+\frac{1}{2}f_{bi})$	f_{bi}	$f_{a<i} + \frac{1}{2}f_{ai}$	$f_{bi}(f_{a<i}+\frac{1}{2}f_{ai})$
15	9	91.5	823.5	17	95.5	1,623.5
14	7	77.5	542.5	11	87.5	962.5
13	18	67.5	1,215.0	9	75.0	675.0
12	11	57.5	632.5	11	60.5	665.5
11	9	48.0	432.0	8	50.5	404.0
10	6	38.5	231.0	11	43.0	473.0
9	9	28.5	256.5	9	35.5	319.5
8	6	22.0	132.0	4	28.0	112.0
7	11	17.5	192.5	5	19.5	97.5
6	5	13.0	65.0	4	11.5	46.0
5	1	9.5	9.5	3	8.5	25.5
4	1	7.0	7.0	2	7.5	15.0
3	6	5.5	33.0	1	4.0	4.0
2	1	3.5	3.5	3	.5	1.5
1	0	1.0	0.0	2	.0	.0
Σ_{15}	100		4,575.5	100		5,424.5
Σ_5	54		3,645.5	56		4,330.5
Σf_{jw}	46			44		

$$p_{a>b} = \frac{4{,}575.5}{10{,}000} = .458 \qquad p_{b>a} = \frac{5{,}424.5}{10{,}000} = .542$$

Or, from the first five ranks,

$$p_{a>b} = \frac{3{,}645.5}{10{,}000 - (46)(44)} = \frac{3{,}645.5}{10{,}000 - 2{,}024} = \frac{3{,}645.5}{7{,}976} = .457$$

Or

$$p_{a>b} = \frac{3{,}645.5}{3{,}645.5 + 4{,}330.5} = \frac{3{,}645.5}{7{,}976.0} = .457$$

will be explained later. The proportion matrix obtained from complete ranks would be like Table 7.4 in the preceding chapter.

Computation of the Scale Values. From this point on, the work is essentially like that for the treatment of pair comparisons. Assuming either Case V or Case III, a Z matrix is derived, and the columns of Z are averaged to obtain scale values M_j. The final scale values for the 15 actors, after a linear transformation, are listed in column 4 of Table 8.7.[1] A meaningful zero for

[1] For information on linear transformations in general, see Chap. 3, and on linear transformations as applying to this kind of use, see Chap. 7.

the scale of actors had been established by using a successive-categories method with the same observers and the same stimuli. The categories were defined in such a way that on the resulting scale a zero point could be located that represented the lower limit of liking for actors. The original scale values from this procedure are given in column 1 of Table 8.7. The first step was to make a linear transformation on this distribution which would achieve a standard deviation of 2.0. This gave the values in column 2 of Table 8.7, whose mean is 4.78. This became the standard or common scale into the terms of which scale values for the actors by all other solutions were transformed. The transformation equation is of the form $R_c = a + bR_j$, for which the coefficients are given at the bottom of Table 8.7 for each case. The transformations not only give every set of scale values found for the actors a meaningful zero point but also a much better basis for comparing directly the scaling results from the different approaches.

It would not be necessary, of course, to go so far as to find R_c. Without the successive-categories results being available, we might leave the final values in some form such as R_j or $10R_j$. One could convert the results from different solutions to a common scale without having knowledge of a meaningful zero point. One would then choose an arbitrary mean as well as an arbitrary standard deviation.

Scale Values Assuming a Composite Standard. The treatment about to be proposed is based on the writer's process for dealing with pair comparisons. The basic assumption again is that each stimulus is judged in comparison with the group as a whole. The group as a whole then becomes a composite standard *CS*, with which every stimulus is compared. It is from the proportions of judgments given to every stimulus as compared with the *CS* that linear scale values are derived. This is even more reasonable in the ranking method than with pair comparisons, since in the ranking method the whole series of stimuli is laid out for observation and each stimulus is placed according to its position in the entire scheme. Since the writer's procedure was first adapted to pair comparisons, let us approach its application to ranked data in the same manner, assuming for the moment that we are dealing with comparative judgments.

Each time a stimulus S_j is assigned to a rank value R_i, it is automatically judged definitely greater than $R_i - 1$ other stimuli and may be said to have received this many choices. If we include stimulus S_j itself, as it is included in the composite standard, we must add half a choice. The number of choices then becomes $R_i - .5$ for each placement of S_j. Each stimulus is placed N times. At each rank value the number of choices for S_j equals $f_{ji}(R_i - .5)$. Summing for all rank values 1 through n, we have the total number of choices given by

$$C_{j>cs} = \Sigma[f_{ji}(R_i - .5)] = \Sigma f_{ji}R_i - .5\,\Sigma f_{ji}$$

or

$$C_{j>cs} = \Sigma f_{ji}R_i - .5N \tag{8.5}$$

The total number of comparisons implied for each stimulus is Nn, from which we have

$$p_{j>cs} = \frac{\Sigma f_{ji}R_i - .5N}{Nn} \tag{8.6}$$

TABLE 8.5. DERIVATION OF SCALE VALUES FOR THE 15 ACTORS BY MEANS OF THE COMPOSITE-STANDARD METHOD, WHEN THE ACTORS WERE COMPLETELY RANKED

	J	K	H	M	D	G	F	N	I	L	E	O	A	B	C	Σ
$\Sigma f_{ji}R_i$	452	516	679	707	735	737	739	774	784	819	880	976	1,023	1,062	1,117	12,000 = $N\Sigma R_i$✓
.5N	50	50	50	50	50	50	50	50	50	50	50	50	50	50	50	750 = .5Nn✓
$C_{j>cs}$	402	466	629	657	685	687	689	724	734	769	830	926	973	1,012	1,067	11,250 = $N\Sigma R_i$ − .5Nn✓
$p_{j>cs}$	.268	.311	.419	.438	.457	.458	.459	.483	.489	.513	.553	.617	.649	.675	.711	7.500 = .5n✓
$z_{(j>cs)}$	−.619	−.493	−.204	−.156	−.108	−.106	−.103	−.043	−.028	+.033	+.133	+.298	+.383	+.454	+.556	−.003✓
R_j	.000	.126	.415	.463	.511	.513	.516	.576	.591	.652	.752	.917	1.002	1.073	1.175	9.282 = .619n✓
R_c*	.9	1.7	3.5	3.8	4.1	4.1	4.1	4.5	4.6	5.0	5.6	6.7	7.2	7.7	8.3	71.8✓

* $R_c = 6.335R_j + 0.86$.

Applying this formula to the data on actors (Table 8.2), we have the solution given in Table 8.5. The operations in each line of this table have appropriate checks, as shown. Transformation of scale values to the final ones R_c was performed by the equation given at the bottom of the table. Reference to columns 4 and 5 of Table 8.7 will show that except for one discrepancy of 0.1, the scale values R_c by this procedure are identical with those from the complete pair-comparison solution. This very high agreement is largely due to the limited range of psychological values for these stimuli. Under these conditions an enormous amount of labor can be saved by utilizing the *CS* method.

Some Variations in Scaling from Ranks

We have just seen the two main approaches to the scaling of stimuli beginning with rank-order data. In both cases the data were derived by having n objects assigned to all n ranks. There are a number of experimental situations in which something less than complete ranking is conveniently obtainable. For such instances we need to make a few modifications of the scaling methods already described.

Scaling from the First k Ranks. There are some practical situations in which the number of stimuli may be too large in view of inadequate interest and perhaps also inadequate discriminating power of the observers. Interest in the most preferred objects may be high and their separations relatively larger. Better cooperation and more dependable judgments may then be obtained from the judges if one asks them merely to select the best five or ten objects and to rank only those selected. We then have data on the first k ranks out of a possible n ranks. The rank-frequency matrix of Table 8.1 is cut off at the row for r_k. It is still possible to scale the objects by modifications of the two procedures just described. Because of their practical importance those procedures will be described and illustrated by means of the data on actors so that we can compare the final results with those obtained by using all the ranks. In either approach, the pair-comparison solution or the *CS* solution, it is necessary to assume Thurstone's Case V. If Case V does not apply, the stimuli with greater dispersions are likely to pile up choices in undue proportion relative to their true scale positions.

The Pair-comparison Solution. By reasoning similar to that involved in the derivation of proportions of comparative judgments from rank information, we can arrive at formulas for estimating similar proportions from the first k ranks. It will be found that formula (8.4) will need to be modified just a little.

When there are k ranks, the lowest rank value assigned to any stimulus will be $n - k + 1$. Let this lowest rank value be called R_v, where $v = n - k + 1$. The stimuli that O does not include in his first k ranks have undifferentiated values less than R_v. The frequency with which stimulus S_j is not ranked we shall call f_{jw}, where $w < v$. This frequency belongs to a broad category R_w whose stimuli are judged less than those that are given ranks, but within which we have no information about relative quantities.

The number of choices that S_j receives in comparison with any other stimulus S_k is estimated by the equation

$$C_{j>k} = \sum_{i=v}^{n} [f_{ji}(f_{k<i} + \tfrac{1}{2}f_{ki})] \tag{8.7}$$

where it must be kept in mind that the summation is only for the top k categories of R_i. In applying formula (8.7), we go through the same operations as in applying formula (8.3), except that we stop with rank value R_v. In Table 8.4, using only the first five rows of products, for the case where $k = 5$, we arrive at the numbers of choices denoted as Σ_5 at the bottom of the table. A few more of such sums are given for other pairs of stimuli in Table 8.6. Although it is found eventually that the two proportions $p_{j>k}$

TABLE 8.6. NUMBER OF CHOICES EACH STIMULUS RECEIVED IN COMPARISON WITH EVERY OTHER STIMULUS AS INFERRED FROM INCOMPLETE RANK-ORDER DATA. DATA WERE FOR 15 ACTORS WHO WERE COMPLETELY RANKED BY EACH OF 100 OBSERVERS*

	A	*B*	*C*	*D*	*E*	*F*
A		4,330.5	4,992.5	2,609.0	2,968.5	1,672.5
B	3,645.5 7,976.0		4,629.5	2,410.0	2,764.5	1,568.0
C	3,452.5 8,445.0	3,882.5 8,512.0		2,317.0	2,631.0	1,444.0
D	4,355.0 6,964.0	4,686.0 7,096.0	5,445.0 7,762.0		3,277.0	1,947.0
E	4,271.5 7,240.0	4,595.5 7,360.0	5,338.0 7,969.0	2.763.0 6,040.0		1,888.5
F	4,877.5 6,550.0	5,132.0 6,700.0	6,015.0 7,459.0	3,103.0 5,050.0	3,611.5 5,492.0	

* This table is given only in part to illustrate the procedure. With each number of choices in the lower-left half is given the sum of the two values for each pair of stimuli. This sum represents the total number of judgments the pair is assumed to have had.

and $p_{k>j}$ are complements, it is well for checking purposes to solve for both using formulas (8.7) and either (8.8) or (8.9).

In finding $p_{j>k}$, the total number of comparisons implied is equal to $N^2 - f_{jw}f_{kw}$. Every time S_j is not ranked (placed in category R_w), there are f_{kw} comparisons *not* made with S_k. There are f_{jw} such occasions, and hence the deduction of the product $f_{jw}f_{kw}$ from the N^2 comparisons implied when ranking is complete. The proportion of the time that the judgment is $S_j > S_k$ is therefore

$$p_{j>k} = \frac{\sum_{i=v}^{n} [f_{ji}(f_{k<i} + \tfrac{1}{2}f_{ki})]}{N^2 - f_{jw}f_{kw}} \tag{8.8}$$

This formula is applied at the bottom of Table 8.4.

There is a second way of estimating the total number of pair comparisons implied in this solution. Since $p_{j>k}$ and $p_{k>j}$ should be exactly complementary, the sum of the numbers of choices given to the two should equal the total number of comparisons. Such sums are given in Table 8.6. They serve as a check on the computation of the denominator of formula (8.8), but the two do not always exactly agree. When they do not agree, the better formula for estimating a proportion for a pair of stimuli is

$$p_{j>k} = \frac{C_{j>k}}{C_{j>k} + C_{k>j}} \tag{8.9}$$

It is not necessary to illustrate with complete tables the calculation of scale values by this approach. The final values are shown in Table 8.7, transformed into the common scale R_c. We find that the results are in very good agreement with those found from the complete rankings. The correlation between the two sets of values is .996. Such a high relationship might be taken to indicate that Case V is quite justified, but examination of some of the data in detail tends to indicate some variation in the tails of the distributions for different actors and some differences in over-all rank orders. For example, in the five-ranks solution actor D tends to rise in relative scale value and actor I tends to fall.

A Composite-standard Solution. The clue to the composite-standard approach when we have only the first k ranks of n objects is given by equation (8.9). The rationale given by the author (3) for the particular case of first choices (where ranking is limited to $k = 1$) also applies here. Let us say that the stimulus to be scaled is S_j, which receives a number of choices C_j. Each stimulus in turn is S_k, with numbers of choices C_k. By analogy to equation (8.9),

$$p_{j>k} = \frac{C_j}{C_j + C_k} \tag{8.10}$$

This equation is not identical with (8.9). In (8.9) only the comparison of S_j and S_k is concerned. In (8.10) C_j pertains to the comparison between S_j and all others and C_k pertains to the comparison between S_k and all others. There is a total number of choices T to be shared by the n stimuli so that $\Sigma C_k = T$.

We have n equations like (8.10) for k varying from a to n. In order to find the proportion of the time that S_j is chosen in preference to all stimuli combined, we sum the numerators of those n equations to find the total number of choices for S_j and sum the denominators to find a comparable estimate of the number of comparisons. Thus, we have

$$p_{j>cs} = \frac{nC_j}{\Sigma(C_j + C_k)} \tag{8.11}$$

Equation (8.11) can be simplified as follows. The denominator can be written as $nC_j + \Sigma C_k$. But $\Sigma C_k = T$, the total number of choices. With these substitutions we have

$$p_{j>cs} = \frac{nC_j}{nC_j + T}$$

Dividing numerator and denominator by n, we have

$$p_{j>cs} = \frac{C_j}{C_j + \frac{T}{n}} \tag{8.12}$$

We still have the task of evaluating C_j for each stimulus. As in the derivation of formula (8.5), we will assume that when S_j is placed at rank value R_i it has received $R_i - .5$ choices over all others and itself, hence $R_i - .5$ choices over the composite standard. At each rank value the number of choices is $f_{ji}(R_i - .5)$. Summing over all k categories, we have

$$C_j = \sum_{i=k}^{n} [f_{ji}(R_i - .5)] = \sum_{i=k}^{n} f_{ji}R_i - .5 \sum_{i=k}^{n} f_{ji}$$

from which
$$C_j = \sum_{i=k}^{n} f_{ji}R_i - .5N_k \tag{8.13}$$

where N_k is the sum of all frequencies in the k categories for stimulus S_j.

Formulas (8.12) and (8.13) were applied to all actors and the final scale values R_c (see Table 8.7) are in close agreement with those found by other methods. They correlate .996 with those found by the pair-comparison treatment of the data from complete ranks. Table 8.7 shows, in general, that scale values are more similar when derived from the same basic data. Hence, in this problem, at least, the kind of treatment of data makes less difference than what data are used and how they were experimentally derived. The scale values derived from the successive-categories judgments agree slightly less well with all those derived from rank-order judgments. There is a spurious overlap of data for the scalings based on 15 versus 5 ranks, of course, which would tend to improve the similarity of solutions in those two cases. If only 5 ranks were called for in a separate collection of data, the two results might not agree so well.

The Method of First Choices. The method of pair comparisons grew out of Fechner's original *Wahlmethode* or "method of choices." It is better named the "method of first choices," since by the method as Fechner used it, the relative values of objects were determined by the numbers of judges who gave each object first choice when presented among several. From the discussions thus far it should be apparent that such numbers are useful only for ranking purposes and are not linear scale values. In the context of the problem of the first k ranks we see that the method of first choices is the limiting case in this general category, the case where $k = 1$.

This being true, scaling that starts from numbers of first choices can proceed on the basis of formulas (8.10) and (8.12). It would be absurd to attempt to scale the 15 actors using only the frequencies in rank 1. These frequencies range from 0 to 17, and proportions based on such scanty information would be highly unstable. The method of first choices demands a relatively small number of stimuli and a relatively large number of judgments per stimulus. The ratio N/n indicates the average number of choices per stimulus when the restriction is to first choices. It might be a good rule to limit the application of scaling procedures to situations in which N/n is not less than 50. Even then, if any frequencies are very small scaling would be questionable. Actually, the method of first choices is a very inefficient one, since it yields so little information for the number of judges involved. It is

TABLE 8.7. SUMMARY OF THE SCALE VALUES OBTAINED BY THE DIFFERENT METHODS FOR THE 15 ACTORS

Actor \ Methods	(1) Successive categories (original)	(2) Successive categories (standardized)	(3) Normalized ranks	(4) Pair comparisons (all 15 ranks)	(5) Composite standard (all 15 ranks)	(6) Pair comparisons (5 ranks only)	(7) Composite standard (5 ranks only)	Actor
J	.21	1.0	.8	.9	.9	1.3	1.0	*J*
K	.48	2.3	1.7	1.6	1.7	1.4	1.3	*K*
H	.90	4.3	3.4	3.5	3.5	3.5	3.5	*H*
M	.95	4.5	3.8	3.8	3.8	3.5	3.6	*M*
D	.70	3.3	3.8	4.1	4.1	5.4	5.4	*D*
G	.80	3.8	4.3	4.1	4.1	3.5	3.5	*G*
F	.71	3.4	4.1	4.1	4.1	3.9	4.0	*F*
N	1.07	5.1	4.5	4.5	4.5	4.7	4.9	*N*
I	.79	3.8	4.8	4.6	4.6	3.9	3.9	*I*
L	.91	4.3	5.0	5.0	5.0	5.1	5.1	*L*
E	1.20	5.7	5.7	5.6	5.6	5.9	6.0	*E*
O	1.66	7.9	6.9	6.7	6.7	7.2	7.0	*O*
A	1.53	7.3	7.1	7.2	7.2	7.0	7.2	*A*
B	1.41	6.7	7.6	7.7	7.7	7.4	7.3	*B*
C	1.75	8.3	8.1	8.3	8.3	8.0	7.9	*C*
Σ	15.07	71.7	71.6	71.7	71.8	71.7	71.6	
M	1.00	4.78	4.77	4.78	4.79	4.78	4.77	
σ	.42	2.00	2.00	2.00	2.00	2.00	2.00	
a	.....	.00	−7.01	+0.88	+0.86	+1.31	+1.04	
b	.....	4.746	2.357	6.019	6.335	4.957	6.024	
r_{m4}	.....	.992	1.000	....	1.000	.996	.996	

best adapted to instances of popular voting, as for candidates, color preferences, and popularity of paintings. The efficiency of this method could be easily improved by asking for at least a second and a third choice. The smaller the number of judges, the more information we need from each one. It could also be improved by asking for last choices (or last few ranked choices) as well as for top choices.

The Method of Triads. The method of triads is essentially a limited rank-order method when used to evaluate stimuli. Each of *n* stimuli is presented in a group of three to O, who is to put the three in rank order. If all possible triads are formed, the method approaches pair comparison in its experimental operations. Each ranking of three stimuli can be decomposed into three pair-comparison judgments. The number of triads possible among n stimuli is $(n - 2)(n - 1)n/6$. While each triad yields three times as many comparative judgments as a pair, the triad method requires $(n - 2)/3$ times as many triads as the pair-comparison method requires pairs. Beyond an n of 11 the triad method is less efficient than pair comparisons, unless something is done to reduce the sampling by triads. This can be done, since the same pair actually appears in $n - 2$ triads. A systematic selection of triads would cover all pairs an equal number of times and at the same time not overtax the observers.

Other Computational Methods. Since rank-order data can be so readily transformed so that scaling may proceed as in the method of pair comparisons, any procedure that applies to the latter will also be adaptable to scaling stimuli judged in rank order. For example, the procedures of Guttman (6) and of Lienau (10) apply. The same comments made concerning those methods in the preceding chapter also apply here.

Saffir (11) recommends that rank-order judgments be treated statistically like judgments in successive intervals (see Chap. 10). This requires the assumption that rank positions represent stable scale levels. Ranks are defined experimentally by comparative judgments, whereas in the method of successive categories there are other guides to O to aid him in maintaining quantitatively stable boundaries between intervals.

Some Evaluations

The Scaling Procedures. Of the various scaling procedures discussed in this chapter, the pair-comparison approach based on complete ranking is the most defensible. It also requires the greatest amount of labor. It is based on the same logical foundations as the scaling from actual pair-comparison judgments. It requires no assumption concerning the form of distribution of the set of stimuli involved. It does require the assumptions underlying the law of comparative judgment, with the relaxations of Thurstone's Case III, at least, and usually those of Case V. There can be no chi-square test of internal consistency, in view of the restrictions on the comparative judgments, which are sometimes called *pseudo comparative judgments*. This most complete scaling procedure is best used when the number of stimuli is small (not more than 15 and preferably not more than 10). It should usually presuppose a large N, preferably not less than a hundred.

Experience has shown that the less laborious scaling procedures give results so very close to those from the complete pair-comparison treatment that some of them are easily justified substitutes. They are particularly welcome when the number of stimuli is large. The composite-standard principle is even more defensible in the treatment of rank-order judgments than in that of pair comparisons. O's simultaneous exposure to all stimuli of the series should emphasize and support the functioning of an adaptation level. More than in the case of pair comparisons should the placement of each stimulus be determined by the standard, which is the average of all the stimuli.

The normalized-rank process is the simplest and most direct of all to apply. It can be used with almost any number of observers; it does not require a large N. The defense for its use depends upon the reasonableness of the assumption of normality, or near normality, of the distribution of the particular sample of stimuli being judged. The assumption of normality in this connection is favored by the fact that the number of stimuli is not too small and that the stimuli are of such a nature that one would expect a tendency to normality of distribution. To qualify, the stimuli should be living organisms randomly selected from an unbiased population or they should be the products of organisms, such as drawings, handwriting samples, compositions, and the like. No lower limit for size of sample can be specified. Irregularities in distributions from normally distributed populations may be evident even when a very large sample is drawn. The important thing is how much risk of error the investigator runs in applying the model of the normal distribution to his data, and how much risk he is willing to take in order to utilize a relatively simple solution. The worst that can happen is failure to achieve a scale of exactly equal units. Any such scaling probably only approaches equality of units, sometimes more, sometimes less. The important thing is for the investigator to be wary of conditions he can know about which might favor departure from normality. Sometimes preliminary inspections of stimuli or trial runs will tend to indicate something about the probable shape of the distribution on the continuum in question.

When the number of stimuli is small and also the number of observers, the best one should expect from the data is a consensus ranking of the stimuli. That is, one must be satisfied with ordinal evaluations of the stimuli. The pooled rank order can be determined by means or medians of rank values, but the sums of the ranks are less likely to give tied composite ranks.

Comparisons with Other Methods. The chief competitors to the method of rank order are those of pair comparisons and of ratings. In more general terms the latter can be extended to include all those methods known under the rubric of "single stimuli" but more appropriately called methods of successive categories.

Compared with Pair Comparisons. From the standpoint of ease and economy of time on the part of the judges, the ranking method is far superior to pair comparisons. It is obviously much easier to rank 20 stimuli than to judge 190 pairs. The dynamic interrelations apparently existing throughout any series of stimuli, although probably present to some extent in pair comparisons, are of great significance in rank judgments. The favorable and unfavorable aspects of these influences have already been pointed out. As for the scale positions obtained from the two methods, the one type is as valid as the other. The fact is borne out by Barrett (1) who concluded that the results from both are extremely valid when the scale values are correlated with objective criteria. Since she used the rank-difference method of correlation, a method that depends upon rank positions, the issue is left somewhat uncertain as to which of the two methods gave the more valid results. Hevner (7) found that the two methods give almost identical results with samples of handwriting, the ranking method making a better showing when tests of internal consistency were applied.

Compared with Rating-scale Methods. When evaluating 40 jokes for the degree of humor, Conklin and Sutherland (2) found rating-scale methods superior to the method of ranking. The former gave a higher self-correlation and a smaller variability in the scale values. No data are available for comparing the two methods applied to other types of stimuli. The rating-scale methods, however, have certain practical advantages over both pair comparisons and ranked judgments, to be mentioned in Chap. 11.

Problems

1. Using Data 8*A*, compile a frequency matrix similar to that in Table 8.2. Make all checks.

DATA 8*A*. RANKS ASSIGNED TO 12 MUSICAL SELECTIONS BY 20 DIFFERENT JUDGES*

O	*A*	*B*	*C*	*D*	*E*	*F*	*G*	*H*	*I*	*J*	*K*	*L*
1	12	11	9	8	6	7	10	5	3	2	4	1
2	12	10	7	6	11	4	8	9	5	2	1	3
3	11	12	8	5	6	10	9	4	2	3	1	7
4	12	9	11	10	8	4	7	6	5	1	2	3
5	12	10	11	7	5	9	4	8	6	2	3	1
6	11	8	12	6	10	4	7	5	9	2	3	1
7	12	10	11	7	9	8	5	6	2	4	3	1
8	12	9	11	8	6	5	4	3	10	2	7	1
9	12	10	11	8	6	4	7	9	5	2	3	1
10	11	12	8	9	7	5	10	6	3	1	2	4
11	12	10	11	7	9	4	5	3	6	2	8	1
12	11	7	9	10	12	8	4	5	3	2	1	6
13	12	10	11	7	4	9	8	5	3	2	6	1
14	12	11	9	10	6	8	5	7	1	3	4	2
15	12	6	11	8	7	10	9	5	3	4	2	1
16	11	12	8	10	7	6	5	4	3	9	2	1
17	12	8	11	5	10	9	7	6	3	2	4	1
18	11	12	10	8	6	9	4	3	2	7	1	5
19	12	10	8	6	9	11	5	1	7	4	3	2
20	12	11	9	10	6	4	8	5	7	2	3	1

* A rank of 1 is highest.

2. Using normalized rank values, compute mean scale values for the 12 stimuli, M_c.

3. Extracting the necessary information from the frequency matrix of Prob. 1, estimate the proportion of the time stimulus *H* was preferred to stimulus *E*. Do the same for the proportion of preferences of *E* over *H*. Make an actual count of preferences of the 20 *O*s from the original table of ranks, and determine the proportions from this information.

4. Apply the composite-standard method to the determination of scale values, after the manner of the solution in Table 8.5.

5. Using linear-transformation equations, convert the scale values obtained in Probs. 2 and 4 to new values having means of 5.0 and standard deviations of 2.0.

6. Compute the coefficient of correlation between the two sets of scale values.

Answers

2. Stimuli	*A*	*B*	*C*	*D*	*E*	*F*	*G*	*H*	*I*	*J*	*K*	*L*
M_c	2.3	3.2	3.45	4.3	4.45	4.75	5.0	5.7	6.15	6.7	6.7	7.3

3. $p_{h>e} = .79$; $p_{e>h} = .21$; by actual counts, $p_{h>e} = .80$ and $p_{e>h} = .20$.

4. Stimuli	*A*	*B*	*C*	*D*	*E*	*F*	*G*	*H*	*I*	*J*	*K*	*L*
R_j	.00	.72	.74	1.23	1.29	1.42	1.49	1.76	1.95	2.34	2.27	2.57

5. Equations: $R_{c1} = 1.34M_c - 1.70$; $R_{c2} = 2.77R_j + .90$.
6. $r = .995$.

References

1. Barrett, M. A comparison of the order of merit method and the method of paired comparisons. *Psychol. Rev.*, 1914, **21**, 278–294.
2. Conklin, E. S., and Sutherland, J. W. A comparison of the scale of values method with the order of merit method. *J. exp. Psychol.*, 1923, **6**, 44–57.
3. Guilford, J. P. Scale values derived from the method of choices. *Psychometrika*, 1937, **2**, 139–150.
4. ———. The computation of psychological values from judgments in absolute categories. *J. exp. Psychol.*, 1938, **22**, 32–42.
5. ———. *Fundamental Statistics in Psychology and Education*, 2d ed. New York: McGraw-Hill, 1950.
6. Guttman, L. An approach for quantifying paired comparisons and rank order. *Ann. math. Statist.*, 1946, **17**, 144–163.
7. Hevner, K. An empirical study of three psychophysical methods. *J. gen. Psychol.*, 1930, **4**, 191–212.
8. Hull, C. L. The computation of Pearson's *r* from ranked data. *J. appl. Psychol.*, 1922, **6**, 385–390.
9. ———. *Aptitude Testing*. Yonkers, N.Y.: World, 1928.
10. Lienau, C. C. Discrete bivariate distribution in certain problems of statistical order. *Amer. J. Hyg.*, 1942, **33**, 65–85.
11. Saffir, M. A. A comparative study of scales constructed by three psychophysical methods. *Psychometrika*, 1937, **2**, 179–198.
12. Strong, E. K. Psychological methods as applied to advertising. *J. educ. Psychol.*, 1913, **4**, 393–404.
13. ———. Application of the 'order of merit method' to advertising. *J. Phil. Psychol., sci. Meth.*, 1911, **8**, 600–606.
14. Thurstone, L. L. Rank order as a psychophysical method. *J. exp. Psychol.*, 1931, **14**, 187–201.

CHAPTER 9

SCALING FROM INTERVAL AND RATIO JUDGMENTS

The methods of this chapter make perhaps the most demanding assumptions concerning human observational powers. Some of the methods take for granted that the observer can successfully equate intervals or distances between responses to stimuli. The basis for interval scaling is the report of the observer that observed supraliminal differences are equal. Other methods of this chapter rest upon the observer's supposed powers to say when one stimulus appears to be some multiple of another or some fraction of another. The operations of observation of this kind constitute the basis for deriving psychological ratio scales.

The methods that will be discussed in this chapter fall into two general groups, as forecast by the title and by the opening paragraph. Under the general heading of "Interval Judgments" there are methods for equating two intervals at a time and for equating several at a time. The traditional method of *equal sense distances* comes under the first of these two categories. This method usually involves the principle of *bisection*, but in a broad sense it includes any method of interval matching where two intervals are involved. The method of *equal-appearing intervals* is the unique procedure of equating intervals where more than two are involved. The possibility of scaling intervals as such based upon comparative judgments of differences has not been very much explored, but should be given attention.

Under the general heading of "Ratio Judgments" we have two somewhat different approaches. On the one hand we tell the observer what ratio he is to achieve by selecting or varying stimuli. He is to find a stimulus one-half as great as another, or one-third, or one-fifth, etc., in the method of *fractionation*. Or he is to find a stimulus that is twice as great as another, or three times, or five times, etc., in the method of *multiple stimuli*. On the other hand, O may be presented with two stimuli and he is told to report, in effect, how many times as great the one is than the other, as in the method of *constant sums*. In more general terms, two or more stimuli are presented to O who is instructed to divide a total number of points, say a hundred, among the stimuli. The main principle of the method is that O reports by estimating observed ratios which probably are not very simple ones.

Methods Based on Interval Judgments

Equal Sense Distances. The method of equal sense distances requires O to bisect a given distance on a particular psychological continuum. Given two sound intensities, S_1 and S_3, the latter being of greater magnitude, O has the problem of finding a stimulus S_2 such that the interval $S_3 - S_2$ equals subjectively the interval $S_2 - S_1$. Because the equating of intervals is so often approached by the operation of bisection, the method has sometimes been called the method of bisection. There are other ways of equating two intervals, the method of bisection being only one.

The method has been of great interest for various reasons at different times. First, the discovery that it was possible to measure supraliminal distances greatly extended the bounds of psychological measurement. Psychophysics needed no longer to be content with measuring thresholds alone. Second, the method was very soon put to use in testing the validity of

TABLE 9.1. RECORD SHEET FOR OBSERVATIONS IN THE BISECTION OF A BLACK-WHITE INTERVAL BY THE METHOD OF MINIMAL CHANGES

S_v	*WR*		*WL*				*WR*				*WL*				*WR*				*WL*				*WR*	
	d	*a*	*a*	*d*	*a*	*d*	*d*	*a*	*d*	*a*	*d*	*a*	*a*	*d*	*a*	*d*	*a*	*d*	*d*	*a*	*d*	*a*	*a*	*d*
34											+													
32						+					+													
30						+					+													
28				+		+	+				+			+				+						
26				+		+	+				+			+		+		+						
24	+			+		+	+			+	+			+		+		+						+
22	=			+	+	+	+		+	=	+			+		+		+			+			+
20	=			+	=	+	+		+	=	+			+		+		+			+			+
18	=	+		+	=	+	+		+	−	+			+		+		+	+		+			+
16	=	=	+	=	=	=	+		=	−	+			+		+	+	+	+	+	+			+
14	=	−	=	=	−	=	=	+	−	−	=		+	+	+	+	=	=	+	=	+		+	+
12	−	−	−	=	−	=	=	=		−	=	+	=	=	−	=	=	=	+	=	=	+	=	+
10		−		=	−	−	−	−		−	=	−	=	=	−	=	−	=	=	−	=	=	=	=
8		−		=	−			−		−	−	−	−	−	−	−	−	−	=	−	−	−	−	=
6		−		−						−		−			−		−		−	−		−	−	−
4										−		−			−		−					−	−	
2												−											−	
PSE	18	16	14	12	18	14	13	12	16	21	12	11	11	11	13	11	13	12	9	13	11	10	11	9

S_v measured in degrees of white; *WR* = white on the right; *WL* = white on the left.

Fechner's law. This test is easily described. If it is true that the equation $R = C \log S$ holds for the quantitative relationship between a certain scaled psychological quantity R and a corresponding stimulus aspect S, then the bisecting stimulus quantity S_2 should equal the geometric mean of quantities S_1 and S_3. This follows from the nature of logarithms (see Chap. 3). Third, the method also furnished a device for checking up on the assumption that *DL*'s on the same scale are equal. If a *DL* as measured in one part of a continuum is really equivalent to a *DL* found in another part of the same continuum, then two equal sense distances should contain the same number of such units.

An Illustrative Experiment. The experiment to provide illustrative data from the method of equal sense distances was on the bisection of an interval of brightness. Stimulus S_3 was a white disk, S_1 was a black disk, and S_v was composed of adjustable sectors of white and black, varied in terms of per cent of white. The disks were in order of brightness, in close proximity in a horizontal row. In half the series of observations the white disk was on the right (condition *WR*) and in the other half the white disk was on the left (condition *WL*). The middle stimulus was altered serially by minimal changes (2 per cent white added or detracted). The results are recorded in Table 9.1, where one can see the order of ascending and descending series as well as the sequence of *WR* and *WL* conditions. A plus sign means the middle stimulus was too light to be halfway and a minus sign means it was too dark.

Determination of the Bisecting Stimulus. The bisecting stimulus is obviously best determined as a mean of the *PSE* estimates.[1] But first, as in treat-

TABLE 9.2. SUMMARY OF THE ANALYSIS OF VARIANCE OF THE DATA ON BISECTION OF THE BLACK-WHITE INTERVAL

Source	Sum of squares	Degrees of freedom	Estimate of variance	F	Significance
Time (T)	53.6	2	26.8	3.63	$P > .05$
Position (P)	15.1	1	15.1	2.05	$P > .05$
Direction (D)	9.4	1	9.4	1.27	$P > .05$
Interaction ($T \times P$)	17.5	2	8.75	1.19	$P > .05$
Interaction ($P \times D$)	0.0	1			
Interaction ($T \times D$)	0.7	2	0.35		
Interaction ($T \times P \times D$)	18.2	2	9.1	1.23	$P > .05$
Within cells	88.5	12	7.38		
Total	203.0	23			

ing such data in Chap. 5, we are concerned about the homogeneity of the observations. Can we regard them as having come from the same universe, in spite of the space variation and the direction-of-series variation? There is also a question of whether there has been any systematic shift of *PSE* from early to late trials. Inspection of Table 9.1 shows a slight tendency for the *PSE* to be lower in the later series.

To test for homogeneity, the data were treated as representing a three-way factorial design. There is insufficient space here to go through the solution in detail. Statistics books emphasizing analysis of variance will explain the solution of such a problem. We have in Table 9.2 the summary table of the F ratios. Besides having F ratios for each of the three variations of conditions, we have also F ratios for three simple interactions and for the complex interaction of time with position with direction. Time refers to early series versus middle versus late; position refers to the place of the greater whiteness right versus left; and direction refers to ascending versus

[1] The *PSE* here is that stimulus value which divides a psychological interval into two equal portions.

descending series. The results give every appearance of homogeneity, since no F was significant beyond the .05 point. We may therefore treat all 24 estimates of the *PSE* in one sample.

The mean *PSE* is found to be 12.96 (in units of per cent of white). The standard deviation is 2.91 and the standard error of the mean is 0.61, both in the same units. As with the problem on *DL*'s for grays discussed in Chap. 5, we need a better unit of stimulus illumination. Assuming that each 1 per cent of black gives off 1 unit of light intensity and each 1 per cent of white gives off 25 such photometric units, we proceed to transform the mean *PSE* into a value on such a scale of units. It is found that 12.96 per cent white and 87.04 per cent of black give off 411.04 such units.

Testing Fechner's Law. Will the bisecting gray have a stimulus value that is the geometric mean of the two terminal stimuli? The terminal stimuli, with 100 and 0 per cent of white, have stimulus values of 2,500 and 100 photometric units, respectively. Their product is 250,000 units, the square root of which is 500 units. The obtained bisecting stimulus with 411 units

TABLE 9.3. SUMMARY OF THE SCALING OF THE WHITE-BLACK VARIATION OF STIMULATION BY MEANS OF THE BISECTING METHOD

Scale values	1	2	3	4	5
Percentage W	0.00	6.38	12.96	24.58	100.00
Percentage B	100.00	93.62	87.04	75.42	0.00
Photom. units*	100.00	232.12	411.04	689.92	2,500.00
log photom. units	2.0000	2.4031	2.6138	2.8388	3.3979

* Photometric unit = 1 per cent black; 1 per cent white = 25 units.

is somewhat lower than the geometric mean. The discrepancy looks large in these terms but not quite so large in terms of per cent of white; 500 photometric units corresponds to 16.67 per cent of white. The deviation of this from the *PSE* is 3.71 per cent, which is about six times the standard error of the mean *PSE*. From this one instance alone we would conclude that Fechner's law was not supported by this bisection. We shall see some supporting evidence for this conclusion later.

Scaling by Means of Successive Bisections. The principle of bisection of intervals can be applied to the scaling of stimuli over wide ranges of the S continuum. Having bisected a rather wide interval to start with, one can bisect in turn the two intervals formed, which results in four presumably equal intervals and five stimulus values marking off the equally spaced psychological intervals.

This procedure was applied following the determination of the stimulus bisecting white and black in the illustration above. The two additional bisecting stimuli were at 24.58 per cent white for the upper interval and 6.38 per cent white for the lower interval. In terms of photometric units these results are equivalent to 689.92 and 232.12, respectively. These results, along with the others, are summarized in Table 9.3. There the interval values from 1 to 5 are assigned to the five stimuli. From these five widely spaced values we can get a better idea of whether Fechner's law closely describes these data. If we plot the psychological-interval values against log S, which in this case is log photometric units, we can see whether the regression is linear. Reference to Fig. 9.1 will show that it definitely is not. The three points in the central region are very close to a linear relationship but the two end points are much out of line.

These limited results should not be taken as a sufficient test of the applicability of Fechner's law to the brightness continuum. One would certainly want to explore more thoroughly the regions near the ends of the curve.[1] A more systematic job of scaling would have been to start with more limited ranges of brightness, perhaps three of them, one overlapping the next to some extent. The three sets of five equidistant points obtained can be fitted together in the same scale, as demonstrated by Stevens and Volkmann (22).

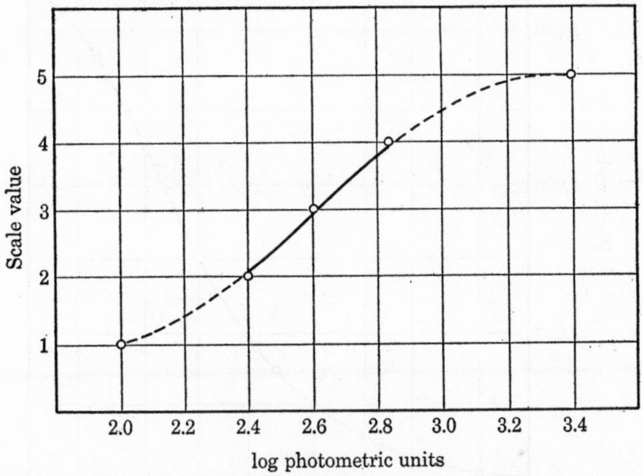

FIG. 9.1. Psychophysical relationship of brightness, as scaled by the method of bisection, and the logarithm of the stimulus.

It is probably best not to carry successive bisections to more than four intervals in a set, because any errors affecting the first bisection are contributory to results in the second bisection. To go beyond the second bisection means a danger of piling error upon error.

A Test of Internal Consistency. In successive bisections as described above, we have five stimulus values involved, the terminal ones being S_5 and S_1. The first bisecting stimulus is S_3 and the subsequent ones are S_4 and S_2. Having determined S_4 and S_2, we can next have O bisect the interval $S_4 - S_2$. If the results are internally consistent, this bisecting stimulus, which we may call S'_3, should equal S_3.[2]

Such a test of internal consistency was made with the brightness experiment used as an illustration above. Using only 12 series for the consistency test, the mean was found to be 14.83 per cent of white. This is to be com-

[1] Much more thorough experiments by Hanes have shown, however, that the regression of R on log S tends to be S-shaped (10, p. 449; 11, p. 722), as it is in Fig. 9.1.

[2] Such a test was evidently first applied by Gage (5). Newman, Volkmann, and Stevens (19) have also applied it to the scaling of loudness.

pared with the mean of 12.96 when the interval $S_5 - S_1$ was bisected. Testing the difference between these means for significance, we find that Student's t is equal to 2.12, which is barely significant at the .05 level. We may say that the test of internal consistency is moderately satisfying.

Variations of the Method. The method of equal sense distances as illustrated above made use of the bisecting principle and also of the operations of the method of minimal changes. Neither is an essential aspect of the method. As in the method of equivalents, in which we seek equivalent stimuli, our goal is to establish subjective equality, except that here it is equality of intervals. Thus, we could use the operations of the method of average error

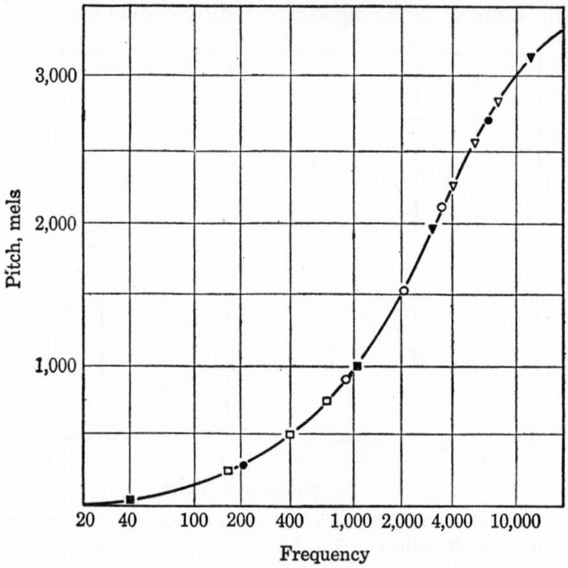

FIG. 9.2. Psychophysical relation of pitch, in mels, to frequency of sound wave, as determined by the method of equal sense distances. (*After Stevens and Volkmann, Amer. J. Psychol.*, 1940, **53**, 336, *by permission of the editor and authors.*)

wherever O can manipulate the variable stimulus, and this approach would be the most economical, as usual; or we could use the operations of the method of constant stimuli.

Instead of bisecting an interval, we could select an interval $S_3 - S_2$ and have O determine an equal interval $S_4 - S_3$ or an equal interval $S_2 - S_1$ or even an equal interval $S_6 - S_5$. In any of these cases the one interval serves as a standard. In the other interval any terminal stimulus not identical with a terminal stimulus in the standard could become S_v.

Another substitute for bisection would be in the form of trisection, or quadrisection, or higher degrees of division. Stevens and Volkmann asked Os to subdivide a pitch interval into four equal parts by manipulating a tuning apparatus (22). Three stimulus ranges were used: 40 to 1,000 c.p.s., 200 to 6,500 c.p.s., and 3,000 to 12,000 c.p.s. The results from the three sets of observations were fitted together as shown in Fig. 9.2. The pitch level corresponding to 1,000 c.p.s. was arbitrarily given the value of 1,000 units on the psychological scale and the unit was called a *mel*. Since the plot of the frequency scale in Fig. 9.2 is logarithmic, the curve's departure from a straight line shows how much the relationship of pitch to frequency deviates from Fechner's law. Having established an interval scale for pitch, the investigators were able to demonstrate two interesting things. The first was that

TABLE 9.4. FREQUENCIES WITH WHICH SPOT-PATTERN STIMULI WERE PLACED IN EACH OF NINE SUCCESSIVE CATEGORIES SPACED AT EQUAL-APPEARING INTERVALS

Stimulus values (*S*)	Scale values (*R*)									Statistics	
	1	2	3	4	5	6	7	8	9	*Mdn*	*Q*
15	14	18	7	1	..	..	..	..	..	1.83	.59
16	16	19	3	2	..	..	..	..	..	1.71	.56
17	7	18	11	4	..	..	..	..	..	2.22	.64
19	8	18	9	3	2	..	..	..	..	2.17	.67
20	3	12	14	3	6	2	..	..	..	2.86	.87
22	1	11	14	12	2	..	..	..	..	3.07	.76
24	..	3	12	14	9	2	..	..	..	3.86	.76
26	..	2	9	18	9	2	..	..	..	4.00	.61
28	..	..	2	20	17	1	..	..	..	4.40	.54
30	..	..	..	26	11	3	..	..	..	4.27	.49
32	..	..	2	10	16	9	3	..	..	5.00	.71
35	..	..	..	8	17	14	1	..	..	5.21	.62
37	..	..	..	8	18	10	4	..	..	5.17	.64
40	..	..	..	2	14	14	10	..	..	5.79	.72
43	..	..	..	..	12	19	9	..	..	5.92	.55
46	..	..	..	2	6	18	14	..	..	6.17	.59
49	..	..	..	..	2	14	23	1	..	6.67	.56
53	..	..	..	..	..	10	25	5	..	6.90	.40
56	..	..	..	..	..	12	22	6	..	6.87	.49
60	..	..	..	..	..	5	22	11	2	7.18	.52
64	..	..	..	..	..	..	14	20	6	7.80	.54
69	..	..	..	..	..	..	7	17	16	8.26	.60
74	..	..	..	..	..	..	6	20	14	8.20	.54

the psychological sizes of an octave and an interval of a fifth are not constant but increase with frequency up to the level of about 4,000 c.p.s., after which they decrease. The second finding was that there seems to be a direct, linear relationship between the pitch of a sound and the distance of excitation along the basilar membrane.

Method of Equal-appearing Intervals. It is not a long jump from the division of a large psychological interval as marked off by two selected stimuli into a few equal-appearing components to the procedure in the method of equal-appearing intervals. In the latter, the range covered is usually greater and the ends may or may not be anchored by means of landmark stimuli. In the typical application of the method, O is given a number of stimuli that he is instructed to sort into piles such that steps between neighboring ordered piles seem to him to be equal. It is necessary that O be able to manipulate the stimuli, whose duration is indefinite or which can be repeated at O's desire. This limits the method to stimuli in the form of objects that can be seen, hefted, or felt.

An Experiment Illustrating Equal-appearing Intervals. The experiment used to illustrate the method of equal-appearing intervals is on the perception of the density of spot patterns. The stimuli were designs on 5-in. squares of cardboard. On each card was drawn a square 2.5 × 2.5 in., within which were small spots ranging from 15 through 74 in number, in

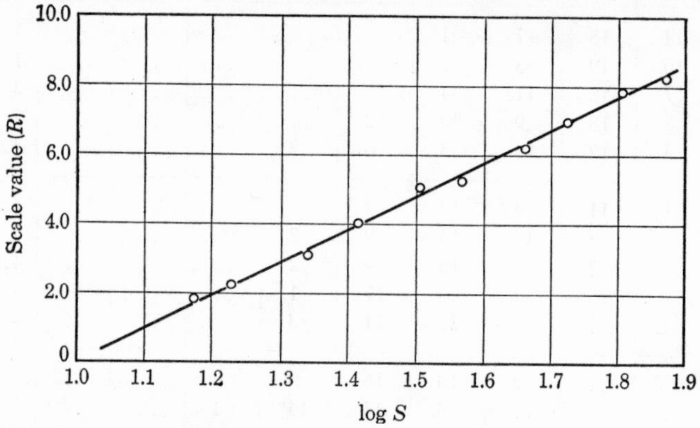

FIG. 9.3. Linear regression of psychological values of "numerousness" of perceived spot patterns as a function of logarithm of number of spots, as determined by the method of equal-appearing intervals.

roughly a geometric series. The pack of cards contained 4 such sets of 25 cards each. O sorted the deck 10 times in 9 ordered piles, attempting to keep the interpile distances psychologically equal. The frequency with which the card of each S value was placed in each category provides the data, which are recorded in Table 9.4.

Scaling Judgments in Equal-appearing Intervals. The scaling from judgments in equal-appearing intervals is very simple. Accepting the main assumption on which the method rests, that O can keep his intervals psychologically equal, we accept the category values as interval-scale values and therefore treat them statistically as such.

In a matrix such as that in Table 9.4, we have in each row a frequency distribution on the psychological interval scale for a given stimulus. The psychological value R for each stimulus is a mean or median of that distribution. When the frequency distributions are not truncated, the mean is better. When distributions are truncated, medians are better. The data in Table 9.4 were obtained without permitting O to place any stimuli below the lowest category or above the highest category; hence there is some truncation and medians have been computed throughout. The measures of dispersion are the semi-interquartile ranges Q. When distributions are not truncated by the end restrictions, the standard deviation would be computed as a better index of dispersion.

Testing Applicability of Fechner's Law. If Fechner's law applies to these data, the regression of R on $\log S$ should be linear. To make the illustration less cumbersome, let us select 10 stimuli from the list in Table 9.4, covering the range rather evenly. The selection is shown in Table 9.5, with corresponding logarithms of S and with psychological values R. The plot of the relationship of R to $\log S$ is shown in Fig. 9.3. The regression is obviously linear and the fit appears to be very good. Applying a least-square solution, we find that the equation is $R = 9.41 \log S - 9.36$. The coefficient of correlation between R and $\log S$ is .998.

TABLE 9.5. SELECTED STIMULI FROM TABLE 9.4, THEIR LOGARITHMS, AND THEIR CORRESPONDING PSYCHOLOGICAL SCALE VALUES

S	$\log S$	R
15	1.1761	1.83
17	1.2304	2.22
22	1.3424	3.07
26	1.4150	4.00
32	1.5051	5.00
37	1.5682	5.17
46	1.6628	6.17
53	1.7243	6.90
64	1.8062	7.80
74	1.8692	8.20
Σ	15.2997	50.36
M	1.52997	5.036

The Fechner law is generally stated as $R = C \log S$, without any Y intercept; here we have an intercept of -9.36. Perhaps this needs to be explained. The answer is to be found in the fact that to satisfy the equation $R = C \log S$, S must be measured in terms of the absolute threshold as the unit. We need $\log S/S_0$ rather than $\log S$. It was shown in Chap. 2 that S_0 can be estimated from the experimental data such as we have here by applying equation (2.13), which reads

$$R = C \log S + a$$

where the parameter a is needed to take care of the unit and can be evaluated as an outcome of the least-square solution. From it we can also determine an estimate of the absolute threshold S_0 by the relation $a = -C \log S_0$. We know C and a from the least-square solution, so that

$$-9.36 = -9.41 \log S_0$$

from which

$$\log S_0 = \frac{-9.36}{-9.41} = .995$$

From the antilogarithm, $S_0 = 9.9$, or approximately 10 spots.

This result may come as a surprise, in that it would seem that the smallest number of spots on a card that could be seen is one. But remembering the kind of judgment that *O* was called upon to make and consequently the kind of perceptual continuum involved, the absolute threshold should be somewhere in the neighborhood of the span of apprehension for "numerousness." Taves (23), who investigated perception of spot patterns below the range involved here, found that at about 7 spots there was a transition from one kind of judgment to another. Whether the discrepancy between 7 and 10 here is important is hard to say. The observer who sorted the cards may have had an unusually high span of apprehension.

Some Common Applications of the Method of Equal-appearing Intervals. The most common practical uses of the method of equal-appearing intervals have been in the scaling of such material as samples of handwriting or drawings, when there are far too many to be handled by the method of pair comparison or by the ranking method, and the scaling of opinions used in the preparation of attitude scales.

As early as 1910, Thorndike (24) had asked 40 judges to sort 1,000 samples of penmanship into 11 equally spaced piles, preliminary to the development of a permanent scale that should have a small number of standard samples spaced at equal psychological units of excellence. It is worthy of note that he made two practical suggestions. He advised that samples beyond the entire range of those we are interested in scaling be introduced so as to prevent truncated distributions for the latter. He also advised starting with a very liberal number of samples, eliminating as scaling proceeds those that *O* believes to fall near the boundaries of categories. This should tend to sharpen the precision of each category, keeping the steps more discrete and making clearer the comparison of samples with categories. Hollingworth (15) used the method in evaluating 39 jokes. He found the procedure quicker, less monotonous, and less fatiguing than the method of ranking. Hillegas (14) used the method along with others in preparing his scale for rating English compositions.

The calibration of statements of opinion to be used in attitude scales, using the method of equal-appearing intervals, was first proposed by Thurstone (25). The procedure for developing attitude scales will be treated in connection with the general discussion of test construction (see Chap. 15).

Evaluation of the Method. There can be little question of the efficiency of the method of equal-appearing intervals, in terms of time and effort required on the part of observers and the investigator. A large number of stimuli can be judged and the amount of statistical computation is at a minimum. If we are willing to accept the operation of equating intervals by inspection as a basis for interval scaling, we have in this method a very acceptable approach to psychological measurement of a relatively high order.

There has been much distrust of the method, however. Thorndike (24) found that the method gave scale values that were not in close agreement with those obtained by pair comparisons. Hevner (13) has found that intervals among the greater stimuli tend to be underestimated as compared with those among the lesser stimuli. Guilford (8) has shown that when a pair-comparison treatment is given to the spot-pattern data used as an illustration in this chapter, it showed relatively greater units among the higher intervals in the method of equal-appearing intervals, in agreement with Hevner's finding. The scale values found for the spot patterns by the pair-comparison treatment did not verify Fechner's law. The regression of R on $\log S$ was one of positive acceleration. This was also true when the scaling was by the method of successive categories, which is to be described in Chap. 10.

When two methods give discordant results, it is not always easy to decide which is at fault. If one decides to adopt a purely operational point of view, one accepts the results for what they are and lives with the discrepancies. If one believes that there should exist a bridge between one set of operations and another, due to an underlying singleness of "truth," one will seek for sources of error. If one adopts the first of these two points of view, one will conclude that Fechner's law holds for R values found for the spot-pattern observations by the operations of the method of equal-appearing intervals and that the law does not hold for R values found by other statistical operations on the same data. If one takes the second point of view, one will say that there cannot be two sets of psychological quantities and that one method of estimating them is faulty.

From the second point of view, the answer may be found in the fact of varying discriminal dispersions. Ament (1) had found many years ago that in a bisected interval the higher of the two segments contained fewer *jnd*'s than the lower. But, as Newman (18) and others have pointed out, *jnd*'s are not always equal units, and Thurstone has shown the reason for this on the basis of his law of comparative judgment.[1] The facts of unequal discriminal dispersions may be the key to the understanding of many such discrepancies. The fact that the data of Table 9.5 fulfil the Fechner law should necessarily not be taken as a vindication of the validity of scaling by the method of equal-appearing intervals. We have numerous instances to show that the psychophysical function is not of the form of Fechner's law. The appropriate attitude to take toward scaling by the method of equal-appearing intervals, then, is one of reserved judgment. If one wishes to make a check on the equality of intervals, one has available several treatments of such data which will be described in the next chapter.

Comparative Judgments of Intervals. It has already been shown that intervals can be matched and equated by various familiar psychophysical methods. The statistical treatment of interval judgments has been in accordance with the operations of those methods. Since intervals have been treated in a manner parallel to the treatment of stimuli, the suggestion naturally arises to extend this parallel to include the use of comparative judgments of intervals. This opens up the possibility of applying to intervals the methods of pair comparison, ranking, and their variations.

Whether the law of comparative judgment applies to the perception of intervals has not been demonstrated, but presumably this could be done, at least in a limited way. It is a statistical principle that if distributions of two quantities are normal, the distribution of their differences is normal. The principle should extend to the distribution of differences between differences.

[1] For a discussion of this, see Chap. 2.

It is probable, however, that this application of the law of comparative judgments would be restricted to Case III, and perhaps to Case V. Intercorrelations of stimuli that serve as terminals of the intervals would affect not only the correlations of intervals but also their dispersions in complex ways. Variations in dispersions of terminal stimuli might not be so troublesome.

Methods Based on Ratio Judgments

In the methods of ratio judgments, an observer is asked to report his evaluations in one of two general ways. He selects or produces a stimulus that bears some prescribed ratio to a standard stimulus or he is given two or more stimuli and is asked to state what ratios are apparent among them. In the former case, we have the *method of fractionation* and the *method of multiple stimuli.* In the first of these, the stimulus *O* selects may bear the (psychological) ratio of 1/2, 1/3, 1/5, or 1/10 to the standard; in the second, the stimulus selected is some multiple of the standard—double, treble, quintuple, etc. In the second general case, in which *O* reports observed ratios, we have variations of the *constant-sum method.*

The Method of Fractionation. The method of fractionation will be illustrated by reference to an experiment that was carried out according to a design similar to that described by Harper and Stevens (12) with one important modification. The problem was to determine the quantitative relationship of psychological weight to physical weight within the range that can be conveniently lifted by an arm movement. The essential conditions of the experiment will now be described.

A Fractionation Experiment with Lifted Weights. Ten standard stimuli were selected, the weights ranging from 40 to 2,000 g. in steps roughly approaching a geometric series. Because it was not possible to provide so large a range of weights in containers of equal dimensions, two overlapping standard series (known hereafter as "small" and "large") were chosen, with five weights each. The heaviest standard weight in the small series was identical in weight with the lightest standard in the large series. The small-series weights were in ointment boxes 5.0 cm. in diameter and 1.7 cm. thick, and the large-series weights were in ointment boxes 10.5 cm. in diameter and 6.7 cm. thick. The standard-weight values are listed in Table 9.6. The comparison series consisted of two ranges, one for each standard series. For the small series, they were: 20, 24, 28, 34, 40, 50, 63, 78, 100, 110, 120, 138, 150, 165, 175, 185, and 200. For the large series, they were: 150, 165, 175, 185, 200, 210, 245, 300, 350, 410, 475, 550, 630, 700, 790, 900, 1,000, 1,125, 1,250, 1,400, and 1,550. Both series were roughly geometric. The Harper and Stevens procedure provided six comparison weights to go with each standard. Preliminary experiments showed that the observer's judgments may well be biased by the selection of these limited ranges. It is better to use one long, continuous series of comparison stimuli for all standards of the same character.

Each of 20 *O*s was instructed to find a weight in the comparison series that seemed to him to be half as heavy as the standard. Half of the *O*s started with the lightest standard and half with the heaviest standard and all *O*s worked serially through the list of standards. Half of the *O*s judged the large series first and half the small one.[1] We therefore have 20 judgments of S_h (the half-stimulus) corresponding to each standard S_s.

There are several possible ways of determining the best estimate of the weight judged half as heavy as each standard. One could compute means or medians of the distributions of comparison weights selected or one could convert the comparison-weight values to log *S* and then find means or medians. The latter procedure gives either geometric means or geometric medians. The values given in Table 9.6 are geometric medians. Since further work with these data will be done mostly on log *S*, it is better to average log *S*. Since in this small sample distributions are not regular and extreme cases are common, medians are better to use than means.

Establishing a Psychological Scale for Weight. Having 10 paired observations, as in Table 9.6, each pair consisting of a standard stimulus value and its corresponding half-stimulus, we can proceed to derive a function relating psychological weight to physical weight. A graphic approach will be described first.

TABLE 9.6. TEN STANDARD-WEIGHT STIMULI AND THE GEOMETRIC MEDIAN OF WEIGHTS JUDGED TO EQUAL ONE-HALF OF EACH STANDARD

	Standard weight (S_s)	Median weight judged half as heavy (S_h)
Small series	40	23.3
	100	51.6
	150	83.3
	200	119.9
	300	165.0
Large series	300	173.2
	550	324.0
	900	543.0
	1,400	801.9
	2,000	1,134.0

In Fig. 9.4 we have points plotted to represent the 10 paired observations. The plot is made on log-log paper because of the large range of *S* values and because of their logarithmic distribution. It is clear that the plot is linear and that the data from the two series of weights fall nicely into line. We will treat them as one set.

The correlation of log S_h and log S_s is so nearly perfect that a straight line can be drawn readily by inspection without much apparent error. It

[1] It would be desirable to give *O* experience in lifting all the weights he is to use in the experiment before any observations are recorded. The intraserial effects upon judgments of ratios have not been investigated as yet. Presumably they would be less apparent with ratio judgments than with categorical and comparative judgments, but this is yet to be determined.

must be remembered, however, that a small error among the larger log values is reflected in a large error in terms of grams. For careful work, therefore, the graphic procedure is not recommended.

From the plotted line in Fig. 9.4 we can determine an estimate of half-stimulus for any S value we choose. The first step in forming the psychological scale is to choose a unit. This is an arbitrary matter. We will follow the lead of Harper and Stevens, adopting the psychological weight corresponding to a stimulus of 100 g. as the unit. This unit they called a *veg*, which they report as coming from an old Norse word meaning "to lift" (12). We now have one pair of related psychophysical values; $S = 100$ g. and V (for veg) $= 1.0$. Other pairs we can find by use of the regression in Fig. 9.4. The weight corresponding to 2 vegs is found by locating 100 on the S_h axis

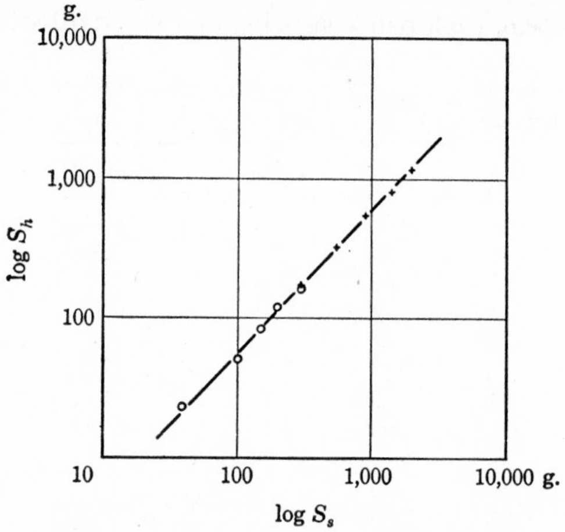

FIG. 9.4. Relationship of half-stimulus S_h to standard stimulus S_s in a log-log plot, as determined by the fractionation method.

and finding the corresponding stimulus on the S_s axis that should feel twice as heavy. This appears to be approximately 180 g.; exact reading on the logarithmic scale is not easy. We can now find a weight S that corresponds to 4 vegs in a similar manner. It appears to be approximately 320 g. The weight corresponding to 8 vegs is approximately 560 g. We could go on, doubling vegs each time, within the limits of the line on the chart. Working in the other direction from 1 veg, corresponding to 100 g. on the S_s scale is an S_h value of approximately 54. The corresponding psychological weight is .5 veg. A quarter veg is found to correspond to approximately 29 g., and ⅛ veg to correspond to approximately 15.2 g.

Having a number of paired V and S values we can now plot the relationship of the two. It would be much better to derive such a relationship algebraically, however, a solution that will be described next.

The algebraic solution begins with the 10 pairs of S_s and S_h values shown in Table 9.6. Those values are transformed into logarithms to achieve the linear relationship seen in Fig. 9.4. A linear function is derived by least-square procedures with which the student is familiar. The resulting equation is $\log S_h = 1.0105 \log S - .2699$. The goodness of fit to the linear function is indicated by a correlation coefficient of .999.

The procedure for deriving pairs of V and S values uses the equation just stated. The results are shown in Table 9.7. The steps are as follows. Beginning with a $\log S$ of 2.0000, at the level of 1 veg, the direct use of the equation, when 2.0000 is substituted for $\log S$, gives 1.7511 for the value of $\log S_h$. This $\log S_h$ corresponds to .5 veg (see the first column of Table 9.7). Substituting in the same equation in turn this newly found value for $\log S$, we find a new $\log S_h$ value of 1.4996. This corresponds to .25 veg. Substituting

TABLE 9.7. DETERMINING CORRESPONDING PSYCHOLOGICAL WEIGHTS IN VEGS AND PHYSICAL WEIGHTS IN GRAMS, USING THE FUNCTIONAL RELATIONSHIP $\log S_h = 1.0105 \log S - .2699$

V	$\log S$ (X)	S	$\log 10V$ (Y)	Y'	$Y - Y'$
.125	1.2454	17.6	.0969	.0779	+.0190
.25	1.4996	31.6	.3979	.3918	+.0061
.5	1.7511	56.4	.6990	.7022	−.0032
1	2.0000	100.0	1.0000	1.0095	−.0095
2	2.2463	176.3	1.3010	1.3136	−.0126
4	2.4900	309.0	1.6021	1.6144	−.0123
8	2.7312	538.5	1.9031	1.9122	−.0091
16	2.9699	933.1	2.2041	2.2068	−.0027
32	3.2061	1607	2.5051	2.4984	+.0067
64	3.4399	2754	2.8062	2.7871	+.0191
Σ	23.5795		14.5154		+.0015
M	2.3580		1.4515		+.00015

this value in the equation, we find a $\log S_h$ of 1.2454, which corresponds to .125, or ⅛, veg. The antilogs for the newly obtained logarithms are found to be 56.4, 31.6, and 17.6 g., respectively, corresponding to .5 veg, .25 veg, and .125 veg (see the third column of Table 9.7).

We have just seen that by successive halving of vegs and finding the corresponding half-stimuli we arrive at pairs of V and S values below 1 veg. We can also double vegs successively, starting with $V = 1$, and find doubled-stimulus values. Our equation, which gives $\log S_h$ as a function of $\log S$, must be solved for $\log S$ in order to estimate in the opposite direction. The fact that the correlation between $\log S_h$ and $\log S$ is so close to 1.0 permits us to do this. Solving the equation for $\log S$, we have $\log S = .9896 \log S_h + .2671$. Apply this first to the $\log S_h$ that equals 2.0000, and we find that $\log S$ equals 2.2463 and the corresponding antilog is 176.3 g. Apply the same equation to a $\log S_h$ of 2.2463, and we find that $\log S$ equals 2.4900, from which the corresponding weight is 309.0 g. In terms of vegs, we have doubled to 2 and then to 4. Continuing with similar steps, we finally arrive at a V of 64 and a weight of 2,754 g. The halving and doubling steps have been carried in both directions from 1 veg far enough to cover the range of stimuli used and a bit more.

Having the 10 pairs of V and S values given in Table 9.7, we can now examine their functional relationship. Plotting V as a function of S, we find a curve with positive acceleration. Harper and Stevens (12) found that a function of the type $\log V = a + \log (1 + \log S)$ fit their data very well. A plot of $\log V$ as a function of $\log (1 + \log S)$ for the data in Table 9.7 shows an obvious curvature; hence this function does not apply to our illustrative data. A plot of $\log V$ against $\log S$, however, yields a relationship with only a trace of curvature (see Fig. 9.5). The best-fitting line has the equation $\log V = 1.2345 \log S - 2.4595$ and the correlation is .9999.[1] Coefficients of

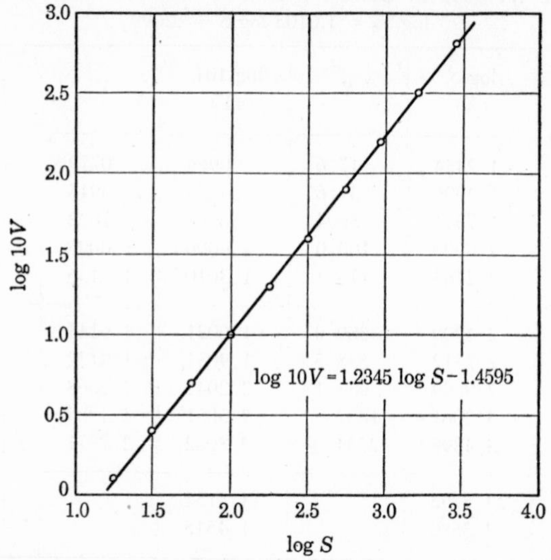

FIG. 9.5. Relation of log 10V to log S for data derived by the fractionation method.

correlation are not sufficiently sensitive to detect minor, systematic departures from linearity, however. Using the linear equation given, we find the predicted log 10V values (called Y' in Table 9.7) and their discrepancies from the obtained log 10V values. In the last column of Table 9.7 it will be seen that there is a systematic trend away from strict linearity. For practical purposes, however, we may say that within the range studied, which is just about the entire range for this type of lifting act, a function of the type $\log V = a + b \log S$ is very descriptive. Taking antilogarithms of the obtained equation, we find that the dependence of V on S can be stated as follows: $V = .003471 S^{1.2345}$.

Other Applications of the Fractionation Method. Quite a number of studies that have employed the method of fractionation have been reported, mostly within the past decade. In 1941, Taves (23) applied it to a study of what he

[1] In Table 9.7 we have used log 10V instead of log V, in order to avoid negative logarithms. This merely adds the constant 1.0 to both sides of the equation:

$$\log 10V = 1.2345 \log S - 1.4595$$

called "numerousness." The stimuli were dot patterns with numbers of dots ranging from 2 to 180 in the standard series. There was a discontinuity in the relationship of S_h to S. Up to about 7 dots S_h was characteristically $\frac{1}{2}S$. Above that limit S_h generally exceeded $\frac{1}{2}S$, the relationship being linear with a slope of .646.

The phenomenon of discontinuity reported by Taves has been found by others, for example by Reese (21). Reese's *O*s were judging flashing lights varying in rate from .5 to 14 per sec. The discontinuity occurred for all *O*s and at about the same level on the scale. Discontinuity, here or elsewhere, indicates that the basis of judgment is distinctly different for higher versus lower levels on the same stimulus scale. It is more likely to occur where the task offers opportunities to use different methods at different ranges or even forces *O*s to do so.

Other types of stimuli to which the fractionation method has been applied include taste intensities, which were investigated by Lewis (16). Hanes (10, 11) investigated the scaling of brightness of lights, giving considerable attention to methodology. Gregg (7) made a study of short temporal intervals by means of the same procedure. Besides the major objective of developing subjective scales of various kinds, these investigators have sometimes been interested in determining the subjective sizes of *jnd*'s, which can be done once subjective scales have been established. It is not uncommon to find that the subjective sizes of *jnd*'s vary systematically with *S*.

There have also been suggestions of new psychological units for the various scales. For a unit of perceived time Gregg suggests a unit called a *temp*, which is defined as equivalent to physical time of 1,000 milliseconds (7). For brightness of lights, Hanes suggests the unit *bril*, one hundred of which are equivalent to one millilambert (10). He found that in comparison with Troland's data, 1 bril is equivalent to 1.61 *jnd*'s, and that Troland's integrated *jnd* scale and the bril scale are linearly related. For the perception of numerousness Taves coined the unit term *numer* (23). Beebe-Center and Waddell (2) define a unit of psychological taste intensity, the *gust*, as that impression corresponding to a 1 per cent solution of sucrose.

The Method of Multiple Stimuli. The method of multiple stimuli has not been used very much. It would seem to be a natural check on scaling results with the fractionation method to reverse the ratios as a test of validity. If the scaled results do not agree by the two approaches, one or both of them lack full trustworthiness. In two or three studies such comparisons have been made, using both fractionation and multiple-stimuli methods. In a study by Geiger and Firestone (6) in which sounds were judged, ratios of 1/2, 1/4, 1/10, 1/100, 2, 4, 10, and 100 were used. There were some discrepancies in scaling derived from the two methods, the greatest discrepancies being with the ratios 1/2 and 2. Ham and Parkinson (9), using ratios of 1/2, 1/3, 1/5, 2, 3, and 5 with judgments of loudness, obtained very good agreements. Hanes (11), in a study of brightness, used ratios of 1/2, 1/3, 2, and 3. The four resulting functions were very similar, but agreements between results from the fractional and multiple methods were best near the central portions of the ranges. In general the *O*s found multiple judgments easier to make, but this depended somewhat upon the type to which they became accustomed first. The judgment of multiple 3 was found to be more difficult than that of the multiple 2.

Evaluation of the Fractionation and Multiple-stimulus Methods. Experience with these two methods is still too limited to permit a decision as to their validity. Since the results to be derived from them are purported to achieve the highest level of measurement, one should be particularly sensitive to any defects that they may have. Reproducibility of types of psychophysical functions in results from different experimental sources is some indication of their soundness. Hanes (11) points out that such reproducibility can be achieved but that there are marked individual differences. It is apparently quite easy for an observer to fall into the stimulus error, making his ratio judgments correspond closely with physical ratios. Hanes also reports that variabilities of fractional and multiple judgments are of the same order of magnitude as those found in matching for equality, a fact that indicates something about reliability of such judgments but not, of course, about their validity. With further use of the methods in more areas of observation we should be in a much better position to decide concerning their validity and their range of applicability.

The Constant-sum Method. The fundamental principle of the constant-sum method was proposed by Metfessel (17) in 1947 for the purpose of obtaining psychological values on ratio scales.[1] Like the methods of fractionation and multiple stimuli, it requires the observer to report upon observed ratios. Instead of specifying a certain ratio that *O* is to achieve, *O* must name the ratio he thinks exists between two or more stimuli. *O* may be presented with two stimuli at a time or with more than two. The typical judgment is to divide a total of 100 points as he thinks they should be divided to represent the several objects in a set. If *O* states that stimuli *A* and *B* should receive 75 and 25 points, respectively, then the ratio of *A* to *B* is 3.0 and the ratio of *B* to *A* is .33. If *O* divides 100 points among *A*, *B*, and *C* giving them 20, 30, and 50 points, respectively, the ratios are $A/B = .67$, $A/C = .40$, and $B/C = .60$. The reciprocal ratios B/A, C/A, and C/B would equal 1.5, 2.5, and 1.67, respectively. Assuming that the observations are correct within sampling errors, the stimuli are thus placed at appropriate distances from a zero point. Letting any one stimulus have the value of unity we can readily scale the others.

Constant-sum Judgments with Pairs of Stimuli. A routine procedure for scaling stimuli from constant-sum judgments has been elaborated by Comrey (4). The n stimuli to be scaled may be presented in pairs, obtaining judgments on N occasions from the same *O* or obtaining judgments from N *O*s at one occasion each. Let us see how the judgment and scaling operations apply to series of lifted weights.

In an experiment that we may use as an illustration, 10 weights were selected covering a range from 40 to 2,000 g. A series in small ointment

[1] In 1944, Toops mentions casually a "method of bids" which he recommended for obtaining judgments of relative weights to be given by expert observers to aspects of a criterion (28). The major operational step in obtaining judgments is the same for the two methods.

boxes included the weights 40, 100, 150, 200, and 300 g. A series in large boxes included the weights 200, 250, 400, 900, and 2,000 g. To avoid the size-weight illusion, the stimuli were paired for observation only within each series. Twenty *O*s gave one judgment each of every pair, there being ten pairs in each series. The numbers of points assigned to each weight in its several pairings were summed for all *O*s and these results appear in systematic arrangement in Table 9.8. The sum of points for any pair of weights should equal $100N$, where N is the number of *O*s. Thus, the sums for weights 300 and 200 when those two were judged together are 1,217 and 783, which equal 2,000.

It will be noted that the stimuli are listed in descending order of magnitude. If one were dealing with stimuli for which physical values were unknown, it would still be important to place them in descending order. This can be done by summing columns and rearranging stimuli in the order of those sums, in both columns and rows. Besides seeing that every corresponding pair of sums totals 2,000, another check is to see that the total for the entire table equals 100 times N times the number of pairs. The number of pairs is $n(n-1)/2$, in this case 10. The total for the entire table is 20,000.

The next step in the direction of scaling is to determine the psychological ratio of each member of a pair to its mate. This ratio is given by the simple relationship

$$R_{jk} = \frac{\Sigma P_{jk}}{\Sigma P_{kj}} \tag{9.1a}$$

for the ratio in one direction, and by

$$R_{kj} = \frac{\Sigma P_{kj}}{\Sigma P_{jk}} \tag{9.1b}$$

for the ratio in the other direction, where ΣP_{jk} = total number of points given to stimulus J when paired with stimulus K (where $K \neq J$), and ΣP_{kj} = total number of points given to stimulus K when paired with stimulus J (where $J \neq K$).

Applying these equations to the pair 200 and 300 g., letting K be 300 g., we find R_{kj} to be 1.554 and R_{jk} to be .643, as can be seen in the second section of Table 9.8. The values in this part of the table may be checked by determining whether R_{jk} in each pair is the reciprocal of R_{kj} or whether the product of the two equals unity.

The next subgoal in this scaling process is to estimate the ratio of the psychological value for each stimulus to the value for the stimulus next smaller in the series. We can see that the ratio of the response for stimulus 300 to that for stimulus 200 is 1.554. This was determined by a direct comparison of the two. The ratio for the comparison of stimuli 200 and 150 was 1.245; that for the comparison of stimuli 150 and 100 was 1.475; and that for the comparison 100 to 40 was 2.091. These values appear just below the diagonal cells in the second section of Table 9.8. We also have some indirect evidence of these same ratios, and it will be seen that in restricting ourselves to the direct ratios we have not used all the data available. If for the moment we call the five stimuli A, B, C, D, and E, in descending order of magnitude, we

TABLE 9.8. DERIVATION OF RATIO-SCALE VALUES IN VEGS FROM SUMS OF POINTS GIVEN TO EACH STIMULUS PAIR

I. SUMS OF POINTS ASSIGNED (ΣP_{kj} AND ΣP_{jk})

	Stimulus weights (S_k)					
	300	200	150	100	40	
300		783	644	423	199	
200	1,217		891	648	350	
150	1,356	1,109		808	495	
100	1,577	1,352	1,192		647	
40	1,801	1,650	1,505	1,353		
ΣP_k	5,951	4,894	4,232	3,232	1,691	20,000✓

II. RATIOS OF CORRESPONDING PAIRS (R_{kj} AND R_{jk})

	Stimulus weights				
	300	200	150	100	40
300		.643	.475	.268	.110
200	1.554		.803	.479	.212
150	2.106	1.245		.678	.329
100	3.728	2.086	1.475		.478
40	9.050	4.714	3.040	2.091	

III. RATIOS OF NEIGHBORING PAIRS ($R_{k(k-1)}$)

	300/200	200/150	150/100	100/40		Check sum
300		1.354	1.772	2.436		5.562
200	1.554		1.676	2.259		5.489
150	1.692	1.245		2.061		4.998
100	1.787	1.414	1.475			4.676
40	1.920	1.551	1.454	2.091		7.016
Σ	6.953	5.564	6.377	8.847		27.741✓
$M = P_{k(k-1)}$	1.738	1.391	1.594	2.212		6.935✓
$cP_{k(k-1)}$	8.524	4.905	3.526	2.212	1.000	
V_k*	3.854	2.217	1.594	1.000	.452	
S_k	300	200	150	100	40	

* $V_k = \dfrac{cP_{k(k-1)}}{2.212}$.

have in the first column of part II of Table 9.8 the ratios A/B, A/C, A/D, and A/E. We have in the second column the ratios B/A, B/C, B/D, and B/E. We have the basis in this information for three additional, but indirect, estimates of the psychological ratio A/B. It is given in turn by the following ratios of ratios: A/C to B/C, A/D to B/D, and A/E to B/E. These ratios of ratios all reduce algebraically to A/B. In terms of a formula,

$$R_{k(k-1)} = \frac{R_{kj}}{R_{(k-1)j}} \tag{9.2}$$

where $R_{k(k-1)}$ = an estimate of the ratio of the psychological impression for stimulus S_k to that for the next smaller stimulus S_{k-1}
R_{kj} = same as above, where j varies from 1 to n, but $j \neq k$
$R_{(k-1)j}$ = ratio of stimulus S_{k-1} to each other stimulus S_j

The estimates of ratios corresponding to neighboring stimuli are given in Table 9.8, part III. Thus, in the first column, 1.554 is the direct ratio. The second value, 1.692, comes from the ratio of 2.106 to 1.245 (see part II, corresponding columns and row). The third value, 1.787, comes from the ratio of 3.728 to 2.086, and so on.

The ratios in the columns of part III are averaged to obtain best available estimates of the psychological ratios corresponding to neighboring stimuli. Let us call the means $P_{k(k-1)}$. Each mean is based upon $n - 1$ observations as they are obtained here. There might be some argument for weighting the directly observed ratio twice. This, in effect, would make use of the diagonal cells. In the ΣP table (part I) we could justifiably assume the diagonal sums to be 1,000. In the R_{kj} table (part II) we could assume the diagonal values to be 1.000. These would give us, in effect, duplicates of the direct estimates of $R_{k(k-1)}$. We will carry through the computations, however, without double weighting of the direct estimates. We do not actually have two independent estimates of each direct ratio. Had we introduced pairs of identical stimuli for judgment, we would have the additional empirical data for the nth estimate of $R_{k(k-1)}$ for each stimulus.

The next step is to assign the value of 1.000 to the lowest stimulus, namely, 40 g. The psychological weight for stimulus 100 is then 2.212, since the ratio corresponding to 100/40 is 2.212. This is in turn multiplied by 1.594, the ratio corresponding to the stimulus ratio 150/100, to give 3.526 for the value of stimulus 150. Carrying the successive multiplications of the $P_{k(k-1)}$ values step by step, we arrive at the scale values $cP_{k(k-1)}$, a symbol indicating values found by multiplicative cumulation. Following Harper and Stevens's suggestion that the psychological weight corresponding to 100 g. be the unit and be called 1 veg, we need to make a final adjustment. This is a matter of dividing each $cP_{k(k-1)}$ value by 2.212, the value $cP_{k(k-1)}$ corresponding to 100 g. The veg values V_k are given in the next to the last row of Table 9.8, part III.

By operations similar to those in Table 9.8, scale values were obtained for the weights in the large series. With the unit arbitrarily chosen corresponding to the lightest stimulus in the series, 200 g., the $cP_{k(k-1)}$ values are as given in the second row of Table 9.9. In the first row of that table are given the

TABLE 9.9. COMBINING THE PSYCHOLOGICAL-WEIGHT VALUES, FROM THE TWO SERIES OF STIMULUS WEIGHTS, ON A SINGLE VEG SCALE

	Stimulus weight								
	2,000	900	400	300	250	200	150	100	40
V_s				3.854		2.217	1.594	1.000	.452
$cP_{k(k-1)}$	12.767	4.847	1.927		1.178	1.000			
V	28.304	10.746	4.272	3.854	2.612	2.217	1.594	1.000	.452

V_s = vegs assigned to the weights in the "small" series, from Table 9.8.
$cP_{k(k-1)}$ = cumulative ratios obtained from the "large" series.
V = final or combined series of psychological weights in veg units.

veg values V_s for the small series. Our problem now is to bring the two sets of scale values into a common scale. There is one weight in common to the two series, namely, the 200-g. weight. It has a value of 2.217 on the scale of vegs as determined in the small-series results. We therefore multiply each of the $cP_{k(k-1)}$ values from the large series by this constant. The last row

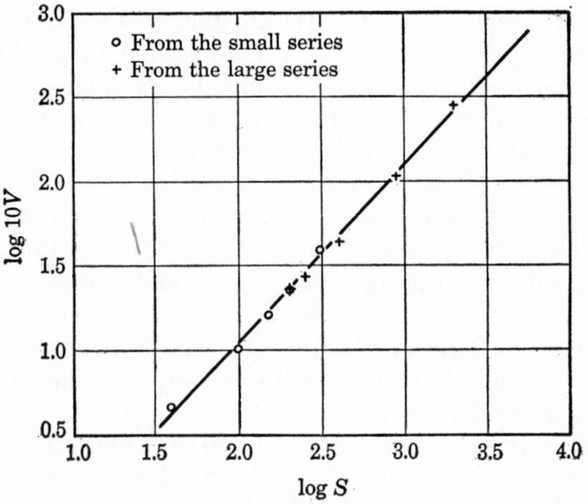

FIG. 9.6. Relation of log $10V$ to log S from data derived by the constant-sum method.

lists the numbers of vegs for weights in the two series on a common scale whose unit is 1 veg.[1]

Figure 9.6 shows that the relationship of log V to log S is essentially linear so that a function of the type $V = CS^k$ is descriptive. Applying a least-square solution to the logarithms, we find an equation relating the logarithms: $\log V = 1.0637 \log S - 2.0982$. Taking antilogs of both sides, we find the equation $V = .00797S^{1.0637}$. The coefficient of correlation between log V and log S is .998.

Constant-sum Judgments with Five Stimuli. In another illustrative experiment, the observer was called upon to judge five weights in a set, assigning a total of 100 points to the five stimuli. The weights, in small and large series,

[1] Where scalings from two different series are to be integrated, it would be better experimental procedure to have more than one stimulus in common.

as before, ranged from 40 to 2,000 g., but with some variations that give a more even distribution in a geometric series. The 10 weights are listed in Table 9.10. The second column in that table presents the total number of points assigned to each stimulus by 20 *O*s. Accepting these values as representing a ratio scale, we next adopt the veg unit, which is a psychological impression corresponding to a stimulus of 100 g. The sums of points for the small series are readily converted to veg units by division of all sums by

TABLE 9.10. LIFTED-WEIGHT DATA WHEN SETS OF FIVE STIMULI WERE JUDGED BY THE CONSTANT-SUM METHOD

	Weights (S)	Sums of points (ΣP)	Ratios (R)	Vegs (V)
Small series	40	91.5	.4854	.4854
	100	188.5	1.0000	1.0000
	150	337	1.7878	1.7878
	200	548	2.9071	2.9071
	300	835	4.4297	4.4297
Large series	300	89.5	1.0000	4.4297
	550	176.5	1.9721	8.7358
	900	330	3.6872	16.3332
	1,400	567	6.3352	28.0630
	2,000	837	9.3520	41.4266

188.5 [see column 3 in Table 9.10]. The stimulus 100 does not appear in the large series; therefore we adopt a temporary unit corresponding to the weight 300. This gives a new set of ratio values for the large series, presented in the last half of column 3. Since the weight 300 appears in the light series with the psychological value of 4.4297, we multiply all the new values in the large series by that constant to achieve a common unit with the small series. The veg values for all 10 weights appear in the last column of Table 9.10.

The relationship of vegs to grams is again nonlinear, with slight positive acceleration. The regression of log V on log S is clearly linear with a least-square equation, $\log V = 1.1760 \log S - 2.2692$. In nonlogarithmic form the equation is $V = .00538S^{1.176}$. The correlation between log V and log S is .998.

Some Evaluation of the Constant-sum Method. The two applications illustrated above show that by judgments of stimuli either two at a time or five at a time, a set of psychological values for lifted weights can be achieved which bears the same *type* of functional relationship to S. The constants in the equations in the two cases are not the same but they are similar. The two experimental operations also achieve relationships similar to that obtained by the fractionation method. For more ready comparison, the three equations are repeated here:

Method	Equation
Fractionation (halving)	$\log V = 1.2345 \log S - 2.4595$
Constant sum (two stimuli)	$\log V = 1.0637 \log S - 2.0982$
Constant sum (five stimuli)	$\log V = 1.1760 \log S = 2.2692$

The constants in the equation for the five-stimuli judgment come closer to those in the equation for the fractionation method. This may or may not be a significant fact.[1]

Comparison of the two experimental conditions, two versus five stimuli, in other respects shows that the *O*s find the two-stimuli arrangements much easier to apply. There are one or two systematic effects apparent in the data from both conditions. In both there is a tendency (not confined to the constant-sum method) for *O*s to favor rounded numbers ending in multiples of 10, 5, and possibly 2. In the two-stimuli arrangement, there seems to be a constant error, as shown in part III of Table 9.8. This is for the estimates of the same ratio (A/B, B/C, etc.) to increase as one goes farther away from the direct estimate in each column. The reasons for this are not apparent. In the application of either stimulus arrangement, it is probable that the method will apply better to visual stimuli that can be presented simultaneously, and this would become more important as the number of stimuli in a set increases.

It is apparent that more methodological research is needed on the techniques of the constant-sum method. There is a question, for example, of how it may be adapted to stimuli whose psychological scale is bipolar. The problem of bipolar scales might be solved by working separately in the two directions from the zero point, avoiding the mixing of stimuli from both sides of the scale. The same restriction applies to the application of the fractionation method. And yet, in marketing situations, it may be natural for an observer to decide how many times one article is worth in economic value than another when he actually dislikes one of them. The mathematical meaning of such a ratio must be different than for one between things on the same side of a psychological scale. In fact, the whole question of ratio judgments is in need of better quantitative rationalization as an important step in their exploitation.

Problems

1. From Data 9*A* compute the mean bisecting stimulus. Determine whether this stimulus is nearer the geometric mean or the arithmetic mean of the terminal stimuli S_1 and S_3.

DATA 9*A*. JUDGMENTS OF BISECTING STIMULI FOR AN INTERVAL OF LOUDNESS OF A MOMENTARY NOISE. STIMULUS INTENSITIES WERE 6.18 AND 23.42 FOR S_1 AND S_3, RESPECTIVELY OBSERVATIONS WERE OBTAINED BY THE METHOD OF MINIMAL CHANGES

S_1 first		S_3 first	
a	*d*	*a*	*d*
11.9	11.6	11.2	12.6
14.3	13.6	12.9	11.6
14.3	13.2	12.6	13.2
14.0	12.9	13.6	12.6
14.0	12.9	11.9	13.2
14.7	14.0	13.6	14.0

[1] All these equations would require minor readjustments in the last term to ensure that 1 veg corresponds to 100 g.

2. Make a test of Fechner's law using Data 9*B* by relating mean category values (R) to log S. For a shorter problem, use only alternate stimuli, including the first and last. Estimate the absolute threshold S_0 from the equation relating R to S.

DATA 9*B*. ELEVEN STIMULUS WEIGHTS WHEN JUDGED BY THE METHOD OF EQUAL-APPEARING INTERVALS GAVE THE FREQUENCY DISTRIBUTIONS PRESENTED BELOW. EACH WEIGHT WAS JUDGED 105 TIMES (THREE TIMES EACH BY 35 *O*s)

Stimulus (S), g.	Category values (R)													
	2	3	4	5	6	7	8	9	10	11	12	13	14	15
50.0		9	27	35	17	12	4	1						
53.5			16	37	15	23	11	2	1					
57.5			10	10	28	29	18	8	1	1				
61.5			1	13	22	15	30	20	3	1				
66.0				5	13	15	23	30	15	4				
71.0					4	20	19	26	22	14				
76.0			1		3	5	11	23	40	20	2			
81.5					1	1	12	19	30	29	13			
87.5						1	3	17	11	35	29	6	1	2
94.0								4	9	31	43	15	2	1
100.0								4	5	11	56	22	5	2

3. From Data 9*C* derive an equation relating half weights S_h to standard weights S.

DATA 9*C*. MEDIANS OF WEIGHTS JUDGED HALF AS HEAVY AS THEIR RESPECTIVE STANDARD WEIGHTS; 20 OBSERVATIONS WERE THE BASIS FOR EACH MEDIAN

Standard weight	Median half weight
40	26.2
100	53.5
200	109
400	226
900	490
2,000	1,000

4. From the equation derived in Prob. 3, determine stimulus weights S corresponding to vegs ranging from 0.25 to 32 by multiples of 2.

5. From the corresponding weights S and their veg equivalents V of Prob. 4, derive an equation relating V to S.

Answers

1. $M_{s_2} = 13.10$; $\sigma = 0.94$; $\sigma_M = 0.20$; $GM = 12.0$; $AM = 14.8$.
2. Equation:* $R = 23.22 \log S - 33.23$; $p_{rs} = .999$; $S_0 = 27.0$.
3. Equation: $\log S_h = .9515 \log S - .1361$; $S_h = .731\, S^{.9515}$; $p_{ss_h} = .999$.
4. Weights corresponding to vegs 0.25 to 32: 35.1, 58.5, 100.0, 176, 318, 593, 1,142, 2,272.
5. Equation: $\log V = 1.4515 \log S - 1.3438$; $V = .00453\, S^{1.4515}$; $p_{vs} = .999$.

REFERENCES

1. AMENT, W. Über das Verhältnis der ebenmerklichen zu den übermerklichen Unterschieden bei Licht- und Schallintensitäten. *Phil. Stud.* (*Wundt*), 1900, **16**, 135–139.

* Based on all eleven stimuli.

2. Beebe-Center, J. G., and Waddell, D. A general psychological scale of taste. *J. Psychol.*, 1948, **26**, 517–524.
3. Boring, E. G. Delboeuf disks and the Kirschmann photometer. *Amer. J. Psychol.*, 1917, **28**, 279–280.
4. Comrey, A. L. A proposed method for absolute ratio scaling. *Psychometrika*, 1950, **15**, 317–325.
5. Gage, F. H. The measurability of auditory sensations. *Proc. Roy. Soc.*, 1934, **116B**, 103–119.
6. Geiger, P. H., and Firestone, F. A. The estimation of fractional loudness. *J. acoust. Soc. Amer.*, 1933, **5**, 25–30.
7. Gregg, L. W. Fractionation of temporal intervals. *J. exp. Psychol.*, 1951, **42**, 307–312.
8. Guilford, J. P. The computation of psychological values from judgments in absolute categories. *J. exp. Psychol.*, 1938, **22**, 32–42.
9. Ham, L. B., and Parkinson, J. S. Loudness and intensity relations. *J. acoust. Soc. Amer.*, 1932, **3**, 511–534.
10. Hanes, R. M. A scale of subjective brightness. *J. exp. Psychol.*, 1949, **39**, 438–452.
11. ———. The construction of subjective brightness scales from fractionation data: A validation. *J. exp. Psychol.*, 1949, **39**, 719–728.
12. Harper, R. S., and Stevens, S. S. A psychological scale of weight and a formula for its derivation. *Amer. J. Psychol.*, 1948, **61**, 343–351.
13. Hevner, K. An empirical study of three psychophysical methods. *J. gen. Psychol.*, 1930, **4**, 191–212.
14. Hillegas, M. B. A scale for the measurement of quality in English compositions. *Teach. Coll. Rec.*, 1912, **13**, No. 4.
15. Hollingworth, H. L. Judgments of the comic. *Psychol. Rev.*, 1911, **18**, 132–156.
16. Lewis, D. R. Psychological scales of taste. *J. Psychol.*, 1948, **26**, 437–446.
17. Metfessel, M. A proposal for quantitative reporting of comparative judgments. *J. Psychol.*, 1947, **24**, 229–235.
18. Newman, E. B. The validity of the just noticeable difference as a unit of psychological magnitude. *Trans. Kans. Acad. Sci.*, 1933, **36**, 172–175.
19. ———. Volkmann, J., and Stevens, S. S. On the method of bisection and its relation to the loudness scale. *Amer. J. Psychol.*, 1937, **49**, 134–137.
20. Pratt, C. C. Bisection of tonal intervals larger than the octave. *J. exp. Psychol.*, 1928, **11**, 17–26.
21. Reese, T. W. The application of the theory of physical measurement to the measurement of psychological magnitudes, with three experimental examples. *Psychol. Monogr.*, 1943, **55**, No. 251.
22. Stevens, S. S., and Volkmann, J. The relation of pitch to frequency. *Amer. J. Psychol.*, 1940, **53**, 329–353.
23. Taves, E. H. Two mechanisms for the perception of visual numerousness. *Arch. Psychol. N.Y.*, 1941, **37**, No. 265.
24. Thorndike, E. L. Handwriting. *Teach. Coll. Rec.*, 1910, **11**, No. 2.
25. Thurstone, L. L. Attitudes can be measured. *Amer. J. Sociol.*, 1928, **33**, 529–554.
26. ———. Fechner's law and the method of equal appearing intervals. *J. exp. Psychol.*, 1929, **12**, 214–224.
27. Titchener, E. B. *Experimental Psychology*, Vol. II, Pts. I and II. New York: Macmillan, 1905.
28. Toops, H. A. The criterion. *Educ. psychol. Measmt.*, 1944, **4**, 271–297.
29. Urban, F. M. Ueber die Methode der gleichen Abstufungen. *Arch. ges. Psychol.*, 1931, **80**, 291–312.

CHAPTER 10

THE METHOD OF SUCCESSIVE CATEGORIES AND OTHER SCALING METHODS AND PROBLEMS

There remain to be discussed one important scaling method, some minor scaling methods, and some special scaling problems. Most attention will be given to the *method of successive categories*, also called the *method of successive intervals*. Like other methods, this one is characterized by certain experimental operations for obtaining judgments and by a variety of ways in which responses can be scaled.

Three infrequently used methods will be mentioned briefly: the *method of similar reactions*, or the *method of similar attributes*, the *method of balanced values*, and the *unfolding method*.

An interesting scaling problem, one that promises to become increasingly important, is that of *multidimensional psychophysics*, with its methods of *multidimensional scaling*. By such procedures it is possible to determine how many psychological dimensions are involved in a certain class of judgments and to achieve scaling on two or more dimensions from the same judgments. A second general problem is that of the degree of objectivity (versus subjectivity) of judgments and the more penetrating problem of the psychological content of the objectivity. A third interesting problem is concerned with the *prediction of choices* from knowledge of measurements. In terms of the goal achieved, prediction of choices is a complete reversal of scaling. In scaling we are given judgments from which to derive measurements; in predicting choices we are given information about measurements from which to predict judgments.

The Method of Successive Categories

With respect to the experimental operations of obtaining judgments, the method of successive categories is a very general one. In principle it includes what has been called the *method of single stimuli* as well as all *rating methods* in which categorical judgments are made. Essentially, the experimental operation is that of judging each of several stimuli as belonging in one of a limited number of categories differing quantitatively along a defined continuum. No assumption is made concerning the psychological equality of category intervals. It is assumed only that the categories are in correct rank order and that their boundary lines are stable except for sampling errors. The scaling problem is to estimate the values of the categories, or of their limits, along the psychological continuum, and from these reference values to derive interval-scale measurements of stimuli.

A Typical Experiment. For illustrative purposes we have data derived from the judgments of 15 well-known male motion-picture actors[1] by each of approximately 100 male students. It was determined first that the *O*s knew most of the actors sufficiently well to say how well they liked the acting of each actor on a scale of seven categories. The categories were defined for *O* as follows:

A. Like his acting exceedingly well.
B. Definitely like his acting.
C. Like his acting somewhat.
D. Do not particularly like or dislike his acting.
E. Dislike his acting somewhat.
F. Definitely dislike his acting.
G. Dislike his acting intensely.
N. Do not know him as an actor.

The frequency with which each actor was placed in every category was ascertained. The frequencies were then transformed into cumulative proportions, which are shown in Table 10.1.

TABLE 10.1. CUMULATIVE PROPORTIONS FOR JUDGMENTS OF 15 ACTORS IN 7 SUCCESSIVE CATEGORIES

Actor	Successive categories						
	1	2	3	4	5	6	7
A	.000	.010	.010	.050	.290	.810	1.000
B	.010	.030	.080	.160	.410	.740	1.000
C	.010	.010	.020	.080	.260	.630	1.000
D	.052	.104	.219	.427	.656	.875	1.000
E	.000	.000	.021	.155	.505	.784	1.000
F	.040	.050	.110	.350	.710	.950	1.000
G	.010	.040	.110	.300	.680	.890	1.000
H	.011	.022	.088	.363	.648	.890	1.000
I	.000	.030	.110	.360	.630	.870	1.000
J	.060	.140	.290	.560	.790	.960	1.000
K	.010	.042	.146	.490	.750	.938	1.000
L	.010	.030	.091	.303	.606	.788	1.000
M	.010	.020	.082	.347	.571	.908	1.000
N	.010	.041	.071	.235	.551	.837	1.000
O	.010	.030	.061	.172	.333	.646	1.000
Σ	.243	.599	1.509	4.352	8.390	12.516	15.000

Scaling Theory for Successive Categories. The key to scaling stimuli by means of judgments in successive categories was discussed in Chap. 2. Before proceeding further here the reader may do well to return to an examination of Fig. 2.7 and to the discussion connected with it. The critical

[1] The actors are the same ones used to illustrate rank-order methods in Chap. 8.

assumption is that the distribution of responses to a stimulus is normal on the psychological continuum. There is also the implicit assumption that momentary judgments (placements in categories) are perfectly correlated with momentary responses (psychological quantities).

If we were to assume that the categories do actually represent equal psychological intervals, the frequency distributions of stimuli are obviously often not normal. In Fig. 10.1 we have the distribution for actor *G*, which, on such a scale, is negatively skewed. Some other distributions would be positively skewed. Skewing is largely a function of whether the mean is on the upper or lower side of the middle category. More fundamentally, in these data, it is a function of inequality of scale units. It happens that the category widths in these results increase systematically as we go up the scale, as seen

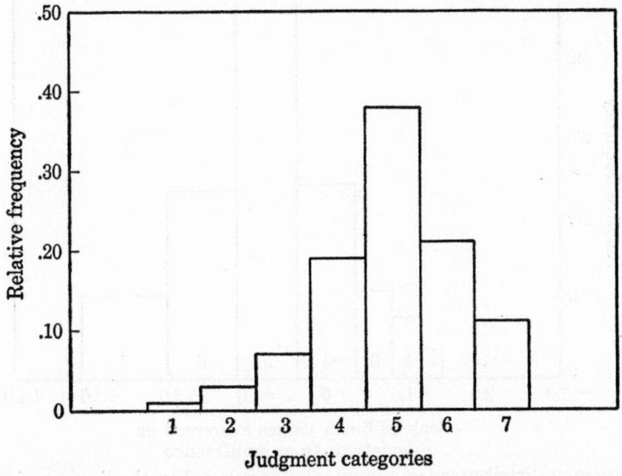

FIG. 10.1. Frequency distribution for actor *G* based on the assumption that the categories of judgment represent an interval scale.

graphically in Fig. 10.2. The distribution of actor *G* in the latter figure is much more symmetrical, due to the fact that the categories are given their proper widths as determined by the scaling processes to be described. The distribution is still not completely normal because of the coarseness of the "yardstick" with its limited number of divisions. The assumed normal distribution shown in Fig. 10.5 shows how the judgments for actor *N* would be distributed if we subdivided the categories infinitely. The *area* in each segment under the normal curve corresponds to the proportion of judgments in each of the seven categories. The description of the scaling processes will show how we arrive at the positions of the categories and their limits in Fig. 10.5.

Scaling the Category Limits. There are a number of routes by which we can go from the cumulative-proportion matrix, as in Table 10.1, to estimates of scale values on an interval scale and to estimates of dispersions of stimuli. Two of these approaches to scaling will be described in some detail and others will be characterized. One general principle of successive-categories scaling is to determine values for the limits of the categories. These limits are essentially liminal values by analogy to limens found in the method of constant stimuli. Another general principle is to determine a single scale value for each category.

Some Historical Background. We shall begin with the first general approach—that of determining liminal values. The investigator first to seek a solution to the problem in this way was Urban (27). In 1933, Urban utilized some spot-pattern data such as were described in Chap. 9 to make tests of the Weber and Fechner laws. His effort at scaling was limited to these purposes. Saffir (22), in 1937, published an article in which he compared scale values obtained by pair comparisons, rank order, and by judgments in successive categories. His scaling in the latter method followed

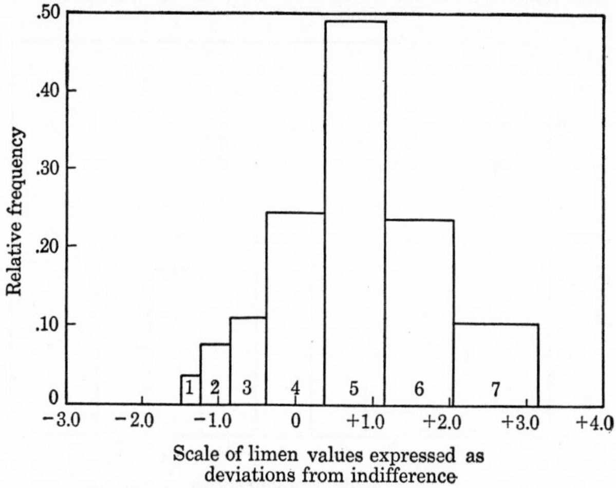

FIG. 10.2. Frequency distribution of judgments for actor *G* on the limen scale, with zero at the indifference point.

an unpublished procedure devised by Thurstone, who called the procedure the "method of successive intervals." Mosier (18) shortly proposed more economical methods of computation based on the Thurstone processes.

Subsequent to the Saffir publication, three investigators proposed methods of scaling categorical judgments, apparently independently. Guilford proposed a method in 1938 that he called the "method of absolute scaling" (11). Attneave (2) described his "method of graded dichotomies" in 1949. Garner and Hake (9) described essentially the same procedures in 1951, in connection with a new approach to the problem through information theory. All these procedures are very similar, with minor innovations here and there. The processes of scaling to be described in the following paragraphs take cognizance of all the suggestions.

Estimation of Liminal Values. Since we have assumed that the frequency distribution of judgments of each stimulus is normal on an interval scale, we have a basis for scaling, starting with frequency data. The cumulative proportions given in Table 10.1 are taken to represent the areas under the unit normal distribution curve below the upper limits of the respective category intervals. We find the linear distances of those limits from the means of the actors, therefore, by looking up the corresponding deviates in the tables of the normal curve. For illustrative purposes we have only six of the actors represented in Table 10.2 and in subsequent tables. Ordinarily, if one decides to do the scaling of the categories by using only a few of the distributions of judgments, one would select stimuli for which distributions extend throughout all categories. Selection was made otherwise here in order to show how scaling is handled when distributions are not complete. For the proportions given in Table 10.1 for the six selected actors, the corresponding deviate values are found in Table 10.2.

In each row of Table 10.2 the deviates pertain to the distribution of a single actor. Each deviate z_j, where subscript j stands for any particular actor, may be regarded as the distance of an upper category limit or limen

TABLE 10.2. DISTANCES, IN z UNITS, OF UPPER CATEGORY LIMITS (LIMENS) FROM MEAN OF EACH OF SIX ACTORS

Actor	Successive categories					
	1	2	3	4	5	6
B	−2.326	−1.881	−1.405	− .994	− .228	+ .643
C	−2.326	−2.326	−2.054	−1.405	− .643	+ .332
I		−1.881	−1.226	− .358	+ .332	+1.126
J	−1.555	−1.080	− .553	+ .151	+ .806	+1.751
K	−2.326	−1.728	−1.054	− .025	+ .674	+1.538
N	−2.326	−1.739	−1.468	− .722	+ .128	+ .982
Σz_j	−10.859	−10.635	−7.760	−3.353	+1.069	+6.372
		− 8.754				
$(\Sigma z_j)_c - (\Sigma z_j)_{(c-1)}$		2.105	2.875	4.407	4.422	5.303

from the mean for that actor. The means for different actors will naturally vary. There are also differences in dispersions, some genuine and some due to sampling errors. Because of differences in means and in standard deviations, the deviates in any one column are far from equal. We have as many scales as there are stimuli, each with its own unit and origin. The next problem is to extract from all this information a single set of values for the upper limits. There is a possibility of evaluating every limit except the upper one for category 7 and the lower one for category 1. These are unscalable because the corresponding proportions are 1 and 0, respectively, whose deviates are infinite.

Some investigators advise us not to utilize any deviates corresponding to proportions below .05 or above .95. To do so, however, discards much useful information where information is scarce anyway. This writer has used deviates for proportions as low as .01 to advantage, for some purposes, as will be seen in the current illustrations. The decision to use or not to use extreme deviates depends upon the number of judgments for each stimulus and whether the tail values fall in line with the others. Whether they do fall in line can often be determined graphically, as we see in procedures described later (see Fig. 10.3).

As usual, some kind of averaging is employed to reduce a number of estimates of a limen to a single value. If we may assume that the dispersions of the stimuli are equal except for sampling errors, it is obviously justifiable to average results from the different distributions. If the matrix of deviates were complete, with no cell values indeterminate, we could simply sum the columns and find means. These means would serve as common scale values for upper category limits. If there are vacancies in the Z matrix (Table 10.2), it is a clearer procedure to determine as many estimates as we can of category widths by subtracting the deviates by pairs down neighboring pairs

TABLE 10.3. COMPUTATION OF MEAN SEPARATIONS BETWEEN NEIGHBORING UPPER CATEGORY LIMITS AS ESTIMATES OF CATEGORY WIDTHS, AND THREE LIMEN SCALES

Actor	Successive categories				
	2	3	4	5	6
B	.445	.476	.411	.766	.871
C	.000	.272	.649	.762	.975
I		.655	.868	.690	.794
J	.475	.527	.704	.655	.945
K	.598	.674	1.029	.699	.864
N	.587	.271	.746	.850	.854
Σd	2.105✓	2.875✓	4.407✓	4.422✓	5.303✓
$M_d = w$	.421	.479	.734	.737	.884
$L_c = cw$	.421	.900	1.634	2.371	3.255
M_c*	.210	.660	1.267	2.002	2.813
A_c†	−1.057	−.607	.000	+.735	+1.546

* M_c = midpoint of category limits.
† A_c = absolute category value with zero at midpoint of indifference category.

or columns. Thus, the width of interval 2 based on the results for actor B is equal to $-1.881 - (-2.326) = .445$. Other estimates of the width of interval for category 2 are recorded in the first column of Table 10.3. The same is done for other categories through category 6. Let all such differences be denoted as d. We have five d values for interval 2, and six for each of the others. The sums of the interval distances are given in the first row at the bottom of Table 10.3. A good check on the accuracy of these sums is to find the corresponding differences between sums of the columns in Table 10.2. The latter differences must take into account the varying numbers of complete pairs of deviates for each interval. The means of the columns in Table 10.3 give us the average estimates of category widths, which are denoted as w.

Having the estimates of distances across the intervals, we can cumulate them to provide scale values of the five limits of the categories on an interval scale. These limit values are designated as L_c in Table 10.3. It should be remembered that these values apply to the upper limits of the intervals. If we want single values to represent the categories, the best we can do from the information we have is to take the midpoints of the intervals. This is done most simply by finding arithmetic means of successive pairs of limens, assuming that the lower limit of interval 2 has a value of zero. The midpoints of intervals are shown as M_c in Table 10.3. They are more representative of the categories than are the limens. Like the limens they are on an interval scale with an arbitrary zero, which is on the boundary between categories 1 and 2.

In this particular experiment our scale is actually a bipolar one with a meaningful zero point presumably at the middle of category 4, which was defined in the terms "do not particularly like or dislike his acting." Deducting the midpoint scale value for category 4, which is 1.267, from each of the midpoints, we can thus make a shift of zero point to a meaningful position.

Determining Scale Values and Variabilities for Stimuli. Using any of the limen scales we have, based upon the values L_c, M_c, or A_c, we can proceed in several ways to assign numerical values to the actors. With the first scale, which utilizes the limens L_c, the numerical values are attached to the upper limits of the categories. These values are well adapted to the computation of medians for the actors. Each actor's scale value is the median of his frequency distribution on the L_c scale. The second and third scales, with values M_c and A_c, are better adapted to the computations of means for stimuli.

There are severe limitations, however, to the possibility of computation of means. For one thing, some of the distributions of judgments are markedly truncated. Truncation does not preclude the computation of a median unless more than 50 per cent of the frequencies fall in an end category. In addition to the truncation problem there is the fact that it is impossible to assign values to judgments falling in categories 1 and 7. The ends of scales derived in this manner are always open. We are therefore limited to the use of medians, except for the few stimuli that may have no frequencies in the end categories. The interpolated medians are shown in the first column of Table 10.4.

Estimates of variability of the stimuli are also possible in terms of the same scales, with similar limitations mentioned above. The direct computation of the standard deviation for a stimulus is precluded by the fact that terminal categories have no assigned values and by the fact of truncation. We are ordinarily limited to the use of the semi-interquartile range Q as the index of variability. Q will not apply when more than 25 per cent of the judgments fall in an end category whose limits have not both been evaluated. The Q values for the six actors were not computed because some distributions were of this type. We shall see later how standard deviations can be estimated as measures of variability of the actors.

A word of caution should be given concerning the use of both medians and Q's in the evaluation of stimuli on the limen scale. Where the number of categories is small, as in the illustrative problem, linear interpolations may lead to gross errors. The use of these two statistics is not recommended unless a distribution covers at least nine categories. We shall see later that there are better ways of determining scale values for stimuli judged in categories, even when the number of categories covered is small. We shall also see that it is possible to evaluate the terminal categories so long as some of the stimuli have been placed in them.

Transformation to a Common Scale. In previous chapters it was the practice to convert obtained psychological values to a scale with a common zero (a zero that has psychological meaning, if possible) and a common variance for a particular group of things evaluated. We shall follow that policy here, for the same six actors will be evaluated by several different approaches.

TABLE 10.4. INTERPOLATED MEDIANS OF THE SIX ACTORS AND THEIR TRANSFORMED VALUES

Actor	Median	A_j*	R_{c1}†
B	2.612	1.345	5.3
C	2.944	1.677	6.6
I	2.016	.749	2.9
J	1.471	.204	.8
K	1.662	.395	1.5
N	2.252	.985	3.8
Σ	12.957	5.355✓	20.9✓
M	2.1595	.8925✓	3.48✓
σ		.512	2.02✓

* $A_j = Mdn - 1.267.$

† $R_{c1} = \dfrac{2A_j}{\sigma_{A_j}} = 3.906A_j.$

Checks: $5.355 = 12.957 - (6)(1.267)$

$.892 = 2.159 - 1.267$

$\sigma_R = 2.00$

The medians in Table 10.4 can be shifted into reference to a meaningful zero point by deducting the constant 1.267. This gives corresponding values on the A_c scale, which are denoted as A_j in Table 10.4. Desiring a standard deviation of 2.0 on the common scale, we need to multiply each A_j by the factor $2/\sigma_{A_j}$. The result is in terms of the values R_{c1} in Table 10.4.

A Test of Internal Consistency. In order to arrive at the medians in Table 10.4 we have gone through some elaborate procedures that were based on assumptions. We can do something to check up on the applicability of those assumptions to these data. Edwards and Thurstone (8) have presented a procedure for determining to what extent the obtained medians and category-limit values can be used to reproduce the original frequency distributions. The operations involved are illustrated in Table 10.5.

The medians are reproduced in the first column of Table 10.5. The upper-limen values are listed in a row at the top of the table. The internal-consistency test is analogous to that for the method of pair comparisons (see Chap. 7). We first determine the distance of each limen from the median for each actor by direct subtraction. This gives the expected deviates z'_j. A good check on the computations in this table is to find means of the columns and the differences between neighboring pairs of means. These differences should equal the previously obtained widths of the intervals, w.

From the deviates we find in the normal-curve tables the corresponding expected proportions p'. These are listed in Table 10.6. We are interested

TABLE 10.5. DEVIATIONS OF MEAN UPPER CATEGORY LIMITS (LIMENS) FROM THE MEDIANS OF THE ACTORS—EXPECTED DEVIATES, z'

		Successive categories					
		1	2	3	4	5	6
Limens:		.000	.421	.900	1.634	2.371	3.255
Actor	*Mdn*						
B	2.612	−2.612	−2.191	−1.712	− .978	− .241	+ .643
C	2.944	−2.944	−2.523	−2.044	−1.310	− .573	+ .311
I	2.016	−2.016	−1.595	−1.116	− .382	+ .355	+1.239
J	1.471	−1.471	−1.050	− .571	+ .163	+ .900	+1.784
K	1.662	−1.662	−1.241	− .762	− .028	+ .709	+1.593
N	2.252	−2.252	−1.831	−1.352	− .618	+ .119	+1.003
$\Sigma z'_j$		−12.957	−10.431	−7.557	−3.153	+1.269	+6.573
$M_{z'_j}$		− 2.1595	− 1.7385	−1.2595	− .5255	+ .2115	+1.0955
w'			.421✓	.479✓	.734✓	.737✓	.884✓

TABLE 10.6. EXPECTED PROPORTIONS p' DERIVED FROM THE DEVIATIONS z' OF TABLE 10.5

Actor	Successive categories					
	1	2	3	4	5	6
B	.005	.014	.043	.164	.505	.740
C	.002	.006	.020	.095	.283	.622
I	.022	.055	.132	.351	.639	.892
J	.070	.147	.284	.565	.816	.963
K	.048	.107	.223	.489	.761	.944
N	.012	.034	.088	.268	.547	.842

in the departures of these proportions from the original, experimentally obtained proportions p of Table 10.1. A matrix of such discrepancies is computed, and also a mean for all discrepancies. For the problem at hand, the mean discrepancy, disregarding algebraic signs, is .021.

A Statistical Test of Significance. This mean discrepancy seems very small and one might be satisfied with it as indicating a good fit. But we cannot be very confident without some kind of statistical test of significance. Such a test is proposed by analogy to that of Mosteller (20) for pair-comparison data. The Mosteller test, as described in Chap. 7, involves transforming both the obtained and expected proportions into angular values θ whose sampling distributions are said to be normal. Formula (7.8), which reads

$$\chi^2 = \frac{N\Sigma(\theta - \theta')^2}{821}$$

applies to this situation. For the actor data the sum of the discrepancies squared is 371.0858. The number of observers may be taken as 100 for practical purposes, although in this experiment a few of the actors were not rated by the full 100. None was rated by less than 91. Overlooking this circumstance, the chi square was found to be 45.20 The number of degrees of freedom is 25, determined as follows. The complete matrix of discrepancies includes 6 × 6, or 36, values. The number of parameters used to obtain the expected proportions was 11, including 6 medians and 5 category limits (the limit of zero being an arbitrary, terminal one). With 25 degrees of freedom a chi square of 45.20 is significant beyond the .01 point.

In some scaling problems of this type the degrees of freedom often exceed 30, which is the greatest number given in the Table E in the Appendix. For a case of more than 30 *df* interpretation can be made through the use of the function

$$\sqrt{2\chi^2} - \sqrt{2(df) - 1} \tag{10.1}$$

which may be interpreted as a t ratio.

A number of things could lead to a significant chi square, since there have been several assumptions involved. Chief among these assumptions are normality of distributions and equivalence of dispersions. We shall find evidence later that the distributions are probably normal but that the dispersions are not equal.[1]

Estimation of Standard Deviations. Two methods will be described for estimating standard deviations for stimuli, on the psychological scale. Both depend upon the regression of the deviate values for each stimulus upon a common scale. One common scale will be that of the limens and the other will be that of one selected stimulus. By an extension of the process in either case we also have the opportunity to make scale-value estimates of the actors. We shall take advantage of that opportunity.

Regression of Stimulus Distributions on the Limen Scale. If we plot the deviate values for each actor, as given in Table 10.2, as a function of the limen values L_c, we obtain straight-line regressions, some of which are illustrated in Fig. 10.3. The fact that such a regression is linear on the limen scale is evidence of normality of distribution for the single stimulus. The regressions are linear for all six actors. The slope of each regression line is the reciprocal of the standard deviation for the actor, when the *SD* is expressed in units of the limen scale. This is consistent with the role of the standard deviation found in the method of constant stimuli, as described in Chap. 6. In that connection the standard deviation was computed by a least-square

[1] The use of chi square here, as in Chap. 7, assumes independence of proportions and hence zero correlations among stimuli.

solution to find the slope of the regression line. Here we shall use a slightly different procedure.

In connection with the method of constant stimuli it may be remembered that there has been some debate as to whether we should use the regression of z on S (or log S) or the regression of S on z. The same problem arises here and perhaps more seriously because the correlations between the two variables z and L are probably lower. What is more serious, the correlations vary

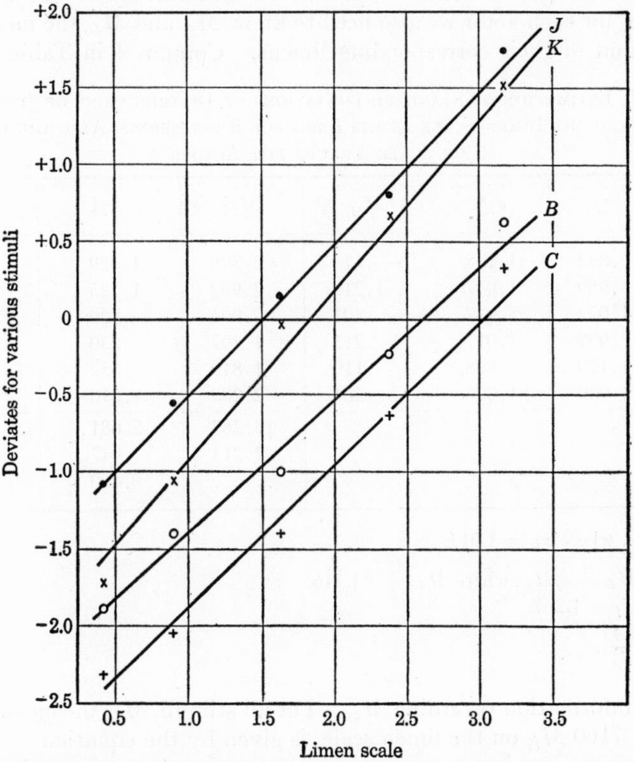

FIG. 10.3. Regression of z values for each of four stimuli S_j on the common limen scale.

from stimulus to stimulus and in the least-square solution this would be a contributing element to variations in standard deviations. The best solution seems to be to eliminate from the customary regression coefficient the correlation term, which leaves us with merely the ratios of the standard deviations of z and L to indicate slope.[1] The ratio σ_{z_j}/σ_L gives the slope of the regression of a particular stimulus scale on the limen scale and the ratio σ_L/σ_{z_j} gives the slope of the regression of the limen scale on a particular stimulus scale. It is the latter that gives us the estimate of the standard deviation of a particular stimulus on the limen scale.

Table 10.7 gives in its second column the standard deviations of z_j for each actor. The ratio σ_L/σ_{z_j} for each actor gives an estimate of his standard

[1] See the discussion of linear transformation in Chap. 3.

deviation σ_j. The σ_j values appear in column 3 of Table 10.7. They range from 1.138 for actor B to .868 for actor K. Such values indicate the degree of homogeneity of agreement of opinion about an actor. The greater the standard deviation, the greater the difference of opinion.

Use of Regressions in Scaling Stimuli. The mean or median for an actor corresponds to a z_j value of zero in his own distribution. By means of the regression lines illustrated in Fig. 10.3 we can find the point on the limen scale that corresponds to a z_j of zero on the stimulus scale. In addition to knowing σ_j for each actor we also need to know M_{z_j} and M_L, the means of the deviates and of their corresponding limens. Column 4 in Table 10.7 pro-

TABLE 10.7. ESTIMATION OF STANDARD DEVIATIONS OF DISTRIBUTIONS OF JUDGMENTS OF ACTORS, USING THE LIMEN SCALE AS THE BASIS FOR REGRESSIONS; ALSO THE ESTIMATION OF SCALE VALUES FOR ACTORS

Actor	z_j	σ_j*	M_{z_j}	M_j†	A_j‡	R_{c2}§
B	.892	1.138	− .773	2.596	1.329	5.4
C	.969	1.047	−1.219	2.992	1.725	7.0
I	1.072	.947	− .401	2.096	.829	3.4
J	.998	1.017	+ .215	1.497	.230	.9
K	1.170	.868	− .119	1.819	.552	2.3
N	1.009	1.006	− .564	2.283	1.016	4.1
Σ				13.283	5.681✓	23.1✓
M				2.214	.947✓	3.85✓
σ				......	.490	1.99✓

* $\sigma_j = \dfrac{\sigma_L}{z_j}$, where $\sigma_L = 1.015$.

† $M_j = M_L - \sigma_j M_{z_j}$, where $M_L = +1.716$.

‡ $A_j = M_j - 1.267$.

§ $R_{c2} = \dfrac{2A_j}{\sigma_{A_j}}$.

vides the information regarding M_{z_j}. For all stimuli, M_L, the mean value for L, is + 1.7160 M_j, on the limen scale, is given by the equation

$$M_j = M_L - \sigma_j M_{z_j} \tag{10.2}$$

Applying formula (10.2), we obtain the values given under the heading of M_j in Table 10.7. These values should be very comparable with the medians interpolated previously. There is considerable resemblance but more discrepancy than one would like to see. The values obtained from the regression method are the more to be trusted, since they are free of the coarse-grouping source of error that plagues the interpolated medians. They are also computed from *all* the data. In order to get the scale values of actors in terms of the common scale with standard deviation of 2.0, a linear transformation is performed on M_j to arrive at the R_{c2} values in the last column of Table 10.7.

Testing the Variances for Homogeneity. The variations in σ_j in Table 10.7 are not very great. They cluster fairly closely and roughly about 1.00. It is possible that their variations are after all a matter of sampling fluctuations. To obtain further light on this point, we can make a statistical test of homogeneity and arrive at a conclusion whether the true dispersions are probably unequal. Such a test is applied to the variances ($V_j = \sigma^2_j$) in Table 10.8.

TABLE 10.8. COMPUTATION OF CHI SQUARE FOR THE TEST OF HOMOGENEITY OF VARIANCES ESTIMATED FOR THE ACTORS

Actor	V_j	$\log V_j$
B	1.2950	.11227
C	1.0962	.03989
I	.8968	$\bar{1}$.95265
J	1.0343	.01465
K	.7534	$\bar{1}$.87703
N	1.0120	.00518
Σ	6.0877	.00167
$\bar{V}_j$	1.0146	
$\log \bar{V}_j$	.00626	

Taking the number of observations to be equal for all stimuli, we can apply the formula[1]

$$\chi^2 = 2.3026(N - 1)[k \log \bar{V}_j - \Sigma \log V_j] \qquad (10.3)$$

where 2.3026 = a constant required when common logarithms are used in the equation instead of natural logarithms
N = number of observations for each stimulus
k = number of stimuli
V_j = variance for each stimulus
$\bar{V}_j$ = mean of variances for all stimuli

Applying formula (10.3), assuming that $N = 100$, we have

$$\chi^2 = 2.3026(99)[(6)(.00626) - .00167] = 8.18$$

The number of degrees of freedom is $k - 1 = 5$. A chi square of 8.18 with 5 degrees of freedom is significant between the .20 and .10 points. We may conclude that the standard deviations for these six stimuli could well have arisen by chance from a population in which dispersions are equal. A test of significance of all 15 standard deviations, however, showed chi square to be significant well beyond the .01 point.

Standard Deviations from Regressions on a Selected Stimulus. Instead of using the limen scale, as in earlier paragraphs, to serve as the common scale, or in the advance of deriving it, we can estimate standard deviations by using regressions of the various stimulus scales on that of an arbitrarily chosen stimulus. We would do well to select for this purpose a stimulus whose frequency distribution covers the whole range of categories fairly well and one that has no obvious irregularities. For this purpose we might select actor *G*. *G*'s scale then becomes the common one. The only information needed

[1] This statistical test is described in more detail by Snedecor (23, p. 250).

is of the kind given in Table 10.2. The deviates of each stimulus in turn are related to the deviates for stimulus G.

Plotting of all the regression lines will show whether distributions are normal. Linearity is again the test of normality. Strictly speaking, it tells us whether all distributions are similar in form to that of the stimulus chosen for the common scale. If they are all of the same form, it is likely that that form is normal.

Letting the standard deviation for actor G be equal to unity, the ratio of each other standard deviation to that of G will express its size on the common scale whose unit is σ_g. Again the choice is made to derive an estimate of σ_j by the ratio $\sigma_{z_g}/\sigma_{z_j}$ rather than by a least-square solution. A worktable like that of Table 10.7 would be appropriate. The work will not be shown here, but the resulting standard-deviation estimates for all 15 actors are given as σ_{j2} in Table 10.15. As in the preceding method of estimating σ_j from regressions, we can obtain new estimates of means here also. By linear transformation these are converted to standard-scale values called R_{c3}, which are given in Table 10.14.

The Use of Standard Deviations in Scaling. The derivation of the limen values in the process described earlier ignored differences among standard deviations. If we decide that the standard deviations are not equal, we know that we were averaging distances coming from scales whose units were different. This is evidently not important when the matrix of deviates is complete, or nearly so. The averaging of estimates of intervals also averages units, and thus the unit of the limen scale is an average of the units of all stimuli. If all stimuli are represented in all averages, the relative values of the mean intervals are not violated. These considerations point to the importance of having stimuli with rather completely overlapping dispersions in scaling categorical judgments. Such distributions are needed, at least, to establish the liminal values. If not all distributions cover all categories, or nearly so, we may select for scaling purposes stimuli that have such distributions.

It might be expected that by using the information about dispersions we could improve upon the scaling. For example, we could equate the units of all stimulus scales before averaging interval widths. This was done for the actor data, the operations not being shown here. The complete deviate matrix corresponding to Table 10.2 was transformed by dividing each row through by its corresponding σ_j. This should equate all dispersions and all units. The limens thus obtained, however, while differing somewhat numerically from the previous ones, were perfectly correlated with them. The test of internal consistency gave a slightly smaller chi square but it was significant at the .01 point. In this test 14 more degrees of freedom were lost because 15 more parameters were used in scaling, one being used to establish the scale unit. In view of the perfect correlation of the limens, with and without using the standard deviations, the extra labor of scaling with them seems not worth while in this problem. There may well be other problems in which the standard deviations differ more and/or in which the stimulus ranges cover the categories less completely so that variations in σ_j would need to be considered in scaling.

Scaling the Categories. The second main principle in the scaling of categorical judgments aims at a value representative of each category, a central value rather than a limiting value. Although it was shown how we could derive midpoint values from the limens, such a procedure is not completely satisfactory because it leaves the terminal categories unevaluated. We will now consider a procedure that arrives at the central category values directly and this includes all categories, so long as we have judgments in all.

The principle is to obtain the mean of the cases falling within each category. By assuming a normal distribution and by knowing the proportion of all judgments for a stimulus falling in a category and below the category, we

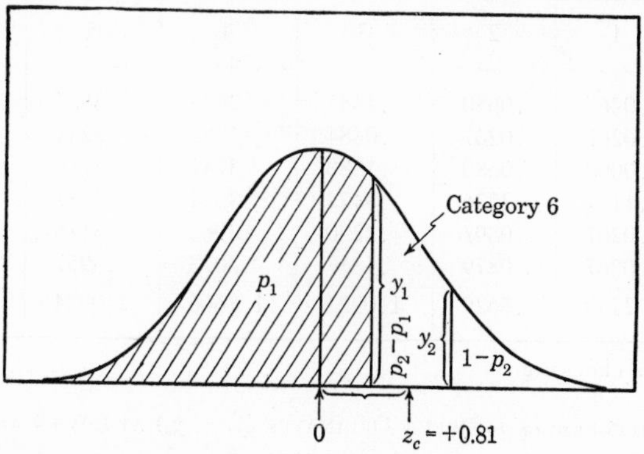

FIG. 10.4. Illustration of ordinates and proportions connected with category 6 in the assumed normal distribution for actor *G*.

can compute the category mean. The mean of a certain segment of cases in a normal distribution is given by the formula

$$z_c = \frac{y_1 - y_2}{p_2 - p_1} \tag{10.4}$$

where z_c = a category mean value measured in standard-deviation units
y_1 = ordinate in a unit normal distribution at lower limit of a category interval
y_2 = ordinate at upper limit of same interval
p_1 = proportion of all judgments below lower limit
p_2 = proportion below upper limit

Figure 10.4 illustrates the quantities defined in equation (10.4). It will be seen that $p_2 - p_1$ in the equation equals the proportion of judgments within the interval.

Scaling the Categories. In scaling the categories, let us use the same six selected stimuli. The work of applying formula (10.4) in such a wholesale fashion is conveniently done in worktables like Tables 10.9 through 10.12. In Table 10.9 we have the ordinates, from the normal-curve tables, corresponding to the upper limits of the categories. This arrangement is convenient since these values parallel exactly the cumulative proportions of Table 10.1. These ordinates are the y_2 values for the categories in whose columns they appear and they also serve as the y_1 values for the categories immediately above.

Table 10.10 includes the differences $y_1 - y_2$. For category 1 we take y_1 to be zero and for category 7 we also take y_2 to be zero. A check of the computations in Table 10.10 is to see that the sum of each column equals the difference between neighboring sums in Table 10.9.

TABLE 10.9. ORDINATES y_2 IN A UNIT NORMAL DISTRIBUTION AT THE UPPER LIMITS OF CATEGORIES FOR EACH OF SIX ACTORS

Actor	Successive categories					
	1	2	3	4	5	6
B	.0267	.0680	.1487	.2433	.3887	.3244
C	.0267	.0267	.0484	.1487	.3244	.3776
I	.0000	.0680	.1880	.3741	.3776	.2115
J	.1191	.2226	.3423	.3944	.2882	.0862
K	.0267	.0897	.2290	.3988	.3178	.1222
N	.0267	.0879	.1357	.3073	.3957	.2463
Σy_2*	.2259	.5629	1.0921	1.8666	2.0924	1.3682

*Used later in checking.

TABLE 10.10. DIFFERENCES BETWEEN ORDINATES $(y_1 - y_2)$ AT LOWER AND UPPER LIMITS OF CATEGORIES*

Actor	Successive categories						
	1	2	3	4	5	6	7
B	−.0267	−.0413	−.0807	−.0946	−.1454	+.0643	+.3244
C	−.0267	.0000	−.0217	−.1003	−.1757	−.0532	+.3776
I	.0000	−.0680	−.1200	−.1861	−.0035	+.1661	+.2115
J	−.1191	−.1035	−.1197	−.0521	+.1062	+.2020	+.0862
K	−.0267	−.0630	−.1393	−.1698	+.0810	+.1956	+.1222
N	−.0267	−.0612	−.0478	−.1716	−.0884	+.1494	+.2463
$\Sigma(y_1 - y_2)$	−.2259✓	−.3370✓	−.5292✓	−.7745✓	−.2258✓	+.7242✓	+1.3682✓

* Assuming ordinates of zero at the lower limit of category 1 and the upper limit of category 7.

Table 10.11 gives the proportions within the categories, $p_2 - p_1$. These can be found from the matrix like Table 10.1 or from the original proportions from which Table 10.1 was derived, if cell proportions have been computed preparatory to Table 10.1. A check on the computations in Table 10.11 is to cumulate the sums of the columns to see whether the final sum equals k, the number of stimuli.

The final steps are shown in Table 10.12. The cell entries are found by dividing cell entries in Table 10.10 by corresponding cell entries in Table 10.11. Every row of Table 10.12 represents a set of category means as derived from the distribution for a single stimulus. These are summed in the columns, and means of differences are found between neighboring categories. These differences are cumulated to form a scale with values cw_c. To locate a meaningful zero point, we deduct the cw_c value for category 4

TABLE 10.11. PROPORTION OF JUDGMENTS IN EACH CATEGORY ($p_2 - p_1$) FOR EACH ACTOR

Actor	Successive categories						
	1	2	3	4	5	6	7
B	.010	.020	.050	.080	.250	.330	.260
C	.010	.000	.010	.060	.180	.370	.370
I	.000	.030	.080	.250	.270	.240	.130
J	.060	.080	.150	.270	.230	.170	.040
K	.010	.032	.104	.344	.260	.188	.062
N	.010	.031	.030	.164	.316	.286	.163
$\Sigma(p_2 - p_1)$	.100	.193	.424	1.168	1.506	1.584	1.025
$c\Sigma(p_2 - p_1)$	.100✓	.293✓	.717✓	1.885✓	3.391✓	4.975✓	6.000✓

TABLE 10.12. MEANS OF CATEGORIES DETERMINED FOR EACH OF SIX ACTORS ON THE STANDARD SCALE FOR EACH ACTOR, AND TWO CATEGORY SCALES (cw_c AND C)

Actor	Successive categories						
	1	2	3	4	5	6	7
B	−2.670	−2.065	−1.614	−1.182	− .582	+ .195	+1.248
C	−2.670	....	−2.170	−1.672	− .976	− .144	+1.021
I	....	−2.267	−1.500	− .744	− .013	+ .692	+1.627
J	−1.985	−1.294	− .798	− .193	+ .462	+1.188	+2.155
K	−2.670	−1.969	−1.339	− .494	+ .312	+1.040	+1.971
N	−2.670	−1.974	−1.593	−1.046	− .280	+ .522	+1.511
Σz_c	−9.995	−9.569	−9.014	−5.331	−1.077	+3.493	+9.533
		−7.302	−6.844				
Σd_c	....	2.693	2.725	3.683	4.254	4.570	6.040
$M_{d_c} = w_c$	....	.673	.545	.614	.709	.762	1.007
cw_c	.000	.673	1.218	1.832	2.541	3.303	4.310
C*	−1.83	−1.16	− .61	.00	+ .71	+1.47	+2.48
C^2	3.3489	1.3456	.3721	.00	.5041	2.1609	6.1504

* $C = cw_c - 1.832$.

from all cw_c values. These differences we call C. We also have the C values squared in Table 10.12 convenient for use in computing standard deviations of stimuli.

Scaling the Stimuli. We find by this method that every category has a value. Using these in conjunction with the obtained proportions given in

Table 10.11, we can readily find the mean C value for each actor. The mean is given by the simple equation

$$M_{j_c} = \Sigma p_i C_i \qquad (10.5)$$

where p_i = proportion in category I and C_i = scale value of category I. The standard deviation of any distribution can be found by the formula

$$\sigma_{j_c} = \sqrt{\Sigma p_i C^2_i - (\Sigma p_i C_i)^2} \qquad (10.6)$$

where p_i and C_i are the same as defined above. The means and standard

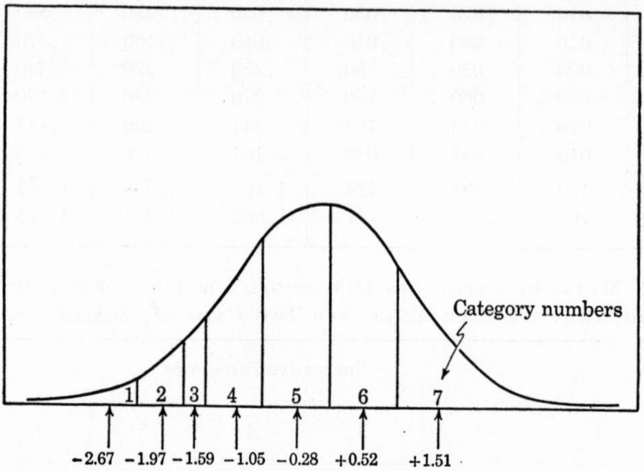

FIG. 10.5. Normalized distribution for actor N with category limits obtained from Table 10.3 and category means from Table 10.12.

deviations for the six actors, denoted as M_{j_c} and σ_{j3}, are listed in Table 10.13. By linear transformation the means are converted to the common scale with standard deviation of 2.0.

TABLE 10.13. MEANS AND STANDARD DEVIATIONS FOR THE SIX ACTORS AND STANDARDIZED SCALE VALUES, AS DETERMINED FROM ORIGINAL FREQUENCIES APPLIED TO THE CATEGORY VALUES DERIVED IN TABLE 10.12

Actor	M_{j_c}	σ_{j3}	R_{c4}*
B	1.235	.996	5.5
C	1.565	.868	7.0
I	.783	.955	3.5
J	.218	1.023	1.0
K	.496	.888	2.2
N	.976	.956	4.4
Σ	5.273		23.6
M	.879		3.93✓
σ	.447		2.00✓

$$* \; R_{c4} = \frac{2M_{j_c}}{\sigma_{M_{j_c}}} = 4.474 M_{j_c}.$$

There may be a few small inaccuracies in the means found in this manner because of truncation in some of the distributions. Figure 10.6 shows a distribution for actor *B*, for example, that is seriously truncated at the upper end. The effect of such a truncation on the mean is apparently not very serious here, as will be seen by comparing the R_{c4} values with corresponding values found by three other methods in Table 10.14. The correlations of R_{c4} with other *R* values are approximately .99. Truncation has more effect on estimation of standard deviations, as will be seen in Table 10.15. There the standard deviations for actors *A*, *B*, *C*, and *O*, whose means are highest, are consistently underestimated as compared with standard deviations from other methods. Similar errors were not found for the lowest-ranking actors because even for the lowest actor, *J*, there was no appreciable truncation, as

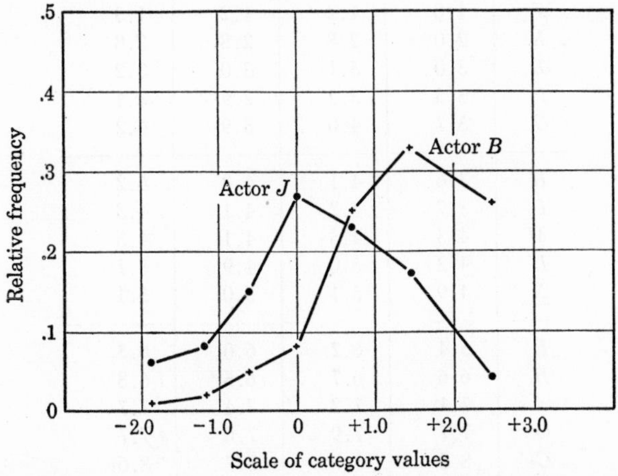

FIG. 10.6. Frequency distributions for actors *J* and *B* on the category scale, with zero at the indifference point.

will be seen in Fig. 10.6. The presence of truncation, then, may preclude good estimates of standard deviations by this approach. One might expect errors of coarse grouping to be appreciable, which might suggest Sheppard's correction. But where the error of this kind is probably rather uniform for all stimuli, there would be no immediate advantage in applying such a correction. There would also be the question whether Sheppard's correction would be properly applied, since midpoints of class intervals are not involved.

Estimation of Standard Deviations by Use of Regressions. If satisfactory estimations of the *SD* cannot be made by the procedure described above, one can resort to the use of regressions, as we saw in connection with limen values. One could use the regression of the category values as obtained from each stimulus on the *C* values, or else on the category values as obtained for a selected stimulus. The steps would be the same as those described in earlier paragraphs. The regressions would be based on data in Table 10.12 where everything is in terms of central category values instead of limiting values. The writer used actor *G*'s distribution again as the common basis for a scale against which to find regressions of other actors' distributions. The resulting estimates of standard deviations are given as σ_{j4} in Table 10.15. They are apparently more in line with other estimates than are the standard deviations σ_{j3}.

Pair-comparison Treatment of Categorical Judgments. The writer has elsewhere (11) developed procedures for the derivation of pseudocomparative judgments from judgments in successive categories. These procedures are so similar to those described in connection with the method of rank order in Chap. 8 that space will not be needed here to show how they apply to categorical judgments. In the method of rank order there are as many ranks (or categories) as there are stimuli. In the method of successive categories there are usually fewer categories than stimuli. In both methods ranking is the basic judgment. The main difference is that in the method of successive categories there are many ties, whereas in the method of rank order there are none. Letting each category be treated as a rank position, we can apply formulas (8.4) and related equations to estimate the proportion of the time stimulus S_j is virtually judged greater than stimulus S_k. In fact, formula (8.4) was developed originally to apply to data in successive categories (11) and in Chap. 8 was adapted to use with ranks. Assuming a composite

TABLE 10.14. SUMMARY OF STANDARDIZED SCALE VALUES FOR THE 15 ACTORS AS OBTAINED BY DIFFERENT PROCESSES

Actor	R_{c1}†	R_{c2}‡	R_{c3}§	R_{c4}‖
J	1.0	1.2	1.2	1.3
K	2.0	2.8	2.8	2.8
D	3.0	3.1	3.0	3.2
F	3.3	3.2	2.9	3.4
G	3.7	4.0	3.9	4.2
H	3.6	4.1	4.0	4.2
I	3.7	4.2	4.1	4.3
M	4.3	4.3	4.1	4.5
L	4.2	5.0	4.9	5.1
N	4.9	5.1	5.0	5.4
E	5.4	6.2	6.0	6.5
B	6.6	6.7	6.5	6.8
A	7.1	7.2	7.4	7.7
O	7.7	7.9	7.6	7.7
C	8.2	8.7	8.7	8.6
M	4.58	4.91	4.81	5.05−
σ	2.01	2.00	2.00	1.99
r_{k4}*	.988	.997	.996	

* r_{k4} = correlation of each R_c value in turn with R_{c4}.
† R_{c1}, from interpolated medians on the limen scale.
‡ R_{c2}, from regressions of z_j on the limen scale.
§ R_{c3}, from regressions of z_j on z_g.
‖ R_{c4}, computed means on the category scale.

standard, we can use formula (8.6) for scaling, with considerable reduction of labor, as usual.

The chief limitation to the application of pair-comparison treatment to successive-category data is that incident to the breadth of the category intervals and the resulting large numbers of tied judgments. The pair-comparison treatment scales the stimuli but gives no direct information concerning the scaling of the categories or their limits. The full pair-comparison treatment would also be prohibitive in terms of labor, for we are likely to resort to the successive-categories method when the number of stimuli is large. The composite-standard approach would therefore be a common solution if the pair-comparison methods are invoked for the scaling of categorical data.

TABLE 10.15. SUMMARY OF ESTIMATES OF STANDARD DEVIATIONS OF ACTORS OBTAINED BY FOUR PROCESSES

Actor	σ_{j1}*	σ_{j2}†	σ_{j3}‡	σ_{j4}§
A	.86	.89	.71‖	.88
B	1.18	1.24	1.02‖	1.15
C	1.08	1.27	.88‖	1.16
D	1.24	1.29	1.17	1.22
E	.84	.88	.87	.87
F	.88	1.00	.91	1.02
G	.97	1.00	.95	1.00
H	.90	.97	.94	.98
I	.98	1.02	.98	.98
J	1.05	1.10	1.04	1.08
K	.90	.92	.91	.94
L	1.06	1.10	1.06	1.08
M	.89	.96	.93	.97
N	1.04	1.09	.98	1.06
O	1.31	1.36	1.05‖	1.22

* σ_{j1}, from regression of z_j on the limen scale.

† σ_{j2}, from regression of z_j on z_g.

‡ σ_{j3}, computed from frequencies distributed on the category scale.

§ σ_{j4}, from regression of category means z_{jc} on those for actor *G*, z_{gc}.

‖ Underestimated because of truncation of distribution.

Some Evaluation of the Method of Successive Categories. The experimental operations for obtaining judgments in successive categories are so simple and economical from the standpoint of both investigator and observers that from this point of view the method has everything in its favor. The interval-scaling procedures involve considerable effort, but no route to the achievement of interval-scale psychological measurements is an easy one. If interval-scale values are wanted, therefore, the approach through this method has much to recommend it. The dependence upon normality of distribution is a critical condition, but since the assumption of normality can be checked experimentally there is little risk involved.

Of the two major scaling principles—scaling limits versus scaling categories—the second is to be preferred. The fact that it can provide evaluations of the two end categories and hence of the entire range is decidedly in its favor. If limiting values of categories must be known, they can be determined by a moderate amount of extra work. Whatever method of scaling the categories or their limits is followed, it is probably wise to utilize a few well-selected stimuli for the purpose. Once a scale is set up on the basis of these stimuli, any other stimulus judged in the same context can also be evaluated and its relative dispersion determined. Graphic devices will be suitable and will save much work, as usual. Probability graph paper would obviate the need for looking up deviates, for some purposes. Graphic procedures are also good ways of checking, since they provide quick information of what the data are like, and whether assumptions are satisfied. Dunlap (6) has provided a graphic method of determining the mean deviates of segments of the unit normal distribution from knowledge of percentages within the categories, and Leverett (16) has provided tables for the same purpose.

Three Unique Scaling Methods

Three methods should be mentioned because they present unique experimental operations and scaling principles. None has received much attention or has been applied very much since it was proposed; yet they seem to offer promising possibilities. They are described here only in principle and in bare outline with the hope that they will not only persist among the family of scaling methods but possibly receive more attention.

The Method of Similar Reactions (Similar Attributes). The *method of similar reactions*, also called the *method of similar attributes*, was developed by Thurstone in connection with the study of attitudes (24). As stated in Chap. 9 (and as described in Chap. 15), Thurstone's chief method of scaling propositions or statements of opinion along an attitude continuum has been the method of equal-appearing intervals. In this connection the need for some indication of the relevance of an opinion for the particular continuum became apparent. It was from this need that the method of similar reactions came about.

If two statements scaled on the same continuum receive almost identical values and if they are both relevant to the continuum, they should function almost alike when offered to subjects for endorsement. That is, those individuals who endorse the one should be expected also to endorse the other and those who reject the one should also reject the other. Two such statements not endorsed together or rejected together as one would expect probably do not reflect the same underlying attitude continuum. One or both may be irrelevant.

Similarity of reaction—endorsement or rejection—is also related to quite another condition—the degree of remoteness of two statements on the scale. Suppose that two selected statements *are* both relevant but not at the same value on the scale. The principle should be true that the farther apart the two statements, the less will they elicit the same reaction—endorsement or rejection—from the same individuals. If the statements are sufficiently far apart there may be none who endorse the one who also endorse the other.

In this principle lies the possibility of scaling. The greater the proportion of similar reactions to two propositions, the nearer they are on the scale, and the smaller the proportion of similar reactions to them, the farther apart they are. By assuming normality of distribution of reaction to a proposition, a mathematical relationship between such a proportion and a corresponding scale separation can be stated. Among all pairs of a set of relevant stimuli experimental proportions of similar reactions can be obtained and interpair scale separations can be estimated, as from pair-comparison judgments. From these scale separations the scaling of single statements can be achieved.

A test of internal consistency is available. Like that in connection with pair-comparison scaling processes, one works backward from scale values to interpair separations to proportions of similar reactions to be expected and compares the latter with the experimentally obtained ones. This test is very important in view of the fact that the apparent interpair separations and the proportions from which they were obtained are determined by irrelevancy of statements as well as by actual scale differences. If the internal-consistency test is satisfied, we may assume that all the statements belong on the same continuum; there is only one dimension of psychological variation.

In one application of the method, Guilford (10) attempted to evaluate the degree of introversion or extraversion indicated by reactions to questionnaire items. The test of internal consistency was by no means satisfied, indicating that the items vary simultaneously along more than one dimension of personality. The use of factor analysis in other studies demonstrated this more clearly. One should therefore have some assurance that one is dealing with items that vary along a single continuum before attempting to scale by the method of similar reactions.

A problem in experimental psychology in which the principle of scaling of similar reactions might apply is that of equivalent stimuli. In learning studies, the degree of confusion of stimuli exhibited by the learner might well furnish data for scaling by the same processes. The presence of more than one dimension of similarity could be detected by tests of internal consistency. It is likely that in this situation more than one dimension of psychological variation does exist. The problem of determining the dimensions is one of multidimensional psychophysics. Several attempts have been made to solve this problem, some of which will be mentioned later in this chapter. It will be suggested in the next section how the method of similar reactions can be used as a step in the direction of arriving at underlying dimensions.

The Method of Balanced Values. A well-rationalized method of finding scale values with reference to a real zero point has been described by Horst (14). It may be called the *method of balanced values*. In addition to asking for pair comparisons, as in the form "I would rather have S_1 than S_2," Horst asks for judgments of the type "If I could have S_1, I would be willing to take S_9." In the former case, S_1 and S_2 are relatively near together on the continuum so that neither is preferred to the other 100 per cent of the time. In the latter case, the two are on opposite sides of the indifference point, which is taken as the absolute zero, S_1 being pleasant and S_9 being unpleasant. The two are sufficiently well balanced to avoid proportions of positive responses equal to 0 or 1.00. When the two are equidistant from zero, $p = .50$.

When $p < .50$, then $S_1 + S_9$ is a negative value, S_9 being more unpleasant than S_1 is pleasant. When $p > .50$, then $S_1 + S_9$ is a positive value, with S_1 more pleasant than S_9 is unpleasant. From the scale separations and differences obtained from the two types of judgments, a least-square solution gives scale values with reference to the indifference point.

The Unfolding Method. Probably the most recent newcomer to the family of scaling methods is Coombs' *unfolding method* (4, 5). The scale values obtained by this method are regarded as being on something better than an ordinal scale but as not achieving the equality of units required for an interval scale. One may begin with such judgments as would be obtained under the instruction "Rank these opinions in the order of the extent to which they are acceptable to you." If the opinions belong on a scale of psychological attitude, the rankings tell how far (in ranks) each opinion is from the observer's own position on the scale. They do not tell in which direction from that position each opinion lies; the unfolding process is designed to take care of that, and from this fact the method gets its name. It is too early to say whether the method will have sufficient advantages, unique to itself, to win general support and use. Because it does not aspire to interval-scale values, which so many other procedures seem to supply, it would need compensating advantages to ensure it an acceptable status among scaling methods.

Multidimensional Scaling

The Dimensional Problem. In previous discussions of scaling methods it has been generally assumed that we are dealing with only one psychological continuum or dimension at a time. In the case of simpler psychophysical judgments, the dimension of response is fairly well recognized and it is known to parallel some well-defined physical mode of variation. Although the stimuli judged may themselves be multidimensional, *O* can more or less successfully isolate the one dimension in which we are interested. By control of the stimulus we attempt to keep constant variations in any but the one physical dimension that uniquely parallels the response dimension in question. When it is impossible thus to isolate a physical dimension, we instruct the observer to restrict his criteria for responses to only one of the response correlates. For example, variations in wave frequency of sound stimuli carry with them variations in both pitch and loudness. We may ask *O* to restrict his judgments to pitch or to loudness.

It is in the judgments of more complicated stimuli and of stimuli whose physical dimensions are not well known, and in judgments of psychological qualities for which there are no recognized corresponding physical dimensions, that the question about dimensions arises. We may define a psychological continuum that we think is unique and yet upon close examination it turns out to be a complex of two or more dimensions. If we ask for affective judgments on a continuum of pleasant-unpleasant, the resulting scale values may actually represent variations on a composite continuum. This is even more true when we ask for what we call "aesthetic" judgments. There may be a number of reasons why an object is judged beautiful or not beautiful, each reason, if it is fundamental and general, and aesthetic in nature, being a different dimension of beauty.

General Importance of the Problem of Dimensions. In quantifying impressions, or responses to objects, the basic source of psychological variations lies in their similarities and their differences. Objects can be similar to other objects for a number of reasons and objects can be different from other objects also for a number of reasons. The problems of similarity and of difference come up at many points in psychology. A problem very basic to studies of perception, learning, and thinking is that of *equivalence of stimuli.* This is brought out most clearly in the form of the gradient of stimulus generalization which has been investigated extensively by Hull and his students. It is manifest most clearly in the general problem of transfer effects in learning. It is a prominent feature of studies of retroactive inhibition. A satisfactory investigation of the Skaggs-Robinson hypothesis requires the specification of dimensions of similarity of stimuli.

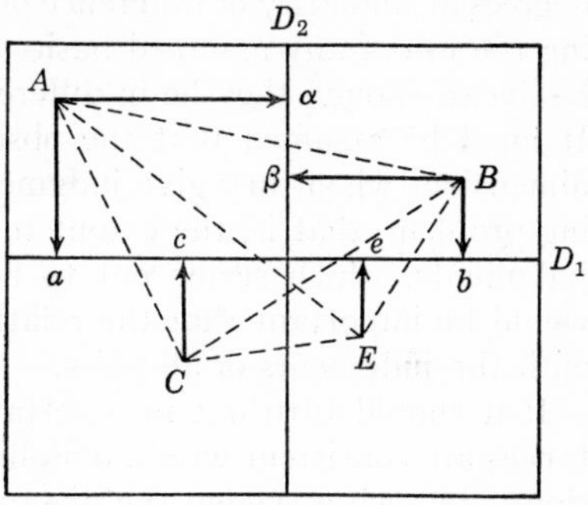

FIG. 10.7. An example of four stimuli represented quantitatively in two-dimensional psychological space.

The problem is also important in the field of attitude measurement. In the preparation of a scale of statements of opinion, a dimension of attitude is specified without knowledge, or even without expectation, that it is a simple and irreducible one. The number of definable social attitudes is potentially enormous. For the sake of economy it would be desirable to consider the possibility of accounting for all of them in terms of simple combinations of a number of basic dimensions. Stated in this form, the problem of attitude measurement is like that of psychological testing in general and the problem has been attacked from the direction of factor analysis. In attitude measurement we can attack the problem either at the point of scale development or at the point of using the scales for determining individual differences. In the former approach we have multidimensional scaling; in the latter we have factor analysis. The objective of the two approaches is the same—to discover the underlying dimensions of a more complex variable.

Multidimensional Scaling Theory. In the space available to us in this chapter it will be possible only to give an introduction to the ideas involved in multidimensional scaling. The theory and procedures include considerable dependence upon matrix algebra, which it is not assumed the student knows. The procedures would also require many pages to illustrate. It is important for the beginning student in psychometrics at least to be aware of the problem and of the general principles of its solution.

We have already noted the problem. The problem can be seen more dramatically by means of a diagram such as that in Fig. 10.7. In this diagram we have two basic dimensions of variation D_1 and D_2, represented as being independent. Four objects, A, B, C, and E, show variations in both of these dimensions. If we could successfully define dimension D_1 and if observers could give us judgments of the four objects without influences from their variations in D_2, we could arrive at the proper scale values a, b, c, and e, for the objects, on dimension D_1. By a separate isolation of the property represented by D_2 we could arrive at four scale values α, β, γ, and ϵ on axis D_2. But suppose that the properties D_1 and D_2 are either not clearly definable or known or that the observer cannot isolate them sufficiently.

The key is to use the interstimulus distances d_{ij}. With four stimuli we have six linear interstimulus distances. These distances represent degrees of similarity or difference. If we ask observers to give judgments merely as to degrees of similarity or difference between all pairs of stimuli, without specifying the use of any assumed basic properties or criteria, the distances should be linear, though they lie in different directions in the plane of the diagram. It must be assumed that the observers are affected by variations in both dimensions when they give judgments of similarity. There is also a weighting problem, that is, the extent to which each dimension contributes to the judgments, which seems not to have received much attention as yet. It would be important that the relative weights remain uniform in connection with the judgments of all pairs.

If it should turn out in a certain experiment that the interstimulus distances are consistent with a one-dimension scale, the system is of one dimension. In such a system the distance AB plus the distance BC should equal the distance AC, where A, B, and C are in order of magnitude. Where the distance AC is less than the sum of the distances AB plus BC, a second dimension is called for. With only three stimuli not more than two dimensions would be needed to represent the interstimuli distances, since they lie in a two-dimensional plane. With four stimuli, such as in Fig. 10.7, we have the possibility of a third dimension, but all the interstimulus distances can be consistently accounted for in two dimensions. The dimensionality of a set of stimulus points is the smallest number of dimensions that will account for all the interstimulus distances with internal consistency.

The essence of the theory is that a collection of similar stimuli may be represented as a set of points in n-dimensional space. For any particular set of stimuli, the dimensionality is ordinarily not known in advance and must be discovered as one outcome of the experiment. The other important outcome is in terms of the scale values for the stimuli on each of the underlying dimensions discovered.

The Scaling of Interstimulus Distances. The major experimental step in multidimensional scaling is to determine the interstimulus distances d_{ij}. This starts much like a one-dimensional scaling process by which the distances are measured comparably on a temporary linear scale. Such a scale is illustrated in Fig. 10.8, representing the six distances shown in Fig. 10.7 laid out on a one-dimensional scale.

Judgment Methods for Stimulus Distances. There are several scaling methods, similar to those for scaling stimuli, that have been applied to the scaling of distances between stimuli. These will be briefly mentioned.

Richardson, who first undertook in 1938 to solve the multidimensional scaling problem, introduced the *method of triads* (21). The stimuli are presented in groups of three, and *O* reports which two are most alike and which two are most different. From this information we have the three distances judged in rank order and we have three comparative judgments concerning those *distances*. The distances are then treated as if by the method of pair comparisons, assuming that the law of comparative judgment applies to distances as it does to stimuli.

Torgerson (26) recommends the *complete method of triads*. In the Richardson method of triads, three comparative judgments are deduced from two explicit judgments. In the complete method of triads every triad is presented for judgment three times. If the three stimuli in a triad are designated as *A*, *B*, and *C*, on each presentation one stimulus is singled out and the observer is asked to say which of the other two is the more like it.

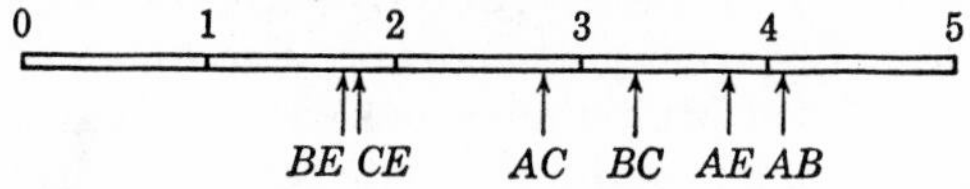

FIG. 10.8. A scaling of linear distances between pairs of stimuli in terms of a common linear scale.

The *method of tetrads*, also described by Torgerson, is essentially a simple application of the method of pair comparisons to stimulus distances. Every *pair* of stimuli is paired with every other *pair*. In other words, *O* is presented with pairs of pairs and judges which pair has greater similarity. As in the triadic methods, the results are treated as comparative judgments, assuming the law of comparative judgment.

Klingberg (15) used as one of his experimental procedures the method of *multidimensional rank order*. With each stimulus in turn as a standard, the remaining $n - 1$ stimuli are to be placed in rank order with respect to their degree of similarity to the standard. These rank-order judgments may be treated after the manner of the several processes described in Chap. 8.

The scaling procedure described in the first part of this chapter also applies to the measurement of interstimulus distances, and we have the method of *multidimensional successive categories*. Attneave has so applied the method (3). The categories of judgment are worded in terms of degree of similarity.

An experimental procedure not resting directly upon judgments may be called the *method of confusion*. Attneave (3) also applied this method. Subjects first partially learned associations between cue objects and response words, where the words were distinctly different so as to avoid confusion among them, but the objects varied by reasonably small steps along two dimensions. One set of objects was composed of squares varying in size and in brightness. Another set was composed of triangles varying in size and in shape. The degree of psychological similarity of each pair of objects within a set was indicated by the number of confusions, where a confusion was defined as giving a word that belonged to one object in response to some other object. A confusion score was obtained for every pair of objects. The results from this more objective method were not entirely satisfactory. The scores for distances along only one dimension were not consistent with those involving both dimensions. The scores had a curved regressional relationship to the scale separations found by the method of successive categories.

The *method of similar reactions*, mentioned earlier in this chapter, would seem to have a good application in this connection. In fact, the results from the confusion method could possibly well be treated as we treat data from the method of similar reactions. Perhaps such treatment would yield distances that have linear relationships to those found by other scaling methods.

Scaling Procedures. The first procedure proposed for determining the dimensionality of a set of observations and for obtaining projections of stimuli on different dimensions was that of Young and Householder (29). Attneave (3) has described procedures that apply in the limited situation in which we know the dimensions and have a few stimuli that vary in one dimension only. Torgerson (26) has developed a set of computing procedures for solving the dimensionality and scaling problems, starting with mutual distances among stimuli. The average investigator will probably find Torgerson's treatment generally applicable and easiest to follow.

Some Typical Results of Multidimensional Scaling. A number of studies have been made in which one of the chief interests was in the methodology of multidimensional scaling. Richardson (21) applied the procedures of Young and Householder (29) to judgments of colors of constant hue but differing in brightness and saturation. The results were consistent with the Munsell evaluations of the colors. Klingberg (15) made a study of the mutual friendliness of seven great powers before World War II, as judged by experts on international relations. He found that a three-dimensional system accounted well for all the mutual international distances except for Japan, which seemed to require a fourth dimension. He could interpret the three dimensions as "dynamism" (attitudes insistent upon change); "communism" (opposition to or fear of); and "belligerency" (readiness to fight).

Attneave (3) used several dimensions, usually two in each experiment. One set of stimuli was composed of parallelograms differing in length of base and in angularity, with one also differing in color. Other objects were squares differing in size and in brightness and triangles differing in size and in shape. Torgerson (26) used colors of constant hue but differing in brightness and in chroma in a two-dimensional situation, and a series of grays in a one-dimensional situation. In both experiments the multidimensional scaling methods detected the appropriate number of dimensions and the scaling of the grays agreed very closely with a scaling by pair comparisons.

An Evaluation of Multidimensional Scaling. The need for a method such as multidimensional scaling is quite clear. While many of the dimensions of sensory variation have been discovered and defined, they have been found by dint of many years of research and much argument. There are several areas of sensory psychology in which the dimensions have stubbornly refused to yield to analysis. It is now hopeful that they may be brought to light by the scaling procedures just discussed. There are probably many other useful dimensions to be found in other perceptual aspects of behavior. The needs for multidimensional scaling in the whole field of perception are very great, to say nothing of the fields of affective, emotional, and aesthetic reactions and the field of attitude research.

The solution of the problem, in the procedures of Young and Householder and of Torgerson, is well under way. The computational processes are as yet very laborious; perhaps this cannot be avoided. There are still a number of questions to be answered with respect to the methodology and to its application. For example, Attneave (3) found that the interrelationships of the distances among pairs of stimuli were not consistent in Euclidian space. In Euclidian space it should be true that the square of the linear distance between a pair of stimuli should equal the sum of the squares of the differences between the projections of the two on the common dimensions. In a single plane this is easy to see as the Pythagorian theorem. In Fig. 10.7, for example, the square of the distance AB should equal the square of the distance ab plus the square of the distance $\alpha\beta$. In Attneave's results it was more nearly true that the interstimulus distance, such as AB, was equal to the sum of the two projections, such as ab and $\alpha\beta$. Torgerson (26) believes, however, that this result was a function of Attneave's special selection of stimuli. Attneave had avoided stimuli that varied in both dimensions simultaneously. That is, one dimension only was varied while the other was held constant. There is also the possibility that the dimensions in Attneave's experiments were too obvious for observers.

Attneave (3) raises several pertinent questions. One is whether we shall have to take into consideration the observers' relative discriminatory abilities in the various dimensions. Others are whether we shall have to consider possible cases of interaction of dimensions and cases of discontinuities. The problem of differential weighting of dimensions was mentioned earlier. Attneave suggests a way of estimating weights when the stimulus dimensions are known and can be measured, and he believes that a multiple-regression solution is contributory to fuller interpretation of results.

There is a very basic problem concerning the nature of judgments of similarity and difference. There is some evidence that the two kinds of judgments are not merely opposite in direction but depend upon different criteria and different neural mechanisms (29). From evidence presently available, it is probably better to rely on judgments of similarity in multidimensional scaling.

These problems are not prohibitive. Their solutions call for considerable work on methodology as such before multidimensional scaling procedures are put into extensive use where dimensions are unknown. It is possible that the methods of factor analysis can be invoked in some circumstances to achieve information concerning the dimensions and the extent to which observers are affected by them. Such an application of factor analysis to aesthetic judgments will be described in the next section.

Objectivity of Judgments

A problem that has engaged the attention of a few investigators is that concerning the objectivity versus the subjectivity of judgments. In the context of psychophysical judgments, objectivity is defined as the extent of agreement among observers. This meaning of objectivity lends itself to the possibility of measurement, for the extent of agreement among a group of observers can be determined experimentally. The operational problem is to achieve some means of quantifying the amount of agreement. This entails further qualification of the meaning of objectivity, and there have been several such qualifications suggested, in accordance with operations proposed for measurement.

The Variance Approach to an Index of Objectivity. In 1908, Wells (28) proposed the principle that the degree of objectivity in judgments of a certain kind applied to a given stimulus should be measured by the ratio of the amount of variability typical *within* individuals to the amount of variability *between* individuals. If an observer A judged a certain stimulus k times on different occasions and if N individuals from the same population judged the same stimulus on one occasion, we have two samples. It is possible to estimate the amount of variability for the single individual and also for the group. If objectivity is high, the size of the index of variability between individuals should be small relative to that within the individual and conversely, if objectivity is low, the variability within the individual should be small relative to that between individuals. Averages of such values would be obtained for a number of stimuli of a similar kind and for a number of *O*s who judged each stimulus a number of times under the same instruction.

In a rough sort of way Wells's procedure is suggestive of the analysis-of-variance statistics developed many years later. In the context of analysis of variance we would substitute ratios of variances for ratios of indices of variability, and we would note that Wells's ratio is more like the reciprocal of the familiar F ratio and that it is used for a quite different purpose. Borrowing an idea from analysis of variance, we see that we could derive indices of *within* and *between* variance from a complete matrix of judgments, each of N *O*s making k judgments on each stimulus. The objectivity-subjectivity ratio ($1/F$) would usually lie between zero and 1.0.

Correlation Approaches to Indices of Objectivity. Two proposed methods for indicating the amount of objectivity in judgments are based on ratios of coefficients of correlation. They differ only in the way in which the coefficients of correlation are experimentally derived.

Hollingworth's Correlation-ratio Method. In 1913, Hollingworth (13) derived a measure of objectivity by a ratio of an index of *group agreement* to an index of *individual agreement* or *personal consistency*. The index of group agreement was found by correlating each *O*'s judgments with the means of judgments for the group. The indices for all *O*s could be averaged to obtain a more stable figure. The index of personal consistency was found by self-correlations with repeated judgments of the same stimuli. A mean of these would supply a more stable value for use in the objectivity ratio.

The use of such a ratio is interesting and novel and with important modifications the principle seems sound. Hollingworth's index of group agreement is undoubtedly inflated for two reasons: (1) inclusion of the *O*'s judgments in the composite with which they are correlated and (2) the greater reliability of average judgments than of judgments of single individuals. The indices of personal consistency were based on judgments of single individuals only. There is also the serious question of the legitimacy of using correlation coefficients in ratios for this purpose, since their scale is not a ratio scale. The use of squares of the coefficients would be justified, since they indicate proportions of variance accounted for. A better index of group agreement could be derived as an average intercorrelation of all individuals. A modified rank-order coefficient of correlation can be used for this purpose, when the judgments for each O can be rank-ordered. It reads

$$\bar{p} = 1 - \frac{k(4N + 2)}{(k - 1)(N - 1)} + \frac{12S^2}{k(k - 1)N(N^2 - 1)} \tag{10.7}$$

where $\bar{p}$ = average intercorrelation among individual judges
k = number of judges
N = number of stimuli
S = sum of the ranks for any stimulus

Adams's Objectivity-Subjectivity Ratio. In order to correct some of the weaknesses in Hollingworth's method, Adams (1) used a new index of group consistency. It is based on the correlation of one O's judgments with those of two other Os, respectively, who are selected at random. By his method Adams found relatively high O/S ratios for judgments of stimuli such as weights, lines, areas, and numbers of X's, and relatively low O/S ratios for stimuli such as advertising appeals and personality traits.

A Factor-analysis Approach to Objectivity. The use of correlation coefficients, as in the Hollingworth and Adams procedures, suggests another and more comprehensive theory of judgments as well as a more analytical procedure. This theory conceives of the variances that different O's judgments have in common as having more than one possible source in terms of underlying dimensions. At this point the problem comes close to that of multidimensional scaling. The goal, however, is rather different. A factor analysis of judgments arrives at a list of common underlying variables and indications as to how much each O's judgments are determined by each source. Multidimensional scaling arrives at a list of underlying dimensions also, but the additional information is in the form of measurements for stimuli on those dimensions. Whether the two methods will arrive at the same dimensions is still to be determined.

Let us assume that any one judgment of a stimulus, given by a specified individual under a certain instruction, is a function of the positions of that stimulus on one or more underlying dimensions of psychological variation. To the extent that the judgment made by another observer is determined by the same scale positions, the two judgments will agree. Disagreement (subjectivity) arises in part from the fact that different dimensions enter into the determination of the judgments of the two Os or the fact that they give different weights to the same dimensions. To the extent that the two Os are affected similarly by the same dimensions, their judgments will agree, and this will show itself in terms of the coefficient of correlation between the judgments of the two.

Determiners acting similarly on judgments of two or more Os contribute to what is called *common-factor* variance in factor analysis. They contribute to objectivity of judgment. These same determiners will also contribute to self-correlation for repeated judgments of each O, since they operate to affect each O's judgments similarly on different occasions. The same O's self-consistency is affected, in addition, by determiners operating in his judgments on both occasions but not operating in other Os. Such determiners contribute to what is called *specific* variance in factor analysis. In addition to the common-factor variance and specific variance there is always some error variance in *O*'s judgments. The total variance in any *O*'s set of judgments, then, is regarded as composed of three sources: common-factor, specific, and error, whose contributions are additive. A quantitative judgment is regarded as a linear combination of weighted contributing quantities, of which some are shared person to person, some are consistent with each person on different occasions, and some vary from person to person as well as from occasion to occasion.

The proportion of any *O*'s variance that is objective in any set of judgments depends upon the extent to which his judgments are determined by common factors. His proportion of common-factor variance is known as his *communality*. His proportion of specific variance is known as his *specificity*. His specificity represents that portion of his total variance that is subjective in judgments of a certain type. This subjective contribution to his judgments plus his common-factor variance make up the proportion of *true variance* in his judgments. The proportion of true variance in any set of measurements defines their reliability. A reliability coefficient indicates the portion of the total variance that is true variance or nonerror variance. The error components vary from occasion to occasion as well as from person to person.[1]

Factor analysis enables us to segregate and to estimate the proportions of these sources of variance for each individual in his judging of a certain set of stimuli under a certain instruction. Furthermore, it enables us to break down the common-factor variance into components or dimensions, and the psychological nature of these dimensions can often be interpreted.

Guilford and Holley (12) applied the factor-analytic approach to the study of aesthetic preferences. Twelve *O*s judged the artistic values of 107 designs and pictures on the backs of playing cards. Each of the *O*s judged the objects twice under each of two different instructions by the method of successive categories. There were altogether four different instructions: *G* (general), "Judge on the basis of general impression"; *C* (color), "Judge on the basis of color effect"; *D* (design), "Judge on the basis of artistic pattern or design"; and *T* (theme), "Judge on the basis of subject matter, theme, meaning, or topic." Two factor analyses were made, based on the intercorrelations of 12 *O*s in each case, so that no *O* appeared more than once in each analysis. As a result we have five common factors with each *O*'s proportion of variance in each factor. From the repeated judgments we have estimates of reliability and from these values and the communalities we also know the specificities and the proportions of error variance.

Table 10.16 presents a summary of the results for five *O*s on the two occasions for each. These were selected to illustrate various features discussed above. We can say that observer *A* on the first occasion, A_1, had half the variance in his judgments determined by factor I. This factor was interpreted as a love of adventure and romance. An additional 9 per cent of his variance was determined by other common factors, none to any great extent. Of his total variance, 88 per cent was true variance and 12 per cent was error

[1] For a more complete discussion of factor theory and of reliability, see Chap. 13.

variance. The difference between his reliability coefficient and his communality indicates that 28 per cent of his variance was consistent in his two trials but was unique to him. On his second occasion, A_2, this observer gave a somewhat similar pattern of common-factor variance, except that variance in factor I fell somewhat and variance in factor III rose (in the negative direction). Factor III was interpreted as a masculinity-femininity interest variable, a bipolar factor. The negative signs before A's two loadings in this factor indicate a slight influence of feminine interests, greater the second time than the first, in spite of the fact that A was a male. His instruction had

TABLE 10.16. SEGREGATION OF DIFFERENT SOURCES OF VARIANCE IN SO-CALLED AESTHETIC JUDGMENTS, AS REVEALED BY FACTOR ANALYSIS

O	Sex	Instr.*	a^2_1	a^2_2	a^2_3	a^2_4	a^2_5	h^2_j	r_{jj}	a^2_s	a^2_e	OI
A_1	M	T	.51	.00	(−).08	.01	.00	.60	.88	.28	.12	.68
A_2	M	D	.35	.01	(−).22	.05	.01	.64	.77	.13	.23	.83
B_1	F	C	.02	.66	(−).22	.01	.00	.91	.91	.00	.09	1.00
B_2	F	T	.00	.92	.00	.00	.00	.92	.94	.02	.06	.98
C_1	F	G	.00	.00	(−).46	.01	.00	.47	.86	.39	.14	.55
C_2	F	C	.00	.02	(−).26	.07	.16	.51	.82	.31	.18	.62
D_1	M	D	.04	.31	.01	.01	.04	.41	.79	.38	.21	.52
D_2	M	C	.00	.20	.03	.33	(−).01	.57	.73	.16	.27	.78
E_1	F	T	.00	.01	(−).06	.30	.33	.70	.85	.15	.15	.82
E_2	F	C	.00	.00	.03	.00	.44	.47	.69	.22	.31	.68

* Instructions: G = general; C = color; D = design; T = theme. The symbols a^2_1, . . . , a^2_5 are contributions of factors to total variance. h^2_j = communality; a^2_s = specificity; a^2_e = error variance; and OI = objectivity index = h^2_j/r_{jj}.

changed from emphasis on theme on the first occasion to emphasis on design on the second. Feminine interests were shown by preference for delicacy of line and coloring as well as for social situations such as teas, parties, and dances.

Observer B had strongest contributions from factor II, which was interpreted as a design factor. This dimension was also bipolar, with positive loadings indicating preference for simple, conventional designs and negative loadings indicating preferences for complicated and realistic designs. One striking thing about observer B is that her entire true variance was devoted to common factors, with practically zero indications of subjectivity in her judgments. Furthermore, except for a variance proportion of .22 in the sex factor on the first occasion, her judgments were almost entirely determined by design. Curiously enough, neither of her instructions were to judge design. It was a general finding that instructions were almost impotent in producing changes in dimensions stressed by the observers. The reason was probably that the instructions did not direct attention along the lines of the factors actually found. There were three theme factors, no color factor, and one design factor. This was a special design factor and there are probably other design factors.

Factor IV was interpreted as an interest in wealth, luxury, and play, and factor V as a love of the outdoors. It is thus seen that what were intended to be aesthetic judgments turned out to be very complex. Only one of the factors, factor II, design, can justifiably be called an aesthetic factor. The others reflect nonaesthetic interests and possibly basic motives, although each factor may not have been reduced to its ultimate dimensions.

The observers can be compared for degree of objectivity by noting their communalities h^2_j, which vary from .41 to .92. They can be compared with respect to subjectivity by noting their specificities a^2_s, which vary from .00 to .39. Means of both these statistics for a group of *O*s would give an over-all idea concerning proportions of objective variance versus subjective variance for these kinds of stimuli. In this experiment several instructions had been imposed, however. Averaging would ordinarily be done under each type of instruction separately.

The observers can be compared on another basis that leaves out of the picture the error variance a^2_e. Considering only the objective and subjective proportions of variance, the ratio of h^2_j to r_{jj} tells the proportion of the true variance that is objective. Let this ratio be an *objectivity index* (*OI*). For the five observers of our illustration the *OI* indices are given in the last column of Table 10.16. The range is from 1.00 for observer-occasion B_1 to .52 for observer-occasion D_1. The same *O* may vary in *OI* index from one occasion to another, as did *A*, *D*, and *E* here. Part of this might be due to the change in instruction; we do not know. At any rate, this kind of index is available as a by-product of a more important general study of the psychological contributions to judgments as carried out through factor analysis.[1]

Prediction of First Choices

As indicated in the introduction to this chapter, the act of predicting choices from known scale values is a reversal of the scaling problem. In Chap. 7 we saw one example of this kind of operation, in connection with the internal-consistency check on scale values found by pair comparison. In that connection, however, we had the limited objective of predicting the choice of *two* stimuli. We shall now consider a broadening of that operation to include the prediction of proportions of first choices among three or more stimuli. There is much interesting theory involved and a practical method for approximating proportions of first choices exists.

The problem has many practical implications. In the field of retailing, many alternative objects of a class—suits, shoes, neckties, and many articles of different brands—are presented for customer selection. Judges of art contests and of other types of competitions are faced with the problem of making first choices. In the realm of politics, voters select one of several candidates for whom to vote. While public-opinion polling is usually conducted in the

[1] It should be said that the effectiveness and validity of this procedure depend upon the adequacy of the factor-analysis solution. This problem can be appreciated after study of Chap. 16.

form of preferential judgments which yield direct evidence of winning candidates, there is much to be learned from the principles governing the reaction known as a first choice.

Thurstone's Rationale of the Problem of First Choices. As in connection with so many other aspects of modern psychophysical problems, Thurstone has been the first to provide a rational basis for the approach to prediction of first choices (25). The following discussion will follow rather closely his line of reasoning.

The Role of Discriminal Dispersion. Thurstone has developed two major theorems concerning choice as a function of scale position and discriminal dispersion. It is obvious that the mean scale position of an object relative to that of another object would have an important bearing upon the majority of choices. It has not been so obvious that when more than two objects are

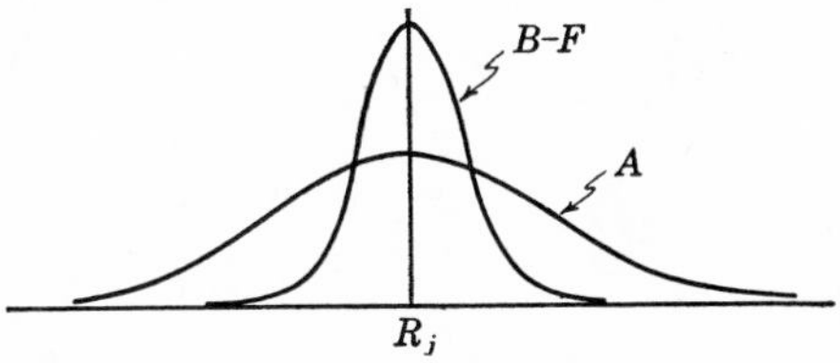

FIG. 10.9. Two discriminal dispersions with equal means and with wide dispersion for stimulus A and equal, narrow dispersions for stimuli B through F.

presented for choices their discriminal dispersions also have a very important bearing on the outcome.

Let us consider, as Thurstone does, six stimulus objects, A to F, all of the same mean scale value. Let stimulus A have a much wider dispersion than the other five, whose narrower dispersions are equal. Figure 10.9 illustrates this situation. If a pair of these stimuli, including A and one other, is presented for choice in a population of observers, the distributions being symmetrical, each would receive .5 of the choices. If all six stimuli are presented for selections of individuals in the same population, what will be the outcome? Object A will receive half the choices and the other half will be divided evenly among the other five. It is clear from the diagram that there are many individuals who rate A higher than any of the other five, and A will receive their votes, regardless. In the two-stimulus choice these *very* favorable voters are balanced by a like number of very *unfavorable* voters who would be certain not to select A. But the latter individuals, in the six-choice situation, will divide their votes among the other five stimuli. This outcome can be generalized by saying that when three or more objects are of equal scale value but of different scale dispersions, the stimulus having the greatest dispersion will receive the most choices.

Let us consider a second type of situation, which is illustrated in Fig. 10.10. Two stimuli I and J have equal means, but I has a definitely wider dispersion. The third stimulus K has a narrow dispersion and a much lower scale position. Note that the dispersions of J and K do not overlap. When these three stimuli are presented in pairs, the proportion preferring I to J would be .5; the proportion preferring J to K would be 1.0; and the proportion preferring

I to *K* would be something less than 1.0. When the three are presented together for preference, the result would be .5 of the choices to *I*, .5 to *J*, and .0 to *K*. Those who would prefer *K* to *I* will vote for *J*, for no one votes for *K* in preference to *J*. The introduction of stimulus *K*, then, does nothing to the relative preferences for *I* and *J*.

Consider, next, the case in which the dispersion for *K* does overlap that of *J* as well as that of *I*, as it did before. Now when the three stimuli are presented for choices, there will be the curious outcome that *I* receives the most votes. Now stimulus *K* can compete with *J* and pull votes away from it. It needs to pull only a few more away from *J* than it does from *I* in order to

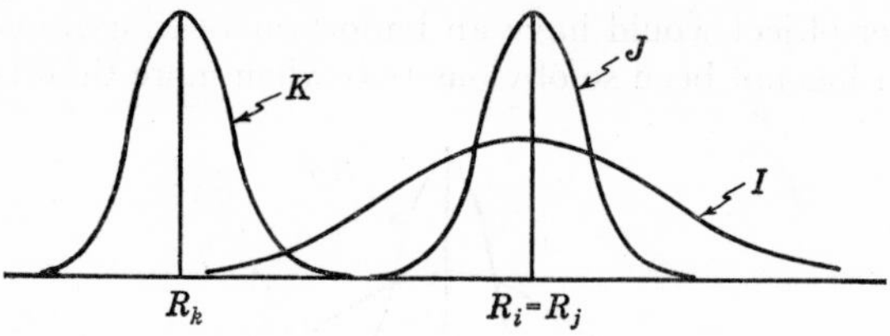

FIG. 10.10. Discriminal dispersions for three stimuli, *I*, *J*, and *K*, those for *J* and *K* not overlapping.

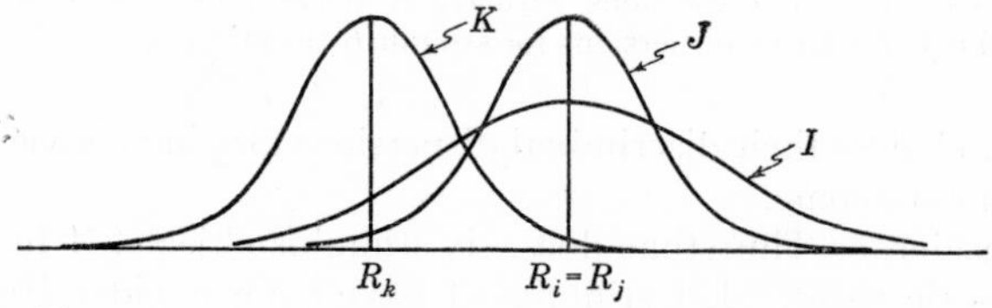

FIG. 10.11. Three discriminal dispersions for stimuli *I*, *J*, and *K*, all overlapping.

give *I* the advantage over *J*. Again, when stimuli of equal scale value are competing with one or more others, the one with the widest dispersion wins out. Thurstone points out that this case is like that of two leading candidates for political office, with a dark-horse candidate brought into the picture. Under such circumstances, it would appear that a leading candidate could afford to come out flatly on issues if the enemies he thus makes are offset by a like number of equally strong friends.

Concluding Remarks. Thurstone (25) has provided a computing procedure by which, knowing the frequency distributions of stimuli in the same successive categories, we can predict the proportion of first choices each stimulus would receive. This procedure is not described here, since it is quite possible to obtain samples of first-choice judgments experimentally, as was remarked earlier. Where such information is available, it would be more satisfactory to use than estimates made indirectly. Where the expense or the lack of time makes direct evidence too costly or impractical, and where the appropriate data are already available, the estimation procedures may be brought into use.

It would appear, however, that the most important benefits of developments in connection with the problem of predicting first choices are their theoretical implications. It is quite possible that other theorems could be deduced from the same source. When correlations as well as dispersions and means are brought into the picture, additional ideas may become deducible. As Thurstone has indicated, many problems of merchandising and of politics, in particular, may be illuminated by such fundamental principles of choices.

A System of the Psychophysical and Scaling Methods

Now that all the psychophysical and scaling methods have been described, it will be enlightening to take a look at an organized system of the methods. There are several ways of classifying the methods, one of which will be presented here. The chief basis of classification will be the objective of the investigator; whether, in his operations of measurement, he seeks to achieve the main properties of the four levels of measurement defined in Chap. 1. He may be interested in determining the equality or equivalence of stimuli, which is the main objective of the nominal scale. He may be concerned with the establishment of the rank order of stimuli or of classes of stimuli, which is the main objective of the ordinal scale. He may be aiming at the erection of a scale of equal units, thus to achieve an interval scale. Finally, he may want a scale of equal ratios, an absolute scale where zero means a genuine limit.

In achieving any of these objectives there are two general approaches. This fact provides us with the second main principle for classifying the methods. The first approach is through the use of direct observation. The judgments are made concerning the quantitative psychological property that we desire to measure. By inspection, two stimuli are observed to be equal or not equal. By inspection, stimuli are placed in complete rank order or in successive categories. By inspection, two intervals between pairs of stimuli are judged to be equal, or, if unequal, one is judged greater than the other. By inspection, ratios of stimuli can be evaluated and compared.

The second general approach does not stake everything on direct observation. The methods that come under this approach may be preferred because there is mistrust of the ability of observers to render the various types of judgments dependably. This approach stresses *probability* as a means of reaching the objectives of measurement. Stimulus S_k may be regarded as equal or equivalent to S_j if S_k is selected as equivalent more often than others. It is equated by using the mode or some other central-tendency statistic applied to a distribution of matchings. Two stimuli are also regarded as equivalent if one is judged greater than the other as often as it is judged less than the other. Rank orders are also established by the proportions of judgments. A stimulus judged greater than another more than 50 per cent of the time is given a higher value on the scale. Intervals between stimuli are regarded as equal if the pairs of stimuli spanning them are judged one greater than the other a certain proportion of the time. This is strictly true, of course, only when Thurstone's Case V prevails. When it does not, we can often make the necessary adjustments. Intervals, as such, can also be compared directly, and their differences can be derived from the proportion of judgments stating that one exceeds the other.

TABLE 10.17. A SYSTEM OF THE PSYCHOPHYSICAL AND SCALING METHODS

Main objective	Methods depending upon direct observation	Methods depending upon probabilities
Determination of equality (equivalence) of stimuli	Average error Minimal changes (equivalents)	Constant stimulus differences Pair comparisons
Determination of rank order	Rank order Successive categories Rating methods	Pair comparisons Unfolding
Determination of equality of intervals	Just noticeable differences Equal sense distances Equal-appearing intervals	Pair comparisons Rank order Triads Tetrads Successive categories Similar reactions Balanced values
Determination of ratios	Fractionation Multiple stimuli Constant sum	(Ratio comparison)*

* A method in the process of being tried out.

Table 10.17 presents an outline of the system of psychophysical and scaling methods constructed along the lines just proposed. The table should serve both an orientation and a summarizing purpose. Some methods appear more than once because they are used for different purposes and have different statistical operations applied to their results. The arrangement is also suggestive of gaps that the future will surely fill.

Problems

1. Scale the categories used in judgment of vegetables in obtaining Data 10*A*, basing your scaling on five similar distributions for vegetables: beets, broccoli, Brussels sprouts, cabbage, and cauliflower. Let zero coincide with category 4.

2. With the category values obtained in Prob. 1, compute means and standard deviations for the eight vegetables in Data 10*A*.

3. Plot the deviate values for the categories as obtained from three or more of the vegetables used for scaling, against the averaged scale values of the categories. Draw conclusions concerning normality of distributions.

4. Determine the limen values between categories using the same five stimuli as in Prob. 1, and set up a limen scale, with zero at the midpoint of category 4.

5. Determine the medians and Q values for the 10 stimuli on the limen scale derived in Prob. 4. Estimate standard deviations from the Q values.[1] Compare medians and standard deviations with means and standard deviations found in Prob. 2.

6. By linear-transformation methods described in this chapter, using regressions of z values for each stimulus on either the category scale or the limen scale, estimate the standard deviations and means for the eight stimuli.

7. Make a statistical test of the homogeneity of variances among the eight stimuli.

[1] From the relation in a normal distribution, $\sigma = 1.4826Q$.

DATA 10*A*. RELATIVE-FREQUENCY DISTRIBUTIONS FOR CATEGORICAL JUDGMENTS GIVEN BY 237 COLLEGE MEN REGARDING LIKING FOR 8 VEGETABLES

Vegetable	Category*								
	1	2	3	4	5	6	7	8	9
Beets	.131	.050	.097	.072	.156	.186	.122	.135	.051
Broccoli	.253	.089	.088	.106	.135	.122	.080	.064	.063
Brussels sprouts	.228	.139	.114	.089	.139	.110	.038	.075	.068
Cabbage	.148	.088	.148	.059	.181	.173	.076	.064	.063
Carrots	.017	.038	.050	.055	.068	.160	.139	.266	.207
Cauliflower	.207	.071	.060	.076	.172	.119	.110	.075	.110
Corn	.004	.013	.008	.008	.033	.059	.089	.295	.468
Turnips	.375	.177	.080	.110	.135	.042	.030	.025	.026

* The categories were defined as follows:

1. I would rather go without a vegetable than eat this.
2. I would accept this only if there were no other choice.
3. I don't like this but will eat it on occasion.
4. I neither like this vegetable nor do I dislike it.
5. I like this vegetable now and then.
6. I usually like this vegetable.
7. I like this more than I like most vegetables.
8. This is among the vegetables I like best.
9. This is one of my top favorites.

Answers

1. Categories 1 to 9 have the following C values: −1.63, −0.93, −0.65, 0.00, +0.30, +0.71, +1.06, +1.43, and +2.13.

2. Means of vegetables 1 to 8, respectively: +0.29, −0.11, −0.16, +0.06, +1.01, +0.15, +1.58, −0.64. Standard deviations: 1.11, 1.21, 1.20, 1.13, 0.93, 1.27, 0.71, and 1.06.

4. Upper category limits: 0.000, 0.286, 0.574, 0.783, 1.187, 1.599, 1.906, and 2.361. To place the zero at the midpoint of category 4, deduct 0.678 from each limit.

5. Medians of the stimuli: +0.49, +0.03, −0.06, +0.23, +1.17, +0.31, +1.66, −0.48. Estimated standard deviations: 0.93, (1.10), 0.96, 0.87, 0.77, 1.13, (0.57), (0.90). (Values in parentheses were estimated from one tail of the distribution only.)

6. From regressions on the limen scale:

σ_j: 0.87, 1.07, 1.09, 0.90, 0.87, 1.12, 0.97, 1.04.

M_j: +0.40, +0.04, −0.01, +0.23, +1.07, +0.53, +1.85, −0.49.

7. Chi square equals 68.4, well beyond the .01 point.

REFERENCES

1. ADAMS, H. F. An objectivity-subjectivity ratio for scales of measurement. *J. soc. Psychol.*, 1930, **1**, 122–130.
2. ATTNEAVE, F. A method of graded dichotomies for the scaling of judgments. *Psychol. Rev.*, 1949, **56**, 334–340.
3. ———. Dimensions of similarity. *Amer. J. Psychol.*, 1950, **63**, 516–556.
4. COOMBS, C. H. Psychological scaling without a unit of measurement. *Psychol. Rev.*, 1950, **57**, 145–158.
5. ———. *A Theory of Psychological Scaling.* Ann Arbor, Mich.: Engineering Research Institute, University of Michigan, 1952.

6. Dunlap, J. W. An abac for determining the mean deviation of a class from the general mean. *Psychometrika*, 1938, **3,** 41–44.
7. Edwards, A. L. The scaling of stimuli by the method of successive intervals. *J. appl. Psychol.*, 1952, **36,** 118–122.
8. ——— and Thurstone, L. L. An interval consistency check for the method of successive intervals and the method of graded dichotomies. *Psychometrika*, 1952, **17,** 169–180.
9. Garner, W. R., and Hake, H. W. The amount of information in absolute judgments. *Psychol. Rev.*, 1951, **58,** 446–459.
10. Guilford, J. P. An examination of a typical test of introversion-extroversion by means of the method of similar reactions. *J. soc. Psychol.*, 1933, **4,** 430–443.
11. ———. The computation of psychological values from judgments in absolute categories. *J. exp. Psychol.*, 1938, **22,** 32–42.
12. ——— and Holley, J. W. A factorial approach to the analysis of variances in esthetic judgments. *J. exp. Psychol.*, 1949, **39,** 208–218.
13. Hollingworth, H. L. *Experimental Studies in Judgment.* New York: Science Press, 1913.
14. Horst, P. A method for determining the absolute affective value of a series of stimulus situations. *J. educ. Psychol.*, 1932, **23,** 418–440.
15. Klingberg, F. L. Studies in measurement of the relations among sovereign states. *Psychometrika*, 1941, **6,** 335–352.
16. Leverett, H. M. Table of mean deviates for various portions of the unit normal distribution. *Psychometrika*, 1947, **12,** 141–152.
17. Likert, R. A technique for the measurement of attitudes. *Arch. Psychol. N.Y.*, 1932, **22,** No. 140.
18. Mosier, C. I. A modification of the method of successive intervals. *Psychometrika*, 1940, **5,** 101–107.
19. ———. A psychometric study of meaning. *J. soc. Psychol.*, 1941, **13,** 123–140.
20. Mosteller, F. Remarks on the method of paired comparisons: III. A test of significance for paired comparisons when equal standard deviations and equal correlations are assumed. *Psychometrika*, 1951, **16,** 207–218.
21. Richardson, M. W. Multidimensional psychophysics. *Psychol. Bull.*, 1938, **35,** 659.
22. Saffir, M. A. A comparative study of scales constructed by three psychophysical methods. *Psychometrika*, 1937, **2,** 179–198.
23. Snedecor, G. W. *Statistical Methods.* Ames, Iowa: Iowa State College Press, 1946.
24. Thurstone, L. L. Theory of attitude measurement. *Psychol. Rev.*, 1929, **36,** 222–241.
25. ———. Prediction of choices. *Psychometrika*, 1945, **4,** 237–253.
26. Torgerson, W. S. A theoretical and empirical investigation of multidimensional scaling. Princeton, N.J.: Educational Testing Service, 1951.
27. Urban, F. M. The Weber-Fechner law and mental measurement. *J. exp. Psychol.*, 1933, **16,** 221–236.
28. Wells, F. L. A statistical study of literary merit. *Arch. Psychol. N.Y.*, 1907, **1,** No. 7.
29. Young, G., and Householder, A. S. Discussion of a set of points in terms of their mutual distances. *Psychometrika*, 1938, **3,** 19–22.

CHAPTER 11

RATING SCALES

Of the psychological-measurement methods that depend upon human judgment, rating-scale procedures exceed them all for popularity and use. Although, generally speaking, rating methods belong logically under the heading of the method of successive intervals, their many forms and the many problems arising in their construction and use demand special treatment in a chapter. Their greatest popularity is in connection with the fields of applied psychology, but they also enjoy wide use in many types of basic research. They are used in the evaluation of individuals, their reactions, and their products, as well as in the psychological evaluation of stimuli. The great ease with which they can be administered gives them unusual appeal.

This chapter will attempt to give the rating methods a meaningful and appropriate place among psychometric methods, pointing out some of the measurement problems raised in connection with ratings. It will describe types of rating scales commonly in use, giving some attention to how they are constructed, their strong and weak points, and their variations. It will point out the many sources of error involved in ratings and what to do about some of them. It will mention some statistical difficulties and some of the special conditions that bear upon the use of ratings.

Forms of Rating Scales

The forms of rating scales in common use fall into five broad categories: *numerical*, *graphic*, *standard*, *cumulated points*, and *forced choice*. Any such classification must necessarily be a very loose one, based on shifting principles. The types are all alike in that they call for the assignment of objects by inspection, either along an unbroken continuum or in ordered categories along the continuum. They are alike in that the end result is the attachment of numbers to those assignments. They differ in the operations of placement of objects, in the kind and number of aids or cues, and in the fineness of discrimination demanded of the rater. They differ in other respects which will be brought out as each type and its variants are described.

Numerical Scales. In the typical numerical scale, a sequence of defined numbers is supplied to the observer. *O* assigns to each stimulus an appropriate number in line with these definitions or descriptions. One example of such a scale that the author has used in obtaining ratings of the affective values of colors and odors is as follows:

10 Most pleasant imaginable
9 Most pleasant
8 Extremely pleasant
7 Moderately pleasant

6 Mildly pleasant
5 Indifferent
4 Mildly unpleasant
3 Moderately unpleasant
2 Extremely unpleasant
1 Most unpleasant
0 Most unpleasant imaginable

Some "numerical" scales actually carry no numbers for *O* to use in making his judgments. *O* reports in terms of the descriptive cues and the experimenter assigns numbers to them. An example would be the following scale for judging weights:

Very heavy
Heavy
Medium
Light
Very light

To these cues the integers 1 through 5 are usually assigned. It is probable, however, that if the experimenter wants to achieve greater equality of psychological intervals between categories, he will do well to attach the numbers for *O* to use. If the data are to be scaled by procedures described in Chap. 10, this practice of having *O* assign the numbers is of little importance.

There are many problems connected with the construction of numerical scales, with their use, and with the errors and statistical issues involved, but for the most part these are held in common with other types of scales and will therefore be treated later. There are one or two issues that are rather unique to numerical scales that will be mentioned here.

The Use of Negative Numbers. An affective scale, such as was illustrated above, is a bipolar one. The continuum represents variations in the direction of two opposite extremes. For this reason some investigators place a zero at the indifference category and negative numbers below it. This may be a more natural scale to some *O*s who are versed in algebra but it may be unnatural, if not bewildering, to less sophisticated *O*s. Another danger is that it may tend to suggest a break in the scale and thus destroy what should be continuity. Having negative numbers with which to deal has its nuisance value for the investigator. For these reasons the use of negative rating numbers is not recommended.

Anchoring an Affective Scale. It might seem that the two end descriptions in the illustration of the affective scale given above would be useless; that no rater would make use of the end categories. In general, it is good policy not to describe terminal categories so extremely that no rater will utilize them. There are two reasons for including the terminal descriptions illustrated, however. One is that some *O*s do actually use them. In the course of their judging a series of stimuli they may come across one that is obviously more extreme than any they have placed in category 9 or category 1. If no more extreme category were available, they would be forced to judge this stimulus equal to others to which they know it is not equal. Thus the end categories, defined as they are, serve as extensions that are occasionally needed. The other reason is a more subtle one. Such terminal categories serve as "anchors" for the whole scale. Hunt and Volkmann (26) have demonstrated that the addition of such a category at either end serves to spread the entire distribution of ratings more in the direction of that category. Greater dispersion is thus achieved. There is a general tendency for *O*s to avoid terminal categories (and along with this to shift all judgments slightly toward the middle of the range) in any case. If categories 0 and 10 were not included, *O*s would tend to avoid categories 1 and 9 and thus to shorten the range of ratings. Thus if an investigator wants an effective scale of nine points, he must provide room to expand beyond those nine points or he may end up with something less than a nine-point scale.

Evaluation of Numerical Scales. Numerical scales are among the easiest to construct and to apply, and the simplest in terms of handling the results. if the rater takes his numbers seriously and if he can apply number properties directly to his observations of the rated phenomena, the ratings should themselves represent measurements of a high order. This is probably too much to assume of any rater, however, although Michels and Helson (35), from reasoning connected with their development of consequences of the adaptation-level concept, have supported the idea of interval and ratio properties of ratings, even when categories are not numbered. An empirical check upon the interval and ratio properties of ratings can be made by methods suggested in preceding chapters.

Numerical ratings are often rejected in favor of other types because it is believed that they are more vulnerable to many biases and errors. In fact, other types were devised for the purpose of overcoming some of those biases and consequent errors. It depends a great deal upon the kind of stimuli rated and the continuum in question. It is also possible that if as much attention were given to the construction of numerical scales as is given to the construction of other types, numerical scales would be found satisfactory in a great variety of situations.

Graphic Scales. The graphic type of rating scale is probably the most popular and the most widely used. It takes on numerous variations as to format, for there are many ways in which one can display a straight line and combine with it the various cues to aid the rater. The line can be segmented in units or it can be continuous. If segmented, the number of parts can be varied. It can be placed horizontally or vertically. Some examples of earlier formats follow:

The first is a self-rating form reproduced from Laird's Personal Inventory C2.

In social conversation how have you been?	___ ___ talkative	___ ___ an easy talker	___ ___ talked when necessary	___ ___ preferred listening	___ ___ refrained from talking

The second sample is a form very frequently employed:

Is he slow or quick thinking?

____

Extremely slow	Sluggish Plodding	Thinks with ordinary speed	Agile-minded	Exceedingly rapid

FELS PARENT BEHAVIOR RATING SCALE NO. 7.1. Solicitousness for Child's Welfare

Serial Sheet No. (Anxious—Nonchalant)

1	2	3	4	5	6	7	8	9	10	Number
										Period of observation
										Rater
										Age in months at end of period
										Child

Rate the parent's tendency to display overconcern for the child's well-being. Is the parent readily excited to overt anxiety all out of proportion to the importance of the situation? Or is the parent markedly calm, cool, and nonchalant, even in the face of critical danger to the child?

Consider the parent's net behavior, regardless of the motives behind it. Include only behavior which is a potential stimulus to the child, impinging more or less directly upon his awareness. Include concern for both physical and mental health and comfort.

– Given to severe, irrational anxiety on largely imaginary grounds. Readily panicked.

– Chronic anxious tension over child, but more "jittery" than panicky. Given to "hunting for trouble."

– Shows considerable anxiety when child is in any danger, but seldom loses rational control.

– Somewhat solicitous, but minimizes hazards. Frequently shows concern, but without losing perspective.

– Rarely worried or solicitous beyond needs of situation and responsibility as parent. Attitude more like that of teacher or nurse.

– Nonchalant and seemingly unconcerned even in major matters. So unsolicitous as to appear neglectful or irresponsible.

FIG. 11.1. A graphic rating form from the Fels Research Institute's *Parent Behavior Rating Scale*. (*Reproduced by permission of Dr. L. W. Sontag, Director, The Fels Research Institute.*)

The Fels Behavior Rating Scale. A relatively new form of graphic rating scale was designed by Champney (10) for the evaluation of aspects of a child's home environment. It is known as the Fels Behavior Rating Scale, a sample of which is reproduced in Fig. 11.1 for the trait of "Solicitousness for Child's Welfare." This scale has several novel features that could well be adopted in many graphic scales; in fact, some of them in nongraphic scales as well.

One of the striking features, in contrast to older forms, is that the rating lines are in the vertical direction. As Champney remarks (10, p. 139), "By some unhappy accident the graphic rating scale got started in the tradition of the yardstick rather than the thermometer." One of the difficulties with the horizontal line has been that there is room only for very short cues. Furthermore, a cue cannot be located at a point but must be spread along the line, and consequently its scale position is much in doubt. Both of these difficulties are overcome in the use of a vertical line. Cues may be long enough to be much more meaningful and they can be localized at points along the scale.

Another feature is that only one trait is rated on a page, with parallel lines for rating 10 objects on the same trait. It is commonly advised that a rater should rate all members of a group in one trait before going on to another trait, when this is possible. Yet few scales provide for this practice. This procedure is said to do much to counteract the well-known "halo effect." A more general benefit is that it calls for a comparison of individual objects in the same trait. Rank ordering can be brought into play to help locate each object properly. There are recognized administrative difficulties in applying scales in this parallel manner, but with ingenuity they can often be overcome.

Other good features of this form of scale will be mentioned in a later general discussion that applies to all types of scales. Still other features that apply to the graphic type will be mentioned in the following discussion of considerations in the construction of graphic scales.

General Practices in Connection with Graphic Scales. Experience has shown that certain rules are favorable to effective graphic ratings. Not all of these are very decisive, and on some there is contradictory opinion. Thus, perhaps, they should be regarded as issues rather than as rules.

1. Each trait should occupy a page by itself, or some other arrangement should be made so that a number of objects are rated in a trait before going on to the next trait.

2. The line should be at least 5 in. long, but not much longer. It should be long enough to allow for the finest discriminations that raters can give, keeping in mind the width of the raters' pencil marks. It should not be so long that the unity of the continuum is disrupted for the rater. Long lines also probably lead a rater to cluster his marks rather than to spread them continuously.

3. The line should have no breaks or divisions. On this there seems to be difference of opinion, for both kinds of lines, continuous and broken, are used. A continuous line emphasizes the continuity of the trait variable; a broken line may suggest discontinuity or qualitative categories which may tend to increase the degree of complexity of the variable. In scoring, a continuous line may be segmented into any number of units one wishes, and the divisions may be placed where one prefers. With divided lines the investigator is left very much with the divisions prearranged and with the way in which the rater has utilized them.

4. The "good" or "high" ends of the lines should be in the same direction. It has

often been urged that the "good" and "poor" ends of scales be alternated in a somewhat random fashion. The reason for this would be to help counteract a response set on the part of the rater to mark somewhat consistently toward one end of all lines, depending upon his tendencies of halo effect and leniency. The practice might be appreciably effective in controlling these errors. To the knowledge of the writer this has never been demonstrated. It has been the writer's experience, on the other hand, that the mixing of high and low quantities is very confusing, even to experienced raters, and that errors of marking happen often enough possibly to jeopardize the validity of the ratings. Clerical errors in scoring may also be induced by this practice. It is suggested that the constant errors of halo and leniency be controlled by other techniques and that the rule as stated at the beginning of this paragraph be followed.

5. For unsophisticated raters, the "good" end should be placed first. In vertical scales, having the "good" end at the top is natural for everybody. In horizontal scales, having the "good" end at the left violates the conventional order found in the mathematical coordinate system. In rating people, however, the ordinary rater likes to think of the good qualities first, as Bryan and Wilke (6) found in connection with the rating of speakers. Whether this practice favors the leniency error is not known. The good will of raters is a condition worth some attention, provided the price is not too high.

6. Descriptive phrases or cues should be concentrated as much as possible at points. This is very easy on vertical scales. With horizontal scales the use of fine print is helpful. Stacking the words up in a column is another device used.

7. The cues need not be equally spaced along the line; in fact, they should often not be. If the cues themselves have been psychologically scaled, their spacing is thereby determined. There are sometimes reasons for distortion in spacing in an effort to counteract common biases in ratings. To counteract the leniency error, the cues on the favorable side may be more widely spaced and more numerous than those on the unfavorable side. To counteract a tendency to bunch ratings too near the middle of the scale, the steps between cues near the middle may be somewhat enlarged.

8. Do not use end cues so extreme in meaning that they will never be applied. To do so discourages using the entire length of the line and favors the central-tendency error.

9. Set the end cues at a little distance from the ends of the line. This is to allow room for needed expansion, should the need arise, as it frequently does. Try to anticipate how much room will be needed so that the entire line will be used at some time.

10. In the case of bipolar traits, the neutral or indifferent cue is ordinarily at the center of the line, but this may often be modified, as indicated by rule 7, for example.

11. In scoring, use a stencil that divides each line into sections to which numerical values are assigned. The divisions need not be equal; they may be altered to help counteract systematic biases in ratings or to normalize distributions of scores. With continuous rating lines the number of steps can be adapted to suit one's wishes. The question of the optimal number of scoring steps will be discussed later.

12. With segmented lines for rating, do not call for any finer discriminations than will be used in scoring.

Evaluation of Graphic Scales. The virtues of graphic rating scales are many; their faults are relatively few. Among the advantages frequently cited in their favor are the facts that they are simple and easily administered; they are interesting and require little added motivation; they are quickly filled out; and they do not require the rater to bother with numbers. These features the rater finds attractive. From the point of view of the investigator, the graphic scale provides opportunity for as fine discrimination as that of which the rater is capable and the fineness of scoring can be as great as desired. As for disadvantages, there are none that do not apply to most other types of scales, except for somewhat greater labor of scoring in connection with some formats.

Standard Scales. The rating scales that come in this category are distinguished by the fact that they present to the rater a set of standards. The standards are more than ordinary cues and are usually objects of the same kind to be rated, with preestablished scale values. In its best form, this type is like the scales for judging the quality of handwriting. These scales provide several standard specimens that have previously been calibrated on a common scale of excellence by some scaling method such as equal-appearing intervals or pair comparison. With the set of standards at hand, a new sample of handwriting can be readily equated to one of the standards or judged as being between two standards. Other rating-scale forms that conform more or less to this principle are the *man-to-man* scale and the *portrait-matching* scale.

The Man-to-man Scale. The man-to-man scale is now mainly of historical interest only. It was developed for use in connection with military personnel and has seen little use elsewhere. The procedure for development of such a scale is probably worth keeping in the record, however; therefore a very brief description will be given here. It is possible that with ingenious improvements it could still be very useful in certain situations.

As applied to military purposes, five qualities were selected for rating. Each superior officer was asked to write down the names of 12 to 25 officers whom he knew very well. He was then asked to arrange them in rank order for each one of the five traits. The highest man in each ranked list was then chosen to represent the top position in that scale and the lowest in rank to represent the lowest point on the scale. The middle man occupied the third point on the scale, and two men midway between the extremes and the median were chosen for the second and fourth positions.[1] The scale with its five landmarks was then complete, and *O* could place any officer who came up for his judgment on the scale by merely comparing him with the five key men already selected. A certain officer's "yardstick" for leadership might look as follows:

Leadership: Initiative, force, self-reliance, decisiveness, tact, ability to inspire men and to command their obedience, loyalty, and cooperation.

Highest	Captain Spence	15
High	Lieutenant Moore	12
Middle	Captain Travers	9
Low	Lieutenant Johns	6
Lowest	Lieutenant Conrad	3

The advantages that have been claimed for the man-to-man scale are three:

1. It gets away from the mere assignment of abstract numbers to an individual's traits.
2. A rather permanent "yardstick" is set up. *O*'s standards will therefore not shift from day to day.
3. If all judges use the same men in their "yardsticks," the ratings of different judges will be comparable in absolute as well as in relative amounts.

[1] Note that this procedure aims at an ordinal scale only.

Disadvantages often pointed out are:

1. In practice, two raters' scales are rarely exactly alike, even if they know the same men.
2. The distances between men on the scale are probably not equal.
3. Willful overestimation and underestimation of an individual are still possible when the scale is used.
4. The original scales are very difficult to make, and the student of psychophysical method will see that they are very crudely made. Better psychometric methods could, of course, be used.

Portrait Matching. A portrait-matching technique was developed by Hartshorne and May (22) in connection with their studies of character. In constructing a set of standards (verbal portraits) for the selected trait of helpfulness, several steps were taken. First, a large number of statements were collected concerning manifestations of helpfulness. Each statement was written on a separate card, and the cards were placed in rank order by seven judges. Ten sketches were made up, each from statements of about the same average rank. The ten sketches or portraits were rank ordered by 48 observers, from which scale values were derived for them. An example of a portrait with a scale value of 7 follows:

B is always thoughtful for others around him and sees many opportunities for little kindly acts without waiting to be asked. On occasion he would take risks to help anyone in danger, and he always makes his own convenience and pride a secondary consideration. He is not greatly interested, however, in remote needs unless they are serious and appealing.

In using the portraits, the rater reads a certain sketch and then names all the individuals to whom it seems to apply. The same individual may be named in connection with more than one portrait. The individual's final rating is the mean of all the portrait values that have been applied to him from all raters. The portrait standards can also be applied in the usual manner, that is, given this individual, which portrait most clearly applies to him.

In the portrait-matching technique we depart from a strict scale-of-standards type of rating, since the "standards" are not objects of the kind to be rated but are merely standardized and calibrated descriptions. This is one example of the looseness of the categories of classification of rating methods. Certain rating forms in the group to follow have features in common with the portrait-matching technique, for example, the guess-who technique. The unique features of the present category—standards scales—are first, the use of calibrated standards, and second, the use of the standard values as the basis for scoring.

Evaluation of the Standards-scale Procedures. Much of what was said in evaluation of the man-to-man scale also applies to the portrait-matching technique. The development of a scale of standards is something of a task. The portrait-matching process avoids the charge of subjectivity that applies to the man-to-man procedure, but it does not provide realistic standards in the form of objects. Granted a good set of objective standards that have wide application, as in the case of handwriting scales, the standards-scale approach to measurement has considerable merit.

Rating by Cumulated Points. The unique, common feature of the next group of rating procedures is in the method of scoring. The score for an object or individual is the sum or average of a number of points, weighted or unweighted. In this respect there is a resemblance to psychological tests composed of items, but there the resemblance ends, for the derivation of points is from human judgments.

The Check-list Method. Typical of this type of rating procedure is the check list. Hartshorne and May (22) used a check list as a basis for evaluating children with respect to character. A list of favorable and unfavorable personal qualities was drawn up and 80 trait names were selected. Examples are:

Cooperative	Stingy
Cruel	Obliging
Thoughtful	Inconsiderate
Unselfish	Callous
A shirker	Humane
Charitable	Greedy

Each rater checked every term in the list that he thought applied to a child. The child's score was the algebraic sum of the weights, +1 for every favorable trait applied and −1 for every unfavorable trait.

Check-list methods are conveniently applicable to the evaluation of the performance of personnel in a job assignment. Where the job is a complex activity involving a large number of minor subgoals or routine operations that can be separately scored, the cumulation of points for successes is a natural approach to quantification. Where based on actual observation, rather than on memory or general impression, and where success or failure is readily distinguishable, the procedure becomes one of testing rather than rating.

The check-list items may be in multiple-choice form rather than what is essentially true-false form as already described. Items like the following have been used to describe the performance of personnel in their work assignments:

Cooperates with others	His relations with the public are	His volume of work output is
__ enthusiastically	__ outstanding	__ great
__ willingly	__ creditable	__ more than average
__ indifferently	__ acceptable	__ average
__ grudgingly	__ poor	__ less than average
__ defiantly	__ detrimental	__ not acceptable

With a large number of such items simple weights of +1, 0, and −1 would probably suffice. With a limited number of items more variation in weights would be desirable. In either case, what weights should be attached to each response could be determined empirically after study of frequency distributions for the responses to each item and also their correlations with some criterion. In this form, the rating procedure is strongly reminiscent of personality inventories, the main difference being that the items are answered by another person.

The Guess-who Technique. The guess-who method of rating was designed also by Hartshorne and May, for use particularly with child raters (22). For this purpose, short portraits each composed of only one or two statements were constructed. Two examples are:

> Here is one who is always picking on others and annoying them.
> Here is one who is always doing little things to make others happy.

Each child was told to list all his classmates who fitted each description, mentioning the same child as many times as necessary. It would be possible to calibrate these short portraits in the same manner as in the portrait-matching procedure and to score by averaging the scale values of the descriptions applied to each child. The Hartshorne and May procedure did not include this scaling step, however. It simply treated each description as being favorable or unfavorable and each favorable description applied to a child earned a point for him toward a total score.

This is perhaps a good place to raise a question that pertains to both the portrait-matching and the guess-who technique. Both have been applied with the instruction for the rater to find the individual to match the description, which is in contrast to the usual instruction to find the description or trait to match the individual. If the first of these two instructions is used, the investigator should by all means supply the rater with the names of all those being rated, any one of whom could be matched to the description, and those names should be prominently at hand. He should not let the rater depend upon his memory of the individuals and their names. There is the more pertinent question, involving the psychology of judgment, whether finding individuals to match a trait is a better metric procedure than finding traits to match an individual. The problem may be worth investigation.

The Use of Scaled Check-list Items. A number of investigators have proposed that check-list items be scaled and that their scale values enter into the scoring of rated individuals (17, 30). Uhrbrock has published a list of 724 statements often made concerning employees, with their scale values and measures of dispersion, from which could be selected lists of appropriate length and content to serve as check-list rating instruments (58). Some examples of his statements are:[1]

Statement	Scale Value	Variance
Is outstanding in every way	10.6	1.05
Has real creative ability	9.6	1.34
Is very energetic	8.5	1.95
Has a pleasing personality	8.0	3.60
Is nearly always well prepared	7.0	2.15
Is a good routine worker	6.0	1.25
Usually lets other people do the talking	5.0	.95
Is always asking for advice	4.0	1.00
Is conceited	3.2	1.36
Aims just to "get by"	2.6	1.95
Is inclined to make trouble	2.0	1.35
Is a complete failure	1.0	.01

[1] Reproduced from *Person. J.* by permission of the editor.

These statements were scaled by the method of equal-appearing intervals with judgments of 20 foremen. There is no pretense that these statements and the larger list from which they came represent a single psychological continuum. They were scaled under the common instruction "If this statement were made about a person, how good do you think the person would be as a *foreman* in this Company?"

Used in a check-list rating device, such statements could be weighted +1 if favorable and applied to the ratee and weighted −1 if unfavorable and applied. But having gone to the trouble of scaling the statements one would like to make use of the information thus provided to improve accuracy of measurement. Some investigators have recommended that the score of a ratee should be the median value of all the statements checked as applying to him. This mode of scoring is consistent with that for attitude scales, which were the model for this type of rating instrument. But, as Jurgenson (27) has pointed out, there is a fallacy in this procedure. It works well with attitude scales whose statements are homogeneous as to content, and also presumably homogeneous in reference to a uniform psychological continuum. When few statements pertain to the same dimension, as in the list quoted from Uhrbrock, the use of a median of scale values may lead to gross errors.

When statements are relatively homogeneous, as in attitude scales, the ones checked for a ratee are usually bunched in some narrow range about the measure of central tendency. In the list quoted above, however, it is quite possible to check items on both sides of the neutral point for the same person. Thus, the same person could be described as "has real creative ability," "lets other people do the talking," and "is inclined to make trouble." For all such people the medians would tend to be near the middle scale value. One might expect a distribution of scores for a large sample of individuals to regress drastically toward the middle value. Of those individuals who obtain only favorable descriptions, the one who received only a few checks among the very top values would have the highest median. Others with a greater variety of virtues would have lower medians, as Jurgenson has pointed out (27). A suggestion will be made later for a scoring method that avoids this error.

Evaluation of Check-list Ratings. Check-list instruments are relatively new and would seem to be growing in favor. Their simplicity of administration is one of their strongest points. In terms of quantitative judgment they require the minimum discrimination on the part of raters. One might say that for each item the rater has only a two-step scale. Only cases near the rater's limen should be difficult for him to judge. Scoring is also very easy, at least where items are weighted merely +1 and 0. The chief application is to very complex variables, such as the value of an employee to his organization, and in this connection it is possible by the check-list approach to cover a large area of traits in a short time. The check-list type of instrument can be adapted to the assessment of a unique variable such as a single trait of personality. In this use it becomes essentially a personality inventory answered for another person. When the items are of specific actions that are observed by the rater, the check list becomes essentially an achievement or proficiency test and its score has the status that would be accorded to that type of measurement.

There are a number of faults in the check-list method, but many of them are easily remedied. The procedure of asking the rater merely to check the items or statements that apply is wide open to various kinds of response biases. It would be much better to require the rater to make a response to every item. He checks it one way if the item applies and another way if it does not. Since there is often resistance to this forced-choice type of item, it is probably best to allow the use of a "doubtful" or "don't-know" category of response, urging that it be used very sparingly. This will not remove all response biases, but it will help to avoid a large "does-not-apply" category of response which has many different meanings.

Requiring one of two, or three, responses to every statement will also help to solve the scoring problem. Every response should have a weight.[1] If the response is favorable (and this includes the response "No" to an unfavorable quality as well as a response "Yes" to a favorable quality), it should have a weight greater than some neutral value. If the response is unfavorable (including the response "No" to a favorable quality), it should be given a weight less than the same neutral value. It is better to derive differential weights empirically by correlating each response to each statement with some suitable criterion. The weight for a "doubtful" response could be determined empirically also. On an a priori basis it could be weighted either midway between the other responses or the same as the unfavorable response, or somewhere between. See Chap. 15 for item-weighting methods.

Forced-choice Ratings. The forced-choice technique was developed in recent years primarily for the purpose of rating personnel. The rater is asked, not to say whether the ratee has a certain trait or to say how much of a trait the ratee has but to say essentially whether he has more of one trait than another of a pair. One of the members of the pair is valid for predicting some total quality and the other is not, both appearing about equally favorable to most people, or about equally unfavorable. According to Travers (55) the basic idea originated with Horst and was put into practice by Wherry, first in the form of a personality inventory and later in the form of a rating instrument.

Like the man-to-man rating form, the forced-choice rating device was introduced to meet problems arising in the evaluation of Army officers. The efficiency reports in use for this purpose for many years were most striking examples of the leniency error. Distributions were very skewed negatively, with about half the officers often being rated in the top category, "superior" (47). This made for good discrimination of very small proportions of worst officers at the lower extreme but gave no basis for discriminating small proportions of the best. The forced-choice method was invoked to meet this situation.

Construction of a Forced-choice Rating Instrument. Several well-recognized steps are followed in the development of a set of items for a forced-choice rating instrument. Briefly, they are:[2]

[1] This includes weights limited to 0 and 1.

[2] The steps are described in detail by Sisson (47).

1. Descriptions are obtained concerning persons who are recognized as being at the highest and lowest extremes of the performance continuum for the particular group to be rated.

2. Descriptions are analyzed into simple behavior qualities, stated in very short sentences or phrases or by trait names, which may be called elements. Elements are used to construct items.

3. Two values are determined empirically for each element; a *discrimination value* and a *preference value*. The discrimination value is an index of validity[1] and the preference value is an index of the degree to which the quality is valued by people like the raters who will use the instrument.

4. In forming an item, elements are paired. Two statements or terms with about the same high preference value are paired, one of which is valid and the other not. Both should have "face validity" for the rater, *i.e.*, the rater should think that they are both favorable for superior performance in the group rated. Two statements or terms with about equally low preference value are also paired, one being valid and the other not.

5. Two pairs of statements, one pair with high preference value and one with low preference value, are combined in a tetrad to form an item. The reason for this kind of combination is that although the average rater will not object to picking one of two favorable descriptions for a person whom he knows, he sometimes balks at picking one of two unfavorable descriptions. Sometimes a fifth, neutral, description is added to form a pentad, but this is less common. An example of a tetrad follows:

__ careless
__ serious-minded
__ energetic
__ snobbish

The traits "serious-minded" and "energetic" would have been found to have equal preference value because they were applied about equally often as favorable traits in describing the type of personnel for whom the scale was developed. The trait "serious-minded," however, was found to be valid, since it was applied to the high criterion group significantly more often than to the low criterion group. The traits "careless" and "snobbish" were found equally unpopular but "careless" discriminates the low from the high criterion group.

6. The instruction to the rater is prepared. The rater is to react to each tetrad as an item, saying which one of the four best fits the ratee and which one of the four is least appropriate.

7. An experimental form of the instrument is tried out in a sample for which there is an outside criterion, for the purpose of validating the responses when the descriptions are set up in this form. Discriminating responses are determined, and, if desired, differential weights are assigned.

8. A scoring key is devised, based on the results in step 7. Ordinarily, a valid, favorable trait marked as most descriptive of the ratee receives a positive weight, also a valid, unfavorable trait judged as least descriptive.

Theory of the Forced-choice Technique. It is supposed that the rater's general tendency to rate too high or too low and his halo tendencies will be counteracted by pairing of descriptions as noted above. It is supposed that irrelevant descriptions serve as "suppressor variables" that will operate to depress the rater's personal biases. This can best be explained by saying that if the rater is dominated by a desire to make the ratee look good and to avoid making him look bad, in using an ordinary check-list device he could

[1] As determined by an item-analysis procedure (see Chap. 15).

check a large number of favorable traits and avoid checking unfavorable ones, thus piling up a good-looking score. In the forced-choice device, however, it is thought that under the same kind of set the rater is likely to mark the irrelevant traits as often as the relevant ones, since he presumably has no inkling as to which favorable and unfavorable traits receive weights toward the score. Choosing irrelevant traits adds nothing toward the score, which is equivalent to depressing the score, and hence the "suppression" feature.

The irrelevant descriptions will operate in this fashion if on the whole they average as high as the relevant descriptions in apparent validity and if the ratees have average equal status in the irrelevant qualities. These two assumptions should not be overlooked. If the rater who wants to mark only favorable traits knows nothing concerning validity of the elements, he is in the position of the heavy guesser in a true-false test. His scores will be heavily weighted with chance and hence are unreliable.

Preferred Item Forms with Forced Choices. Highland and Berkshire (23) have made an extensive study of forced-choice rating forms in connection with rating instructors. Six different kinds of items were tried out:

Form A. Two statements per item, both favorable or both unfavorable; rater selects more (less) descriptive statement.

Form B. Three statements per item, all favorable or all unfavorable; rater selects the most and least descriptive statements.

Form C. Four statements, all favorable; rater selects two most descriptive statements.

Form D. Four statements, all favorable; rater selects the most descriptive and the least descriptive.

Form E. Four statements, two favorable and two unfavorable; rater selects the most and least descriptive.

Form F. Five statements, two favorable, two unfavorable, one neutral; rater selects most and least descriptive.

The Highland-Berkshire study included results on odd-even reliability of scores; validity against a criterion of rank ordering of the instructors; susceptibility of scores to biasing (with raters told to assure ratees high scores); and popularity of the rating form from the point of view of raters. The findings showed that forms E and F yielded some of the highest coefficients of reliability. Forms C and D tended to give the highest validity coefficients. Forms C and B showed the least tendency to bias. Forms C and A were most popular with the raters and forms B and D were least popular. Everything considered, form C was regarded as best.

Evaluation of the Forced-choice Technique. When the new Army officer-rating form was used in comparison with the old form, it was claimed that the new form[1] was superior in several respects (3, 47). The scores were less correlated with the military ranks of the officers rated. The rater knows the rank of the officer he rates, and it was supposed that this knowledge greatly influenced scores on the old form. Discriminations were found to be somewhat better at both ends of the distribution for the new form. The distribution of scores for the new form was leptokurtic, which means greater extension of ratings in the tails but poorer discrimination in some central part of the

[1] Only two of several parts of the new form were actually of the forced-choice type.

range. The distribution was reported to be less skewed, but there was decidedly less change in this respect than one would have the right to expect. It was also reported (3, 47) that the new form gave more valid scores against a performance criterion in new samples. Taylor and Wherry (53) report that in a study comparing graphic ratings with forced-choice ratings the leniency error seemed reduced in the latter. This conclusion was based upon the fact that mean scores increased more for graphic ratings in going from a situation in which raters knew that the results were to be used only for experimental purposes to a situation in which raters knew that the ratings affected the ratee's records. It was also found, however, that graphic ratings made after the rater had made forced-choice ratings tended to shift downward in making the same change of situation.

There has been some criticism of the forced-choice technique. It is recognized that the research work involved in constructing a scale of this type is considerable and that each device must be constructed for a particular purpose for use in a particular population. Even so, if it can be demonstrated that the expected benefits follow, the price may not be too great. As yet, the demonstrated gains have been unspectacular and we do not know whether when the novelty of the new form wears off raters will again drift back into undesired habits shown with older rating forms. The naming of the technique may be unfortunate from the public-relations point of view. Even though the forcing is tempered by the use of the tetrad and pentad types of items and is therefore comparable with items in any multiple-choice test, many raters do not like to be told that they are being forced. The name of the technique can, of course, be withheld. It could readily be changed.

It is not certain that the forced choice overcomes the biases it was supposed to correct. Astute raters can probably decide which of some pairs of matched descriptions are actually more relevant or valid. Highland and Berkshire (23) found that when raters were instructed to make a ratee look good, averages of scores increased from one-half to three-quarters of a standard deviation. No studies have been made to show how many of the relevant traits average raters can detect. Proponents of the method do not claim complete disguise of items and complete control of personal biases, but they do claim reduction in consequent errors (3).

From the standpoint of measurement theory the forced-choice technique poses an interesting problem. The irrelevant descriptions pertain to traits of personality as well as the relevant ones. The judgment of the rater gives a partial rank ordering of four traits *within the individual.* The scores that are to be derived from such judgments are to represent differences *between individuals.* Evaluations of traits within a person are a form of measurement that Cattell has called "ipsative" measurement (9). Measurements expressed in terms of individual differences are "normative" measurements. The question to be asked here concerning the forced-choice technique is to what extent the ipsative properties of the judgments are carried over into the scoring of individuals. The leptokurtic distribution of scores might be a consequence of this very thing.[1] To a large extent the item analysis based

[1] The possibility of a large element of guessing on the part of the rater, mentioned above, may also be responsible.

on the tetrad items should do much to bridge the gap to normative measurement. It is questionable whether this bridge is completely successful.

Problems in Rating-scale Construction and Use

Constant Errors and Their Control. The use of ratings rests on the assumption that the human observer is a good instrument of quantitative observation, that he is capable of some degree of precision and some degree of objectivity. His ratings are taken to mean something accurate about certain aspects of the object rated. While forced to have much confidence in quantitative human judgments, we must be ever alert to the weaknesses involved and to the many sources of personal biases in those judgments. From time to time in preceding paragraphs reference has been made to such well-known errors in ratings as the *error of leniency*, the *error of central tendency*, and the *halo effect*. We will now examine these concepts more closely and consider some other sources of bias.

The Error of Leniency. This error was named from the very obvious fact that raters tend to rate those whom they know well, or in whom they are ego-involved, higher than they should. This is presumably a constant tendency regardless of trait. Some raters, to be sure, are aware of this failing and they may consequently "lean over backwards" and as a result rate individuals lower than they should. It would be best to recognize a general type of error which would include those individuals who can justifiably be called "easy raters," and on the other hand those individuals who for some reason can be called "hard raters." In other words, the preference here is to use the term "leniency error" to apply to a general, constant tendency for a rater to rate too high or too low for whatever reasons. When rating is too low, the constant error is one of negative leniency.

Since a positive leniency error is by far the most common one, some investigators take steps to anticipate it and to arrange scales to help counteract it, as in the following sample:

Physical health:

poor	fair	good	very good	excellent

Only one unfavorable descriptive term is given and most of the range is given to degrees of favorable report. The investigator evidently anticipates a mean rating somewhere near the cue "good" and a distribution symmetrical about that point.

The Error of Central Tendency. One of the reasons for the error of central tendency is that raters hesitate to give extreme judgments and thus tend to displace individuals in the direction of the mean of the total group. This is perhaps more common in rating individuals whom the raters do not know very well. It is for this reason that a recommendation was made earlier in connection with graphic scales that the intermediate descriptive phrases be spaced farther apart. In a similar manner in the numerical type of scale, the strength of the descriptive adjectives may be adjusted so as to counteract the error of central tendency. Greater differences in meaning may be introduced between steps near the ends of the scale than between steps near the center.

The Halo Effect. A constant error to which every judge falls victim is called the halo effect. First mentioned by Wells (60), the error was given its name by Thorndike (54). In the words of Rugg (42, p. 37), "We judge our fellows in terms of a general mental attitude toward them; and there is, dominating this mental attitude toward the personality as a whole, a like mental attitude toward particular qualities."

One result of the halo effect is to force the rating of any trait in the direction of the general impression of the individuals rated and to that extent to make the ratings of some traits less valid. Another result is to introduce a spurious amount of positive correlation between the traits that are rated. Because of this fact, ratings in which the halo effect has not been in some way canceled out or held constant should never be used in an attempt to find the intercorrelation of traits. The halo effect is not unlike the stimulus error of psychophysics. It involves irrelevant criteria with which judgments are contaminated. Perhaps it can never be fully avoided, but experience has shown us where it is most likely to be found, and we can therefore know where to suspect its influence and where to avoid it. According to Symonds (51) it is more prevalent:

1. In a trait that is not easily observable.
2. In a trait that is not frequently singled out or discussed.
3. In a trait not clearly defined.
4. In a trait involving reactions with other people.
5. In a trait of high moral importance. This involves the so-called traits of character.

Certain devices that have been used to help counteract the halo effect have already been mentioned. They include the practice of rating one trait at a time on all ratees, facilitated by having one trait per page rather than one ratee per page, and the practice of the forced-choice technique. Other remedies will be mentioned later.

A Logical Error in Rating. Newcomb (38) has pointed out an error in rating whose effect is not unlike the halo effect. This error is due to the fact that judges are likely to give similar ratings for traits that seem logically related in the minds of the raters. We may therefore call it a *logical error.* When several raters estimated the proneness of each of 30 boys to certain *types* of behavior, the intercorrelations of the traits averaged .493. When objective records were kept by these same raters, based upon observed behavior, the intercorrelations averaged only .141. The difference is attributed to "logical presuppositions in the minds of the raters" (38, p. 289). Like the halo effect, this error increases the intercorrelation of traits, but for a different reason. In the halo effect it is the apparent coherence of qualities in the same individual, whereas in the logical error it is the apparent logical coherence of various traits irrespective of individuals. The latter error can be avoided in part by calling for judgments of objectively observable actions rather than abstract, and hence semantically overlapping, traits.

A Contrast Error. Murray has pointed out a kind of bias which yields what he called a contrast error (37). By this he means a tendency for a rater to rate others in the opposite direction from himself in a trait. This showed up particularly in connection with the trait of "need for orderliness." Raters who themselves were high in orderliness tended to see others as being less orderly than they were, and raters low in orderliness tended to see others as being more orderly than they were, as indicated by excesses of low and high ratings. The phenomena of reaction formation and of projection, pointed out by the psychoanalysts, would lead one to expect such attitudes toward some traits.

There is good logical reason to expect the opposite kind of bias in the case of some traits and to expect other kinds of attitudes toward those traits. For example, a person who is exceptionally cooperative might let his tolerance blind him to evidences of uncooperativeness in others. There is also a common human tendency to expect others to be like ourselves and to be surprised at times to find they are different. It is proposed here that there should be recognized a more general class of errors involving the rater's attitudes toward specific traits. Sometimes the bias is one of contrast but sometimes it may be the opposite.

A Proximity Error. A new kind of rating error, apparently little suspected, has been discovered by Stockford and Bissell (49). Like the logical error and the contrast error, it injects undue covariances among rated trait variables. The reason for this source of spurious correlation is the nearness in space or in time for the rating of two traits. Adjacent traits on a rating form tend to intercorrelate higher than remote ones, their degrees of actual similarity being presumably equal. Stockford and Bissell found the average intercorrelation of adjacent traits to be .66. With increasing degrees of remoteness the average intercorrelations systematically dropped until with five or more intervening traits the average intercorrelation was .46. When the order of the traits was rearranged in random fashion and new ratings obtained, the same general results were found under the new arrangement.

This error is another reason for not placing very much faith in intercorrelations of ratings as information concerning intercorrelations of traits. The error might be counteracted to some extent by placing similar traits farther apart and the more obviously disparate ones closer together. Even better would be the practice of rating one trait at a time, separating traits by greater time intervals.

Minimizing Errors by Training Raters. Various experiences with ratings tend to show that the most effective method for improving ratings in many ways is to train raters carefully. This also applies to the counteracting of constant errors. The rater who knows about the existence of the different kinds of errors can be on the lookout for them and can take steps to counteract them. Training that includes practice followed by group discussions seems to be most effective.

A Rationale for Errors of Rating. The problems of rating biases and their effects upon ratings will become clearer if we envisage them in terms of mathematical and statistical forms. Let us make the following definitions and assumptions:

X_{ijk} = a rating of person I in trait J by rater K

X_{ijt} = the "true" value of person I in trait J

X_{ijke} = the total error in rating X_{ijk}

Let us assume the simple, summative equation

$$X_{ijk} = X_{ijt} + X_{ijke} \tag{11.1}$$

We thus have an obtained rating expressed as a linear combination of two major components.

The total error X_{ijke} can be further broken down into components which it is simplest to assume are independent, additive contributions. Some of these components can be identified as follows:

X_{kl} = rater K's "leniency" error, defined as broadly as above, *i.e.*, it is his tendency to overvalue or to undervalue ratees in general

X_{ki} = rater K's "halo" error in connection with person I; his general tendency to overvalue or undervalue ratee I for any reason. We may regard this as a contribution to interaction variance—interaction between rater and ratee

X_{kj} = rater's rater-trait interaction error; this component represents K's general tendency to overvalue or undervalue a certain trait in others. The "contrast" error is one example of it

X_{ijkr} = a residual error made by rater K in rating person I. It includes everything in X_{ijke} not identified otherwise

We may now state an equation giving the total error as a simple summation of the identified components:

$$X_{ijke} = X_{kl} + X_{ki} + X_{kj} + X_{ijkr} \tag{11.2}$$

We may also restate equation (11.1) in expanded form:

$$X_{ijk} = X_{ijt} + X_{kl} + X_{ki} + X_{kj} + X_{ijkr} \tag{11.3}$$

It will be noticed that this equation does not express all the kinds of errors that have been mentioned. The error of central tendency is one of those not represented. One reason is that the errors included in the equation are simple increments, positive and negative, while the central-tendency effect is not simply such an increment. It is likely that the error of central tendency can be largely accounted for in terms of X_{ijkr}. The logical and proximity errors are not included because they, too, are not in the form of simple increments. Their main effects are to inflate correlations between ratings of traits, not to produce constant errors that can be segregated simply in a summative equation.

The Estimation of Error Contributions to Ratings. It will be demonstrated next that it is possible within the context of a single rating situation to estimate the amount of each kind of constant error in equation (11.2) and to eliminate it from the ratings obtained in the given situation. The errors so identified and so eliminated are relative to the particular rating situation. We shall therefore refer to the errors as X'_{kl}, X'_{ki}, and X'_{kj} in the special context. The equation will read:

$$X_{ijk} = X'_{ijt} + X'_{kl} + X'_{ki} + X'_{kj} + X'_{ijkr} \tag{11.4}$$

where the "true" value is also relative to the limited context.

As a simple illustration, consider the ratings of Table 11.1. The ratees were seven scientists in a research organization who were rated on eight traits having to do with creative performance.[1] Five of the traits are included in this illustration. The three raters were senior scientists in the same group who knew their fellows best. We have in Table 11.1 the data for

TABLE 11.1. RATINGS OF SEVEN INDIVIDUALS IN FIVE TRAITS, AS GIVEN BY THREE RATERS

Rater / Ratee	Trait *A*			Trait *B*			Trait *C*			Trait *D*			Trait *E*		
	α	β	γ	α	β	γ	α	β	γ	α	β	γ	α	β	γ
1	5	6	5	5	5	5	3	4	5	5	6	7	3	3	3
2	9	8	7	7	7	7	5	5	5	8	7	7	5	2	5
3	3	4	3	3	5	5	3	3	5	7	6	5	1	6	5
4	7	5	5	3	6	3	1	4	3	3	5	3	3	5	1
5	9	2	9	7	4	7	7	3	7	8	2	7	5	3	7
6	3	4	3	5	4	3	3	6	3	5	4	5	1	2	3
7	7	3	7	7	3	7	5	5	7	5	5	5	5	4	7

a three-way factorial design without replications. Variations are over rater, trait, and ratee.

In Table 11.2 we have the summaries of three analysis-of-variance solutions treating the data of Table 11.1 as two-way factorial designs. In the three solutions we have ratings treated as replications across individuals, traits, and raters, respectively. The F ratios indicate that differences between traits are significant beyond the .05 point in one solution and beyond the .01 point in the other; differences between individuals are significant beyond the .01 point in both solutions in which these were tested; but differences between raters are not significant. Differences between raters would indicate variations from rater to rater in relative leniency errors. Of the simple interaction variances, that between rater and trait was insignificant; that between rater and individual was significant beyond the .01 point; and that between individual and trait was insignificant. There is no way of testing for significance of the triple interaction, of rater with trait with individual, since there are no replications within such combinations and hence no way of estimating residual or error variance. Using the triple interaction variance as an estimate of error variance, the same conclusions as given above were obtained with respect to simple differences and interactions. We may therefore conclude that of the errors represented in equation (11.2) only the relative halo effect is statistically significant.

We will next be concerned with the attempt to estimate the amounts of each kind of constant error X'_{kl}, X'_{ki}, and X'_{kj} of the kinds defined in equation (11.4). If we can deduct the three sources of error variation, we should have left $X'_{ijt} + X'_{ijkr}$. The variance remaining in such values would be made up to a larger degree of the true-value contribution. Since reliability of measures is defined as the proportion of true variance in them, the ratings

[1] The data were incidental to a project on aptitudes of high-level personnel which was supported financially by the Office of Naval Research under contract N6onr-23810.

should then be more reliable and their possibility of correlating with other measures should be increased. Hence there would be also the possibility of increased validity.

If we were interested in ratings as estimates of population values, we would not attempt to estimate the contributions to error that prove to be

TABLE 11.2. SUMMARY OF ANALYSIS OF VARIANCE OF RATINGS OF SEVEN INDIVIDUALS IN FIVE TRAITS AS GIVEN BY THREE RATERS

I. IGNORING INDIVIDUAL DIFFERENCES

Source	Sum of squares	Degrees of freedom	Variance	F	P
Between raters (R)	9.05	2	4.52	1.35	$>.05$
Between traits (T)	46.53	4	11.63	3.47	$<.05$
Interaction ($R \times T$)	12.96	8	1.62	.48	$>.05$
Within sets	301.71	90	3.35		
Total	370.25	104			

II. IGNORING DIFFERENCES BETWEEN TRAITS

Source	Sum of squares	Degrees of freedom	Variance	F	P
Between raters (R)	9.05	2	4.52	2.26	$>.05$
Between ratees (I)	94.92	6	15.82	7.91	$<.01$
Interaction ($R \times I$)	98.68	12	8.22	4.11	$<.01$
Within sets	167.60	84	2.00		
Total	370.25	104			

III. IGNORING DIFFERENCES BETWEEN RATERS

Source	Sum of squares	Degrees of freedom	Variance	F	P
Between ratees (I)	94.92	6	15.82	6.25	$<.01$
Between traits (T)	46.53	4	11.63	4.60	$<.01$
Interaction ($I \times T$)	51.47	24	2.14	.85	$>.05$
Within sets	177.33	70	2.53		
Total	370.25	104			

statistically insignificant but would allow those contributions to add to errors X'_{ijkr}. Although only the constant error X_{ki} proved significant in the illustrative problem, we will proceed to make corrections for all three in order to show how it is done.

In order to determine the variations of ratings when rater and ratee are combined, we start with a matrix of arithmetic means for rater-ratee combinations, as in Table 11.3. Each mean in the body of Table 11.3, part I, is based on five observations. The variations among these means include the simple influences of rater differences and ratee differences which we must remove to find the rater-ratee interaction effects. The last column in part I shows the deviations of rater means from the grand mean. These deviations are X'_{kl}, the raters' constant errors. The last two rows of Table 11.3, part I,

TABLE 11.3. ESTIMATIONS OF THE CONTRIBUTIONS TO THE INTERACTIONS OF RATER WITH RATEE AMONG THE RATINGS OF SEVEN PERSONS BY THREE RATERS; FIVE TRAITS WERE INVOLVED

I. MEANS OF RATEES DERIVED FROM RATINGS BY DIFFERENT RATERS

Raters \ Ratees	1	2	3	4	5	6	7	All ratees	X'_{kl}
α	4.20	6.80	3.40	3.40	7.20	3.40	5.80	4.89	+.05
β	4.80	5.80	4.80	5.00	2.80	4.00	4.00	4.46	−.38
γ	5.00	6.20	4.60	3.00	7.40	3.40	6.60	5.17	+.33
All raters.	4.67	6.27	4.27	3.80	5.80	3.60	5.47	4.84	.00
d_i	−.17	+1.43	−.57	−1.04	+.96	−1.24	+.63		

II. MEANS CORRECTED FOR RATER ERRORS X'_{kl} AND FOR RATEE DEVIATIONS d_i

Raters \ Ratees	1	2	3	4	5	6	7	All ratees
α	4.32	5.32	3.92	4.39	6.19	4.59	5.12	4.84
β	5.35	4.75	5.75	6.42	2.22	5.62	3.75	4.84
γ	4.84	4.44	4.84	3.71	6.11	4.31	5.64	4.84
All raters...	4.84	4.84	4.84	4.84	4.84	4.84	4.84	4.84

III. CONTRIBUTIONS OF INTERACTIONS OF RATER AND RATEE: HALO ERRORS X'_{ki}

Raters \ Ratees	1	2	3	4	5	6	7	Σ
α	−.52	+.48	−.92	− .45	+1.35	−.25	+ .28	−.03
β	+.51	−.09	+.91	+1.58	−2.62	+.78	−1.09	−.02
γ	.00	−.40	.00	−1.13	+1.27	−.53	+ .80	+.01
Σ	−.01	−.01	−.01	.00	.00	.00	− .01	−.04

show individual differences over all traits and raters. The deviations d_i (from the grand mean, 4.84) of individual means, in all traits combined, may include halo effects on which raters agree. The interaction errors that will be estimated are actually *relative* halo effects. They are the subjective contributions to the ratings within the context of these raters, traits, and ratees. Within this context the various rater means and trait means represent the base of "objectivity."

In part II of Table 11.3 we have the adjusted means of the rater-ratee combinations. The adjustment is a double one, eliminating the inter-rater differences and inter-ratee differences. From the mean in each cell of part I of Table 11.3 are deducted the corresponding deviations X'_{kl} and d_{i}. For example, the value in the first row and column is equal to

$$4.20 - (+ .05) - (- .17) = 4.32$$

This procedure ensures that the adjusted means for all raters and for all ratees will equal 4.84, the grand mean. Except for two cells in part II all the rater-ratee means still deviate from the grand mean. It is in these deviations that we find evidence of the amounts of interaction of rater and ratee, or the relative halo errors. The deviations of these adjusted means from the grand mean are given in part III of Table 11.3. They range from -2.62 to $+1.58$. The most striking deviations indicate that rater α tends to overvalue ratee 5; rater β tends to overvalue ratee 4 and to undervalue ratees 5 and 7; and rater γ tends to undervalue ratee 4 and to overvalue ratee 5. Considering individuals, there is most difference of opinion concerning numbers 4 and 5, with rater β tending to disagree with both α and γ.

In order to estimate interaction errors of the rater-trait type we go through a similar process, as in Table 11.4. Here, however, we average by combinations of raters and traits, ignoring individual differences among ratees. The steps are analogous to those in Table 11.3 and therefore will not be described in detail. The end result in part III of Table 11.4 shows generally smaller deviations than in the previous interaction errors. We should expect this from the fact that the rater-trait interaction variance proved to be not significant. If the deviations were significant, we could say that rater α is most affected by the traits he rates and that he tends to see the ratees as higher in trait A and lower in traits C and E than do other raters.

Finding Adjusted Ratings. Having estimated the amounts of the three kinds of errors—X'_{kl}, X'_{ki}, and X'_{kj}—we can use them to help find better evaluations of the ratees, with *adjusted* ratings somewhat freed from those sources of error. If we deduct these three components from the others in equation (11.3), we have left a combination that is largely true variance. The adjustment process is described by the equation

$$X'_{ijk} = X_{ijk} - X'_{kl} - X'_{ki} - X'_{kj} \qquad (11.5)$$

When this equation is applied to the original ratings of Table 11.1, we obtain the adjusted ratings of Table 11.5.

To illustrate the adjustment process for one rating, for example the rating of individual 1 in trait A by rater α, we have

$$X'_{1A\alpha} = 5.00 - .05 - (-.52) - .66 = 4.81$$

Another example for individual 7 in trait A by rater β would be

$$X'_{7A\beta} = 3.00 - (-.38) - (-1.09) - (-.48) = 4.95$$

The adjusted ratings in Table 11.5 have had removed the inter-rater differences. This is shown by the fact that within each trait the means for the three raters are equal, within rounding errors. The means differ from trait to trait because we have not removed trait differences, as such. The inter-trait differences as shown here should be relatively freed of the influences of errors for which adjustments were made. The individual differences within sets of seven values in Table 11.5 are somewhat reduced as compared with

TABLE 11.4. ESTIMATION OF THE CONTRIBUTIONS TO THE INTERACTIONS OF RATER WITH TRAIT AMONG THE RATINGS OF SEVEN PERSONS BY THREE RATERS; FIVE TRAITS WERE INVOLVED

I. MEANS OF RATINGS BY RATER COMBINED WITH TRAIT

Raters \ Traits	*A*	*B*	*C*	*D*	*E*	All traits	X'_{kl}
α	6.14	5.29	3.86	5.86	3.29	4.89	+.05
β	4.57	4.86	4.29	5.00	3.57	4.46	−.38
γ	5.57	5.29	5.00	5.57	4.43	5.17	+.33
All raters....	5.43	5.14	4.38	5.48	3.76	4.84	.00
d_t	+ .59	+ .30	− .46	+ .64	−1.08		

II. MEANS BY RATER AND TRAIT, CORRECTED FOR RATER ERROR X'_{kl} AND FOR TRAIT DEVIATIONS d_t

Raters \ Traits	*A*	*B*	*C*	*D*	*E*	All traits
α	5.50	4.94	4.27	5.17	4.32	4.84
β	4.36	4.94	5.13	4.74	5.03	4.84
γ	4.65	4.66	5.13	4.60	5.18	4.84
All raters......	4.84	4.84	4.84	4.84	4.84	4.84

III. CONTRIBUTIONS OF INTERACTIONS OF RATER AND TRAIT; REACTION ERRORS X'_{kj}

Raters \ Traits	*A*	*B*	*C*	*D*	*E*	Σ
α	+.66	+.10	−.57	+.33	−.52	.00
β	−.48	+.10	+.29	−.10	+.19	.00
γ	−.19	−.22	+.29	−.24	+.34	−.02
Σ	−.01	−.02	+.01	−.01	+.01	−.02

the original ratings, but there is considerable variance remaining, now much more due to true individual differences.

Effects of Adjustments of Ratings upon Their Intercorrelations. What effects should the adjustments have upon correlations of the ratings? We have the possibility of computing rater intercorrelations, which indicate the internal consistency among raters. Such correlations have usually been

TABLE 11.5. ADJUSTED RATINGS OF SEVEN INDIVIDUALS IN FIVE TRAITS; ERRORS OF LENIENCY, X'_{kl}, OF HALO, X'_{ki}, AND OF RATER-TRAIT INTERACTION, X'_{kj}, HAVE BEEN REMOVED FROM THE ORIGINAL RATINGS OF TABLE 11.1

Rater / Ratee	Trait *A*			Trait *B*			Trait *C*			Trait *D*			Trait *E*		
	α	β	γ	α	β	γ	α	β	γ	α	β	γ	α	β	γ
1	4.8	6.4	4.9	5.4	4.8	4.9	4.0	3.6	4.4	5.1	6.0	6.9	4.0	2.7	2.3
2	7.8	9.0	7.3	6.4	7.4	7.3	5.0	5.0	4.8	7.1	7.6	7.3	5.0	2.3	4.7
3	3.2	4.0	2.9	3.8	4.4	4.9	4.4	2.2	4.4	7.5	5.6	4.9	2.4	5.3	4.3
4	6.7	4.3	6.0	3.3	4.7	4.0	2.0	2.5	3.5	3.1	3.9	4.0	3.9	3.6	1.5
5	6.9	5.5	7.6	5.5	6.9	5.6	6.2	5.7	5.1	6.3	5.1	5.6	4.1	5.8	5.1
6	2.5	4.1	3.4	5.1	3.5	3.4	3.8	5.3	2.9	4.9	3.7	5.4	1.7	1.4	2.9
7	6.0	5.0	6.1	6.6	4.4	6.1	5.2	6.2	5.6	4.3	6.6	4.1	5.2	5.3	5.5
Mean.......	5.41	5.47	5.46	5.16	5.16	5.17	4.37	4.36	4.39	5.47	5.50	5.46	3.76	3.77	3.76

regarded as indices of rating reliability but sometimes as rating validity (10). We also have the possibility of computing the intercorrelations of traits, in which case we have indices of the independence of the variables as rated. In both types of correlations we deal with a population of individuals.

The removal of inter-rater differences should have no influence upon either type of correlation. All this adjustment does is to shift the means and zero points for the ratings a constant amount within sets. The covariances are unaffected. The removal of the rater-trait interaction errors should have no effect upon the intercorrelations of raters when the inter-rater correlation is within traits. It should have no effect upon the intercorrelations of traits when the intertrait correlation is within raters. The adjustment for rater-ratee interaction should affect both types of correlation. Since the halo effect tends to increase intercorrelations of traits and to decrease intercorrelations of raters, the adjustment should have effects in the opposite directions. The adjusted ratings should yield lower correlations between traits and higher correlations between raters.

Tables 11.6 and 11.7 show that this is essentially what happened in the case of the illustrative data. The average intercorrelation of raters was .23

TABLE 11.6. SUMMARY OF INTERCORRELATIONS BETWEEN RATERS FOR ADJUSTED AND UNADJUSTED RATINGS

Trait	Unadjusted ratings				Adjusted ratings			
	$r_{\alpha\beta}$	$r_{\alpha\gamma}$	$r_{\beta\gamma}$	$\bar{r}_z$	$r_{\alpha\beta}$	$r_{\alpha\gamma}$	$r_{\beta\gamma}$	$\bar{r}_z$
A	.11	.92	−.16	.47	.63	.96	.60	.80
B	−.26	.64	−.11	.13	.40	.70	.77	.64
C	−.13	.84	−.37	.23	.67	.75	.42	.63
D	−.06	.74	−.29	.20	.50	.54	.50	.51
E	−.32	.55	−.08	.07	.27	.38	.56	.41
$\bar{r}_z$	−.22	.78	−.20	.23	.56	.74	.58	.62

before the ratings were adjusted and .62 after they were adjusted.[1] It was a striking result that rater β correlated rather consistently negatively with both raters α and γ before adjustment. The reason lies in halo errors in opposite directions, as shown in part III of Table 11.3. After adjustments are made for halo errors, the correlations between rater β and the others are all positive and average .56 and .58. These limited results show how seriously biased the intercorrelations between raters may be for unadjusted ratings.[2]

Table 11.7 shows that for two raters, α and γ, the correlations between

TABLE 11.7. SUMMARY OF INTERCORRELATIONS BETWEEN TRAITS WITH RATINGS ADJUSTED AND UNADJUSTED

Rater	Rating*	r_{ab}	r_{ac}	r_{ad}	r_{ae}	r_{bc}	r_{bd}	r_{be}	r_{cd}	r_{ce}	r_{de}	$\bar{r}_z$
α	U	.64	.58	.32	.94	.87	.51	.79	.77	.68	.31	.70
	A	.34	.22	−.06	.87	.71	.19	.58	.62	.32	−.11	.42
β	U	.85	.29	.82	−.29	−.08	.61	−.04	.18	−.61	.14	.25
	A	.78	.28	.77	.31	.26	.55	.16	.26	.01	.13	.40
γ	U	.78	.73	.48	.62	.91	.66	.88	.54	.92	.51	.74
	A	.65	.56	.20	.34	.82	.43	.72	.03	.79	.04	.52

* U = unadjusted ratings; A = adjusted ratings.

traits tended to drop materially after adjustment but for rater β the average tendency was in the opposite direction. Rater β had some tendency for negative correlations between a few of the traits. It is likely that these were spurious correlations brought about by strong halo errors in opposite directions. The adjustments of β's ratings tended to lower his high positive trait intercorrelations and to change his negative trait intercorrelations to positive. It is likely that his trait intercorrelations of adjusted ratings come nearer to representing his conceptions of trait similarities. At any rate, his average intertrait correlation after adjustment is similar to those of the other raters (.40 compared with .42 and .52). The trait-intercorrelation means for raters α and γ were very similar before adjustment also (.70 and .74).

Linear Transformations of Ratings. Where distributions of ratings of the same set of objects made by different raters differ with respect to mean and standard deviation, it is possible to convert them to equivalent distributions in these respects by applying linear transformations. We could adopt the mean and standard deviation of one of the rater's distributions to become the common scale, or we could arbitrarily choose any mean and standard deviation we desired. If we do not apply the adjustment procedures described above, under what circumstances would it be advantageous to apply linear transformations?

In averaging the ratings from a number of raters to obtain a single value for

[1] Coefficients were transformed to Fisher's Z before averaging and means were transformed back to r.

[2] It must not be expected that results so largely in line with expectations will always occur. In small samples, particularly, unexpected things can happen.

a given ratee in a given trait, the differences in means call for no correction. As was pointed out above, the relative leniency errors have no bearing upon the intercorrelations of ratings as between raters or as between traits. The same is true of the correlation of ratings with an outside criterion. If we do not apply a linear transformation, the mean of the composite ratings will deviate from the mean we would obtain after making such transformations to the extent of the mean of the relative leniency errors.

Variations in dispersion, however, do have some bearing upon contributions to variance of the composite ratings. Each rater's contribution to the composite will be proportional to the standard deviation of his ratings. This is a weighting problem. Each rater's ratings are automatically weighted in proportion to the size of his dispersion.[1] Unless the variation in raters' standard deviations is large, the weighting problem is probably not serious. Errors thus introduced into the composites of ratings would probably be trivial in comparison with other errors such as halo effect. If larger standard deviations are due to these large errors, however, the need for reducing the weight of ratings containing such errors becomes important. To the extent that large standard deviations indicate better discrimination of true variance we should want greater weight to be attached to the ratings.

Incomplete Matrices of Ratings. The discussions of adjusted ratings and of linear transformations thus far have implied complete matrices of ratings. By this we mean that every rater gave a rating to every individual in every trait. Frequently it happens in an investigation or in personnel practice that each rater can know and rate only part of the sample. Under this circumstance each rater's errors are confined to his own group of ratees. Ratees may benefit or be discriminated against unduly because they happen to be in a certain group.

There is no simple, generally applicable solution to this problem. To the extent that any two or more raters have ratings in common sufficient to make the kind of study of ratings that was described above, something can be done to make adjustments. Linear transformations taking care of differences in means as well as differences in standard deviations would become important in this kind of situation. If one is willing to make assumptions concerning comparability of subgroups of ratees, one extends the possibility of making inferences about the amounts of errors of different kinds.

The Number of Steps to Be Used in a Rating Scale. In the construction of several of the types of rating scales a common question concerns the number of rating and scoring categories to use. This problem has received considerable attention and much empirical investigation. In a survey of 54 teacher-rating scales, Boyce (4) found that some of them had as few as 2 steps while others had as many as 7, with 4 being the most popular number. Conklin (12) found from 2 to 20 steps had been used in various forms of scales. Scott's man-to-man scale had 5 main divisions which were subdivided into 3 each, making a total of 15 units. Lund's scale used in judging degrees of belief and of desire contained 21 steps (32).

There are several logical considerations. If we use too few steps, the scale

[1] For a further discussion of this type of weighting problem, see Guilford (19, p. 460); see also Chaps. 14 and 15 of this volume.

is obviously a coarse one, and we lose much of the discriminative powers of which raters are capable. On the other hand, we can grade a scale so finely that it is beyond the raters' limited powers of discrimination. The fineness will also depend upon the willingness of raters to make the effort to use the discriminative powers they have. With willing and cooperative raters we can appropriately call for finer discriminations than we can from unmotivated raters.

There has been some empirical evidence on the answer to this question. Conklin (12) concluded after analysis of some 23,000 ratings that for untrained raters the maximum number of steps should be *five* for a single (unipolar) scale and *nine* for a double (bipolar) scale. Symonds (50) concluded that the problem is primarily one of reliability. Starting from the empirical fact that the average of inter-rater correlations is in the region of .55 to .60, he concluded that *seven* steps is optimal. At this level of reliability, more than seven categories increases the reliability (inter-rater correlation) by an amount that is so small that it does not pay for the extra effort involved. Fewer steps may be used, he advised (52, p. 79), if the trait is rather obscure and if the raters are untrained and only moderately interested, or if a number of ratings of different aspects of the thing rated are to be combined. In the check-list technique, in which each aspect is often rated on a two-point scale, summing a large number of ratings may lead to relatively high reliability of total scores.

Champney and Marshall (11) have demonstrated that the Symonds conclusion is by no means the whole story. Their findings lead to the recommendation that when the rater is trained and interested, the optimal number of units may be as many as three times seven. Symonds had based his conclusion in part on the fact of the effect of coarse grouping (few broad categories) on coefficients of correlation. The effect of errors of grouping on coefficients of correlation is a percentage change, and the coarser the grouping, the greater the percentage of reduction. The smaller the coefficient of correlation with very fine grouping, the smaller is the net change. Thus, when reliabilities of ratings (from a fine scale) are relatively low, one could well tolerate the loss that coarse grouping involves.

Champney and Marshall found that the loss was definitely more than that accounted for by the grouping error, however. Using the Fels graphic scale, in which the line is 90 mm. long, they scored the same ratings with various numbers of steps from 1 to 45 mm. in width. As the fineness of scoring increased, the average intercorrelation of ratings increased with negative acceleration until it reached a maximum and then decreased slightly. In other words, there was an optimal fineness of scale above which as well as below which intercorrelations tended to be smaller.

The reasons for this can best be explained in terms of the illustration given by Champney and Marshall. The line scale could be scored either in centimeter units or millimeter units, giving either one-digit scores or two-digit scores. Are the second-digit contributions meaningful measurements? In one simple experiment second digits were picked at random and added to the rounded centimeter scores. The correlations dropped distinctly below that for the centimeter one-digit scores. The two-digit millimeter scores as given by the raters correlated higher than the centimeter scores, showing that the extra digit added some true variance which contributed to the correlations. The millimeter scores were not as reliable in this sense as scores with units of 2 and 3 mm., however. The conclusion was that the extra digit obtained from the raters adds both true and error variance. More generally, as finer divisions are made, additional true variance is added; but this becomes decreasingly important, while the addition of random errors becomes increasingly important. The optimal point of refinement is passed when there is a balance in the addition of true versus error variance.

We are left, therefore, without being able to set up any hard and fast rule concerning the number of scale divisions to use. The optimal number is a matter for empirical determination in any situation. Fortunately, there is a wide range of variation in refinement around the optimal point in which reliability changes very little. It can be said, however, that the number 7 recommended by Symonds is usually lower than optimal and it may pay in some favorable situations to use up to 25 scale divisions.

Distributions of Ratings. When a rater assigns ratings to a number of objects of a class, the frequency distribution is likely to show peculiarities attributable to the rater. This is demonstrated by the fact that distributions of the same objects from different raters often vary markedly. The strong negative skewing that is clearly attributable to the error of leniency has already been mentioned. There are other departures from the symmetrical, unimodal form of distribution that one might expect. Some distributions are distinctly bimodal and some are multimodal or "saw-toothed." We do not ordinarily have good evidence as to the true form of distribution of the objects rated, but if they are randomly selected human individuals, we should at least expect unimodal distributions.

In a study of distributions of ratings of colors, color combinations, odors, odor combinations, musical intervals, and poems judged as to affective value, Guilford and Jorgensen (20) found many striking examples of bimodal distributions. Some raters gave clearly unimodal distributions and others clearly bimodal distributions for the same set of stimuli. The proportion of the raters giving bimodal distributions varied from .48 for poems to .82 for musical intervals. If a rater gave a bimodal distribution for single colors, he also gave a bimodal distribution for color combinations. The tendency to bimodality was greater when numerical scales were used than when graphic scales were used. When the graphic scale was segmented, the distributions were more likely to be bimodal than when the lines were continuous. With a numerical scale, the point of lowest frequency was at the indifference category, though this low frequency was very rarely zero. With graphic scales, the point of lowest frequency deviated from the indifference category in many instances.

The interpretation of these findings is not completely clear, but there is no doubt that there is considerable distortion of the scale going on. Assuming that the true distribution of psychological values is unimodal, those raters who yield bimodal distributions are the ones at fault. The result is usually a severe contraction of the scale in the region of indifference. It appears that some observers take indifference to be a point instead of a range with the width of one category. This habit might be met by eliminating an indifference category in numerical scales and by not mentioning indifference in a graphic scale except as attached to a point. If, in spite of such efforts to overcome bimodality of distribution, it occurs when the investigator has reason to believe it should not, he can reevaluate the scale categories by a procedure proposed by Guilford and Jorgensen (20) or by treating the ratings as in the methods of handling successive categories, as described in Chap. 10.

Multimodal Distributions of Ratings. Multimodal distributions of ratings are likely to occur in the use of graphic scales because raters bunch their ratings near the descriptive cues. An example is a scale used by the Army Air Forces Training Command on which aviation students expressed their degrees of preference for training as bombardier, navigator, and pilot. There was a segmented line of nine units provided for each of the three types of training, with five descriptive cues placed at odd-numbered segments. The distributions of ratings of 1,000 students for training as bombardier and as navigator were as follows (frequencies are percentages):

Scale category	1	2	3	4	5	6	7	8	9
Bombardier	3.1	2.6	15.6	8.0	20.3	7.3	20.5	15.6	7.0
Navigator	7.6	4.2	17.6	7.6	16.8	7.2	15.1	15.1	8.8

The exceptional high frequencies at the rating of 8 can be explained by the fact that 80 per cent gave a rating of 9 to pilot training and avoided matching that level for other types of training. The general effect is to reduce a nine-point scale in large part to a five-point scale. Remedies would possibly be to give a cue to *every* segment of line, or to run cues across breaks, or to use continuous lines and to place them in the vertical position after the manner of the Fels type of scale.

Prescribed Distributions. Much can be done to avoid peculiar distributions of ratings by giving raters training. If they are informed that unimodal, and perhaps normal, distributions are to be expected, they should tend to conform in that direction. The instruction might be made even more explicit by telling the rater what percentage of his ratings of a group of objects should be expected in each category. If all raters conform to the same distributions, their ratings should be much more comparable. Where individual raters depart distinctly from the prescribed distribution, it would be easier to detect their constant errors.

The Construction of Definitions and Cues. A trait to be rated should ordinarily be introduced with a trait name and a definition, and there should be cues. Within reasonable limits, nothing should be left undone to give the rater a clear, univocal conception of the continuum along which he is to evaluate objects and to give all raters the same conception. The name of the trait is primarily useful as a label. Used without definition and without cues, it could be very misleading. Even with the qualifications and specifications provided by definition and cues, it should be carefully chosen.

Definitions should be stated as much as possible in operational terms. A good example of this is seen in the Fels Parent Behavior Rating Scale, a sample of which is given in Fig. 11.1. The trait name chosen for this particular scale is "Solicitousness for Child's Welfare (Anxious—Nonchalant)." The title includes or is immediately followed by two terms describing the opposite poles of the continuum. The instruction in Fig. 11.1 contains defining elaboration. This instruction attempts to anticipate questions a rater is likely to ask when he actually gets into the acts of observation and rating. Such details cannot always be anticipated without a preliminary tryout with the scale, preferably by the investigator himself as rater.

Requirements for Good Cues. Rating-scale cues have the double purpose of supplementing and reinforcing the definition of the continuum and of providing anchors or mileposts to guide the rater in making quantitative judgments. In order to serve these functions, they must be very carefully written, carefully selected, and carefully placed. Champney (10), in a study of cues, has listed some excellent criteria to which one should give attention in constructing scales. The listing of criteria below draws heavily upon his recommendations.

1. *Clarity.* Use short statements, in simple, unambiguous terminology.
2. *Relevance.* The cue should be consistent with the trait name and its definition as well as with other cues. Avoid bringing into a cue any implications of other traits. Such a slip is all too easy to make without realizing it.
3. *Precision.* A good cue applies to a point or a very short range on the continuum. There should be no doubt about its rank position among other cues and if possible it should not overlap them in quantitative meaning. This implies our being able to localize the cue at a point on a scale.
4. *Variety.* The use of the same terms in all or many of the cues may fail to differentiate them sufficiently. Vary the language used at different scale levels.
5. *Objectivity.* Stay clear of terminology implying ethical, moral, or social evaluations, unless dealing specifically with such types of traits. Cues with implications of good or bad, worthy or unworthy, and desirable or undesirable should generally be avoided.
6. *Uniqueness.* The cues for each trait should be unique to that trait. Avoid using cues of a very general character, such as "excellent," "superior," "average," "poor," and the like. In a rating scale for evaluating speakers, for example, Bryan and Wilke (6) use the following kinds of cues in answers to questions:

How would you describe the speaker's flow of words?

Fluent	Easy	Unimpeded	Hesitant	Labored

To what extent did you find the speech interesting?

Absorbing	Stimulating	Passable	Dull	Boring

Empirical Evaluation of Cues. In order to satisfy some of the criteria just mentioned, it is sufficient to exercise ordinary practices of good editing. The best editing, however, will not ensure that all the criteria are satisfied. If the use of a scale justifies the effort, considerable experimental work should go into the development of cues, their selection, and their placement. After writing, editing, and selecting a much larger number of cues than one needs, one should submit them to expert judges to evaluate along the continuum. The method of equal-appearing intervals or the graphic rating method could be used to advantage. From the statistical results one can determine whether each statement or term is precise and what its mean scale position is. Correlation studies will answer the question of psychological relevance.

Supplementary Ratings. Sometimes it is desirable to call upon the rater for additional, qualifying information. This has the twofold utility of calling to the attention of the rater the need for being meticulous in making his ratings and of telling the investigator something about the dependability of the ratings. It is obvious that not all raters are capable of evaluating all individuals of a group equally well on all traits. Where information is seriously lacking or insufficient, the investigator would like to be informed so that he may eliminate ratings or weight them less. When the rater is required to evaluate the dependability of his own ratings, he may give more serious attention to the basis for his judgments and hence be more careful in making the ratings.

Some rating instruments include a category designated as "Don't know," or "No chance to observe," with each trait. These categories may be overworked by the disinterested rater who wants to "get it over with" as soon as possible. For the serious rater they give some relief from the compulsion to guess when he does not want to do so. Some scales provide space for the rater to offer sketchy reports of actual observations which support the quantitative judgment he gave. The investigator can perhaps decide from this report whether the rater had in mind the proper continuum.

The amount of supplementary information called for will depend upon the circumstances. Disinterested raters will tolerate only a minimum. Even interested raters may lose in motivation if it is overdone. The point of balance between the addition of care and of useful information and loss of care and of taste for the rating task would have to be decided for each situation.

Some Peculiarities of Ratings

Some Characteristics of Raters. A wealth of experience with rating scales has taught us much about raters and their peculiarities in addition to others already mentioned. These additional peculiarities are listed below. In each case an attempt is made to refer to the investigator who deserves credit for making the suggestion.

1. Individuals differ in the capacity to judge others, but there is no such thing as a general judicial capacity (Hollingworth, Wells).
2. Raters disagree because they observe the individuals in different types of situations (Remmers, Plice, Arlett, Dowd, Webb).
3. Two ratings by the same rater are no more valid than one (Slawson). The reason for this is apparently that a rater repeats the same constant errors a second time, and the means of his ratings therefore deviate just as far from the truth as do the single judgments.
4. Raters do much better if interested in the ratings they make (Conrad).
5. Raters should have sufficient time for making the ratings (Conrad).
6. Raters do better if they have educational and professional backgrounds similar to those of the ratees (Conrad).
7. The ability of any rater to rate a specified trait should be determined (Conrad). The correlation of his ratings with a pool of ratings by others is the accepted test.
8. The good judge of self is more intelligent and more observing than the good judge of others (Adams).
9. The good judge of self tends to be happier, less irritable, more sympathetic and generous, and more courageous than the good judge of others (Adams).

10. The good rater is not necessarily self-consistent (Hollingworth), nor is the self-consistent rater necessarily a good rater (Slawson).

11. For certain admirable traits there is a positive correlation between possession and the ability to judge. The reverse of this is true in general for undesirable traits (Hollingworth).

12. One who knows himself best also judges others better in certain traits (Hollingworth).

13. Raters do better if carefully trained with respect to the distribution of abilities, the nature of the scale, and cautions against errors such as the halo effect, central tendency, overrating, prejudice, and the logical error.

14. Raters tend to rank themselves in a group less accurately than they rank others (Shen). This is largely due to the systematic errors of the rater.

15. Raters tend to overestimate themselves in most traits and to underestimate themselves in few (Shen).

16. Raters do not always overestimate themselves in desirable traits (Shen).

17. There are individuals who overestimate themselves in all traits and others who underestimate themselves in all traits (Shen).

18. Men are more lenient in their ratings than women (Hart, Olander).

19. Raters rate their colleagues, fellow students, or fellow teachers higher than they rate others (Cattell, Remmers, Plice).

20. Self-ratings are too high on desirable traits and too low on undesirable traits (Hollingworth, Shen, Tschechtelin).

21. There is a tendency to overrate members of the same sex as compared with members of the opposite sex (Kinder).

22. In self-ratings, superior individuals underestimate themselves and inferior individuals overrate themselves, the latter having the greater error (Hoffman).

23. Parents overrate their children as a rule, but they may underestimate very superior children.

24. Personally selected raters, selected by those who are to be rated, tend to rate an individual higher than he rates himself (Uhrbrock).

25. The assurance of a rater is of some importance. Judgments of which he is very sure are much more reliable than ordinary ratings (Cady).

26. Ratings may be influenced by the raters knowing the purpose for which they are to be used. To avoid this error, ratings should be secured with the raters in ignorance of their use and if possible at a time in advance of the situation demanding their use (Paterson).

27. Different raters use different criteria in judging the same trait. For this reason it is sometimes desirable to ask the rater to state the bases upon which his own judgments are made.

28. The leniency error is much greater when the rater must confront the ratee with results of the ratings. Stockford and Bissell (49) found a mean change from 60 to 84 under this condition.

29. The error of leniency is less for ratings made on descriptive scales than for those made on evaluative scales (Stockford and Bissell).

30. Length of acquaintance leads to substantial errors of leniency. Stockford and Bissell (49) found that length of acquaintance with employees correlated .64 with ratings of acceptability of personality. It also correlated to the extent of .65, on the average, with a number of traits when the scale was evaluative and to the extent of .42 when the scale was descriptive.

31. The influence of length of acquaintance upon ratings correlates negatively with the *IQ* of the rater. In general, the correlation was $-.46$; in a trained group it was $-.68$, and in an untrained group, $-.30$ (Stockford and Bissell).

32. Training reduces the effect of length of acquaintance. The mean correlation of this variable with ratings in a trained group was .32 and in an untrained group .48 (Stockford

and Bissell). Taken together with point 31, the indication is that those of higher *IQ* gain more in this respect by training.

33. Intelligence of raters is related to the reliability of ratings. *IQ* correlated .33 with reliability coefficients (reratings); .52 in a trained group and .20 in an untrained group (Stockford and Bissell).

Concerning Differences between Traits. The recommendations given so far have applied more specifically to constant errors in the raters and other common errors that occur no matter what traits are being rated. There are also certain facts that apply to some traits and not to others. Some traits are more easily observed and judged than others. Some are more objective and different judges are more likely to agree upon them than they do upon other more subjectively estimated traits. The experiences of various investigators will now be summarized briefly.

Hollingworth (25) found close agreement among raters upon the following traits: *efficiency*, *originality*, *perseverance*, *quickness*, *judgment*, *clearness*, *energy*, and *will*. There was fair agreement upon *mental balance*, *breadth*, *leadership*, *intensity*, *reasonableness*, *independence*, *refinement*, *physical health*, and *emotions*. There was poor agreement upon such traits as *courage*, *unselfishness*, *integrity*, *cooperativeness*, *cheerfulness*, and *kindliness*. Shen (45) found the best agreement upon *scholarship*, *leadership*, and *intelligence* and the poorest agreement upon *judicial sense*, *punctuality*, and *tact*. Miner (36) found good agreement for the traits of *energy*, *leadership*, *general ability*, and *reliability*. Tschechtelin (56) found that children in grades 4 through 8, also teachers, rated most reliably (rerating) traits of *punctuality*, *intelligence*, *friendliness*, and *working well with others*. They rated less reliably traits of *popularity*, *depression*, *dependability*, and *sympathy*.

Stockford and Bissell (49) found that the trait of *dependability* was rated with highest rerating reliability among several traits on which employees were rated (average $r = .78$) and *cooperation* was rated with least reliability ($r = .49$). There was greatest inter-rater agreement on ratings of *quality of work* ($r = .70$) and least on ratings of *cooperation* ($r = .04$).

A few rules concerning traits can be gleaned from experience:

1. Traits should be described univocally, objectively, and specifically (Paterson, Kingsbury).

2. A trait that is to be rated should not be a composite of a number of traits that vary independently (Freyd).

3. Each trait should refer to a single type of activity or to the results of a single type of activity (Paterson).

4. Traits should be grouped according to the accuracy with which they can be rated (Paterson).

5. In describing traits, avoid the use of general terms such as "very," "extreme," "average," or "excellent" (Freyd).

6. Traits should be judged on the basis of past or present accomplishments rather than upon what the raters regard as future promise (Paterson).

7. In self-ratings there is no trait in which all individuals overestimate or all underestimate themselves.

8. Finally, do not use scales for traits on which reliable or more objective data can be obtained (Paterson). It would be unwise to depend upon ratings of health when medical records are obtainable, or to use ratings on intelligence when mental tests are available.

General Evaluation of Rating Methods

As compared with their nearest rivals, pair comparisons and the method of rank order, the rating-scale methods have certain definite advantages and the results often compare very favorably with those from more accurate methods. The advantages may be listed as follows:

1. Ratings require much less time than either pair comparisons or ranking methods.
2. The procedure is far more interesting to the observers, especially if graphic methods are employed.
3. Rating-scale methods have a much wider range of application.
4. They can be used with psychologically naïve raters who have had a minimum of training.
5. They can be used with large numbers of stimuli. Even the method of ranking becomes difficult and irksome when there are more than 30 to 40 stimuli.
6. Some investigators in experimental aesthetics maintain that the best judgments are made when stimuli are presented singly, that comparative judgments destroy the aesthetic attitude.

Certain empirical studies made to compare the different scaling methods also demonstrate the worth of ratings. Symonds (51) concludes that under ordinary conditions ratings give results as reliable as those obtained from the ranking method.[1] Conklin and Sutherland (13) in a study of jokes found that ratings gave smaller mean deviations, in other words, were less variable from one judge to another, than did rankings. The reliability of the ratings was given by a coefficient of .79 as compared with a reliability of .73 for rankings. Since the humor of a joke may so quickly wear off with repetition, one can readily see why single presentations should give more stable results.

Marsh and Perrin (33), in a study of the validity of ratings, correlated them with more objective criteria. The judges observed the subjects while they performed certain tasks and then made their judgments without knowing the test scores. The ratings for intelligence correlated .78 with test scores. A like coefficient for the aiming test was .36; for a card-sorting test it was .68. Judgments of head size correlated with actual size to the extent of .76. Ratings of some human traits and performances thus have a satisfactory degree of validity. The degree of validity of ratings varies for different traits, as we should expect.

Concerning the status of ratings as measurements, it is best to regard most of them as being at about the same level as values found by methods of successive intervals in general. In other words, they achieve the status of ordinal measurements and only approach that of interval measurements. By various methods of correction and scaling, like any successive-interval data, they can be transformed more or less successfully into interval measurements if we wish to take the trouble. When they are condemned because of the many sources of bias and error to which they are vulnerable, the answer is that many of these sources are to some degree controllable, the effects can become known, and we can apply corrections and scaling procedures. In view of the many pressures to evaluate human beings in all sorts of variables

[1] Problems of reliability of ratings will be treated in Chap. 14.

and in view of the lack of better procedures, the rating method promises to find welcome use for many years to come.

Problems

1. From Data 11*A* estimate the relative errors of leniency, halo, and contrast by procedures described in this chapter. State all the conclusions you can from the results.

DATA 11*A*. RATINGS GIVEN TO SIX WELL-KNOWN MEN IN PUBLIC LIFE IN THE UNITED STATES. EACH WAS RATED ON FOUR TRAITS BY FOUR RATERS.* A VERTICAL, GRAPHIC SCALE WAS USED. COMPARISONS WERE TO BE MADE WITH ALL MEN IN PUBLIC LIFE

Rater / Ratee	Trait *A*				Trait *B*				Trait *C*				Trait *D*			
	α	β	γ	δ	α	β	γ	δ	α	β	γ	δ	α	β	γ	δ
1	7	6	8	7	8	2	8	7	5	1	8	2	5	0	10	5
2	7	7	6	7	7	6	6	6	6	6	9	1	5	6	8	2
3	6	6	4	5	8	9	8	6	10	5	9	8	9	5	10	6
4	8	8	6	6	9	10	3	1	8	8	7	6	9	7	4	4
5	8	5	6	7	9	5	4	4	5	1	4	1	9	1	3	1
6	5	4	3	3	7	8	1	0	7	7	8	4	7	8	0	0

* Ratees 1 to 3 are Republicans and 4 to 6 are Democrats. Raters α and β are Democrats and raters γ and δ are Republicans, all being graduate students in psychology.

The traits:

A. Intelligence (defined in terms of *IQ*, where 5 represents the decade 120–129).
B. Honesty (defined as telling the truth; freedom from deception or trickery).
C. Friendliness (defined as cordiality and warmth).
D. Generosity (defined as giving credit; putting others before himself).

2. Adjust the ratings for rater β for all traits and also the ratings of trait *B* given by all raters, removing the three sources of error discovered in Prob. 1.

3. Intercorrelate the four traits as given by rater β, for the adjusted and unadjusted ratings. Point out all noteworthy findings.

4. Intercorrelate the four raters, using the ratings they gave for trait *B*, both adjusted and unadjusted. Point out all noteworthy findings.

Answers

1. Leniency errors:

Rater:	α	β	γ	δ
Error:	+1.55	−0.24	+0.26	−1.58

Halo errors:

Ratee:	1	2	3	4	5	6
Error:	−3.07	+0.55	−0.63	+1.99	−1.32	+2.49

Contrast errors:

Trait:	*A*	*B*	*C*	*D*
Error:	+0.20	+0.97	−0.76	−0.43

2. Sums of β's ratings in traits:

A	*B*	*C*	*D*
36.3	35.6	33.9	31.1

Sums of ratings by all raters equal 35.6.

3. Mean intercorrelation (using Fisher's *Z* method):

Unadjusted ratings: .76
Adjusted ratings: .34

4. Mean intercorrelation (Fisher Z method):
   Unadjusted ratings: .10
   Adjusted ratings: .51

REFERENCES

1. ADAMS, H. F. The good judge of personality, *J. abnorm. and soc. Psychol.*, 1927, **22,** 172–181.
2. ARLETT, A. H., and DOWD, C. E. Variability among a group of judges in rating character traits in children. *Psychol. Bull.* 1926, **23,** 617–619.
3. BAIER, D. E. Reply to Travers' "A critical review of the validity and rationale of the forced-choice technique." *Psychol. Bull.*, 1952, **48,** 421–434.
4. BOYCE, A. C. Methods of measuring teachers' efficiency. *Fourteenth Yearbook nat. Soc. Stud. Educ.*, 1915, Pt. II.
5. BRADSHAW, F. F. The American Council on Education rating scale. *Arch. Psychol. N.Y.*, 1930, **18,** No. 119.
6. BRYAN, A. I., and WILKE, W. H. A technique for rating public speeches. *J. consult. Psychol.*, 1941, **5,** 80–90.
7. CADY, V. M. The estimation of juvenile incorrigibility. *J. Delinqu. Monogr.*, 1923, No. 2.
8. CATTELL, J. McK. *American Men of Science*, 2d ed. New York: Science Press, 1910.
9. CATTELL, R. B. Psychological measurement: ipsative, normative, and interactive. *Psychol. Rev.*, 1944, **51,** 292–303.
10. CHAMPNEY, H. The measurement of parent behavior. *Child Develpm.*, 1941, **12,** 131–166.
11. ——— and MARSHALL, H. Optimal refinement of the rating scale. *J. appl. Psychol.*, 1939, **23,** 323–331.
12. CONKLIN, E. S. The scale of values method for studies in genetic psychology. *Univ. Ore. Publ.*, 1923, **2,** No. 1.
13. ——— and SUTHERLAND, J. W. A comparison of the scale of values method with the order of merit method. *J. exp. Psychol.*, 1923, **6,** 44–57.
14. CONRAD, H. S. The bogey of the "personal equation" in ratings of intelligence. *J. educ. Psychol.*, 1932, **23,** 147–149.
15. ———. The personal equation in ratings: I. An experimental determination. *J. gen. Psychol.*, 1932, **41,** 267–293.
16. ———. The personal equation in ratings: II. A systematic evaluation, *J. educ. Psychol.*, 1933, **24,** 39–46.
17. FERGUSON, L. W. The development of a method of appraisal for assistant managers. *J. appl. Psychol.*, 1947, **31,** 306–311.
18. FREYD, M. The graphic rating scale. *J. educ. Psychol.*, 1923, **14,** 83–102.
19. GUILFORD, J. P. *Fundamental Statistics in Psychology and Education.*, 2d ed. New York: McGraw-Hill, 1950.
20. ——— and JORGENSEN, A. P. Some constant errors in ratings. *J. exp. Psychol.*, 1938, **22,** 43–57.
21. HART, H., and OLANDER, E. Sex differences in character as indicated by teachers' ratings. *Sch. & Soc.*, 1924, **20,** 381–382.
22. HARTSHORNE, H., and MAY, M. A. *Studies in Service and Self-control.* New York: Macmillan, 1929.
23. HIGHLAND, R. W., and BERKSHIRE, J. R. A methodological study of forced-choice performance rating. *Research Bull.* 51–9, 1951. San Antonio, Tex.: Human Resources Research Center.
24. HOFFMAN, G. J. An experiment in self-estimation. *J. abnorm. and soc. Psychol.*, 1923, **18,** 43–49.

25. Hollingworth, H. L. *Judging Human Character.* New York: Appleton-Century-Crofts, 1922.
26. Hunt, W. A., and Volkmann, J. The anchoring of an affective scale. *Amer. J. Psychol.*, 1937, **49,** 88–92.
27. Jurgensen, C. E. A fallacy in the use of median scale values in employee check lists. *J. appl. Psychol.*, 1949, **33,** 56–58.
28. Kinder, V. S. Through our own looking glass. *Sch. & Soc.*, 1925, **22,** 533–536.
29. Kingsbury, F. A. Analyzing ratings and training raters. *J. Person. Res.*, 1922, **1,** 377–383.
30. Knauft, E. B. Construction and use of weighted checklist rating scales for two industrial situations. *J. appl. Psychol.*, 1948, **32,** 63–70.
31. Knight, F. B., and Franzen, R. H. Pitfalls in rating schemes. *J. educ. Psychol.*, 1922, **13,** 204–213.
32. Lund, F. H. Emotional and volitional determinants of belief. *J. abnorm. and soc. Psychol.*, 1925, **20,** 63–81, 174–196.
33. Marsh, S. E., and Perrin, F. A. C. An experimental study of the rating scale technique. *J. abnorm. and soc. Psychol.*, 1925, **19,** 383–399.
34. Martin, L. J. An experimental study of Fechner's principles of aesthetics. *Psychol. Rev.*, 1906, **13,** 142–219.
35. Michels, W. C., and Helson, H. A reformulation of the Fechner law in terms of adaptation-level applied to rating-scale data. *Amer. J. Psychol.*, 1949, **62,** 355–368.
36. Miner, J. B. Evaluation of a method for finely graduated estimates of abilities. *J. appl. Psychol.*, 1917, **1,** 123–133.
37. Murray, H. A. *Explorations in Personality.* New York: Oxford University Press, 1938.
38. Newcomb, T. An experiment designed to test the validity of a rating technique. *J. educ. Psychol.*, 1931, **22,** 279–289.
39. Paterson, D. G. Methods of rating human qualities. *Ann. Amer. Acad. Pol. and soc. Sci.*, 1923, **110,** 81–93.
40. Remmers, H. H., and Plice, M. J. Reliability of ratings at Purdue University. *Industr. Psychol.*, 1926, **1,** 717–721.
41. Richardson, M. W., and Kuder, G. F. Making a rating scale that measures. *Person. J.*, 1933, **12,** 36–40.
42. Rugg, H. O. Is the rating of human character practicable? *J. educ. Psychol.*, 1921, **12,** 425–438, 485–501; 1922, **13,** 30–42, 81–93.
43. Scott, W. D., Clothier, R. C., and Mathewson, S. B. *Personnel Management.* New York: McGraw-Hill, 1931.
44. Shen, E. The influence of friendship upon personal ratings. *J. appl. Psychol.*, 1925, **9,** 66–68.
45. ———. The reliability coefficient of personal ratings. *J. educ. Psychol.*, 1925, **16,** 232–236.
46. ———. The validity of self-estimates. *J. educ. Psychol.*, 1925, **16,** 104–107.
47. Sisson, E. D. Forced choice—the new Army rating. *Person. Psychol.*, 1948, **1,** 365–381.
48. Slawson, J. The reliability of judgments of personal traits. *J. appl. Psychol.*, 1922, **6,** 161–171.
49. Stockford, L., and Bissell, H. W. Factors involved in establishing a merit-rating scale. *Personnel*, 1949, **26,** 94–118.
50. Symonds, P. M. On the loss of reliability in ratings due to coarseness of the scale. *J. exp. Psychol.*, 1924, **7,** 456–461.
51. ———. Notes on rating, *J. appl. Psychol.*, 1925, **9,** 188–195.
52. ———. *Diagnosing Personality and Conduct.* New York: Appleton-Century-Crofts, 1931.

53. TAYLOR, E. K., and WHERRY, R. W. A study of leniency in two rating systems. *Person. Psychol.*, 1951, **4,** 39–47.
54. THORNDIKE, E. L. A constant error in psychological ratings. *J. appl. Psychol.*, 1920, **4,** 25–29.
55. TRAVERS, R. M. W. A critical review of the validity and rationale of the forced-choice technique. *Psychol. Bull.*, 1951, **48,** 62–70.
56. TSCHECHTELIN, S. M. A. A 22-point personality rating scale. *J. Psychol.*, 1944, **18,** 3–8.
57. UHRBROCK, R. S. Rating tendencies of personally selected judges. *J. educ. Psychol.*, 1932, **23,** 594–603.
58. ———. Standardization of 724 rating scale statements. *Person. Psychol.*, 1950, **3,** 285–316.
59. WEBB, E. Character and intelligence. *Brit. J. Psychol. Monogr., Suppl.*, 1915, No. 3.
60. WELLS, F. L. A statistical study of literary merit. *Arch. Psychol. N.Y.*, 1907, **1,** No. 7.

CHAPTER 12

PRINCIPLES OF JUDGMENT

From time to time in previous chapters something was said concerning peculiarities of human judgment, particularly as they affect the operations of certain methods of measurement. This was true especially in connection with the method of constant stimuli and with the various rating-scale procedures. In Chap. 2 an important distinction was made between the response continuum and the judgment continuum involved in a psychophysical experiment or in a scaling situation. It was pointed out that there are indications of occasional failure of the two continua to correspond in a one-to-one fashion. It is now time to supply better support for this conclusion and to consider the many ways in which judgments are affected by the various determining conditions, often regardless of the particular measurement method involved.

Throughout most of the chapter, the most striking impression will undoubtedly be to the effect that all human judgments are relative. Without recognition of this relativity we are due for many a puzzling experience and we shall be plagued by many apparent inconsistencies. Although the factual evidence is far from complete, it is possible to arrive at some degree of order in terms of general theory of judgment and in terms of general principles. The last part of the chapter will be devoted to Helson's *adaptation-level* theory, which at present comes closest to a general explanatory basis for phenomena of psychophysical judgment.

Judgment Time and Confidence

The subjects of judgment time and of confidence in judgments are treated together because many research studies have shown interest in both and have related the two phenomena.

Judgment Time. In Chap. 6, judgment time was considered as a possible substitute for the psychophysical judgment in determining a limen by the method of constant stimulus differences. It was rejected chiefly on the grounds that it has correlated with the stimulus difference much lower than has the proportion of correct judgments. The phenomenon of judgment time is interesting in its own right, however, as a psychological variable related to other variables.

Johnson (21) found that as the variable stimulus S_v approached the point of subjective equality (*PSE*) from below, the judgment time increased with positive acceleration. As S_v increased above the *PSE*, the judgment time decreased with negative deceleration. The maximum judgment time tended to be at the *PSE*. These relationships are of the general type illustrated in Fig. 12.1. Johnson also found that judgment times tended to be three to four times as long under instructions to emphasize accuracy. Flynn (7) verified Johnson's results, concluding that judgment time decreases as the stimulus difference ΔS increases, in a function of hyperbolic form.

Cartwright (3) proposed the general hypothesis that judgment time will be at a maximum at the boundary between categories of judgment or at the boundary of a range of sensory equivalence. His results tended to support strongly his hypothesis. For example, in one experiment the *O*s were exposed a number of times to angles ranging from 60 to 100 degrees in steps of 10 degrees. They later had recognition tests with angles ranging from 10 to 160 degrees. The hypothesis led to the prediction of maximum judgment times near angles of 60 and 100 degrees. The average distance between the point of maximum judgment time and the limen was only 4 degrees. In another experiment, the *O*s were taught to respond with the color names

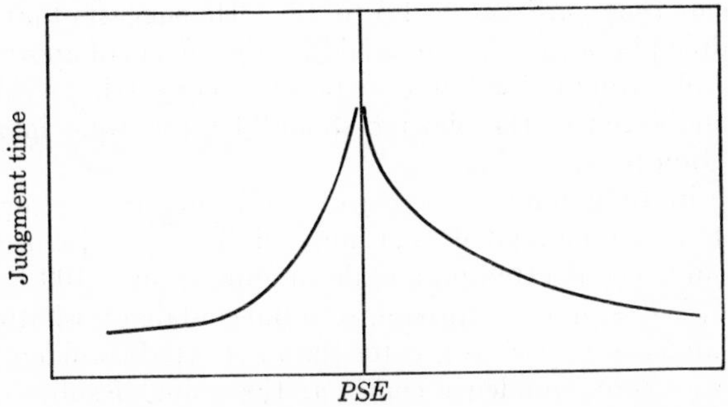

FIG. 12.1. Relationship of judgment time to a stimulus difference $S_v - S_s$.

"red," "blue," and "purple" when angles of 50, 90, and 130 degrees were exposed. In later recognition tests, which essentially amounted to judgments in successive categories, it was found that maximal judgment times came very near the limens separating the color categories. Cartwright's principle accounts for the usual finding that equality judgments average longer than judgments of greater or less, by the fact that they cover a shorter range between two limens that are not very far apart. The principle also accounts for the usual finding that the use of three categories of judgment yields longer average judgment times than the use of two. As the number of categories increases or as category intervals become shorter, judgment times should tend to increase.

Postman and Zimmerman (55) put Cartwright's hypothesis to a test in the field of attitude measurement. They predicted that decision time should be longest for statements toward which *O* is relatively indifferent in the sense that he would be equally willing to accept or reject them. In the experiment, oral responses of "Yes" or "No" were timed for every statement of opinion administered to *O*. Each *O* was later asked to rate his response to each statement on a scale from 0 (strong disagreement) through 5 (indifferent) to 10 (strong agreement). For the composite of responses of 28 *O*s, the mean decision time showed a regular regression as a function of rated intensity.

Below the indifference point and above it two equations, respectively, describe the relationship:

$$\log y = .45 + .15x$$
$$\log y = .62 + .13x$$

where y = a decision-time index T/M_t (where T = actual decision time and M_t = mean decision time for each O) and x = intensity rating. It was assumed that the indifference point is at the border between the two ranges of statements accepted and rejected and hence is a psychological limen.

Dashiell (6) studied the same kind of phenomenon in connection with affective judgments of colors. He predicted that the farther apart colors are on the affective scale, the shorter will be the judgment time in making a comparative judgment. In a list of seven colors judged by pair comparisons, as the rank difference of affective values in pairs decreased from 6 to 1, the mean judgment time varied from 1.3 to 2.1. He suggests that the relationship was modified because it was overlaid by the effects of another factor, the distance of a color from the indifference point. The farther a color's affective value from indifference, the shorter should be the time in obtaining an affective reaction to it.

Confidence in Judgments. Degree of confidence in the correctness of a judgment is found to be related to stimulus difference. Johnson (21) found that when confidence is rated on a scale ranging from -100 (complete confidence that S_v is less than S_s) through zero (no confidence whatever) to $+100$ (complete confidence that S_v is greater than S_s) rated confidence is an ogive function of S_v. Zero confidence comes at the point of subjective equality, not at S_s. The slope of such an ogive is lower than that for the psychometric function relating judgments of "greater" to S_v. Under instructions for speed in making judgments, the regression became irregular. The means of the confidence ratings were about the same under both speed and accuracy instructions.

Felt Difficulty of the Judgment Task. Related to the degree of confidence in a judgment is the felt difficulty of a task. The two should be negatively and very substantially related. In a study of felt difficulty, Guilford and Cotzin (13) used a series of lifted weights as the standard scale with which the difficulties of making comparative judgments of sounds could be matched. It was ascertained that a geometric series of weights yielded a linear series of felt difficulty in lifting, as one should expect from Fechner's law. In three judgment tasks, O was called upon to judge small differences in pitch, in loudness, and in time intervals. He would judge 10 differences of equal size and then find a weight that seemed equally difficult to lift. The auditory stimulus differences were evaluated objectively for psychological difficulty by scaling them from the proportions of wrong judgments. One result was that the felt difficulty of a judgment, as indicated on the weight scale, bore a logarithmic relationship to the objectively scaled difficulty of the stimulus difference. Another result was that the same objectively scaled difficulty level for the three kinds of auditory stimuli was matched with the same felt difficulty in terms of lifted weights. This shows that felt difficulty was on a common scale for the three tasks. The results pointed to the conclusion that problems of felt difficulty of tasks, and hence also problems of confidence, cannot be understood without reference to a number of variables, among which are ability level of the observer, his level of motivation, his degree of effort, and his sets for speed and accuracy.

Relation of Confidence to Judgment Time. The fact of correlation of judgment time with confidence has been known for many years. In recent years the nature of the relationship has been more clearly determined. Volkmann (79) proposed to describe the relationship by means of the hyperbolic equation

$$T = a + \frac{b}{2C - 1} \qquad (12.1)$$

where T = judgment time, C = measured degree of confidence, and a and b are constants. Johnson (21) proposed an exponential relationship for the same purpose, in the equation

$$T = a\,(10)^{b(1-C)} \qquad (12.2)$$

where the symbols are as defined in (12.1).

In an experiment on recognition of visual patterns varying in similarity, Seward (64) found the Pearson product-moment correlations between judgment time and confidence rating to vary from .37 to .81 with a mean of .65 for 22 individual *O*s. We can definitely conclude that confidence and judgment time are functionally related, but the relationship is not a highly dependable one. It is possible that Seward's correlations would have been higher had the nonlinearity been taken into account, however. In view of the mathematical equation proposed above, we may say that either variable, judgment time or confidence, changes most rapidly at lower levels of the other.

The Time-order Error

When stimuli are presented for comparative judgments, it is often apparent, by one sign or another, that the second of a pair is systematically judged greater than we should expect or less than we should expect. To take the most common example, when the standard is given first and the variable second, the indications are that the standard is underestimated or overestimated; usually it is underestimated. When the standard is compared with itself, there is an excess of greater judgments for the second stimulus, which means that the standard (first stimulus) seems less by comparison. This is a negative *time-order error*, or *TOE*. If there were an excess of judgments "less," the *TOE* would be regarded as positive. Judgments of the other variables are in line with the ones for the standard compared with itself.

There have been two important theories specifically designed to account for the time-order error, particularly the negative *TOE*. Koehler's *sinking-trace theory* assumes that the second of two stimuli gives a *fresh* neurological impression of the second stimulus that is present for comparison with a *sinking* neurological trace of the impression made by the first stimulus (31). Lauenstein's *assimilation theory* assumes that the trace from the first stimulus assimilates to whatever level of excitation exists between the two moments of stimulation for the stimuli compared (32). We shall not be concerned with the validity of either theory here except to point out that they have instigated a great deal of useful research, that both are inadequate to account for all the facts, and that a more comprehensive principle or set of principles is needed to make the facts intelligible. We are concerned here with putting some degree of order into the facts, with attention to their implications for measurement.

Measurement of the Time-order Error. One common way in which the size of the *TOE* is measured in an experiment has already been indicated. It is the simple difference $PSE - S_s$. The decision as to whether the error is negative or positive is determined by the algebraic sign of the difference. For the data in Table 12.1, S_s is 200 g., the *PSE* is 199.11, and consequently the *TOE* is 199.11 − 200 = −0.89 g.

TABLE 12.1. PROPORTIONS OF JUDGMENTS "GREATER" FOR EACH OF SEVEN WEIGHTS WHEN COMPARED WITH A STANDARD OF 200 G.

Weights S_v	185	190	195	200	205	210	215
p_G	.052	.146	.200	.517	.846	.853	.934
z_j	−1.63	−1.05	−.84	+.04	+1.02	+1.05	+1.51

Another common indicator of the extent of the *TOE* is in terms of the *per cent difference.* This means the difference in percentage of judgments "less" and judgments "greater" in the experiment. In equation form,

$$D\% = \frac{100(L - G)}{L + G} \tag{12.3}$$

where L = number of judgments "less" for all stimuli combined and G = number of judgments "greater." This type of measure has been used in most of the experiments to which reference will be made in subsequent paragraphs.

As an example of the use of this measure let us apply it to the data of Table 12.1. The proportions of judgments "greater" in that table were obtained after a division of the "doubtful" judgments proportionately to judgment categories "greater" and "less." The sum of the proportions of "greater" judgments is 3.548, which means that out of a total of 700 judgments originally given, 354.8 were "greater" and 345.2 were "less." Applying formula (12.3), we obtain

$$D\% = \frac{100(345.2 - 354.8)}{345.2 + 354.8} = -1.4$$

The *TOE* in these data is thus indicated by the difference of 1.4 per cent and the error is negative.

Neither of these methods of measuring a *TOE* is ideal. The first, which utilizes a physical scale, is meaningful in the context of psychophysics and will serve when a clearly parallel physical scale is available. It is another instance in which we state psychological values in terms of a related physical scale. The second procedure is independent of a physical scale but is faulty in that a percentage of judgments is not a measure on a linear scale. Percentages and proportions of judgments are usually taken to represent areas.

To avoid the criticisms made of the two methods of measuring a *TOE*, it is suggested that we resort to a strictly psychological scaling, stating the extent of the error in terms of psychological distances. The seven stimulus weights of Table 12.1 can be psychologically scaled by assuming Thurstone's law of comparative judgment, Case V. The deviates corresponding to the proportions in Table 12.1 are given in the last row of that table. They may be taken as the psychological values of the seven weights. One estimate of the *TOE* is the distance of the psychological value of a weight of 200 g. from the origin of this scale. We note that at the weight of 200 g. the corresponding deviate is +.04. This value might be taken as an estimate of the *amount* of *TOE* (we would need to reverse its algebraic sign, since the error is negative), but we can do better by using all the data. To use this one value would stake everything on one observed proportion. We can use all the data by fitting a regression line to the relation of z_j to S_v. This may be done by the least-squares fit or by a linear transformation or by other approximation methods described in Chap. 3. Using the linear-transformation method, we find that the line crosses the 200-g. level at a z value of +.10. We may say that *TOE* is −.10 standard-deviation units. The interpretation is that on this standard-deviation scale, weights tend to feel .10 units lighter when they are the first of two being compared.

Where Time-order Errors Are Found. The pervasiveness of the phenomenon of *TOE* is quite evident. It has been found in the judgments of many kinds of stimuli and in making many kinds of judgments. It has been studied extensively in judgments of loudness of sounds and of heaviness of lifted weights. Philip (47), Stott (65), and Woodrow (84) have found it in judgments of time intervals. Marchetti (34), McClelland (35), and Tresselt (69, 70) have found it in judgments of lines, circles, and squares. Postman (50) predicted that a *TOE* would not be found in judgments of pitch, and did not find it in that connection. His prediction was based on the Stevens hypothesis that pitch and loudness judgments would behave differently because variations in pitch depend upon a shifting to other neural elements, whereas variations in loudness depend upon quantitative changes in the same elements. Several other investigators, including Tresselt (73) and Wada (82), however, have found ample evidence for a *TOE* in the variable of pitch. Fodor and Happich (8) found the *TOE* phenomenon in connection with taste stimuli. Beebe-Center (2) and Danzfuss (5) have found it in affective judgments of odors, tones, and tone combinations.

Conditions upon Which the Time-order Error Depends. Like many a phenomenon, the *TOE* varies in direction and in size under varying conditions. It is not by any means a simple and uniform kind of event. Among the most important conditions affecting it are general level of stimuli; range of stimuli applied; time interval between stimuli; experience of the observer in the experiment; background stimuli; and other incidental conditions.

General Level of Stimuli. Woodrow (83) found, when weights were applied by the method of pair comparisons, that in the region of 130 to 140 g. the

TOE was zero. Above that range it was negative and below that range it was positive, in a systematic manner. This type of finding was verified by Needham (42) in judgments of loudness. Subsequently, Bartlett (1) made a very systematic study of this principle. He set up a geometric series of 100 weights in steps of $4(1.03)^{n-1}$, where n is the number of the weight in the series. The *TOE* was approximately zero in the range from about 40 to 70 in the weight series. Below weight 40 the *TOE* was positive and with increasing magnitude. Above weight 70 the *TOE* was increasingly negative, though this regression was less marked than that for positive errors. Figure

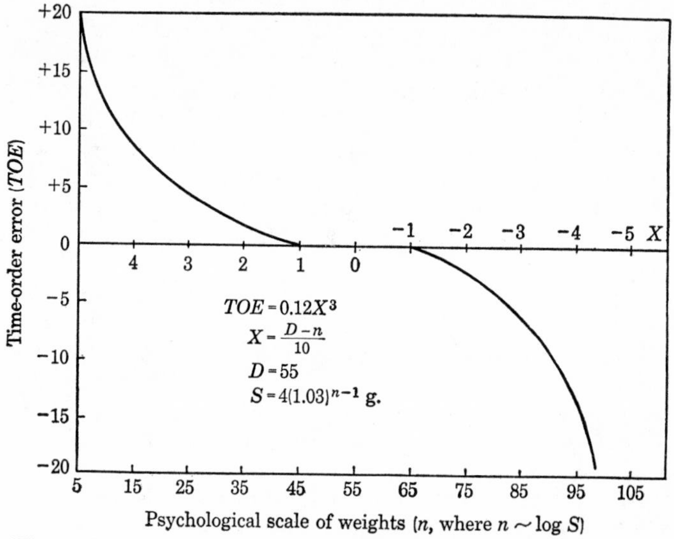

FIG. 12.2. Time-order error as a function of the position of the stimulus in a series. (*After R. J. Bartlett.*)

12.2 shows the type of regressions of *TOE* on log S obtained by Bartlett. He proposed to describe the relationships by the equation

$$R = 0.12X^3 \tag{12.4}$$

where R = amount of *TOE* in terms of steps in this weight scale and

$$X = \frac{D - n}{100}$$

[where D = a central value (presumably the midpoint of the range of zero *TOE*) and n = the weight number]. Bartlett found that some data on visual judgments obtained by Hecht could also be described well by this type of function.

Bartlett's hypothesis concerning the principle is that the impression of the first stimulus (he uses the word "image" rather than "impression") regresses toward the central value of all the stimuli in the experiment. This interpretation is probably in the right direction and places the *TOE* in the larger framework of shifting impressions in general to be discussed in this chapter.

Marchetti (34) found only positive time errors for judgments of line lengths, with lines as long as 8 ft. This raises the natural question of whether there is an indifference point somewhere above 8 ft., above which the *TOE* for line length would become negative. Our common range of experiences with lines certainly goes well above 8 ft.; thus such a neutral point would be within the realm of possibility.

The Range of Stimuli Applied. Bartlett (1) also found that the range of stimuli with zero *TOE* is not constant, but depends upon how far the stimuli of the experiment extend. When his series was extended up to a weight of 121 and later to a weight of 130, the regressions of *TOE* on *n* were of the same shape but started to depart from a *TOE* of zero at weights 77 and 88, respectively. When the highest weight was 100, the highest weight with zero *TOE* was at 70. The extension of the weight series at its upper end had no appre-

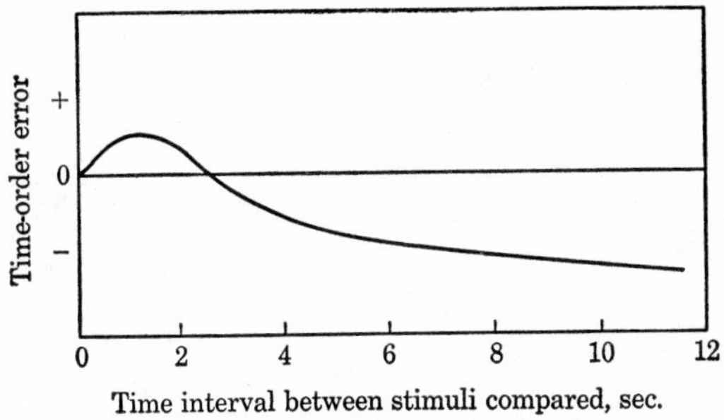

FIG. 12.3. Time-order error as a function of the time interval between the stimuli being compared.

ciable effect on the *TOE* function at the lower weight levels. Although no other investigator seems to have reported similar findings for the *TOE*, in this respect, there have been a number of reports of similar happenings when categorical judgments are used. This fact also puts the *TOE* into the general class of systematic changes of impressions.

The Time Interval between Stimuli. There have been many studies of the trend of the *TOE* as the time interval between pairs of stimuli is varied. Koehler (31) had found that when the interval is from 1 to 3 sec. the *TOE* is typically positive. With increasing time intervals, at least up to 12 sec., the error goes over on the negative side. The typical relationship is shown in Fig. 12.3. Both Wada (82) and Needham (40) have verified this functional relationship. This function does not prevail under all conditions, as we shall soon see.

Experience of the Observer in the Experiment. As an observer proceeds to give more judgments in the same experiment, the relation of the *TOE* to time interval changes radically. Koehler (31) found the trend to become less marked and less regular after 3 hr. of experimentation. Needham (40) found that after 8 to 9 days of the experiment, presumably 1 hr. each day, the functional relationship was almost completely reversed, with a negative *TOE* during short intervals and a positive *TOE* during longer intervals. Needham attributes the changes to learning but also concludes that there are many determiners for the direction and size of *TOE*. His *O*s reported that the task of judging was different under short versus long intervals, the details concerning those differences remaining unknown. It is possible that with continued practice with the same stimuli and the same time interval the *TOE* would tend toward zero.

Background Stimuli and the Time-order Error. Some of the most revealing studies of the *TOE* have been concerned with the effects of background stimulation. Background stimuli here include those impinging upon *O* simultaneously with the comparison stimuli or those interpolated between or those extrapolated before or after.

One of the first interpolation studies was reported by Guilford and Park (14). The standard was a weight of 200 g. Three interpolated weights of 100, 200, and 400 g. were introduced midway in the interval between S_s and S_v, which was constant at 7 sec. The *TOE*'s were negative in all cases except one, most strongly so with the interpolated stimulus of 100 g. and least with the interpolated stimulus of 400 g.

Lauenstein (32) and Pratt (56) found similar results in judgments of sounds. Tresselt (70), using lines and squares as stimuli, exposed in a tachistoscope, investigated the hypothesis that the tachistoscope frame would affect the *TOE*'s for the long lines and large squares more than those of short lines and small squares and would affect the *TOE*'s of squares more than of lines. The reason was that the frame was more similar in size and in form to the square and to the larger line or square. Her hypothesis was upheld strongly only in the case of the large squares, whose average *TOE* was +.44. The average *TOE* for the small squares was −.40 and for both long and short lines it was −.12. McClelland (35) found no difference in *TOE* whether judgments of lines were made in complete darkness or in a lighted room where nonexperimental lines are visible. He found the error less negative when the line was framed by a large outline square.

In a somewhat different study, with continuous background tones, Tresselt (73) found negative *TOE*'s regardless of the relation of the background pitch to that of the tones compared. The tones compared were near a standard of 521 c.p.s. The background tones were of 100, 250, 1,000, and 2,000 c.p.s., in series of experiments *A*, *B*, *D*, and *E*, respectively. In series *C* there was no background tone. The average *TOE*'s were as follows:

Series	*A*	*B*	*C*	*D*	*E*
TOE	−.90	−1.50	−2.63	−1.83	−1.10

The results are not in line with those previously found but the continuity of the background tone may be responsible.

Philip (47) both interpolated and extrapolated (before and after) a greater and a lesser stimulus with each pair of temporal durations to be judged. The standard was a light flash of 1.01 sec. duration and the background stimuli were of 0.78 and 1.39 sec. duration (*L* and *G*, respectively). In general, the *TOE* was negative with background stimulus *L* and positive with *G* when *L* and *G* precede S_s and S_v or when *L* and *G* are interpolated between them.

The reverse tended to be true when *L* and *G* followed S_s and S_v. There was some indication that the set of the observer was important, particularly his direction of attention in looking at the three stimuli.

We have one study on the effect of time interval upon the *TOE* under the condition of background stimulation. Needham (44) found that when louder (*L*) and weaker (*W*) background stimuli were interpolated and time intervals varied up to 8 sec., the effects of background stimuli on the *TOE* tend to decrease. The *TOE*'s tend to approach each other and even to become reversed.

Although we have a considerable number of facts concerning the effects of background stimulation on the *TOE*, there is little in the way of unifying principles under which to order them. The experiments need to be extended systematically over a much wider range and with combinations of other conditions. The effects of background stimulation upon categorical judgments have been investigated and the results of these studies will be mentioned later. Again, it may be said that it is probable that the conditions of the *TOE* are in common with those affecting judgments in general and that we shall understand why the *TOE* behaves as it does when we arrive at more general principles of judgment.

Effect of the Psychophysical Method Used. Postman (51) compared the *TOE*'s obtained by the method of average error and the method of constant stimulus differences. The judgments were of loudness and the time interval between pairs of tones was varied from 0 to 6 sec. The usual type of relationship between *TOE* and time interval was found by the method of constant stimuli. By the method of average error, however, the constant error was uniformly positive, averaging 1 decibel (db.). The author's conclusion was that the error by the latter method is not a genuine *TOE*. Although, as it was stated (51), the *O*s judged on a different basis in the method of average error, it would seem that in terms of all other specifiable operations this constant error is a species of *TOE*. The specific condition or set of conditions that makes the difference in the two results is simply not identified.

Karlin (29) predicted that the *TOE* would be greater when there are three categories of judgment in the method of constant stimuli than when there are two. This proved to be the case when the "equal" judgments were divided proportionately but not when they were divided evenly between "greater" and "less."

Effect of Stimulus-cessation Gradient. McClelland (35) has recently discovered another condition that appears to have a bearing upon the size and direction of the *TOE*. He found that the *TOE* for judging visual lines was negative when the exposure of lines was effected by turning on and off a light but was positive when the exposure was by shutter arrangement, other conditions being the same. The chief difference is the rate at which the stimulus begins and ends, the shutter arrangement giving the sharper gradient of change. His hypothesis is that the second stimulus is compared with the most recent impression of the first stimulus, which is one of decreasing quantity. This possibility is something to consider in connection with other experiments where negative *TOE*'s are found.

Scale Formation and Revision

In this section we shall be concerned with the problem of how, when he encounters an experimental set of stimuli to be judged, an observer adjusts to the task. We shall be particularly concerned with the situation in which he makes absolute (categorical) judgments. But we shall see that events similar to those described when he makes comparative judgments (for example, events occurring in connection with the time-order error) also occur in connection with absolute judgments. It was pointed out in Chap. 7 that so-called relative judgments partake of properties of so-called absolute judgments. The reverse is also true. Both types of judgment are affected alike by certain conditions. In brief, any observer who is inexperienced with judging a certain set of stimuli goes through a period of adjustment to the task and we find the pattern of his judgments determined by his experiences in judging these and similar stimuli and by other circumstances surrounding the experiment.

Anchoring of Scales. It has been known for a long time that judgments in categories tend to shift somewhat systematically consequent to certain changes in determining conditions. This has presented a twofold challenge. One problem is to find methods of tying a scale down so that the meanings of particular judgments are relatively fixed. Another problem is a more general one of determining the principles that account for the shifting of a scale as the stimulating conditions are varied. These problems have led to a number of investigations having to do with the effects of so-called "anchor stimuli."

Anchor stimuli have been introduced in various ways. To a list of stimuli that have been under observation may be added one or more stimuli lying beyond either end (or both ends) of the range used in the experiment. When they are so added, O may be asked to judge them along with those already in the series or he may not be asked to judge them. In the latter case, he may be exposed to each one in turn with no greater relative frequency than each of the regular stimuli or he may be exposed to an anchor stimulus alternately with every other stimulus applied. When he does not judge anchor stimuli, they serve about the same function as what were called "background" stimuli in the preceding section.

Some investigators have also referred the term *anchor stimuli* to those added *within* the range of the experiment. It has even been suggested that every stimulus in the experiment serves the function of an anchor stimulus, whether intended as such or not, in view of its appreciable effect upon the total pattern of judgments. From these comments the reader will see that the concept of an anchor stimulus itself has needed anchoring and the psychological problem goes beyond the mere addition or use of a special stimulus called an *anchor*.

Effects of Anchor Stimuli. The typical anchor experiment has given O some experience judging stimuli within a certain range and then has added one anchor stimulus beyond one end of the range. For example, Postman and Miller (54) used a series of time-interval stimuli of 250, 375, 500, 750, and 1,000 milliseconds (msec.) to be judged on a five-point scale. The anchor stimuli were, in turn, 1,000, 1,150, 1,400, and 1,500 msec. When used, each anchor stimulus was inserted just before the stimulus to be judged. The same five-point judgment scale was to be used after the introduction of the anchor stimulus.

The results from this kind of experiment are in rather good agreement as to general conclusions. These can be stated in the form of principles derived primarily from the experiments of Volkmann (80), Hunt and Volkmann (20), Rogers, (62), McGarvey (36), and Cohen (4), as well as Postman and Miller (54).

1. A scale extends toward an anchor stimulus that is outside the stimulus range. Figure 12.4 represents the essential facts concerning the shifting of a scale due to the presence of an anchor stimulus. Assume a five-point scale of successive categories of somewhat different widths. The limens can be expressed in terms of physical values by reference to

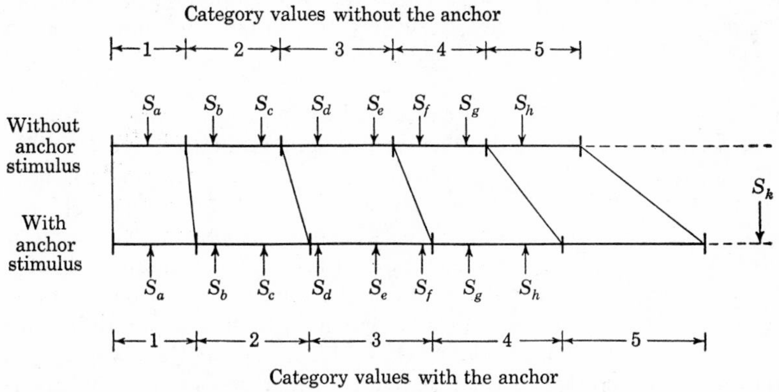

FIG. 12.4. Illustration of the change in a judgment scale following the introduction of an anchor stimulus above the range of experimental stimuli.

stimulus values that come at the division points between categories. Stimuli S_a to S_h are allocated to positions within the categories as shown. When the anchor stimulus S_k is introduced, the shifting is expressible as a raising of the limens (in terms of stimulus values) or a lowering of scale values of stimuli (none achieves a category value of 5). Other principles to be mentioned next are also illustrated in Fig. 12.4.

Several subsidiary principles qualify the first general statement:

a. The farther the anchor stimulus from the stimulus range, the greater the shift.

b. The more remote the anchor stimulus, the less the *increment* of shift. By this is meant that the shifting effect shows diminishing returns.

c. The closer the stimulus to the anchor, the greater is its shift on the scale.

d. The extension of the scale toward the anchor stimulus is never complete. An exception to this may be when *O* is instructed to judge the anchor stimulus along with the others.

e. One effect of the extension is to broaden the categories.

2. The end of the scale without an anchor stimulus remains fixed. Only in rare instances does this end of the scale "pull loose" from its mooring.

3. An anchor may be moved so far from the stimulus range that the shifting of the scale reaches a "breaking point." In this event the limens fall back, but not completely.

4. An imagined stimulus may also serve as an anchor.

5. The anchorage effects are not dependent upon specific instruction to modify scales.

6. Anchors *within* the stimulus range, when not balanced around a central stimulus value, have effects like those outside the range.

7. Anchorage effects apply to many kinds of judgments. Among those to which they have been found to apply are judgments of lifted weights (62), slants of lines (62, 80), time intervals (54), affective values of odors (4) and of colors (20), and judgments of desirability of behaviors and of importance of traits for occupations (36).

Learning in Scale Formation. The extension of anchorage effects to anchor stimuli *within* the stimulus range suggests the need for a more general view of the problem. The present conception is that *O* goes through a period of adjustment to any scale, with or without anchor stimuli, and the adjustment is a phenomenon of learning. Experiments have been instituted to determine how the phenomena of learning apply to scale formation, a subject that will next engage our attention.

In 1942, Tresselt and Volkmann (75) proposed the hypothesis that the principles of judgment are the principles of conditioning. An individual's scale is therefore a function of stimulations of a similar nature that he has experienced in the past and it is subject to change with new experiences. From this it should be expected that a group of individuals who are subjected to the same experiences should gravitate toward the same scale of evaluations. When 120 *O*s were exposed to a series of weights, ranging from 11 to 560 g., that they judged only once in different sequences, the *O*s did tend toward a common scale. Judgments were in three categories, "heavy," "medium," and "light." There was a very wide dispersion of weights judged "medium" in the first trial, but this dispersion decreased, more rapidly at first and then more slowly approached a minimum. There was some evidence of discontinuity at about the fourth and fifth weights lifted. About 60 per cent of the *O*s noticed a change in their own standards coming at about these positions in their series of experiences in the experiment.

Johnson (22) approached the problem by varying systematically the composition of a set of stimuli used in an experiment. In an experiment with 10 lifted weights ranging from 20 to 100 g., he administered positively and negatively skewed distributions of stimuli in two different sets. With two categories of judgments he determined limens under the two conditions. The means of limens were 29.6 for the series with concentration of lighter weights (positive skew) and 70.3 for the series with concentration of heavier weights (negative skew). One might predict these limens to be very close to the geometric means of the series, if Fechner's law applies to the weights. They were both lower than the geometric means, which were 32.6 and 77.7. Johnson attempted to account for the discrepancies by making a modification in Fechner's law to take into account another feature of conditioning, the *generalization gradient.* This concept as applied to the psychophysical-judgment situation means that the same response (judgment category) spreads over a range of stimulus magnitudes with one particular magnitude most typical of it. More will be said concerning the application of this concept to psychophysical judgments in later paragraphs. Sufficient to say here that with his correction Johnson predicted limens of 30.7 and 67.9, respectively, which are nearer the obtained limens.

Johnson tested his hypothesis with other biased distributions of weight stimuli (22), with judgments of distances of pennies from a wall at which they had been tossed (24), and with judgments of pitch of sounds (26). Sometimes one limen (from two-category judgments) was predicted and obtained and sometimes more than one limen (three or more categories of judgment). In general, Johnson's equation predicted the limens more often too high than too low. There was some tendency to predict the lower limens too low and the higher limens too high. The errors of prediction were greater than one might be willing to tolerate in some experiments, in spite of the fact that the coefficient of correlation between 29 predicted and obtained limens for pitch was .97. An incidental finding was that a limen could be predicted better from more recent experiences than from an average including more remote experiences (26).

The Transition from One Scale to Another. It is possible to trace the transition from one scale to another as *O* gains more experience with the new set of stimuli. In making the change from one set of stimuli to the other, *O* keeps the same judgment categories. Johnson (27) proposed the hypothesis that the limen at any moment during the transition should be a weighted average of the two limens existing before and after the transition. In terms of an equation,

$$L_n = \frac{wL_1 + nL_2}{w + n} \tag{12.5}$$

where L_n = limen after n trials with new series
L_1 = limen before transition
L_2 = limen after transition
w = weight given to first limen relative to weight of one trial in new series

Johnson interprets w psychologically as the contribution of the experience in the first series to impeding adaptation to the second series.

In an experiment with judgments of pitch, for example, Johnson (27) would expose *O* to a set of higher-pitched tones (numbered 10 to 18 in his quarter-octave series) several times, to be judged in two categories. He then exposed a set of lower-pitched tones (steps 1 through 9) to be judged in the same two categories. The predicted shift was from a limen of 14 to one of 5. The mean limen for the first three trials was actually 13.83 and for the last three trials 5.07. The weight w, as empirically determined, was 0.13, indicating the relatively small effect of the old impressions in preventing a change to the new standards. The type of progress in learning is indicated by the curve in Fig. 12.5, where the rapid adjustment to a new series is very clear. Figure 12.5 is based upon experiments in which the shift was from a lower to a higher set of pitches. With a shift in this direction there was more resistance to change, the rate being shown by a resistance weight (w) of 0.96 and by the fact that at the seventh trial the limen was still a whole unit (quarter octave) below 14.0.

When the number of exposures (for judgment) of the first set of stimuli was varied for different *O*s, with 1, 2, 3, and 5 exposures, the weight w (for a shift upward) was 0.36, 0.65, 0.96, and 1.22, respectively. Since the more recent experiences should be more potent than the earlier ones, one should hardly expect a w greater than 1.00. The fact that it does happen to exceed 1.00 must mean that there is some extra predisposing resistance against permitting the limen to climb to the predicted level. The background of experience prior to the experiment should be taken into consideration, as we shall see in the next experiments to be reported.

Although the results in general appear to fit the curve described by equation (12.5) well enough to support strongly Johnson's hypothesis, as he points out, there are obvious discrepancies here and there suggestive of minor discontinuities, perhaps due to insightful events. It is of incidental interest to add here that there are individual differences in resistance to change of scale. This suggests that the constant w might be used as a score of some personality trait in the area of perseveration or rigidity. It would be useful for such a purpose, however, to the extent that all tested individuals have had considerable past experiences of the kind employed in the test. Tresselt and Becker (74), however, did not find positive evidence of relation of line-drawing tendencies and temperament traits as measured by inventories.

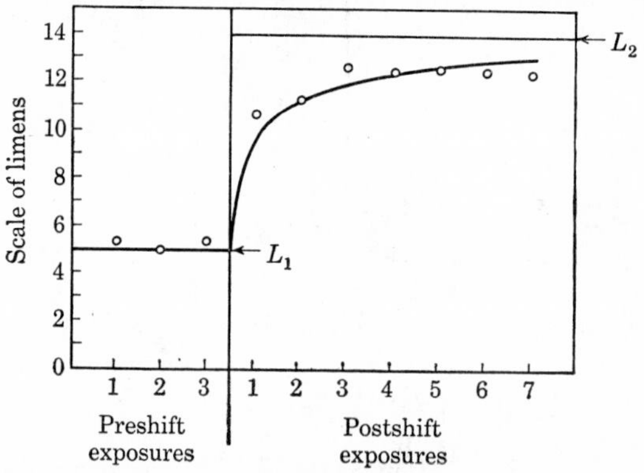

FIG. 12.5. Transition of a limen after change to a new set of stimuli, described as a learning function. (*After D. M. Johnson. J. exp. Psychol.*, 1949, **39**, 851–860. *By permission of the American Psychological Association.*)

Effects of Previous General Experience. In an investigation performed earlier than Johnson's learning study just cited, Tresselt (71) had found essentially the same general results using series of lifted weights. It was noted that one or two *O*s resisted changes to a new scale, giving "light" judgments to almost all stimuli. It was found that one of these *O*s belonged to a weight-lifting club in which he had been accustomed to lifting weights of from 100 to 300 lb. In a subsequent investigation Tresselt (72) specifically studied the effects of previous experience by using 36 professional weight lifters and 36 professional watchmakers as subjects. The results show that the means of weights that the professional weight lifters called "medium" were systematically higher than those for students. There was one exception. After lifting two or three weights, the professional weight lifters seemed to realize their maladaptation to the series and they overcorrected, but they later reverted to their typical constant error. The means of weights judged "medium" by the watchmakers were not very different from those of the students. They also showed the "overcompensatory reaction" at about the third weight lifted. Both groups showed decreasing variability of categorical judgments as they gained more experience with the experimental weights. In her interpretations Tresselt suggests that the better adaptation of the watchmakers was due to the fact that their previous experiences in lifting had not been nearly so similar to the task in the experiments as had been the experience of the weight lifters. We should have expected the negative transfer effects to be greater for the professional weight lifters. We may conclude that similar pre-experimental experiences may have a marked effect upon scale formation. We may expect that where previous experience is effective, the central tendency of the new scale will lie in the direction of that experience, and the more biased the former experience the more slowly will the new center approach the "normal" center.

Judgment and the Stimulus-generalization Gradient. Reference was made earlier to the fact that the principle of the stimulus-generalization gradient can be applied to psychophysical judgments. This idea has been suggested by Cartwright (3), Johnson (22), and others. Figure 12.6 repre-

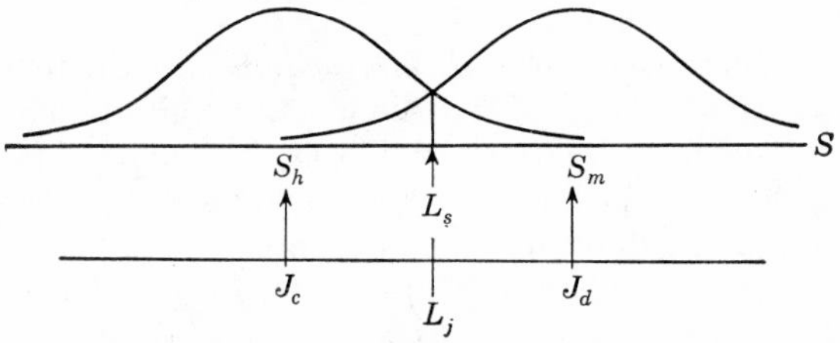

FIG. 12.6. Two stimulus-generalization gradients corresponding to two categorical judgments.

sents the general picture of this application to the categorical psychophysical judgment. We have there two judgments, J_c and J_d, separated by a limen L_j represented on the judgment scale. The most common stimulus giving rise to the judgment J_c is S_h and the most common stimulus to elicit the judgment J_d is S_m. There is a range of stimuli eliciting J_c in diminishing relative frequency as a function of distance from S_h. Another range elicits J_d with diminishing frequency as a function of distance from S_m. The two ranges overlap with similar frequencies at L_s.

This picture suggests one or two other related ideas. It is reminiscent of Fig. 2.3, which represents similar relationships between stimuli and quantities on the response continuum. The parallel is only superficial, however, for the relationships involved differ in two important respects. In Fig. 12.6 we have the judgment continuum instead of the response continuum. If the judgment and response continua are perfectly correlated in an experimental situation, then we can substitute the response continuum in Fig. 12.6. If we do that, however, there is still the difference that in Fig. 2.3 we are dealing with the regression of R on S, whereas in Fig. 12.6 we are dealing with the regression of S on J. The similarity suggests, however, that in Fig. 2.3 we have essentially what may be called *response-generalization gradients* representing ranges of equivalent responses to particular *stimuli*. In Fig. 12.6 we have *stimulus-generalization gradients* representing ranges of equivalent stimuli that elicit particular *responses*.

From the standpoint of methodology, the picture in Fig. 12.6 suggests another principle for determining a limen on the S scale. The principle is based on the solution to the problem of predition of categories from measurements (see Guilford, 12, pp. 371*ff*.). Space will not be taken to describe the application of that principle here. The essence of the principle is that the limen L_s comes at an S value at which the probability of the S being in the one judgment category equals that of the S being in the other category. There are graphic as well as algebraic solutions to this problem (12). We would start with a matrix of frequencies such as that in Table 9.4. In scaling the stimuli represented there, we used the distribution of frequencies of observations of each stimulus over the various judgment categories. These distributions are in the *rows* of the table. We could also deal with the frequency distributions in the *columns*. These distributions represent the kind of distributions pictured in Fig. 12.6. Each cell in Table 9.4 shows how frequently, relatively, each stimulus is placed in a specified judgment category, and how frequently, relatively, each judgment category is applied to a specified stimulus.

The Shape of the Stimulus-generalization Gradient. Up to this point we have not considered the shape of the stimulus-generalization gradient in the psychophysical-judgment situation. Johnson (22) assumed the gradient on either side of the mode to be linear. This would be the simplest assumption. He has used this assumption in explaining preferences for number "judgments" in sequences of consecutive numbers. He regarded the number series as a highly generalized series of stimulus-generalization gradients (25).

Figure 12.6 shows the double gradient as a normal distribution. Logically, if the response-generalization gradient is normal, as Thurstone assumes, for linear, or nearly linear, regressions over the short ranges of S and R involved in a single gradient, it would seem, intuitively, that the stimulus-generalization gradient should also be normal. We have some experimental evidence on this point, though it is not conclusive. Philip (46) attempted to determine the shape of the gradient by having 11 stimuli judged in 11 successive categories. The stimuli varied in the relative proportions of spots of two colors. Eleven examples of double gradients (some of them incomplete) could be derived from the data. These were superimposed and averaged in order to obtain a single, general picture of the stimulus-generalization gradient. The result was a slightly skewed and slightly leptokurtic distribution, not departing very markedly from normal.

More recently Postman (53) studied the same problem by means of a recognition-memory test for six-letter nonsense words. Twenty-four such words were exposed to learners. In the recognition test 6 words were identical with 6 that had been exposed, 6 had five letters in common, 6 had 4 letters in common, 6 had 3 in common, and the remaining 24 had an average of 1.3 letters in common. The percentage of recognitions (correct and incorrect) at each degree of similarity was given as follows:

Degree of similarity.......	6	5	4	3	1.3
Per cent recognized........	95.5	85.3	61.2	40.0	30.1

The trend looks much like half of a normal distribution curve. It is probably a good hypothesis that under common conditions the double gradient that marks off the range of equivalent stimuli is somewhat normal in form. Probable exceptions will be noted.

Special Conditions Affecting the Stimulus-generalization Gradient. There are several indications in the experimental results that continued practice reduces the range of equivalence (3) and this should modify the distribution in the direction of leptokurtosis. This principle could be predicted from the facts of conditioning. Special instructions may also be effective in narrowing the range (3). If the stimuli are multidimensional, equivalence may depend upon more than one dimension unless the instructions clearly and effectively specify the use of only one dimension. As *O* successfully isolates one dimension, his range of equivalence should decrease. The sharpness of the gradient is also influenced by background stimuli and by context in general. For example, Cartwright (3) presented the word "huge" in two sentences: "Yesterday I saw a huge man," and "Yesterday I saw a huge building." *O* was given in turn 10 other words each of which he could accept or reject as a substitute for "huge." The words were immense, grand, great, vast, colossal, large, magnificent, big, mighty, and massive. *O* tended to accept a wider range of words when describing a building than when describing a man. The range of equivalence was greater in the one context than in the other.

Cartwright (3) predicted that in the sphere of attitudes an individual who is extreme on an attitude continuum will have a sharper gradient for that end than for the opposite end. For example, a radical person should rate few people in his own category and more in the conservative, and vice versa. An extremely radical *O* and an extremely conservative *O* were each given the names of 20 people who ranged widely in attitude on this continuum and who were given rank positions on it. For the radical *O*, the radical category covered 7.5 rank positions while the conservative category covered 10. For the conservative *O*, the conservative category covered 5.2 ranks and the radical category 8.5. The generality of this phenomenon is unknown, but it is interesting that it could be correctly deduced for at least one attitude continuum from conditioning and psychophysical principles.

The Need for the Concept of a Judgment Continuum. It should be abundantly clear by this time that there is not a unique and universal connection between any stimulus and any average categorical judgment. Within the larger frame of reference of an entire stimulus continuum the same set of judgment categories sometimes applies to one general level on the stimulus continuum and sometimes to another. The same tone in the context of one range of tones is readily called "very high" in pitch and in the context of another range of tones is readily called "very low." A weight of 200 g. may be called "very, very heavy" in a range of weights 20 to 200 g., while it may well be called "very light" in a range from 200 to 2,000 g. It is not likely that the response *R*, in terms of actual feeling of weight, changes as much as the change in judgment indicates, though it probably changes somewhat.

When an average category judgment changes by a certain amount in response to a given stimulus, it is difficult to say how much of the change is in

R and how much is in *J*, these being on separate continua, response and judgment continua, respectively. It is likely that whenever there is a major scale revision, the observer undergoes adjustments of both his relations of *R* to *S* and his relations of *J* to *R*. Following a drastic change of stimulus levels, the judgment categories remaining the same, at first the normal modal relations of *R* to *S* are disturbed as well as the preceding relations of *J* to *R*. The modal relations of *R* to *S* may return to nearly "normal" rather quickly as the effects of the most recent experiences wear off and a new system of *J*-to-*R* relationships is established. This also means a somewhat stabilized set of relationships between *J* and *S*, as Johnson (27) has shown experimentally, within the limits of the gradients of equivalent stimuli.

The methodological implication is that any *O* should be given some practice trials during which he is permitted to develop a somewhat stabilized series of response levels and of judgments more uniquely related to them. The data from such preliminary trials should not be used unless it can be shown that they do not differ significantly from the body of the data that follows. The designing of experiments should also take into account the possibilities of systematic shifts which may serve to conceal other systematic differences that constitute the major subject of investigation.

Some Special Conditions of Judgment

Before we attempt to generalize concerning the phenomena of judgment described in preceding sections and to arrive at more general principles or a comprehensive theory of psychophysical judgment, we should consider some additional determiners of judgment. Some of these are rather incidental conditions having only methodological significance, while others are of more general psychological interest.

Goodfellow (11, p. 34) has aptly said, "A sensory threshold is a function of the total personality and the total environment and not merely of the particular stimulus upon which the observer is asked to make a judgment." Not all of the conditions of the environment and of personality are reflected to an appreciable degree in the results, but we need to know which ones are significantly effective and which ones are not.

Environmental Conditions. Some of the more important environmental conditions have been mentioned in the preceding discussions, including the composition of the stimulus series, background stimuli, and other contextual stimuli. Some of the effects were noted in terms of time-order errors, shifting limens, and modified stimulus-generalization gradients. More subtle and less-suspected conditions may also be effective, such as which experimenter operates the experiment and whether the experimenter is in the same room or in a separate one (9, 11); the instruction to the observer (9); the "atmosphere" within which the experiment is made (23); the rate of onset of stimulation (11); and simultaneous stimulation of other sense organs (11). The effects reported in connection with these conditions have been varied and are not always reproducible. They are things possibly to be considered in any experimental situation.

Physical Condition of the Observer. Some surprising results have been found concerning the effects of physical conditions upon limens. Goodfellow

(11) found that limens were lower (sensitivity greater) after *O*s had been kept awake all night than after 12 hr. of sleep and rest in bed. Sensitivity was found to be greater after a 12-mile hike. Sensitivity was also found increased during muscular tension, and when the tests were made on a finger the effects were similar when the tension was in the finger or in remote muscle groups.

Motivation and Suggestion. When the observer is specially motivated, his limens are likely to be lower (9). Extra encouragement is sometimes sufficient to produce apparently increased sensitivity (11).

Although some common tests of suggestibility have utilized judgments of small sensory differences, little thought has been given to the effect of suggestion on limens. Goodfellow (9) has shown that the effects may be very appreciable. When *O*s were told that the hand lotion on their fingertips would increase sensitivity, obtained limens were lower. When *O*s were told that alcohol removed the sensitizing drug, limens went back to "normal." When other *O*s were told that the lotion was applied merely to prevent chafing, the limens remained unaffected. When *O*s were given drinks of Sanka and of other coffee without knowledge that one had been decaffeinated, limens were lowered under both conditions. After *O*s were told they were getting Sanka, limens returned to normal. One psychologist who took measurements of his own auditory threshold every morning believed that he had no variations from day to day and found none. When the calibration of the audiometer was changed from day to day without his knowledge, he showed genuine variations, in keeping with the changed calibrations! Senders and Sowards (63) have found that *O*s tend to give different judgments in proportion as they are told to expect them. The sophisticated experimenter will learn the appropriate lessons from all these results.

Judgment Habits and Sets. When psychophysical judgments, or other human or animal responses of a simple alternative sort, are made to impossible tasks, it is usually assumed that the choice of responses will be unbiased, that is to say, in the nature of a "chance" event. Guessing is presumed by the investigator to occur at random in order that he may take advantage of mathematical models based on assumptions of random events. Experience shows that the assumption of randomness may not always be justified and that in some instances the outcomes show marked departures from such a state of affairs.

An example of this is an experiment by Goodfellow (10), who asked students to make guesses as to whether a coin had fallen heads or tails. On the first throw the over-all proportion of "heads" responses was .80. On the second throw the proportion of "heads" responses was still above the a priori probability—it was .57. On the third throw the majority of responses swung in the opposite direction, there being a proportion of .44 "heads" responses.

Earlier than the Goodfellow experiment, Preston (59) had given his *O*s the task of judging many differences all of zero. There were 14 pairs of weights, all of 100 g. Judgments were to be in three categories: *G* (greater), *E* (equal), and *L* (less). Preston's chief concern was the extent to which *O* repeats himself in successive judgments. For the three judgments there are nine possible immediate sequences of two: *LL*, *LE*, *LG*, *EL*, *EE*, *EG*, *GL*, *GE*, and *GG*. He found that not only does *O* tend to avoid giving the sequences *LL*,

EE, and *GG*, but he also tends, though less clearly, to avoid such sequences as *LEL* and *LGL*, in other words repeating the same judgment for two or three occasions following. Preferred sequences beginning with *L*, *E*, and *G* were *LG*, *EG*, and *GE*. It will be noted, incidentally, that these three sequences not only avoid repetition but also work toward a negative time-order error.

Other investigators have found results supporting those of Preston, among them Goodfellow (10) and Philip (45). There has been some suggestion that the avoidance of repetition of the same judgment is an instance of Thorndike's refractory-phase hypothesis (66). A study of Preston and Zeid (61) throws doubt on the Thorndike hypothesis as necessarily applying to a sequence of choices. The experiment was a maze that offered the possibility of sequences of as many as five right or left turns. Such repetitive sequences were taken *more* often than expected by chance.

The best explanation for the avoidance of runs of judgments, when this occurs, seems to be a mental set against runs. A similar avoidance of simple alternations occurs. Goodfellow offered *O*s sequences of five guesses as to how a coin fell (10). He found not only avoidance of runs and of alternations but of other obviously systematic patterns, such as symmetrical ones. His hypothesis was that in such circumstances *O* recognizes the situation as a chance affair and he has learned enough about games of chance in the past to know that *regular* sequences of outcomes are unlikely. He regulates his sequences of judgments accordingly. The avoidance of alternations has been found by others (59), except that in the maze situation Preston and Zeid found runs and alternations *more* frequent than by chance expectation (61). This can be accounted for by the fact that the maze does not seem to the observer to be a gambling situation. The Goodfellow hypothesis seems to be generally acceptable, with limitations.

The Role of Difficulty of Judgment. All investigators find that it is when the level of difficulty in an experiment is high that mental sets are most effective in producing biased results. Faced with what seems to be an impossible judgment task, *O* will grasp at anything that seems to be an aid. For example, Thornton (67) found that in photographs a smiling person is likely to be rated as more honest than one not smiling. A person wearing glasses is likely to be rated higher for intelligence, dependability, industriousness, and honesty. Such effects were found to be less when the rater saw the ratee personally than when pictures were used (68).

Implications for Methodology. The effects of suggestion and of habits or sets seem to be the most serious ones from the point of view of well-controlled experimentation. Although we have definite evidence for the *O*'s tendency to control the proportions of his judgments in categories, to avoid regular sequences, and to use secondary cues and self-imposed sets of various kinds, we should not generalize too sweepingly from the few experiments. While typical *O*s may behave in the ways that Goodfellow found in a sequence of five judgments in a coin-tossing situation, they may behave differently in judging in a situation that is not so obviously a chance affair and where the sequence of stimuli is a long one.

From a statistical point of view this is a serious question. For if the peculiar judging habits found by Goodfellow and others hold generally in psychophysical experiments, we have much interdependence of observations, and consequently sampling statistics will not apply. Verplanck, Collier, and Cotton (78) found that in making long series of visual judgments there were signs of interdependence of judgments as remote as the eleventh position. They, also, asked for judgments of liminal stimuli only, however.

Senders and Sowards (63), who studied long series of judgments in a psychophysical setting, found results differing conspicuously from those of Goodfellow. They extracted out of long series of responses as many sets of sequences of four or five as possible and studied their contents. Runs of the same response were quite common, as well as symmetrical patterns, such as were rare in the Goodfellow results. Their conclusion is that in the ordinary psychophysical experiment there need be little concern about biased sequences brought about by the set to avoid system. They recommend, however, that *O* should never be told the over-all proportion of each kind of judgment to expect and that there should be an adequate proportion of easy judgments and no protracted runs of very difficult judgments, so that *O* maintains confidence that he is actually observing and not guessing. This advice appears to be very sound. It is likely that in an experiment that follows these precautions judgments may be assumed to be independent and hence this fundamental requirement for statistical analysis may be regarded as satisfied.

Regression Phenomena

Central Tendency. A number of investigators have reported a phenomenon found in judging many kinds of stimuli under a variety of conditions and methods—a tendency for stimuli to be judged in the direction of a central region or point. Consider, for example, a recent experiment of Turchioe (76). Observers were asked to reproduce three different standard time intervals of 780, 1,010, and 1,390 msec. The averages of reproductions were 840, 1,014, and 1,200, respectively. Thus there was little error in connection with the middle standard, but the matching stimulus for the short standard was too large and that for the long standard was too small.

Hollingworth (18) is credited with discovering and naming the central-tendency phenomenon in 1909. He was working with reproductions of hand movements over linear distances. Within each series of standards used on any one day, *O* developed a system of positive and negative constant errors. The system had a neutral point on the stimulus scale at which there was neither overestimation nor underestimation. Below the neutral point there was overestimation and above it there was underestimation. With the standard stimuli in three sets ranging from 70 to 250 mm., 30 to 150 mm., and 10 to 70 mm., the neutral points were roughly near 120, 65, and 35, respectively. We have in the central-tendency phenomenon something that behaves very much like the time-order error discussed earlier in this chapter. It is likely that both will be explained by the same principle or principles.

Central Tendency as a Statistical Regression. One very promising conception of the central-tendency phenomenon is a recent suggestion of Johnson (28). He proposed the idea that the *averages* of judgments of stimuli in a series must show some regression toward the central tendency of that series because of imperfect discrimination. This is easiest to see in connection with stimuli judged in successive categories. If discriminations were perfect, a stimulus would always receive the same judgment, for there would be no discriminal dispersion. The mean of psychological impressions and of judgments for this stimulus would be as far from the mean of all stimuli in the series as each and every impression or judgment of that stimulus is. When there is imperfect discrimination and some dispersion on the R continuum, like any predicted value, the mean R and the mean judgment regress toward the mean of the series.

This can be illustrated by means of the problem of judgments of actors used in Chap. 10. For every actor there was considerable dispersion of

TABLE 12.2. ESTIMATION OF TRUE (UNREGRESSED) SCALE VALUES T_j OF THE 15 ACTORS FROM OBTAINED (REGRESSED) SCALE VALUES M_j

Actor	M_j	σ_j	T_j
A	1.447	.706*	2.66
B	1.280	1.016*	2.09
C	1.617	.881*	3.25
D	.598	1.169	− .25
E	1.224	.868	1.90
F	.643	.914	− .10
G	.788	.947	.40
H	.788	.945	.40
I	.813	.983	.48
J	.239	1.040	−1.49
K	.518	.914	− .53
L	.964	1.058	1.00
M	.847	.928	.60
N	1.016	.975	1.18
O	1.438	1.053*	2.63
Σ	14.220	14.397	14.22
M	.948	.960	.948
σ	.375		1.29

* Underestimates.

judgments, as we can see from the standard deviations in Table 12.2. We have reproduced in Table 12.2 the mean scale values of the 15 actors and their standard deviations as computed by the category-value method of scaling. If a central-tendency effect has occurred, the mean scale values have much less spread than the original or actual values of the actors. We can thus think of two variables: (1) the scale of the *true* spacing of the actors, on which the dispersion of the 15 actor values is greater than that of the 15 obtained scale values, and (2) the scale of the 15 *obtained* means. Let us call the true scale values T_j and the obtained ones M_j. It is as if we had a prediction problem, or correlation problem, of the relationship of the obtained scale values to the true scale values. The "predictions" are made from the true scale values T_j. The predictions are the means M_j. The dispersions of the single judgments A_j around these means represent the distributions of errors of prediction.

Correlation between True Values and Single Judgments. As indicated in Chap. 3 and in statistical textbooks (12, p. 397), the extent of the regression is indicated, inversely, by the size of the correlation coefficient. The correlation that describes the regression under consideration here is that between single judgments and the true scale values T_j, or between the single judgments and the mean scale values M_j. We may assume that the obtained mean scale values, although showing less dispersion, are perfectly correlated with the true scale values.[1] We could actually compute the correlation between the single judgments A_j and means M_j, using category values such as those in Table 10.12 and cell frequencies such as those in Table 10.11, but there is a much shorter way of estimating this correlation in this situation.

The total variance of all the single judgments in the sample may be regarded as composed of two components: that contributed by sums of squares *within* actors (nonpredicted variance) and that contributed by sums of squares *between* actors M_j (predicted variance). The larger the latter is relative to the former, the greater the correlation between M_j and the single judgments. This correlation is the ratio of the standard deviation of the means M_j to the standard deviation of all single judgments combined. The square of this correlation coefficient gives the proportion of the total variance in the *sample* that is contributed by the variations in means M_j. In terms of a formula,

$$r_{at} \doteq \frac{\sigma_m}{\sigma_a} \tag{12.6}$$

where r_{at} = correlation between single judgments A_j and true values T_j
σ_m = standard deviation of means M_j, in other words, the standard deviation of "predicted" judgments
σ_a = standard deviation of all single judgments combined

The entire distribution of single judgments of the 15 actors would be found in a table such as Table 10.11.

It should be pointed out that in applying the Pearson product-moment r here, the usual assumptions must be satisfied, including that of homoscedasticity. Homoscedasticity means equality of discriminal dispersions, in other words, as applied here, Thurstone's Case V. We have evidence that the standard deviations of the actors are not homogeneous, in spite of the relatively narrow range of standard deviations (see Table 12.2), but we proceed to use these data as an illustration, for want of better data.

The total variability of the single judgments is indicated by σ_a, which equals 1.289. The variability of the obtained means is indicated by σ_m, which is .375. The ratio σ_m/σ_a gives us .291 as the estimate of the correlation r_{at}. From this we find the standard error of estimate to be

$$\sigma_{at} = 1.289\sqrt{1 - .0847} = 1.233$$

[1] A possible exception will be noted later.

The average dispersion that we should expect *within* actors is thus 1.233. The mean of the standard deviations actually computed (see Table 12.2) is .960, which is somewhat smaller. There are two reasons for this discrepancy, the first more certain than the second. The first is that some of the computed standard deviations are underestimations due to truncation of distributions at the upper ends. The second reason may be lack of homoscedasticity.

Figure 12.7 shows graphically the situation we have been discussing with respect to the actor data. The slope of the regression line is determined by the correlation of .291. Dotted lines have been drawn at vertical distances of 1.233 (the standard error of estimate) from the regression line. At any true scale value we may select, there is assumed to be a normal distribution whose mean is at the regression line and whose standard deviation is σ_{at}.

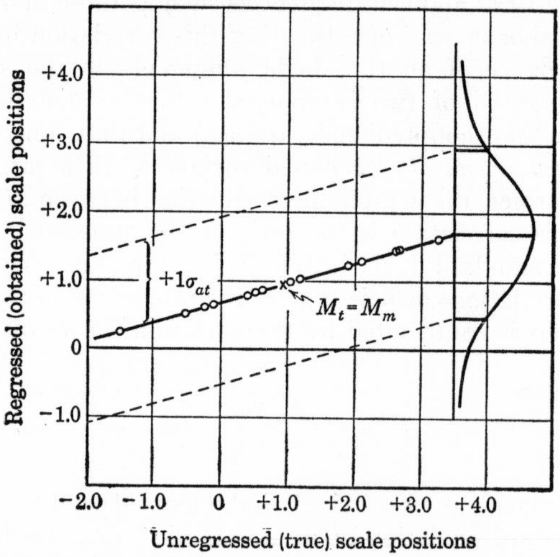

FIG. 12.7. Regression of estimated scale values toward the mean of all stimuli.

Estimating True Scale Values. It is of some interest to see what the 15 true scale values may be like, since they have a much wider dispersion than the 15 obtained scale values M_j. We have used these M_j values to represent measurements of the 15 actors. The estimation of the true scale values can be carried out as follows. We have assumed the means and the true scale values to be perfectly correlated. We may also assume that the means of the two sets of scale values, true and obtained, are equal. The regression line pivots about these means. The correlation being perfect, all we need is a linear-transformation equation. This involves the ratio of the two standard deviations for true and obtained scale values. We know that $\sigma_m = .375$. We will assume that $\sigma_t = \sigma_a = 1.289$. The justification for this is that in the limiting case where $r_{at} = 1.0$, A_j is perfectly "predicted" from T_j. Under this condition $\sigma_t = \sigma_a$. The ratio of the two standard deviations σ_a/σ_m equals 3.436, which also equals $1/r_{at}$. The transformation equation becomes

$$T_j = 3.436(M_j - .948) + .948 = 3.436M_j - 2.309$$

where the first .948 is the mean of the M_j values and the second is M_t.

The estimated true values for the 15 actors are given under T_j in Table 12.2. It is readily noticed that whereas no M_j value is negative, four of the T_j *are* negative, two of them definitely so. This leads to the conclusion that although two actors may have been definitely on the unpopular side of the indifference point, the regression effect has put them on the popular side in the process of scaling! If this interpretation is correct, one should use caution in accepting obtained scale values involving a supposedly genuine psychological zero point unless discriminations are very good.

Limitations to the Regression Treatment. There are evidently a number of limiting conditions to the application of the regression model, as used in the illustration above. The condition of homoscedasticity was not satisfied in the actor data, and it will not be satisfied generally except where Thurstone's Case V prevails. Homoscedasticity had to be assumed with evidence to the contrary in this particular illustration. If there is demonstrated homoscedasticity, the assumption of linearity may be easy to accept. When there are systematic discrepancies among the dispersions of stimuli, however, there may be real departures from linearity. When there is linearity, but when dispersions differ significantly, stimuli having greater dispersions may have regressed more toward the mean than stimuli having smaller dispersions. This would mean lack of perfect correlation between the true and obtained (mean) scale values. Assuming that the amounts of regressions are unequal for different stimuli, one could perhaps use the information concerning dispersions to make slight corrections in obtained scale values.

It seems likely that a regression effect does occur and that the statistical operations involved provide us with additional quantitative information. It is possible that the coefficient of correlation, for example, can be used as an index of sensitivity. The index of determination r^2 would be a better value to use because of its additive properties. It would indicate the proportion of the variance in the single judgments that can be called "true" variance, *i.e.*, variance that is determined by the true scale values. The coefficients k and k^2 would also indicate the amount of regression and the amount of error of observation, respectively. The standard error of estimate of an obtained scale value would also be an over-all index of errors of observation.

Adaptation Level

There has been only one serious attempt to arrive at a single general principle that would account for the many phenomena of judgment mentioned in this chapter. This is the concept of *adaptation level*, which seems to be most promising as an underlying and unifying principle. The idea originated with Helson (16), who discovered it first in connection with judgments of visual qualities. As a principle, the adaptation-level concept is not confined to judgments of sensory properties but applies, by analogy, at least, to very complex perceptual events. We have heard much in recent years from social psychologists concerning "frames of reference" and "contexts." It is likely that the concept of adaptation level provides more rigorous patterns for the description of such phenomena.

Origin of the Adaptation-level Concept. Helson first arrived at the adaptation-level idea in studies of color constancy, color contrast, color conversion, and adaptation (15). The concept can best be explained by reference to his experimental design. Before Helson's experiments the color phenomena just mentioned were regarded as somewhat unrelated events. Conflicting results on colors had been obtained, such as shifts from a color-constancy event to a color-contrast event with a very slight change in conditions. Helson conceived of the general color problem as involving three experimental variables: the color object, its background, and the nature of the illumination. He therefore proposed to vary each of these variables over wide ranges in many combinations. The background color (under standard illumination) was varied in three steps, white, gray, and black, with reflectances of .03 (3 per cent), .26, and .80, respectively. The object colors varied in a larger number of steps, ranging in reflectance from .03 to .80. For every combination of background and object color, there were four different illuminants described as red, green, yellow, and blue.

In very brief and general terms, the results were as follows. An object with reflectance level above that of its background took on the hue of the illuminant. An object with reflectance level below that of its background took on a hue complementary to that of the illuminant (color contrast). An object of about the same reflectance level as its background tended to be seen in its natural color, that is, as achromatic and of appropriate brightness level (color constancy). One systematic exception to the last rule was that the object color giving the constancy response tended to be less extreme than the background stimulus level. The general conclusion was that the color-constancy event, at least for achromatic stimuli, would occur when the object viewed was at the adaptation level of the moment and that the adaptation level is a function of many stimulus conditions.

Adaptation Level in Lifted Weights. Helson generalized the conclusions concerning color phenomena to other perceptual activities and tested the applicability of the adaptation-level concept to judgments of lifted weights. In one experiment *O*s judged five weights, varying from 200 to 400 g., in nine successive categories, the middle category being "medium." One set of judgments was made without an anchor stimulus, one with an anchor of 900 g., and one with an anchor of 90 g. The measure of the adaptation level (A) was given in terms of the stimulus scale and was defined as that stimulus weight that is judged on the average as being neither heavy nor light. Above A, weights tend to be judged heavy; below it they tend to be judged light. The adaptation level thus becomes the point of reference for the psychological scale. It corresponds to a psychological zero point in a bipolar scale of quantitative meanings. Helson's results with weights yielded adaptation levels of 248 (without an anchor stimulus), 357 (with the 900-g. anchor), and 186 (with the 90-g. anchor). These were near the predicted adaptation levels. The method of prediction of A will be described next.

Some Mathematical Formulations of the Adaptation Level. Let us consider first the kind of adaptation level that pertains to a particular experimental situation. Within the context of a single experiment, with series of systematically repeated and ordered stimulations of the same kind, a single adaptation level may be presumed to prevail. On the psychological continuum, the quantity corresponding to the adaptation level is an arithmetic mean of the responses to the stimulations presented during the experiment.

The prediction of the adaptation level from the stimulus quantities depends upon what function of S, $f(S)$, is assumed. If we assume that $f(S)$ is the familiar Fechnerian function, A is predicted to be a geometric mean of the stimuli used. If the frequency with which each stimulus is applied is not the same for all stimuli, this must be taken into account. In most experiments, stimuli to be judged are applied equally often. If some are background or anchor stimuli and others are judged, a distinction must be made and appropriate weights must be applied. The equation that Helson found most adequate to predict the adaptation level for the color results was of the form (16):

$$A = K(B^3{}_o\bar{B})^{1/4} \qquad (12.7)$$

where A = adaptation level
K = a constant
B_o = background reflectance
$\bar{B}$ = geometric mean of reflectances of stimuli exposed on background

Some General Equations for Adaptation Level. In the typical experimental situation, besides the series stimuli that are being judged there are other stimuli that help to determine significantly the adaptation level. There are background stimuli, as in the brightness experiment cited above, and other contextual stimuli. There may be a standard stimulus, or there may be anchor stimuli, or there may be others that are present for more incidental reasons. We must not leave out of account similar stimuli predating the experiment. In an earlier section ample evidence was cited to show that experiences previous to the experiment have appreciable effects. While it was also pointed out that O adapts rather quickly to the level of stimuli prevailing in an experiment, the adaptation may not be complete. For these reasons we need to consider the possible effects of preexperimental adaptations, if we are going to have a comprehensive frame of reference for the adaptation level and to allow for failures to predict it from experimental data only. Michels and Helson (37) have taken into account the preexperimental, residual effects in the formulation of their theory.

We may think of the chief determiners of the adaptation level during an experiment (strictly for one sitting of observations) as being (1) the residual effect of all pertinent, previous experiences, (2) the contextual stimuli, and (3) the experimental stimuli. As a basis for further discussion, let us adopt the following definitions:

A_p = the adaptation level at the time the experiment begins, where the subscript stands for "past" or "previous"
A_c = the adaptation level that would be set up by the contextual stimuli only, where the subscript stands for "contextual"
A_r = the adaptation-level resulting from the joint effects of past and contextual stimulation
A_e = the adaptation level resulting from all three sources of determination, including the stimuli being judged
S_i = a stimulus being judged in the experiment
$\bar{S}_i$ = a geometric mean of S_i; $\bar{S}_i$ may also be regarded as the adaptation level that would be determined by the experimental stimuli only

Following Helson's general principle that the adaptation level is a weighted geometric mean of all stimuli affecting it, we have the general equation

$$A_e = A^m{}_p A^n{}_c \bar{S}^e{}_i \tag{12.8}$$

where m, n, and e = weights to be applied to the logarithms of the stimulus effects A_p, A_c, and $\bar{S}_i$, respectively, their sum being unity. By requiring that $m + n + e = 1$, we eliminate the need for a constant multiplier for the product on the right of (12.8). The exponents may be easily remembered by associating m with memory, n with neighbor, and e with experimental. In logarithmic form the equation reads

$$\log A_e = m \log A_p + n \log A_c + e \log \bar{S}_i \tag{12.9}$$

An expression for the quantity A_r can be written in an equation following the same principle:

$$A_r = A^h{}_p A^d{}_c \tag{12.10}$$

where the exponents h and d differ from the corresponding ones in equation (12.8) and their sum is also equal to unity. Using A_r in place of the first two terms in the function in (12.8), we have

$$A_e = A^q{}_r \bar{S}^b{}_i \tag{12.11}$$

where $q + b$ also equals 1.0. Both (12.10) and (12.11) can, of course, be written in the logarithmic form of equation (12.9).

Where there are no contextual stimuli significantly determining A_e, one term of (12.8) drops out and we have

$$A_e = A^x{}_p \bar{S}^y{}_i \tag{12.12}$$

Where the influence of past experience may be regarded as negligible, or where after considerable experience in the experiment we may assume that adjustment to a new adaptation level is virtually complete, the exponent x would be very close to zero. In the first few trials with S_i, weight x may be large relative to y. As learning proceeds, y gains in value relative to x. If equation (12.12) is put in logarithmic form, it will be seen that it is very similar to the learning equation of Johnson (27), given earlier in this chapter as equation (12.5). His limens are essentially measures of adaptation levels and his resultant limen is expressed as a weighted mean of the limens (adaptation-levels) before and after (complete) experimental learning. As x approaches zero in (12.12), y approaches 1.0 and the adaptation level A_e becomes the geometric mean of S_i, as it should.

Experimental Determination of an Adaptation Level. There are a number of ways in which an adaptation level prevailing during an experiment can be determined by experimental and computational operations. With two categories of judgment applied to single stimuli, the limen serves as one estimate. If there are three or more categories of judgment and one of them is a neutral category (medium, equal, indifferent, etc.), the mean of stimuli placed in that category may be used as a very simple, but also sometimes very rough, index of adaptation level. A much better approach, and one that uses all the data, is to fit judgment data to some function of S by a least-square solution and from the result determine what stimulus value A_e corresponds to the neutral point on the R scale derived from the judgments. Such a solution will now be illustrated.

Fechner's Law and the Adaptation Level. The function of S that one thinks of first is the Fechner logarithmic relationship. Its application in determining an adaptation level is consistent with the principle of using geometric means in the equations above. Where it is demonstrated that the Fechner law does not apply sufficiently well, some other function $f(S)$ should be used and some revision in the equations given above would have to be made, accordingly.

Michels and Helson (37) have shown that we need a significant change in the application and interpretation of Fechner's law, in view of adaptation-level theory. In the traditional application, the Fechner equation applies when the unit of the S scale is the absolute threshold S_0. The equation by the Michels-Helson revision reads

$$R = C \log \frac{S}{A} \tag{12.13}$$

In expanded form,

$$R = C \log S - C \log A \tag{12.14}$$

Letting $-C \log A = K$, we have

$$R = C \log S + K \tag{12.15}$$

which is in form for solution by least-square procedures. In order to apply this general equation to empirical data, we need to assume that from judgments we have psychological values of R on an interval scale.

A Least-square Solution for the Adaptation Level. To illustrate the least-square solution for A_e, we will utilize some data given by Helson (17). Five weights, ranging from 200 to 400 g. by equal steps, were judged, on lifting, in nine verbally described categories: very, very light; very light; light; medium-light; medium; medium-heavy; heavy; very heavy; very, very heavy. Numerical values from 10 through 90 were given in steps of 10 to these categories. We will assume that the judgment scale, as numbered, represents an interval scale for R.

Table 12.3 presents paired values for S_i and mean judgment R. Carrying through the usual operations of fitting a line to the regression of R on $\log S_i$, we find that the constants in the equation are $C = 94.54$ and $K = -155.38$, so that the equation reads $R = 94.54 \log S_i - 155.38$.

From the equation just derived, we solve for the value of $\log A$ corresponding to R_a, which is the psychological scale value corresponding to the neutral judgment. Substituting R_a and A_e in equation (12.15), we have

$$R_a = C \log A_e + K$$

Solving for $\log A_e$, we have

$$\log A_e = \frac{R_a - K}{C}$$

TABLE 12.3. LEAST-SQUARE SOLUTION FOR THE DETERMINATION OF THE ADAPTATION LEVEL WHEN JUDGMENTS ARE GIVEN IN CATEGORIES ON AN INTERVAL SCALE

S_i	$\log S_i$ (X)	R (Y)	X^2	XY	Y^2	R'
400	2.6021	91	6.7709	236.7911	8,281	90.6
350	2.5441	85	6.4724	216.2485	7,225	85.1
300	2.4771	79	6.1360	195.6909	6,241	78.8
250	2.3979	71	5.7499	170.2509	5.041	71.3
200	2.3010	62	5.2946	142.6620	3,844	62.2
Σ	12.3222	388	30.4238	961.6434	30,632	
M	2.46444	77.6	6.08476	192.32868	6,126.4	

Substituting the known values for R_a, K, and C,

$$\log A_e = \frac{50 + 155.38}{94.54} = 2.17241$$

from which $A_e = 148.7$. The adaptation level prevailing during the course of this experiment was 148.7 g. This is well below even the lowest stimulus weight, the most important reason for which is that two anchor weights of 90 and 133 g. were lifted before every weight S_i was lifted and judged.

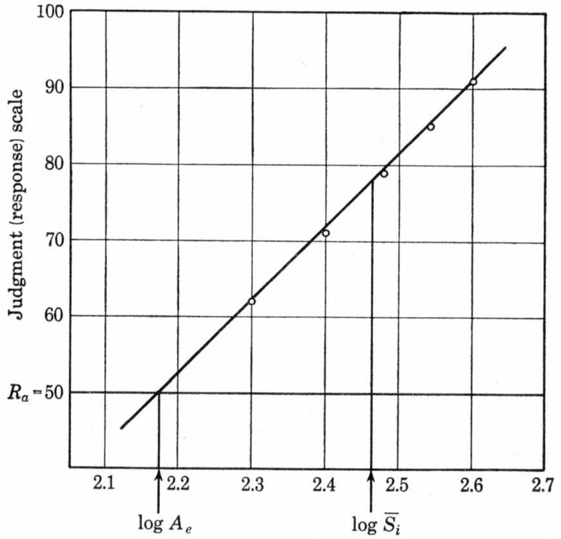

FIG. 12.8. Line of best fit to the relationship between means of categorical judgments and logarithms of stimulus weights, from which the logarithm of the adaptation level is estimated.

Figure 12.8 shows the line of best fit relating R to S_i for the Helson data, and it shows how the value of $\log A_e$ corresponds to a psychological value R_a at the neutral point on the scale. It is apparent that the fit is excellent. This can also be seen in the last column of Table 12.3, where the predicted R

values, R', are given. They are very close to the obtained values, R. The excellent fit lends confidence to the process of extrapolation that was required to determine the value of A_e in these data. It also supports the assumption of Fechner's law, with the Michels-Helson modification.

Estimation of Weights of Determiners of Adaptation Level. Without having more data than those used in our illustration, it would not be possible to estimate the values of the three weights represented in equation (12.8), that is, weights m, n, and e. There are too many unknowns for the number of equations we can obtain from the data. It is possible, however, to estimate two of the weights from the data we have, if we are willing to make an assumption. That is, to assume that weight m is zero, which is to say that experience previous to that in the experiment has no bearing upon the obtained A_e. We would have remaining from equation (12.8) the relationship

$$A_e = A^n{}_c \bar{S}^e{}_i$$

where $n + e = 1$. In logarithmic form this equation reads

$$\log A_e = n \log A_c + e \log \bar{S}_i$$

in which it must be remembered that A_c is a geometric mean of the contextual (anchor) stimuli and $\bar{S}_i$ is a geometric mean of the experimental stimuli S_i. For the sake of simplicity in what follows immediately, let

$$\log A_e = E$$
$$\log A_c = C$$

and

$$\log \bar{S}_i = I$$

The equation in logarithmic form just cited reads

$$E = nC + eI$$

The three values E, C, and I are known from the experiment. They are:

E = 2.17241 (from the least-square solution)
C = 2.03904 (log of the geometric mean of 90 and 133 g.)
I = 2.46444 (from Table 12.3; log of the geometric mean of all experimental stimuli)

We also have the equation $n + e = 1$, by definition. The two equations involving n and e are therefore

$$2.03904\,n + 2.46444\,e = 2.17241$$
$$n + e = 1$$

the solution of which gives $n = .6865$ and $e = .3135$. The ratio of the former to the latter is 2.19.

We may now say that the anchor stimuli as a group must be weighted more than twice as much as the experimental stimuli as a group in predicting the experimental adaptation level A_e. In terms of numbers of lifting acts, the anchor stimuli were lifted two times as often as the experimental stimuli. The ratio of n to e might therefore have been expected to be about 2.0, provided anchor stimuli as a class have equal importance with judged stimuli as a class in determining adaptation level, the number of lifts being the same for the two classes.

The fact that the ratio n/e is slightly greater than 2.0 is a little surprising, but it may be because we have not taken into account determiner A_p from previous experience. It would be possible to estimate the importance of A_p by introducing into the experiment other anchor stimuli, and also the condition with no anchor stimuli. Having this additional information and the fact that $m + n + e$ must equal 1, we could estimate all the parameters of equation (12.8), thus covering the situation including the anchor stimuli. By this approach we would have to assume that the contribution of A_p is the same whether anchor weights are present or not.

An Evaluation of the Adaptation-level Concept. The treatment of this important subject of the adaptation level has been necessarily kept to the minimum essentials, due to limitations of space and to the involved nature of some aspects of the subject. Adaptation-level theory is still in the process of development, but already it has demonstrated considerable power to explain many facts and principles of psychophysical judgment as well as other psychological phenomena. It provides the relativity that psychophysics, in particular, has needed for so long. It accounts for many types of failure of data to conform to constancy criteria, failures that Gestalt psychologists have been among the first to point out but for which they have been slow to suggest satisfactory remedies.

Among the important problems mentioned in this chapter on which the adaptation-level concept throws considerable light are the effects of anchor stimuli and of other contextual stimuli; the asymmetry of judgments of a series of stimuli; the effects of irregular distribution of stimuli in a series; the effects of an observer's personal experiences before the experiment and his adjustment to a new set of stimuli; the central-tendency phenomenon; and the time-order error. Helson (16) has demonstrated with illustrations how the adaptation-level concept accounts for data in which such phenomena occur. We have space here for only a few comments to show intuitively how the concept applies.

Anchor stimuli and other contextual stimuli applied during the course of the experiment receive weight toward the determination of the adaptation level, as the mathematical development in previous discussion has shown. An anchor stimulus above the range of stimuli to be judged effects a raising of the adaptation level. Judging the stimuli with reference to a higher adaptation level results in fewer judgments above the neutral category, consequently a shift of scale and of the limen.

The finding that in a series of comparison stimuli the *PSE* is characteristically below the middle of the range is consistent with the fact that the geometric mean of those stimuli is below their arithmetic mean. All such instances of asymmetry of judgments can be traced to the dislocation of the adaptation level from the center of the stimulus range. As the standard stimulus is moved up or down within the series, the adaptation level follows it, as indicated by movement of the *PSE*. Skewing the distribution of stimuli in a series effects corresponding changes in the resulting limen, as Johnson (22) has shown.

The effects of previous experiences within the universe of the stimuli of the experiment, as demonstrated by Tresselt (71, 72) are nicely accounted for in terms of adaptation-level theory. Although previous experience is usually informal and uncontrolled, and its amount and direction are unknown to the experimenter, the effects upon an experiment can be estimated by the use of equations given in this chapter, while accounting for other effects. In a controlled experiment, Johnson (27) demonstrated systematic changes in the limen as the result of new experiences with stimuli. It was pointed out in earlier pages how his equation describing the change of limen can be readily interpreted as a shifting of the relative weights of the old (residual) experiences versus the new (experimental) experiences involved.

The phenomenon of central tendency is explained in part by the adaptation-level concept. The well-established tendency is for judgments to center about a neutral point as a pivot. This neutral point is at the adaptation level, which is an average value. The phenomenon of movement of judgments toward this point, however, seems best explained, at present, in terms of Johnson's (28) concept of regression. The regression is regarded as being due to lack of perfect discrimination and it can be described by the principles of correlation and statistical regression toward a mean.

One aspect of the time-order error (*TOE*) is well accounted for by the adaptation level. This is the dependence of the error upon the general level of stimulation. When a judgment is given on a comparison stimulus, that stimulus is being compared not only with the standard but also with the adaptation level. If the comparison stimuli are in general above the adaptation level, the *TOE* should be negative, with the usual excess of "greater" judgments. If the comparison stimuli tend to be lower than the adaptation level, the *TOE* should be positive, with an excess of "less" judgments. These effects have been well demonstrated by Bartlett (1), Woodrow (83), and others. The effects of contextual stimuli on the *TOE* are in line with their effects on the adaptation level. The relations of time interval between stimuli to the *TOE* are not entirely clear. The best substantiated phenomenon is the switch from a positive to a negative *TOE* at about 3 sec. This may be a significant indication as to temporal aspects of the adaptation level and its effects.

It may be that further developments of adaptation-level theory will bring in certain time parameters to advantage. Philip (48) has introduced into the logarithmic adaptation-level equation the time interval between pairs of stimuli being compared, apparently with meaningful results. The expression of all pertinent time relations in the equation runs the risk of enlarging the number of unknowns intolerably, but where their inclusion means better prediction they should be given serious consideration.

The applications of adaptation-level theory beyond psychophysics depend upon demonstrations of the broader generality of the theory. It is probable that many a problem in behavior will be approachable in a more rational manner if the adaptation-level concept is applied.

Problems

1. Estimate the size of the time-order error involved in Data 12*A*, using three methods described in this chapter (500 judgments are involved).

DATA 12*A*. PROPORTIONS OF JUDGMENTS "GREATER" GIVEN TO FIVE STIMULUS WEIGHTS IN COMPARISON WITH A STANDARD OF 100, THE STANDARD BEING LIFTED FIRST

S_v, g.	94	97	100	103	106
p	.06	.22	.59	.92	.98

2. Using Data 12*B*, which were derived from Data 9*B*, determine the correlation between the "true" psychological values of the weights and the single judgments. The standard deviation σ_a is found from the combined distribution of all frequencies in Data 9*B*. What does r_{at} tell concerning these data?

DATA 12*B*. MEANS AND STANDARD DEVIATIONS FOR THE 11 STIMULUS WEIGHTS REPRESENTED IN DATA 9*B*. VALUES ARE ON THE EQUAL-APPEARING-INTERVAL SCALE ON WHICH JUDGMENTS HAD BEEN MADE

S	M_j	σ_j
50.0	5.11	1.31
53.5	5.87	1.38
57.5	6.65	1.45
61.5	7.30	1.47
66.0	8.15	1.50
71.0	8.80	1.41
76.0	9.49	1.36
81.5	10.05	1.28
87.5	10.94	1.43
94.0	11.63	1.07
100.0	12.05	1.11

3. Compute the standard error of estimate of obtained from true values and compare it with the mean of the standard deviations for the 11 stimuli, σ_j.

4. Estimate the true psychological values for the weights T'_j. Compute their mean and standard deviations, and check them by making the appropriate comparisons.

5. Compute the adaptation level indicated by Data 12*C*, using a least-square solution, assuming the Michels-Helson modification of Fechner's law. The "medium" category had a numerical value of 50.0.

DATA 12*C*. AVERAGE JUDGMENTS (*J*) OF 5 STIMULUS WEIGHTS (*S*) USING A RATING SCALE OF 10 TO 90 POINTS, EACH WEIGHT BEING LIFTED FOLLOWING A 900-G. ANCHOR STIMULUS*

S	M_j
200	19.5
250	34.5
300	47.3
350	54.3
400	63.5

* Adapted from Helson, H., Adaptation-level as frame of reference for prediction of psychophysical data. *Amer. J. Psychol.*, 1947, **60,** 1–29.

6. Assuming that only the anchor and experimental stimuli are effective in producing the adaptation level, estimate the relative weights to be assigned to these two sources. Interpret the weights you find.

Answers

1. From the *PSE*, $TOE = -0.87$ g.; $D\% = -10.8$; in terms of *SD* units, $TOE = -0.27$.
2. Correlation $r_{at} = .856$; $r^2_{at} = .733$.
3. $\sigma_{at} = 1.345$; mean of $\sigma_j = 1.343$.
4. Mean of estimated true values is 8.73; $SD = 2.60$.
5. $A_e = 321.5$; equation: $J = 144.586 \log S - 312.504$.
6. Weight for experimental stimuli S_i: $e = .9126$. Weight for anchor stimulus: $n = .0874$.

References

1. Bartlett, R. J. Measurement in psychology. *Advancement of Sci.*, 1939, 1–20.
2. Beebe-Center, J. G. *The Psychology of Pleasantness and Unpleasantness.* New York: Van Nostrand, 1932.
3. Cartwright, D. C. Relation of decision-time to the categories of response. *Amer. J. Psychol.*, 1941, **54,** 174–196.
4. Cohen, N. E. The relativity of absolute judgments. *Amer. J. Psychol.*, 1937, **49,** 93–100.
5. Danzfuss, K. Die Befühlsbetönung einiger unanalysierten Zweiklänge, Zweitonfolgen, Akkorde und Akkordfolgen bei Erwachsenen und Kindern. *Phil. u. psychol. Arb.*, 1923, **5,** 1–87.
6. Dashiell, J. F. Affective value-distances as a determinant of esthetic judgment-times. *Amer. J. Psychol.*, 1937, **50,** 57–67.
7. Flynn, B. M. Pitch discrimination. The form of the psychometric function and simple reaction time to liminal differences. *Arch. Psychol. N.Y.*, 1943, **39,** No. 280.
8. Fodor, K., and Happich, L. Der Bedeutung der Zeit zwischen zwei Vergleichreizen bei Bestimmung von Unterschiedsschwelle. I. Untersuchungen am Geschmaksorgan. *Arch. ges. Physiol.*, 1922, 197.
9. Goodfellow, L. D. Sources of error in psycho-physical measurements. *J. gen. Psychol.*, 1940, **23,** 197–200.
10. ———. The human element in probability. *J. gen. Psychol.*, 1940, **23,** 201–205.
11. ———. Significant incidental factors in the measurement of auditory sensitivity. *J. gen. Psychol.*, 1946, **35,** 33–41.
12. Guilford, J. P. *Fundamental Statistics in Psychology and Education,* 2d ed. New York: McGraw-Hill, 1950.
13. ——— and Cotzin, M. Judgment of difficulty of simple tasks. *Amer. J. Psychol.*, 1941, **54,** 38–52.
14. ——— and Park, D. G. The effect of interpolated weights upon comparative judgments. *Amer. J. Psychol.*, 1931, **43,** 589–599.
15. Helson, H. Fundamental problems in color vision: I. The principle governing changes in hue, saturation, and lightness of non-selective samples in chromatic illumination. *J. exp. Psychol.*, 1938, **23,** 439–476.
16. ———. Adaptation-level as frame of reference for prediction of psychophysical data. *Amer. J. Psychol.*, 1947, **60,** 1–29.
17. ———. Adaptation-level as a basis for a quantitative theory of frames of reference. *Psychol. Rev.*, 1948, **55,** 297–313.
18. Hollingworth, H. L. The central tendency of judgment. *J. Phil., Psychol., sci. Meth.*, 1910, **7,** 461–468.
19. Hunt, W. A., and Flannery, J. Variability in the affective judgment. *Amer. J. Psychol.*, 1938, **51,** 507–513.

20. ——— and VOLKMANN, J. The anchoring of an affective scale. *Amer. J. Psychol.*, 1937, **49,** 88–92.
21. JOHNSON, D. M. Confidence and speed in the two-category judgment. *Arch. Psychol. N.Y.*, 1939, **34,** No. 241.
22. ———. Generalization of a scale of values by the averaging of practice effects. *J. exp. Psychol.*, 1944, **34,** 425–436.
23. ———. A systematic treatment of judgment. *Psychol. Bull.*, 1945, **42,** 193–224.
24. ———. How a person establishes a scale for evaluating his performance. *J. exp. Psychol.*, 1946, **36,** 25–34.
25. ———. Technique for analysis of a highly generalized response pattern. *Psychol. Rev.*, 1946, **6,** 348–364.
26. ———. Generalization of a reference scale for judging pitch. *J. exp. Psychol.*, 1949, **39,** 316–321.
27. ———. Learning function for a change in the scale of judgment. *J. exp. Psychol.*, 1949, **39,** 851–860.
28. ———. The central tendency of judgment as a regression phenomenon. *Amer. Psychologist*, 1952, **7,** 281.
29. KARLIN, L. The influence of equality judgments on the constant error. *J. exp. Psychol.*, 1951, **42,** 300–301.
30. KAY, L. W. The relation of personal frames of reference to social judgments. *Arch. Psychol. N.Y.*, 1943, **40,** No. 283.
31. KOEHLER, W. Zur Theorie des Sukzessivvergleichs und der Zeitfehler. *Psychol. Forsch.*, 1923, **4,** 115–175.
32. LAUENSTEIN, O. Ansatz zu einer physiologischen Theorie des Vergleichs und der Zeitfehler. *Psychol. Forsch.*, 1932, **17,** 130–177.
33. LONG, L. A study of the effect of preceding stimuli upon the judgment of auditory intensities. *Arch. Psychol. N.Y.*, 1937, **30,** No. 209.
34. MARCHETTI, P. V. Time-errors in judgments of visual extents. *J. exp. Psychol.*, 1942, **30,** 257–261.
35. MCCLELLAND, D. C. Factors influencing the time error in judgments of visual extents. *J. exp. Psychol.*, 1943, **33,** 81–95.
36. MCGARVEY, H. R. Anchoring effects in the absolute judgment of verbal materials. *Arch. Psychol. N.Y.*, 1943, **39,** No. 281.
37. MICHELS, W. C., and HELSON, H. A reformulation of the Fechner law in terms of adaptation-level applied to rating-scale data. *Amer. J. Psychol.*, 1949, **62,** 355–368.
38. NASH, M. C. An experimental test of the Michels-Helson theory of judgment. *Amer. J. Psychol.*, 1950, **63,** 214–220.
39. NEEDHAM, J. G. The time-error as a function of continued experimentation. *Amer. J. Psychol.*, 1934, **46,** 558–567.
40. ———. The time error in comparison judgments. *Psychol. Bull.*, 1934, **31,** 229–243.
41. ———. Rate of presentation in the method of single stimuli. *Amer. J. Psychol.*, 1935, **47,** 275–284.
42. ———. Contrast effects in judgments of auditory intensities. *J. exp. Psychol.*, 1935, **18,** 214–226.
43. ———. The effect of the time interval upon the time error at different intensive levels. *J. exp. Psychol.*, 1935, **18,** 530–543.
44. ———. Interpolation effects with different time intervals. *J. exp. Psychol.*, 1935, **18,** 767–773.
45. PHILIP, B. R. Repetitive and alternative responses and sequences of errors in the discrimination of color mass. *J. exp. Psychol.*, 1942, **31,** 202–218.
46. ———. Generalization and central tendency in the discrimination of a series of stimuli. *Can. J. Psychol.*, 1947, **1,** 196–204.

47. ———. The effect of interpolated and extrapolated stimuli on the time order error in the comparison of temporal intervals. *J. gen. Psychol.*, 1947, **36,** 173–187.
48. ———. The frame of reference concept. *Can. J. Psychol.*, 1949, **3,** 73–79.
49. ———. The effect of general and specific labeling on judgmental scales. *Can. J. Psychol.*, 1951, **5,** 518–528.
50. Postman, L. The time error in auditory perception. *Amer. J. Psychol.*, 1946, **59,** 193–219.
51. ———. Time error as a function of the method of experimentation. *Amer. J. Psychol.*, 1947, **60,** 101–108.
52. ———. Retroactive inhibition and psychophysical judgment. *Amer. J. Psychol.*, 1947, **10,** 367–377.
53. ———. The generalization gradient in recognition memory. *J. exp. Psychol.*, 1951, **42,** 231–235.
54. ——— and Miller, G. A. Anchoring of temporal judgments. *Amer. J. Psychol.*, 1945, **58,** 43–53.
55. ——— and Zimmerman, C. Intensity of attitude as a determinant of decision time. *Amer. J. Psychol.*, 1945, **58,** 510–518.
56. Pratt, C. C. The time error in psychophysical judgments. *Amer. J. Psychol.*, 1933, **45,** 292–297.
57. ———. Time-errors in the method of single stimuli. *J. exp. Psychol.*, 1933, **16,** 798–814.
58. Preston, M. G. The effect of interpolated time intervals upon the contrast effects. *J. exp. Psychol.*, 1936, **19,** 706–715.
59. ———. Contrast effects and the psychophysical judgments. *Amer. J. Psychol.*, 1936, **48,** 389–402.
60. ———. Contrast effects and the psychometric functions. *Amer. J. Psychol.*, 1936, **48,** 625–631.
61. ——— and Zeid, P. M. Observations on sequences of choices made at five successive choice points. *J. exp. Psychol.*, 1943, **32,** 275–290.
62. Rogers, S. The anchoring of absolute judgments. *Arch. Psychol. N.Y.*, 1941, **37,** No. 261.
63. Senders, V. L., and Sowards, A. Analysis of response sequences in the setting of a psychophysical experiment. *Amer. J. Psychol.*, 1952, **65,** 358–374.
64. Seward, G. H. Recognition time as a measure of confidence. *Arch. Psychol. N.Y.*, 1928, **16,** No. 99.
65. Stott, L. H. Time-order errors in the discrimination of short tonal durations. *J. exp. Psychol.*, 1935, **18,** 741–766.
66. Thorndike, E. L. The refractory phase in associative processes. *Psychol. Rev.*, 1927, **34,** 234–236.
67. Thornton, G. R. The effect on judgments of personality traits of varying a single factor in a photograph. *J. soc. Psychol.*, 1943, **18,** 127–148.
68. ———. The effect of wearing glasses upon judgments of personality traits of persons seen briefly. *J. appl. Psychol.*, 1944, **28,** 203–207.
69. Tresselt, M. E. The time-errors in visual extents and areas. *J. Psychol.*, 1944, **17,** 21–30.
70. ———. Time errors in successive comparison of simple visual objects. *Amer. J. Psychol.*, 1944, **57,** 555–558.
71. ———. The influence of amount of practice upon the formation of a scale of judgment. *J. exp. Psychol.*, 1947, **37,** 251–260.
72. ———. The effect of the experience of contrasted groups upon the formation of a new scale of judgment. *J. soc. Psychol.*, 1948, **27,** 209–216.
73. ———. Time-errors in successive comparisons of tonal pitch. *Amer. J. Psychol.*, 1948, **61,** 335–342.

74. ——— and Becker, M. Scales of judgment and personality correlates. *J. gen. Psychol.*, 1950, **43**, 221–230.

75. ——— and Volkmann, J. The production of uniform opinion by non-social stimulation. *J. abnorm. soc. Psychol.*, 1942, **37**, 234–243.

76. Turchioe, R. M. The relation of adjacent inhibitory stimuli to the central tendency effect. *J. gen. Psychol.*, 1948, **39**, 3–14.

77. Turner, W. D. Intra-serial effects with lifted weights. *Amer. J. Psychol.*, 1931, **43**, 1–25.

78. Verplanck, W. S., Collier, G. H., and Cotton, J. W. Nonindependence of successive responses in measurements of the visual threshold. *J. exp. Psychol.*, 1952, **44**, 273–282.

79. Volkmann, J. The relation of time of judgment to certainty of judgment. *Psychol. Bull.*, 1934, **31**, 672–673.

80. ———. Anchoring of absolute scales. *Psychol. Bull.*, 1936, **33**, 742–743.

81. ———, Hunt, W. A., and McGourty, M. Variability of judgment as a function of stimulus-density. *Amer. J. Psychol.*, 1940, **53**, 277–284.

82. Wada, Y. Der Zeitfehler beim Sukzessivevergleich der Tonhöhe. *Jap. J. Psychol.*, 1932, **7**, 505–538.

83. Woodrow, H. Weight discrimination with a varying standard. *Amer. J. Psychol.*, 1933, **45**, 391–416.

84. ———. The effect of practice upon time-order errors in the comparison of temporal intervals. *Psychol. Rev.*, 1935, **42**, 127–152.

85. ——— and Stott, L. H. The effect of practice on positive time-order errors. *J. exp. Psychol.*, 1936, **19**, 694–705.

86. Woodworth, R. S. *Experimental Psychology.* New York: Holt, 1938.

CHAPTER 13

THEORY OF PSYCHOLOGICAL TESTS

No other contribution of psychology has had the social impact equal to that created by the psychological test. No other technique and no other body of theory in psychology has been so fully rationalized from the mathematical point of view. One can also say that of all devices used in psychological research, none is so commonly utilized as a psychological test of some kind, whether the investigator is undertaking a study that is primarily experimental or primarily statistical. The experimentalist who undertakes a laboratory experiment on learning, motivation, or thinking necessarily comes out with test scores of some kind.

It will be impossible to do justice to this large subject in the space of three chapters. Whole books have been devoted to the subject, none of which gives complete coverage. The three chapters here will merely attempt to serve as a useful introduction to the subject, providing the basic quantitative ideas involved and describing the more common techniques for dealing with test problems. Where some of the more important problems have had to be slighted, reference is made to sources where more extensive information may be obtained.[1]

Problems of Measurement by Tests

Selection of Test Problems. This chapter will present the major theories that attempt to give testing a rational basis. We shall find that there are currently several distinct approaches to the subject. All of them contribute useful ideas basic to test practices, and the deductions to which they lead are in general agreement. They have to do with the statistical and psychological meanings of test scores. They consider the general question of what it is that test scores measure and how well they measure it. They recognize the fundamental aim of all testing, which is the evaluation of individuals and of individual performances on continua representing definable psychological traits and functions. They take advantage of the usefulness of rigorous mathematical thinking as a means of arriving at dependable deductions concerning test properties and test results.

Chapter 14 will be devoted to the most commonly known properties of tests—reliability and validity. These subjects will not be limited to one chapter or confined to tests, however. In Chap. 13 the concepts of reliability and validity will loom large in the discussion of test theory. In Chap. 15 the

[1] An indication of the rapid strides made in the psychological-test field is seen in a comprehensive bibliography by Goheen and Kavruck (7). Of more than 2,500 titles from the years 1929 to 1949 on tests and statistics, a majority have to do with tests.

achievement of reliability and validity in constructing tests will be important goals for the techniques described. The problems of reliability and validity extend beyond the limits of test procedures; they apply to all measurement methods—to ratings and to scale values in general as well as to test scores. It will be emphasized that there is a distinction between reliability and validity as defined in theory and reliability and validity as estimated in test operations. Thinking about reliability and validity of measurements will be much clearer if this distinction is kept in mind. It will also be emphasized that there are several meanings to reliability and to validity. Common synonyms for reliability include: *dependability*, *consistency*, and *stability*. Each means something somewhat different as applied to measurements. Even the same term has slightly different meanings as applied to different measurement operations. Common synonyms for validity include *relevance*, *discrimination value*, and *predictive value*. The goal implied in each case is different and the corresponding index of validity is estimated by different operations. Chapter 14 will stress the operations by which the different kinds of reliability and validity may be estimated from empirical data.

Chapter 15 will be devoted to some of the more common problems connected with test development, including attitude scales and personality inventories. The production of a new test is a complex task, involving many kinds of skills and many operations. Again, because of limitations of space, only the essential details and those bearing on measurement aspects will be covered. The art of item writing cannot be treated except by incidental references. Most attention will be given to the techniques of item analysis, as they are used to maximize certain desired properties of tests—the form and level of score distribution as well as reliability and validity.

The Major Theoretical Problems. In the setting of psychological measurement in general, measurement by means of tests arouses some questions. Given a set of test scores from the same test applied under comparable external conditions to a group of examinees from a specified population, what sort of measurements do we have? Do they qualify as ratio measurements? Most probably not, and this deficiency is not very important. Do they qualify as interval measurements? We saw in the first chapter that this *is* very important, if we are to have full logical justification for applying most of the statistical and mathematical operations that are commonly used with test scores. Do we even have completely correct ordinal measurements? This question can well be asked in view of the fact that on second administration of the same test or on administration of an apparently comparable form of the same test there are some changes in rank ordering of individuals. How does theory of test measurements cope with these questions?

In addition to the question of what level of measurement is achieved by means of tests, there are other problems. Test scores, in a general sense, are quantitative descriptions of some aspect or aspects of human behavior. Behavior that is exhibited under prescribed conditions may be quantified in a variety of ways. For example, the oration of a speaker might be evaluated in terms of the average loudness of his voice, the average pitch level, the variability in either pitch or in loudness, the rate of speaking in words or syllables per unit of time, the frequency of gestures, their extent of movement, and so on. There are many other possible "dimensions" of his performance that might be singled out for quantification. The question of choice of dimensions is an important problem. The choice is usually determined by accessibility of the aspect observed, its susceptibility to quantitative description, and its relevance for the purposes for which the measurements are taken.

The most common type of test is that composed of items, each item presenting its own task. The score has been the number of "correct" responses in a limited time. The items may cover a range of difficulty or they may be concentrated at one level of difficulty. In the latter case, the score depends upon the probability of the examinee's passing items at that particular level. Some examinees have a greater probability than others and hence they are assumed to have higher levels of ability than others or more of a certain trait. If each item is of a different level of difficulty, some can pass more difficult items than others and hence obtain a higher score. The time limit that is ordinarily imposed for convenience in group testing provides another source of variance in the scores, in that different examinees work at different rates of speed. Without proof, it is not appropriate to assume that rate of work is closely correlated with ability to master items at different difficulty levels. The relative contributions of speed and power in time-limit tests are usually unknown. This question is avoided in completely speed tests (no examinee has time to attempt all items) and in completely power tests (every examinee has a chance to attempt every item). The great majority of tests fall between these extremes, and we shall see that there are serious questions concerning what a test measures when speed versus power is emphasized. Also, the fact that not all examinees attempt every item imposes troublesome statistical problems all along the line.

Most test theory has been aimed at the understanding of a test composed of items. Almost all test theories assume that scores can be conceived as composites of one kind or another. It is rather obvious that when we sum the number of correct responses to obtain a score the total-test score is a summation of the item scores. Each item is appropriately conceived as a part test, even though its range of scores may be limited to two—zero and one. We shall see that there are other ways of conceiving of the total score as a composite of contributing parts where the "parts" are in more abstract terms. The oldest and most commonly conceived breakdown is in terms of a "true" and an "error" component. A more recent development in theory conceives of the "true" component as being a summation of contributions from common and specific factors. This is the approach through factor theory. We shall see how all these summative-component ideas offer contributions to the understanding of measurements by means of tests.

Types of Test Scales

Physical Measures of Psychological Variables. Many tests, more often in the experimental setting, yield measurements of performance on physical scales. More often than not this is a time measurement. This man runs the hundred-yard dash in 10.8 sec.; that one completes 50 simple addition problems in 6.5 min.; and still another reads a long paragraph in 4.8 min. Such tasks fall into the category of work-limit tests. Since the measuring scale used is in physical units, it might be assumed that the scores are on a ratio scale. But remembering that these scores are really used to indicate quantities of psychological performance and hence psychological ability, the neatness of the physical values is very deceiving. We probably have neither equal psychological units nor a meaningful zero point. Zero time, of course, would mean superlatively good (also impossible) performance; thus no psychological zero point has been established.

There can be no debating the equality of the time units, as such, but does an increment of time when the performance is rapid mean the same psychological change in ability as the same increment when the performance is slow? We have no assurance that it does. In Chap. 7 it was pointed out that Hull and others came to mistrust latent times of responses as indices of habit strength or reaction potential. Psychological equality of units there, as elsewhere, is essential if we are to establish the correct kind of functional relationship between the *psychological* variable in which we are interested and some other variable. The use of physical measurements enables us to make certain statements about performances, but those statements remain in the realm of physical discourse and do not permit sure psychological conclusions.

Mental-age Scales. A very common time scale used in psychology is the mental-age scale. In spite of severe criticisms [for example, by Richardson (22) and Gulliksen (11)] mental-age scales continue to be used. As Richardson points out, mental-age intelligence scales, as psychological measures, fail to meet many of the requirements of measurement. They have no real origin, no equal units, and they measure a composite whose psychological components differ from one level to another. The age at which zero ability occurs is unknown and is probably before birth, which is taken to be the origin in mental-age scales. The regression of mental ability on chronological age is in all probability not linear, which destroys equality of psychological units.

From the mental-age calibration of test items one would get the impression that the psychological distance from a fourteen-year-old test to a fifteen-year-old test is equivalent to the distance between a nine-year-old test and a ten-year-old test. Such an impression is almost surely erroneous. The items that compose a mental-age scale are selected on the basis of their correlations with chronological age. Probably all functions and abilities vary with chronological age during childhood. The result is that the item selected may measure any changing function, intellectual or not. Very much depends upon the judgment of the test maker to keep items in the general intellectual domain. It is likely that different functions are changing most rapidly at different ages. The consequence is that different kinds of items will correlate higher with age at different age levels. In any case, since all or most functions are changing at any age, items that correlate with more different abilities will probably correlate higher with the age criterion. The consequence is selection of items measuring several psychological functions.

Summational Psychological Scores. We have just seen that measures of psychological traits in physical units do not necessarily give us anything better than ordinal measurements. Are there any other types of scores that do any better? The most common type of test score is the summational type, as indicated earlier. It rests on the summation of counted responses in a keyed category—right responses or wrong responses. The problem of weighting responses need not concern us here. Conclusions we draw concerning summated item scores whose weights are equal will apply in principle to summated item scores whose weights are unequal.

Any evidence that summated scores provide interval-scale measurements is incomplete and the conclusions are controvertible. It would help us a great deal if we could know the shape of the frequency distribution of our tested population on an ideal scale for the dimension measured by the test. The fact that we so often obtain a frequency distribution of scores that approaches normality is not crucial evidence of equality of units. If we knew that the population *is* normally distributed on the trait, the occurrence of a normal obtained-score distribution would be sufficient evidence. When we have a randomly selected sample from a homogeneous population, we feel some confidence in assuming normality of distribution on psychological-trait continua. Then having a normal distribution of obtained scores, we proceed as if the units were equal. This is more true when the test is a long one (at least 30 to 40 items) and the mean is near the center of the score range.

A few experimental studies have attempted to derive information concerning equality of units, though the evidence is always indirect. A study of Grossnickle (8) will be cited as an example. Grossnickle applied the operations of scaling examinees by the method of pair comparisons and then related such scale values to summation scores for the same individuals. She administered a vocabulary test to 100 examinees. With the papers in rank order for total score, she combined successive groups of 5 to compose 20 "individuals." She assumed that each test item "judged" the "individuals" in comparison with each other. If "individual" A had more correct responses to item 10 than "individual" B had, item 10 judged A greater than B, and so on. When the proportion of the time that each "individual" was judged as greater than another individual had been determined, scaling proceeded by the procedures described in Chap. 7, assuming Case V. The plots of the z values were linear, indicating normality of dispersions of "individuals" and the slopes were approximately equal to 1.0, indicating equality of dispersions. The important finding for us here is that the scale values of the "individuals" obtained by pair comparisons bore a linear relationship to the summation scores for the same "individuals." If the equality of unit for the pair-comparison scaling be accepted, in view of the logical grounds on which that scaling rests, we can accept the equality of unit for the summation scores on the same test. At least there were no systematic shifts in size of unit. Generalizing to other tests and other populations must be exercised with caution.

When obtained-score distributions are not normal when we have a right to expect them to be, we may well suspect the inequality of units. When distributions are skewed and we can account for the skewing on the basis of known features of the test—its being much too easy or too difficult for the population involved—we may resort to one of the common scaling procedures developed for handling test scores in order to approach equal units. There are other important motives for scaling test scores, of course, such as the desire for a common mean and a common standard deviation. In meeting the latter objective, the normalizing step may or may not be applied. A common form of distribution has its definite advantages, and the familiarity with the Gaussian distribution and the many kinds of operations that such a distribution makes possible give that form definite appeals.

The writer has discussed at length the processes of scaling test scores elsewhere (9) and therefore will not take space to repeat descriptions of them here. The most common scale is the *T scale*, in which distributions are normalized with means of 50 and standard deviations of 10. Less well known is the writer's *C scale*, on which distributions achieve a mean of 5 and a standard deviation of 2. A variant of this is the *stanine scale* with a slightly lower standard deviation due to the fact that the two tail categories at either end of the distribution are combined to make 9 steps rather than 11. Canfield has proposed a 10-step *sten scale* (1) which has some unique advantages.[1]

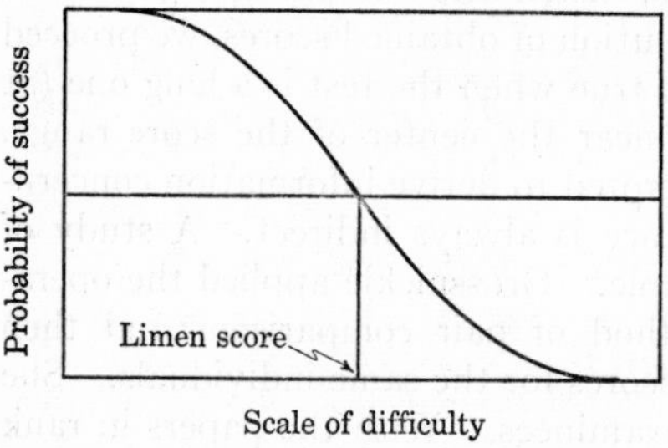

FIG. 13.1. A limen score—the level of difficulty at which the examinee's probability of success is .5 on the psychometric function relating probability of success to difficulty.

Limen Scores. It should not be surprising to suggest that sensory limens may be used as measures of individual differences in sensitivity. In some tests, in fact, we have the alternative of using either a limen or a summation score as the measure of an examinee's status. For example, some of the Seashore tests of musical talent—pitch discrimination, loudness discrimination, and time discrimination—could be scored either way. The simpler summation scoring is used with those tests, but the question could well be raised as to whether a limen score might not be better.

The limen score has a broader application than that to sensory tests. It can be applied to any test whose items have been calibrated on a scale, such as a scale of difficulty. Let us say that we have a vocabulary test composed of 25 items at each of seven levels of difficulty on a scale of equal units. For any person who attempts these items the probability of passing items at successive levels of difficulty is a continuous, descending function. The relationship usually found between proportion of items passed and difficulty level is ogival, as shown in Fig. 13.1, which represents the hypothetical case. Consistent with psychophysical principles, the score for the individual is that level of difficulty at which the probability of passing is .50.[2] The operations for finding the limen may be any of those described in connection with the constant methods in Chap. 6.

Mosier (17) has rationalized the test-taking situation in a manner that is analogous to the theory of the psychophysical-judgment situation, showing that the same principles apply to both. He has also made a study of limen scores in relation to summation scores (18). For one test he found that the

[1] For a general discussion of test-scaling procedures, see Flanagan's treatment (13).

[2] Where no item is passed by chance.

limen scores had a reliability of .88 and corresponding summation scores had a reliability of .94. The linear correlation between the two kinds of scores equaled 1.016 when corrected for attenuation. If we may regard Mosier's limen scores as having been based on better measurement principles and procedures, we may place greater confidence in his summation scores as representing interval measurements. It is not safe to say how far we may generalize from his finding, but there are others.

In a similar study, Lorr (16) found that a limen score had a reliability coefficient of .94, which equaled that for the corresponding summation scores. He presented proof, however, that the limen score is a linear function of z scores derived from the proportions of correct responses in the total test. Now if all examinees attempt all items the *proportion* correct is a linear function of the *number* correct. This means that the latter, which is a summation score, would not be a linear function of the limen scores.[1] In Lorr's results, however, the plot of proportion-correct score against limen score was practically linear with a correlation that would appear to be not far from 1.0. The reason for a linear result contrary to his proof that the regression should be ogival was probably that the range of z scores was only from -1.28 to $+0.84$. In this limited range an ogive approaches linearity. In spite of Lorr's proof, therefore, we have further evidence that in practice the less laborious and more commonly used summation score can be linearly related to the limen score.

Glaser (5) has approached the estimation of limen scores in an indirect way. The procedure was essentially (1) to administer the test twice with an appropriate time interval between; (2) to determine on which items each examinee changed his responses; and (3) to score the test in terms of the average item-difficulty level for the range of changed responses. The range of changed responses is assumed to be an indicator of the examinee's transition zone on the difficulty (or ability) scale. The average of the item values in this range would be a rough approximation to the limen. The correlations of such scores with corresponding summation scores were high, but not as high as for genuine limen scores as found by others. For a vocabulary test the correlation was .78; for a mathematics test, .79; and for a space test, .83.

Consistency Scores. There has been considerable interest in very recent years in personal variability in measured ability. It is sometimes pointed out that we should know not only the examinee's characteristic level on a scale of ability but also his degree of consistency in performing near that level. It is possible that individuals differ systematically from one another in their consistency as well as in their level of performance. If this is so, we can obtain additional, useful information about individuals. If a certain examinee is quite consistent, his level of performance will be quite predictable. If another examinee is markedly inconsistent or variable about his mean, he

[1] It is not unlikely that many learning scores that are in terms of proportion correct and number correct have an actually ogival relationship to the psychological variable of habit strength. It is possible that a better learning score would be a proportion transformed to a z value. It is also possible that some ogive-shaped learning curves actually represent linear psychological-change functions.

is to that extent unpredictable in this ability. Usual test practices seem to operate on the assumption that all examinees are equally predictable.

The psychophysical model as represented in Fig. 13.1 suggests immediately one way of determining each examinee's degree of consistency, or conversely his degree of variability. The latter would be indicated by the standard deviation of his psychometric function on a trait continuum. Mosier arrived at this concept from his psychophysical rationale of testing (17) and called the index *epsilon*. The epsilon scores that he obtained in his study, however, proved to have a reliability of only .55. Lorr (16), using a similar approach, found a reliability figure of .64. Thus it does not seem that examinees are very consistent in their inconsistencies of this kind. Judging by these two attempts, it appears that much effort goes into the determination of scores whose reliabilities are intrinsically low.

There is the larger psychological question whether such personal variability is specific to different tests or is a more general trait that would be found common to a variety of tests. One is also reminded of the clinical interest in "spread" of performance, which is usually detected over a variety of tests. There are thus intermingled problems of variability over time as well as over difficulty levels and over different abilities. The psychological meanings of none of these phenomena are as yet very clear. They represent a challenge of unsolved measurement problems.

Glaser has approached the measurement of consistency from another direction (4, 5, 6). The essentials of the method include administering a test two or three times, repeating it after appropriate time intervals. The score is the number of responses changed. The reliabilities of the change scores reported were generally low, ranging from .51 to .72 in three tests (vocabulary, mathematics, and space) (6). Intercorrelations of consistency scores from the three kinds of tests ranged from .09 to .20 (4), indicating great specificity of the psychological variable measured.

Correlations of the several consistency scores with the corresponding regular (level) scores for the same tests revealed a serious restriction effect when extreme obtained level scores approached the possible limits. It is very easy to see that those who get all answers correct, or nearly all, cannot possibly have a very high change score; neither can those who get none or almost none right. Only in the middle range of level scores can change scores be maximal. The result is a curved regression of consistency scores of this type as a function of level scores. If the distribution of level scores is negatively skewed, the (linear) correlation of consistency scores with level scores will be negative; if the distribution is positively skewed, the correlation will be positive; if the distribution is symmetrical, the linear correlation will approach zero. This is what Glaser found (4).

Lorr tried a still different kind of consistency score, based on the difference between first and second total scores from two administrations of the test (16). The correlation between this score (taken as either algebraic or as absolute differences) and the epsilon score[1] was insignificant. It is thus apparent that no consistency score yet proposed has achieved sufficient reliability or generality. Possibly this describes the psychological fact that

[1] Based on precision of the psychometric function of difficulty.

there is no very dependable and general trait of consistency of the kind sought by these investigators.

Theory of Test Scores

In this section we shall consider several rational, quantitative approaches to the understanding of test scores. The mathematical models selected for this purpose make possible the various statistical operations by which test scores can be meaningfully manipulated. They show the way to the production of better tests to suit various purposes, to a better understanding of what tests actually measure, and to the evaluation of test results.

In most of what is said here, as well as elsewhere in these chapters on tests, we will assume that we are dealing with tests composed of items and that the probability of chance success in responding to items is extremely small. While this would seem to rule out many kinds of tests, including that most popular form, the multiple-choice test, the conclusions that are reached will merely need some modification to take care of such forms. Other restrictive assumptions will be mentioned as needed.

The Rationale of Test Reliability. Under the concept of reliability we are concerned about the accuracy with which a score represents the status of an individual in whatever aspect the test measures him. It is generally recognized that most scores are fallible, that they are not free from error. The most important step toward the fruitful understanding of reliability came with the statement of a very simple equation. This equation, which expresses the idea that an obtained score may be conceived as a simple, summative combination of a true component and an error component, reads

$$X_t = X_\infty + X_e \tag{13.1}$$

where X_t = obtained test score
X_∞ = true component
X_e = error component[1]

The true component X_∞ and error component X_e are conceived as quantities on the same scale as that of the obtained scores X_t. There are several ways of defining the true component or true score. One is to say that X_∞ is the score this individual would have obtained under ideal conditions or with a perfect measuring instrument. Another is that X_∞ is the mean of obtained scores from a very large number of independent administrations of the same test to a particular person. This procedure would be a physical impossibility, but this potential experimental approach provides a basis for quasi-operational definition of a true score. The error component or error score is an increment (positive or negative) that is a function of conditions at a particular occasion of test administration to a particular person. The contributing factors to error scores are many. Sometimes we can identify some of them, but usually they are unknown determiners of variation.

Certain additional assumptions are usually made concerning true and error scores, to simplify the thinking that follows from the model supplied by equation (13.1). One assumption is that errors are as likely to be

[1] The symbols used here are intended to be consistent with those in Guilford (9).

negative as positive and that in a large population their mean is zero. This assumption is not necessary but is very convenient. Another assumption is that in a large population errors are uncorrelated with true scores. That is, there is no tendency for individuals with high true scores to have either more positive or more negative error scores. Still another assumption is that there is no correlation between error scores in one form of a test and error scores in a parallel form of the same test. These three assumptions may be clearly stated in the form of equations:

Assumption I: $M_e = 0$ (M_e = mean of errors) (13.2)

Assumption II: $r_{\infty e} = 0$ ($r_{\infty e}$ = correlation of true and error scores) (13.3)

Assumption III: $r_{e_1 e_2} = 0$ (e_1 and e_2 = error scores in forms 1 and 2 of the same test) (13.4)

Contributions to Obtained Mean and Variance. From equation (13.1) and the assumptions that go with it, we can make statements concerning the contributions of true and error components to the mean and variance of obtained scores. Since the mean of the sums of unweighted components is equal to the sum of the means, we can say that

$$M_t = M_\infty + M_e = M_\infty \tag{13.5}$$

In other words, the mean of the obtained scores equals the mean of the true scores. This is one advantage of assumption I. In any one limited sample, however, M_e may not equal zero, in which case the obtained mean will not equal exactly the true mean.

When summed components are uncorrelated, by another principle, the variance of a sum of unweighted measures is equal to the sum of the variances. We can therefore state the equation

$$\sigma^2_t = \sigma^2_\infty + \sigma^2_e \tag{13.6}$$

We see here the advantage of assumption II. Had we assumed nonzero correlation for $r_{\infty e}$, we should have to add to equation (13.6) the covariance term $2r_{\infty e}\sigma_\infty\sigma_e$, which would complicate the picture from here on.

Assumption III will not concern us further for the present. It is basic to development of ideas concerning reliability when parallel tests are used.

Logical Definition of Reliability. We are ready now to define reliability in terms of the concepts just developed. Briefly, *reliability is the proportion of true variance in obtained test scores.* This can be stated in equation form:

$$r_{tt} = \frac{\sigma^2_\infty}{\sigma^2_t} \tag{13.7}$$

where r_{tt} = the coefficient of reliability. It is expressed as a self-correlation of the obtained test scores. The term "self-correlation" is merely an idea for which there is no direct, experimental operation. In the next chapter we shall see how there are many alternative operations for *estimating* r_{tt}. If we knew the size of the true variance σ^2_∞, we could, of course, compute the reliability of obtained scores by equation (13.7).

Since the total and component variances are related as in equation (13.6), we have another approach to the expression of reliability. From equation (13.6) we know that $\sigma^2_\infty = \sigma^2_t - \sigma^2_e$. Substituting this difference in (13.7), we have

$$r_{tt} = 1 - \frac{\sigma^2_e}{\sigma^2_t} \tag{13.8}$$

This is a useful transformation, since it is possible to obtain from experimental data information concerning the amount of error variance as well as σ^2_t, and thus to estimate reliability.[1]

Estimation of True Variance. It is possible operationally to obtain an estimate of the extent of the true variance in a set of scores if the coefficient of reliability and total variance are known. Solving equation (13.7) for the true variance, we have

$$\sigma^2_\infty = r_{tt}\sigma^2_t \tag{13.9}$$

Since r_{tt} never exceeds 1.00, the true variance is almost always smaller than the obtained variance. Taking square roots of (13.9), we have an estimate of the standard deviation of true scores:

$$\sigma_\infty = \sigma_t \sqrt{r_{tt}} \tag{13.10}$$

The Standard Error of Measurement. By other operations we can solve equation (13.8) for the variance and the standard deviation of the errors in scores. We then have the two equations

$$\sigma^2_e = \sigma^2_t(1 - r_{tt}) \tag{13.11}$$

and

$$\sigma_e = \sigma_t \sqrt{1 - r_{tt}} \tag{13.12}$$

Of the last four equations, (13.12) has been found most useful and has been given the special name of *standard error of measurement.* It is also often called the *standard error of obtained scores.* It is a rather direct indicator of the probable extent of error in any score in the set to which it applies. We will see next how the same statistic is determined from another approach.

The Index of Reliability. Recall that reliability was defined as the proportion of true variance in scores. We can also put this statement in the form more common in prediction problems by saying that reliability is the proportion of the variance in obtained scores determined by or accounted for by variance in true scores. This puts the matter in terms of predicting obtained scores from true scores. It is quite reasonable to think of obtained scores as having a linear regression on true scores. Such a relationship is indicated in Fig. 13.2.

To say that r_{tt} represents the proportion of variance in the obtained scores determined by variance in the true scores places r_{tt} in the category of *coefficient of determination,* which is a coefficient of correlation squared (see Chap. 3). The correlation coefficient that has been squared in this case is $r_{t\infty}$, the

[1] By what is known as the Rulon formula [see formula (14.3)].

correlation between obtained and true scores. This statistic is known as the *index of reliability*. In terms of equations,

$$r_{tt} = r^2_{t\infty} \tag{13.13}$$

and

$$r_{t\infty} = \sqrt{r_{tt}} \tag{13.14}$$

The standard error of estimate of obtained from true scores is given by the usual form of equation

$$\sigma_{t\infty} = \sigma_t \sqrt{1 - r^2_{t\infty}} \tag{13.15}$$

From the definitions given above and from equation (13.13), it will be seen that this standard error of estimate is identical with the standard error of measurement of equation (13.12). Either indicates the extent of the error probable in X_t for any given true score X_∞. If we assume a normal distribution of errors at every true-score level, we can draw inferences concerning the probability of errors of different sizes. For any given obtained score, then, we can draw conclusions concerning the probable limits of corresponding true scores. The question concerning whether errors of measurement are always uniform at all true-score levels will arise later. The question whether the regression of obtained scores on true scores is always linear will also arise later in this chapter.

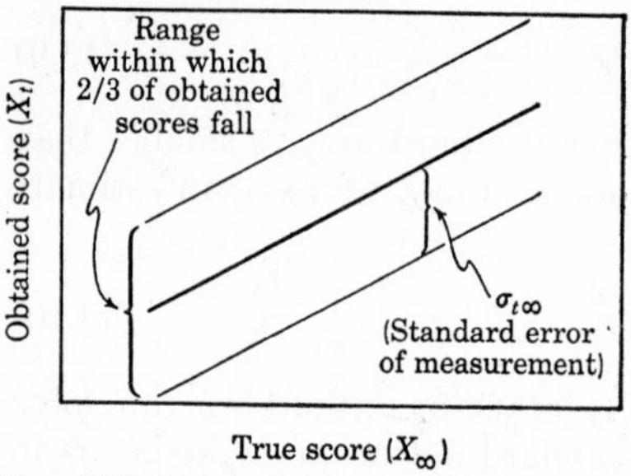

FIG. 13.2. Regression of obtained scores on true scores, with parallel lines drawn at vertical distances of one standard error from the regression line.

Effect of Length of Test on True and Error Variances. It is common knowledge that the longer the test is made (under certain limitations), the more reliable it is. We shall now see how this happens.

Let us first take the simple case in which a test is doubled in length (with appropriate doubling in time). In order to predict what will happen to the variances and to reliability, we must make certain assumptions. We say that the new parts of the lengthened test must be homogeneous with those already present. By "homogeneous" we mean that the new items not only resemble the old ones in form and kind of content but are also of equal difficulty, and have equal intercorrelation with one another and with the old items. In the case of doubling a test, the operation is like adding scores from two parallel forms. Parallel forms, as defined by Gulliksen (11), have equal means, equal variances, and equal intercorrelations between all pairs of forms.[1] We will proceed on the basis of combining two parallel forms.

The variance of *obtained* scores for a test of doubled length is given by the equation

$$\sigma^2_{2t} = 2\sigma^2_t(1 + r_{tt}) \tag{13.16}$$

[1] The intercorrelation of two parallel forms is equivalent to the reliability of either of them.

From this it can be seen that the greater the reliability, or proportion of true variance, the greater the variance of the composite score. If the component tests had zero intercorrelation (which may be taken as r_{tt} in this case), the variance of the composite would be just two times the variance of each component. If the intercorrelation were perfect, doubling the length would quadruple the variance.

The proof of equation (13.16) is very simple. The variance of the sum or composite of two unweighted measures X_1 and X_2 is

$$\sigma^2{}_c = \sigma^2{}_{x_1+x_2} = \sigma^2{}_1 + \sigma^2{}_2 + 2r_{12}\sigma_1\sigma_2$$

By assumption, $\sigma_1 = \sigma_2 = \sigma_t$, and $r_{12} = r_{tt}$; therefore

$$\sigma^2{}_{2t} = 2\sigma^2{}_t + 2r_{tt}\sigma^2{}_t = 2\sigma^2{}_t(1 + r_{tt})$$

The *true* variance for the test doubled in length is given by the equation

$$\sigma^2{}_{2\infty} = 4\sigma^2{}_\infty \tag{13.17}$$

In terms of the parallel-forms pattern,

$$\sigma^2{}_{2\infty} = \sigma^2{}_{\infty 1} + \sigma^2{}_{\infty 2} + 2r_{\infty 1\infty 2}\sigma_{\infty 1}\sigma_{\infty 2}$$

Since true variances in the two components are equal and the correlation of true scores is 1.0,

$$\sigma^2{}_{2\infty} = 4\sigma^2{}_\infty$$

Thus, we conclude that regardless of the reliability of a test, doubling its length quadruples its true variance. Unless a test has perfect reliability, its true variance increases at a more rapid rate than its total variance. In this lies the secret of increased reliability with increased length. We shall see that what happens to the error variance also helps.

The error variance of a test doubled in length is given by the equation

$$\sigma^2{}_{2e} = 2\sigma^2{}_e \tag{13.18}$$

Here we take into account assumption III mentioned earlier: that errors in two parallel forms of a test are uncorrelated. This means that the error variance in the composite is merely a sum of error variances in the two components; hence equation (13.18). This also means that error variance increases more slowly than either true or total variance, so long as there is any true variance at all.

The Spearman-Brown Prophecy Formula. The original formula given in defining reliability [equation (13.7)] also applies to the composite scores, except that here we want the ratio of true to total variance in the test of double length. Putting in ratio the terms of equations (13.17) and (13.16), we have

$$r_{22} = \frac{\sigma^2{}_{2\infty}}{\sigma^2{}_{2t}} = \frac{4\sigma^2{}_\infty}{2\sigma^2{}_t(1 + r_{tt})}$$

where r_{22} = reliability of a test of doubled length. This equation can be simplified as follows:

$$r_{22} = 2\left(\frac{\sigma^2_\infty}{\sigma^2_t}\right)\frac{1}{1 + r_{tt}} = 2r_{tt}\,\frac{1}{1 + r_{tt}}$$

from which

$$r_{22} = \frac{2r_{tt}}{1 + r_{tt}} \tag{13.19}$$

This is the Spearman-Brown formula applied to the doubling of a test in length. For the general case, in which a test is increased in length by the multiple n, the reasoning is the same. For a composite made up of a simple sum of n parallel forms, the three kinds of variance can be shown to be as follows:

$$\sigma^2_{nt} = n\sigma^2_t[1 + (n - 1)r_{tt}] \qquad \text{(total variance)}$$
$$\sigma^2_{n\infty} = n^2\sigma^2_\infty \qquad \text{(true variance)}$$

and

$$\sigma^2_{ne} = n\sigma^2_e \qquad \text{(error variance)}$$

Thus it is clear that in the lengthening process the true variance increases n times as rapidly as the error variance. By developments like those when $n = 2$ above, we find the generalized Spearman-Brown formula to be

$$r_{nn} = \frac{nr_{tt}}{1 + (n - 1)r_{tt}} \tag{13.20}$$

It should be added that n need not be an integer and that it may be less than 1.0. It is any ratio of the altered test length to the original length. It should also be pointed out that the application of this formula rests on the assumptions that were made in deriving it. In the next chapter we shall see how much departure from these special conditions can be tolerated.

The Rationale of Test Validity. Validity is concerned with the question of *what* a test measures. While there are certain relationships between reliability and validity of test scores, we need an extension of the rationale given above for reliability in order to account for the facts of validity. Most commonly, the degree of validity is indicated by some correlation coefficient. When the test is used to predict performance in some life situation, validity is often described in terms of a correlation between the test and some measure of performance in the life situation. This correlation, and others, must be logically accounted for. A very good approach is through factor theory, the rudiments of which will now be explained.

Fundamental Factor Theory. Multiple-factor theory may be said to build on the theory already presented. It accepts the division of obtained-score variance into true and error components. The essentially new step is to assume that the true variance can be further broken down into additive components. These components are *common-factor* variances plus possible *specific variance.* The common-factor variances are shared by other tests, just as true variance is shared by two parallel forms of the same test. The specific-variance component, so far as our information goes, is unique to this particular test. It is a part of the true variance and is therefore shared by two forms of the same test.

If we express each of these contributors in terms of a component score, we may write the basic equation

$$z_t = az_a + bz_b + cz_c + \cdots + qz_q + sz_s + z_e \tag{13.21}$$

where z_t = total test score in standard form

$a, b, c, \ldots, q$ = coefficients or weights to be applied to the various component scores (where there are q common factors)

$z_a, z_b, z_c, \ldots, z_q$ = standard scores in common factors A to Q

z_s = standard score in the specific component, with its weight s

z_e = standard score for the error component

It is to be understood that this equation applies to the score of a single examinee in a given test. For simplicity, we will assume that the common factors and the specific and error components are mutually independent, making possible the deduction of simple, additive equations.

Each term in equation (13.21), if no coefficient is zero, contributes to the total variance of the obtained scores. Expressing each contribution to total variance that is provided by a component, weighted as it is, we may write the second basic equation for factor theory:

$$\sigma^2_t = \sigma^2_a + \sigma^2_b + \sigma^2_c \cdots + \sigma^2_q + \sigma^2_s + \sigma^2_e \tag{13.22}$$

where each term on the right represents each weighted component's contribution to total-score variance. Dividing all terms by the total variance, we have an expression for the proportion of the variance contributed from each source:

$$\frac{\sigma^2_t}{\sigma^2_t} = \frac{\sigma^2_a}{\sigma^2_t} + \frac{\sigma^2_b}{\sigma^2_t} + \frac{\sigma^2_c}{\sigma^2_t} + \cdots + \frac{\sigma^2_q}{\sigma^2_t} + \frac{\sigma^2_s}{\sigma^2_t} + \frac{\sigma^2_e}{\sigma^2_t} = 1.00$$

Substituting simpler terms for the proportions,

$$1.00 = a^2_x + b^2_x + c^2_x + \cdots + q^2_x + s^2_x + e^2_x \tag{13.23}$$

where $a^2_x, b^2_x, \ldots, q^2_x$ = proportions of variance contributed to scores in test X by common factors A to Q, respectively, and s^2_x and e^2_x = proportions contributed by specific and error components, respectively. The reliability of a test can now be expressed as a sum of proportions of true variance:

$$r_{tt} = 1 - e^2_x = a^2_x + b^2_x + c^2_x + \cdots + q^2_x + s^2_x \tag{13.24}$$

Communality, Specificity, and Uniqueness. In addition to reliability, we can define three other concepts in terms of proportions of variance in test scores. *Communality* is defined as the proportion of common-factor variance in the scores. In equation form, and symbolizing communality by h^2,

$$h^2_x = a^2_x + b^2_x + c^2_x + \cdots + q^2_x \tag{13.25}$$

Communality is the proportion of true variance minus the proportion of specific variance, or

$$h^2_x = r_{tt} - s^2_x \tag{13.26}$$

The proportion of specific variance in a test is known as its *specificity*, which is symbolized by s^2_x. The specificity plus the proportion of error variance is called the *uniqueness* of a test. In equation form, symbolizing uniqueness by u^2_x,

$$u^2_x = s^2_x + e^2_x \tag{13.27}$$

Another relationship that can be stated concerning uniqueness is that it is the complement of communality; thus

$$u^2_x = 1 - h^2_x \tag{13.28}$$

Uniqueness includes everything that this test does not have in common with any other known measure.

Factor Theory and Validity. We made this excursion into basic factor theory in order to find a logical foundation for validity. Thus far we have seen only that this depends upon the test's common-factor variance or its communality. We will now be more specific concerning this statement. There is another theorem in factor theory to the effect that *the correlation between two tests is the sum of the cross products of their common-factor coefficients or factor loadings.* We must next define *factor loading.* Each common-factor term in equation (13.23) gives the proportion of total-score variance determined by that factor. Each term is therefore properly regarded as a coefficient of determination. That is why the terms are represented as squares. The square roots of these terms, namely, a_x, b_x, . . . , q_x, are the factor loadings. When factors are uncorrelated, as we have assumed them to be, factor loadings are also the coefficients of correlation between the respective factors and the total score. Also, because of the statistical independence of the factors, we may use them as the weights for the factors, as in equation (13.21).

To return to the statement that a correlation between two tests is the sum of cross products of factor loadings, we may state the same idea by means of the equation

$$r_{xy} = a_x a_y + b_x b_y + c_x c_y + \cdots + q_x q_y \tag{13.29}$$

If either test X or Y has a zero loading in any one of these common factors, that factor contributes nothing to their intercorrelation. The larger the factor loadings in factors that the tests have in common, the greater their intercorrelation. This same equation applies to the correlation of a test with a practical criterion. The criterion measure can also be expressed in terms of factors and factor loadings. Unless test and criterion have at least one factor in common, the test will have zero validity for predicting that criterion.

The Univocalness of Tests. Factor theory has highlighted a very serious fault in psychological tests. This is the fact that any test that measures more than one common factor to a substantial degree yields scores that are psychologically ambiguous and very difficult to interpret. What is worse, almost all tests have a complexity greater than one, that is, they measure more than one common factor. It is this situation that has led critics of psychological tests like Thomas to say, "Mental testing fails to provide scientific measurement of human abilities . . . because its results are so far incapable of fulfilling the essential conditions of scientific quantification"

(24, p. 83). One of the essential conditions of measurement that Thomas has in mind is that of univocalness of meaning of scores. In the simple case where two common factors A and B are measured to about the same degree by a test, we never know whether a certain substantial score is achieved by reason of a large amount of factor A in the individual or a large amount of factor B or by a substantial amount of both. The same score can be obtained from many different combinations of ability in factors A and B. From this score alone we cannot decide which combination occurs.

The situation is not hopeless. A big step toward the solution of the problem is to determine what each common factor is contributing to the scores that one uses. Something can be done toward the purification of tests by building up their leading common factors at the expense of secondary ones. More specific steps will be described in Chap. 16. For the purposes of practical predictions, ambiguous tests have definitely served useful purposes, even when their factorial compositions have been unknown. Practical testing operations can proceed on a much more enlightened basis, however, when their factorial contributors are known, and certain vocational operations, such as classification of personnel, demand univocal test scores.

The Test Score as a Composite of Item Scores. Another approach to test theory is to regard a score as a summation of item scores. When a score is the number of correct responses to items, there are direct relationships between total-score statistics—including mean, standard deviation, reliability, and validity—and the statistical properties of the items from which the score is derived.

The Item-score Matrix. If we administer a test of n items to each of N examinees, we can express the results in an item-score matrix. An example is given in Table 13.1. There is a column for every item I and a row for

TABLE 13.1. ITEM-SCORE MATRIX

Examinees	Items: a	b	c	d	.	.	.	i	.	.	.	n	$\sum_{i=1}^{n} s_i = X_t$
1	1	0	1	0	0	0	0	0	0	0	0	0	2
2	1	1	1	0	0	1	0	0	0	0	0	0	4
3	1	1	1	1	0	0	0	0	0	0	0	0	4
4	1	1	0	1	1	0	0	1	0	0	0	0	5
5	1	1	1	1	1	0	0	0	0	0	0	0	5
.	1	1	1	0	1	1	1	0	0	0	0	0	6
.	1	1	1	1	1	1	1	0	0	0	0	0	7
j	1	1	1	1	0	1	1	1	1	1	0	0	9
.	1	1	1	1	1	1	1	1	1	1	1	0	11
N	1	1	1	1	1	1	1	1	1	1	1	1	12
$\sum_{j=1}^{N}$	10	9	9	7	6	6	5	4	3	3	2	1	$65 = \Sigma X_t$
$M_i = p_i$	1.0	.9	.9	.7	.6	.6	.5	.4	.3	.3	.2	.1	$6.5 = M_x$

every examinee J. Every examinee attempts every item, and each item score s_{ji} is either 1 or 0. The sum of the item scores in each row gives the total score for the examinee of that row. The sum of the item scores for each column gives the number of examinees who passed that item. Thus, the item matrix is a source of information for describing items as well as describing examinees. Dividing each item-score sum for columns by N, we find the proportion of examinees who pass the corresponding item, p_i. The proportion who pass each item is a simple standard way of describing the difficulty of the item. It is actually the mean of scores for items, and the lower the mean, the more difficult the item.

The Mean of Test Scores as a Function of Means of Item Scores. It will be noted that the sum of the item means p_i equals the mean of the total scores for examinees. To emphasize this fact, we shall put it in equation form:

$$M_x = \Sigma M_i = \Sigma p_i \tag{13.30}$$

where M_x = mean of total scores in test X
M_i = mean of scores in each item
p_i = proportion of examinees passing the item

The Variance of Test Scores as a Function of Item Statistics. Since the test score is a summation of unweighted components, we can estimate its variance from item statistics by the formula for the variance of sums. The information needed includes the variances and the covariances of the items. The variance of item I is given by the equation

$$\sigma^2_i = p_i q_i \tag{13.31}$$

where p_i = proportion passing the item and $q_i = 1 - p_i$. From this, the standard deviation of an item is simply

$$\sigma_i = \sqrt{p_i q_i} \tag{13.32}$$

The general expression for a covariance between two variables is

$$C_{12} = r_{12}\sigma_1\sigma_2$$

The covariance for items I and J would be

$$C_{ij} = r_{ij}\sqrt{p_i q_i p_j q_j}$$

With as many covariance terms as there are *pairs* of variables included in the summation, the general formula for the relation of σ^2_t to item variances and covariances is

$$\sigma^2_t = \Sigma p_i q_i + 2\Sigma r_{ij}\sqrt{p_i q_i p_j q_j} \quad (\text{where } j > i) \tag{13.33}$$

where $p_i = p_a, p_b, p_c, \ldots, p_n$ in turn, and r_{ij} = correlation between each item in turn and every other item (where subscript j is a numerically higher value than i). The correlation coefficient needed for item intercorrelation in equation (13.33) is a product-moment coefficient. Since the item-score distributions are point distributions with only two values, 0 and 1, the product-moment coefficient here is a phi coefficient.

There are a number of interesting and fruitful deductions to be drawn from equation (13.33). The first of these is that the greater the item variances, the greater the test-score variance. An item variance is maximum when $p = q = .5$. In other words, item variance, and hence test-score variance, is dependent upon difficulty level of the item. The greatest test-score variance occurs when items are of median difficulty for the examinees tested. Furthermore, it is greatest when *all* items are at this level of difficulty.

A second deduction is that the test-score variance is greater when item intercorrelations are greater, for high r_{ij} values increase the covariance terms, which enter into the summation producing the total variance σ^2_t. The maximum contribution of the covariance terms would come when all r_{ij} values are 1.00. Because of certain properties of the phi coefficient, high intercorrelations of items require a uniform difficulty level. This level need not be at $p = q = .5$, but it must be uniform. The maximum phi between two variables is indicated by the equation

$$\phi_{\text{max.}} = \sqrt{\frac{p_j q_i}{q_j p_i}} \qquad (\text{where } p_i \geqq p_j \geqq .5) \qquad (13.34)$$

where p_i = the largest marginal proportion in a 2×2 contingency table and p_j = the larger marginal proportion in the other variable. Here p_i or p_j, or both, might be the proportion failing an item. Only when $p_i = p_j$ will the product under the radical equal 1.0; otherwise $\phi_{\text{max.}}$ will be less than 1.0. Thus, only when items are of equal difficulty can phi coefficients be at their positive maximum. The farther apart two items in difficulty, the lower their product-moment correlation has to be.

Relation of Score Reliability to Item Statistics. If the items of a test are of equal difficulty and their intercorrelations are equal, we have essentially parallel items. Being of equal difficulty, their means and standard deviations are equal. In connection with a collection of items approaching this condition, we could apply the S-B (Spearman-Brown) formula of equation (13.20) to the average item intercorrelation $\bar{r}_{ij}$ to estimate the reliability of the total scores. To apply this formula for this purpose, however, we should need to compute all the item intercorrelations, which would mean computing $\frac{n(n-1)}{2}$ phi coefficients. We shall see shortly how the mean item intercorrelation may be estimated.

Using the same relationship in reverse, knowing the degree of reliability of total scores, we can estimate the average item intercorrelation. Using the S-B formula with the ratio $1/n$, it becomes, by rearrangement,

$$\bar{r}_{ij} = \frac{r_{tt}}{n + (1 - n)r_{tt}} \qquad (13.35)$$

This is not as useful as the reverse application of the Spearman-Brown formula, for we rarely have interest in knowing $\bar{r}_{ij}$ for its own sake while we usually want to know r_{tt}. There are occasions on which one would like to estimate r_{tt} from knowledge of $\bar{r}_{ij}$, provided one knows the latter statistic.

Fortunately, it can be estimated from correlations of items with total score, and the latter are usually obtained in the ordinary operations of item analysis.

Richardson (21) has demonstrated that under the condition of parallel items, the average item intercorrelation is related to the average item-total correlation by the equation

$$\bar{r}_{ij} = \bar{r}^2_{it} \tag{13.36}$$

where $\bar{r}_{ij}$ = average intercorrelation between items (where each r_{ij} is a ϕ coefficient) and $\bar{r}_{it}$ = average correlation of items with total score (where r_{it} is a point-biserial coefficient). This means that the term $\bar{r}^2_{it}$ may be substituted in the S-B formula to estimate r_{tt} with n equal to the number of items. While we never have a test of completely parallel items, the formulas just given will serve to make rough estimates when the condition of parallel items is approached.

Relation of Score Reliability to Item Covariances. It can be shown that for reliability of the internal-consistency type, in other words for homogeneity of parts within a test, r_{tt} depends entirely upon the covariance terms of equation (13.33). This means, in turn, that reliability depends entirely upon the item intercorrelations. The estimation of r_{tt} from $\bar{r}_{ij}$, just mentioned, is a good indication of this proposition. Since item intercorrelations depend upon the range of item difficulties, as demonstrated above, reliability will be highest when difficulties are uniform.

Relation of Score Distributions to Item Statistics. The means, standard deviations, and intercorrelations of items in a test have very important bearings upon the shape of the total-score distribution. It is well known that as the average item mean becomes higher (items easy), the score distribution becomes negatively skewed, and as the average item mean becomes lower, (items difficult) the score distribution becomes positively skewed. If items are of medium difficulty for the population tested, the distribution becomes symmetrical.

The effects of item intercorrelations are more subtle. Their chief effect is upon kurtosis. As item intercorrelations increase, the distribution of total scores grows flatter, from mesokurtic to platykurtic, to rectangular, to bimodal, and finally U-shaped. With perfectly correlated items of medium difficulty, half the examinees would make perfect scores and half would make zero scores, for a person who passed one item would pass them all and a person who failed one item would fail them all.

If all one wanted to accomplish with a test were to separate two groups, this would be the kind of item intercorrelation to seek to achieve. The proportion to be separated in the upper group would determine the difficulty level of items to be included. There is a general principle that a test discriminates best at the level of ability corresponding to the level of difficulty emphasized in the items. This principle holds also when item intercorrelations are not perfect. As the item intercorrelations decrease from 1.0, distributions begin to fill in near the middle. A test of perfect reliability would discriminate two groups perfectly but would give us no discrimination between individuals within each group. The maximum number of discriminations would be made in a rectangular distribution. Under that condition there would be the smallest number of ties and the least doubt concerning rank order. From this point of view, and if an ordinal scale will do for one's purposes, a rectangular distribution would be the type at which to aim. This goal would be achieved when the items are moderately intercorrelated, for example, with r_{ij} about .50, in which case r_{it} would be about .70, and r_{tt} would be less than 1.00.

Relation of Validity to Item Statistics. The validity of a composite of item scores, like any composite used to predict a criterion measure, depends upon both the correlation of the items with the criterion and the item intercorrelations. The most apparent principle is that the greater the item-criterion correlations and the lower the item intercorrelations, the greater the validity of the total score. The optimal validity of a total score would be attained with different weighting for each item, in accordance with multiple-correlation principles. When items are weighted equally, as they usually are, validity will be something short of optimal.

Humphreys (10, p. 890) has shown that with items of uniform level of difficulty, the correlation of total score with criterion is estimated by the equation

$$r_{tc} = \frac{\bar{r}_{ic}}{\bar{r}_{it}} \tag{13.37}$$

where r_{tc} = correlation between test score and criterion
$\bar{r}_{ic}$ = average correlation between item and criterion
$\bar{r}_{it}$ = average correlation between item and total score

Thus, the validity coefficient, under these conditions, equals the ratio of the mean item-criterion correlation to the mean item-total correlation. For high validity, $\bar{r}_{ic}$ should be relatively large and $\bar{r}_{it}$ relatively small. Thus, when a test is used alone to predict a criterion, it has a better chance of being valid when it is of low internal consistency. The reason is that the factorial complexity of a criterion is usually great, and a single test that incorporates more of the common factors of that criterion would bring more terms into equation (13.29) and thus pile up a larger validity coefficient. In the language of information theory, items with lower intercorrelations have less redundancy; they duplicate one another in prediction less than items with higher intercorrelations. If one's goal is to increase validity without regard to internal-consistency reliability, the selection of items with high r_{ic} and low r_{it} is the essential operation to apply.

Other aspects of the relations of both reliability and validity to item properties will be discussed in Chap. 14.

Test Scores as a Function of Ability. Recently Lord (15) has approached test theory from a somewhat different point of view. There is insufficient space here to follow his development in any detail, but certain of his conclusions will be pointed out, particularly where they add new ideas.

Lord's starting point, one might say his basic postulate, is that in a test of ability, the probability that an examinee will respond correctly to a certain item is a normal ogive function of ability. The greater an examinee's ability, the greater his probability of answering the item correctly; and the function is the cumulative normal curve. This idea is reminiscent of psychophysical theory and is not new as applied to tests. It is in Lord's deductions from this postulate that we find new ideas concerning tests.

Figure 13.3 shows the ogive functions for four different items. These functions differ in both mean and dispersion on the ability scale. Items *A* and *B* require the least ability for liminal performance (ability at which probability of success is .5), and *D* requires the most ability. Item *B* has the greatest dispersion (and lowest precision), and items *A* and *D* have the greatest precision.[1] Precision is positively related to the correlation of the item with ability (biserial *r* or tetrachoric *r*, in this case, since our interest is in the relation of *what the item measures* to the ability represented on the base line). An item with perfect positive correlation would have infinite precision (a vertical line), and an item with zero correlation would have zero

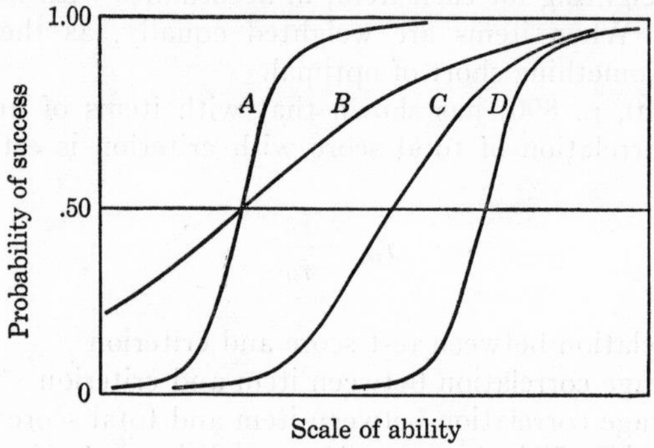

FIG. 13.3. Four ogives showing the increase in the probability of success in test items with increase in ability of the individual.

slope (a horizontal line). A highly reliable test will contain items with a relatively narrow range of limens and of dispersions. In other words, the ogives will cluster within a limited range of ability and will have similar slopes.

The Regression of Scores on Ability. The relationship of scores obtained from a test to the ability measured by the items is described by the equation (15, p. 11)

$$M_{s \cdot c} = \Sigma p_i \qquad (13.38)$$

where $M_{s \cdot c}$ = average score of examinees at ability level *c* and p_i = probability that the examinee at ability level *c* will answer item *I* correctly. If we sum the probabilities for all items at each of several successive, selected ability levels, the regression of these sums on ability will probably not be a straight line. The regression is the sum of *n* ogive regressions, each of which is, of course, nonlinear. If the items are of approximately the same difficulty level and of relatively uniform precision, the curvature in their sum is quite marked. In practice, however, when a test is of moderate difficulty for the population tested and when items have some spread in difficulty level and in precision, the relationship of scores to ability approaches linearity. This is particularly true when the item intercorrelations are low (tetrachoric *r*'s

[1] For a definition of "precision" in this connection, see Chap. 6.

below .20), as they usually are. If a test is too easy or too difficult, yielding a skewed score distribution, the regression of scores on ability is very likely to be curvilinear. Normalizing such a distribution should help to improve linearity of regression and consequently should work toward interval-scale measurement.

Thus, the picture painted by Lord may not be very serious when testing conditions are favorable for overcoming curvilinear relationship of scores to ability and when certain corrective procedures are applied. It should also be pointed out that Lord's rationale rests on the assumption that the test measures but one common factor; it is a univocal test. His development also leaves out of account the multiple-choice test. Since most tests depart from this highly specialized situation, the generality of applications from his theory is restricted. He has done an important service, however, in showing under what conditions we may expect equality of units and under what conditions we may not.

Homogeneity and Heterogeneity of Tests. In recent years there has developed a relatively independent body of theory which emphasizes the concepts of homogeneity and heterogeneity of tests. A perfectly homogeneous test is described by Loevinger (14) as one that measures the same common factor in all individuals and in all its items. A perfectly heterogeneous test is one whose items are statistically independent; each measures something that no other item measures. From a more operational point of view, we would find that when a perfectly homogeneous test is administered, if all items were arranged in order of increasing difficulty, each examinee would pass all items up to a certain point and fail all items thereafter. In a perfectly heterogeneous test, with the items arranged in order of difficulty, the items passed would appear at random in the sequence.

Loevinger was not the first to stress the importance of consistency of performance on items as a requirement for measurement. Walker (27) in 1931 pointed out that ideally a score X should represent correct responses to the first X easiest items. A test in which all item-score patterns are of this sort he called *unig*. Departure from ideal patterns he called *hig*. In Table 13.1 we find that examinees 3, 5, 7, and 9 gave perfectly unig patterns; the other score patterns show some degree of hig. The greater the degree to which patterns tend toward the unig condition, the more homogeneous the test.

Loevinger presents a general equation for an index of homogeneity (14, p. 31). It reads

$$H_t = \frac{V_t - V_h}{V_m - V_h} \tag{13.39}$$

where H_t = homogeneity index of a test
V_t = variance of total test scores
V_m = variance of a perfectly homogeneous test having the same distribution of item difficulties as the test in question
V_h = variance of a perfectly heterogeneous test having the same item characteristics

This formula recognizes that the degree of homogeneity of which a test is capable will depend upon its distribution of item difficulties. It also recognizes that even a perfectly heterogeneous test with the same item characteristics has some variance. The index, then, is a ratio of the increase in variance of this particular test over that for a test otherwise similar but with zero item intercorrelation to the difference between a test with perfect item intercorrelations and one with zero intercorrelations. This is not a computing formula; it merely states a principle. Loevinger provides a computing formula for approximating this index (14, p. 32), which is reproduced in Chap. 14. She also provides formulas for indicating homogeneity of an item with total score and with another item.

Others who have emphasized the item-score pattern in relation to total scores include Guttman, well known for his advocacy of *scale analysis*, which is based on homogeneity principles. He believes that items represent a scale of measurement only to the extent that one is able to reproduce response patterns from total scores. His theories and techniques will receive mention in connection with attitude-scale construction in Chap. 15.

Discrimination Theory. In the last-mentioned theoretical approach there is not much implication of concern about equality of units and about the goal of an interval scale for scores. Still another approach, which takes a similar attitude toward measurement, emphasizes a test's capability for discriminating between individuals. It recognizes that there is insufficient logical or experimental support for believing that obtained scores bear a linear relation to ability. It accepts rank ordering as the chief goal in testing and aims at maximizing discriminations. The chief exponents of this approach are Ferguson (3) and Thurlow (25).

Individuals are discriminated when they obtain different scores and they are not discriminated when they obtain identical scores. The relation between any two examinees' scores is either one of difference or one of equality. The total number of possible relations of pairs of examinees in a sample of N examinees is $N(N - 1)/2$, which can also be written $(N^2 - N)/2$. The number of *equality* relations occurring among these pairs is

$$\frac{\Sigma f^2_i - \Sigma f_i}{2}$$

where f_i = frequency of cases receiving each score. Σf_i equals N. The number of *difference* relations occurring is

$$\frac{(\Sigma f_i)^2 - \Sigma f^2_i}{2}$$

The sum of these two quantities is equal to $(N^2 - N)/2$, since only these two kinds of score relationships exist.

The number of differences is at a maximum when all frequencies are equal. They are equal when each is $N/(n + 1)$, where n is the number of items. This could happen in practice, of course, only when N is a multiple of $n + 1$. In a rectangular distribution the number of differences is

$$\frac{N^2 - \dfrac{N^2}{n+1}}{2}$$

Ferguson also presents a coefficient of discrimination, which expresses the ratio between the number of discriminations a test actually provides and the maximal number that such a test *could* provide (3, p. 67). The formula for the coefficient is

$$\delta = \frac{N^2 - \Sigma f^2_i}{N^2 - \dfrac{N^2}{n+1}} = \frac{(n+1)(N^2 - \Sigma f^2_i)}{nN^2} \tag{13.40}$$

where δ = coefficient of discrimination
N = number of individuals in sample
f_i = frequency at each score
n = number of items in test

This coefficient varies from zero, when all individuals make the same score, to 1.0 when the distribution is rectangular. While the size of this coefficient depends upon the degree of intercorrelation of items, it also depends upon other properties of the test. We saw previously that when item intercorrelation is moderately high the score distribution becomes rectangular. Further increase in item intercorrelation bring bimodal and finally U-shaped distributions as well as higher reliability. The coefficient of discrimination is greatest when the distribution is rectangular, and it decreases with bimodal and U-shaped distributions. Discriminations are admittedly poorer in the latter instances, except at restricted score levels. Thus, maximal discrimination all along the line is best only when the test is short of perfect reliability.

It is interesting that the theory from this approach comes to much the same conclusions concerning the optimal item composition for a test as those from other approaches. These conclusions agree that the best items are those of medium difficulty and of a narrow range of difficulty. There is agreement on the desirability of high item intercorrelations, though the discrimination approach warns us more clearly against carrying this goal too far. Thus, something short of perfect reliability of the internal-consistency variety is optimal for numerous and widespread discriminations.

A word of warning is perhaps necessary lest too much weight be placed on discriminations as such. There is also the question as to what the discriminations mean and whether they are likely to be stable, that is, in the same directions, in a parallel form of the test or in a repetition of the same test. It is reassuring that the high number of discriminations depends upon high item intercorrelations, a condition that should tend to guarantee a similar kind of discrimination along the line. The question of the *kind* of discrimination and whether it is what we want takes us over into the problem of validity on which the theory has nothing to say.

Speed and Power Problems

In the practice of group testing it is sometimes essential, or at least it is very convenient, for every examinee to be allotted the same limited working time on a test. This fact, particularly, has raised many questions concerning the effect of working time upon scores and upon measurement. There is the practical question concerning the optimal time limit to be adopted for the test, where optimal is defined in terms of some value judgment in the light of some psychological-measurement goal. There are the more fundamental questions concerning what psychological qualities are measured when time is liberal versus when time is short. The problems of time cannot be divorced from the problems of difficulty, as we shall see. There has been some theory aimed at these problems and very recently some experimental and factor-analytical investigations have been aimed at their solution.

Theory of Relationships of Speed and Power. There seems to have been a working hypothesis that speed and power, as descriptive variables of psychological performance, are relatively interchangeable, that we can measure the same abilities either by determining how many units of work can be produced per unit of time or by determining the level of difficulty that can be mastered in liberal time. This would mean that an individual could obtain the same score (number of successful acts—responses to items) under different combinations of time and difficulty levels so long as the product of time times difficulty were constant. This picture of the relationships is undoubtedly much too simple.

Probability of Success in Relation to Difficulty and Time. Thurstone made the first attempt at a rationale of this problem in 1937 (26), an attempt which does not seem to have been followed up but which would seem to be promising. His reasoning was essentially as follows. He defined the power of an individual as that level of difficulty of tasks at which his probability of success is .5 when given infinite time. In practice, infinite time is all the time the examinee will take. It is true that the amount of time he will take depends upon his motivation, but we will assume a high level of desire to complete the task, such as we usually assume in connection with testing of abilities. Along with this definition of power is the assumption that the probability of success is a descending ogive function of difficulty. This is not a new assumption, for we saw it represented in Fig. 13.1. Here, however, we may extend the assumption by adding "within a constant time interval."

Figure 13.4 (first diagram) represents the assumed relationship of probability of success to difficulty level when time varies ($T_1, T_2, \ldots, T_\infty$). At infinite time the median of the psychometric curve comes at difficulty level A, which by definition is the measure of this individual's power in this kind of task. At decreasing time limits, the ogive moves to the left on the difficulty scale. One may assume that the precision of the curve remains the same for this kind of task and this individual. The slope and shape of the curve are matters for experimental determination. There may be changes in both slope and in skewness. The diagram assumes symmetry, that the inflection point is at the median.

Success as a function of time (for the same individual in the same kind of task) is pictured in the second diagram of Fig. 13.4, at different difficulty levels ($D_1, D_2, \ldots, D_8$). At some moderate difficulty level Dj we may assume that the regression of probability of success upon time is of the ascending ogive form. For easy items the probability curve has very high precision, but as difficulty increases, the precision of the curves decreases. The main reason for this is that zero time imposes a limit. At zero time the probability of success is zero. Some difficult tasks are mastered with probability less than .5 even after long time intervals. There are some tasks so difficult that the individual has no probability of solving them, even in infinite time. Their functions would lie along the base line at $p = 0$.

The important practical implication of these hypotheses is in the form of deductions concerning the effect of limited time on psychological measurement. Would the ordinary summation scores yield the appropriate measures of individuals when there is a time limit to the test? The measurement of the individual's power in the task was defined as his limen score in infinite time. We saw that under power conditions of testing there is almost a perfect correlation between summation scores and limen scores in the same test. In Fig. 13.4, diagram 1, we see that the limen score decreases systemati-

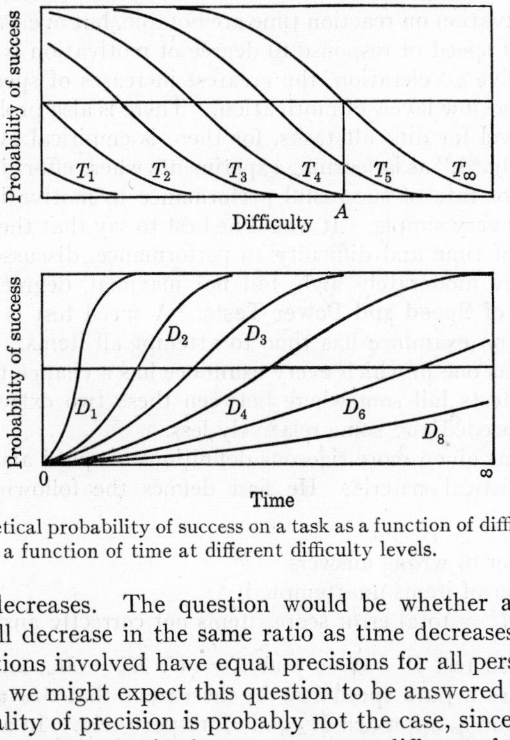

FIG. 13.4. Hypothetical probability of success on a task as a function of difficulty at different time limits and as a function of time at different difficulty levels.

cally as time decreases. The question would be whether all individuals' limen scores will decrease in the same ratio as time decreases. If the psychometric functions involved have equal precisions for all persons and at all difficulty levels, we might expect this question to be answered in the affirmative. But equality of precision is probably not the case, since there is much empirical evidence that obtained scores measure different factors as speed versus power is emphasized. The individual's power in a task, as defined, is a quantity independent of his speed of work. It is best measured under power conditions and estimates of it from scores obtained under conditions that limit time are made with some risk, depending upon how severe the time limitation is.

There have been a few studies bearing directly or indirectly on Thurstone's theory of the difficulty-time manifold in relation to success, most of them providing some support. In a study by Philip (20), for example, difficulty of a psychophysical judgment was varied by making color-spot patterns more or less alike, the observer being asked to judge differences. Exposure times were varied from .133 to .668 sec. At each level of difficulty, errors were S-shaped functions of exposure time. A study of Hunter and Sigler (12) demonstrated similar effects in an investigation of span of apprehension, in which difficulty was controlled by varying the illumination level.

Relation of Speed and Power to Motivation. Thurstone (26) also speculated concerning the effects of motivation upon probability of success as difficulty and time vary. One conclusion was that increased motivation has no effect upon power but may increase speed. Trying hard to master an item will not increase the probability of success in infinite time, but if the individual can master it at all, he can do so in shorter time. It is likely that the easier the task, the greater relatively the effect of increased motivation. In the easiest tests the task becomes essentially one of reaction time. The effects of motivation on reaction time are notable, but even with simple tasks the relation of speed of response to degree of motivation is probably one of sharply negative acceleration, the greatest increases of speed being noticed from changes at low levels of motivation. There is also probably an optimal motivation level for difficult tasks, for there is empirical evidence that one may "try too hard," as in learning experiments where effort is varied. Thus, the relations of rate of successful performance to motivation are not very well known or very simple. It would be best to say that the rationale stated for relations of time and difficulty to performance, discussed above, apply when there are moderately high, but not maximal, degrees of motivation.

Definitions of Speed and Power Tests. A speed test is often defined as one in which no examinee has time to attempt all items. A power test is often defined as one in which every examinee has a chance to attempt every item. Most tests fall somewhere between these two extremes; some relatively more speeded and some relatively less.

Gulliksen has given more rigorous definitions of speed and power tests, in terms of statistical criteria. He first defines the following symbols (11, p. 230):

W = number of wrong answers
U = number of items unattempted
$X = W + U$ = total error score (items not correctly answered)

In a pure speed test $W = 0$ so that $X = U$, $M_x = M_u$, and $\sigma_x = \sigma_u$. Any test approaches a pure speed test to the extent that M_w and σ_w approach zero and M_u and σ_u approach M_x and σ_x, respectively. In a pure power test M_u and σ_u equal zero, and M_w and σ_w equal M_x and σ_x, respectively. To the extent that any test approaches these conditions it is a power test. A hard-and-fast line between speed and power tests is not possible to fix. Gulliksen (11, p. 233) offers the criterion that if the ratio σ_w/σ_x is very small the test is essentially a speed test and if the ratio σ_u/σ_x is very small the test is essentially a power test. These statements assume that there have been essentially no omitted items.

Speed and Power Factors in Time-limit Tests. Some investigations of time-limit tests throw considerable light on what is measured as time is varied. All show that there are speed factors distinct from power factors.

Davidson and Carroll (2) factor-analyzed separately speed scores and "level" or power scores derived from the same tests. They also related the same factors to time-limit scores as obtained under the standard administration of the same tests. The speed score for a test was the number of items attempted, disregarding errors. The power score was number of correct answers when all items were attempted. The results showed a *general* speed factor common to the speed scores and related to some extent to some of the time-limit scores. Some of the well-known common factors were found in the analysis of the power scores. Corresponding to one of these factors, a reasoning factor, there was a speed-of-reasoning factor in the analysis of speed scores. The time-limit scores were related to different degrees to the various speed and power factors, some more to the one kind and some more to the other.

Myers (19) administered three forms of a figure-analogies test, each form being given in three ways, with 10, 20, and 30 items, respectively, administered in 12 min. In the power tests (10 items), 97 to 100 per cent of the examinees completed the items. In the speed tests (30 items) 30 to 41 per cent completed the items. The effect of speed conditions on various scores was studied— the number of items attempted, the number of right answers, the number of omissions, and the number of wrong answers. A factor analysis of each form of the test showed two "factors," one recognized as speed and the other as power.[1] Both the number-attempted and the number-right scores under speed conditions measured the speed "factor." The number-attempted score means different things for different individuals. Some examinees make no responses until they feel confident of the answer, while others record an answer even when they know they are guessing. In a speed test, too, differences in motivation level may have an important bearing on the number of answers recorded. Thus, speed conditions where items are not very easy open the door to many uncontrolled determiners of individual differences in scores.

Tate (23) approached the speed versus power problem experimentally. His major problem of investigation was to determine whether there is a factor of mental speed that is independent of power and independent of the kind of task in which it is measured. Tate used four kinds of tasks, including tests of arithmetic reasoning, number series, sentence completion, and spatial relations. The items were at three difficulty levels. At the easy level, 3 to 11 per cent failed the items; at the moderate level, 17 to 40 per cent failed; and at the difficult level, 42 to 61 per cent failed. The items were administered individually, and the response time to each item was recorded separately. This is an important condition, since in the group administration of tests, although total working time is controlled, each examinee regulates his own timing within a test. One interesting feature of Tate's treatment of results was that conversion of his working-time scores into log-time measures resulted in normal distributions.

Several of Tate's findings are noteworthy (23, p. 373). With difficulty and accuracy (proportion correct) controlled, there were still very large

[1] The term "factors" is in quotation marks here because each factor is probably a composite of several.

differences in speed scores. *Correlations between speed scores (accuracy and difficulty controlled) and power scores were approximately zero for all kinds of items.* A power score was defined as the sum of difficulty levels for items passed by the individual. With accuracy controlled, persons fast at one level of difficulty tend to be fast at other levels. With accuracy controlled, persons fast on one kind of task tend to be fast on others. Speed is less affected by difficulty level than by kind of items. Thus, it appears that speed of work is a relatively stable personal trait somewhat related to kind of task but not fully determined by kind of task or level of difficulty. Tate's conclusion was that there is a general speed factor and also speed factors specific to each kind of task. The psychological nature of these speed factors is unknown, but it is a good hypothesis that they represent motivational and temperament variables as well as or instead of abilities.

The implications of speed and power for reliability and validity of tests and for item analysis and other test features will be discussed in the chapters to follow.

Problems

1. In test *K*, the *SD* of obtained scores is 12.0, and the *SD* of true scores is 10.0. Find:
   a. The *SD* of error components of the obtained scores.
   b. The reliability of the obtained scores.
   c. The index of reliability.
   d. The standard error of measurement.
2. The reliability of test *L* is .85, and the *SD* of obtained scores is 8.0. Find:
   a. The proportion of error variance.
   b. The index of reliability.
   c. The standard error of measurement.
   d. The *SD* of true scores.
3. For a test parallel to test *L* of Prob. 2, but three times as long, find:
   a. Variance and *SD* of total scores.
   b. Variances of true and error components.
   c. Coefficient of reliability.
4. For each test in Data 13*A*, find:
   a. Its communality, specificity, uniqueness, and proportion of error variance.
   b. Its factor loadings.

DATA 13*A*. PROPORTIONS OF TOTAL VARIANCE IN THREE TESTS ATTRIBUTABLE TO EACH OF FOUR COMMON FACTORS AND RELIABILITY COEFFICIENTS

Test	Factor				r_{tt}
	A	*B*	*C*	*D*	
G	.49	.16	.00	.25	.90
H	.36	.00	.00	.36	.82
J	.00	.64	.25	.00	.95

5. Compute intercorrelations of tests *G*, *H*, and *J*, in so far as those intercorrelations are determined by factors *A* to *D*.
6. From the item-score matrix in Data 13*B*, find:
   a. Person scores.

b. Item means.
c. Item variances and their sum.
d. Total-score mean as a function of item means.
e. Total-score variance, from total scores.
f. The covariance component of the total-score variance.

DATA 13*B*. MATRIX OF ITEM SCORES IN A 10-ITEM TEST TAKEN BY 8 PERSONS

	Item									
Persons	*a*	*b*	*c*	*d*	*e*	*f*	*g*	*h*	*i*	*j*
1	0	0	0	0	0	0	0	0	0	0
2	1	0	0	1	0	0	0	0	0	0
3	1	1	1	0	1	0	0	0	0	0
4	1	1	1	1	0	0	1	0	0	0
5	1	1	1	0	1	1	0	0	0	0
6	1	1	1	1	0	1	0	1	1	0
7	1	1	1	1	1	1	1	1	0	0
8	1	1	1	1	1	1	1	1	1	1

7. Estimate the maximum (phi) correlation possible between selected pairs of items in Data 13*B*:
a. Items *e* and *f*.
b. Items *b* and *h*.
c. Items *a* and *i*.

Answers

1. (*a*) $\sigma_e = 6.63$; (*b*) $r_{tt} = .694$; (*c*) $r_{t\infty} = .83$; (*d*) $\sigma_{t\infty} = 6.63$.
2. (*a*) .15; (*b*) $r_{t\infty} = .92$; (*c*) $\sigma_{t\infty} = 3.10$; (*d*) $\sigma_{\infty} = 7.38$.
3. (*a*) $\sigma^2_{3t} = 518.4$, $\sigma_{3t} = 22.8$; (*b*) $\sigma^2_{3\infty} = 489.6$, $\sigma^2_{3e} = 28.8$; (*c*) $r_{tt} = .94$.
4. (*a*)

	h^2	s^2	u^2	e^2
G	.90	.00	.10	.10
H	.72	.10	.28	.18
J	.89	.06	.11	.05

(*b*)

	A	*B*	*C*	*D*
G	.7	.4	.0	.5
H	.6	.0	.0	.6
J	.0	.8	.5	.0

5. $r_{gh} = .72$; $r_{gj} = .32$; $r_{hj} = .00$.
6. (*a*) 0, 2, 4, 5, 5, 7, 8, 10.
(*b*) .875, .750, .750, .625, .500, .500, .375, .375, .250, .125.
(*c*) .109, .188, .188, .234, .250, .250, .234, .234, .188, .109. $\Sigma p_i q_i = 1.984$.
(*d*) $\Sigma p_i = 5.125$.
(*e*) $\sigma^2_t = 9.109$.
(*f*) $9.109 - 1.984 = 7.125$, where $1.984 = \Sigma p_i q_i$.
7. Maximum correlations: (*a*) $\phi_{ef} = 1.00$; (*b*) $\phi_{bh} = .745$; (*c*) $\phi_{ai} = .655$.

References

1. Canfield, A. A. The "sten" scale—a modified C-scale. *Educ. psychol. Measmt.*, 1951, **11**, 295–297.
2. Davidson, W. M., and Carroll, J. B. Speed and level components in time-limit scores: A factor analysis. *Educ. psychol. Measmt.*, 1945, **5**, 411–427.
3. Ferguson, G. A. On the theory of test discrimination. *Psychometrika*, 1949, **14**, 61–68.
4. Glaser, R. A methodological analysis of the inconsistency of response to test items. *Educ. psychol. Measmt.*, 1949, **9**, 727–739.
5. ———. The application of the concepts of multiple-operation measurement to the response patterns on psychological tests. *Educ. psychol. Measmt.*, 1951, **11**, 372–382.
6. ———. The reliability of inconsistency. *Educ. psychol. Measmt.*, 1952, **12**, 60–64.
7. Goheen, H. W., and Kavruck, S. *Selected References on Test Construction, Mental Test Theory and Statistics*, 1929–1949. Washington, D.C.: U.S. Government Printing Office, 1950.
8. Grossnickle, L. T. The scaling of test scores by the method of paired comparisons. *Psychometrika*, 1942, **7**, 43–64.
9. Guilford, J. P. *Fundamental Statistics in Psychology and Education.* 2d ed. New York: McGraw-Hill, 1950.
10. ——— and Lacey, J. I. (eds.). *Printed Classification Tests. Army Air Forces Aviation Psychology Research Program, Report* 5. Washington, D.C.: U.S. Government Printing Office, 1947.
11. Gulliksen, H. *Theory of Mental Tests.* New York: Wiley, 1950.
12. Hunter, W. S., and Sigler, M. Span of visual discrimination as a function of time and visual stimulation. *J. exp. Psychol.*, 1940, **26**, 160–179.
13. Lindquist, E. F. (ed.) *Educational Measurement.* Washington, D.C.: American Council on Education, 1951.
14. Loevinger, J. A systematic approach to the construction and evaluation of tests of ability. *Psychol. Monogr.*, 1947, **61**, No. 285.
15. Lord, F. A theory of test scores. *Psychometr. Mongr.*, 1952, No. 7.
16. Lorr, M. Interrelationships of number-correct and limen scores for an amount-limit test. *Psychometrika*, 1944, **9**, 17–30.
17. Mosier, C. I. Psychophysics and mental test theory: Fundamental postulates and elementary theorems. *Psychol. Rev.*, 1940, **47**, 356–366.
18. ———. Psychophysics and mental test theory: II. The constant process. *Psychol. Rev.*, 1941, **48**, 235–249.
19. Myers, C. T. The factorial composition and validity of differently speeded tests. *Psychometrika*, 1952, **17**, 347–352.
20. Philip, B. R. The relationship of exposure time and accuracy in a perceptual task. *J. exp. Psychol.*, 1947, **37**, 178–186.
21. Richardson, M. W. Notes on the rationale of item analysis. *Psychometrika*, 1936, **1**, 69–76.
22. ———. The logic of age scales. *Educ. psychol. Measmt.*, 1941, **1**, 25–34.
23. Tate, M. W. Individual differences in speed of response in mental test materials of varying degrees of difficulty. *Educ. psychol. Measmt.*, 1948, **8**, 353–374.
24. Thomas, L. G. Mental tests as instruments of science. *Psychol. Monogr.*, 1942, **54**, No. 245.
25. Thurlow, W. R. Direct measures of discriminations among individuals performed by psychological tests. *J. Psychol.*, 1950, **29**, 281–314.
26. Thurstone, L. L. Ability, motivation, and speed. *Psychometrika*, 1937, **2**, 249–254.
27. Walker, D. A. Answer-pattern and score-scatter in tests and examinations. *Brit. J. Psychol.*, 1931, **22**, 73–86; 1936, **26**, 301–308; 1940, **30**, 248–260.

CHAPTER 14

RELIABILITY AND VALIDITY OF MEASURES

In the discussion of psychological-test theories in Chap. 13 much was said concerning the ideas underlying the concepts of reliability and validity. The present chapter will be concerned with problems of reliability and validity as we meet them in practice, as applying not only to tests but to other psychological measurements. We shall not have space to treat all kinds of measurements but shall be limited to the more common ones. It should be said in passing, however, that not enough attention has been given to these problems outside the area of psychological tests, and particularly tests as applied to measurements of individual differences.

We shall find that although the definitions and meanings of reliability and validity as set forth in Chap. 13 remain basic, the operations by which we commonly seek estimates of them involve us in many modified meanings. Measurement conditions are not all standardized according to one pattern of experimental operations, and we are often faced with the necessity of estimating reliability and validity under special conditions. Under the same conditions, too, there are many alternative ways of estimating the amount of true variance. Indeed, there are many ways of defining operationally the meaning of true variance itself. In addition to the many ways of estimating reliability and validity we shall also consider the more common determiners of those properties of measurement in practice.

Approaches to the Estimation of Reliability

The Standard Approaches to Reliability. Traditionally, the textbooks have told us that there are three fundamental types of approach to the estimation of reliability. All of these were designed to answer the question, "What is the self-correlation of this test?" There have been three standard procedures, known loosely as the "split-half," "alternate-forms," and "retest" methods. All have in common the goal of deriving two sets of scores from the "same" test administered to the "same" sample for the purpose of correlation to find r_{tt}. In the case of the split-half method, the Spearman-Brown formula has usually been applied to estimate the reliability of the test of full length from the obtained estimate of correlation of a test of half length.

These major distinctions still hold today, but they are much more rigorously defined and the operations are better controlled. For example, the division of a test into two parts for this purpose is to be accomplished in a way that will ensure that the two resemble each other in certain statistical ways as well as in more superficial and obvious ways. Each should represent faithfully the total test in all significant respects. The use of the Spearman-Brown formula demands this. The principle of fractionation of a test into halves has also been broadened to divisions into thirds or smaller parts, even into single items. The information sought concerns the equivalence of parts for measurement purposes, or the *internal consistency* of the test. Internal-consistency reliability is therefore one of the major classes of reliability, operationally defined.

A retest coefficient of correlation tells us nothing concerning the internal consistency of a test. In fact, the parts or even the items of a test might intercorrelate zero and yet the retest correlation could be high. The key concept for this procedure is that of *stability*. It answers the question concerning how stable or dependable are the measurements over a period of time. High reliability of this kind tells us that the individuals remain rather uniform, or maintain their rank positions in spite of changes, in whatever psychological functions this test measures. A low retest reliability coefficient means that the function or functions measured fluctuate from time to time or the test as an instrument is affected by other things that do fluctuate.

The alternate-forms method bears resemblances to both the internal-consistency approach and the retest approach. The end result is an index of how equivalent the psychological-measurement content of one form of the test is with the content of another. The nearer together the two forms are administered in time, the more nearly is the coefficient an index of internal consistency. The farther apart the two forms are administered in time, the more chance there is for function fluctuations and other incidental fluctuations. In the extreme time-interval case, this is like retesting, except that it is with a different form of the same test. At any rate, the alternate-forms method indicates both equivalence of content and stability of performance.

The definition of the alternate-forms method has been sharpened somewhat in recent years. For example, Thorndike (47) speaks of *equivalent forms*, by which he means tests having identical true variance and no overlap of error variances. An equivalent-forms coefficient will tell the story concerning reliability of either form to the extent that these two conditions are satisfied. If the nature of the true variance differs in the two forms, to that extent the reliability of each will be underestimated. If the error variances in the two are not experimentally independent but overlap, to that extent reliability will be overestimated. Equivalence of forms can be promoted in test construction by seeing that they have similar distributions of item-difficulty indices and of item-total correlations.

Gulliksen (25) speaks of *parallel tests*, which he defines statistically. Parallel tests have equal means, equal variances, and equal intercorrelations with one other. For the purpose of determining whether they are parallel in all these respects, he recommends the construction of at least three forms so that there can be three estimates of intercorrelation. He presents various statistical tests for determining whether these properties of parallel tests have been satisfied (25, Chap. 14). If two or more such forms are to be combined to make a longer test, the Spearman-Brown formula would be applied to estimate the reliability of the longer form. To the extent that the properties of parallel tests are fulfilled, this formula will give an accurate estimate of total-score reliability.

Contributions to True and Error Variance in Different Methods. It is easy to see why the three types of estimate of reliability might give very different coefficients. From the standpoint of theory this is because different components are regarded as error variance in the three cases. Let us consider a few of the important sources of variance affecting a test score and how they may be counted among the sources of true variance in some cases and among the sources of error variance in others.

We hope that a test, regardless of the manner of estimating its reliability, measures some enduring property or properties of individuals. Any such component or components, to the extent that they do endure, would contribute to true variance for any method of estimating reliability. Any growths or declines in these properties during an interval between test and retest administrations might affect retest reliability, and also alternate-forms reliability if the time interval were long enough. If all individuals grew at the same rate or declined at the same rate, however, change in the properties would not affect reliability. It would take *differential* rates of change to lower reliability, in which case the differential changes have contributed to error variance. In deciding how much time interval to use between two forms of a test or two administrations of the same form, one should decide to what extent he wants function fluctuations, and other fluctuations that occur in time, to be taken into account. Some investigators prefer the alternate-form type to the internal-consistency type of coefficient for the reason that they are interested in how much stability to expect of scores over time.

Variations among individuals in test-taking experience in general contribute to "true" variance to the extent that they promote consistency in the two scores. In terms of factor theory (see Chap. 13), such variance contributes nothing to measurement of common factors in which we are interested. The same may be said for more specific test-taking experience. Both of these experiential sources may make an erroneous contribution to reliability of the alternate-form and retest types, but this effect is likely to be blurred with increasing time interval. The differential effects of experience may wear off quickly as all examinees gain more common experience in the present form, or administration, and in the next.

Differences in motivation may be of significant importance in some instances. This has to do both with *level* of motivation, and with *direction* of motivation, that is to say, mental set. It was surmised in Chap. 13 that above a minimal level of effort the variation in motivation probably has little effect on scores. Some individuals, however, either because they find the test very uninteresting and/or because they lack the necessary inducement to do well, may tend to lag behind their true performance and obtain low scores. In the split-half method, particularly with odd-even splits, the effects of motivational deviations such as this should be spread evenly over both parts. This would contribute to "true" variance, but it does not contribute to the variance we want to measure. In the alternate-form approach, to the extent that the same motivation level carries over, this source contributes to true variance also. In the retest approach, the carry-over is less probable.

Under "mental set" comes a variety of things. The understanding that the examinee has of what he is expected to do is one source. His guesses as to what he had better do, perhaps even contrary to the examiner's instructions, are another source. Response sets of various kinds contribute to true variance or detract from it.[1] These frequently contribute to true variance in that they make scores more consistent than they would otherwise be. They do not contribute to the measurement of psychological functions in which we probably have more interest. To the extent that sets change from one test administration to another, this contribution to reliability diminishes. The internal-consistency type of reliability coefficient is less likely to suffer loss from this source.

A number of conditions of the examinee that might come under the general heading of "readiness to work" may have some bearing on the size of the reliability coefficient, such as physical health, condition of rest or of fatigue, and emotional state. All these would be relatively more uniform during a single sitting but would contribute to error variance when there is a time interval sufficiently long for these conditions to change. They would be likely to change in different directions and in different amounts in different examinees. Rather momentary fluctuations of attention, memory, etc., however, could contribute to error variance in the single sitting as well as between sittings and thus contribute to error variance in all approaches. Chance success in multiple-choice items is also a source of error variance in all methods.

The fact of identical content in the retest approach is one of the few contributors to "true" variance in a retest coefficient that cannot contribute to true variance in the other approaches. This is largely dependent upon a kind of item, depending upon specific knowledge or skill for handling that kind of item. In a pitch-discrimination test, items of the same difficulty level are unidentifiable as well as interchangeable. Memory for specific responses made in the earlier administration, where those responses are used again, contributes to true variance. Memory that leads to a change of response, if this means going from a right to a wrong response, or vice versa, contributes to error variance.

Enough has been said concerning the various sources of true and error variance to impress one with the very large number of determiners and with the fact that those sources sometimes increase the reliability coefficient and sometimes decrease it. The choice of which type of reliability estimate to use can often be facilitated by deciding what sources we want to go into error variance and what sources into true variance. The interpretation of a coefficient will also be more enlightened if we keep in mind all the things that might have contributed to its size.

Split-half Methods of Estimating Reliability. There is general agreement that split-half methods of estimating reliability should be applied to power tests only, or to tests that approach the pure-power condition. The specific problems of reliability of speed tests will be discussed later in the chapter. Here it is enough to say that if all parts are to be parallel, all, or nearly all, the examinees must attempt items in the last part as well as in other parts.

[1] See Chap. 15 for a discussion of response sets.

To be parallel parts, the items of the subtests that compose the parts should have items of equal average difficulty, equal spread of difficulty, and equal item intercorrelation, and the same amount of time should be devoted to each.

The Odd-even Method. The odd-even split has been generally favored for several reasons. If items are arranged in order of increasing difficulty, this split ensures parallelism so far as difficulty is concerned. It ensures that approximately the same amount of time will be devoted to each half. It tends to keep testing conditions more nearly constant for the two halves, for it is highly unlikely that conditions either external to the examinee or internal to him will fluctuate systematically with alternating items. This constancy of conditions for the two halves gives a false impression of the amount of true variance in a test, however, for no other predictions from the test scores will be made with so many really extra-test determiners contributing positively to the obtained correlation. This is why some investigators much prefer the alternate-forms method, with a time interval of at least a day between administrations. The change of conditions thus introduced is more like those changes between administration of two different tests or between test administration and measurement of some criterion in validation.

The speed factor is also a very serious contributor to error in r_{tt} as estimated from the split-half method. This cannot be too strongly emphasized, for it is so frequently ignored. If there were no omissions and no errors in responses to the test, the correlation between odds and evens scores would be practically perfect, the maximum difference between pairs of half-test scores being 1 where an odd number of items were attempted. To the extent that there are unattempted items at the end of the test, the speed of work contributes a large part of the half-score variances. We saw in Chap. 13 that speed of work may be independent of power. If it is the power aspect that we want to measure, speed contributes something to true variance that we do not want. To the extent that a test is speeded, an odd-even coefficient is inflated.

In order to illustrate the use of an odd-even r_{tt} along with others, we will use data from the simple test situation represented in Table 14.2. From the matrix of item scores it is easy to extract 10 pairs of odds and evens scores.[1] These are listed in Table 14.1. The correlation r_{oe} is .809. Applying the S-B (Spearman-Brown) formula to this we obtain .894 for the reliability of the total score. This is a trifle higher than estimates we shall see for the same test when other methods are used, but it is very close to the figure estimated by the better-accepted methods.

Mosier (54) offers a short-cut computing formula that will save some effort in computing an odd-even r. It requires the scoring of only one of the parts, let us say the odds-score part, and the total test, which one would score anyway. The formula is

$$r_{oe} = \frac{r_{ot}\sigma_t - \sigma_o}{\sqrt{\sigma^2_t + \sigma^2_o - 2r_{ot}\sigma_o\sigma_t}} \tag{14.1}$$

[1] The estimation of test reliability on such a very small sample is, of course, tolerated only for illustrative purposes.

where r_{ot} = correlation between odds score and total score
σ_o = SD of odds scores
σ_t = SD of total scores

This may be recognized as a special application of the formula for the correlation of one part of a total with the other part when the correlation of a part with the total is known (24, p. 357). By whatever formula the odd-even coefficient is computed, the S-B formula would be applied to estimate the reliability of the total test.

TABLE 14.1. ODDS SCORES AND EVENS SCORES FOR THE TEST DATA IN TABLE 13.1 (ALSO IN TABLE 14.2) PREPARED FOR ESTIMATING RELIABILITY BY THE ODD-EVEN, RULON, AND FLANAGAN METHODS

X_o	X_e	$(X_o - X_e)$ d	d^2	$(X_o + X_e)$ X_t	X^2_t
2	0	+2	4	2	4
2	2	0	0	4	16
2	2	0	0	4	16
2	3	−1	1	5	25
3	2	+1	1	5	25
4	2	+2	4	6	36
4	3	+1	1	7	49
4	5	−1	1	9	81
6	5	+1	1	11	121
6	6	0	0	12	144
Σ 35	30	+5	13	65	517
145	120		Σd^2	ΣX_t	ΣX^2_t
ΣX^2_o	ΣX^2_e				
M 3.5	3.0	+0.5		6.5	
σ^2 2.25	3.00	1.05		9.45	
r_{oe} = .809					

The Spearman-Brown Formula with Unequal Variances. In practice the two standard deviations from half scores are rarely equal. The important practical question is how large the inequality can be without leading to errors when the S-B formula is applied. Cronbach (9) has made some estimates of error in r_{tt} when computed by the S-B formula under these conditions. The effect is to overestimate r_{tt}. The smaller the r_{tt}, the greater the percentage of error. It is safe to conclude from Cronbach's results (9, p. 302) that the error is less than 1 per cent when the ratio of the SD's is not greater than 1.1 and that the error is not greater than 2 per cent when the ratio of SD's is 1.2. If r_{tt} is greater than .60, the size of error is not over 5 per cent, even when the larger SD is 50 per cent larger than the smaller.

Reliability with Unequal Parts. Horst (35) has proposed a formula to use when the parts are definitely of unequal length. Sometimes the nature of the test requires us to face this contingency. The formula is

$$R = \frac{r[\sqrt{r^2 + 4pq(1 - r^2)} - r]}{2pq(1 - r^2)} \tag{14.2}$$

where R = reliability of sum of the two parts
r = correlation between the two parts
p = proportion of total test devoted to one part
$q = 1 - p$

In the special case when $p = q = .5$, Horst's formula reduces to the S-B formula. In every case when two unequal parts are correlated, r underestimates reliability and R will be found larger than r. The more imbalance in the two parts, the greater the difference between r and R.

The Rulon Formula. Rulon (67) has developed a simple formula for reliability of total-test scores that follows closely the basic definition of reliability—that reliability is the proportion of true variance in a test. Rulon's equation, however, actually expresses the complementary statement that reliability is equal to unity minus the proportion of error variance. It is the error variance that Rulon estimates from obtained data.

If two half-test scores, odds and evens or otherwise, are obtained for each examinee, the differences between these scores can be used to indicate the errors of measurement. This is the information to which Rulon's formula applies. It reads

$$r_{tt} = 1 - \frac{\sigma^2{}_d}{\sigma^2{}_t} \tag{14.3}$$

where d = difference between two half scores for an examinee
σ_d = *SD* of those differences
σ_t = *SD* of total scores

This gives the reliability for the *total* score, not for the half scores, and therefore the S-B formula would not be applied. A rough, intuitive reason for this is that each difference is the sum of two equal half errors; the difference therefore belongs to the total test rather than to either half test.

Applying the Rulon formula to the data of Table 14.1, we find there that $\sigma^2{}_d = 1.05$ and $\sigma^2{}_t = 9.45$, the ratio of the two being .111; hence $r_{tt} = .889$. Without applying the S-B formula, we have a figure that is close to the corrected odd-even estimate, which was .894.

The Rulon formula can be applied to parallel forms, in which case the coefficient would indicate reliability of a test composed of the sum of the two forms. If one wanted the reliability for one form only, one would apply the S-B formula with $n = .5$.

The Flanagan Formula. Flanagan (19) gives a formula parallel to Rulon's. It estimates the error variance, in a sense, as the sum of the variances of the two halves. This can be seen in the formula, where the sum $\sigma^2{}_1 + \sigma^2{}_2$ is used in place of Rulon's $\sigma^2{}_d$.

$$r_{tt} = 2\left(1 - \frac{\sigma^2{}_1 + \sigma^2{}_2}{\sigma^2{}_t}\right) \tag{14.4}$$

where σ_1 and σ_2 are the SD's of the two halves, respectively. As in the case of the Rulon formula, this provides an estimate of total-score reliability.

Applying the Flanagan formula to the data from Table 14.1, we have

$$r_{tt} = 2\left(1 - \frac{2.25 + 3.00}{9.45}\right) = .888$$

The Kuder-Richardson Formulas. Dissatisfied with the split-half methods, Kuder and Richardson (44, 65) developed new procedures based on item statistics. There are a great many ways of splitting n items into two sets of $n/2$ items each, from which we might obtain as many different estimates of r_{tt}. In a sense, Kuder and Richardson split a test into n parts of one item each. Just as larger parts must be parallel in order to obtain good estimates of r_{tt} so must the items be parallel in the Kuder-Richardson approach. Furthermore, they assume that all items measure only one common factor; the items are factorially univocal. The basic Kuder-Richardson formula proposed for computing purposes is

$$r_{tt} = \left(\frac{n}{n-1}\right)\left(\frac{\sigma^2_t - \Sigma pq}{\sigma^2_t}\right) \qquad \text{(K-R formula 20)} \qquad (14.5)$$

where n = number of items in test, as usual
p = proportion of correct responses to each item in turn (or proportion of examinees responding in the keyed manner)
$q = 1 - p$

If the reader will refer back to equation (13.33), which expresses the total variance of a test σ^2_t in terms of the summation of item variances pq and covariances $r_{ij}\sigma_i\sigma_j$, formula (14.5) will take on meaning consistent with the basic definition of reliability. The numerator of the term at the right in (14.5) equals the sum of the covariances of the items, and this represents essentially the amount of true variance in the test. The ratio in the term at the right is therefore essentially the ratio of amount of true variance to the amount of total variance. This ratio is multiplied by the ratio $n/(n-1)$, however, something we have not seen thus far. Without this term, r_{tt} could never equal 1.00. Its upper limit would be the reciprocal of $n/(n-1)$, which is $(n-1)/n$. The shorter the test, the more serious this would be. The reason for this limitation is that the term Σpq can never equal zero so long as the items discriminate at all; thus the term at the right cannot equal 1.0.

Applying this K-R formula, which has become known as K-R formula 20, to the data in Table 14.2, we find that the estimate of r_{tt} by this method is .857. $\Sigma pq = 2.03$, $\sigma^2_t = 9.45$, and $n = 12$; therefore

$$r_{tt} = \left(\frac{12}{11}\right)\left(\frac{9.45 - 2.03}{9.45}\right) = .857$$

This figure is noticeably lower than those previously obtained by the various split-half methods. This discrepancy might be attributed to overestimation of r_{tt} by the split-half methods or to underestimation by the use of K-R formula 20. This may be because the conditions required for using K-R formula 20 were not satisfied in these test data. Certainly the items were of widely differing difficulty, which is one reason, also, for differing intercorrelations. This is a serious matter when tests are as short as this, as will be pointed out later.

Variations of the Kuder-Richardson Formula. Because the K-R formula just given requires knowledge of statistics on item difficulty, which entails considerable work, several modified K-R formulas have been proposed.

TABLE 14.2. ITEM SCORES AND TOTAL SCORES OF 10 EXAMINEES IN A 12-ITEM TEST, WITH DATA NEEDED FOR ESTIMATING RELIABILITY BY SEVERAL APPROACHES

	Item												X_t	X^2_t
	a	*b*	*c*	*d*	*e*	*f*	*g*	*h*	*i*	*j*	*k*	*l*		
Persons 1	1	0	1	0	0	0	0	0	0	0	0	0	2	4
2	1	1	1	0	0	1	0	0	0	0	0	0	4	16
3	1	1	1	1	0	0	0	0	0	0	0	0	4	16
4	1	1	0	1	1	0	0	1	0	0	0	0	5	25
5	1	1	1	1	1	0	0	0	0	0	0	0	5	25
6	1	1	1	0	1	1	1	0	0	0	0	0	6	36
7	1	1	1	1	1	1	1	0	0	0	0	0	7	49
8	1	1	1	1	0	1	1	1	1	1	0	0	9	81
9	1	1	1	1	1	1	1	1	1	1	1	0	11	121
10	1	1	1	1	1	1	1	1	1	1	1	1	12	144
R_i	10	9	9	7	6	6	5	4	3	3	2	1	$65 = \Sigma X_t = \Sigma R_i$	$517 = \Sigma X^2_t$
W_i	0	1	1	3	4	4	5	6	7	7	8	9	$55 = \Sigma W_i$	
p_i	1.0	.9	.9	.7	.6	.6	.5	.4	.3	.3	.2	.1	$6.5 = \Sigma p_i$	
p^2_i	1.0	.81	.81	.49	.36	.36	.25	.16	.09	.09	.04	.01	$4.47 = \Sigma p^2$	
$p_i q_i$	.0	.09	.09	.21	.24	.24	.25	.24	.21	.21	.16	.09	$2.03 = \Sigma p_i q_i$	

$M_t = 6.5 \qquad M_p = \bar{p} = .5417 \qquad \sigma^2_t = 9.45 \qquad \sigma^2_p = .0795$

Kuder and Richardson suggest that when item difficulties are very nearly equal, the term Σpq can be approximated by using n times the product of the average p times the average q. The formula reads

$$r_{tt} = \left(\frac{n}{n-1}\right)\left(\frac{\sigma^2_t - n\bar{p}\bar{q}}{\sigma^2_t}\right) \quad \text{(K-R formula 21)} \qquad (14.6)$$

where $\bar{p}$ and $\bar{q}$ are averages of p and q for the n items. This is more convenient than it may appear, for $\bar{p}$ is equal to M_t/n and $\bar{q}$ is equal to $(n - M_t)/n$. Substituting these for $\bar{p}$ and $\bar{q}$ in (14.6), and combining terms, we have

$$r_{tt} = \frac{n\sigma^2_t - M_t(n - M_t)}{(n-1)\sigma^2_t} \qquad (14.7)$$

In other words, we have an estimation formula requiring nothing but total-score statistics M_t and σ_t, along with number of items n.

Applying formula (14.7) to the data from Table 14.2, we have

$$r_{tt} = \frac{12(9.45) - (6.5)(5.5)}{11(9.45)} = .747$$

This estimate of r_{tt} is well below any that have been obtained thus far from these data. It shows clearly what may happen and illustrates the fact that under usual testing conditions K-R formula 21 gives a lower-bound estimate of r_{tt} and this will be lower than that from formula 20.

Tucker's Modified K-R Formula. To meet the demand for a simplified K-R formula 20 and yet to avoid the inaccuracies of K-R formula 21, Tucker (77) has developed a modified K-R formula. It reads like K-R formula 21 with another term added:

$$r_{tt} = \left(\frac{n}{n-1}\right)\left(\frac{\sigma^2{}_t - n\bar{p}\bar{q} + n\sigma^2{}_p}{\sigma^2{}_t}\right) \tag{14.8}$$

where $\sigma_p = SD$ of the proportions of correct responses. The variance $\sigma^2{}_p$ can be computed by the formula

$$\sigma^2{}_p = \frac{\Sigma p^2}{n} - \bar{p}^2 \tag{14.9}$$

where $\bar{p}$ = the mean of the proportions of correct responses for all items. In the data of Table 14.2 we find that $\sigma^2{}_p = .0795$, which we can apply in (14.8):

$$r_{tt} = \left(\frac{12}{11}\right)\left(\frac{9.45 - (12)(.2483) + (12)(.0795)}{9.45}\right) = .857$$

This gives a result, in this particular case, identical with that from formula 20. It is definitely an improvement over the result from formula 21. But as applied here, it requires about the same amount of item-statistics information as the use of formula 20. Tucker suggests that without knowing the item means p, and without computing their variance, we can make some rough guesses concerning the variance $\sigma^2{}_p$. If p ranges from .0 to 1.0 in a rectangular distribution, according to Tucker's estimate (77) the variance of p is .083. If p has the same range but in a normal distribution, the variance of p is .028. The distribution of p in the illustrative problem (see Table 14.2) is almost rectangular. Had we used the rough estimate of .083 instead of the obtained one of .0795, the resulting r_{tt} would have been only a trifle higher (.861). Even when item means have not been computed, one can get a rough idea concerning their amount of spread and whether their distribution probably approaches the normal or the rectangular form. Using this rough information, one can make a guess as to the variance $\sigma^2{}_p$. It is recommended that Tucker's correction be applied instead of using K-R formula 21.

K-R Formulas When Items and/or Responses Are Weighted. Dressel (15) has provided a modification of the K-R formula to apply when items are weighted differently in scoring. The K-R formulas given thus far apply when every right answer receives an item score of 1. For a test where right answers receive various positive scores and all wrong responses receive zero, Dressel's formula reads

$$r_{tt} = \left(\frac{n}{n-1}\right)\left(\frac{\sigma^2_t - \Sigma w^2{}_i p_i q_i}{\sigma^2_t}\right) \tag{14.10}$$

where w_i = weight assigned to the right response to item I and other symbols are as previously defined. Dressel also gives formulas that apply when scoring formulas are used, weighting wrong responses and omissions differently. Ferguson (18) extends the K-R formula to include the situation in which items each have more than two weights, for example, weights of -1, 0, and $+1$.

Accuracy of the K-R Formula 20. Since the derivation of the K-R formula rests on the assumptions of a unifactor test and parallel items and since we rarely encounter tests of that kind, it is important to see how much accuracy is lost in applying the formula more generally. Brogden (4) made a thorough and systematic study of this by setting up artificial tests with widely varying composition. Item means (p) varied from .03 to .97; item intercorrelations (tetrachoric) varied from .2 to .8; n varied from 9 to 153; and distributions of p varied by being normal, rectangular, and skewed. Reliabilities were estimated by the K-R formula 20 and by a more accurate K-R formula 2, which was taken as the source of unbiased estimates of r_{tt}. In general, the results from formula 20 showed little bias. There was more bias when tests were short (9 to 18 items) and when intercorrelations were high (.6 to .8). The conclusion was that under usual testing conditions the bias will be very small. Brogden's conclusions apply to formula 20 [formula (14.5) above] and not to the less exact formula 21. It is generally agreed that none of the K-R formulas should be used if there is much speeding involved in a test. This limits their use to power tests or those very close to that category.

The reader may well wonder why the K-R formula 20 can give fairly accurate results, even in long tests, in spite of apparent violation of the several limiting assumptions. This is possibly explained by the fact that Gulliksen (25, p. 224) has arrived at formulas identical with the K-R formulas starting with only the assumption that intercorrelations of items are equal to reliabilities of items. This is, of course, one of the conditions for a test measuring a single common factor. But this condition also probably applies when each item measures to about the same extent a weighted combination of more than one common factor. The constant combination is in effect a unity. If the common factors are distributed very unevenly among the items, as Wherry and Gaylord (80) have shown, the r_{tt} as estimated from the K-R formulas will be reduced in size.

The Analysis-of-variance Approach to Reliability. Since so much of the statistical thinking concerning reliability is put in terms of variances, it is not surprising that the estimation of reliability can be made by a more conventional analysis-of-variance approach. Several investigators have proposed this kind of approach, among whom are Jackson (39), Hoyt (37), and Alexander (2). Like the K-R approach, this one starts from the item level.

The data in Table 14.2 are set up for application of Hoyt's method. He regards the matrix of item scores as a two-way factorial design for analysis of variance without replications. Hoyt's basic formula for reliability is

$$r_{tt} = 1 - \frac{V_r}{V_e} = \frac{V_e - V_r}{V_e} \tag{14.11}$$

where V_r = variance for remainder sum of squares and V_e = variance for examinees.

The various sums of squares are computed by the formulas

$$\sum d^2{}_e = \frac{\Sigma X^2{}_t}{n} - \frac{(\Sigma X_t)^2}{nN} \tag{14.12}$$

where $\Sigma d^2{}_e$ = sum of squares for examinees
X_t = total score for each examinee
n = number of items
N = number of examinees

$$\sum d^2{}_i = \frac{\Sigma R^2{}_i}{N} - \frac{(\Sigma X_t)^2}{nN} \tag{14.13}$$

where $\Sigma d^2{}_i$ = sum of squares for items, R_i = number of correct responses for item I, and other symbols are as previously defined.

$$\sum x^2{}_t = \frac{(\Sigma R_i)(\Sigma W_i)}{(\Sigma R_i) + (\Sigma W_i)} \tag{14.14}$$

where $\Sigma x^2{}_t$ = total sum of squares, W_i = number of wrong responses to item I, and other symbols are as previously defined. The sum of squares for remainder is given by

$$\Sigma x^2{}_r = \Sigma x^2{}_t - \Sigma d^2{}_e - \Sigma d^2{}_i \tag{14.15}$$

The various sums of squares computed for the illustrative data in Table 14.2 are given in the first column of values in Table 14.3. The degrees of freedom[1] for each variance term are given in the next column, and the variances in the last column. Applying equation (14.11), we have

TABLE 14.3. SOLUTION FOR THE VARIANCES IN A SHORT TEST PREPARATORY TO ESTIMATION OF RELIABILITY

Source of variance	Sum of squares	Degrees of freedom	Variance
Examinees	7.875	9	.875
Items	9.492	11	.863
Remainder	12.425	99	.126
Total	29.792	119	

$$r_{tt} = \frac{.875 - .126}{.875} = .857$$

[1] Degrees of freedom for persons is $N - 1$; for items, $n - 1$; and for remainder, $Nn - N - n + 1$.

The result is identical with that from the K-R formula 20. In fact it can be shown algebraically that it should be. This may mean that two good methods confirm one another and that the best estimate we can get of reliability for this test is about .86, or it may mean that the Hoyt method, like the K-R method, gives a biased result (underestimation) in a short test. At any rate, it is safe to say that the reliability of this test is probably not lower than .86.

The analysis-of-variance approach can also be applied effectively to data from alternate forms and from retesting. In these instances the power of the methods of analysis of variance can be brought to bear on the segregation of variances of different sources and the meanings of the resulting coefficients can be rather definite. There is insufficient space to describe the various computing techniques here. For descriptions of them the reader is referred to the articles by Jackson (40) and Alexander (2). In the application to this type of reliability studies in the experimental-laboratory situation in particular, the articles of Melton (52) and Grings (22) will be informative. We shall see later how the approach applies to ratings.

Generalized Formulas for Reliability. One or two attempts have been made to bring a number of the various formulas under a common generalized equation. Cronbach (9) proposes his coefficient alpha, the formula for which is

$$\alpha = \left(\frac{n}{n-1}\right)\left(1 - \frac{\Sigma V_i}{V_t}\right) \qquad (14.16)$$

where V_i = variance of part I of a test, the size not specified
V_t = variance of total scores
n = number of parts

The parts can be as small as single items, in which case we have the K-R formula 20, or as large as halves, in which case we have Flanagan's formula. In the latter case, the factor 2 in formula (14.4) is now seen to be the ratio $n/(n-1)$ (which appears in so many of the formulas), where $n = 2$. Thus, Flanagan's formula, being the simplest of all in the alpha family and the easiest to apply, is recommended where attention has been given to making the two halves parallel. The Rulon formula will give as good results under the same conditions.

Horst (32) provides a generalized formula for r_{tt} that applies when several measures of the same person by means of comparable test parts (forms or other replications) are available. He shows that the K-R and S-B formulas are special cases of his general formula. For computing purposes, his formula is uneconomical; therefore it will not be reported here.

Guttman (27) presents a family of formulas that apply to a single administration of a test, all of which, he concludes, give lower-bound estimates of r_{tt}. Some of these are identical with formulas we have already seen, particularly with variations of the K-R formula. Other investigators, beginning with other assumptions, do not agree that all of these are lower-bound coefficients. We have seen above, how, for example, the odd-even and perhaps the Rulon and Flanagan formulas possibly lead to overestimates of r_{tt}. Guttman's claim to superiority for his formulas is that they rest on much less restrictive assumptions.

Some Special Reliability Formulas. There remain to be considered some less well-known formulas, and also formulas providing indices somewhat different from r_{tt}. There are ways, other than by the K-R formula, of estimating reliability of a total score from item statistics. There is some interest in having an index of reliability that is independent of test length, for as the same test increases homogeneously in length, its r_{tt} increases according to the S-B formula. The comparison of tests as to reliability is therefore not fully satisfactory if they differ much in length or in testing time. There are indices of reliability stemming from the homogeneity and discrimination theories mentioned in Chap. 13.

Reliability Estimated from Item Intercorrelations. There are occasions in which one would like to forecast the reliability of a new test in advance. This can be done, to a rough approximation, if we know certain item statistics for the items going into the new test. One procedure is suggested by a discussion in Chap. 13. If we know the correlation of each item with a total score that is of the same nature as that of the new test, we can apply formula (13.36) to estimate the average item intercorrelation and then apply the S-B formula (13.20) to estimate the reliability for the sum of n items.

Gulliksen (25, p. 378) suggests another approach, using the formula

$$r_{tt} = \left(\frac{n}{n-1}\right)\left[1 - \frac{\Sigma\sigma^2_i}{\Sigma(r_{it}\sigma_i)^2}\right] \tag{14.17}$$

where σ^2_i = item variance = p_iq_i
r_{it} = correlation of item with total score, a point-biserial r
n = number of items

Having in mind the K-R formula, it would appear that the term $\Sigma(r_{it}\sigma_i)^2$ is a forecast of the total-score variance for the test.

It has been the experience of the writer that both the Gulliksen formula and the use of the S-B formula on average item intercorrelations, particularly the Gulliksen formula, tend to underestimate the reliability later derived by orthodox methods. These rough estimates will serve to support such decisions as the dropping of a test that looks unpromising, the lengthening or shortening of a test, or the application of another item analysis to improve it. Such an estimate of reliability should never be reported as final information. In both cases, much depends upon good estimates of r_{it}, since this changes according to the nature of the total test of which the items are going to be a part, whereas σ_i is a property of the item only and is relatively independent of the whole in which it is a part.

Reliability Indices Independent of Test Length. In order to obtain indices of reliability of different tests on a more comparable basis, we may resort to several different devices. One would be to use the S-B formula to predict reliability for all tests when n is some arbitrarily fixed quantity, for example, 10, 50, or 100 items. Adoption of a large n like 50 or 100 would give small differences in r_{nn} among the more reliable tests. One meaningful length would be the length when $n = 1$, in other words, one-item tests. The index would then be approximately equivalent to the average item intercorrelation, if the range of item intercorrelations is small. Putting the ratio $1/n$ in place of n in the S-B formula, we come out with the equation

$$\bar{r}_{ij} \doteq \frac{r_{tt}}{n + (1 - n)r_{tt}} \tag{14.18}$$

Conceiving of this quantity as the alternate-forms reliability of an item, the index might be referred to as *reliability per item.*

Woodbury (81) introduces for this purpose the concept of *standard length,* with a parameter τ related to reliability but independent of test length. His formula is

$$\tau = \frac{n(1 - r_{tt})}{r_{tt}} \tag{14.19}$$

where n = number of items (or other units) and r_{tt} = reliability coefficient at length n. Tau varies from zero, when r_{tt} = 1.0, to ∞ when r_{tt} = .0. Thus, the smaller the tau coefficient, the better the test.

Loevinger's Coefficient of Homogeneity. The theory of homogeneous versus heterogeneous tests was discussed in Chap. 13. The chief rival to the reliability coefficient coming from this approach is Loevinger's (48) *coefficient of homogeneity,* which, with symbols consistent with others of this chapter, reads

$$H_t \doteq \frac{N(\Sigma X^2_t - \Sigma X_t) + \Sigma R^2_i - (\Sigma X_t)^2}{2N(\Sigma iR_i - \Sigma X_t) + \Sigma R^2_i - (\Sigma X_t)^2} \tag{14.20}$$

where H_t = coefficient of homogeneity
N = number of examinees in sample
X_t = total-test score
R_i = number of correct responses to ith item
i = ordinal number of item where items are arranged in increasing order of difficulty

Loevinger advises that this formula gives an approximation only and should be used with 100 or more examinees. As an illustration, however, let us apply it to the data of Table 14.2. We then have

$$H_t \doteq \frac{10(517 - 65) + 447 - 4{,}225}{20(307 - 65) + 447 - 4{,}225} \doteq .699$$

This coefficient is much lower than any of the reliability coefficients reported above for the same data. This is very characteristic. Thorndike (47), for example, reports that for a test for which r_{tt} was .90 by the K-R formula H_t was only .30. Coefficient H_t is designed to vary from .0 when a test is completely heterogeneous to +1.0 when a test is completely homogeneous.

It appears to be the consensus that the goal of approximating completely homogeneous tests is a will-o'-the-wisp and that many a test with low H_t can still be highly reliable and useful. When this coefficient is used, the standards of accepting or rejecting tests on the basis of it have to be very different from those associated with r_{tt}.

The Index of Discrimination. Ferguson's *index of discrimination* formula given in Chap. 13 (13.40) is suitable for computing purposes. Applying it to the data of Table 14.2, we have

$$\delta = \frac{13(100 - 14)}{12(100)} = .932$$

This rather high figure reflects the fact that the frequency distribution of total scores is almost rectangular.

The Usefulness of a Coefficient of Reliability. A coefficient of reliability is the most common fact reported concerning a test and certainly it is much easier to obtain than is a coefficient of validity or a factor loading. Reliability is the minimum information one should have concerning a test, but it is certainly not the most useful information. If it is quite high, it can sometimes give the test user a false sense of security. For example, should one feel very comfortable about a test whose r_{tt} is .90 but whose proportion of variance in the factor one wishes to measure is only .30? As the writer has urged elsewhere (23), factor loadings should become indispensable facts to know about a test. What the scores mean and what we can predict from them is entirely restricted to the relevant factors.

What, then, is the importance of knowing a coefficient of reliability? It is safe to say that in developing the vast majority of tests constructed today the makers strive toward internal consistency. The coefficient r_{tt} indicates how well the test constructor has approached that goal. In new areas of test construction, particularly, one does not know whether a test of a new type has any internal consistency at all. A spread of scores is no indication, since the spread may be due entirely to error variance. This last statement is reasonable when we remember that each individual could decide the answer to every item (in a multiple-choice test) by the throw of a die and still there would be a dispersion of scores.

There are certain tests and measures concerning which reliability is the most important thing to be known. Achievement examinations are usually regarded as self-validating in the sense that they were tailored to measure the outcomes of well-identified objectives in training or education. They serve as their own criteria. To know their accuracy of measurement in terms of an index of reliability, then, is of first importance, for, assuming the selection of relevant material, accuracy is the only question to be raised. Tests used in clinical diagnosis should also be known to have a very substantial degree of reliability. Tests used in personnel classification and in vocational guidance should also be highly reliable. In the latter instances it is differences between scores that count, as in the ups and downs in a profile. We shall see that difference scores are almost always lower in reliability than the test scores from which they come, sometimes very much lower. It depends upon the ratio of the reliabilities of the separate scores to their intercorrelations.

As to how high reliability coefficients should be, no hard-and-fast rules can be stated. For research purposes, one can tolerate much lower reliabilities than one can for practical purposes of diagnosis and prediction. We are frequently faced with the choice of making the best of what reliability we can get, even though it may be of the order of only .50, or of going without the use of the test at all. For some purposes, even a test of low reliability adds enough to prediction to justify its use, particularly when used in a battery along with other tests.

It is sometimes said that reliability is important because it contributes to validity and that validity is the important goal. The relationships between reliability and validity are by no means simple and not always direct. If a test is found to be valid because it predicts some practical criterion, if we add to it more of the same kind of true variance, making it more reliable, we also add to its validity. If we are attempting to predict a criterion that is very complex factorially, the best way to improve the test's validity is to bring in additional common factors that are also in the criterion, thus increasing validity but lowering internal-consistency reliability. As pointed out in Chap. 13, to maximize validity of a test, we must often lower internal consistency.

One additional instance in which it is important to know the reliability of a measure is that of validating a test against a practical criterion. It is very important to know the reliability of the criterion. Only in this way can we determine how much effective prediction we are getting. If the criterion has a reliability of only .30, no test or battery of tests can correlate very much with it. Correction of the validity coefficients for attenuation would be needed to tell us just how much of the true variance in the criterion we are accounting for.

Special Problems of Reliability

The preceding section dealt primarily with ways of estimating reliabilities of tests. There is still something to be said concerning the way in which reliability depends upon various determining factors, such as speed of work, range of ability, and chance success by guessing. There are also certain special kinds of measures of which we want to know reliabilities, such as composite measures, differences, and ratings. These and other problems will have our attention in this section.

The Standard Error of Measurement. The standard error of measurement was introduced in Chap. 13 as an index of the extent of dispersion of error components in scores. The usual computing formula [to repeat formula (13.12)] is

$$\sigma_{t_\infty} = \sigma_t \sqrt{1 - r_{tt}}$$

We must now consider some of the peculiarities and limitations of this statistic in practice.

The usual interpretation given to a standard error of measurement (*SEM*) is like that for any standard deviation. For our little illustrative test, where $\sigma_t = 3.07$ and let us say the $r_{tt} = .89$,

$$\sigma_{t_\infty} = 3.07 \sqrt{1 - .89} = 1.00$$

We may say that for any particular true score the odds are 2 to 1 that the obtained score will not deviate more than one unit from it. A departure of two units from the true score would be expected in one case in about twenty. Such deductions assume equal dispersions of errors at all score levels and normality of dispersions of errors. The most serious questions have been raised concerning equality of errors at all score levels.

Gulliksen concludes (25, p. 124) that the *SEM* should be constant for all score levels when the score distribution is not skewed and when kurtosis is 3 (distribution is normal). Thorndike points out (47, p. 605) that if items have been concentrated for selection at a certain difficulty level, the *SEM* will be smallest at that level. Lord (51) points out that in many a distribution the dispersion of errors will be smallest at the tails of the distribution and that the *SEM* is at best an average value. From the comments of Thorndike and Lord one might draw the general conclusion that the error dispersions are usually smallest where the population is spread thinnest by the test.

Mollenkopf (53) has investigated systematically the effects of skewness and variations in kurtosis on the *SEM*. He concluded that slight skewing could be tolerated but not departures in kurtosis from 3. Since most distributions depart somewhat from normality, he recommends that the *SEM* be determined for at least ten score levels and reported. Green (21) suggests a method for determining the significance of differences among *SEM* values at different score levels. It is the writer's conclusion that in view of the very limited use made of the *SEM* the extra work implied by Mollenkopf and Green is not justified. If one wishes to be sure of the size of an *SEM* and of its constancy when a score distribution departs notably from normality such refinements may be in order.

Item-difficulty Conditions Optimal for Reliability. At one or more places in Chap. 13 it was concluded that concentration of item difficulty near $p = .5$ is a favorable condition for high reliability. This conclusion needs some modification, in the light of recent work by Brogden (3), Tucker (76), and Cronbach and Warrington (11). Item intercorrelations have some bearing upon how much concentration of difficulty should be exercised. With perfectly correlated items and with items all at difficulty level .5, we have what Cronbach and Warrington call an "inflexible" test, with discriminations excellent at the .5 level but dropping off rapidly on both sides of the median score. This is to be expected in a U-shaped distribution of total scores that would result. The higher the intercorrelation of items, then, the more need there is for some dispersion as to difficulty of items, unless discrimination at one score point is all that one wants. For the kind of items found in practice, with much lower than perfect intercorrelations, the rule still stands that reliability is promoted by concentrating difficulty of items at .5, especially in short tests. In long tests, let us say of more than 30 items, some spread of item difficulty is desirable even when item intercorrelations are not high. If difficulty is widespread, the distribution of difficulty is better if flat, approaching rectangular form.

Best Difficulty Levels in Multiple-choice Tests. The comments made in the last paragraph pertain to tests in which chance success is not a factor. When chance success is a factor, the proportion passing an item is greater than the proportion who actually know the answer, so that items appear to be easier than they are. One might expect that the optimal difficulty level when chance is a factor would be such that the proportion of right answers *corrected for chance* would be .50. This would mean a two-choice item with an uncorrected proportion of .75 and a five-choice item with an uncorrected proportion of .600. Such is not the case. Cronbach and Warrington (11) conclude that optimal discrimination for a multiple-choice item comes at a level easier than median difficulty *after correction for chance*. The reason is that chance reduces reliability most in the lower score levels where much guessing occurs. This lower level of scores near the chance level is therefore to be avoided. Lord (50, p. 189) demonstrates that r_{tt} will be maximum when item difficulty is somewhat easier than halfway between the chance level and 1.0. Under ordinary conditions, with item intercorrelations (tetrachoric) from .10 to .30, the optimal level for two-choice items is an *uncorrected* proportion of .85; for three-choice items, .77; four-choice items .74; and five-choice items .69.

Length of Test Required to Achieve a Given Reliability. The Spearman-Brown equation tells us what reliability coefficient to expect after a test has been altered homogeneously in length. By solving that equation for n, we have an equation that tells us the ratio of the new test to the old one which will be needed to achieve some specified reliability in the new one. It is assumed, of course, that we know the reliability in the old length. This formula is

$$n = \frac{r_{nn}(1 - r_{tt})}{r_{tt}(1 - r_{nn})} \tag{14.21}$$

Suppose that the reliability in a test we have is only .35 and that we ask how many times as long the test must be in order to achieve a reliability of .60. Applying the formula,

$$n = \frac{.60(1 - .35)}{.35(1 - .60)} = 2.79$$

The test must be almost three times as long. The lengthening must, of course, be of the same kind of items in every way as those giving the reliability of .35, to make the prediction a success.

Reliability of Speed Tests. The question of effect of speed on reliability has arisen before. We will now face the problem more fully. There have been developed recently some methods for dealing with partially speeded tests. We also know better how much the condition of speed affects r_{tt}, as computed by the usual formulas. Most of the usual formulas are economical, since they apply to the single administration of a test. They do not require two forms or two administrations. We would want to use them as far as we can. The alternate-form method can be made almost as economical as any of the split-half procedures and it can be recommended for use with tests that have any degree of speeding. The experimental operation is to divide the test into two parallel halves, to the best of our knowledge, and to administer them as two separately timed tests, with any relatively short time interval between parts that one wants. The S-B formula can be applied to estimate the reliability of a combination of the two parts.

It has been amply demonstrated that an odd-even coefficient overestimates reliability when there is an appreciable amount of speeding. It should thus be regarded as an upper-bound estimate under this condition. There have been several formulas suggested for finding a lower-bound estimate for a slightly speeded test. One of the simplest of these to apply was proposed by Gulliksen (26) for use with error scores. It reads

$$R_m = R_{xx} - \frac{M_u}{\sigma^2_x} \tag{14.22}$$

where R_m = estimate of reliability of a slightly speeded test
R_{xx} = odd-even reliability coefficient stepped up by use of S-B formula
M_u = mean of number of items unattempted at end of test
σ^2_x = variance of total error score

Gulliksen defines his error score as including all wrong responses plus items skipped. He advises that when the *SD* of the number of unattempted items, σ_u, is much greater than two-tenths to three-tenths of the *SD* of number of items answered wrongly, σ_w, a split-half coefficient is unsafe (25). He also recommends that when the ratio of M_u to σ^2_x is greater than .2 to .3 the test is so speeded that even formula (14.22) should not be used. One should then resort to an alternate-form estimate of reliability. He provides other formulas alternative to (14.22), which may be applied under similar conditions (26). Cronbach and Warrington (10) have developed still another formula which entails considerable computation but which they imply is more accurate than Gulliksen's. They present an index of speededness of a test, which also requires a considerable amount of information not ordinarily available.

Reliability and Range of Ability in the Population. The size of r_{tt} obtained from a sample will depend directly upon the heterogeneity of the population. Heterogeneity in this context stands for the variability of the population on the trait measured. A standard formula has been in use for some time for estimating the reliability of a test when used in a population of one *SD* from knowledge of its reliability in a population with different *SD*. It reads

$$r_{uu} = 1 - \frac{\sigma^2_k(1 - r_{kk})}{\sigma^2_u} \tag{14.23}$$

where r_{uu} = reliability coefficient for the population in which it is unknown
σ_k = *SD* in the population for which reliability is known
r_{kk} = known reliability
σ_u = *SD* in the population for which reliability is unknown

The validity of the use of this formula rests on the important assumption that the standard error of estimate is constant for all levels of scores in both populations. This means that the score distribution in both ranges should be approximately normal and should not be truncated in either case.

Reliability of Multiple-choice Tests. Because of the element of chance success in responding to multiple-choice items, we expect them to be less reliable than completion items, or other forms in which chance success is unimportant.

A number of studies by Remmers and his associates (13, 62, 63) have shown that with increasing number of alternative responses in tests with multiple-choice items, reliability increases. In fact the increases in r_{tt} can be predicted by use of the S-B formula, letting the ratio of alternative responses k be substituted for n. This was true for two to five alternatives, with some overprediction for seven. It was true in a vocabulary test, an arithmetic test, and an attitude inventory. The important condition is that the added alternatives be "parallel" with the original ones. One thing this means is that on the whole all wrong alternatives are equally attractive to examinees. In connection with this problem, Thorndike points out that a multiple-choice item behaves as if it were composed of $k - 1$ two-choice items where k varies from 2 to 5 (47).

Other studies, for example by Plumlee (61), do not show as much gain in reliability with increasing number of alternative responses. Much depends upon the *difficulty* of the multiple-choice test, as Lord (51) points out. The easier the multiple-choice test, the less important is chance success. The optimal difficulty levels, as recommended by Lord, were mentioned earlier. From the properties of the S-B formula, we stand to gain much more from increasing the number of alternatives when a test is short.

Reliability of Composite Scores. The reliability of a composite score is a function of the reliabilities of its components, their dispersions, their intercorrelations, and the respective weights assigned to them. Mosier (55) presents the formula

$$r_{ss} = 1 - \frac{\Sigma w^2{}_j\sigma^2{}_j - \Sigma w^2{}_j\sigma^2{}_j r_{jj}}{\Sigma w^2{}_j\sigma^2{}_j + 2\,\Sigma w_j w_k \sigma_j \sigma_k r_{jk}} \tag{14.24}$$

where r_{ss} = reliability of a sum of components
w_j = weight assigned to any component J
w_k = weight assigned to any other component K
σ_j, σ_k = *SD*'s of components J and K, respectively
r_{jj} = reliability coefficient for any component J
r_{jk} = intercorrelation of components J and K (where subscript k is numerically greater than subscript j)

If the test scores have been scaled to a common standard deviation, all sigma terms may be omitted from (14.24).

Some interesting deductions can be drawn to serve as principles of test-battery construction. The reliability r_{ss} can equal 1.00 only when every r_{jj} also equals 1.00. If all intercorrelations r_{jk} are zero, the reliability of the composite will be a weighted mean of the reliabilities of the components. This is an unlikely contingency, but the deduction emphasizes the fact that intercorrelations of components contribute to total reliability of the composite. It is well known, however, that high intercorrelations of components detract from validity of the composite. Where validity is at stake for a composite, we would therefore not strive toward high composite reliability but the reverse. Where composite scores are to be used for differential prediction, we would want high reliability.

Reliability of Difference Scores. Differential prediction in practice is based in principle on difference scores such as the difference $X_j - X_k$. It is important to know the reliability of such a score because it comes from two fallible scores and the error variances from them summate. Mosier (47) has presented the following formula for the reliability of a difference score obtained from two total scores:

$$r_{dd} = \frac{r_{jj} + r_{kk} - 2r_{jk}}{2(1 - r_{jk})} \tag{14.25}$$

where r_{dd} = reliability of the difference $X_j - X_k$
r_{jj}, r_{kk} = respective reliabilities of X_j and X_k
r_{jk} = intercorrelation of X_j and X_k

Some deductions from this formula are rather obvious. If the intercorrelation is as great as the mean of the reliabilities, r_{dd} is zero; there is then no reliability in the difference scores. If r_{jk} is zero, the reliability of the difference scores equals the mean of r_{jj} and r_{kk}. This dramatically emphasizes the need for univocal, uncorrelated scores in differential prediction.

Reliability of Profiles. A profile of scores represents a number of intertest differences and the dependability of quantitative judgments based on the profile will depend upon the reliabilities of those differences. It might be well to estimate r_{dd} for every pair of scores, or at least for those differences upon which most interpretation and weight are placed. For a single, over-all index of these reliabilities, Mosier (47) offers the following formula:

$$r_{pp} = \frac{\bar{r}_{ii'} - \bar{r}_{ij'}}{\sqrt{(1 - \bar{r}_{ij})(1 - \bar{r}_{i'j'})}} \tag{14.26}$$

where $\bar{r}_{pp}$ is the coefficient of reliability for a profile, $\bar{r}_{ii'}$ is the mean reliability (alternate forms or retest) for scores entering into the profile, subscripts i and j indicate different test scores, subscripts i' and j' indicate second measures by the same tests, and $\bar{r}$ indicates mean correlation. Thus the formula is a summarization of the reliabilities of difference scores among all pairs of tests.

Reliability of Ratio Scores. Another way to express a difference between two test scores is to use their ratio. Cronbach (7) has developed formulas for estimating the reliabilities of ratio scores.

Reliability of Scores of Subjectively Scored Tests. When the scorer's judgment enters into the scoring of tests, we have a double problem of reliability. In addition to the usual errors of measurement that apply to the test content itself, we have errors contributed by the biases of the scorer. If we did nothing to separate these errors, we might sometimes conclude that the content reliability of such a test is low when it is the reliability of the scorer that is at fault. Gulliksen (25) has suggested a method and a formula for effecting the separation so that we may know how much of the unreliability to attribute to the test as such. His formula is

$$r_{cc} = \frac{r_{x'_1x''_2}}{\sqrt{r_{x'_1x'_2}r_{x''_1x''_2}}} \tag{14.27}$$

where x' and x'' are scores on two forms of the test and subscripts 1 and 2 stand for two readers. The required experimental operations include administration of two forms of the test to the same sample, determination of correlations between the two forms as read by different readers, and correlations between readers' scores for the same form. The numerator can be a mean of four estimates, $r_{x'_1x''_2}$, and the like. The reader reliabilities in the denominator set the upper limit for reliability of the test. If reader agreement is indicated by a mean inter-reader correlation of .80, the top correlation for the numerator of equation (14.27) is .80.

Reliability of Ratings. There are some who prefer to estimate reliability of ratings by use of rerating data, and certainly this is a meaningful type of reliability. Except for the trouble of a replication, it is an easy procedure to employ. There are serious dangers of correlation of what should be errors, however, due to the memory of the raters.

Most investigators seem to prefer the operation of correlating ratings obtained from different raters as the approach to reliability of ratings. There may be common biases among raters, but this source of error correlation is probably smaller than in re-ratings. One has to assume that raters involved in the reliability study are interchangeable. Since raters with similar types of information are generally utilized for this purpose, this assumption is not unreasonable.

Reliability by the Intraclass Correlation. The most recently suggested method of estimating reliability for ratings has been described by Ebel (16). If each of k raters has rated N persons on some trait on one occasion, we have the possibility of obtaining intercorrelations of ratings of the N persons from all possible pairs of the k raters. This suggests the use of the statistic known as the intraclass correlation, which gives essentially an average intercorrelation. Ebel's formula is

$$\bar{r}_{11} = \frac{V_p - V_e}{V_p + (k - 1)V_e} \tag{14.28}$$

where $\bar{r}_{11}$ = reliability of ratings for a single rater
V_p = variance for persons
V_e = variance for error
k = number of raters

Ebel's symbols have been changed to be more consistent with those used previously in this chapter.

It should be noted that this gives the mean reliability for *one* rater. The reliability of the mean of k ratings for each person would be greater. For this, Ebel (16) gives the formula

$$r_{kk} = \frac{V_p - V_e}{V_p} \tag{14.29}$$

where the symbols mean the same as in (14.28). This gives the reliability for mean ratings from k raters. One could arrive at the same result by applying to the reliability for one rater the S-B formula to predict reliability for a measure k times as long. Experience to be cited shortly supports this step very well.

We will now see how Ebel's formulas are applied. The data of Table 14.4 represent the ratings of seven persons by three raters in a certain trait. For the purpose of determining the variances among persons and among raters, we sum rows and columns and square the sums.

TABLE 14.4. RATINGS OF SEVEN PERSONS MADE BY THREE RATERS FOR A CERTAIN TRAIT, PREPARED FOR DETERMINING VARIANCES USED IN ESTIMATING RELIABILITY OF RATINGS

Person	Rater				
	A	B	C	ΣX_p	$(\Sigma X_p)^2$
1	5	7	5	17	289
2	9	8	8	25	625
3	4	5	3	12	144
4	7	6	6	19	361
5	8	2	9	19	361
6	3	4	4	11	121
7	6	3	7	16	256
ΣX_r	42	35	42	$119 = \Sigma X$	$2,157 = \Sigma(\Sigma X_p)^2$
$(\Sigma X_r)^2$	1,764	1,225	1,764	$4,753 = \Sigma(\Sigma X_r)^2$	
ΣX^2	763		$\frac{(\Sigma X)^2}{kN} = 674.33$		

The sum of squares for persons is

$$\sum d^2{}_p = \frac{(\Sigma X_p)^2}{k} - \frac{(\Sigma X)^2}{kN} \tag{14.30}$$

The sum of squares for raters is

$$\sum d^2{}_r = \frac{(\Sigma X_r)^2}{N} - \frac{(\Sigma X)^2}{kN} \tag{14.31}$$

The total sum of squares is

$$\sum x^2{}_t = \Sigma X^2 - \frac{(\Sigma X)^2}{kN} \tag{14.32}$$

And finally, the sum of squares for remainder or error is

$$\Sigma d^2{}_e = \Sigma x^2{}_t - \Sigma d^2{}_p - \Sigma d^2{}_r \tag{14.33}$$

It is the sums of squares from equations (14.30) and (14.33) that we need for use in formula (14.28). The sums of squares are given in Table 14.5, their

TABLE 14.5. COMPUTATION OF THE VARIANCES NEEDED TO ESTIMATE RELIABILITY OF THE RATINGS GIVEN IN TABLE 14.4

Source	Sum of squares	Degrees of freedom	Variance
From persons...........	44.67	6	7.445
From raters............	4.67	2	*
From remainder.........	39.33	12	3.2775
Total................	88.67	20	*

* Variance not needed and not computed.

degrees of freedom, and the two variances we need, V_p and V_e. From formula (14.28),

$$\bar{r}_{11} = \frac{7.445 - 3.2775}{7.445 + (3 - 1)(3.2775)} = .298$$

This is the reliability for one rater. For the three raters combined or for the averages of their ratings, formula (14.29) gives

$$r_{33} = \frac{7.445 - 3.2775}{7.445} = .560$$

Applying the S-B formula to the r_{11} of .298 gives us the same result. The agreement is not always as close as this.

It is not uncommon to have incomplete sets of ratings because not all raters can judge all persons. Thus k will vary from person to person. To meet this contingency, Ebel (16) recommends the use of a formula of Snedecor's for estimating an average k that may be used:

$$\bar{k} = \left(\frac{1}{N - 1}\right)\left(\sum k - \frac{\Sigma k^2}{\Sigma k}\right) \tag{14.34}$$

where k varies from person to person and N is number of persons.

An Average Rank-order Correlation among Ratings. Another approach to the average intercorrelation of k individuals' ratings is to apply formula (10.7). This formula applies when we can convert the ratings of N persons into a complete rank order for each of k raters. When the judgments have been obtained by the method of rank order, the formula is especially convenient.

In Table 14.6 we have the rank positions of the seven persons as given by three raters. Applying formula (10.7), we have

$$\bar{r}_{11} = 1 - \frac{3(28 + 2)}{(2)(6)} + \frac{(12)(1{,}142)}{(3)(2)(7)(48)} = .30$$

The Spearman-Brown formula may be applied to this to estimate reliability for a larger number of raters.

Applicability of the Spearman-Brown Formula to Ratings. Of the many studies in which the applicability of the S-B formula has been primarily or secondarily under investigation, most of them show that the formula predicts changes in reliability as the number of raters is varied over rather wide ranges. The nature of the objects rated has varied, but the results are essentially the same (6, 66, 70). The application may not be as accurate as in connection with tests, but it gives results sufficiently accurate for considerable usefulness. It definitely shows the same principle that applies with tests, namely, that most gains in reliability come from multiplying raters when initial reliability is low, and that in adding raters the law of diminishing returns sets in very rapidly. There is usually much to be gained by adding the first two or three raters, but not much after reaching five.

TABLE 14.6. SAME SEVEN PERSONS AS IN TABLE 14.4 RANKED FOR RATINGS AS ASSIGNED BY EACH OF THREE RATERS, PREPARATORY TO COMPUTING AN AVERAGE RANK-DIFFERENCE CORRELATION

Person	Rater				
	A	B	C	S	S^2
1	3	6	3	12	144
2	7	7	6	20	400
3	2	4	1	7	49
4	5	5	4	14	196
5	6	1	7	14	196
6	1	3	2	6	36
7	4	2	5	11	121
Σ	28	28	28	84	$1,142 = \Sigma S^2$

$a=3, N=7$

Reliability of Categorical Data. The interest in reliability of categorical data has to do with the consistency with which cases will fall in the same category. Guttman (28) has treated this problem at some length, giving formulas for determining lower-bound estimates from a single experimental trial, as well as for other types of estimates. There is no indication that there has been much experience with these procedures; thus it is too early to evaluate them. In the polling situation, Dodd and Svalastoga (14) have suggested that the per cent of "Don't-know" responses can be taken as an index of instability of responses in other categories. In one study they found this index correlated .91 with the percentage of changed answers when respondents were given an opportunity to change their votes.

GENERAL PROBLEMS OF VALIDITY

When used without qualification and when used in the practical setting, the term *validity* refers to the degree to which test scores or other measures predict some practical criterion measures. The problems of determining practical validity we shall leave to the next section. Here we shall face some more preliminary or basic problems. We shall consider some different meanings of validity, how it is distinguished from reliability, and how it depends upon reliability.

Meanings of Validity. In a broad sense, validity has to do with the question of what test scores measure and what they will predict. A score is valid for predicting anything with which it correlates, where "anything" does not include the score itself, for a self-prediction has to do with reliability. When two tests show an intercorrelation greater than zero, the "what" that one of them measures is identical, at least in part, with the "what" that the other measures. In Chap. 13 we saw that what a test measures, in common with other tests and other measures, is in the form of common factors. Common-factor variance, then, is the basis for validity. This variance, which is called communality, plus some specific variance make up the true variance which is the source of reliability. The correlation of a test with each common factor (a common-factor loading) is its coefficient of validity for measuring that factor. A test may have a validity (factor loading) of .50 for measuring the factor of numerical facility and a validity of .60 for measuring reasoning. The practical validity of a score, indicated by the correlation between the score and some practical criterion measure, is also dependent upon common factors in the test and criterion. The factor loadings of a test are discovered from the way in which that test correlates with other tests. Thus, the key to the definition of validity goes back to the operation of intercorrelation.

Validity by Assumption. There are some measures whose validity is taken for granted, for example, achievement-test scores. This means that it is assumed that the scores measure what we want them to measure. In order to justify this step, we must be clear as to the objectives to be achieved during learning and as to the kinds of items it takes to indicate the realization of those objectives. If a man is learning to fly an airplane, the measure of his degree of skill in this performance must indicate how well he flies an airplane in relation to other pilots. Any criterion measure that is adopted without further question for the purpose of validating a test is assumed to be valid. It is true that one can often question the validity of a criterion, and it should be questioned more often than it is. Nevertheless, there comes a time when enough satisfaction is felt with the suitability of a criterion to lead to its adoption.

The validity of some nonachievement tests is also often taken for granted. This was more often true formerly than now. But even now, many a test is put into use because it "looks as if it measures trait *Q*," or it was designed to measure some hypothesized trait *L* and therefore it must measure trait *L*. The door of factor analysis is always open to anyone who feels sufficient scientific curiosity or who has developed sufficient professional conscience to test such a hypothesis. It is a sobering experience to find that a test that looks so good for measuring a certain trait that it "could not miss" proves on correlation analysis to measure some quite different factors. Mosier (56) reports that two tests of alphabetizing ability, both of which looked like real aspects of the job task but of different form, intercorrelated just zero. What is worse, their correlations with a criterion of actual alphabetizing on the job were only .09 and .00. One might suspect these essentially zero correlations were due to low reliabilities of tests and criterion, but the reliabilities for the tests were .81 and .89 and for the criterion .40.

Intrinsic Validity. The degree to which a test measures what it measures may be called its *intrinsic validity*. This definition can also be stated in terms of how well the obtained scores measure the test's true-score components. This validity is indicated by the square root of the proportion of true variance, in other words, the square root of its reliability. Another name for this statistic is the *index of reliability*, as defined in equation (13.14). Lord has demonstrated (50) that this is also the curvilinear correlation between test scores and the ability that they measure. This index of validity makes practical sense only when the test measures a single common factor and when its communality is as great as its reliability—a very unlikely occurrence. It makes theoretical sense under somewhat broader conditions. Since it is directly and closely related to reliability, the same conditions that affect reliability will also affect intrinsic validity.

Relevant Validity. The degree to which a test measures factors that are common to other measures may be called its *relevant validity.* The index of relevant validity is the square root of the test's communality (h^2), in other words, h. This is parallel to the intrinsic validity just mentioned, the difference being that specific variance is permitted to enter into the estimation of intrinsic validity but not into relevant validity. The two are identical when specific variance is zero. The coefficient h indicates the upper limit of a test's correlation with any other measure and hence a limit to its validity coefficient indicating practical validity. To the extent that h is underestimated, however, it represents a lower-bound estimate to relevant validity.

Face Validity. The term *face validity* has many meanings and has been loosely used. It is best restricted to the fact that a test "looks" valid, particularly to those who are unsophisticated, in test practices. Since, as was indicated above, looking valid, by itself, is no guarantee of any form of genuine validity, even to experienced psychologists, one can have little confidence in such information. This is why some psychologists facetiously refer to the acceptance of some tests as a matter of "faith validity." Apart from any confidence in superficial appearance, or lack thereof, it is sometimes said that for the sake of good public relations it often pays to make a test appear relevant to the layman who takes it or who has any administrative decisions to make concerning it. A more scientifically and professionally justifiable reason for face validity is to make it palatable to the examinee. If he feels that a test is relevant, he will be likely to have increased motivation in taking it, and uniformly high motivation is an important testing condition.

Correction for Attenuation. Intercorrelations of tests, and of tests with criteria, are restricted in size because of the amount of error variance in each, where error variances are uncorrelated. This is as it should be if we want the coefficient of correlation to indicate how well one fallible measure can be predicted from another fallible measure. If, however, we want to know how much the true variances are related and how well they can be predicted, we must take into account the reliabilities of the measures.

Complete Correction for Attenuation. If we want to know the correlation between the true component in X, which we will call X_∞, and the true component in Y, which we will call Y_ω, we apply the formula for full correction for attenuation:

$$r_{\infty\omega} = \frac{r_{xy}}{\sqrt{r_{xx}r_{yy}}} \tag{14.35}$$

where $r_{\infty\omega}$ = correlation between true components of X and Y

r_{xy} = obtained correlation between X and Y

r_{xx}, r_{yy} = reliability coefficients of X and Y

The type of reliability estimate to use for this purpose has been a much-debated subject. A good general rule is to use the type of estimate that treats as error those things that one decides should be treated as error, as

Johnson (42) has pointed out. Since the intercorrelation r_{xy} is usually obtained with some time interval between tests, the reliability coefficients should entail a similar interval. This allows any intervening events and changes to operate to produce error variance. Certainly, there is no condition in the administration of two different tests that can be comparable to the condition applying for an odd-even reliability estimate. Neither is there identity of content in the two different tests, comparable with that in the retest condition. The type of estimate left is that of alternate forms, with appropriate time interval.

If complete correction for attenuation gives a coefficient close to 1.0 (within sampling error), one should conclude that one has in X and Y essentially two forms of the same test. Their entire true-variance components are in common.

Correction in the Criterion Only. In predicting criterion measures from test scores, one should not make a complete correction for attenuation. Correction should be made in the criterion only. On the one hand it is not a fallible criterion that we should aim to predict, including all its errors; it is a "true" criterion or the true component of the obtained criterion.

On the other hand, we should not correct for errors in the test, because it is the fallible scores from which we must make predictions. We never know the true scores from which to predict. We should obtain a very erroneous idea of how well we are doing with a selection test or composite score if the reliability of criterion measure were only .30, which can very well happen, and if no correction for attenuation were made. If the uncorrected validity coefficient r_{xy} were .20, the correlation corrected for errors in the criterion would be .36, or almost doubled. (It would be more appropriate to compare coefficients of determination in this instance, however. These coefficients are .13 and .04, which indicates that the variance in common is tripled.) The formula for a one-way correction is

$$r_{x\omega} = \frac{r_{xy}}{\sqrt{r_{yy}}} \qquad (14.36)$$

where $r_{x\omega}$ is the correlation with correction in Y only and other symbols are as defined above. This type of correction should be used much more than it is, even though it requires an estimate of criterion reliability. The latter should be regarded as indispensable information even if the correction is not made.

Errors in Correction for Attenuation. Johnson (41) has issued a timely warning concerning reliance on coefficients corrected for attenuation. It should be common knowledge that there are sampling errors in r_{xy} and that these should therefore be reflected in a corrected r. If this were the only thing to be concerned about, the matter would not be unusually serious. But Johnson has demonstrated that a coefficient of correlation fluctuates owing to errors of measurement as well as errors of sampling. In an experiment with two artificial tests, each in several forms, in which the "true" correlation was approximately .59 and the reliabilities averaged approximately .90, the obtained r_{xy} coefficients ranged from .45 to .64, with a mean of

.53. N was relatively small, being 55. Six of the obtained coefficients were actually greater than the "true" correlation. Had such coefficients, or even some of the other higher ones, been used in formula (14.35), the corrected coefficient would have been greater than 1.00. This should be a warning to use large samples, reducing sampling errors as much as possible, and also to interpret with reservations corrected validity coefficients when reliabilities are low.

Procedures of Validation

This section will be concerned with the operations for estimating validity. It will not be possible to go into all the various alternative devices for indicating success in prediction in the personnel operations. We shall be limited to those procedures that yield validity coefficients, for they remain the point of reference for all validation methods. References will be made to criterion problems, multiple prediction of criterion measures, and the needs for and the methods of cross validation.

General Standards for Validation Studies. Jones (43) has recently performed a real service by making a survey of validation studies as they have been made in the past. Of 2,100 studies reported between 1906 and 1948, after eliminating reports considered completely inadequate, only 427 remained. Only 46 of these were regarded as satisfactory (with the exception that follow-up studies were lacking). Only 17 were satisfactory except for lack of estimates of criterion reliability. Only 8, or .4 of 1 per cent, were satisfactory in all respects. Jones also presents some excellent requirements for a good validation study, to which the reader is referred (43, p. 223). They incorporate what should be recognized as merely the specifications for good experimental design applied to this kind of problem. Many of Jones's requirements will be reflected in the following discussions.

Criterion Measures. The key to a successful validation study is a good criterion measure or combination of criterion measures. When one knows in advance that a validation study will be made in connection with certain tests, especially if the tests were designed to meet a specific prediction problem, the first goal should be the achievement of a good criterion. Without this, in such a study, there is little point in further efforts at test construction. It is sometimes recommended that as much time should be spent on the development of the criterion as on the development of the tests. This means doing the hard things first; at least it means not relegating them to a minor place. When one is aiming at factorial validity, however, the goal is to develop tests for general purposes and an immediate validation against practical criteria is not essential. A correlation study of some kind *is* necessary, however, and is the alternative to a practical validation study.

The story of the criterion problem in the personnel situation is now a very long one, longer than can be told here. Some thoughtful articles by Toops (75), Lauer (46), Rundquist and Bittner (68), Brogden and Taylor (5), Adkins (1), and Cureton (47) should be read by those who wish to improve their techniques of practical validation. Toops discusses the various kinds of criteria available, pointing out some of the features of the industrial situation that affect them, and giving rules for procedures dealing with them.

Lauer suggests a number of principles for improving criteria. Rundquist and Bittner report some experiences in the use of ratings as criteria. Brogden and Taylor discuss the steps essential to the development of criterion measures and some of the biases and errors that offer pitfalls. Adkins deals with criteria in the civil-service situation. Cureton considers in much detail some basic problems of quantifying behavior in the development of criterion measures.

Factor Analysis of Criterion Measures. For those who prefer to pursue validation studies with as much enlightenment as possible, the factor analysis of criterion measures is a profitable approach. Knowledge of the reliability of criterion measures is minimum information. Knowledge of their factor loadings provides considerable additional information. There are several operations that this makes possible. Where there are several criterion measures to be considered for use, such information tells us which ones are likely to be more relevant and how they should or should not be combined, and if combined how they should be weighted. It also tells us what tests should be included in a battery to predict the criteria and enables us to predict validity of a test in advance, through the use of formula (13.29). It, furthermore, tells us where a test battery is weak, where an important factor in the criterion is represented insufficiently by the battery. If the communality of the criterion is definitely lower than its reliability, we have a challenge to identify the "specific" variance as possibly due to other common factors not yet taken into account. The operation of factor analysis of criterion measures would be to intercorrelate them with good tests of all the probable common factors and with one another.

The factor-analysis approach has been taken by a number of investigators, among them Fruchter (20), who analyzed criteria in connection with 14 specialty courses in the U.S. Air Force technical training. Ryans (69) analyzed criterion data on teacher behavior in order to determine the dimensions of teacher performance in the elementary grades. Newman and others (58) analyzed twice criterion measures in the U.S. Coast Guard Academy with consistent results. In each case the information derived, although not all factors may have been in the form of basic personality variables, could hardly fail to be very informative if not immediately useful.

Multiple Predictions. Problems of multiple prediction arise because either the scores from which predictions are made may be from a single test or from several or the criterion measures predicted may come from a single variable or from several. The usual situation is a multiple predictor and a single criterion measure. In this case, the single criterion measure may be a composite score. Whether the criterion is singly derived or is a composite, the usual procedure is to derive a multiple-regression equation, with weights that will maximize the correlation between predicted and obtained criterion measures. The procedures for this are described in most statistical textbooks.

Some Limitations to Multiple-regression Equations. Perhaps there are still some psychologists who would prefer to combine predictive measures in an intuitive fashion in predicting a criterion. Studies in which this approach has been used as compared with the multiple-regression approach almost invariably show superiority for the latter. The multiple-regression approach has its limitations, however. Cureton (47, p. 690) voices the opinion that it has been badly misused and misinterpreted, in educational research particularly. It must be admitted that there are pitfalls in the way of the user of multiple-regression methods. Under the appropriate conditions their use can be very effective.

First to be considered is that these methods rest on the assumption of linear regressions among the measures going into the equation. As Mosier points out (47, p. 785), when the entire range of ability is taken into account, the regressions of a criterion on scores of ability are probably quite commonly nonlinear. For example, take the regression of performance in some task not requiring a great deal of intelligence on a score for intelligence when morons and imbeciles are included in the range. Above a minimal level, let us say at about 100 on the *IQ* scale, the regression may be horizontal and for upper levels of *IQ* might even decline. The reason that linear regressions are so often found is that among those who compete, or whom we will permit to compete, in some economic or social activity, the range is shortened so that within the remaining levels of ability the regression is practically linear. It is a very rare test that is appropriate for all levels of ability; it is tailored for and used in relatively limited ranges in which regressions can be linear so far as we can ordinarily detect. In the case of interest and temperament scores, however, Guilford (74) has pointed out the actual and potential existence of many curvilinear regressions, perhaps because greater ranges are involved. At any rate, it behooves the investigator who employs multiple-regression procedures to assure himself that his regressions are linear. Where regressions are linear, it is generally conceded that the multiple-regression method is superior to the multiple-cutoff method. Even if some regressions are nonlinear, it is possible by transformations to reduce them to rectilinear form and then use multiple-regression methods.

Linear Restraint. It is a common experience to find that after three or four of the most valid tests have been combined in an equation to predict a criterion, adding more tests rarely improves prediction. This is said to be due to the phenomenon of *linear restraint.* It has been commonly recognized that the outcome just described is likely to happen when the intercorrelations of predictors are substantial. The intercorrelations mean that the predictors have common factors, but the significant thing is that the first three or four tests cover all the common factors that this battery has for predicting this criterion. There are said to be as many linear restraints as the difference between the number of tests and the number of common factors involved. One way of reducing the number of restraints is to combine tests that intercorrelate high with one another, and to let them enter the battery as one variable. If two tests that intercorrelate very highly are permitted to enter the equation separately, the one that correlates with the criterion less, even though the difference is small, is likely to acquire a zero weight, possibly even a small negative weight. In another sample, if the two validity coefficients were reversed in order of size, even slightly, their beta weights might swing just as decisively in the opposite direction. Cureton (47, p. 692) recommends that multiple-regression procedures be applied after removing as many of the restraints as possible. If we do not remove them, the regression weights may be shifted markedly in unfortunate directions.

Shrinkage. The problem of shrinkage is also important. The multiple-regression procedures, in maximizing multiple correlation, take advantage of any correlated errors or specific variations, giving an overoptimistic picture of predictive value of the weighted-composite score. The weights and the correlation apply to this particular sample. In a new sample from the same population, the weights would be likely to yield predictive values that correlate with the criterion less than the multiple R in the sample from which the weights were obtained. Shrinkage formulas for R do not ordinarily tell the full story of this loss in correlation. The best indication of shrinkage is actually to use the results from a new sample. This means cross validation, which will be discussed later.

Prediction of Multiple Criteria from Multiple Scores. When the criterion consists of several different measures, we have a new and very complicated prediction problem. Hotelling (36) first solved this problem statistically by deriving for the tests combining weights that would predict best the most predictable weighted-composite criterion. Horst (29), Edgerton and Kolbe (17), and Kurtz (45) followed with related procedures. Wherry (78) proposed an approximation method, which proved to be more efficient than Hotelling's when there are more than five variables. Thomson (72, 73) and Peel (59) have proposed more simplified and generalized procedures. All of these would require too much space for adequate description here. Hsü has made the novel suggestion (38) that a multiple-regression equation be derived for each test in turn with the various criterion measures as predictors. The multiple R would then indicate the validity coefficient for the test. There is the reverse possibility, of predicting each criterion measure from a weighted composite of the tests. This keeps the direction of the regression in the usual form, treating criteria as dependent variables.

Weighting Tests by Their Lengths. The regression weight of a test in a multiple-regression equation is inversely proportional to its standard deviation. Its standard deviation is in turn related in some degree to its length. The beta weight, which also enters into the test's operating weight in the equation, is indirectly related to the test's length. Horst (30) conceived the idea of making the tests of a battery each of such a length that they can be combined for predicting a particular criterion by using equal weights. This means a simple, unweighted sum of scores. Such optimal lengths would be appropriate for this particular purpose but would have to be altered to predict some other criterion.

A related problem has been under investigation, in which the main goal is to find the optimal lengths for tests to maximize the multiple R when the total testing time is fixed. Among the investigators of this problem are Horst (31, 33), Long and Burr (49), and Taylor (71). Where total testing time is inflexible (which does not seem likely to be common), these methods should contribute to the formation of an efficient battery. The problem seems at the present time to be somewhat academic.

Cross Validation. The importance of cross-validation studies following the derivation of a multiple-regression equation was mentioned above. The need for such studies is even greater in connection with item analyses; hence the subject will be treated at greater length in Chap. 15. Here a few procedures will be pointed out in connection with test batteries.

Mosier (57) has recently pointed out several kinds of cross validation depending upon the experimental design. The typical design is very simple. Multiple-regression weights are determined for tests in one sample from the population and are then used in a second sample to determine how well the composite score predicts the criterion as compared with the multiple *R* in the first sample. If there is too much difference (and here a test of statistical significance of a deviation in *R* may be in order), one may well question the weights and develop a revised equation. If the drop in *R* is small and insignificant, one may accept the new value as a verification of the weights and also as a more realistic index of validity for the population.

A modification of this design is known as a double cross validation. In this case a set of weights is derived in each of two samples from the same population independently and is then applied to the other sample for checking purposes. This means a double validation study, which should yield much more information. If, fortunately, weights are in the same general rank order from the two samples, one has the satisfaction of confirmation. If they are somewhat different, further experimental and statistical work is needed to improve them. The double cross validation requires no larger total sample than the single cross validation, but does, of course, entail more statistical work. If the available number of examinees is very large, one need not stop at two samples, but might well effect a triple or even larger cross-validation design.

Sometimes the cross validation extends somewhat beyond the particular population. Having established weights in one population, we may want to know whether they are also effective in a different population in which they might be expected to apply without intolerable shrinkage. The shift may be from one sex to the other; from one age group to another; or from one industrial organization to another. Such transfer of weights is desirable when it will apply. It saves developmental studies of weights in each and every new kind of personnel. In this fashion we learn about the extent to which the weights may be generalized. Very often weights are adapted from one population to another without such a checkup. While this is better than acting without *any* information and on merely hypothesized or intuitive assumption of validity, the new validation of the weights is highly desirable. Somewhat the same remarks may be made also when a new criterion is involved in the new situation, whether from the same population or from a new one. Where an answer is sought concerning the range of generality of applicability of a battery with its regression weights, the conducting of parallel weighting and cross-validation studies is desirable.

Special Problems of Validity

There remain a few minor problems of validity to be discussed, including the relation of validity to the length of test, the relation of validity to range or heterogeneity of sample, and an incidental validation procedure.

Relation of Validity to Length of a Test. Since validity depends upon reliability and since reliability depends upon test length, validity also depends upon test length. The relationships here implied rest on the assumption of parallel content in all parts of the test, long or short. The longer the test, the more reliable it is, and, the longer the test, the more valid it is. The Spearman-Brown formula covers the relationship of length to reliability; it is also involved, but less simply, in the relation to validity. In terms of factor theory, as the homogeneous lengthening increases true variance at the expense of error variance, it also increases in the same ratio the proportions of common-factor variance and hence the common-factor loadings, which are the basis of validity. The validity of a test increased in length n times is given by the equation

$$r_{nx \cdot y} = \frac{r_{xy}}{\sqrt{\frac{1 - r_{xx}}{n} + r_{xx}}} \tag{14.37}$$

where $r_{nx \cdot y}$ = correlation of variable Y with test X increased by ratio n
r_{xy} = correlation of Y with X in original length
n = ratio by which length of X is changed
r_{xx} = reliability of X

As with increases in reliability with lengthening of a test, most is gained in r_{xy} when r_{xx} is small and when n is large. It can be less clearly seen, but validity changes with length less rapidly than does reliability.

Validity of a Test of Infinite Length. If a test is made infinitely long, its reliability becomes perfect but its variance still includes some specificity. It cannot under this condition achieve perfect validity. By making n indefinitely large in equation (14.37) we can see what the upper limit of validity becomes:

$$r_{\infty x \cdot y} = \frac{r_{xy}}{\sqrt{r_{xx}}} \tag{14.38}$$

Comparison of this equation with (14.35) and (14.36) will show that this is what it would take to correct a validity coefficient for attenuation in the test only. This would imply the prediction of fallible criterion measures from true test scores, which would be impossible and useless from the practical point of view. Yet equation (14.38) has an important meaning and it has a usefulness in another way. It tells us the maximum validity we could expect with great amounts of lengthening. The key to this is the index of reliability, $\sqrt{r_{xx}}$. The nearer it is to 1.0, the less effect will lengthening of any extent have on validity. We thus have an answer to the question, "Would it pay to lengthen this test to gain validity?" A practical use is that the equation gives us *an index of validity that is independent of test length.* The potentialities with regard to validity for tests of different lengths can be directly compared by means of this statistic.

Validity for Increased Length in Both Test and Criterion. When both variables are increased in length the prediction of their correlation is

$$r_{nx \cdot my} = \frac{r_{xy}}{\sqrt{\left(\frac{1 - r_{xx}}{n} + r_{xx}\right)\left(\frac{1 - r_{yy}}{m} + r_{yy}\right)}} \tag{14.39}$$

where X is increased n times and Y is increased m times and the symbols are parallel to those in (14.37).

Lengthening Needed to Achieve a Given Validity. Solving equation (14.37) for n, we have an expression for the ratio by which a test must be lengthened to achieve a specified validity. The resulting equation is

$$n = \frac{1 - r_{xx}}{\dfrac{r^2_{xy}}{r^2_{nx \cdot y}} - r_{xx}} \tag{14.40}$$

where the symbols are as defined in equation (14.37). A little study of this formula will show that it has limitations with respect to the values that can be assigned meaningfully to $r_{nx \cdot y}$. The meaningful upper limit of $r_{nx \cdot y}$ is equivalent to $r_{\infty x \cdot y}$ that we would find from equation (14.38).

Effect of Range of Ability on Validity. In a general way, we can see intuitively that as the range of ability in the selected population decreases, the possibility for high correlations between tests and criteria decreases. The limiting case would be the lower limit of range, at which all persons are of the same ability, in which case the correlation would shrink to zero. It can also seem reasonable that an intelligence-test score may correlate zero with a criterion for success in a simple, mechanical task like armature winding, within the range of those who engage in that activity. If one were to bring in persons both of higher and lower intelligence, the correlation might become appreciable.

In personnel selection the investigator is perpetually facing the problem of restriction of range in his experimental samples. The applicants from whom selection is made may vary over a substantial portion of the range of ability. But because of possible selection on the basis of the test or composite score itself, or on the basis of other measures that are correlated with it, validation must be done within a more limited range. The validity figures one wants to know are those pertaining to the entire range of applicants from whom selection is made. This problem has been solved with some degree of satisfaction, with formulas designed for correction of correlation coefficients for restrictions of range. Their application is limited to the type of restriction known as a truncation, that is, with rather clean-cut selection of cases above a certain cutoff score. Because the formulas and their explanations are space consuming and because they are available in statistical textbooks (24, 25) they will not be given here.

Validation by the Nomination Technique. For the case in which the criterion measures must be based upon human judgment and where only the extremes of a criterion group can be separated with confidence from the rest, Peters (60) has proposed the nominating technique. His method is to define the trait continuum for selected persons of a group who know all members well and who are to serve as observers. Each observer is asked to select the highest and lowest members in the trait variable. The number of nominations from each observer is presumably a constant. Those persons nominated three times (this could be another arbitrary number) for either highest or lowest group are used in the validation sample. It is assumed that the regression is linear and that the extreme criterion groups selected represent the tail areas under the normal curve. The correlation under these circumstances is a special biserial r, with the formula

$$r_b = \frac{(M_2 - M_1)p_2p_1}{(p_1y_2 + p_2y_1)\sigma_x} \tag{14.41}$$

where M_2 and M_1 = mean test scores in highest and lowest groups, respectively

p_2 and p_1 = proportions of total group nominated in the highest and lowest groups, respectively

y_2 and y_1 = ordinates in unit normal distribution curve corresponding to p_2 and p_1, respectively

σ_x = standard deviation of entire sample of scores

Needless to say, this technique should be used with hesitation where there is suspicion of curved regression. A check on this might be made by comparing the mean test score of the excluded middle group with M_1 and M_2. If it approaches an even division of the difference between M_1 and M_2, the assumption of linearity is supported.

Peters (60) supplies with this formula an equation for estimating the standard deviation of r_b on the assumption that the population correlation is zero:

$$\sigma_{r_b} = \frac{\sqrt{p_1p_2}}{(p_1y_2 + p_2y_1)\sqrt{N}}\sqrt{p_1 + p_2} \tag{14.42}$$

This would be used in testing the null hypothesis when r_b is small.

Problems

1. Compute an odd-even estimate of reliability for the test in Data 13*B*. What is the ratio of σ_e to σ_o? What bearing does this have on the result?
2. Apply the Rulon and Flanagan formulas to estimating reliability for Data 13*B*.
3. Apply the various Kuder-Richardson formulas, including Tucker's version, to estimating r_{tt} for Data 13*B*.
4. Apply Hoyt's analysis-of-variance formula to the estimation of reliability for the same test.
5. Apply Ferguson's discrimination index to Data 13*B*.
6. In a test of 40 items the coefficient of reliability is .83. What is the most probable reliability of a test having 90 comparable items? Of a test having 200 comparable items?
7. In Prob. 6, how many comparable items would be required to attain a reliability of .90? Of .95?
8. A test was given to 300 individuals with the result that r_{tt} = .88 and the *SD* was 11.5. In a selected sample of 50 individuals from the same group, the *SD* was 9.6. What is the probable coefficient of reliability for the latter group?
9. Determine the reliabilities of difference scores obtained from the following pairs of tests:

   Tests *A* and *B*: r_{aa} = .90, r_{bb} = .80, and r_{ab} = .30.

   Tests *C* and *D*: r_{cc} = .80, r_{dd} = .70, and r_{cd} = .65.
10. Apply the Ebel method of estimating reliability of ratings to Data 11*A*, trait *A*, determining reliability both for one rater and for a combination of four raters.

11. A test in mathematics has a reliability of .85 and a test in English has a reliability of .75. The intercorrelation of the two tests is .45. Estimate the degree of intercorrelation if:

a. The mathematics test alone is made perfectly reliable.
b. The English test alone is made perfectly reliable.
c. The intrinsic amount of correlation of the traits measured is to be known.
d. The maximum amount of correlation is made possible.

12. A test has a validity coefficient of .50 and a reliability coefficient of .90. The criterion has a reliability coefficient of .70. Estimate the validity coefficient indicating how well the true variance in the criterion is being predicted. What is the maximum amount of validity that could exist in this situation?

13. Show in terms of factor theory why a coefficient of correlation corrected for attenuation does not become 1.00.

14. A certain test composed of 25 items has a validity coefficient of .55 and a reliability coefficient of .85. Estimate the validity if:

a. The test were doubled in length.
b. The test were composed of 80 comparable items.
c. The reliability of the test were .70 (instead of .85) and doubled in length.

15. How many items must a 25-item test (with validity of .60 and reliability of .70) have in order to achieve a validity of (*a*) .65; (*b*) .70; (*c*). 70 (if reliability were .50 instead of .70)?

Answers

1. $r_{oe} = .86$; $\sigma_e/\sigma_o = 1.12$.
2. Rulon $r_{tt} = .92$; Flanagan $r_{tt} = .92$.
3. K-R (20) $r_{tt} = .87$; K-R (21) $r_{tt} = .81$; Tucker $r_{tt} = .87$.
4. Hoyt $r_{tt} = .87$.
5. Ferguson $\delta = .93$.
6. When $n = 2.25$, $r_{nn} = .917$; when $n = 5.0$, $r_{nn} = .961$.
7. When $r_{nn} = .90$, $n = 1.84$, which means 74 items. When $r_{nn} = .95$, $n = 3.89$, which means 156 items.
8. $r_{uu} = .828$.
9. For A and B, $r_{dd} = .79$; for C and D, $r_{dd} = .29$.
10. $r_{11} = .662$; $r_{44} = .887$.
11. (*a*) .488; (*b*) .520; (*c*) .564; (*d*) .564.
12. .598; .630.
14. (*a*) .572; (*b*) .581; (*c*) 597.
15. (*a*) 49; (*b*) 216; (*c*) 53.

REFERENCES

1. ADKINS, D. C. Principles underlying observational techniques of evaluation. *Educ. psychol. Measmt.*, 1951, **11**, 29–51.
2. ALEXANDER, H. W. The estimation of reliability when several trials are available. *Psychometrika*, 1947, **12**, 79–99.
3. BROGDEN, H. E. Variation in test validity with variation in the distribution of item difficulties, number of items, and degree of their intercorrelation. *Psychometrika*, 1946, **11**, 197–214.
4. ———. The effect of bias due to difficulty factors in product-moment item intercorrelations on the accuracy of estimation of reliability. *Educ. psychol. Measmt.*, 1946, **6**, 517–520.
5. ——— and TAYLOR, E. K. The theory and classification of criterion bias. *Educ. psychol. Measmt.*, 1950, **10**, 159–186.
6. CLARK, E. L. Spearman-Brown formula applied to ratings of personality traits. *J. educ. Psychol.*, 1935, **26**, 552–555.

7. Cronbach, L. J. The reliability of ratio scores. *Educ. psychol. Measmt.*, 1941, **1**, 269–278.
8. ———. Test "reliability": Its meaning and determination. *Psychometrika*, 1947, **12**, 1–16.
9. ———. Coefficient alpha and the internal structure of tests. *Psychometrika*, 1951, **16**, 297–334.
10. ——— and Warrington, W. G. Time-limit tests: Estimating their reliability and degree of speeding. *Psychometrika*, 1951, **16**, 167–188.
11. ——— and ———. Efficiency of multiple-choice tests as a function of spread of item difficulties. *Psychometrika*, 1952, **17**, 127–147.
12. Cureton, E. E. Symposium: The need and means of cross validation. II. Approximate linear restraints and best predictor weights. *Educ. psychol. Measmt.*, 1951, **11**, 12–15.
13. Denney, H. R., and Remmers, H. H. Reliability of multiple-choice measuring instruments as a function of the Spearman-Brown prophecy formula, II. *J. educ. Psychol.*, 1940, **31**, 699–704.
14. Dodd, S. C., and Svalastoga, K. On estimating latent from manifest undecidedness. *Educ. psychol. Measmt.*, 1952, **12**, 467–471.
15. Dressel, P. L. Some remarks on the Kuder-Richardson reliability coefficient. *Psychometrika*, 1940, **5**, 305–310.
16. Ebel, R. L. Estimation of the reliability of ratings. *Psychometrika*, 1951, **16**, 407–424.
17. Edgerton, H. A., and Kolbe, L. E. The method of minimum variation for the combination of criteria. *Psychometrika*, 1936, **1**, 183–187.
18. Ferguson, G. A. A note on the Kuder-Richardson formula. *Educ. psychol. Measmt.*, 1951, **11**, 612–615.
19. Flanagan, J. C. A proposed procedure for increasing the efficiency of objective tests. *J. educ. Psychol.*, 1937, **28**, 17–21.
20. Fruchter, B. Ability patterns in technical training criteria. *J. appl. Psychol.*, 1952, **36**, 381–384.
21. Green, B. F., Jr. A test of the equality of standard errors of measurement. *Psychometrika*, 1950, **15**, 251–257.
22. Grings, W. W. The evaluation of experimentally controlled criteria. *Psychol. Bull.*, 1952, **49**, 333–338.
23. Guilford, J. P. New standards for test evaluation. *Educ. psychol. Measmt.*, 1946, **6**, 427–438.
24. ———. *Fundamental Statistics in Psychology and Education.* 2d ed. New York: McGraw-Hill, 1950.
25. Gulliksen, H. *Theory of Mental Tests.* New York: Wiley, 1950.
26. ———. The reliability of speeded tests. *Psychometrika*, 1950, **15**, 259–269.
27. Guttman, L. A basis for analyzing test-retest reliability. *Psychometrika*, 1945, **10**, 255–282.
28. ———. The test-retest reliability of qualitative data. *Psychometrika*, 1946, **11**, 81–95.
29. Horst, P. Obtaining a composite measure from a number of different measures of the same attribute. *Psychometrika*, 1936, **1**, 53–60.
30. ———. Regression weights as a function of test length. *Psychometrika*, 1948, **13**, 125–134.
31. ———. Determination of optimal test length to maximize the multiple correlation. *Psychometrika*, 1949, **14**, 79–88.
32. ———. A generalized expression for the reliability of measures. *Psychometrika*, 1949, **14**, 21–31.
33. ———. A note on optimal test length. *Psychometrika*, 1950, **15**, 407–408.

34. ———. Optimal test length for maximum battery validity. *Psychometrika*, 1951, **16,** 189–202.
35. ———. Estimating total test reliability from parts of unequal length. *Educ. psychol. Measmt.*, 1951, **11,** 368–371.
36. HOTELLING, H. The most predictable criterion. *J. educ. Psychol.*, 1935, **26,** 139–142.
37. HOYT, C. Test reliability estimated by analysis of variance. *Psychometrika*, 1941, **6,** 153–160.
38. HSÜ, E. H. A note on and some suggested methods for the determination of the validity coefficient. *J. educ. Psychol.*, 1948, **39,** 304–307.
39. JACKSON, R. W. B. Reliability of mental tests. *Brit. J. Psychol., Gen. Sec.*, 1939, **29,** 267–287.
40. ———. Note on the relationship between internal consistency and test-retest estimates of the reliability of a test. *Psychometrika*, 1942, **7,** 157–164.
41. JOHNSON, H. G. An empirical study of the influence of errors of measurement upon correlation. *Amer. J. Psychol.*, 1944, **57,** 521–536.
42. ———. Test reliability and correction for attenuation. *Psychometrika*, 1950, **15,** 115–119.
43. JONES, M. H. The adequacy of employee selection reports. *J. appl. Psychol.*, 1950, **34,** 219–224.
44. KUDER, G. F., and RICHARDSON, M. W. The theory of the estimation of test reliability. *Psychometrika*, 1937, **2,** 151–160.
45. KURTZ, A. K. The simultaneous prediction of any number of criteria by the use of a unique set of weights. *Psychometrika*, 1937, **2,** 95–101.
46. LAUER, A. R. Improvement of test criteria. *Iowa Acad. Sci.*, 1947, **54,** 239–241.
47. LINDQUIST, E. F. (ed). *Educational Measurement.* Washington, D.C.: American Council on Education, 1951.
48. LOEVINGER, J. A systematic approach to the construction and evaluation of tests of ability. *Psychol. Monogr.*, 1947, **61,** No. 285.
49. LONG, W. F., and BURR, I. W. Development of a method for increasing the utility of multiple correlations by considering both testing time and test validity. *Psychometrika*, 1949, **14,** 137–161.
50. LORD, F. M. The relation of the reliability of multiple-choice tests to the distribution of item difficulties. *Psychometrika*, 1952, **17,** 181–194.
51. ———. A theory of test scores. *Psychometr. Monogr.* No. 7, 1952.
52. MELTON, A. W. The methodology of experimental studies of human learning and retention. *Psychol. Bull.*, 1936, **33,** 305–394.
53. MOLLENKOPF, W. G. Variation of the standard error of measurement. *Psychometrika*, 1949, **14,** 189–215.
54. MOSIER, C. I. A short cut in the estimation of split-halves coefficients. *Educ. psychol. Measmt.*, 1941, **1,** 407–408.
55. ———. On the reliability of a weighted composite. *Psychometrika*, 1943, **8,** 161–168.
56. ———. A critical examination of the concepts of face validity. *Educ. psychol. Measmt.*, 1947, **7,** 191–205.
57. ———. Symposium: The need and means of cross-validation. I. Problems and designs of cross-validation. *Educ. psychol. Measmt.*, 1951, **11,** 5–11.
58. NEWMAN, S. H., FRENCH, J. W., and BOBBITT, J. M. Analysis of criteria for the validation of selection measures at the United States Coast Guard Academy. *Educ. psychol. Measmt.*, 1952, **12,** 394–407.
59. PEEL, E. A. Prediction of a complex criterion and battery reliability. *Brit. J. Psychol., Statist. Sec.*, 1948, **1,** 84–94.
60. PETERS, C. C. A technique for correlating measurable traits with freely observed social behaviors. *Psychometrika*, 1941, **6,** 209–219.

61. Plumlee, L. B. The effect of difficulty and chance success on item-test correlation and on test reliability. *Psychometrika*, 1952, **17**, 69–86.
62. Remmers, H. H., and Ewart, E. Reliability of multiple-choice measuring instruments as a function of the Spearman-Brown prophecy formula, III. *J. educ. Psychol.*, 1941, **32**, 61–66.
63. ——— and House, J. M. Reliability of multiple-choice measuring instruments as a function of the Spearman-Brown prophecy formula, IV. *J. educ. Psychol.*, 1941, **32**, 372–376.
64. Richardson, M. W. The relation between the difficulty and the differential validity of a test. *Psychometrika*, 1936, **1**, 33–49.
65. ——— and Kuder, F. The calculation of test-reliability coefficients based upon the method of rational equivalence. *J. educ. Psychol.*, 1939, **30**, 681–687.
66. Rosander, A. C. The Spearman-Brown formula in attitude scale construction. *J. exp. Psychol.*, 1936, **19**, 486–495.
67. Rulon, P. J. A simplified procedure for determining the reliability of a test by split-halves. *Harv. educ. Rev.*, 1939, **9**, 99–103.
68. Rundquist, E. A., and Bittner, R. H. Using ratings to validate personnel instruments: A study in method. *Person. Psychol.*, 1948, **1**, 163–183.
69. Ryans, D. G. A study of criterion data (a factor analysis of teacher behaviors in the elementary school). *Educ. psychol. Measmt.*, 1952, **12**, 333–344.
70. Smith, F. F. Objectivity as a criterion for estimating the validity of questionnaire data. *J. educ. Psychol.*, 1935, **26**, 481–496.
71. Taylor, C. W. Maximizing predictive efficiency for a fixed total testing time. *Psychometrika*, 1950, **15**, 391–406.
72. Thomson, G. The maximum correlation of two weighted batteries. *Brit. J. Psychol., Statist. Sec.*, 1947, **1**, 27–34.
73. ———. Note on the relations of two weighted batteries. *Brit. J. Psychol., Statist. Sec.*, 1948, **1**, 82–83.
74. Thurstone, L. L. (ed). *Applications of Psychology*. New York: Harper, 1952.
75. Toops, H. A. The criterion. *Educ. psychol. Measmt.*, 1944, **4**, 271–297.
76. Tucker, L. R. Maximum validity of a test with equivalent items. *Psychometrika*, 1946, **11**, 1–13.
77. ———. A note on the estimation of test reliability by the Kuder-Richardson formula (20). *Psychometrika*, 1949, **14**, 117–119.
78. Wherry, R. J. An approximation method for obtaining a maximized multiple criterion. *Psychometrika*, 1940, **5**, 109–115.
79. ———. Symposium: The need and means of cross validation. IV. Comparison of cross-validation with statistical inference of betas and multiple R from a single sample. *Educ. psychol. Measmt.*, 1951, **11**, 23–28.
80. ——— and Gaylord, R. H. The concept of test and item reliability in relation to factor pattern. *Psychometrika*, 1943, **8**, 247–264.
81. Woodbury, M. A. On the standard length of a test. *Psychometrika*, 1951, **16**, 103–106.

CHAPTER 15
TEST DEVELOPMENT

This chapter will consider some of the more statistical aspects of test development. It cannot deal with all facets of the subject. It will mention some of the problems and operations connected with the construction of tests, referring the reader to sources on the more detailed subjects of types of items, item writing, and item editing. The subject of item analysis will occupy our attention for the greater part of the chapter, followed by a discussion of scoring problems and a treatment of attitude-scale construction.

Introduction to Test Construction

When one sets out to construct a test, there are several considerations that will determine one's approach and operations. It will depend upon one's philosophy of testing in general and of testing in the particular area and upon the use of the test to be produced. It will depend upon the kind of test, whether it is an aptitude test or an achievement test; and if it is an achievement test, whether the setting is an academic one or a technical one. It will depend upon whether the test is an instrument for purposes of research or of personnel operations. If it is an aptitude test, or a test of temperament, or interests, or attitudes, it will depend on whether the test is designed for general purposes or some specific purpose. It will also depend upon the medium of the test, whether it is of printed form, of apparatus form, or of motion-picture form. All these considerations have overlapping and interacting bearings on the production of the test. Back of it all will be certain psychological theories as to the nature of human personality and of its significant and measurable dimensions. There will be many steps in common, regardless of these background conditions, especially if the test is of the printed type and more particularly if it is a test of ability. The greatest part of the emphasis in this chapter, as in the previous ones, will be on the printed test of abilities. As usual, many of the principles developed to apply to such tests are readily transferred to other types.

Sources of Information on Test Construction. The chief, recently published sources of information on how to construct printed tests include books written or edited by Adkins (3), Guilford and Lacey (54), Lindquist (79), Stuit (102), and Travers (107), and also articles by Adkins (1, 2). The book and articles by Adkins emphasize testing in the civil-service setting. Most of these publications include discussions of how to write and edit items. On the same subject there are articles by Anstey (5) and by Mosier, Myers, and Price (89). A discussion of construction of apparatus tests will be found in Lindquist (79). Melton's volume (85) on *Apparatus Tests* is largely devoted to test construction. The relatively new field of motion-picture tests has been treated for the first time in book form by Gibson (41).

The Rational versus the Empirical Approach. If one asks where ideas for tests come from, the answer is usually one of two kinds. Either the test is developed to measure some ability or other trait that is hypothesized as being a significant dimension of personality, without regard to immediate use of the test, or it is developed to predict or to evaluate the performance of some kind of personnel in a particular life situation. In the former case, the test is thought to have general applicability because its scores describe something significant about persons in the population for which it was designed, and perhaps in similar populations. These descriptions are expected to be useful for many purposes, and to discover these uses is a matter of practical validation. In the second case, the personnel-testing situation, the test is tailored to satisfy a certain specific use in a limited kind of application. The difference is somewhat the same as that between basic and applied research, and in both cases the distinction is not always complete.

In the case of the general-purpose test, the success of the test depends upon whether some meaningful and significant psychological variable of individual differences has been identified and quantified. A rational approach for this purpose is offered by factor theory and the operations of factor analysis. It is not enough to hypothesize that trait X should be a unique mode of variation among individuals and then to assume that a test that looks as if it measures trait X really does so. Factor analysis is an excellent way of checking up on all such hypotheses. It establishes empirically (or fails to do so) that such a trait does exist and that this is the way to measure it; it also shows how well this test measures it. Once the factor is established and its general psychological nature is identified, it is possible to develop other tests to measure it and to verify the fact that they do so. Such a prediction is a rigorous test of a hypothesis of this kind.

In developing a test to meet a specific personnel problem, one can also use the knowledge about factors as far as it will go. Predicting that factors P, Q, and R seem involved in the performance on the job is a rational way to begin. Such predictions are best made after observations of what individuals actually do on the job. Flanagan (36) has recommended that a job analysis for the purpose of psychological inspection begin by listing the kinds of behaviors the personnel on this job actually exhibit. To determine significant behaviors, he proposes his technique called *critical incidents*. This involves asking persons who are in the best positions to observe for reports of behaviors they have noted that led to failure and other behaviors that they have noted that led to unusual success. After assembling such reports, noting common behaviors in either the failure or success list, one can make psychological abstractions of the traits probably involved. Here the factor concepts should be very useful in so far as they are known.

There are times when a test maker resorts to an almost purely empirical approach. This is much more likely to happen in the personnel-testing situation than in the basic-research situation. An example of a test made by the empirical approach is the Biographical Data Blank developed by Army Air Force psychologists during World War II (54). Without any measures of temperament or interests, of known validity, for the selection and classification of men for pilot training or navigator training, the approach that promised possible quick results was to find out what items of biographical information would predict which students would pass and which ones would fail. The approach is a "shotgun" type of procedure. A list of some 150 items concerning a man's past life, most of them factual in nature, was administered to hundreds of trainees before they entered preflight school. After they had completed primary flying training, every response to an item was correlated with the pass-fail dichotomy used as the criterion. Items correlating significantly with the pilot criterion were saved for use in obtaining a score to predict pilot-training success. Items correlating significantly with the navigator criterion were scored for predicting navigator success. No great attention was paid to whether a keyed response was reasonable or not; if it predicted, it was usually scored accordingly. The total scores proved to be relatively valid and useful. The reasons were not known, and one could adopt the point of view that so long as the scores worked no question need be asked. The pilot and navigator scores were later factor analyzed along with other scores, and reasonable explanations were found for their validities. The pilot-score variance had represented in it some small variances in factors known as *mechanical knowledge*, *psychomotor coordination*, *perceptual speed*, and *socioeconomic background*. The navigator-score variance had some small contributions from factors of *numerical facility*, *perceptual speed*, and *socioeconomic background*. All these factors could be much better measured by other tests, making the biographical-data scores unnecessary and providing a much more meaningful measurement operation.

There are some dangers in a purely empirical approach, as Travers points out (108). Granting that the empirical approach yields quicker results, he cites an example in which it also led to some serious biases. An attempt was made to predict success of research scientists in administrative positions. The biographical-background qualities that correlated positively with the dichotomy of more and less successful administrators included the qualities of having a rural background and coming from a family of skilled craftsmen. Those correlating negatively included the qualities of having a large-city background and coming from a retail-merchant family. These correlations made little sense until it was discovered that the observers who had judged the experimental group as successful tended to have anti-Semitic attitudes. To score an instrument in line with the correlations would have perpetuated the same bias. Thus it can be clearly seen that the criterion one uses against which to validate items may include other important differences in addition to the ones we want to predict. If the empirical approach is used, it is very important to control the selection of cases in the criterion group, avoiding irrelevant variances. Even then, if an item acquires a scoring weight that is unreasonable, it should be suspect and not used until its validity is appropriately rationalized.

Pretesting of Tests. The pretesting of a new test is very important wherever that is possible. In addition to providing data for an item analysis and consequent information concerning items, which will be discussed in the next section, pretest results tell us much about other aspects of a test. Pretesting helps us to discover weaknesses in the instructions and in the format and to establish a reasonable time limit and a desirable length of test. Conrad recommends (79) three preliminary test administrations. The first one, for which a sample of 100 examinees will suffice, is for the purpose of uncovering the gross defects. It is desirable that the test constructor himself administer this preliminary form. The second administration is primarily for item analysis, for which ideally the number of examinees should be about 400. The third administration would be of the "final" form as a kind of "dress rehearsal," to catch any obvious minor defects that may have evaded detection before and to determine reliability. The amount and kind of pretesting will depend upon several considerations; thus the steps mentioned above need not be followed religiously for all tests. The steps advised by Conrad, however, will be generally recognized as representing good workmanship in test construction.

Item Analysis

Objectives and Uses of Item Analysis. The typical item analysis of a test of ability yields two kinds of information. It provides an index of item difficulty and an index of validity, where the term *validity* is used in a very broad sense. The index of validity may mean how well the item measures or discriminates in agreement with the rest of the test or how well it predicts some external criterion. The most common indices used are p_i, the proportion of examinees who pass the item, and either some measure of correlation of the item with an external criterion, r_{ic}, or the correlation of item with total score (internal criterion), r_{it}. The correlation r_{ic}, of item with an external criterion, is less often computed. The intercorrelations of items, r_{ij}, are even less often computed. None of these statistics would be computed just for their own sakes; it is what we can do, knowing them, that counts. The first major objective of an item analysis, then, is to obtain objective information concerning the items we wrote for the test.

This information is valuable for several reasons. It provides the opportunity to check up on the test writer's subjective judgment in selecting the items to compose the test. No matter how expert the item writer or the item critic or editor, such checks are still desirable, and the expert would be the first to welcome them. By experience with such checking the test writer learns to improve in his art. He learns how examinees react to items in general and to the items of each test in particular. In multiple-choice tests he learns which distracters (wrong answers) or misleads are not functioning, as shown by their relative unpopularity. He gains new insights into the kind of item that does best in this kind of test and thinks of new hypotheses concerning the nature of the ability being measured. He learns where and how items need to be rewritten.

The most common use of the item-analysis data is in the selection of best items to compose the final test form. Starting with a surplus number of items, the writer can save the ones that look best in terms of item statistics. The selection enables the writer to modify the test in the direction he wants. Several properties of the total score depend upon the properties of the items that compose it: the mean, variance, form of score distribution, reliability, and validity. These features can be controlled, within the limits of the items available, by selecting items of the right average difficulty level, the right spread of difficulty, and the right degree of intercorrelations, in accordance with principles mentioned in the chapters preceding. As also indicated previously, item statistics can be used to forecast roughly the total-score statistics.

Preparation for Item Analysis. The usefulness of an item analysis and the degree of success achieved with the preliminary test form will depend upon several things under the control of the test maker. The items originally written and selected should be aimed at the kind wanted in the final form, in terms of difficulty level, spread of difficulty, and degree of intercorrelation. If the kind of items wanted in a test are not put there before the item analysis, analysis will not put them there. With ordinary skill to control these properties, one should need not more than 50 per cent more items in the preliminary form than are wanted in the final form. If one wants a range of difficulty in the final form, it is best to include relatively more easy and difficult items, since more of them are usually lost in item analysis. In a multiple-choice test one can also add an additional distracter to each item, thus trying out an extra one, and discard the worst after analysis.

There is no point in item analysis of a test that is designed as a speed test. In fact, only power tests, or those close to power tests, should be so treated. In administration of the form for item analysis, liberal time should be given. Ideally, every examinee should attempt every item. If there must be limited time so that there might be many unattempted items, steps should be taken to remedy the situation. The items might be rotated in different order for different examinees so that every item is in the last part equally often. Additional items not to be analyzed might be included at the end of the test so that "busywork" is supplied for the early finishers while the slow workers are completing the items to be analyzed. There are other possible devices for meeting this problem.

It is more important to analyze aptitude tests than achievement tests. In achievement tests it is sometimes more important to have the items approved by a subject-matter expert than to know their correlation with total score. In either kind of test, the reliability of the total score should be known; otherwise one cannot evaluate properly item-total correlations. If the score reliability is low, there is much heterogeneity and no one item will ordinarily correlate very high with it. A factor analysis or something in that direction is probably a better operation to apply, to determine whether there are possibly clusters of more internally homogeneous items to serve as new criteria for item analysis. If the reliability of the total score is very high (.90 or better), there is little chance of improving the test in this respect. Item-total correlations would not then be needed, but difficulty indices would still be useful for achieving other goals, and possibly also for increasing reliability a bit. There is little point in item analysis of the final form of a test, but if a first item analysis does not yield the kind of test form wanted, and if there is promise of further improvement, a second experimental form, with item analysis, is indicated.

Indices of Item Difficulty. When the item is scored either 0 or 1, the simplest index of its difficulty is its mean item score p. This value is also the empirical probability that the particular population involved will pass the item. It should also be pointed out that p, an average item score, is also an *average* index of difficulty for individuals. As Coombs has pointed out (14), the difficulty of an item varies for different individuals. We do not have accurate information concerning an item's difficulty for an individual. All we know is that if he passes it, the item is less difficult than his ability to cope with it, and if he fails it, is more difficult than his ability to cope with it.

While the statistic p enters into many of the formulas, as we have seen, and and it can be used to rank-order items for difficulty, it is not the best metric

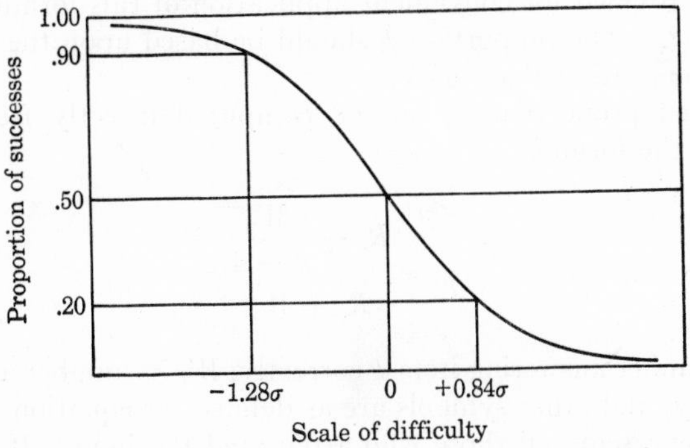

FIG. 15.1. Scale values in terms of normal-curve deviates z as measures of difficulty of items, on the assumption that proportions of correct responses are an ogive function of difficulty in a homogeneous population.

we could use. Two faults make it somewhat unsatisfactory. First, it is inversely related to difficulty and is therefore a *direct* measure of *easiness*. Second, it does not provide a linear scale of measurement; it is not linearly related to ability. The usual assumption is that probability of passing an item is a normal-ogive function of its difficulty and that difficulty is linearly related to ability.

This assumption is the key to possibility of a linear scale for difficulty. Figure 15.1 illustrates the relationship between proportion passing an item and its difficulty value expressed as a standard measure z. Positive z values are taken as corresponding to proportions less than .50 and negative values as corresponding to proportions greater than .50. By this transformation from p to z we have a rational, linear scale of difficulty with the order of values corresponding to increasing difficulty. There are two qualifications that must be mentioned. One is that such difficulty values for the same items (and their corresponding p values) will differ from one population to another, depending upon the means and standard deviations of the ability in those populations. To achieve what Thurstone (104) calls *absolute scaling* of items on a scale of common unit and origin, we can effect linear transformations. The other qualification is that with multiple-choice items or any others in which chance success is an appreciable element, a correction for chance is in order before scaling is carried out.

Correction of Proportions of Correct Responses for Chance. Since chance success inflates the proportion of obtained right answers to an item as compared with the proportion of legitimate right answers, some sort of correction is in order. Guilford (47) proposed that an obtained proportion be corrected by the equation

$$_cp = \frac{kp - 1}{k - 1} \tag{15.1}$$

where $_cp$ = proportion of correct responses corrected for chance success
p = obtained proportion
k = number of alternative responses

Table 15.1 is provided for convenient application of this formula for values of k from 2 to 5. The proportion p should be based upon the number who attempt the item rather than on N.

The corrected proportion $_cp$ can be computed directly from response-count data by the formula

$$_cp = \frac{R_i - \dfrac{W_i}{k - 1}}{R_i + W_i} \tag{15.2}$$

where R_i = number answering item I correctly, W_i = number answering the item incorrectly, and other symbols are as defined for equation (15.1). The denominator represents all those who attempted the item. If there are no unattempted items (in a completely power test), $R_i + W_i = N$, the number in the sample, for all items.

Formula (15.1) was originally designed for items like those in the Seashore tests of musical talent (pitch, loudness, and time discriminations), in which the examinee who guesses among the alternative answers should find them equally attractive. This is an important condition, for the formula rests on the assumption that either an examinee knows the right answer (or knows that the wrong answers are all wrong) or else he guesses at random. In achievement tests, particularly, we know that the responses are not all equally attractive. The examinee may know that one answer is wrong, in which case he guesses among $k - 1$ remaining choices. If he knows that two answers are wrong, he guesses among $k - 2$ remaining choices. From this point of view, because of partial knowledge the odds for chance success are increased; how much we do not know. On the other hand, actual misinformation, which increases the likelihood of avoidance of the right answer, complicates the picture. These departures from random guessing are somewhat compensatory and are individual matters, as a rule, and hence do not completely invalidate the use of the correction formula. The statistic $_cp$ is undoubtedly nearer the correct index of difficulty than is the uncorrected p. A correction is most important when we compare as to difficulty items having different numbers of alternative responses.

Horst (62) proposed an approximate solution to the guessing problem, based on a formula that requires additional response-count information. By reasoning for which there is insufficient space to report here, he derives the principle that the number who actually know the correct answer is equal to the number marking it minus the number marking the most popular incor-

TABLE 15.1. A TABLE TO FACILITATE THE CORRECTION OF THE PROPORTION OF PASSING INDIVIDUALS FOR A TEST ITEM

p Uncorrected proportion	n Number of alternatives				p Uncorrected proportion	n Number of alternatives			
	2	3	4	5		2	3	4	5
.99	.980	.985	.987	.9875	.59	.180	.385	.453	.4875
.98	.960	.970	.973	.9750	.58	.160	.370	.440	.4750
.97	.940	.955	.960	.9625	.57	.140	.355	.427	.4625
.96	.920	.940	.947	.9500	.56	.120	.340	.413	.4500
.95	.900	.925	.933	.9375	.55	.100	.325	.400	.4375
.94	.880	.910	.920	.9250	.54	.080	.310	.387	.4250
.93	.860	.895	.907	.9125	.53	.060	.295	.373	.4125
.92	.840	.880	.893	.9000	.52	.040	.280	.360	.4000
.91	.820	.865	.880	.8875	.51	.020	.265	.347	.3875
.90	.800	.850	.867	.8750	.50	.000	.250	.333	.3750
.89	.780	.835	.853	.8625	.49	.000	.235	.320	.3625
.88	.760	.820	.840	.8500	.48	.000	.220	.307	.3500
.87	.740	.805	.827	.8375	.47	....	.205	.293	.3375
.86	.720	.790	.813	.8250	.46	....	.190	.280	.3250
.85	.700	.775	.800	.8125	.45	....	.175	.267	.3125
.84	.680	.760	.787	.8000	.44	....	.160	.253	.3000
.83	.660	.745	.773	.7875	.43	....	.145	.240	.2875
.82	.640	.730	.760	.7750	.42	....	.130	.227	.2750
.81	.620	.715	.747	.7625	.41	....	.115	.213	.2625
.80	.600	.700	.733	.7500	.40	....	.100	.200	.2500
.79	.580	.685	.720	.7375	.39	....	.085	.187	.2375
.78	.560	.670	.707	.7250	.38	....	.070	.173	.2250
.77	.540	.655	.693	.7125	.37	....	.055	.160	.2125
.76	.520	.640	.680	.7000	.36	....	.040	.147	.2000
.75	.500	.625	.667	.6875	.35	....	.025	.133	.1875
.74	.480	.610	.653	.6750	.34	....	.010	.120	.1750
.73	.460	.595	.640	.6625	.33	....	.000	.107	.1625
.72	.440	.580	.627	.6500	.32	....	.000	.093	.1500
.71	.420	.565	.613	.6375	.31	....	.000	.080	.1375
.70	.400	.550	.600	.6250	.30	....	....	.067	.1250
.69	.380	.535	.587	.6125	.29	....	....	.053	.1125
.68	.360	.520	.573	.6000	.28	....	....	.040	.1000
.67	.340	.505	.560	.5875	.27	....	....	.027	.0875
.66	.320	.490	.547	.5750	.26	....	....	.013	.0750
.65	.300	.475	.533	.5625	.25	....	....	.000	.0625
.64	.280	.460	.520	.5500	.24	....	....	.000	.0500
.63	.260	.445	.507	.5375	.23	....	....	.000	.0375
.62	.240	.430	.493	.5250	.22	....	....	....	.0250
.61	.220	.415	.480	.5125	.21	....	....	....	.0125
.60	.200	.400	.467	.5000	.20	....	....	....	.0000

rect answer. This is reasonable in that by random guessing we should expect incorrect answers to be equally popular and among those marking the most popular mislead in excess of chance expectation are many who know that other responses are wrong. Horst's formula is

$$p_k = \frac{R_i - D_i}{R_i + W_i} \tag{15.3}$$

where p_k = proportion who probably know the right answer
R_i = number answering the item correctly
D_i = number giving the most popular distracter to the item as their answer
W_i = number answering the item incorrectly

If a corrected proportion should come out negative by any of these formulas, this result may indicate overcorrection for some reason. It may also mean misinformation or an overly attractive distracter or some other source of bias. If the departure from chance in the negative direction is statistically significant, it is important to look for the source of the bias.

Other Indices of Difficulty. Other indices of item difficulty have been proposed, some of which will be found described by Gulliksen (56). One additional principle might be mentioned. The item difficulty is calibrated in terms of the total-score level (or other numerical index of ability) at which the individuals of the population have a probability of .5 of success. This is a median or liminal value of the item on an arbitrary scale of ability. A still different procedure suggested by Davis (17) follows the normal-curve principle described above, but makes a linear transformation from the z scale to another that has all positive values and extends from 0 to 100 with a median of 50. The transformation equation is $d = 21.063z + 50$, where d is Davis's index of difficulty. Davis provides a table for finding d directly from p (17).

Difficulty Indices from Extreme Groups. In some methods of item analysis, the correlation r_{it} is often obtained from only part of the sample; it is obtained from those making extreme scores, for example the upper and lower 27 per cents of the sample. The proportion passing for the entire sample is then usually estimated from a combination of the extreme groups. The validity of this procedure depends upon several conditions. One is that the distributions of ability as represented by item and by total score are symmetrical. Another is that the regression is linear. Other conditions are the degree of correlation between item and total score and the distance of p from .50, as shown by Michael and Perry (86). They demonstrate that as r_{it} increases, the proportion p_t as estimated from the tails, each containing $.27N$ cases, underestimates p for the whole sample when it is above .50 and overestimates p when it is below .50. The error is less than .02 when r_{it} is not over .40, but may be as great as .12 when r_{it} is as high as .90. The error is greatest when p is in the region of .75 (or .25). Table 15.2 provides a more accurate estimate of p from p_t for various combinations of r_{it} and p_t. These corrections hold when we have a normal bivariate surface. Davis (79, p. 283) reports a correlation of .98 between p_t estimated from the 27 per cent tails and those from the entire sample. Since the errors in p_t are systematic, there could be a very high correlation between p_t and p in spite of large errors near the extremes of p.

Some Special Problems of Difficulty. Some fairly recent studies have indicated interest in measurement of difficulty from other points of view. Some have to do with the relation of difficulty, as measured above, to stimulus values of items, and some have to do with average subjective impression of difficulty.

Guilford (48) found that for the tests of sensory discrimination in the Seashore musical-aptitude series, when difficulty is scaled (from corrected proportions) in terms of z values, the ease of passing an item is proportional to the logarithm of stimulus difference. One deduction was that if the

TABLE 15.2. ESTIMATION OF PROPORTIONS OF PASSING INDIVIDUALS, p, FOR A TOTAL SAMPLE FROM PROPORTIONS p_t OBTAINED FROM THE TWO TAILS EACH CONTAINING $.27N$ OF THE CASES. FOR A p_t BELOW .5, FIND ITS COMPLEMENT AND THE COMPLEMENT OF THE p CORRESPONDING TO IT

r_{it}	p_t (Proportion estimated from tails each containing $.27N$)							
	.55	.60	.65	.70	.75	.80	.85	.90
.40	.555	.61	.66	.71	.765	.815	.865	.915
.55	.56	.62	.67	.725	.78	.83	.88	.925
.70	.57	.63	.69	.75	.81	.85	.895	.935
.80	.58	.66	.73	.78	.83	.87	.905	.94
.85	.60	.68	.745	.80	.84	.88	.915	.945
.90	.63	.72	.77	.82	.85	.885	.92	.945

sample is very large, no item becomes so easy that every examinee will pass it. Another was that there is no limit to degree of difficulty; with sample large, the (corrected) probability of a right response is not zero so long as stimulus differences are not zero. This is concordant with a statement made in Chap. 6 to the effect that even when an observer is guessing concerning differences he is more likely to be right than wrong.

Reese (95) made a comparative study of objective versus subjective difficulty. Objective difficulty was indicated by the proportion of failures. Subjective difficulty was indicated in two ways. One was by scaling items from judgments by the fractionation method and the other was in terms of proportions of felt failures. In the latter case, E said immediately after completing an item whether he had passed or failed. The items were digit series given in a memory-span test and multiple-choice vocabulary items. In both cases, subjective difficulty from the fractionation method gave an S-shaped regression of difficulty on item value (number of digits and Thorndike *IER* value, respectively). Thus subjective difficulty roughly paralleled objective difficulty. No zero for subjective difficulty could be located, and all the longest digit series seemed equally difficult.

Guilford and Cotzin (53) arrived at somewhat different conclusions in a study that involved matching to felt difficulty of lifting weights. The subjective difficulty of lifting weights was proportional to the logarithm of the weights. The felt difficulty of judging the Seashore items was proportional to the logarithm of their objective difficulty values (scaled from corrected proportions of right responses). Different kinds of tonal items of equal objective difficulty tended to be matched to the same lifted weights, indicating some generality of subjective standards of difficulty.

Indices of Item Validity. We shall interpret validity broadly here to include the relation of an item to the total score of its test. There are numerous indices and procedures for determining item validity. The more common ones fall roughly into four groups. One approach uses a measure of precision, in line with the theory that the probability of passing an item is an ogive function of ability. A second approach stresses the numbers of discriminations of the desired sort that the item is capable of making. It emphasizes the extent to which the item predicts segregation of examinees into those with high versus those with low criterion scores. The third approach, which correlates the item with the criterion score in some way, is probably the most popular one. The fourth approach is by way of analysis of variance.

Psychometric Precision of Items. Ferguson (30) proposed that the processes of the method of constant stimuli be adapted to the study of items. Ferguson first subdivides the sample on the basis of total scores into seven groups, at intervals of $.6\sigma_t$. He next determines the proportion of each subgroup who pass the item. The proportions are usually an ogive function of the ability scale as expressed in the seven subgroups. The procedures for computing a mean and a standard deviation for an item are numerous (see Chap. 6).

Ferguson points out several advantages of this method. It describes the difficulty level and the standard deviation on the same scale. It enables us to state the probabilities of an item being passed at different levels of ability. Finney (33) agrees concerning the virtues of this general approach, but proposes the substitution of his probit-analysis process (see Chap. 6), which has the advantages of better indices of reliability of mean and of standard deviation. Applying this process to some items to which Ferguson had applied the constant process, Finney obtained almost identical results.

It can be predicted that very few test makers will want to devote so much effort to the study of items. If they did, they should probably want to substitute the index of precision h for the standard deviation of the item, since h is *directly* proportional to the degree to which the item discriminates among those above and below its median.[1] Turnbull (109) has proposed a graphic procedure based on the same principles. If one decides to use the constant method, it is recommended that a graphic process using normal probability paper be utilized. Turnbull's process also yields an estimate of correlation of item with criterion, but if a correlation coefficient is what one wants, there are more efficient methods for computing it. The chief value in applying any form of the constant processes would be to establish a graded series of items from which limen scores for individuals are to be derived.

Indices of Discrimination between High and Low Groups. A very common step is to divide the total sample into two groups on the basis of the criterion, not into several as the preceding approach requires. The most obvious

[1] See Chap. 6 for an explanation of the statistic h.

question is whether the two groups, which may be upper and lower halves or quarters or other proportions of equal numbers, behave differently with respect to the item. The simplest index from this source is the difference $p_u - p_l$, where p_u and p_l are proportions of passing examinees in upper and lower groups, respectively. An easily obtained derivative of this difference is $z_u - z_l$, where z_u and z_l are the normal-curve deviates corresponding to p_u and p_l. This method is advocated by Lawshe (71) who prepared a nomograph for graphic solutions. The method is sometimes called the *D* method and the index $D = z_u - z_l$.

Johnson (65) puts the upper-lower difference $p_u - p_l$ in a form more convenient for computing by using the formula

$$ULI = \frac{R_u - R_l}{f} \tag{15.4}$$

where ULI = upper-lower index
R_u, R_l = numbers giving right answer in upper and lower groups, respectively
f = number of examinees in each group

Johnson recommends using 27 per cent in each group, in which case $f = .27N$. He provides a standard error formula for the *ULI*, which reads

$$\sigma_{ULI} = \frac{1}{f}\sqrt{R_u + R_l - \frac{R^2_u + R^2_l}{f}} \tag{15.5}$$

Where the difference $p_u - p_l$ is used as the index, an ordinary critical-ratio test can be applied to determine the significance of the difference in proportions. Mosier and McQuitty (88) have published an abac for graphic solution for the critical ratio in the item-analysis situation. A chi-square test can also be applied to the frequencies R_u and R_l, the results of which would tell the same story as the critical ratio. Guilford has shown (49) that when we know the proportions who pass the item in equal upper and lower criterion groups, the formula for chi square reduces to

$$\chi^2 = \frac{N(p_u - p_l)^2}{4pq} \tag{15.6}$$

where p may be taken as the arithmetic mean of p_u and p_l, and $q = 1 - p$. Fulcher and Zubin (39) have described a machine they devised for automatic computations of chi square in item analysis. Guilford (49) has also presented an abac for determining under limited conditions whether the difference $p_u - p_l$ yields a significant chi square. Davis (79, p. 290) describes a chi test attributed to Cureton, which is especially convenient when samples are small.

The uses of the critical ratio and chi square in item analysis have limitations. These statistics are sampling statistics whose primary purpose is to test hypotheses. It is true that with N constant their relative values can be used to compare the items as to discriminating power. They cannot be used to compare items in this respect where N's differ.

Some methods of item analysis do not divide the sample into two *equal* groups, upper and lower, on the basis of the criterion score. The segregation is on the basis of item score, separating the passers from the failers. From this point on there are several routes to an index of item effectiveness. Most of them are based upon the mean total scores for the two item groups. If we call these means M_p and M_q, for passers and failers, respectively, the simple difference $M_p - M_q$ is an immediate index. If this is zero or if it is so small as to be statistically insignificant, the conclusion can well be that the item is invalid. The greater the difference, the better the item. The rationale for this index is that taking the total score as the criterion measure of ability, the most probable ability of those passing the item, in the least-square sense, is indicated by M_p and the most probable ability of those failing the item is indicated by M_q. This is a simple prediction problem in which a measurement is predicted from category membership (see 51, p. 389).

In computing a critical ratio for the difference $M_p - M_q$, the fact of spurious overlap of item score with total score and the consequent lack of experimental independence of the two makes a slight correction necessary. If the item in question were omitted in computing the means, M_q would remain unchanged, because all the failers have item scores of zero in the item, but M_p would be reduced one unit, because all passers have item scores of 1 in it. The standard deviation σ_p is unaffected, since adding or subtracting a constant from all total scores does not change this statistic. The difference between means to be tested, therefore, is $M_p - M_q - 1$. Everything else proceeds as usual.

A variant of the mean-difference index is what Vernon (110) calls the *d* method. The index is the difference $M_p - M_q$ divided by σ_t, the standard deviation of total scores. Such an index is perfectly correlated with the difference $M_p - M_q$, and would therefore seem to have no advantages and requires an extra computing step. It should be said that Vernon points out (110) that the *d* index favors the selection of items deviating far from median difficulty. This should also be true of the difference $M_p - M_q$. Unless one wanted a test of this type, which is very unlikely, these methods would be among the least preferred.

Index of Homogeneity of Item with Test. Loevinger (80) has proposed an index of homogeneity of an item with total score in keeping with her homogeneity theory (see Chap. 13). A perfectly homogeneous item is such that those passing it all have higher scores than those failing it. A perfectly heterogeneous item is one such that the total scores of those passing and those failing are distributed at random. The index she uses is a modification of one previously developed by Long (82). It reads

$$H_{it} = 1 - \frac{2\Sigma \text{ ``passes'' below or tied with ``fails''}}{PQ - \Sigma \text{ ``passes'' one above ``fails''}} \tag{15.7}$$

where H_{it} = Loevinger's index of homogeneity of item with total score
P = *number* of "passes" regardless of total score
Q = *number* of "fails"

In a completely power test, $P + Q = N$. The numerator shows the amount of confusion among total scores of those who passed the item and those who failed it. If there were none of the passers below or tied with the failers, the numerator would be zero and H_{it} would equal 1.0.

Correlation Indices of Item Validity. Four coefficients of correlation are commonly used to indicate the correlation of an item with a criterion. They are the *biserial r*, *point-biserial r*, *tetrachoric r*, and the *phi coefficient.*

If we are interested in the correlation between the variable that the item measures and the continuous criterion measure, and if we may assume that the thing measured by the item is continuously and normally distributed in the population, the biserial r is the coefficient we want. If the criterion variable is also normally distributed in the population, it can be dichotomized and a tetrachoric r may be computed. If we are interested in how well we can predict the criterion from the item or how much it can contribute to a total score, with its own score limited to 0 and 1, the point-biserial r is the coefficient to compute. The test theory that regards a total score as the summation of item scores assumes this type of correlation. If the criterion is not a continuous variable but a natural division into two groups, the phi coefficient is called for. The phi coefficient may be applied also when the total-score distribution is arbitrarily dichotomized at some cutting score because the test will be used to discriminate at that same level.

1. *The Biserial r in Item Analysis.* The best formula to use for the biserial r in the item-analysis application is

$$r_b = \frac{M_p - M_t}{\sigma_t} \frac{p}{y} \tag{15.8}$$

where M_p = mean criterion score of those passing item
M_t = mean criterion score of all examinees
σ_t = standard deviation of all total scores
p = proportion passing item
y = ordinate in unit normal distribution corresponding to p

Where complete power conditions do not prevail, it would be best to use only statistics based on those who attempted the item. This would mean the M_t and σ_t will vary for some items. The statistics M_p, p, and y differ for all items except by chance.

The standard error for r_b to use in testing for significant departure from a correlation of zero can be estimated by the formula

$$\sigma_{r_b} = \frac{1}{\sqrt{N}} \frac{\sqrt{pq}}{y} \qquad (r_b = 0) \tag{15.9}$$

where σ_{r_b} = standard error of a biserial r of zero, N = number of examinees in the sample, $q = 1 - p$, and other terms are as defined in (15.8).

2. *The Point-biserial r.* The formula for the point-biserial r adapted to item analysis is parallel with formula (15.8). It reads

$$r_{pbi} = \frac{M_p - M_t}{\sigma_t} \sqrt{\frac{p}{q}} \tag{15.10}$$

where symbols are as defined in (15.8) and (15.9). The computation of r_{pbi} involves the same amount of work as for r_b and the same comment concerning using the number attempting each item applies.

Suggestions for computing the biserial coefficients more efficiently have been made by Adkins and Toops (4), DuBois (18), and Siegel and Cureton

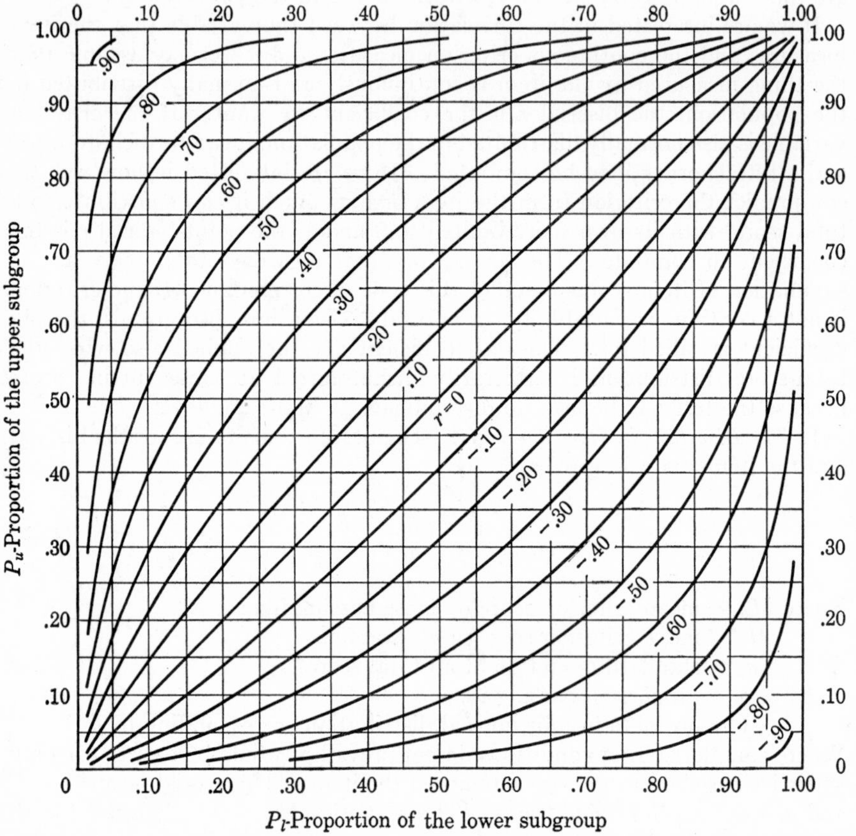

FIG. 15.2. An abac for estimating biserial coefficients of correlation between item and total score when the sample has been restricted to the highest and lowest 27 per cent of the total-score distribution. The proportion of examinees passing the item in the upper criterion group, p_u, is found on the ordinate, and the corresponding proportion from the lower criterion group, p_l, is found on the abscissa. The coefficient r_b is found at the intersection of perpendiculars at these values. Thus, with p_u equal to .75 and p_l equal to .45, $r_b = .31$. (*Adapted from a similar abac by J. C. Flanagan, with his permission.*)

(98). Goheen and Davidoff (43) have presented a graphic method for which all one needs to know for an item is M_p and p. The most efficient method for estimating r_b for an item is to use Flanagan's abac (34). This instrument is designed for use when the middle 46 per cent of the examinees on total score have been eliminated and each tail contains 27 per cent. The only information one needs to use in entering the chart includes p_u and p_l, the proportions passing the item in the upper and lower tails, respectively. The choice of 27 per cent in each tail was determined by Kelley's demonstration

(69) that with this tail proportion the coefficient is most sensitive. On the other hand, this procedure loses 46 per cent of the data. It is recommended that the Flanagan r be used when 100 cases remain in each tail, which means examining a sample of approximately 370. A modified Flanagan chart is given in Fig. 15.2.

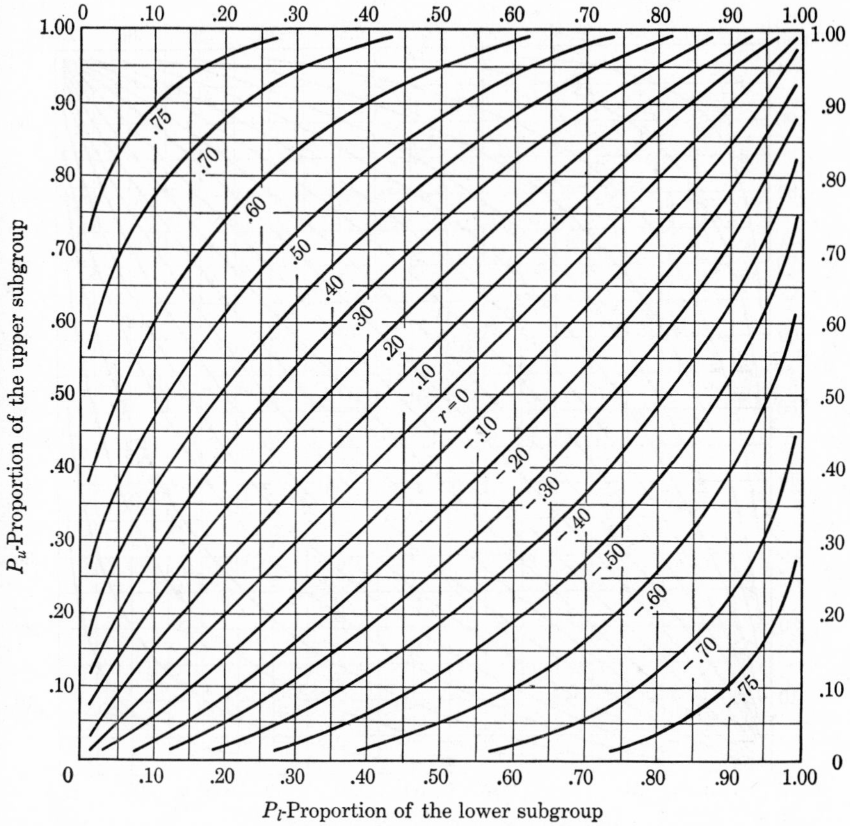

FIG. 15.3. An abac for estimates of the point-biserial r when one variable is divided at the median of the distribution. Used similarly to the abac in Fig. 15.2. (*Prepared by Harvey F. Dingman.*)

Davis (17) has adopted the practice of transforming the Flanagan r into Fisher's Z statistic[1] and then by linear transformation arriving at a correlation index on a scale from 0 to 100. The advantages claimed for this scale are that it has equal units and normal sampling distributions. This makes possible a ready arithmetical averaging of coefficients and also convenient tests of statistical significance.

The correlation r_{pbi} can be estimated from the biserial r by the relationship

$$r_{pbi} = r_b \frac{y}{\sqrt{pq}} \tag{15.11}$$

[1] See Guilford (51, p. 212).

where y, p, and q are as defined in (15.8) and (15.9). Since under the assumptions for computing a tetrachoric r the latter is comparable with r_b, a tetrachoric r can be substituted for r_b in (15.11). The coefficient r_{pbi} can also be estimated from phi, as Michael, Perry, and Guilford (87) have shown, though not so conveniently as by formula (15.11). The most economical estimate of r_{pbi} can be made by using the abac in Fig. 15.3.[1]

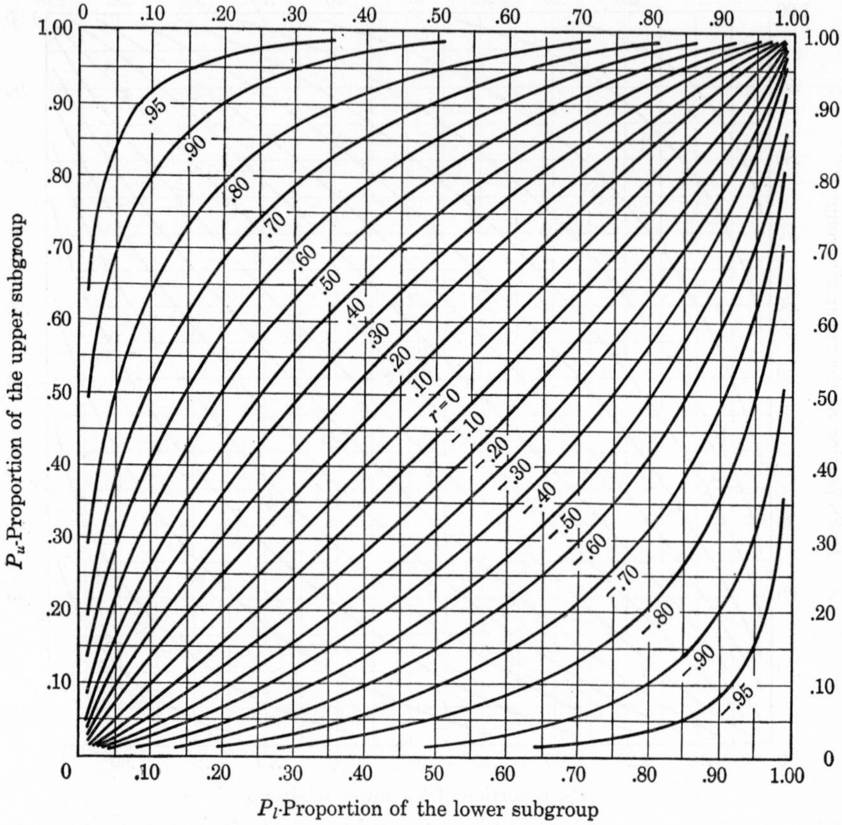

FIG. 15.4. An abac for graphic estimates of the tetrachoric r when one variable has been divided at the median of the distribution. Used similarly to the abac in Fig. 15.2. (*Prepared from the Pearson tables of r_t by Harvey F. Dingman.*)

3. *The Tetrachoric r.* The use of the tetrachoric r in item analysis would be prohibitive without computing aids. There are a number of such aids available. Mosier and McQuitty (88) have prepared an abac designed for use in item analysis, for which only p_u and p_l need to be known. A similar abac is presented in Fig. 15.4. The total-score distribution must be dichotomized at the median. N should be large, preferably as large as 400, due to the large sampling error of r_t.

The standard error of r_t for a correlation of zero can be estimated by the formula

[1] This abac is based upon the relationship given in equation (15.11).

$$\sigma_{r_t} = \frac{1.253}{\sqrt{N}} \frac{\sqrt{pq}}{y} \qquad (r_t = 0) \tag{15.12}$$

where σ_{r_t} equals standard error of a tetrachoric r of zero and other symbols are as defined in formula (15.9).

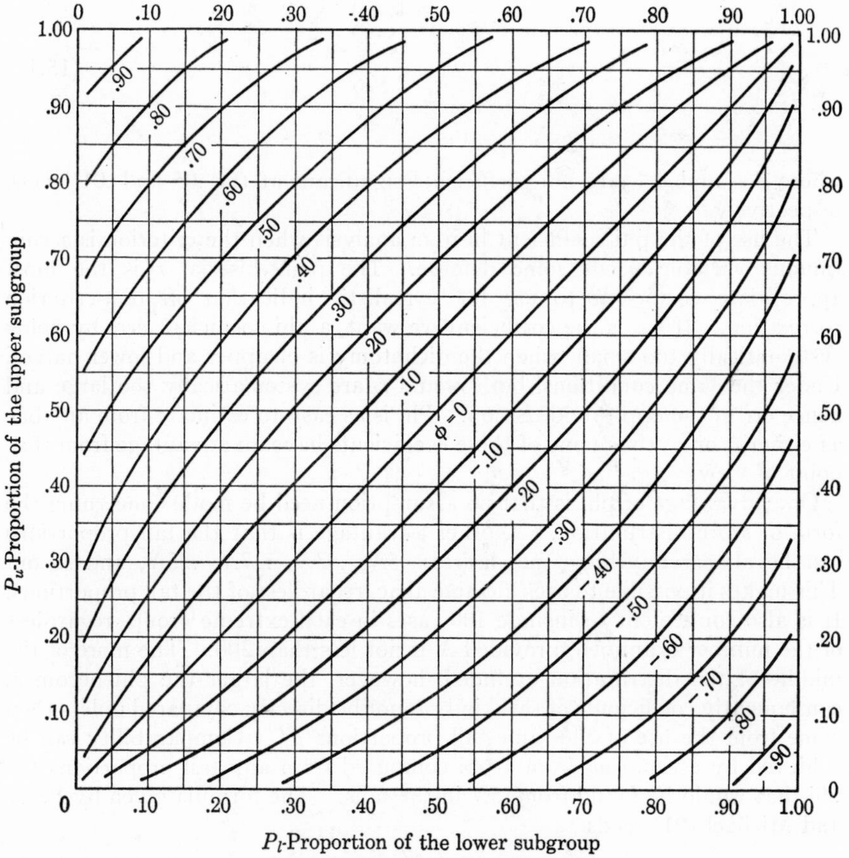

FIG. 15.5. An abac for graphic estimates of the phi coefficient when one variable has an even division of cases in two categories. Used similarly to the abac in Fig. 15.2.

4. *The Phi Coefficient.* In the item-analysis situation, where upper and lower groups are equal in number, Guilford (49) has shown that the formula for the phi coefficient simplifies to

$$\phi = \frac{p_u - p_l}{2\sqrt{pq}} \tag{15.13}$$

where the symbols are as defined previously, particularly with formula (15.6). An abac for solving for phi, given p_u and p_l, is presented in Fig. 15.5. Jurgensen (67) has published tables for facilitating the computation of phi.

A very ready test of the hypothesis of zero correlation can be made through the fact of the close relation of phi to chi square. With one degree of freedom, a chi square of 3.841 is significant at the .05 level and a chi square of 6.635 is significant at the .01 level. Since $\phi^2 = \chi^2/N$, a ϕ significant at either the .05 or the .01 level can be stated by the equations

$$\phi_{.05} = \frac{1.960}{\sqrt{N}} \qquad \phi_{.01} = \frac{2.576}{\sqrt{N}} \tag{15.14}$$

where $\phi_{.05}$ and $\phi_{.01}$ are phi coefficients significant at the .05 and .01 levels, respectively.

The use of the phi coefficient in item analysis when the criterion is a continuous variable needs some defense. The point-biserial r is the most appropriate coefficient to use for a realistic indication of item-criterion correlation. If r_{pbi} is the coefficient we want, a phi coefficient errs by being systematically too small, when the dichotomy is of upper and lower halves. Under the same conditions, both r_b and r_t are systematically too large and hence err in the opposite direction. Phi is as easy to estimate from an abac as either r_b or r_t; thus none of these coefficients have an advantage from that point of view.

One advantage of phi is that no assumption need be made concerning the form of score distribution. Another advantage is that the tail proportions can be almost anything one desires—$.5N$, $.33N$, $.27N$, $.25N$, and so on. This makes it possible to use the same abac, regardless of the tail proportions. It is also convenient to include 100 cases in each extreme group, regardless of the number examined, provided N is not less than 200. The more of the middle of the distribution excluded, however, the larger the phi becomes; consequently coefficients of this kind cannot be directly compared unless they come from the use of the same tail proportions p''. Comparability can be achieved by estimating from a phi computed from any tail proportions the phi that would be found from $.5N$ in the tails. The formula given by Perry and Michael (91) reads

$$\phi_{.5} \doteq \frac{p''}{1.253 y_{p''}} \phi_{p''} \tag{15.15}$$

where $\phi_{.5}$ = phi coefficient to be expected from two halves of the total-score distribution, when

p'' = proportion of sample in each tail for computing $\phi_{p''}$ [by formula (15.13) or from the abac]

$y_{p''}$ = ordinate in the unit normal distribution curve marking off p'' of the cases from the rest

A certain peculiarity of ϕ makes it especially desirable in many situations but also undesirable in others. This is the fact that ϕ can be at its maximum between any two variables only when they are both of equal difficulty, or when $p = p'$, as was pointed out in connection with formula (13.34). Since the criterion is usually dichotomized at $p' = .50$, items of median difficulty can have, and will tend to have, the higher correlations and hence will tend to be selected for retention in the test. Since such items contribute most to internal-consistency reliability, this is a desirable feature of phi. The use of r_{pbi} tends to have the same effect, though to a smaller extent. If one wished to construct a test that would discriminate best at some other level, say at $p = .25$, the criterion group should be dichotomized with 25 per cent in the upper group and 75 per cent in the lower group. Items of the same difficulty level would be favored when phi is the coefficient used. This feature of phi is a disadvantage when we want to retain items of extreme difficulty or when we want to know which of such items are worth saving. Such items could probably be made more valid if their difficulty were moderated in revision.

There are several possibilities for determining which items of extreme difficulty are promising or worth keeping. One method would be to compute a biserial r or a tetrachoric r for such items, since these coefficients are not affected by difficulty level, under ordinary conditions. Some investigators favor computing both phi and either r_b or r_t for each item as a routine practice, for the benefit of the two kinds of information they provide. Another method would be to compute the ratio of phi to the maximum phi that could happen at the particular level of difficulty of the item.[1] The ratio $\phi/\phi_{max.}$ indicates how much of the available range for phi under these conditions is used by the obtained phi. Similar uses of this ratio have been proposed by Johnson (66) and Loevinger (81). Still another method would be to dichotomize the criterion distribution at a different place for each item so that the proportion in the upper criterion group equals the proportion passing the item. This procedure would entail so much labor that either of the other two should be preferred. Perhaps the best solution to this problem is to use the point-biserial r, which has some of the phi coefficient's property of favoring items of moderate difficulty and yet not enough to lead to the discarding of really good items with difficulties away from the median.

Factor Analysis of Items. Where there is doubt concerning the psychological homogeneity of the items or where item-total correlations tend to be low, some steps should be taken to divide the test into subtests, each of greater homogeneity. This assumes that scores with high internal consistency are desired. The best approach, but one that is usually prohibitive, is factor analysis of the items. If the number of items is small, or if one can select a limited number that appear to represent hypothesized factors, an analysis might not be too costly. The coefficient of correlation between items should be the tetrachoric, since it is the nature of common traits in which we are interested in this instance. The use of phi coefficients would introduce variations in correlations due to differences in difficulty levels and hence so-called "difficulty factors." Vernon has applied factor analysis in connection with items (111). He concluded that one could do about as well with ordinary item analysis. But his method of analysis emphasized a single common

[1] The computation of $\phi_{max.}$ is given by formula (13.34). For an abac for giving $\phi_{max.}$, see Guilford (51, p. 344).

factor, the condition in which the factor-analysis approach is not particularly needed in the study of items.

Other devices aimed at the accomplishment of the same general goal short of factor analysis have been suggested. Wherry, Campbell, and Perloff (114) have proposed a method of successive item analyses. The steps are briefly as follows:

1. Find the item-total coefficients.
2. Group the items with highest coefficients to form a new test.
3. Using the new total score, find new item-total coefficients.
4. Add to the new test items that gain in r_{it} and drop those that lose in r_{it}.
5. Continue until results stabilize, that is, r_{it} changes very little.
6. Examine rejected items and form new homogeneous-looking subtests.
7. Repeat steps 3 to 5 in each subgroup.

Lentz and Whitmer (74) earlier proposed a method they called *item synonymization.* The steps were much the same as those just described, that is, successive item analyses with changing criterion scores, except that these investigators begin with a single selected item in building up a "synonymy." The final goal is a set of tests each with high reliability and low correlation with other tests.

Neither of these methods will necessarily produce univocal tests in the sense that each measures only one common factor. In working toward greater reliability, the items selected will have increasing similarity of factor content, but this communality may be a combination of common factors. If one common factor should dominate a test at the start, the test would probably change toward greater purity for that factor as the items are successively analyzed. But the chances are against this kind of situation. Where one is not particularly concerned about univocal scores, these methods should still achieve the practical goal of reliable and relatively independent scores.

Analysis of Variance in Item Analysis. In 1938, Lev (76) proposed that the operations of analysis of variance be adapted to item analysis. Baker (6) followed with a step-by-step outline of the procedures involved. The chief advantage claimed is that the method extracts the utmost amount of information from the data. The labor involved is great, and unless more than ordinary use is to be made of the information obtained, this procedure cannot be highly recommended.

Some Evaluation of Item-analysis Procedures. Some generalizations can be made with respect to the dependability and the comparative values of the different methods of item analysis. First, it can be said that indices of difficulty are much more stable than indices of item validity. From the reports of Gibbons (40) and Carter (11) one may conclude that indices of difficulty are highly consistent from sample to sample even with N as low as 50. Indices of item validity that they reported, however, tend to be much less consistent from sample to sample (correlations of the order of .50 to .60, even with an N of about 400). The type of index of validity used was unlike any described above, for the one investigator, and not stated for the other.

The type of test and of tested population would undoubtedly have bearings on the stability of item indices. In a certain Army Air Force investigation (54), a test was administered to two samples of about 400 each. Item-total correlations were computed by means of the tetrachoric *r*, biserial *r*, point-biserial *r*, phi coefficient based on upper and lower halves and also on the upper and lower 27 per cents, and the Flanagan *r*. The correlation of each index in the two samples was computed and found to range from .79 to .91, the tetrachoric *r* showing the least stability and the phi coefficient (the upper and lower 27 per cents) the most.

As to the item-validity index to use, there is little choice in terms of end results. In the same AAF study just cited (54), the intercorrelations of the indices for the 68-item test ranged from .88 to .98. The larger correlations between indices tended to depend upon which data were used, all of them or the extreme 54 per cent. The items are therefore in approximately the same rank order for validity index, no matter which coefficient is used. The main difference would be that the point-biserial *r* and phi would tend to lead to the selection of items of moderate difficulty, whereas the other indices would not favor any particular difficulty level if the total-score distribution is symmetrical.

Other studies bear out these conclusions concerning the similar item validities from different coefficients, among them being investigations by Lawshe and Mayer (72), Ely (24), and Kuang (70). These studies sometimes included other indices as well, for example, Lawshe's *D* method, per cent difference, and probit analysis. The same items tended to be selected to form shorter tests, regardless of the index used. In terms of reliability of resulting test scores, no method seems significantly and consistently better than others. The size of the tail samples seems to bear no consistent relationship to reliability or to items selected, where this was varied from 10 per cent to 50 per cent.

In terms of labor, the constant method, the probit method, and analysis of variance require by far the greatest time and effort. Methods using evenly dichotomized total-score groups require the least work. Since they give results consistent with costlier methods, they should be preferred. The ready availability of a standard error of an index is important, especially to determine whether the item discriminates significantly better than chance. The most efficient, meaningful, and useful indices, in view of what is ordinarily done with them, are the tetrachoric *r*, ϕ, and the point-biserial *r* estimated as recommended in this chapter. Of these, the point-biserial *r* should usually be preferred if only one coefficient is obtained. The point-biserial *r* has lacked a standard-error formula, but it has been demonstrated recently that for a hypothesized r_{pbi} of zero the same confidence limits may be applied to this statistic that apply to the Pearson product-moment *r* (see Table D in the Appendix).[1]

Some Special Problems in Item Analysis. Most of the methods mentioned above were devised for items answered under power conditions where chance success is almost nil. Unfortunately, there is some speeding in most tests, and some form of multiple-choice item is commonly preferred. We shall

[1] From a personal communication from Dr. Norman C. Perry.

have to consider modifications of item-analysis procedures to meet these conditions. We shall also have to face the fact that when the total-test score is the criterion, the item-total correlation is spurious due to overlap of specific and error variances in the item. There is also the problem of shrinkage. When we select the items with the highest item-total correlations, many of these correlations are inflated from favorable sampling errors; we do not know which ones. In functioning in a new test, such items lead to disappointments in terms of lower total-score reliabilities than we would expect.

Effects of Speed upon Item Indices. In the discussion of indices of difficulty it was pointed out that the proportion passing an item should be the ratio of those passing to those *attempting* it. This appears reasonable and simple, but if there are many unattempted items those nearest the end of the test have the largest number of drop-out examinees. The drop-out examinees tend to have lower total scores; therefore as we approach the end of the test, the population becomes an increasingly different one. It is probably a more able one. With the mean ability level of the population going up, difficulty indices (p) for the last items are not comparable with those attempted by all examinees. They tend to become larger as the population becomes more able. The items thus seem to be easier. If one chooses the other alternative, of making N the base for every proportion p, the value of p becomes progressively smaller for the last items. This apparent increase in difficulty is largely due to the position of an item in the test, rather than to its intrinsic difficulty. The best solution is to use power tests or to use some device to see that all items are about equally often attempted.

Speed in a test also affects item-total correlations, sometimes very drastically. For an item near the end of a test, almost none of the low criterion group may have attempted the item and those who have are not good representatives of their group. Probably all of the upper criterion group have attempted the item. The correlation for this item is based on a different population than that for items attempted by everybody, including the least able. The correlation would probably be biased downward, since the upper portion of the low group who pass the item are more like the upper group than is the entire lower group. If those who did not attempt the item are counted as failing (it is, of course, gross error to say that never having attempted an item is the same as failing it), the correlation r_{it} may be very high, even though there is no genuine correlation between item and total score. This kind of outcome for late items in speeded tests was strikingly demonstrated by Wesman (112). Such a correlation is likely to tell us more about the position of the item in the test than about its intrinsic relation to the criterion. Again, we see the need of power conditions for item analysis.

Effects of Chance Success on Item Analysis. The question of effects of chance on indices of *difficulty* was sufficiently well covered in earlier discussion. We still have to consider the effects of chance success on validity indices, particularly those in the correlation family. The effect on the difference $p_u - p_l$ (as an index of item validity) when the correction formula (15.1) is applied does not change matters so long as the number of alternatives k is constant, for the equation relating ${}_cp$ to p is a linear transformation. The comparisons of such differences between items where k

varies might make some changes in relative item validities. Since k is usually constant within the same test, this is unimportant. The effect of correction for chance upon the D coefficient, where $D = z_u - z_l$, would make some difference, depending upon the nearness of p_u and p_l to .5 and whether they are on the same side of .5 or straddle it.

The effects of chance success on coefficients of correlation have been investigated by Carroll (10). In general, coefficients of correlation are lowered to the extent that chance affects scores. Chance success contributes error variance, and this attenuates intercorrelations, as we saw in Chap. 14. We must penetrate the problem more deeply to understand the effects on item-total correlations. The parameter of item difficulty has much to do with the problem. As item difficulty increases, the amount of guessing increases, and the element of chance success increases in importance. Examinees who know all the answers make perfect scores, and chance success plays no role in them. Examinees who know all except 10 of the answers and who guess on the remaining 10 items will have scores of $n - 10 + e$, where e is a chance increment. We may assume that the distribution of e is binomial, and if the items are of the two-choice type, e varies from 0 to 10, with a mean of 5 and probabilities of the various increments in accord with the binomial expansion. For examinees who may know none of the answers but guess on all of the items, in such a test their scores are expected to give a binomial distribution about a mean of $n/2$. Thus, the more difficult the test for the population, the larger is the element of chance and the lower will be the correlation between that test and anything else.

In item analysis this has several implications. The most obvious one is that in a difficult test where chance is important, we have a less reliable criterion with which to correlate items. The same principle holds for items. For a difficult item, chance has much to do with the proportion passing it, and the lower the proportion who know the answer, the greater is the role of chance.

One remedy might be to correct each proportion that enters into the computation of a correlation coefficient for chance. This would give the estimated proportion of those who know the answer, with the reservations expressed in connection with item-difficulty indices above. Davis (17) recommends this step in connection with his use of the Flanagan r. The same step can be used in connection with r_t from Fig. 15.4. In Table 15.3 we can see what happens to r_t as corrected proportions p_u and p_l are used. The

TABLE 15.3. EFFECTS OF CORRECTING PROPORTIONS OF PASSING INDIVIDUALS IN UPPER AND LOWER GROUPS UPON THE TETRACHORIC r ESTIMATED FROM THEM

	Without Correction				With Correction			
	Pass	Fail	Both		Pass	Fail	Both	
Upper	.40	.10	.50	$p_u = .80$	.30	.20	.50	$_cp_u = .60$
Lower	.30	.20	.50	$p_l = .60$	.10	.40	.50	$_cp_l = .20$
Both	.70	.30	1.00	$r_t = .35$	.40	.60	1.00	$r_t = .62$
	p	q			$_cp$	$_cq$		

uncorrected proportions are .80 and .60, respectively. With correction on the assumption of two-choice items the proportions become .60 and .20.

The r_t without correction is .35; with correction, .62. If the items were of the five-choice type, the correlation would increase from .35 to .40.

Correction for chance success is important in the criterion score as well as in the item. This can be effected by using the ordinary correction equation, which is formula (15.24). This step would be more important when the total range of scores is used than when the middle is left out. Among the above-median scores are some for examinees who got there by lucky guessing. Among the below-median scores are some for examinees who refrained from guessing, even possibly when they should not have done so. With the middle group left out, there is little likelihood of these inversions in true rank order of examinees. This would be one argument for using only tail groups in item analysis, even when scores are corrected for chance. Even when there is correction, overcorrections and undercorrections may throw some examinees on the wrong side of the median.

The corrections suggested in connection with r_t, like the use of r_t in general, imply that we are interested in knowing how much the thing measured by the item relates to the thing measured by the test. The correction in p_u or in p_l is designed to indicate proportions actually knowing the answers. The correlation resulting is an indication of what we might expect to obtain if items were not of the type in which chance success is a contributor to score variances. If we want to know how well this item, fallible as it is, due to the chance element, correlates with this total score, also fallible due to chance, we would correlate without making corrections for chance. When we want to use the point-biserial r as the r_{it} index, for example, because of its realistic descriptive properties, we would not correct for chance, with one possible exception. It would depend upon what total score we want to predict from item scores, the one with or without correction. It can be argued that even if we plan later to use a total score without correction we may want to apply the correction during item analysis in order to achieve the best kind of separation into two criterion groups. Without correction of this kind, we have some bold or lucky guessers among the high group and some timid or unlucky guessers among the low group. We are not particularly interested in selecting items to predict boldness versus timidity in connection with guessing in a test. When the middle group is excluded in item analysis, the question of whether to correct or not to correct the total score becomes rather academic.

Bryan, Burke, and Stewart (8) studied the effects on r_{it} (biserial r) when either total score or item mean was or was not corrected for chance in several achievement tests. Correction of total scores only did not change the average r_{it} index except this was somewhat lower in the more difficult tests. Correction of item proportions increased consistently the average r_{it} indices whether the total scores were corrected or not. In the easier tests, the r_{it} indices were very highly correlated (.94 to .98) before and after correction of total scores, whether the item proportions were corrected or not. For difficult tests, there were much lower consistencies in r_{it} before and after correction of total scores (correlations .64 to .80). The most striking thing about the results is the extent to which test difficulty affects item-analysis results when chance is a factor.

Plumlee (94) made a study of the loss in r_{it} due to chance in five-choice tests as compared with completion tests of parallel contents. The mean coefficients r_b were .08 higher for the completion forms than for the multiple-choice forms. On the basis of predictions based on the effects to be expected from chance, the difference should have been .13. Thus one may conclude that under her conditions the corrections for chance probably overcorrect, and that with five-choice items and with tests not too difficult the need for correction is not very great.

If items are to be intercorrelated when chance is an element, as in preparation for a factor analysis, one should by all means correct for chance before computing tetrachoric r's. The procedure for this is described by Carroll (10).

Correction of Item-total Correlations for Spurious Overlap. When an item is correlated with the total score of which it is a part, the value of r_{it} tends to be inflated. The shorter the test, the greater this inflation is likely to be. Even if all the items correlated actually zero with what the total score measures, and if all item variances were equal, each item would correlate to the extent of $1/\sqrt{n}$, where n is the number of items. Under these conditions, with 25 items r_{it} would be .20 for all items. This is slightly above the .01 confidence level for a sample of good size and it might therefore be taken as indicating a significant correlation if one were not aware of the possible spurious origin.

Zubin faced this problem in 1934 (115) with solutions that do not seem to have been followed up or generally applied. In connection with the critical-ratio method discussed above, his correction for overlap was incorporated in the equation. More recently the writer developed independently equations for applying corrections to r_b and r_{pbi} after they have been computed (52). Since these two coefficients can be estimated in convenient ways described above, these correction formulas will be presented, rather than the Zubin formulas. For the corrected biserial r, we have

$$ {}_b r_{ir} = \frac{r_b \sigma_t - \dfrac{pq}{y}}{\sqrt{\sigma^2_t + \left(\dfrac{pq}{y}\right)^2 - 2r_b\sigma_t \dfrac{pq}{y}}} \tag{15.16} $$

where ${}_b r_{ir}$ = a biserial correlation corrected for spurious item-total overlap and other symbols are as defined in equation (15.8). The expression pq/y is the standard deviation of an item on the scale of which the distribution is normal and on which the means of passers and failers are one unit apart.[1] The ratio pq/y may be found in Table G in the Appendix, for various values of p.

For the corrected point-biserial r, the equation is similar, the difference being that the standard deviation of the item is $\sqrt{pq}$ instead of pq/y.

$$ {}_{pbi} r_{ir} = \frac{r_{pbi}\sigma_t - \sqrt{pq}}{\sqrt{\sigma^2_t + pq - 2r_{pbi}\sigma_t \sqrt{pq}}} \tag{15.17} $$

[1] I am indebted to Dr. Norman C. Perry for this suggestion.

Abacs for the use of formula (15.17) have been published by Guilford (52). The chief contributor to spuriousness in either r_b or r_{pbi} is the ratio of the item variance to the total-score variance. The larger the item variance relative to the total variance, the greater the need for correction. In using these formulas, it should be remembered that the resulting correlation is between the item and the sum of the remaining $n - 1$ items. This may require some minor adjustments when further operations are applied to the correlation data.

Cross Validation in Item Analysis. The need for cross validation is even greater in connection with item analysis than it is in connection with a test battery (68). Shrinkage in correlations is relatively greater with items than with total-test scores because their number is so much larger and more degrees of freedom are lost. The selection of items brings into the revised test many items with chance-inflated correlations, and, the more selectivity, the greater the shrinkage. Cureton (79) cites a minor study in which artificial scores were obtained for 29 "students" by flipping a coin to decide the answer to each of 85 items. The "best" 24 items were selected on the basis of correlations with grade-point averages. The correlation of the "scores" with the criterion was .82. The reliability of the "test" was zero. The validity is, of course, entirely spurious. In a new sample such a correlation would shrink to about zero.

A double cross validation is recommended wherever possible in item analysis. This may reduce the size of N for any one analysis, but by applying a test of significance that uses compound probability the chances of finding significantly correlated items is perhaps better than if one combined sample were used. One also has the confidence provided by finding similar correlations in two samples. The procedure for applying compound probability has been described by Baker (7). First, for each item one finds the probability of so large a deviation from zero correlation occurring in each of the samples. Then one finds a chi square by the formula

$$\chi^2 = -4.605 \log p_1 p_2 \qquad (15.18)$$

where p_1 and p_2 are probabilities of random departures as large as the ones obtained from the two samples, and the logarithm is to the base 10. The general rule for degrees of freedom for this chi square is two times the number of probabilities compounded. Here there are two probabilities; thus there are 4 degrees of freedom. Suppose an item has correlations in two samples of .163 and .116. N is 200 in each sample. With a sample of 200 the standard error of a point-biserial r of zero is approximately .07. The ratios of the two r's to σ_r are therefore 2.33 and 1.66. For t's of these values, we have correlations significant at approximately the .02 and .10 levels, respectively. Applying formula (15.18),

$$\chi^2 = -4.605 \log (.02 \times .10) = 12.429$$

With 4 degrees of freedom, this chi square is significant about midway between the .02 and the .01 levels. We would accept the correlations as significant. Such a statistical test might not be crucial in accepting an item after correlation with total score, since most acceptable items have higher correlations, but it would be very typical after correlation of an item with an outside criterion. Baker (7) has prepared a chart for reading off compound probabilities from two given single probabilities. This has been reproduced in Fig. 15.6, and will serve for most practical purposes in item analysis. It has quite general application to cases in which the same hypothesis is tested in two samples and hence applies to cross-validation studies of test batteries as well as of items.

Item Selection for Tests. Having item information, we use it most commonly to guide us in composing the final form of a test. Besides the obvious goals of maximizing reliability and validity, there are a number of secondary goals. Among them are a good total-score distribution, a rank ordering of

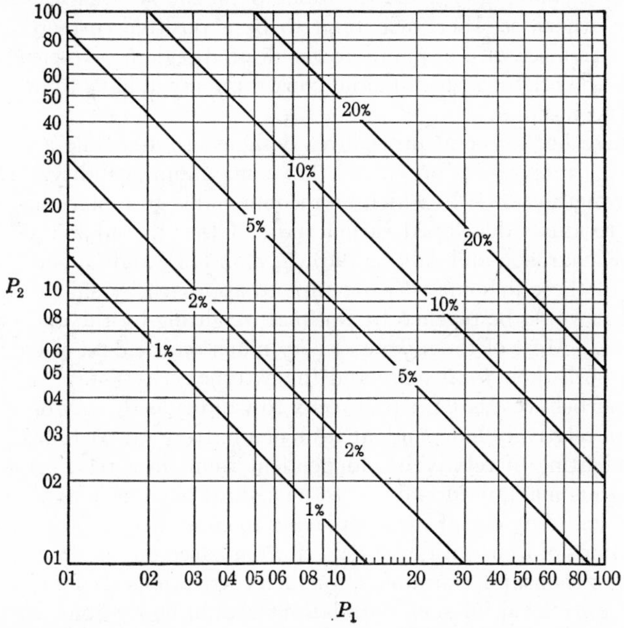

FIG. 15.6. An abac for estimating the compound probability of two experimental probabilities of significance. See the text for instructions for using the abac. (*Reproduced through the courtesy of Dr. Paul C. Baker.*)

items as to difficulty, and a revision of items where improvements are promising. If two parallel forms of a test are to be constructed, the item information offers us an indispensable guide. If we are attempting to arrive at factorially univocal tests, we can also obtain item-analysis data to help achieve this goal. Most of the steps of item analysis described above have been directed at improving internal consistency. Advice concerning good item conditions for high reliability and for desired score distributions has been offered in so many places, both here and in other chapters, that there is nothing of importance to be added in that direction. The other problems just mentioned call for a few comments.

Item Selection for Validity. So far as item analysis is concerned, there are two approaches to increasing or maximizing practical validity of total scores. When each test is to be relatively unique, perhaps univocal, validity is improved as a by-product of increased reliability. No such test by itself will give maximum validity. This goal is to be achieved by combining such tests in appropriate composites, with parts optimally weighted. When a single test is to have maximum validity, we have seen that each item must correlate as high as possible with the external criterion and as low as possible with other items in the test. This goal calls for item analyses against both the total-score criterion and the outside criterion. One then selects items having low correlations with total score and high correlations with the outside criterion. A convenient device for this is to plot each item as a point with projections on a pair of cartesian coordinates, one of which represents r_{it} and the other r_{ic}. It is easy then to see which items are within or nearest to the region of low r_{it} and high r_{ic}. If the items are of the same subject matter and are similar otherwise, there will tend to be a positive correlation between r_{it} and r_{ic} with a scarcity of points in the desired region. To ensure items in this region, the original selection and construction will have to be carried out with this end in mind.

There have been several procedures designed to assemble a collection of items whose composite score would have maximum validity. Horst (64) proposed a method in 1936 which he recommended to replace his method of successive residuals developed earlier (63). Other methods have been suggested by Richardson and Adkins (96), Layton (73), and Gleser and DuBois (42). All of these in some way attempt to approach by shorter procedures the goal that would be reached by optimal weighting by the multiple-regression method. Most of them depend very much on the data of correlation of items with both their total score and the external criterion.

The writer believes that the best route to validity is by way of the optimal weighting of relatively independent tests in a battery rather than a less-than-optimal weighting of relatively independent items in a test. A test whose validity is thus maximized is likely to be a short one and its validity will be very unstable. Any one of the approaches to constructing such a test should use correlations of item with external criterion based on hundreds, preferably on one to two thousand, examinees, for such correlations are inevitably small. The significance level for such correlations should be rigorous, certainly not less extreme than the .01 level and preferably at the .001 level. Otherwise, one would find validity of the total score fluctuating from sample to sample. A cross validation is imperative.

Item Selection for Independence of Tests. In achieving more univocality for a test we can apply a technique that might be called *negative item analysis*. If test G was designed to measure a certain common factor and test H to measure another and the factors are believed to be independent, we should like the correlation between the scores X_g and X_h to be as low as possible. It is quite common to find that scores designed for two factors correlate much higher than we have reason to believe the factors do. In this example, then, we can correlate items in G with score X_h as well as correlate items in H with score X_g. From these results the selection of items would be on the basis of the lowest correlations. We should still be concerned about reliabilities of X_g and X_h; therefore we would also consult the usual correlations r_{ig} and r_{ih}, of items with their respective total scores.

The Preparation of Parallel Forms. Defining parallel forms as tests having equal means, variances, and intercorrelations, we have certain operations with item-analysis data that will tend to produce such forms. The information concerning difficulty and item-total correlations should be sufficient. A practical device suggested by Gulliksen (56) is very helpful. The first step is to plot on cartesian coordinates, one for p and one for r_{it}, a point for each item. If we were going to prepare three parallel forms, the next step would be to look for clusters of three points lying close together in this two-dimensional space. Figure 15.7 is given to illustrate the kind of clustering one looks for. It may not be possible to form all the usable items in triads in this manner, in which case the remaining items must be selected so that the mean r_{it} and mean p are as nearly equal as possible in the three forms.

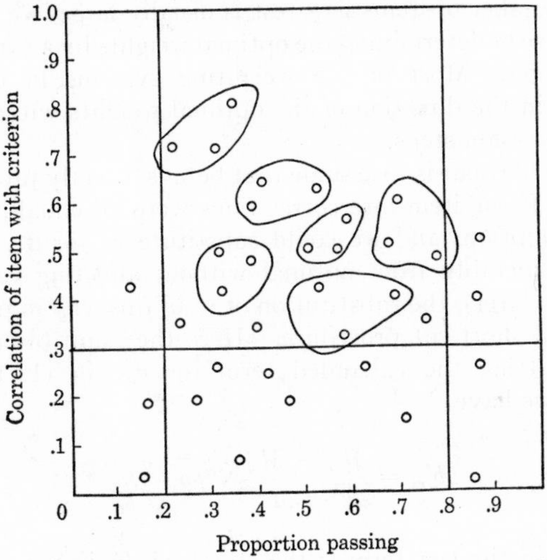

FIG. 15.7. Scatter diagram representing item statistics p and r_{it} ordinarily used in the selection of items, illustrating how items can be selected to produce three parallel tests. The procedure was devised by Gulliksen (56).

One would also make the usual selections on the basis of desired levels of p and of r_{it}.

SCORING PROBLEMS

Three major scoring problems will be discussed briefly in this section. One has to do with the weighting of responses to items; a second pertains to scoring formulas; and a third is concerned with response biases and how to deal with them.

Scoring Weights. Since we have made much of the conception that a test composed of items is essentially a battery of subtests, and since the validity of a composite score may be improved by optimal weighting of its parts, the question of differential weighting of items and of responses arises. Item analysis shows that items are not all equally correlated with a criterion, and that they have unequal variances, and unequal correlations with other items. All such features normally enter the picture when multiple-regression equations are derived.

The Multiple-regression Principle of Weighting. If the multiple-regression principle were applied to items, the weight for an item would be equal to

$$b_{ci} = \beta_{ci} \frac{\sigma_c}{\sigma_i} \tag{15.19}$$

where b_{ci} = optimal weight to be assigned to item I in predicting criterion C
β_{ci} = standard, partial, regression coefficient
σ_c and σ_i = standard deviations of criterion and item, respectively

The beta coefficient would be derived from the correlations of items with criterion and from intercorrelations of items. The weight b_{ci} is directly proportional to the beta coefficient and to σ_c and is inversely proportional to σ_i. Since the number of items in a test is usually large, we do not take the impractical course of determining the optimal weights by a complete multiple-regression solution. Most of the weighting systems in use make some attempt to aim in the direction of the optimal weights without applying all the multiple-regression steps.

One common short cut is to assume that beta is directly proportional to the correlation r_{ci}. If the item intercorrelations were all equal, this would be a reasonable assumption, and we could substitute r_{ci} for β_{ci}. Since weights can depart considerably from optimal without affecting validity seriously (as will be shown later), the substitution of r_{ci} in this way in practice can well be tolerated as a short-cut procedure. Here the point-biserial r should be substituted. Putting the expanded term for r_{pbi} in (15.19) and substituting σ_c for σ_t, we have

$$b'_{ci} = \frac{M_p - M_q}{\sigma_c} \sqrt{pq} \frac{\sigma_c}{\sqrt{pq}}$$

where the $\sqrt{pq}$ in the last term is the standard deviation σ_i. Simplifying, we have

$$b'_{ci} = M_p - M_q \tag{15.20}$$

Thus, it turns out that the weight to assign to item I is the difference of criterion-score means of those passing and those failing the item. This is consistent with the principle of least squares. The best prediction of criterion score for those passing the item is the mean of their scores M_p. The best prediction of criterion score for those failing the item is the mean of their scores M_q. We could give each passer a score of M_p and each failer a score of M_q for this item. The difference between their scores is then $M_p - M_q$. Or, applying the weight in (15.20), we multiply the item score of 1 times the difference $M_p - M_q$ for the passer, and we multiply the item score zero by the same weight for the failer. The difference in scores of passer and failer is $M_p - M_q$ either way. It is the difference between their weighted scores that counts. This is an important principle to remember in connection with weighting.

The writer (50) has derived a similar weight by substituting the phi coefficient for an item instead of r_{pbi} in equation (15.19). The result is the formula

$$b''_{ci} = \frac{p_u - p_l}{pq}$$

where b''_{ci} = an approximated regression weight based on the phi coefficient
p_u, p_l = proportions passing the item (or responding in some specified manner to the item) in upper and lower criterion groups

$$p = \frac{p_u + p_l}{2}$$

$$q = 1 - p$$

Because this weight would range from -4 to $+4$ as phi varies from -1.0 to $+1.0$, and since it is the difference or range of weights that is important, a constant 4 was added to make all weights positive. The weight used in practice is

$$W = \frac{p_u - p_l}{pq} + 4 \tag{15.21}$$

A standard error was developed to test the null hypothesis (a W of 4.0, or a phi of zero):

$$\sigma_{w_o} = \frac{2}{\sqrt{Npq}} \tag{15.22}$$

A t ratio would be estimated by the formula

$$t_{w_o} = \frac{p_u - p_l}{2}\sqrt{\frac{N}{pq}} \tag{15.23}$$

where t_{w_o} = t ratio for testing departure of weight W from the null value of 4.0.

The weight W was designed originally for the purpose of assigning weights to alternative responses to personality-inventory items. In such instruments there are usually more than two alternative responses, in which case the point-biserial r does not apply, particularly to intermediate responses. Suppose the three responses are "Yes," "?," and "No." This is not an item-weighting problem, but a response-weighting problem, provided there are responses in more than two categories, as there almost inevitably are. One can first make the dichotomy of "yes" versus "?-and-no" combined; then between "?" versus "yes-and-no" combined; and finally "no" versus "yes-and-?" combined. The phi coefficient is well adapted to handling these kinds of dichotomies.

An abac is provided in Fig. 15.8 for rapid estimation of weight W graphically. The only information needed to enter the abac is that of p_u and p_l.

Wherry (113) has proposed a weight that appears to have much in common with that given in formula (15.21). French (37) has derived a weight that also helps determine how to key multiple-choice items where the test maker is not sure of the right answers.

Some Principles of Weighting Components. It was pointed out above that weights can depart from the optimal ones and yet not affect validity seriously.

This calls for further comment. Both Burt (9) and Gulliksen (56) have given much attention to the weighting problem and come out with essentially the same conclusions. The effectiveness of weights in changing the essential character of the common-factor variances in scores depends upon several things. It depends first of all upon the *range* of weights assigned to the components (tests or items). This must be qualified by saying that it

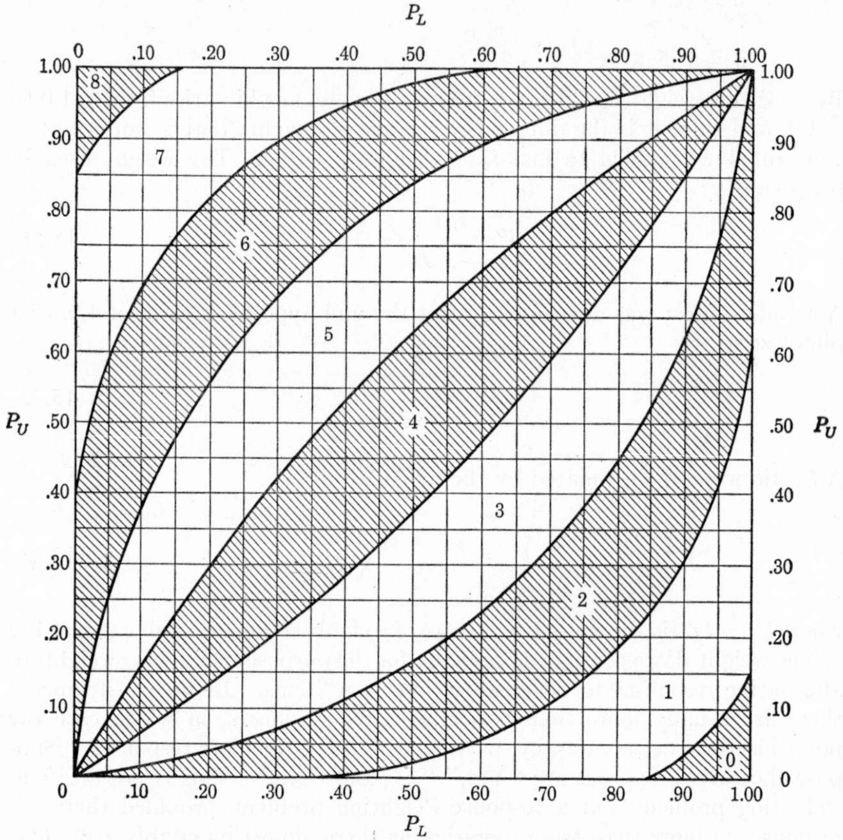

FIG. 15.8. An abac for the graphic determination of scoring weights for responses to items. p_u = proportion responding in the prescribed manner in the upper criterion group, and p_l = similar proportion from the lower criterion group.

depends upon the *range of weights relative to their mean*. The greater this ratio, the greater the possibility that one set of weights will give a composite score that does not correlate high with that from another set of weights. For two sets of weights for the same combination of components, the greater the correlation of weights, the greater the correlation of the composite scores. If the weights correlate perfectly, the composite scores will correlate perfectly. Only by giving some components weights reversed in direction in the two sets could we eliminate correlation between composite scores. The higher the intercorrelations of the components, the greater will two composite scores derived from different weights also intercorrelate. The larger the number of components, the less effective are weights in changing the character of the composite score.

Differential weighting of items is therefore most effective in short tests and usually pays little dividends when there are more than 10 to 20 items. It pays more when the average intercorrelation of items is low. In a long test it matters little what set of weights is used, provided they are of appropriate algebraic sign. Thus weights of 1 for all items in long tests of ability are quite appropriate.

It must not be assumed that applying no weights enables us to escape the weighting problem, for every item in a test weights itself. Its *effective* weight is determined by its variance and its covariances with other items. The application of differential weights has the effect of modifying weights already present.

Empirical Studies of Weighting within Tests. A number of investigations have generally supported the conclusions reached above. Examples are studies by Guilford, Lovell, and Williams (55), by Phillips (92), and by Harper and Dunlap (61). The first two found practically no improvement in reliability of achievement tests as short as 25 items. The third study substituted weights of -1, 0, and $+1$ in 14 keys of the Strong Vocational Interest Blank for Women for the standard weights of -4 to $+4$. The new experimental scores correlated .95 to .99 with the standard scores. Strong (101) objected, however, and found that such new scores led to different counseling in from one-sixth to one-twelfth of the cases as compared to that indicated by the more heavily weighted scores. His correlations between old and new scores were not as high as Harper and Dunlap had found.

Scoring Formulas. The term *scoring formula* usually refers to the practice of giving the number-right score R and the number-wrong score W relatively different weights and summing to obtain a total test score. Actually, there are possibilities, also, of weighting differently the number of omissions O (items reached but not answered) and the number unattempted U (not reached). Interest has been focused on the number of actual errors in view of the chance-success responses in multiple-choice tests. Where speed is an important factor in test administration, some examinees may hurry through doing much guessing, thus adding to their R scores. Or some examinees suddenly realizing that time is nearly up with a number of items still remaining may hastily mark the remaining answers at random. Some correction formulas are designed to counteract to some extent this contribution from guessing and/or to estimate the number of items to which the examinee actually knows the answers. Formulas designed to correct for chance are known as *a priori scoring formulas.* Another class of scoring formulas are designed to maximize validity in predicting some criterion. They are known as *empirical scoring formulas.*

Effects of Chance on Test Scores. Before noting the a priori formulas that have been introduced to correct for chance, we should consider the contributions of chance to scores. It is not sufficiently realized that a multiple-choice test restricts the range of effective measurement by a test. In a 40-item two-choice test, the effective range is from 20 to 40. This leaves a usable range of 21 points instead of the 41 we could have with a completion form. If the two-choice test is relatively easy or relatively difficult, this restricts the effective range still further. A two-choice test must therefore necessarily be a long one. It should be twice as long as a five-choice test, and the latter should be about 25 per cent longer than a completion test. In a five-choice test of 50 items, the most probable chance score is 10, which limits the usable range to 41 points.

When we also take into account the sampling errors of chance scores, we must revise the restricted range still further. The standard error of a chance score, assuming a binomial distribution of error scores, is $\sqrt{npq}$, where n is the number of items, p is the probability of chance success, $1/k$, and q is the probability of a wrong response, $(k - 1)/k$. In a five-choice test with 50 items, the standard error equals $\sqrt{50(.2)(.8)} = 2.83$. If we adopt the .05 level of confidence that an obtained score could not have been derived by chance, the deviation of 2σ is 5.66, or close to 6 points. Adding this to the expected chance score of 10, we have 16 as the lowest probable non-chance score. Our effective range is then 16 to 50.

In considering whether any one individual's score could be a chance score, we have to take into account the number he attempted rather than the total number of items n. This lowers the chance expectancy but increases the standard error of the mean, and hence widens the confidence limit for this individual.

In some tests, chance scores, even some below-chance scores, may be obtained and these fall in line with the higher scores to form the tail of a distribution. This may indicate that wrong responses are serving to measure in reverse somewhat the same functions measured by the correct responses or it may indicate misinformation. There is a strong likelihood, however, that the test is too difficult and the below-chance scores indicate either just chance or some other qualities unknown. It is well, then, to keep a multiple-choice test so easy that not only chance scores are avoided but also those within two standard errors of mean chance expectation.

A Priori Scoring Formulas. The a priori formula most commonly used reads

$$S = R - \frac{W}{k - 1} \tag{15.24}$$

where S = formula score
R = number of right answers
W = number of wrong answers
k = number of alternative responses to each item

This formula and others like it rest on the assumption that the examinee either knows the answer or he responds at random. A similar formula that yields scores perfectly correlated with S is the following:

$$S' = R + \frac{B}{k} \tag{15.25}$$

where B = number of answers left blank = $O + U$ (number omitted plus number unattempted at the end).

The procedure with this formula offers to every examinee the additional points which in the long run he could expect by chance on the unanswered items. Whether formula (15.24) or (15.25) is applied, the examinee should be told about its general nature. He will find the second formula more palatable and more inviting to omit items and he should be induced by it to work more carefully on those he does answer. Neither formula will take care of the personality differences that prompt some examinees to be bold guessers and others to be conservative or timid nonguessers. If an examiner wishes to treat actual omissions differently from unattempted items, he may weight them differently in the scoring formula. That is, the term B/k in (15.25) could be broken into two components weighting the O score differently from the U score.

Lyerly (84) has demonstrated that the traditional formula, (15.24), yields a maximum-likelihood estimate of a "real score." He views the problem as one of sampling among items (when E does not know the answers). Assuming a binomial distribution of this sampling, the most probable real score is the mode of this distribution. The common formula (15.24) gives the mean of such a distribution, which cannot be more than one unit from the mode. To allow for this discrepancy, Lyerly recommends that if S comes out with a fraction, we round to the next higher integer unless $k = 2$, in which case we round to the next lower integer.

When we know that the underlying assumptions are not satisfied, of course, we should not apply formula (15.24). Another occasion on which it would not pay to use this formula is in a power test in which E attempts practically all items. Then R and W would be correlated approximately -1, and S would correlate approximately $+1$ with R. One thing still to be gained under this circumstance, however, would be estimating the number of answers each examinee knows and the average number the group actually knows.

One final warning should be given in the use of scores corrected for chance. The correction extends the range of numerical values and increases the variance of scores, but does not thereby add correspondingly to effective measurement. Correction thus gives a false idea of effective measurement. The scores of a true-false test with the formula $S = R - W$ will have twice the range of the uncorrected scores, but it will be noted that only the even numbers are used. If this score is added to other scores from tests in which chance is much less potent, we automatically weight what is probably an unreliable test more because of its inflated variance. If optimal weighting is effected or if any other process is used in which weights are inversely related to standard deviations, the correction will cause no trouble. One could avoid this possible error in "blind" weighting of tests in combination by modifying the correction formula (15.24) to read

$$S'' = \frac{(k - 1)R - W}{k} \tag{15.26}$$

This would restore variance to the level existing before correcting the scores.

Empirical Weighting of Wrong Responses. When the scores R and W do not correlate very high negatively, there is some chance that the wrongs score measures something other than chance and other than what the rights score measures (in reverse direction). Fruchter (38) has shown by factor analysis of rights and wrongs scores from the same tests that the two may measure different common factors as well as measure the same factors to different extents. Research in the Army Air Forces (54) discovered that the wrongs scores from several clerical-type tests measured a factor of carefulness, whereas the rights scores that were designed to measure carefulness measured other factors.

Where a test is used to predict some specified external criterion, it may pay to treat the scores R and W as if they came from two different tests and to combine them in a multiple-regression equation. If we give score R a weight of 1, the optimal weight for W is given by Thurstone's[1] equation:

$$v = \frac{\sigma_R(r_{CR}r_{WR} - r_{CW})}{\sigma_W(r_{CW}r_{WR} - r_{CR})} \qquad (15.27)$$

where v = weight to be assigned to the wrongs score
R = number of right responses
W = number of wrong responses
C = criterion measure

Since it is the relative value of the weights that is important in a regression equation, we can arbitrarily let the weight for the R score be 1 and then let the weight for the W score, by formula (15.27), be whatever is necessary. The weight v will usually be negative, but may actually become positive where speed is the important parameter in the test.

The multiple correlation of a weighted combination of R and W by equation (15.27) can be estimated by the formula

$$R^2_{C \cdot RW} = \frac{r^2_{CR} + r^2_{CW} - 2r_{CR}r_{CW}r_{WR}}{1 - r^2_{WR}} \qquad (15.28)$$

where the subscripts are as defined in (15.27). Note that this gives the multiple R squared, calling for the square-root operation to find $R_{C \cdot RW}$.

Experience has shown that such a weighting of R and W in predicting a particular criterion may increase the validity of the test from .03 to .06 over that obtainable with R scores alone. The increase over the validity obtained with a priori scores is of the order of .02 to .03. It is also found that the negative weight for W (when a negative weight is called for, and that is almost always) can be varied quite a bit without affecting the multiple correlation, but that there is usually an optimal weight for W. For a two-choice numerical-operations test used to predict a navigator-training criterion, AAF psychologists found that the optimal formula was $R - 3W$. When the test was used to predict a bombardier-training criterion, however, the optimal formula was $R - .5W$. For neither was the a priori formula $R - W$ optimal. Errors in responses were several times as important in predicting navigator success as in predicting bombardier success. It should be added that very large samples, preferably more than 500, are needed in order to establish stable weights in this manner.

[1] See Thurstone (106).

Response Biases and Response Sets. By "response bias" we mean that a response to a test item tends to be altered in such a way that it indicates something other than that which we intended it to measure. The biases in which we are particularly interested here are usually determined by mental sets on the part of the examinee that are other than optimal for ensuring valid measurement by means of the item. Cronbach (15, 16) has done us a great service by his systematic study of response sets and their effects. This subject will concern us in the next few paragraphs.

Kinds of Response Sets. The following list of response sets is essentially Cronbach's, with some difference in terminology and one additional type of set.

1. *The set to gamble.* Whenever clear-cut response alternatives are presented, unless *E* is told to respond to every item, there will be individual differences in caution or lack thereof. Caution is negatively correlated with the rights score to the extent that the gambler adds to his score by chance success. This problem was discussed earlier under the subject of chance.

There are other aspects to the problem when we consider tests of temperament and interest. In many such tests there is a neutral category, such as "indifferent," "uncertain," or "?." Caution, although it may be of a different kind than that in tests of ability, would be expected to favor the use of the neutral category. Cronbach reports (15) that a score based entirely on the number of neutral responses had a reliability coefficient of .73. The writer has found about the same reliability for number of "?" responses in different temperament inventories. Thus the tendency to use the neutral category is a consistent habit. There is considerable true variance in this kind of score. Does it mean caution and caution only? It could mean indecision, or lack of observation, or it could mean a genuinely moderate amount of the trait indicated by the keyed items. It could actually mean that the examinee is inclined in one direction or another on the trait continuum for which the keyed score was designed. The writer has found that when a "?" response is correlated with a criterion for the trait in item analysis it often correlates significantly and sometimes as high as one of the other responses. He therefore gives this response a weight, using formula (15.21). Sometimes the weight *is* neutral, but it is often in the direction of a nonneutral weight. Thus the reliability such as Cronbach reports for a neutral-response-bias score may be loaded very much with variance in common factors we want to measure. It cannot all be attributed to caution or anything else without evidence.

2. *Semantics.* Where the categories of response are such as "agree," "strongly disagree," "dislike," and "sometimes," there is much room for individual interpretations. What one person calls "sometimes," another calls "often," and so on. Resulting constant errors may well cumulate to bias scores to degrees that should cause concern. Very little has been done to establish just how much difference in quantitative meaning such descriptive terms entail or how much they affect scores. The fact that we obtain high reliability coefficients of scores is no assurance of their lack of consequence, for these personal deviations in interpretation probably contribute to true variance. They would detract from validity.

We encounter the same kind of difficulty in the method of constant stimuli (Chap. 6), when doubtful judgments are used, and we find it in the use of rating scales where verbal cues are used to guide the rater. No doubt any method that will serve to stabilize individual interpretations of words will go a long way to improve psychological measurements of different kinds.

3. *Impulsion.* An "impulsion" set is seen operating when there is the alternative for *E* to respond or not to respond; to mark or not to mark. This situation occurs in multiple-choice tests in which, given a model object, *E* is to mark all those in a list that resemble it or are identical with it. *E*s differ in the number of marks that they make. The more marks they make, the greater their chance of hitting the right ones. Unless there is a penalty for errors of commission the score favors the liberal marker. The same kind of bias occurs in using check lists, where each item is to be marked or not marked. It occurs in essay examinations in which the amount written weighs heavily in the mark given.

4. *Acquiescence.* This is the error of the "yes man," at least for the "yes man" of a type. The set is to favor affirmative responses over negative responses. There may be a few negativistic persons who are inclined in the opposite direction. The point here is that each person has some general disposition on this continuum, positive or negative. It is found, however, that more individuals give an excess number of "true" responses in true-false tests, regardless of the actual composition of the test. This has several interesting consequences. For example, the poor student who guesses a great deal makes a good score on the true items but a very poor score on the false items. Sometimes the score based on only the false items correlates extremely high with that on the total test.

The same kind of set may be found in tests answered by "Yes" and "No." The number of "Yes" responses may be excessive on some papers. This may represent the actual situation with respect to this person's status in the traits that are scored, but it may also represent distortions due to the acquiescence set.

5. *Speed versus accuracy.* This is a long-recognized disturber that has received much attention in preceding discussions. There is nothing important that can be added here.

6. *Falsification.* Since the time when temperament and interest inventories became popular, we have had a new source of bias recognized and identified by various terms such as *faking-good* and *sophistication* as well as the term chosen here, *falsification.* The set is motivated by the desire to make a good score or to make a good appearance and to cover up defects and deficiencies. If the examinee has any idea about the kinds of traits being measured, as is more likely to be true of vocational-interest inventories, it has been shown that he can manage to increase certain scores by a judicious choice of responses, without regard to whether those responses describe him or not. In temperament inventories he is not so likely to guess successfully what traits are being scored, but as he comes to each item he may have his own ideas as to which response is more desirable to him or to his examiner. If his ideas of desirability are correlated with any trait key, he can thus increase that score. If his ideas are at random with respect to any trait key,

he may not change his score, but he has added much chance variance to his total scores. If he is applying for or competing for a certain assignment, he will probably think what are the best responses to make to each item in the light of this assignment. He may be very mistaken about the way in which items are actually keyed and might make a poorer score rather than a better one; yet the score he makes does not describe him as it should and is therefore biased.

Many studies have shown that under obvious inducements much biasing of responses and of scores can occur, but no crucial study has been made showing how much actually does occur under normal testing conditions. It must not be supposed that all examinees attempt to make a good impression, for many are honest. There are some who actually "lean over backwards" when reporting upon themselves; there are the soul-searching ones and self-flagellating ones; and there are those who want to appear mentally incapacitated. The user of inventories must be ever alert to the occasions for any of these biases, positive or negative.

Some Principles of Response Sets. Before we attempt to suggest corrective measures for response sets, it is desirable to extract some generalizations. The sources of response sets, like those for sets in general, are varied. Some of the sources in this connection will be implied in what follows.

1. *Sets are consistent and persistent.* While some sets of an examinee may shift from test to test and even from item to item, others represent apparently enduring qualities that can be called personality traits. Some are very persistent over time, and some are consistent from one test to another and from one administration to another of the same test. To the extent that consistency occurs, we find that the sets contribute to increased reliability of total scores. In other words, within the true variance of a test, perhaps even among its common-factor variances, we may find a contribution from one or more of these sets. It is this fact that makes possible the use of tests of ability, which are more objective, to provide, as by-products, scores for temperament traits. Unfortunately, such variance probably occupies a small part of the total-score variance and cannot therefore give an unadulterated index of status in a temperament trait. Perhaps with intentional cultivation this "bias" variance can in some tests be augmented and made to do duty as a measure of temperament.

2. *Response sets make scores more ambiguous.* To the extent that response sets contribute to the true variance of a test they are probably doing so at some expense of the common-factor variance that we intended to bring out in our measurements. Even if there is merely addition of more true variance, it alters the meaning of the score and of its interpretation in use. We should therefore strive to get rid of such biases even if to do so lowers reliability. The test will be a better diagnostic instrument even if the bias variance is replaced by error variance, because the latter is not focused systematically in any direction while the bias variance is.

3. *Response sets operate most in ambiguous and unstructured situations.* When the instructions leave too much to the imagination of the examinee, he invents his own goal and his own task. If each examinee has his own goal and task and if these differ among examinees, we have lost the experimental con-

ditions necessary for meaningful scores. We hear much about the virtues of unstructured tests for diagnostic purposes. Since unstructured tests open very widely the way for personal response sets, and since personal sets lead to ambiguous scores and interpretations, the conclusion is inevitable that the "scores" from unstructured tests are largely uninterpretable. There is a sense in which the unstructured test can be of use, and that is in the direction of the measurement of the sources of response sets when these sources are personality traits. But there must be a structuring of some kind to make the outcome mean anything at all univocal concerning the particular trait we want to measure. In throwing away some of the controls in order to give response sets free play, the projective tester has thrown away controls that he very much needs for interpretable measurement.

4. *Difficult tests open the way to response sets.* In the multiple-choice test it is when the items are difficult for the examinee that he resorts most to response sets. This parallels very closely the situation in psychophysical judgment. When differences in stimuli become so small that it all seems like guesswork, the observer falls into habits that determine his sequences of judgments (see Chap. 12). Since the same test is easy for some and difficult for others, this poses a special problem, but it is not an insoluble problem.

The Control of Response Sets. Some of the facts concerning response sets and the principles just stated almost suggest their own remedies. Some of the specific steps that may be taken to counteract them and their effects are suggested below.

1. *Identify the set.* We are much better prepared to do something about a disturbing response set if we can identify it and can know that it is present. There are various ways of finding indications that a certain suspected set is present. Bias scores can be developed and some have been in use. The Humm "no-count" score, which is the number of "No" responses given to the Humm-Wadsworth Temperament Scale, is used to indicate that the individual is attempting to give "good" answers rather than real answers. For the great majority of the items in that scale the answer "Yes" is in the pathological direction. With the *Minnesota Multiphasic Personality Inventory* there are a number of so-called validating scores used to indicate various types of departures from correct reporting on the part of the examinee. It would be important to factor analyze such scores to determine whether they are actually measuring what they are purported to measure, or to validate them in some other way.

2. *Structure the test sufficiently.* Administering a test is like conducting an experiment. If the outcome is to have meaning, experimental controls must be exerted. There is no escaping this scientific requirement. The administrator should set the goal and define the task for all examinees. This may be accomplished by writing better instructions. It might even be well to warn *E* against certain biases and their unfortunate effects. In administering check lists, one might instruct *E* to mark a stated number of items, or might set upper and lower limits for him.[1]

3. *Use good test forms.* Some item forms are more subject to biases from

[1] For further comments on check lists, see Chap. 11.

sets than others. The multiple-choice form in which E selects one right answer only and in which the alternatives are objectively interpretable seems to be best. Yet, even in multiple-choice tests there have been indications of bias, in the form of slight preference for some answer positions over others, especially for low-scoring individuals. Mosier and Price (90) have provided a system for randomizing the position of the right answer, also of the wrong answers. This should go far to prevent the test maker from hitting, by a position habit of his own, a response pattern that does or does not coincide with the examinee's habits.

Cronbach (16) recommends avoidance of certain item forms including the "yes-no" choice, the "same-different" choice, the "mark-or-not-to-mark" distinction, the categories "like," "indifferent," and "dislike," and of the neutral category in general. The writer can agree that this would remove much of the trouble with response biases, but it would also remove many useful tests because at present there are no good substitutes for some of these response categories. He has not found the indifference category so troublesome if it is given an empirical weight, as indicated earlier.

The forced-choice type of item is also sometimes recommended as a solution to some of the bias problems. Gordon (45, 46) has found slightly higher reliability and validity for inventory scores obtained from forced-choice items than from the usual type. The writer believes, however, that there are better ways of dealing with the same problems and that the forced-choice device introduces some measurement problems that may be worse than those they were intended to correct.[1]

4. *Make multiple-choice tests sufficiently easy.* This advice has been emphasized a number of times. Where a population has considerable variability in the ability tested, it might even be wise to develop two or three tests at different levels of ability. Some preliminary rough testing would determine at which level each individual should be tested and the appropriate test would then be applied to him. By scaling procedures the scores from the three tests could be brought to a common scale. The use of limen scores also suggests itself in this connection.[2]

5. *Use a good scoring formula.* After considering the nature of the test and the score distributions for rights, wrongs, and unattempted items, a favorable a priori formula may be chosen. The best solution would be to obtain factor-analysis information concerning each of these scores and to weight them accordingly. Another good solution, if a known criterion is to be predicted, is to derive optimal weights using formula (15.27).

6. *Use suppressors to remove effects of bias.* Knowing what kind of bias is present, not having been able to prevent it, we may resort to a corrective procedure. This is to use a "suppressor" score to attempt to negate the bias variance in the score. In an inventory in which there may be successful falsification, each trait score might be summed with a "lie" score (the latter with appropriate negative weight) to lower the bias variance. Since this is a difference score, the suppression as well as the trait score should be of high

[1] For a fuller discussion of the forced-choice technique, see Chap. 11.

[2] For a discussion of limen scores, see Chap. 13.

reliability. Even then the difference score will be less reliable than the trait score, but since it is more univocal, it is more interpretable. The same suppression score should not be used in combination with all trait scores, since this would introduce correlation among the corrected trait scores due to a common element. Levine (77) has made the very pertinent suggestion that suppression items be planted in the inventory for use where suppression is needed. They should be item analyzed and those correlating low with the criterion but high with the other trait items should be selected to provide the suppressors for that trait.

7. *Refrain from using tests where biasing sets are invalidating.* One may as well recognize the limitations to the application of tests whose scores can be effectively biased. Before accepting the scores from an inventory in a certain situation, some exploration might well first be instituted to determine whether the examinees can and do successfully bias scores. It may be that in spite of motivation to do so, little effective biasing occurs. Examinees may not be so sophisticated as some believe, and items can be written so as to make alternative responses seem equally attractive or equally unattractive. Schultz (97) administered an attitude-interest inventory to two successive freshmen classes, one before it was admitted to the college and the other after it had been admitted. He found that the students were apparently unable to detect the more valid items and that the inventory score remained valid in the interested (preadmission) group.

Attitude-scale Construction

The construction of attitude scales is treated as a special subject because it presents some unique problems. These problems stem largely from the fact that attitude scales represent more obviously bipolar continua than do any other test scales. Temperament variables are also in the bipolar class, but in measurement they are usually scored as if they were unipolar. The contrast between attitude scales and others is clearer in comparison with scales of ability. In a test of ability, an examinee either passes an item or he does not. Items are either too easy or too difficult for him. In an attitude scale of the Thurstone type, an examinee accepts or endorses opinions at some region on the continuum and rejects those both above and below. There are two turning points or limens on an attitude scale but only one on an ability scale. This situation has suggested the use of a limen score for the examinee on attitude scales, where the limen score is a kind of point of subjective equality between the person's attitude level and the opinion level on the scale. Summation scores are also used to measure attitude levels of individuals, as we shall see. The failure to recognize clearly the distinction between limen scores and summation scores has been a source of some confusion in dealing with attitude scales.

It will be the purpose of this section to describe briefly the three major techniques for attitude-scale construction, those attributed to Thurstone, Likert, and Guttman, to evaluate them, and to bring out various problems connected with attitude scales in general.

Definition of Attitudes. Before we proceed further, it would be well for us to have a definition of the term *attitude.* An attitude is a personal disposition common to individuals, but possessed to different degrees, which impels them to react to objects, situations, or propositions in ways that can be called favorable or unfavorable. The underlying basis in motivation is responsible for the bipolar nature of an attitude continuum. Motivation manifests itself in terms of appetites and aversions, and through experience we develop favorable and unfavorable inclinations toward various objects and classes of objects. The learning phenomena of generalization and discrimination determine the lines along which attitudes form and along which they function. While attitudes are subject to change, their directions and strengths are sufficiently enduring over periods of time to justify treating them as personality traits.

The Thurstone Method of Scale Construction. Thurstone was the first to suggest that social attitudes can be measured by the opinions that individuals will endorse as their own and that opinions can be calibrated (105). The scaling of opinions is necessary in the development of an attitude scale on which persons are to be given limen scores. Each person's characteristic position on the attitude continuum is indicated by the median of the scale values of the opinions that he endorses. This defines a limen score.

The logic behind the use of opinions to measure attitudes is that there is a positive correlation between what people say on a subject and what they will do about it. No one who is at all observing would maintain that the correlation is perfect. All we can say is that to the extent people's actions correlate with their expressed opinions we can predict the former from the latter. Since both opinions and actions are multiply determined, we should not expect the correlation to be high between them. Any single statement of opinion and any single action is extremely unreliable from a measurement standpoint. Since replications add reliability, we use a number of opinions; and to obtain substantial correlation of an opinion score with actions, we should have a number of action episodes. It is only over a long run of opinions and a long run of actions that we should expect the opinion-action correlation to be high, leaving out of account any biases that occur. It is often worth knowing about a person's position on an attitude scale in spite of the low predictability of particular actions. Knowing averages of attitudes of a group is also valuable in dealing with social, economic, and political problems.

Steps in the Scaling of Opinions. The scaling procedure goes roughly as follows. Suppose the question on which we want to develop an attitude scale is that of the importance of college football. First, several groups of people are asked to write down spontaneously what they themselves think of college football. Groups that differ all along the continuum are sought for this purpose in the hope of obtaining all shades of opinion.

From 100 to 200 statements are selected, with an attempt to cover the whole range rather evenly. Statements are edited, and if there appear to be gaps or if more extreme statements seem to be needed, they are written. Several requirements are laid down for the selection of statements. They should be short and to the point. They must be in such a form that the ideas can be accepted or rejected. Acceptance or rejection must mean something about the attitude to be measured. "Double-barreled" statements should be excluded from the list. An example of a double-barreled statement would be, "College football is an aid to athletics in general but it detracts from academic work." Edwards and Kilpatrick (22) add some requirements to the effect that we should avoid statements that could be endorsed by individuals on opposite sides of the indifference point, statements that are factual or that could be taken as such, and statements that could be endorsed by everyone or by no one.

Each statement included for scaling should be typed on a separate card. These statements should be sorted by a large number of judges who themselves represent a wide range of opinion on the subject. Anchor statements may be provided to mark the top and bottom piles, and the middle pile may be labeled as "neutral." If the neutral pile is marked, there should be some really neutral statements in the list, such as, "It really makes no difference to me whether we have college football or whether we do not." If it is suspected that there are more psychological steps on one side of neutrality than the other, a neutral landmark should not be used, or it might be placed to one side of the middle category.

It has been found that the scale values for opinions will not depend upon the attitudes of the judges. This was found by Pintner and Forlano (93) in developing a scale for patriotism and by Eysenck and Crown (25) in developing a scale for anti-Semitism. Farnsworth (26) has found that scaling of opinions may shift with time. Certain opinions on war were judged more pacifistic in 1940–1941 than they had been some 10 years earlier. Fehrer (29) found that the distribution of opinions of various scale levels in the list of those rated has much bearing upon accurate scaling. When items known to have scale values from 3 to 10 on a militarism scale (the three most pacifistic categories of opinions being omitted) were evaluated, they tended to be judged more pacifistic. When opinions from 0 through 7 on the scale were judged, they tended to be rated more militaristic.

The derivation of scale values for the opinions that have been judged in equal-appearing intervals is accomplished by computing medians. The semi-interquartile range Q is computed as an index of dispersion of items on the scale. The end goal is to have approximately 25 items rather evenly spaced on the continuum, or better, to have two alternate forms of this sort. The obtained statistical information will help in selecting the items. The Q values, for example, indicate ambiguity or uncertainty of meaning. Items with largest Q values should be omitted first. The parallel nature of the two forms can be improved by taking into account not only the median and Q of each item but also its content. The question of whether an opinion is relevant or valid for a particular scale is not so easily answered from the data available. This is one of the weaknesses of the Thurstone method. It requires additional information to determine item validity, for example, item intercorrelations and item-total correlations.

Farnsworth (27) has found evidence that judges of opinions do not keep their intervals equal. When this is suspected, one should resort to the category-scaling procedure, described in Chap. 10, or to some other procedure for evaluating the category positions on the scale. If one of the categories is labeled as "neutral," this also provides an empirical method of locating the indifference point on the scale.[1]

Scoring Methods. When the finished attitude scale is administered to individuals to find their attitude scores, the usual procedure has been to ask *E* to check each opinion that applies to him. It is expected that he will mark a limited number of neighboring opinions. A median or mean of the scale values of the opinions he endorses is taken as his score.[2] There is an important bias often pointed out in this connection. It has to do with the number of statements endorsed and the range of the scale covered. Those who mark more statements tend to obtain averages closer to the neutral value. This is a regression phenomenon which affects individuals with extreme scale positions most. When such *E*'s extend their number of opinions marked, they do so mainly by going toward the neutral zone. It is best, therefore, to standardize the number to be marked, restricting *E* to three or five opinions. When he has to limit his choices, he will probably concentrate marks nearest his average.

A question of format of the attitude scale has sometimes arisen, namely, should the items be in order of scale value in the list or should they be in random order. The serial order would be primarily for the convenience of the scorer; it might encourage response biases on the part of the examinee. Dunlap and Kroll (19) found scores equally reliable either way, but since response biases contribute to reliability and still may detract from validity, this does not answer the question.

The Likert Method. Likert (78) proceeded in the development of attitude scales along lines more similar to those of ordinary test development. His items were of the multiple-choice type, with three responses, "Yes," "?," or "No," or five responses, "Strongly approve" through "Undecided" to "Strongly disapprove." His first approach was to scale the response alternatives, using what is called the *category-scale method*, described in Chap. 10, and to use these scale values as weights for responses. He discovered, however, that the integral values 1 to 5 in the five-choice items and 2 to 4 in the three-choice items gave just as reliable scores as the category-scale values, and the two scores correlated essentially perfectly. He therefore used the simpler weights. The direction of the weighting of responses to an item would be determined a priori, from knowledge of its content, which could be checked by item analysis. Each *E* responds to every item, and his score is the sum of the weights assigned to his responses. Thus the score is definitely in the summation category.

Eysenck and Crown (25) have proposed a method of scoring that combines the weights of Likert and the scale values of Thurstone in the form of products. The *opinion* has a Thurstone scale value and each *response* has a Likert weight. The total score for an individual is the sum of such products. Eysenck and Crown have reported that this led to a higher reliability (.94, split-half) than that for scores from the Thurstone method alone (.83) or the

[1] Ferguson (31) summarizes the requirements for a good attitude scale.

[2] Lorge (83) has found the median value to be a slightly more reliable score than the mean value.

Likert method alone (.90). They call this procedure the *scale-product method.* It is a quite common finding that the Likert method leads to scores with higher reliabilities with fewer items than does the Thurstone method.

The Guttman Method of Scale Analysis. Guttman's novel method of scale analysis has been subject to so much legitimate criticism that space will not be taken to describe it in full here. The principles involved and the general nature of the method will be mentioned and the nature of the criticisms. The interested reader will find full descriptions of the method in the book edited by Stouffer (100) and in Guttman's articles (57, 58, 60). Modified procedures have been suggested by Goodenough (44), Suchman (103), and Lessing and Bodine (75).

Scale-analysis Theory. The theory on which scale analysis rests is essentially that of homogeneity, as explained in Chap. 13. Guttman believes that a genuine scale, capable of legitimate measurement, exists when homogeneity is virtually complete. The items should measure one factor only; the scale should be univocal. The writer can heartily agree that this is the goal toward which to strive. From the standpoint of homogeneity theory, two persons receiving the same score should have responded in the same way to all items. Stated in another way, from an individual's score we should be able to predict his responses. There is no particular value in being able to do this, but it is symptomatic of a good scale. The scale-analysis procedure is not so much a method of arriving at this goal of a univocal test, although it helps achieve the kind of scoring toward that end, as it is a method of determining to what extent a scale (in Guttman's sense) has been achieved.

Major Steps in Scale Analysis. Some of the significant steps should be briefly stated. First, the investigator hypothesizes a variable (usually of attitude, although the method applies more broadly than that) that he thinks exists and is worth measuring in connection with his basic-research or practical problems. Suppose that it is decided there is a variable of "fatherliness" in the attitudes of a father toward his children. A large number of descriptive statements can be collected or written that seem to indicate the degree of this quality. This constitutes what Guttman calls a "universe of items." A reasonably small number of items is selected, perhaps twenty or less. Each item is given two or more alternative responses. The items are administered to a group of examinees who respond to every item. A provisional key is set up on an a priori basis for obtaining an experimental score. The examinees are placed in rank order on the basis of this experimental score, and are listed in a column. In each row of the matrix are the item responses of an examinee. The responses to each item have been listed by columns in presumed order of relation to total score. With the examinees in rank order for total score, the question now is whether the responses to each item are in close agreement as they should be in a homogeneous test. That is, those marking the response that should indicate the quality most strongly should be consistently among those with highest total scores. The number of reversals in responses, in deviation from perfect correlation, is counted, and the numbers of such errors are summed for all items. The total percentage of error deducted from 100 per cent gives the *index of reproducibility.* If this is lower than 90 per cent, the decision is that under these scoring conditions a scale does not exist, or if the index is between 85 and 90 per cent, a "quasi scale" exists. The scale of percentages is, of course, a continuous one and these limits are arbitrary.

If the index of reproducibility does not indicate a scale, the matrix of responses is inspected to determine where improvements in nonoverlapping may be effected by combining response categories to an item. With these combinations made, a new scoring key is used to obtain revised total scores and the procedures described above are repeated with these new categories and scores. It can be seen that the combining of categories that do the most good in eliminating errors of reproducibility may capitalize heavily on chance errors, and although the criterion of 90 per cent reproducibility may be eventually met, shrinkage in a new sample would be inevitable.

Evaluation of Scale Analysis. The critics of this method have been many, of whom may be mentioned Festinger (32), Clark and Kriedt (12), Edwards (20), Edwards and Kilpatrick (22, 23), Loevinger (81), Eysenck and Crown (25), and Smith (99). There is much agreement on some of the criticisms. For example, it is pointed out that the criterion of scalability is rarely achieved, even when total scores reach an acceptable level of reliability. The criterion is variously described as "unrealistic," "useless," and even "harmful." Even when the criterion is achieved, it is not certain that we have a univocal score. The score may represent, instead, a rather uniform combination of two or more factors. There is no really effective way of selecting good items by this approach. Much depends upon the investigator's wisdom in regard to the items he puts into the analysis process. The procedures themselves lack rigorous rules for combining response categories and for counting errors of reproduction. Reproducibility is related to response popularity. When responses pile up in one category, reproducibility cannot fail to be high. This sets a lower limit to what is often a restricted range of nonchance reproducibility, a limit that may on occasion be uncomfortably close to the criterion. The method also favors groups of items that turn out to be virtually rewording of the same content, in which case the variable emphasized could well be a specific factor rather than a common factor. Guttman (59) has replied to some of these criticisms, but he has failed to meet them all.

Intensity Analysis. Intensity analysis is not a part of the scale-analysis procedure but may be used as an adjunct to it or to attitude-scaling by other methods. Its aim is to establish an indifference point on the scale. It does this only roughly and with a great deal of effort. The principle is new and interesting. An "intensity" score is derived for examinees who obtain "content" scores at different levels on the attitude continuum. If the response categories to items are five, with the two terminal ones designated as "strongly" or the equivalent and the middle one as neutral, the two extreme responses are combined with a weight of 2, the next two categories combined with a weight of 1, and the middle category is given a weight of zero. The sum of these weights is the person's "intensity score." The intensity scores are recorded in a scatter plot as a function of content or attitude-level scores. The regression of average intensity scores on level scores is usually U-shaped or J-shaped. A minimal intensity-score region can usually be seen. The point of minimum intensity score is taken as the indifference point. As indicated before, this is not very accurately located.

General Evaluation. It would appear that the choice of method to use for the development of an attitude scale lies between the Thurstone and Likert procedures. Which of these should be used depends on what kind of score we want. If we want a limen score, the Thurstone method is required, or an equivalent method. Apparently this approach needs more items to achieve the same degree of reliability as that common for a Likert-type scale. One significant value of a limen score is that from the numerical value one can point to a part of the scale and say that the person who makes this score is likely to endorse opinions in this region and others of like value. When an examinee is permitted to mark as many opinions as he pleases, we also gain some idea of his degree of certainty or his dispersion on the attitude continuum. This possible information seems not to have been used very much. It would require a larger number of items than commonly employed to achieve reliable variability measures. In Chap. 13 we saw that variability scores are typically unreliable.

The Thurstone method lacks good indices of validity of items. For this reason some investigators recommend (22) that an item analysis of the usual kinds be made of the items. Such analyses tend to select items of the more extreme scale positions, which is to be expected. If one is going to use the Thurstone method of scale administration, neutral items would have to be retained in spite of their invalidity.

If one is going to use a summation score, the Likert approach, or any of the common item-analysis procedures, is the one to follow. The responses may be weighted not on a priori basis, but on the basis of item-analysis data, using a weight such as that given by formula (15.21). Such a weight might be substituted for the Likert weight, also, in applying the scale-product method of Eysenck and Crown.

The problem of univocality of scales is no different in connection with attitudes than anywhere else in measurement by means of tests. The route to univocal scores is by way of factor analysis, to which we give full attention in the next chapter, or by way of something equivalent.

Problems

1. Determine a z value for each item in Data 15*A*, as derived from each group. Answer the following questions:
   a. Which group has the higher average ability? Explain.
   b. Which group has the greater dispersion of ability? Explain.
   c. How can the two sets of difficulty indices (z values) be made more comparable?

DATA 15*A*. PROPORTIONS PASSING EACH OF FIVE ITEMS IN TWO GROUPS

	Item				
	A	*B*	*C*	*D*	*E*
Group I	.01	.09	.32	.70	.95
Group II	.08	.30	.54	.83	.96

2. Determine the z indices for the items in Data 15*B*, before and after correcting for chance success. State general conclusions.

DATA 15*B*. ITEMS DIFFERING IN NUMBER OF ALTERNATIVE RESPONSES AND IN PROPORTIONS PASSING

Alternative responses	5	5	3	3	2	2
Proportion passing	.90	.60	.90	.60	.90	.60

3. Estimate the proportions of the entire criterion distribution passing each item in Data 15*C*, using the correlation coefficients for the items given in answer to Prob. 5.

DATA 15*C*. NUMBERS OF EXAMINEES AMONG 100 IN EACH OF TWO GROUPS WHO PASSED EACH ITEM. THE GROUPS WERE THE UPPER AND LOWER 27 PER CENTS OF THE TOTAL CRITERION SAMPLE

	Item			
	G	*H*	*I*	*J*
High 27%	65	69	97	95
Low 27%	42	16	79	25

4. Find Johnson's *ULI* index for items in Data 15*C* and standard errors.
5. Find Flanagan estimates of biserial r's for the items in Data 15*C*.
6. Estimate item-total correlations for the items in Data 15*D* by finding r_t, r_{pbi}, and ϕ from their respective abacs. Decide which correlation coefficients are statistically significant.

DATA 15*D*. PROPORTIONS OF EXAMINEES FROM UPPER AND LOWER HALVES WHO PASSED EACH ITEM ($N = 200$)

	Item			
	L	*M*	*N*	*O*
Upper	.77	.96	.27	.59
Lower	.39	.81	.12	.45

7. Assume that item *M* in Data 15*D* has two alternative responses. Recompute r_t after correcting all proportions for chance success. Do the same for item *O*, assuming three alternatives.

8. Assume that the total score standard deviations for items *L* and *O* in Data 15*D* are 2.0 and 4.0, respectively. Correct the point-biserial r's (obtained for these items in answer to Prob. 6) for part-whole overlap.

9. In an item-validation study in two samples, three items were found to have discrimination indices with the following pairs of probabilities: Item *Q*, .06 and .02; item *R*, .01 and .15; and item *S*, .09 and .08. What are the compound probabilities for significance?

10. Determine scoring weights *W* for the responses to the two items in Data 15*E*. Determine which weights are statistically significantly different from a weight of 4.0.

DATA 15*E*. PROPORTIONS RESPONDING "YES," "?," AND "NO" TO TWO ITEMS IN AN INTEREST INVENTORY. THE TWO GROUPS, COMPOSED OF 100 EACH, WERE UPPER AND LOWER HALVES WITH RESPECT TO TOTAL SCORE

	Item *S*			Item *T*		
	Yes	?	No	Yes	?	No
Upper	.305	.030	.665	.945	.030	.025
Lower	.710	.040	.250	.310	.120	.570

11. Given the following information: $r_{CR} = .50$, $r_{CW} = -.40$, $r_{RW} = -.60$, $\sigma_R = 12$, and $\sigma_W = 3$, where subscripts *R*, *W*, and *C* stand for rights, wrongs, and criterion scores, respectively, find:

a. The optimal weight for wrongs scores, when rights scores are weighted +1.
b. The validity for the score with optimal weighting.

Answers

1.

	A	*B*	*C*	*D*	*E*
I:	+2.33	+1.34	+0.47	−0.52	−1.64
II:	+1.41	+0.52	−0.10	−0.95	−1.75

2.

z:	−1.28	−0.25	−1.28	−0.25	−1.28	−0.25
cz:	−1.15	0.00	−1.04	+0.25	−0.84	+0.84

3. Estimated *p*: .535, .410, .895, .640.
4. *ULI*: .23, .53, .18, .70
   σ_{ULI}: .069, .059, .044, .048
5. Flanagan *r*'s: .24, .55, .40, .73.
6. r_t: .58,* .50,* .35,* .21
   r_{pbi}: .46,* .30,* .24,* .17†
   ϕ: .37,* .23*, .19*, .15†
7. For item *M*, $r_t = .60$; for item *O*, $r_t = .61$.
8. For item *L*, $r_{ir} = .22$; for item *O*, $r_{ir} = .05$.
9. Compound probabilities: $P < .01$; $.01 < P < .02$; $.02 < P < .05$.
10. Item I: *W* = 2,* 4, 6*
    Item II: *W* = 7,* 3,† 1*
11. $v = -1.54$; $R_{c \cdot rw} = .515$.

* Significant beyond the .01 level.
† Significant beyond the .05 level.

REFERENCES

1. ADKINS, D. C. Test construction in a public personnel administration. *Educ. psychol. Measmt.*, 1944, **4**, 141–160.
2. ———. Construction and analysis of written tests for predicting job performance. *Educ. psychol. Measmt.*, 1946, **6**, 195–211.
3. ———. *Construction and Analysis of Achievement Tests.* Washington, D.C.: United States Civil Service Commission, 1947.
4. ——— and TOOPS, H. A. Simplified formulas for item selection and construction. *Psychometrika*, 1937, **2**, 165–171.
5. ANSTEY, E. The *d* method of item-analysis. *Brit. J. Psychol., Statist. Sec.*, 1948, **1**, 167–177.
6. BAKER, K. H. Item validity by the analysis of variance: An outline of method. *Psychol. Rec.*, 1939, **3**, 242–248.

7. Baker, P. C. Combining tests of significance in cross-validation. *Educ. psychol. Measmt.*, 1952, **12,** 300–306.
8. Bryan, M. M., Burke, P. J., and Stewart, N. Correction for guessing in the scoring of pretests: Effect upon item difficulty and item validity indices. *Educ. psychol. Measmt.*, 1952, **12,** 45–56.
9. Burt, C. The influence of differential weighting. *Brit. J. Psychol., Statist. Sec.*, 1950, **3,** 105–123.
10. Carroll, J. B. The effect of difficulty and chance success on correlations between items or between tests. *Psychometrika*, 1945, **10,** 1–19.
11. Carter, H. D. How reliable are the common measures of difficulty and validity of objective test items? *J. Psychol.*, 1942, **13,** 31–39.
12. Clark, K. E., and Kriedt, P. H. An application of Guttman's new scaling technique to an attitude questionnaire. *Educ. psychol. Measmt.*, 1948, **8,** 215–223.
13. Conrad, H. S. Characteristics and uses of item-analysis data. *Psychol. Monogr.*, 1948, **62,** No. 295.
14. Coombs, C. H. The concepts of reliability and homogeneity. *Educ. psychol. Measmt.*, 1950, **10,** 43–56.
15. Cronbach, L. J. Response sets and test validity. *Educ. psychol. Measmt.*, 1946, **6,** 475–494.
16. ———. Further evidence on response sets and test design. *Educ. psychol. Measmt.*, 1950, **10,** 3–31.
17. Davis, F. B. *Item-analysis Data.* Cambridge, Mass.: Harvard University Press, 1946.
18. DuBois, P. H. A note on the computation of biserial *r* in item validation. *Psychometrika*, 1942, **7,** 143–146.
19. Dunlap, J. W., and Kroll, A. Observations on the methodology in attitude scales. *J. soc. Psychol.*, 1939, **10,** 475–487.
20. Edwards, A. L. On Guttman's scale analysis. *Educ. psychol. Measmt.*, 1948, **8,** 313–318.
21. ——— and Kenney, K. C. A comparison of the Thurstone and Likert techniques of attitude scale construction. *J. appl. Psychol.*, 1946, **30,** 72–83.
22. ——— and Kilpatrick, F. P. A technique for the construction of attitude scales. *J. appl. Psychol.*, 1948, **32,** 374–384.
23. ——— and ———. Scale analysis and the measurement of social attitudes. *Psychometrika*, 1948, **13,** 99–114.
24. Ely, J. H. Studies in item analysis 2: Effects of various methods upon test reliability. *J. appl. Psychol.*, 1951, **35,** 194–203.
25. Eysenck, H. J., and Crown, S. An experimental study in opinion-attitude methodology. *Int. J. Opin. Att. Res.*, 1949, **3,** 47–86.
26. Farnsworth, P. R. Shifts in the values of opinion items. *J. Psychol.*, 1943, **16,** 125–128.
27. ———. Attitude scale construction and the method of equal appearing intervals. *J. Psychol.*, 1945, **20,** 245–248.
28. Feder, D. D. Estimation of test item difficulty by averaging highest and lowest quarter performance compared with total population count. *Educ. psychol. Measmt.*, 1947, **7,** 133–134.
29. Fehrer, E. Shifts in scale values of attitude statements as a function of the composition of the scale. *J. exp. Psychol.*, 1952, **44,** 179–188.
30. Ferguson, G. A. Item selection by the constant process. *Psychometrika*, 1942, **7,** 19–29.
31. Ferguson, L. W. The requirements of an adequate attitude scale. *Psychol. Bull.*, 1939, **36,** 665–673.
32. Festinger, L. The treatment of qualitative data by "scale analysis." *Psychol. Bull.*, 1947, **44,** 149–161.

33. Finney, D. J. The application of probit analysis to the results of mental tests. *Psychometrika*, 1944, **9**, 31–39.
34. Flanagan, J. C. General considerations in the selection of test items and a short method of estimating the product-moment coefficient from data at the tails of the distribution. *J. educ. Psychol.*, 1939, **30**, 674–680.
35. ———. Critical requirements: A new approach to employee evaluation. *Person. Psychol.*, 1949, **2**, 419–425.
36. ———. The use of comprehensive rationales in test development. *Educ. psychol. Measmt.*, 1951, **11**, 151–155.
37. French, J. W. A technique for criterion-keying and selecting test items. *Psychometrika*, 1952, **17**, 101–106.
38. Fruchter, B. Differences in factor content of rights and wrongs scores. *Psychometrika*, 1953, **18**, 257–265.
39. Fulcher, J. S., and Zubin, J. The item analyzer: A mechanical device for treating the fourfold table in large samples. *J. appl. Psychol.*, 1942, **26**, 511–522.
40. Gibbons, C. C. The predictive value of the most valid items of an examination. *J. educ. Psychol.*, 1940, **31**, 616–621.
41. Gibson, J. J. (ed.). *Motion Picture Testing and Research. Army Air Forces Aviation Psychology Research Program Reports, Report* 7. Washington, D.C.: U.S. Government Printing Office, 1947.
42. Gleser, G. C., and DuBois, P. H. A successive approximation method of maximizing test validity. *Psychometrika*, 1951, **16**, 129–139.
43. Goheen, H. W., and Davidoff, M. D. A graphical method for the rapid calculation of biserial and point biserial correlation in test research. *Psychometrika*, 1951, **16**, 239–242.
44. Goodenough, W. H. A technique for scale analysis. *Educ. psychol. Measmt.*, 1944, **4**, 179–190.
45. Gordon, L. V. Validities of the forced-choice and questionnaire methods of personality measurement. *J. appl. Psychol.*, 1951, **35**, 407–412.
46. ———. The effect of position on the preference value of personality items. *Educ. psychol. Measmt.*, 1952, **12**, 669–676.
47. Guilford, J. P. The determination of item difficulty when chance success is a factor. *Psychometrika*, 1936, **1**, 259–264.
48. ———. The psychophysics of mental test difficulty. *Psychometrika*, 1937, **2**, 121–122.
49. ———. The phi coefficient and chi square as indices of item validity. *Psychometrika*, 1941, **6**, 11–19.
50. ———. A simple scoring weight for test items and its reliability. *Psychometrika*, 1942, **6**, 367–374.
51. ———. *Fundamental Statistics in Psychology and Education.* 2d ed. New York: McGraw-Hill, 1950.
52. ———. The correlation of an item with a composite of the remaining items in a test. *Educ. psychol. Measmt.*, 1953, **13**, 87–93.
53. ——— and Cotzin, M. Judgment of difficulty of simple tasks. *Amer. J. Psychol.*, 1941, **54**, 38–52.
54. ——— and Lacey, J. I. (eds.). *Printed Classification Tests. Army Air Forces Aviation Psychology Research Program Reports, Report* 5. Washington, D.C.: U.S. Government Printing Office, 1947.
55. ———, Lovell, C., and Williams, R. M. Completely weighted versus unweighted scoring in an achievement examination. *Educ. psychol. Measmt.*, 1942, **2**, 15–21.
56. Gulliksen, H. *Theory of Mental Tests.* New York: Wiley, 1950.
57. Guttman, L. A basis for scaling qualitative data. *Amer. sociol. Rev.*, 1944, **9**, 139–150.

58. ———. The Cornell technique for scale and intensity analysis. *Educ. psychol. Measmt.*, 1947, **7**, 247–279.
59. ———. On Festinger's evaluation of scale analysis. *Psychol. Bull.*, 1947, **44**, 451–465.
60. ——— and SUCHMAN, E. A. Intensity and zero point for attitude analysis. *Amer. sociol. Rev.*, 1947, **12**, 57–67.
61. HARPER, B. P., and DUNLAP, J. W. Derivation and application of a unit scoring system for the Strong Vocational Interest Blank for Women. *Psychometrika*, 1942, **7**, 289–295.
62. HORST, P. The difficulty of a multiple choice test item. *J. educ. Psychol.*, 1933, **24**, 229–232.
63. ———. Item analysis by the method of successive residuals. *J. exp. Educ.*, 1934, **2**, 254–263.
64. ———. Item selection by means of a maximizing function. *Psychometrika*, 1936, **1**, 229–244.
65. JOHNSON, A. P. Notes on a suggested index of item validity: The U-L index. *J. educ. Psychol.*, 1951, **42**, 499–504.
66. JOHNSON, H. M. Maximal selectivity, correctivity, and correlation obtainable in a 2 × 2 contingency table. *Amer. J. Psychol.*, 1945, **58**, 65–68.
67. JURGENSEN, C. E. Table for determining phi coefficients. *Psychometrika*, 1947, **12**, 17–29.
68. KATZELL, R. A. Symposium: The need and means of cross validation. III. Cross-validation of item analysis. *Educ. psychol. Measmt.*, 1951, **11**, 16–22.
69. KELLEY, T. L. The selection of upper and lower groups for the validation of test items. *J. educ. Psychol.*, 1939, **30**, 17–24.
70. KUANG, H. P. A critical evaluation of the relative efficiency of three techniques in item analysis. *Educ. psychol. Measmt.*, 1952, **12**, 248–266.
71. LAWSHE, C. H., JR. A nomograph for estimating the validity of test items. *J. appl. Psychol.*, 1942, **26**, 846–849.
72. ——— and MAYER, J. S. Studies in item analysis: 1. The effect of two methods of item validation on test reliability. *J. appl. Psychol.*, 1947, **31**, 271–277.
73. LAYTON, W. L. The relationship between the method of successive residuals and the method of exhaustion. *Psychometrika*, 1951, **16**, 51–56.
74. LENTZ, T. F., and WHITMER, E. F. Item synonymization: A method for determining the total meaning of pencil-paper reactions. *Psychometrika*, 1941, **6**, 131–139.
75. LESSING, A. K., and BODINE, A. J. Guttman scale analysis by means of IBM equipment. *Educ. psychol. Measmt.*, 1951, **11**, 298–314.
76. LEV, J. Evaluation of test items by the method of analysis of variance. *J. educ. Psychol.*, 1938, **29**, 623–630.
77. LEVINE, A. S. A technique for developing suppression tests. *Educ. psychol. Measmt.*, 1952, **12**, 313–315.
78. LIKERT, R. A technique for the measurement of attitude scales. *Arch. Psychol. N.Y.*, 1932, No. 140.
79. LINDQUIST, E. F. (ed.). *Educational Measurement.* Washington, D.C.: American Council on Education, 1951.
80. LOEVINGER, J. A systematic approach to the construction and evaluation of tests of ability. *Psychol. Monogr.*, 1947, **61**, No. 285.
81. ———. The technic of homogeneous tests compared with some aspects of "scale analysis" and factor analysis. *Psychol. Bull.*, 1948, **45**, 507–529.
82. LONG, J. A. Improved overlapping methods for determining the validities of test items. *J. exp. Educ.*, 1934, **2**, 264–267.
83. LORGE, I. The Thurstone attitude scales: I. Reliability and consistency of rejection and acceptance. *J. soc. Psychol.*, 1939, **10**, 187–198.

84. LYERLY, S. B. A note on correcting for chance success in objective tests. *Psychometrika*, 1951, **16**, 21–30.
85. MELTON, A. W. (ed.). *Apparatus Tests. Army Air Forces Aviation Psychology Research Program Reports, Report* 4. Washington, D.C.: U.S. Government Printing Office, 1947.
86. MICHAEL, W. B., and PERRY, N. C. Errors in estimates of item difficulty obtained from use of extreme groups on a criterion variable. *Educ. psychol. Measmt.*, 1954, **41** (in press).
87. ———, ———, and GUILFORD, J. P. The estimation of a point biserial coefficient of correlation from a phi coefficient. *Brit. J. Psychol., Statist. Sec.*, 1952, **5**, 139–150.
88. MOSIER, C. I., and MCQUITTY, J. V. Methods of item validation and abacs for item-test correlation and critical ratio of upper-lower differences. *Psychometrika*, 1940, **5**, 57–65.
89. ———, MYERS, C., and PRICE, H. G. Suggestions for the construction of multiple-choice test items. *Educ. psychol. Measmt.*, 1945, **5**, 261–271.
90. ——— and PRICE, H. G. The arrangement of choices in multiple choice questions and a scheme for randomizing choices. *Educ. psychol. Measmt.*, 1945, **5**, 379–382.
91. PERRY, N. C., and MICHAEL, W. B. The estimation of a phi coefficient for an entire criterion group from a phi coefficient calculated from the use of the extreme tails of a normal distribution of criterion scores. *Educ. psychol. Measmt.*, 1951, **11**, 629–638.
92. PHILLIPS, A. J. Further evidence regarding weighted versus unweighted scoring of examinations. *Educ. psychol. Measmt.*, 1943, **3**, 151–155.
93. PINTNER, R., and FORLANO, G. The influence of attitude upon scaling of attitude items. *J. soc. Psychol.*, 1937, **8**, 39–45.
94. PLUMLEE, L. B. The effect of difficulty and chance success on item-test correlation and on test reliability. *Psychometrika*, 1952, **17**, 69–86.
95. REESE, T. W. The application of the theory of physical measurement to the measurement of psychological magnitudes, with three experimental examples. *Psychol. Monogr.*, 1943, **55**, No. 251.
96. RICHARDSON, M. W., and ADKINS, D. C. A rapid method of selecting test items. *J. educ. Psychol.*, 1938, **29**, 547–552.
97. SCHULTZ, D. G. Item validity and response change under two different testing conditions. *Research Bulletin.* Princeton, N.J.: Educational Testing Service, 1952.
98. SIEGEL, L., and CURETON, E. E. Note on the computation of biserial correlations in item analysis. *Psychometrika*, 1952, **17**, 41–43.
99. SMITH, R. G., JR. "Randomness of error" in reproducible scales. *Educ. psychol. Measmt.*, 1951, **11**, 587–596.
100. STOUFFER, S. A. (ed.). *Measurement and Prediction.* Princeton, N.J.: Princeton University Press, 1950.
101. STRONG, E. K., JR. Weighted vs. unit scales. *J. educ. Psychol.*, 1945, **36**, 193–216.
102. STUIT, D. B. (ed.). *Personnel Research and Test Development.* Princeton, N.J.: Princeton University Press, 1947.
103. SUCHMAN, E. A. The logic of scale construction. *Educ. psychol. Measmt.*, 1950, **10**, 79–93.
104. THURSTONE, L. L. A method of scaling psychological and educational tests. *J. educ. Psychol.*, 1925, **16**, 433–451.
105. ———. Attitudes can be measured. *Amer. J. Sociol.*, 1928, **33**, 529–554.
106. ———. *The Reliability and Validity of Tests.* Ann Arbor, Mich.: Edwards Bros., Inc., 1931.
107. TRAVERS, R. M. W. *How to Make Achievement Tests.* New York: Odyssey, 1949.
108. ———. Rational hypotheses in the construction of tests. *Educ. psychol. Measmt.*, 1951, **11**, 128–137.

109. TURNBULL, W. W. A normalized graphic method of item analysis. *J. educ. Psychol.*, 1946, **35,** 129–141.
110. VERNON, P. E. Indices of item consistency and validity. *Brit. J. Psychol., Statist. Sec.*, 1948, **1,** 152–166.
111. ———. An application of factorial analysis to the study of test items. *Brit. J. Psychol., Statist. Sec.*, 1950, **3,** 1–15.
112. WESMAN, A. G. Effect of speed on item-test correlation coefficients. *Educ. psychol. Measmt.*, 1949, **9,** 51–57.
113. WHERRY, R. J. Maximal weighting of qualitative data. *Psychometrika,* 1944, **9,** 263–266.
114. ———, CAMPBELL, J. T., and PERLOFF, R. An empirical verification of the Wherry Gaylord iterative factor analysis procedure. *Psychometrika,* 1951, **16,** 67–74.
115. ZUBIN, J. The method of internal consistency for selecting items. *J. educ. Psychol.*, 1934, **25,** 345–356.

CHAPTER 16

FACTOR ANALYSIS

In spite of the great social and scientific usefulness of psychological tests it must be acknowledged that for the most part we have had very inadequate ideas as to what it is they actually measure. The plea is frequently offered in defense of tests that, by analogy, we do not know the whole truth about electricity and yet we do not question the right of the physicist or the engineer to measure it. Let us be ready to recognize that, although the full nature of electricity is not known, some of the real variables of electricity, such as potential, resistance, and inductance, have been isolated and laws of their interrelationships have been stated. The fundamental variables or dimensions of human ability and of human personality in general are still well within the unexplored territory reserved for psychologists. To meet this situation, a statistical approach such as factor analysis is necessary.

If one were to consult an unabridged dictionary in order to find all the terms that are used to describe human personality, including human abilities, in other words, the terms that stand for observable traits, one would find several thousand such concepts. Science, wishing to describe human nature, has at its disposal all these concepts. But to use all of them is very poor economy. Many are synonyms; others overlap to various degrees; others express opposite characteristics. Science, forever motivated to bring order out of chaos, to reduce to the simple that which is complex, wants to know what is the smallest number of concepts with which one can order and describe adequately the multiplicity of phenomena that come under its scrutiny. From the quantitative aspect, what is the smallest number of variables or dimensions of personality that will be adequate to the task?

Wundt saw this problem in connection with feeling and proposed his famous tridimensional theory. The existential psychologists have seen the problem in connection with sensory phenomena, and attributes of colors, of sounds, and of experience in general are the result. The task of isolating the independent aspects of experience has been a difficult one. The task of isolating independent variables in personality is even more difficult. Armchair methods dominated by deductive logic rather than by observation led to the faculty psychologies, traditionally unacceptable to modern psychology. Direct observation has likewise failed to arrive at any set of unitary traits which even approach a universal acceptance. Factor analysis or some similar objective process had to be brought into the search for the unitary traits of personality.

To illustrate the problem in another, more practical way, suppose that we wanted to describe an individual's personality as completely as possible by means of test scores. If we wanted to be sure to omit no aspect of his personality, we should probably have to give him several hundred tests. We should find so many of these tests intercorrelated that we would realize that we had duplicated our efforts perhaps several times over. By studying those intercorrelations, we would find that we could let single tests represent groups of tests in such a way that coverage of traits is not sacrificed. Where each test serves thus for a cluster of tests, we may say that we have an underlying factor. The task of describing the individual is then greatly simplified by having one test do the work of several. Where the factor can be given psychological definition and meaning, we also have a new powerful concept not only for descriptive purposes but also for thinking about human nature.

History of Factor Theory and Factor Methods

Early Conceptions of Mental Ability. Probably the first conception of mental ability is that handed down from the faculty psychologies which regarded mind as having a limited number of distinct and unitary powers. Although very old, this idea has been assumed, at least implicitly, by those who have constructed mental tests. Binet, rejecting the simple sensory and motor tests of Galton and Cattell, proposed to measure the higher functions of memory, imagination, judgment, and the like. Kraeplin, likewise, proposed tests to measure varying losses of the important functions in the insane and in individuals under the influence of drugs and fatigue.

Whipple's classical manual of tests (51) presented a classification under the categories long made familiar as separate functions, or, by implication, faculties. The implication carried the further idea that a memory test measured memory and nothing else and that an association test measured the power of association and nothing else. We know from the way in which tests intercorrelate that this part of the implication is quite untrue. According to this theory two tests of memory should correlate perfectly with each other, allowing for errors of measurement, and a test of memory should correlate zero with a test of judgment or of attention or of perception. This is decidedly not the case. Most tests of mental ability exhibit some degree of positive correlation; often two tests that are classified under the same name exhibit no more correlation than do two other tests supposedly belonging to two different categories of ability. The notion of broad unitary powers which operate singly and in an isolated manner must therefore be discarded.

Even more untenable is the idea that mental ability may be summed up under the one category of "intelligence." This conception is perhaps common to the unobserving layman, who regards individuals as equally bright or dull in everything they do, provided emotion or some other nonintellectual factor does not enter in. The conception of intelligence as a unitary entity was a gift to psychology from biology through the instrumentality of Herbert Spencer. Were this theory true, any two tests of intelligence should correlate perfectly with one another, allowing for errors of observation. Attempts to define this supposed unitary ability have signally failed to satisfy. Whether it is defined as the power to adapt to novel situations, as the power to learn, or as the power to solve the problems of life, the way is left open to analyze intelligence into a number of abilities which, working together, accomplish the result. If it is defined much more narrowly as the ability to do abstract thinking or as the ability to combine experiences, it becomes a more unitary affair, but then many aspects admittedly belonging under the category of mental ability are clearly ignored. Thus all unifactor theories fail to meet the test of accounting for the known facts and the test of universal agreement.

Spearman's Two-factor Theory. No single event in the history of mental testing has proved to be of such momentous importance as Spearman's proposal of his famous two-factor theory in 1904 (43). His logic at that time ran somewhat as follows: First, we may assume that any correlation between two tests implies a factor common to both, plus two specific factors, as indicated in Fig. 16.1*A*. Let the two tests be called a and b, the common factor g, and the two specific factors s_a and s_b, as shown in the diagram. We may then regard tests a and b as two measures of the common element g, with the

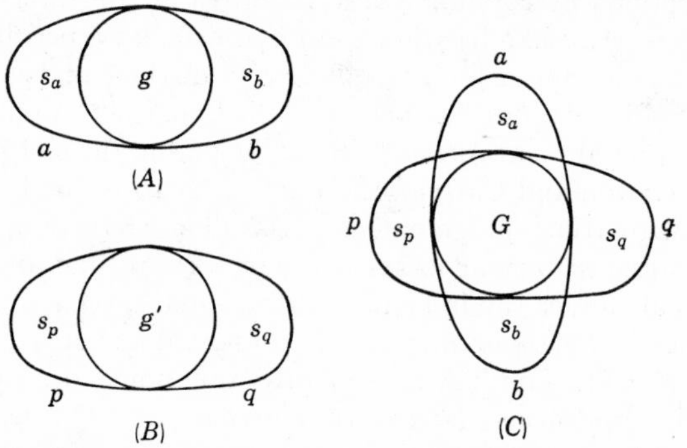

FIG. 16.1. Graphic representation of the common element in correlated tests according to the Spearman theory of one common factor G.

two remainders s_a and s_b. Since a and b are measures of the same ability, we may look upon the correlation r_{ab} as a coefficient of reliability. Now let p and q be two other tests with g' as the common element, as in Fig. 16.1*B*. As before, we may regard r_{pq} as a coefficient of reliability of a measure of g'. Using the formula for the correction for attenuation, we may now estimate the correlation between g and g', since we have two independent measures of each. Applying a formula for correction of a coefficient of correlation for attenuation, we have[1]

$$r_{gg'} = \frac{r_{ap}r_{aq}r_{bp}r_{bq}}{r_{ab}r_{pq}} \tag{16.1}$$

From some experiments which Spearman reports, $r_{gg'}$, so computed, was found to approximate a value of 1.00. This meant that g and g' were practically identical. The factor pattern could be more appropriately sketched as in Fig. 16.1*C*.

In a similar manner we can test whether or not the common factor in one pair of tests is identical with the common factor in any other pair of tests. Spearman was willing to draw the far-reaching conclusion that the common

[1] The numerator of (16.1) is a geometric mean of the four known intercorrelations of measures of g and g'.

element is identical in all tests involving the process of cognition. Every test, then, he thought to be composed of the g factor, which is universal, plus a specific factor that is found in each test alone. We may state Spearman's two-factor pattern in algebraic terms as follows:

$$\begin{aligned} z_1 &= w_1 g + v_1 s_1 \\ z_2 &= w_2 g + v_2 s_2 \\ &\cdots\cdots \\ z_k &= w_k g + v_k s_k \\ &\cdots\cdots \\ z_n &= w_n g + v_n s_n \end{aligned} \tag{16.2}$$

where $z_1, z_2, \ldots, z_k, \ldots, z_n$ = standard scores in tests 1, 2, 3, . . . , n
g = a standard score for the amount of g factor in an individual
$s_1, s_2, \ldots, s_k, \ldots, s_n$ = standard scores in specific factors, 1, 2, 3 . . . , n
w and v = regression coefficients or weights applied to g and the specific in each test

The Criterion of Proportionality. It can be shown that in order to assume the two-factor pattern in a set of tests for which the intercorrelations are known, any two columns of coefficients must be in simple, direct proportion. A table of intercorrelations is known as a *correlation matrix.* A matrix, in general terms, is any table of numbers with columns and rows. One peculiarity about a correlation matrix is that it is symmetrical about its principal diagonal. The coefficients in the upper-right portion are identical with those in the lower-left portion, as in Table 16.1.

TABLE 16.1. INTERCORRELATIONS OF SIX HYPOTHETICAL TESTS HAVING ONE COMMON FACTOR, ILLUSTRATING THE CONDITION OF SIMPLE PROPORTIONALITY IN A CORRELATION MATRIX

	a	*b*	*c*	*d*	*e*	*f*
a		.40	.10	.45	.30	.35
b	.40		.16	.72	.48	.56
c	.10	.16		.18	.12	.14
d	.45	.72	.18		.54	.63
e	.30	.48	.12	.54		.42
f	.35	.56	.14	.63	.42	
	1.60	2.32	.70	2.52	1.86	2.10

Table 16.1 was designed to illustrate a complete condition of proportionality. Let us consider first columns (1) and (2), for tests *a* and *b*. The criterion of proportionality requires that

$$\frac{r_{ac}}{r_{bc}} = \frac{r_{ad}}{r_{bd}} = \frac{r_{ae}}{r_{be}} = \frac{r_{af}}{r_{bf}}$$

The same would, of course, be true of the corresponding rows, since they have identical coefficients due to the symmetry of the matrix. Let us confine our interest to the first two ratios, namely,

$$\frac{r_{ac}}{r_{bc}} = \frac{r_{ad}}{r_{bd}}$$

Multiplying the extremes by the means in this proportion, we have

$$r_{ac}r_{bd} = r_{bc}r_{ad}.$$

Transposing, we have

$$r_{ac}r_{bd} - r_{bc}r_{ad} = 0 \tag{16.3}$$

This is Spearman's famous *tetrad difference*, which became the most acceptable criterion of the two-factor pattern. It can be written for any combination of four tests. If you apply this equation to any such combination of tests in Table 16.1, you will find that all the tetrad differences are exactly zero.

The proportionality in this correlation matrix is much more obvious even to casual inspection if the variables are rearranged in order both in columns and rows. Summing all columns in Table 16.1 gives us the rank order for the general level of correlations for each variable. In Table 16.2 the varia-

TABLE 16.2. SAME INTERCORRELATIONS AS IN TABLE 16.1 WITH VARIABLES REARRANGED SO AS TO SHOW THE PROPORTIONALITY MORE CLEARLY

	d	*b*	*f*	*e*	*a*	*c*
d		.72	.63	.54	.45	.18
b	.72		.56	.48	.40	.16
f	.63	.56		.42	.35	.14
e	.54	.48	.42		.30	.12
a	.45	.40	.35	.30		.10
c	.18	.16	.14	.12	.10	

bles have been arranged in order of the rank of the sums. Now it is clear that in every column and row, the coefficients grade from high to low. Spearman called this *hierarchical order*. In actual practice, with test scores that are attenuated by errors of sampling and measurement, however, the hierarchical order is never as obvious as this. Because of errors of these kinds in the coefficients, he expected tetrad differences to deviate slightly from zero even when the two-factor pattern was regarded as satisfied. When, however, the differences were farther from zero than could be tolerated, the hypothesis of a single common factor in a set of tests had to be abandoned. If you will apply the tetrad-difference equation to coefficients from Table 16.7, you will find many that are substantially different from zero. In that matrix three common factors are involved.

Graphic Illustration of G and S. The two-factor pattern is illustrated graphically in Fig. 16.2*A*, Spearman's *g* factor being shown as the large central circle and the specifics as small circles grouped about *G*. Each ellipse stands for a mental test. The ellipses are permitted to overlap *G* to different extents in order to indicate the fact that some tests are more heavily "loaded" with *G* than others. The amount of correlation between any two tests is determined by the extent to which the two tests are loaded with G. Thus, tests a and b will have a relatively high correlation, since they have much in common in G. Tests a and c will be scarcely correlated at all, since both have small loadings with G.

The Introduction of Group Factors. Tests g and h are exceptions to the rule, for they have in common something besides factor G. Spearman and his students had to admit that in many tables of intercorrelations coefficients may include some correlation over and above that demanded by a single common factor G. They attributed this at first to overlapping s factors, as shown by the overlapping of s_g and s_h in Fig. 16.2A. Tests g and h have a

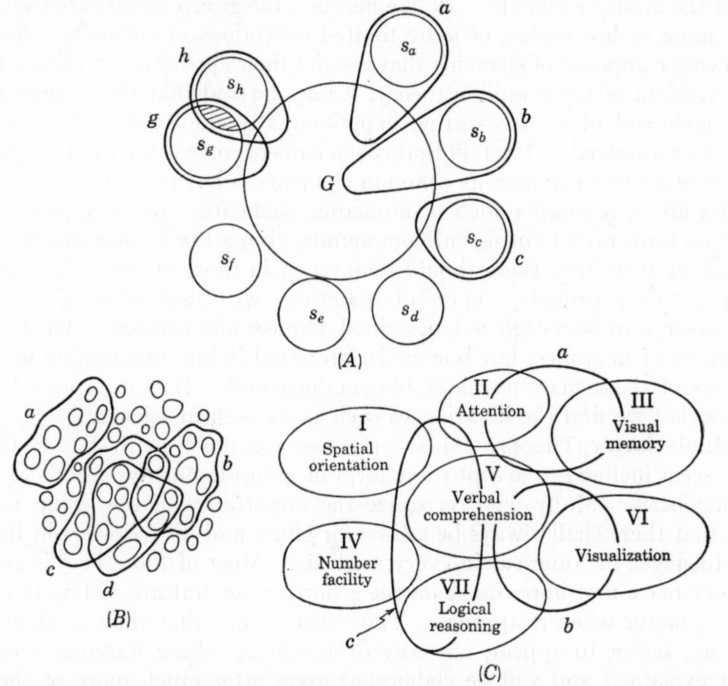

FIG. 16.2. Graphic representation of Spearman's two-factor theory (A), of the sampling theory (B), and of the weighted group-factor theory (C), showing correlated tests.

higher correlation than that attributable to G alone. Such an additional common factor as in tests g and h became known as a *group factor*. Such a factor was found to play a role not only in two tests but also in a number of tests. Among the group factors that Spearman and his associates came to recognize are verbal ability, numerical ability, and possible factors of mental speed, mechanical ability, attention, and imagination.

The Sampling Theory of Mental Ability. There have been a number of thinkers regarding factor theory who have been very reluctant to accept factors, either universal ones like G or group factors, as representing psychological unities. Chief among these is G. H. Thomson (45) who has proposed a sampling theory. This theory is shown graphically in Fig. 16.2B. Each small circle represents a unit of ability, which, though very limited in scope, may enter into a great variety of performances. There are assumed to be a great number of such units and they may be regarded by some as being in the nature of single stimulus-response bonds or associations.

According to the sampling theory, every test samples a certain range of these elementary human abilities; some with a wide range and some a narrow range. The degree of correlation between any two tests depends upon the number of units of ability they have in common. Thomson believes that the abilities combine in such a way as to give correlations approaching the Spearman hierarchical order. He believes in a "general ability" like Spearman's G, but it is not a basic entity. It is a rather constant combination of the ability elements. In like manner, the group factors are combinations, more or less stable, of more limited collections of elements. Specific factors are composed of elements that restrict their appearance to single tests.

In criticism of the sampling theory, it may be said that there seems to be little likelihood of demonstrating experimentally the existence of the elements hypothesized. The fact that coefficients of correlation can be regarded as dependent upon numerous common elements is not proof that correlated abilities are also compounded of numerous elements. If the supposed elements do form rather consistent compounds, giving the appearance of larger psychological unities, there should be interest in those larger unities (group factors). They probably represent something with psychological meaning. They deserve to be recognized, described, named, and utilized. The brain is a complex of neurones, but science is interested in the functioning of great numbers of those neurones in stable combinations. It is in repeated compounds that we find the invariances such as we seek in science.

Multiple-factor Theory. Most of those concerned with factor theory today seem inclined to accept some form of group-factor hypothesis as their working basis. Many who recognize the importance of the group factors insist that there shall always be a G factor (Burt and his followers in Britain and Holzinger in America) in every analysis. Most of those in this general category place first importance on the group factors but are willing to recognize a g factor when it appears. They also believe that their methods will allow a g factor to appear, one way or another. These statements can be better explained and will be elaborated upon after much more of the factorial procedures has been presented. Briefly, the multiple-factor theory holds that the performance on a certain test depends upon one or more common factors, each weighted according to its significance for success in the task.

At this point the reader should review the introduction to factor theory given in Chap. 13, for it presents the basic equations of multiple-factor theory. The first equation (13.21) states a total test score as a weighted summation of common-factor scores (in standard-score form) plus a specific component plus an error component. The weights are known as *factor loadings*. The second equation (13.22) states the total variance of test scores as a simple summation of component variances in the common factors, specific component, and error component. This same equation can also be stated in terms of proportions of total variance, as in equation (13.23). The proportion of common-factor variance is defined as the *communality* of the test and is designated as h^2. Add to this the proportion of specific variance s^2, and we have the proportion of true variance, which equals r_{tt}, the reliability coefficient. The combination of specific and error variance is defined as the *uniqueness* of the test. The uniqueness is the complement of the communality and equals $1 - h^2$. All these simple, summative equations rest on the assumption that the components are uncorrelated.

Table 16.3 presents an example of three tests which involve seven common factors to the extents given by factor loadings. Figure 16.2*C* illustrates the

TABLE 16.3. HYPOTHETICAL FACTOR LOADINGS OF THE THREE TESTS WITH THE SEVEN FACTORS IN FIG. 16.2*C*

Test	Common factor						
	I	II	III	IV	V	VI	VII
a	..	.5	.5	..	.2	..	..
b	..	..	..	..	.4	.6	.2
c	.2	.1	..	.3	.5	..	.4

same situation graphically. Three hypothetical tests are superimposed upon the factors. Test *a* depends upon factors II, III, and V; it draws rather heavily upon II and III but very little upon V. Test *b* draws upon factors V, VI, and VII; test *c* draws upon factors I, II, IV, V, and VII. The amount of correlation between tests *a* and *b* will be very slight; between *a* and *c* it will be larger, but still slight, and r_{bc} will be of significant size. The vacant spaces in the test ellipses may be assumed to comprise other group factors not shown, unique to each test and hence behaving like specifics; they may be assumed to contain also whatever errors of measurement there may be. All intercorrelations will depend upon the weighting of the factors held in common. But note that the common territory between pairs of tests may involve one, two, or more factors, and the degree of correlation will depend upon the loading of the two tests with those common factors.

The Factor-analysis Methods. Since Spearman proposed his criterion of the tetrad difference, a number of procedures for factor analysis have been proposed. All of them start with the same kind of data—a correlation matrix—though some of them can also use a matrix of covariances. Chief among the procedures for extracting factors are the methods of *principal components* of Hotelling (33), of *principal axes* of Kelley (37), of *summation* of Burt (3), and the *centroid method* of Thurstone (49). The first two have much in common, and also the second two. In addition to the process of extracting factors, Thurstone, especially, has provided rotation methods which he insists are necessary for arriving at meaningful factors. Holzinger (32) has designed methods of solving for factors in which he requires that every test yield some relationship to a *g* factor and to one, but only one, group factor. Tryon has developed what he calls a method of *cluster analysis*, which has a different aim than factor-analytic methods, and consequently cannot be classified with them without serious reservations.

The methods of Hotelling and Kelley are undoubtedly more rigorous mathematically and can be applied completely objectively. Without modifications, however, they frequently lead to factors by which one can account for obtained scores and intercorrelations but which are difficult to interpret psychologically. The results also lack invariance, in the sense that they depend upon what particular tests are analyzed together. The Burt and the Holzinger methods impose some arbitrary restrictions, one of which is the requirement of a *g* factor. A *g* factor can always be found, if one insists upon it. But this theoretical bias may well predispose us to quite misleading results.

For all these reasons, only the Thurstone methods of factor analysis will be explained in this chapter. While investigators in England generally follow Burt's leadership in factor-analytic studies, investigators in this country almost invariably use the Thurstone procedures. The Thurstone theory and methods have been developed on the basis of matrix algebra. It will not be assumed in this chapter that the student is familiar with matrix algebra. A few of the fundamental matrix ideas and operations with matrices will be explained briefly, to take advantage of the insights and the economy that they offer.

The Correlation Matrix and the Factor Matrix

The major statistical goal in a factor analysis is to substitute a *factor matrix* for the *correlation matrix*. The correlation matrix has as many columns and rows as there are tests. The factor matrix has as many rows as there are tests but only as many columns as there are common factors. There are almost always fewer common factors than there are tests. The *elements* (numerical values within the matrix) of the correlation matrix are intercorrelations among tests. The elements of the factor matrix are correlations of tests with the factors, where the factors are *orthogonal* (uncorrelated). When the factors are *oblique* (correlated), the elements in the factor matrix may or may not be correlations of tests with factors.

Relation of Correlation Coefficients to Factor Loadings. It was shown in Chap. 13 that the correlation between two tests is regarded in factor theory as the sum of the cross products of their orthogonal, common factors. This was expressed in equation (13.29), which is repeated here with a new number (and new symbols) for convenience:

$$r_{ij} = a_i a_j + b_i b_j + c_i c_j + \cdots + q_i q_j \tag{16.4}$$

where a_i = loading of factor A in test I, a_j = loading of factor A in test J, and so on. Any one or more of the factor loadings might be zero in either test, in which case that common factor would contribute nothing to intercorrelation. In fact, there may be only one factor in common to the two tests. But so long as they have one factor in common, there will be some correlation.

In Table 16.4 may be seen an example of a factor matrix F and a corresponding correlation matrix R. Skip the matrix in the middle for the time being. Matrix F has all the information contained in it that is contained in matrix R. One can be derived from the other. The data are fictitious, where coefficients of correlation are without sampling errors. In practice, we know matrix R from obtained data and we want to find F. Factor analysis proceeds in that direction. In this illustration, however, F was invented for the occasion and from it R was derived. Each coefficient can be computed by applying equation (16.4). Since there are only two common factors, there are only two terms in the equation. The correlation r_{12} is equal to $a_1a_2 + b_1b_2$, which equals $(.9)(.8) + (.0)(.2) = .72$. The correlation $r_{14} - (.9)(.3) + (.0)(.8) = .27$, and so on. The coefficients in parentheses in Table 16.4 are the communalities, which are obtained by the same principle of multiplication. They would not ordinarily be known in obtaining a correlation matrix from scores.

TABLE 16.4. DEMONSTRATION OF HOW A FACTOR MATRIX F, MULTIPLIED BY ITS TRANSPOSE F', GIVES A CORRELATION MATRIX R

F (Factor matrix)

Tests	Factor A	Factor B
1	.9	.0
2	.8	.2
3	.0	.8
4	.3	.8
5	.0	.6
6	.7	.0

×

F' (transpose of factor matrix)

.9	.8	.0	.3	.0	.7
.0	.2	.8	.8	.6	.0

=

R (correlation matrix)

Tests	1	2	3	4	5	6	Tests
1	(.81)	.72	.00	.27	.00	.63	1
2	.72	(.68)	.16	.40	.12	.56	2
3	.00	.16	(.64)	.64	.48	.00	3
4	.27	.40	.64	(.73)	.48	.21	4
5	.00	.12	.48	.48	(.36)	.00	5
6	.63	.56	.00	.21	.00	(.49)	6

$F \times F' = R$

A Correlation Matrix as a Product of Two Matrices. At this point a little matrix algebra is in order. The correlation matrix in Table 16.4 is shown as being the product of the factor matrix F multiplied by its *transpose* F'. Some explanation of matrix terminology is in order.

Some Features of a Matrix. It was said before that a matrix is composed of numbers in columns and rows. Each number, at the intersection of a certain row and a certain column, is known as an *element*. The general symbol for an element is a_{ij}, where the subscripts denote the row and column, respectively. Element a_{35} is in row 3 and column 5. Element a_{62} is in row 6 and column 2. The first number in the subscript indicates the row and the second number the column. In general terms, a matrix can be written as in Table 16.5, where we have m rows and n columns.

TABLE 16.5. A GENERAL MATRIX WITH ELEMENTS a_{ij}

$$\begin{Vmatrix} a_{11} & a_{12} & a_{13} & \cdots & & a_{1n} \\ a_{21} & a_{22} & a_{23} & \cdots & & a_{2n} \\ a_{31} & a_{32} & a_{33} & \cdots & & a_{3n} \\ a_{41} & a_{42} & a_{43} & \cdots & & a_{4n} \\ \cdots & \cdots & \cdots & & a_{ij} & \cdots \\ a_{m1} & a_{m2} & a_{m3} & \cdots & & a_{mn} \end{Vmatrix}$$

The *order* of a matrix is its number of rows and number of columns. In general terms, the order of a matrix is $m \times n$. In Table 16.4, the order of F is 6×2 and the order of R is 6×6. When a matrix is square, we may say that its order is n, since the number of rows equals the number of columns. Thus we may say that matrix R in Table 16.4 is of order 6.

The *transpose* of a matrix is another matrix whose rows contain the same elements as the columns of the matrix of which it is the transpose, and in the same order. Its columns contain the same elements as the corresponding rows in the original matrix, and in the same order. This explains the composition of matrix F' in Table 16.4, and its relations to matrix F. F' is the transpose of F. If you were to attempt to obtain the transpose of R, you would find that R and R' are identical, because of the symmetry in R. This would not necessarily be true of every square matrix. Coming back to F and F', it will be seen that the *order* becomes reversed. F is of order 6×2, whereas F' is of order 2×6.

Matrix Multiplication. We are now ready to see how F multiplied by its transpose equals the correlation matrix R. In such a multiplication, the elements in the first *column* of the product matrix come from the use of the elements in the first *column* of the second matrix (the multiplier). The element in each *row* of the first *column* of R comes from a corresponding *row* of F. Table 16.6 shows the operations for the multiplication of a matrix by its transpose. Note how each element in R is composed. You will find that for every element in R an equation of the type of (16.4) has been called for.

TABLE 16.6. MULTIPLICATION OF A FACTOR MATRIX BY ITS TRANSPOSE TO OBTAIN A CORRELATION MATRIX USING SYMBOLS FOR FACTOR LOADINGS TO ILLUSTRATE THE OPERATIONS INVOLVED

$$\begin{Vmatrix} a_1 & b_1 \\ a_2 & b_2 \\ a_3 & b_3 \end{Vmatrix} \times \begin{Vmatrix} a_1 & a_2 & a_3 \\ b_1 & b_2 & b_3 \end{Vmatrix} = \begin{Vmatrix} (a_1a_1 + b_1b_1) & (a_1a_2 + b_1b_2) & (a_1a_3 + b_1b_3) \\ (a_2a_1 + b_2b_1) & (a_2a_2 + b_2b_2) & (a_2a_3 + b_2b_3) \\ (a_3a_1 + b_3b_1) & (a_3a_2 + b_3b_2) & (a_3a_3 + b_3b_3) \end{Vmatrix}$$

$$F \qquad \times \qquad F' \qquad = \qquad R$$

The rules for matrix multiplication short-circuit the operations so that one need not think of applying equation (16.4) at every step. In writing and speaking, it is considerably shorter to say $F \times F' = R$, where each letter stands for a whole matrix and the times sign indicates a whole system of orderly multiplications and additions. It should be added that, unlike ordinary algebra, a multiplication must take place in a given order. $F \times F'$ is not the same as $F' \times F$. The latter product would give a matrix of order 2×2 and it would not be a correlation matrix such as we want. We shall find that matrix multiplication is useful in many other connections, also a transpose.

The Reduced Correlation Matrix. It should be added that matrix R is a *reduced* correlation matrix. The reason for this is that it represents only the common-factor variances of the tests. Note that in deriving the correlations from common-factor loadings the values appearing in the diagonal cells are the communalities of the tests. The communalities are the proportions of common-factor variance in the tests. This leaves the specific and error contributions to variance out of account. But the correlation coefficients also leave them out of account; thus it is consistent to have communalities in the diagonal cells. The importance of this will become more apparent later. Some factorists place the value 1.00 in every diagonal cell. This introduces specific and error variance, but it does things to the factorial picture which will be pointed out later.

The Number of Common Factors and the Rank of the Correlation Matrix. We have to consider next another very important property of a matrix—its *rank*. This is a key concept to the Thurstone theories. *The number of common factors is equal to the rank of the correlation matrix.* The idea of matrix rank can best be explained by looking into the history of factor analysis.

Thurstone recognized the fact, which had apparently been overlooked before, that when Spearman's tetrad differences are all zero (within the limits of sampling errors), the rank of the matrix is one. There is one common factor because there is a simple, direct proportionality among rows and columns of the matrix. Spearman's tetrads are, in fact, the *first minors* of a matrix. A *minor* is a square submatrix that has been extracted from a larger matrix, with each of its rows taken from the same row of the matrix and each of its columns taken from the same column of the matrix. The minor occupies a rectangular pattern in the matrix. The first minors are of order 2 × 2 or, more briefly, of order 2.

As an example, from Table 16.2, let us select rows *e* and *a* and columns *d* and *f*. The first minor thus formed is

$$\begin{vmatrix} .54 & .42 \\ .45 & .35 \end{vmatrix}$$

A square matrix like this is called a *determinant*, for which a single value can be given. A minor of order 2 may be expressed in the general terms:

$$\begin{vmatrix} a & b \\ c & d \end{vmatrix}$$

The value of this determinant is given by the equation $ad - bc$. This is identical with the tetrad-difference equation as applied to correlation coefficients. Applied to the minor given above from Table 16.2, we have

$$(.54 \times .35) - (.45 \times .42) = .1890 - .1890 = 0$$

Let us take a second minor, of order 3, from the correlation matrix of Table 16.7 where we know that there are two common factors. Let this minor come from rows 1, 2, and 3, and from columns 4, 5, and 6. We have

$$\begin{vmatrix} .27 & .00 & .63 \\ .40 & .12 & .56 \\ .64 & .48 & .00 \end{vmatrix}$$

It is obvious that if you take any first minor from this 3 × 3 determinant, its value is not zero. This indicates that there is more than one common factor present. Let us see whether the selected second minor will equal zero. We will not go into a detailed explanation of how to evaluate determinants of order greater than 2, for the student will not need to do these operations in factor analysis. The evaluation of our 3 × 3 minor is given by the following arithmetic:

$$\begin{vmatrix} .27 & .00 & .63 \\ .40 & .12 & .56 \\ .64 & .48 & .00 \end{vmatrix} = .27\begin{vmatrix} .12 & .56 \\ .48 & .00 \end{vmatrix} - .40\begin{vmatrix} .00 & .63 \\ .48 & .00 \end{vmatrix} + .64\begin{vmatrix} .00 & .63 \\ .12 & .56 \end{vmatrix}$$

$$= .27(-.2688) - .40(-.3024) + .64(-.0756)$$

$$= -.072576 + .120960 - .048384$$

$$= 0$$

When all the minors of order 3 vanish, there are two common factors. When all the minors of order 4 vanish, there are three common factors. By induction it is seen that the number of common factors is one less than the order of the lowest-order minor that will vanish. If the minors of a certain order vanish, all those of higher order will also vanish. The number of common factors equals the rank of the matrix. Thus the rank of a matrix is the order of the highest-order minors that do not all vanish. With one common factor all minors vanish down to and including those of order 2. The highest-order minors that do not vanish have an order of 1. The lower the order of vanishing minors, the simpler the proportionality. There is proportionality, though it may be of a somewhat complicated nature, whenever the rank of a correlation matrix is lower than its order. When its rank equals its order, there are as many factors as tests.

Geometric Interpretation of Factors

The facts of intercorrelations and of factor loadings and their interrelationships and the various concepts, such as communality, specificity, uniqueness, and orthogonality, can be illustrated geometrically. This approach may help the student to gain further insight into factor theory. It is also basic to some of the operations to follow, particularly the phase of factor analysis known as rotation of axes.

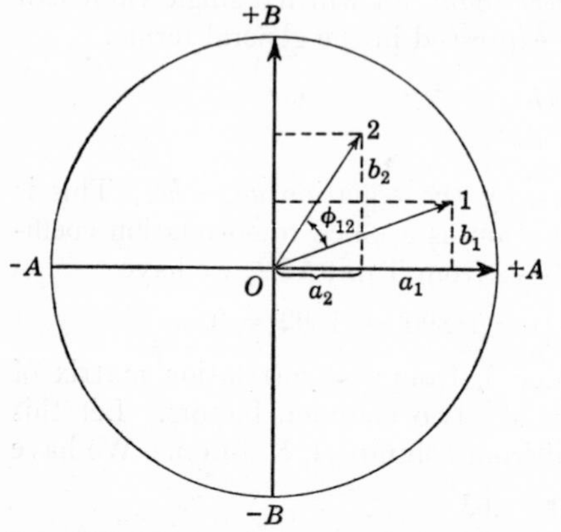

Fig. 16.3. Geometric representation of two tests in a two-factor space. The two vectors A and B represent orthogonal common factors, and the vectors 1 and 2 represent two correlated tests.

Factors and Tests as Vectors. Observe Fig. 16.3. For illustrative purposes we have represented there two common factors A and B and two tests, 1 and 2. Factor A is represented by the horizontal axis in a cartesian coordinate system and factor B by the vertical axis orthogonal to it. The independence of the two factors is shown by this orthogonality, since we may move along axis A, or on a line parallel with it, without at all introducing any change along axis B, and vice versa.

The circle in Fig. 16.3 is drawn with a radius of unity. Tests 1 and 2 are represented as vectors extending outward from the origin O. A vector is a line having a given length and a given direction. The factors are also interpretable as vectors and as taking their start from the common origin. They are of unit length. A factor vector is given unit length because its entire variance is common-factor variance. The test vectors are short of unit length because the space of the plane defined by the two reference axes A and B is a common-factor space. Not all of their variance is common-factor variance. With two common factors we have a space of two dimensions. The unique variances of the tests would have to be represented by additional dimensions, at least one for each test. We shall see very shortly that the length of each test vector is related to its communality.

In the common-factor space we have as many dimensions as there are common factors. A third orthogonal factor would be placed through the origin at right angles to A and B. A fourth factor can be imagined at right angles to these three. A fifth and a sixth and so on could be added without limit. If each factor represents a fundamental variable of human personality, we can say that geometrically personality is represented by an n-dimensional hypersphere, a sphere of n dimensions.

Factor Loadings as Coordinates. Note that from the end of each test vector perpendiculars have been drawn in dotted lines to the two reference axes. The distances from the origin to the points at which these perpendiculars cut the axes are the coordinates of the test vectors. We say that test 1 has a projection of a_1 on axis A, and a projection of b_1 on axis B. The coordinates of test vector 1 are (.8,.3). These coordinates represent the factor loadings of A and B in test 1. Likewise, a_2 and b_2 represent the loadings of A and B in test 2. They are equal to .4 and .6, respectively.

We have found before that the sum of squares of factor loadings gives the communality of a test [equation (13.25)]. Thus $a^2{}_1 + b^2{}_1$ in this two-factor illustration gives the communality for test 1. In Fig. 16.3 it will be noted that a_1 and b_1 are the legs of a right triangle whose hypotenuse is the vector for test 1. From the Pythagorean theorem, h^2 is the square of the hypotenuse, which means that the length of the test vector is equal to h.

Correlations of Tests as Scalar Products. Intercorrelations of tests can also be given a geometric interpretation. This interpretation has proved to be very important in arriving at a method of extracting factors from a correlation matrix. Having defined h geometrically, we can now use it in expressing a coefficient of correlation. Without offering proof here, the following equation derived by Thurstone is given:

$$r_{ij} = h_i h_j \cos \phi_{ij} \qquad (16.5)$$

where r_{ij} = correlation between tests I and J

h_i, h_j = lengths of vectors for tests I and J, respectively

ϕ_{ij} = angle of separation between vectors I and J

The expression on the right is known as a *scalar product*. It can be shown to be related to equations already given for deriving correlations from factor loadings (16.4).

Now the cosine of an angle varies between 1.0 and 0 as the angle varies between 0 and 90 degrees, respectively. According to equation (16.5), if both h's are equal to 1.0, the correlation is determined entirely by the angle of separation of the vectors. Under the same conditions, if they are colinear (angle of 0 degrees), the correlation is 1.0. If they are separated by 90 degrees, the correlation is zero, regardless of the vector lengths. Vectors separated by more than 90 degrees correlate negatively. When the separation is as much as 180 degrees, the correlation approaches −1.0 as the vector lengths approach unity, for then cos ϕ equals −1.0. Most tests of ability are positive or zero, which means that their vectors lie within one quadrant in a plane, or within a cone that does not spread more than 90 degrees in any direction.

Test Configuration and Factor Structure. Equation (16.5) is very important because it demonstrates the fact that the intercorrelations of tests describe the angles of separation between their vectors and also the lengths of those vectors. A set of test vectors is fixed in space and remains invariant with or without any reference axes to give them a reference frame. A collection of test vectors is called a *test configuration*. A test configuration is illustrated in Fig. 16.4*a*. This test configuration describes geometrically the intercorrelations of the correlation matrix for Prob. I in Table 16.7. It is true that we are able to draw this configuration only because of knowing the factor matrix (see Table 16.4) for these tests. But after the configuration was drawn, the reference axes were no longer needed.

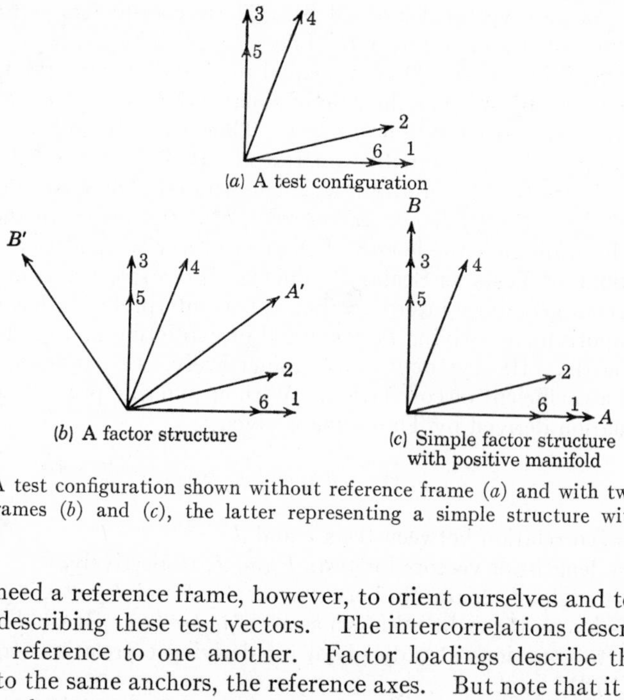

FIG. 16.4. A test configuration shown without reference frame (*a*) and with two different reference frames (*b*) and (*c*), the latter representing a simple structure with positive manifold.

We do need a reference frame, however, to orient ourselves and to provide a way of describing these test vectors. The intercorrelations describe them only with reference to one another. Factor loadings describe them with reference to the same anchors, the reference axes. But note that it would be possible to place two orthogonal axes in the test configuration in an infinite number of ways. All would be equally effective in providing common anchors for the six tests. In the *factor structure* in Fig. 16.4*b* we have a pair of reference axes, A' and B', placed arbitrarily in a certain position. We could write a factor matrix for the six tests in *this* reference frame. The second column would have three positive coordinates (loadings) for tests 3, 4, and 5, and three negative loadings for tests 1, 2, and 6. We would say that factor B' is a bipolar factor, since there are both positive and negative loadings of substantial size.

The Need for Rotation of Reference Axes. You will find later that in extracting factors from a correlation matrix we first introduce an arbitrary reference frame such as that in Fig. 16.4*b*. The position of these axes is a mere accident of the configuration of tests we happen to have in the battery for analysis. The factor matrix for this structure will not duplicate the one with which we started in Table 16.4. The latter had in it no negative projections and a number of zeros. The matrix for the factor structure in Fig. 16.4*b* has no zero loadings and it does have some negative loadings. What remains is to find the position for the reference axes which will reproduce the original factor matrix. For if the original factors stand for some meaningful psychological variables, it is probable that the arbitrary axes A' and B' do not.

The solution is in a rotation of the reference frame, leaving the test configuration invariant, as it will be no matter where we place the axes. Reference to Fig. 16.4 will show that a rotation of less than 45 degrees is needed to get from the structure in *b* to that in *c* which will be found to be the correct one. It is correct in that it reproduces the factor matrix with which we started.

Criteria for Rotation of Axes. In practice we have no knowledge of the "correct" factor matrix. How can we tell when we have achieved the proper rotation? When dealing with tests of abilities, one criterion is that of *positive manifold.* By this we mean that after rotation all the factor loadings are positive, after making allowances for sampling errors. This is because it is hard to imagine a factor of ability being negatively related to excellence of performance in a test. It would mean that the more of a fundamental ability a person has the lower his score would tend to be. The very general empirical finding that tests of ability rarely correlate negatively with one another suggests that the test vectors should not only lie inside a 90-degree spread but that this spread should be in the positive quadrant of the coordinate system.

The criterion of a positive manifold is of limited use, however. It does not apply when we are dealing with genuinely bipolar factors which we often encounter outside the domains of abilities. A more generally applicable criterion known as *simple structure* was devised by Thurstone. This idea will be more fully defined later. Suffice it to say here that when rotation to simple structure is achieved we have a maximal number of zero factor loadings. In Fig. 16.4*c* we have the reference axes rotated orthogonally to a position that yields four zero loadings—tests 3 and 5 for factor A and tests 1 and 6 for factor B. This brings the axes to a place at which the original factor matrix is duplicated. This is because the original factor matrix was designed to satisfy simple structure. Thurstone believes that when simple structure is achieved in rotations the factors have psychological meaning. In other words, simple structure is a principle of order in psychological nature.

Extraction of Factors by the Centroid Method

We are now ready to see how, starting with a correlation matrix, we can arrive at factors and factor loadings. We will use the simple two-factor problem (Prob. I) as a way to begin, since it illustrates the main principles. We shall then solve a three-factor problem in more detail, observing some of the best computing steps with their checks. Both problems are with fictitious data, since it is very difficult to find real data which will not run into complicating features that may tend to confuse as well as enlighten. The student will need to remember as he tries these procedures on actual data that the present illustrations are of somewhat idealized situations. They should serve to demonstrate the principles of factorial procedures, however, on which the student must build as he gains experience in new problems.

General Principles of the Centroid Method. It may be helpful to the beginner to consider the geometric picture of the factor situation. Figure 16.5 shows the assumed factor structure for Prob. I. The test-vector lines are omitted in this picture, only points at the ends of those vectors being shown. Ignore the dotted lines for the moment. The actual factors *A* and *B* provide the main reference frame for the purpose of discussion only. Our first important step is to locate one new reference axis (we will locate the second one later). All the experimental information we have is in the correlation matrix. We must locate the first axis merely from this information.

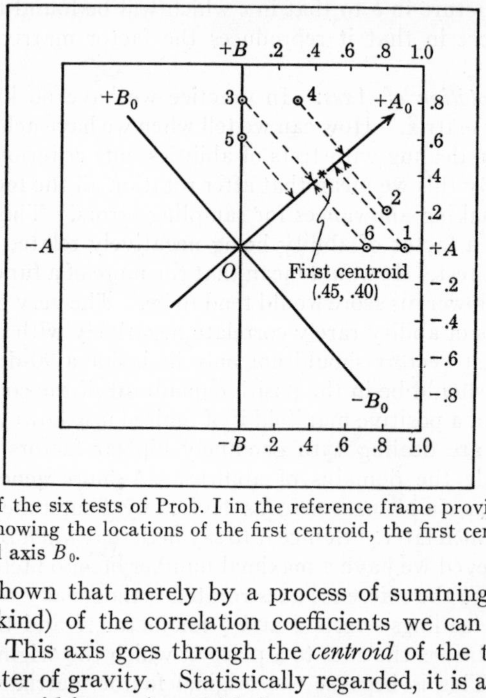

FIG. 16.5. A plot of the six tests of Prob. I in the reference frame provided by the known factors *A* and *B*, showing the locations of the first centroid, the first centroid axis A_0, and the second centroid axis B_0.

It has been shown that merely by a process of summing and of finding averages (of a kind) of the correlation coefficients we can locate the first reference axis. This axis goes through the *centroid* of the test vectors. A centroid is a center of gravity. Statistically regarded, it is a mean. In this problem, the centroid is a point which is at the center of gravity of the six points in Fig. 16.5. This point is determined from the correlation coefficients by a process about to be described.

Here, where we know the relation of the tests to the reference frame *AOB*, it is possible for us to locate the centroid in another way, a much simpler way. In finding the arithmetic mean of values that are on a *single* scale, you add up the linear values and divide by their number. In the present problem, we have values along *two* dimensions. There will be an *A* average and a *B* average. Those two averages give us the coordinates of the centroid of the six tests with respect to the *AOB* reference frame. From the factor matrix in Table 16.4, we find that the sums of the *A* and *B* coordinates are 2.7 and 2.4, respectively. The means corresponding are .45 and .40. In Fig. 16.5

a star has been placed at the point described by these coordinates. The first centroid axis, designated as A_0, is drawn through that point. It will become our first temporary reference axis (before rotation to final position). Since we know that there is only one other common factor in this problem, the second temporary reference axis—the second-centroid-factor vector—can be drawn orthogonal to axis A_0 as shown in Fig. 16.5. This axis becomes B_0.

It will be shown later how axis B_0 is also located through a *second* centroid, using only the information provided by the intercorrelations. Briefly, after extracting the first centroid factor we remove from the correlation coefficients as much of them as is accounted for by factor A_0. This leaves a matrix of *residuals*, which, in this problem, are entirely accounted for by factor B_0.

Extraction of Centroid Factors. We are now ready to extract the first centroid factor. But at the very outset we must be aware of a difficulty that is met in practice but which will not cause any trouble in Prob. I. In a correlation matrix derived from test scores or other experimental measurements, the diagonal cells are empty. It could have been noted when we computed the correlation matrix from the factor matrix (Table 16.4) that in these cells we should have the communalities of the tests. The communalities are the values that are consistent with the correlation coefficients. The coefficients alone can determine the rank of the matrix (and hence the number of common factors). With communalities in the diagonal cells, the rank of the matrix is maintained. Other values in those cells would change the rank of the matrix. More of this later.

In Prob. I we know the communalities and we will take advantage of that fact and use them. In Prob. II, however, we will assume that we do not know them, so that we may see what happens in a genuine factor analysis with empirical data and unknown communalities. The solution of Prob. I is simplified in other ways, but the essential steps are present. The steps are listed under four main stages.

Stage I: *Extraction of the first centroid factor.*

Step 1. With communalities entered in the diagonal cells, sum the columns, entering the sums in the row headed by E. The choice of the symbol E here will be clearer when we get into the solution of Prob. II.

Step 2. Sum the rows and see that they check with the sums of the columns.

Step 3. Sum the sums in row E and those in the check-sum column. See that they agree. This gives the sum of all elements in the matrix, symbolized by T (for grand total).

The first-factor loadings are given by the equation

$$a_1 = \frac{E_j}{\sqrt{T}} = mE_j \tag{16.6}$$

where a_1 = first-centroid-factor loading

E_j = sum of correlations with test J (where J is each test in turn)

T = sum of all coefficients in the correlation matrix

Step 4. Compute the first-factor loadings. Since we are to divide each E by the same value, it is much easier, especially when there are many tests, to find the reciprocal of $\sqrt{T}$ and use it as a constant multiplier. In Table 16.7, $T = 13.05$, $\sqrt{T} = 3.6125$, and $1/\sqrt{T} = .27682$, which is called m. These values should be carried to at least five significant digits. It is important to check m before going further. This is done by using the equation $mT = \sqrt{T}$. The first-factor loadings to three decimal places appear in the last row of Table 16.7.

TABLE 16.7. EXTRACTION OF THE FIRST CENTROID FACTOR FROM THE CORRELATION MATRIX OF PROBLEM I

Test	1	2	3	4	5	6	Check sum
1	(.81)	.72	.00	.27	.00	.63	2.43✓
2	.72	(.68)	.16	.40	.12	.56	2.64✓
3	.00	.16	(.64)	.64	.48	.00	1.92✓
4	.27	.40	.64	(.73)	.48	.21	2.73✓
5	.00	.12	.48	.48	(.36)	.00	1.44✓
6	.63	.56	.00	.21	.00	(.49)	1.89✓
E	2.43	2.64	1.92	2.73	1.44	1.89	13.05✓ $= \Sigma r = T$
$mE = a_1$	.673	.731	.531	.756	.399	.523	3.613✓ $\sqrt{T} = 3.6125$
							$1/\sqrt{T} = .27682 = m$
							$mT = 3.6125$✓

Step 5. Check the last step. The sum of the factor loadings should equal $\sqrt{T}$.

Notice that the first-factor loadings are shown graphically in Fig. 16.5 as projections on axis A_0. They come in the order from test 4 with the highest loading to test 5 with the lowest loading. Cutting through the centroid of the six points as axis A_0 does, it may be expected to give all the points substantial projections on it.

Stage II: *Computation of the first-factor residuals.* The first factor accounts for much of the original intercorrelations. How much it does account for can be seen by applying the general equation (16.4) to the situation of centroid factors. Transposing in equation (16.4), we have

$$r_{ij} - a_i a_j = b_i b_j + c_i c_j + \cdots + q_i q_j \tag{16.7}$$

Symbolizing the terms on the right-hand side of this equation by ρ_{ij}, we have an equation for computing the first-factor residuals:

$$\rho_{ij} = r_{ij} - a_i a_j \tag{16.8}$$

For computing purposes, this is conveniently written

$$\rho_{ij} = r_{ij} + (a_i)(-a_j) \tag{16.9}$$

Step 6. Prepare a worktable like Table 16.8. The body of this table will contain the residuals. In the first column, list in order the first-factor loadings a_1, corresponding to the test numbers in column 2. In the top row, list the first-factor loadings with reversed sign (call them k_1, where $k_1 = -a_1$).

Step 7. Add to each element in matrix R (Table 16.7) the product $(a_1)(k_1)$ from the corresponding row and column in Table 16.8. This operation applies equation (16.9).

Step 8. Sum the columns of residuals and record in the row after Σ.

Step 9. Sum the rows of residuals, and check these with column sums. The column and row sums should be close to zero. This is a check of the work thus far. No algebraic sum at this step should deviate as much as .10 except in large matrices. Such discrepancies as do occur when there have been no errors of computation are due to accumulations of rounding errors.

TABLE 16.8. COMPUTATION OF THE FIRST-FACTOR RESIDUALS AND THE SECOND-FACTOR LOADINGS IN PROBLEM I

$-a_1 = k_1$		−.673	−.731	−.531	−.756	−.399	−.523	$-3.613 = \Sigma k_1$	
a_1	Test	1	2	3	4	5	6	Check sum	Check sum
.673	1	.357	.228	−.357	−.239	−.269	.278	−.002✓	(1.728)✓
.731	2	.228	.146	−.228	−.153	−.172	.178	−.001✓	(1.105)✓
.531	3	−.357	−.228	.358	.239	.268	−.278	.002✓	1.728✓
.756	4	−.239	−.153	.239	.158	.178	−.185	−.002✓	1.152✓
.399	5	−.269	−.172	.268	.178	.201	−.209	−.003✓	1.297✓
.523	6	.278	.178	−.278	−.185	−.209	.216	.000✓	(1.344)✓
Σ		−.002	−.001	.002	−.002	−.003	.000	−.006✓	8.354✓
E		(1.728)	(1.105)	1.728	1.152	1.297	(1.344)	$8.354 + \Sigma \lvert E \rvert = T$	
$mE = a_1$		−.598	−.382	.598	.399	.449	−.465	2.891✓ $\sqrt{T} = 2.8903$	
								$1/\sqrt{T} = .34598 = m$	
								$mT = 2.8903$	

Let us stop to see what we have in the matrix of residuals. In this problem where we know there are only two factors, the situation is simple enough to be represented on a plane. Figure 16.6 shows what has been going on. We know that the second-centroid-factor axis B_0 can go in only one place—through the origin and orthogonal to A_0. We can forecast the second-factor loadings graphically by dropping perpendiculars from the six test points to axis B_0. When we took from the original correlation coefficients those parts accounted for by factor A_0, we took one dimension out of our two-dimensional system, leaving only one dimension, namely, B_0. Consequently, we should actually move the points down to axis B_0. The arrows in Fig. 16.6 indicate this movement. The numbers 1′ to 6′ indicate the positions of the six tests in this one-dimensional system. In it there is a single common factor. The residual matrix represents the positions of the tests along axis B_0. It is from this matrix that we must determine their factor loadings. Here the residuals are like intercorrelations in a one-dimensional or *g*-factor system. You would find that the tetrad differences for these residuals are all zero. In most problems in practice, however, we have more than one common factor and more than one dimension left after extracting the first factor. A simple figure such as we have here could not then describe the situation.

Reflections of Test Vectors. The extraction of the second centroid factor proceeds much like that of the first, with one important difference. Note that if we left the six points 1′ to 6′ just as they are in Fig. 16.6 (and their positions are described also by the residuals), we would find the centroid to be almost exactly zero. Somehow, we will have to get the centroid away from the origin so that we can put a vector through it. Here a neat trick is performed. We reflect some of the test points through the origin, getting all of them on the same side of the origin. From the diagram, we can see that we could reflect tests 1′, 2′, and 6′ or we could reflect the other three. By "reflecting" we mean that each test vector retains its same length but it extends in the opposite direction. You will see that tests on the same side of the origin in Fig. 16.6 have positive residuals while those on opposite sides

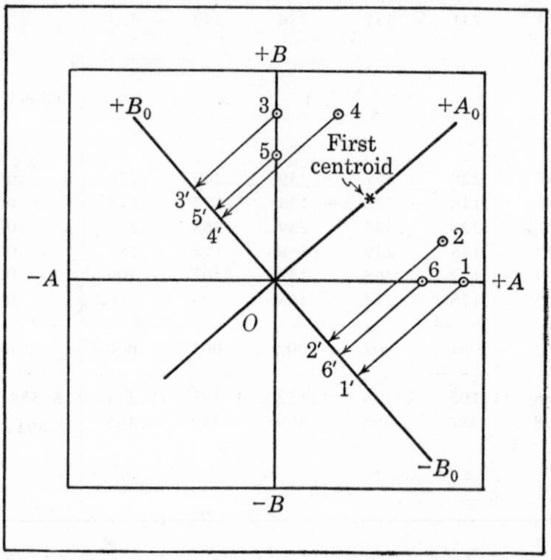

FIG. 16.6. Illustration showing in geometrical terms what happens in the extraction of the first centroid factor in Prob. I.

of the origin have negative residuals. After we reflect either set of three, all residuals should become positive.

Here it is clear as to what combination of test vectors should be reflected. In practice, where there are more than two factors, it is not so easy to decide which ones to reflect. The general policy is to reflect one test vector at a time, note the results, then reflect a second, and so on. We reflect those that promise to do the most good in terms of producing large, positive sums of columns. The greater we can make the grand total T, the more variance we can extract each time. One should certainly keep on until all sums are positive, and this means sums *not including the diagonal values*. With practice one learns what to look for—columns with the greatest number of negative signs or with largest negative residuals. The next solution, of Prob. II, will demonstrate a very automatic procedure which ensures good reflections.

Stage III: *Extraction of the second centroid factor.*

Step 10. Reflect as many test vectors as may be necessary, in line with the preceding discussion. Here let us reflect tests 1′, 2′, and 6′. The result is shown graphically in Fig. 16.7, where we have 1″, 2″, and 6″ now on the positive side of B_0 in appropriate distances. In the table of residuals (Table 16.8), we change algebraic signs in rows 1, 2, and 6, also in columns 1, 2, and 6. Some elements will have double sign changes, coming back to positive when we are all through. After all sign changing, all residuals here will be positive. This is not always the case.

Step 11. Sum the columns and rows, checking the results. Put parentheses around sums for the reflected variables. We will treat all sums as positive in computing the factor loadings, but we must not forget that we have made some temporary changes in signs.

Step 12. Sum the sums, finding $\Sigma|E|$, which is the sum of the *absolute* values of E. This equals T. Find $\sqrt{T}$ and m as in steps 3 and 4 above, and check as in step 5.

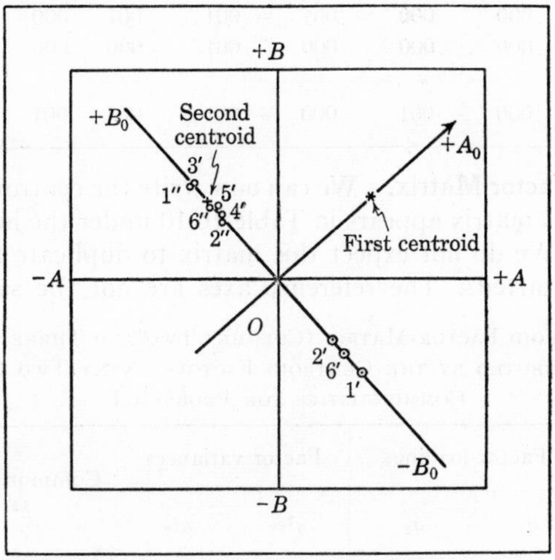

FIG. 16.7. Geometrical illustration of the process of reflection of test vectors before extraction of the second centroid factor in Prob. I.

Step 13. Compute the second-factor loadings by the products mE, listing them in the bottom row of the table. Assign a negative algebraic sign to loadings of tests whose vectors were reflected.

Incidentally, we can now locate the second centroid by finding the average of the loadings, treating them all as positive. It is at a distance of .48 from the origin, as shown in Fig. 16.7. The arithmetic mean of the absolute values of factor loadings tells us how far the centroid is from the origin. This information is of little value except to tell us relatively how much variance we were able to extract.

Stage IV: *Computation of the second-factor residuals.* This process is like that in computing the first-factor residuals in every respect (see Table 16.9). It would not really be necessary here, for we have extracted all the factors there are. We should expect the second-factor residuals to be zero. This step would be desirable in practice, however, even though we feel fairly certain that we will extract no more factors. There is the chance to do some checking as in step 9. We also want to be sure that the residuals are all sufficiently small as to assure us that it does not pay to extract more factors. Table 16.9 shows that the extractions here have exhausted the correlation matrix, except for rare rounding errors.

TABLE 16.9. COMPUTATION OF THE SECOND-FACTOR RESIDUALS IN PROBLEM I

$-a_2 = k_2$		.598	.382	−.598	−.399	−.449	.465	$-.001 = \Sigma k_2$
a_2	Test	1	2	3	4	5	6	Check sum
−.598	1	−.001	.000	.001	.000	.000	.000	.000✓
−.382	2	.000	.000	.000	−.001	.000	.000	−.001✓
.598	3	.001	.000	.000	.000	−.001	.000	.000✓
.399	4	.000	−.001	.000	.000	−.001	.001	−.001✓
.449	5	.000	.000	−.001	−.001	−.001	.000	−.003✓
−.465	6	.000	.000	.000	.001	.000	.000	.001✓
	Σ	.000	−.001	.000	−.001	−.003	.001	−.004

The Centroid-factor Matrix. We can now write the centroid-factor matrix for Prob. I. This matrix appears in Table 16.10 under the heading of "Factor Loadings." We do not expect this matrix to duplicate factor matrix F with which we started. The reference axes are not the same. Both are

TABLE 16.10. CENTROID FACTOR MATRIX (COLUMNS TWO AND THREE), PROPORTIONS OF VARIANCE CONTRIBUTED BY THE CENTROID FACTORS (NEXT TWO COLUMNS), AND COMMUNALITIES FOR PROBLEM I

Test	Factor loadings		Factor variances		Communalities h^2
	a_1	a_2	a^2_1	a^2_2	
1	.673	−.598	.453	.358	.811
2	.731	−.382	.534	.146	.680
3	.531	.598	.282	.358	.640
4	.756	.399	.572	.158	.730
5	.399	.449	.159	.202	.361
6	.523	−.465	.274	.216	.490
		Σa^2_k	2.274	1.438	3.712
			61.3%	38.7%	100.0%

related to the same correlation matrix, however. If we call the centroid matrix C, the product CC' should equal R. It would take a rotation of reference axes to transform matrix C into matrix F. This we will do later.

It is of interest to compute the squares of the centroid-factor loadings, for they tell us the proportions of variance accounted for by each factor in each test and in all tests combined. They also give us, by summing for each test, the communalities of the tests. The latter are given in the last column of Table 16.10. It will be seen that they agree within .001 with those derived from matrix F. In analyzing empirical data, this is an important check, in order to see whether the computed communalities agree with those with which we start extracting the first factor. The sums of the squares of the factor loadings by factors are given at the bottom of Table 16.10. From these we see that the first factor took out over 61 per cent of the variance extracted and the second factor the remaining 39 per cent.

TABLE 16.11. AN ASSUMED FACTOR MATRIX F WITH THREE COMMON FACTORS

Test	Factors			Communality h^2
	A	*B*	*C*	
1	.9	.0	.0	.81
2	.7	.4	.0	.65
3	.0	.8	.3	.73
4	.0	.9	.0	.81
5	.3	.0	.9	.90
6	.0	.0	.8	.64

Extraction of Factors in a Three-factor Problem. We will now extract the centroid factors in a problem having three common factors. This solution will be made more realistic than that for Prob. I in several ways. By extending the repeated cycles to be seen here, the student should be able to apply the steps to a problem with a greater number of factors. The procedure described is based upon Thurstone's "complete centroid" method which was designed with complete checks so that even a clerk who knows nothing about factor theory can carry out a solution. The student may feel that there is too much checking and that the work can be curtailed materially. That is probably true. Until you are practiced in extracting factors, however, it would be well for you to include all the steps given.

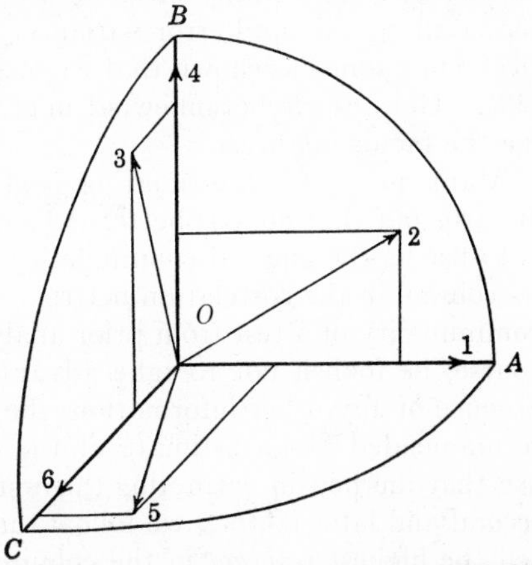

FIG. 16.8. Geometrical illustration of the test configuration and the factor structure involved in Prob. II.

The data for Prob. II are fictitious and somewhat ideal. The factor matrix and communalities are presented in Table 16.11. A three-dimensional diagram shows the factor structure in Fig. 16.8. Tests 1, 4, and 6 are each of complexity one (have variances each in one common factor only) and tests 2, 3, and 5 are of complexity two. No test is of complexity three, though this could happen in practice. Vectors for three tests, 1, 2, and 4, lie in the plane AOB, which means they have no projections on factor C. Tests 3, 4, and 6 have no projections on factor A. Tests 1, 5, and 6 have no loadings in factor B.

We have a neat, orthogonal, simple structure. You will find later that this facilitates very decidedly the rotations to come.

Guessed Communalities. Although we know the communalities in this problem, as we did in Prob. I, we will assume that they are not known, as in a typical research problem. The problem of unknown communalities has been one of the toughest to solve in factor analysis, but it has not proved to be anything more than an annoying inconvenience in practice. We have seen that to maintain the proportionality that exists among the correlation coefficients we must use communalities in the diagonal cells of the correlation matrix. What we do is to make the best guesses of them that we can and proceed as if they were correct. If the correlation matrix is very large, and we may interpret "very large" here to mean 20 or more tests, we need not be very much concerned about making bad guesses of communalities. If the correlation matrix is small, particularly if there are less than 10 to 15 variables, we check up to see how much in error our guesses were by comparing guessed with obtained communalities after the factors have been extracted. If the discrepancies are as large as .10, either positive or negative, we do well to start the extractions all over again, using new guesses based on the computed communalities we found the first time through. More will be said about this later.

If the communalities are overestimated, we are likely to increase the rank of the matrix, which means that there appear to be more common factors than there actually are. In the extreme case, if we put 1.00 in each diagonal cell, the rank of the matrix becomes equal to its order; there will be as many factors as tests. Many of these are, of course, not common factors; they represent specific and error variance. If we underestimate the communalities, Thurstone has shown that we may be involved with imaginary numbers (49). Guesses can be somewhat in error, however, without seriously distorting the factor picture.

Many methods of estimating communalities have been suggested (49). It turns out that none is better than the simplest of them all. This method is to use as the guessed communality for each test the highest coefficient in its column in the correlation matrix. If one has information concerning the communality of a test from prior analysis in a similar battery, one would, of course, be foolish not to take advantage of that information. But in the absence of any other information, the highest r in a column can be strongly recommended as an estimate of the communality of that test. We shall use that method in extracting the first factor in Prob. II. As we extract the second and later factors, we follow the same principle, using in the diagonal cell the highest *residual* in the column, discarding the obtained residual for that cell.

The extracting of the first centroid factor in Prob. II (see Table 16.12) proceeds like that in Prob. I (see Table 16.7), except for the use of guessed communalities in row D. The computation of the first-factor residuals (see Table 16.13) is also like that for Prob. I up to step 7. From there on the routine is different. It will now be described.

Steps in the Complete Centroid Method. These new steps are designed to provide complete checking of computations. One of their chief advantages, however, is that they make decisions as to which test vectors to reflect an automatic procedure.

Step 1. Having recorded the first factor loadings, a_1, in column 1, sum them to find v_1. Sum the k_1 values and see whether $\Sigma k_1 = -\Sigma a_1$, as a check. $\Sigma k_1 = -v_1$.

Step 2. Carry over from the preceding table (Table 16.12) the s_1 values, recording them in the row headed s_1. Sum them after recording, and see that this sum checks with that found previously.

TABLE 16.12. CORRELATION MATRIX FOR PROBLEM II AND EXTRACTION OF THE FIRST CENTROID FACTOR

Test	1	2	3	4	5	6	Check sum	
1		.63	.00	.00	.27	.00	.90✓	
2	.63		.32	.36	.21	.00	1.52✓	
3	.00	.32		.72	.27	.24	1.55✓	
4	.00	.36	.72		.00	.00	1.08✓	
5	.27	.21	.27	.00		.72	1.47✓	
6	.00	.00	.24	.00	.72		.96✓	
s_1	.90	1.52	1.55	1.08	1.47	.96	7.48✓	
D	.63	.63	.72	.72	.72	.72	4.14	
$s_1 + D = E$	1.53	2.15	2.27	1.80	2.19	1.68	11.62✓ $= T$	$\sqrt{T} = 3.4088$
$mE = a_1$	.449	.631	.666	.528	.642	.493	3.409✓	$1/\sqrt{T} = .29336 = m$
								$mT = 3.4088$✓

Step 3. Compute the residuals for test 1, using formula (16.9) as previously. Sum these values and record in the row after s_2. Note that nothing is done with the diagonal residuals at this stage. They would be discarded, having no use here. New diagonal-cell estimates will be made in row D.

Step 4. Find the product k_1v_1 for test 1, and record it in the row provided for it.

Step 5. Find $k^2{}_1$ for the first test, and record in the appropriate cell.

Step 6. Find the sum of $s_1 + k_1v_1 + k^2{}_1$, and record just below those three values. Check to see that the s_2 already recorded agrees with this sum. It should do so with a small rounding error in the third decimal place.

Step 7. With the check in step 6 satisfied, copy the residuals for test 1 in the corresponding *row* of the residual matrix.

Step 8. Sum the row just recorded, and see that the result agrees with s_2 for the same test.

Step 9. Do the same operations described in steps 3 through 8 for the remaining tests. You will have one less residual to compute for each succeeding test. There will be none to compute for the last test, but finish out the column and the checks for that test as for the others.

Step 10. Sum the s_2 values and the check-sum values, and see that the two sums agree exactly.

Step 11. Sum the k_1v_1 values and the $k^2{}_1$ values, and record in the check-sum column. The check for Σk_1v_1 is the product $(-v_1)(v_1)$. They should agree exactly. The exact check for $\Sigma k^2{}_1$ is $\Sigma a^2{}_1$.

TABLE 16.13. FIRST-FACTOR RESIDUALS AND EXTRACTION OF THE SECOND CENTROID FACTOR

	k_1	−.449	−.631	−.666	−.528	−.642	−.493	$-3.409 = -v_1$✓
a_1	Test	1	2	3	4	5	6	Check sum
.449	1		.346	−.299	−.237	−.018	−.221	−.429✓
.631	2	.346		−.100	.027	−.195	−.311	−.233✓
.666	3	−.299	−.100		.368	−.158	−.088	−.277✓
.528	4	−.237	.027	.368		−.339	−.260	−.441✓
.642	5	−.018	−.195	−.158	−.339		.403	−.307✓
.493	6	−.221	−.311	−.088	−.260	.403		−.477✓
	$3.409 = v_1$							−2.164✓
	s_1	.900	1.520	1.550	1.080	1.470	.960	7.480✓
	k_1v_1	−1.531	−2.151	−2.270	−1.800	−2.189	−1.681	$-11.622\ (-v_1)(v_1) = -11.621$✓
	k^2_1	.202	.398	.444	.279	.412	.243	$1.978\ \Sigma a^2_1 = 1.978$✓
	$s_1 + k_1v_1 + k^2_1$	−.429	−.233	−.276	−.441	−.307	−.478	−2.164✓
	s_2	−.429	−.233	−.277	−.441	−.307	−.477	−2.164✓
	$-s_2/2 = A$	.2145	.1165	.1385	.2205	.1535	.2385	1.0820✓
	$+ 6$	−.0065	−.1945	.0505	−.0395	.5565	(.2385)	.6050✓
	$B + 5$	−.0245	−.3895	−.1075	−.3785	(.5565)	(.6415)	.2980✓
	$-2B = C$	.049	.779	.215	.757	−1.113	−1.283	−.596✓ $\Sigma\|C\| = 4.196$
	D	.346	.346	.368	.368	− .403	− .403	$\Sigma\|D\| = 2.234$
	$C + D = E$	.395	1.125	.583	1.125	−1.516	−1.686	$6.430 = T$ 6.430✓
	$mE = a_2$	.156	.444	.230	.444	−.598	−.665	2.537✓ $\sqrt{T} = 2.53574$
								$1/\sqrt{T} = .39436 = m$
								$mT = 2.53573$✓

Step 12. See that $\Sigma(s_1 + k_1v_1 + k^2{}_1)$ equals $\Sigma s_1 + \Sigma k_1v_1 + \Sigma k^2{}_1$.

Step 13. See that Σs_2 approximately equals the values mentioned in step 12.

Step 14. For each test find a value A, which equals $-s_2/2$. This is in preparation for making reflections of some of the test vectors. Carry this step through the check-sum column. Sum the row and check.

Step 15. In row A find the largest positive value. Here it is .2385 for test 6. Record this number in the cell immediately below, in parentheses. This shows that the sum of residuals for test 6 has changed signs but not numerical value.

Step 16. Write +6 at the head of the next row to indicate that test 6 is being reflected. The values in this row are to indicate what the column sums would be after reflecting all signs in the row of residuals for test 6. Each one is found by adding algebraically the A value for a test to the residual in the row for test 6. For example, in the column for test 1, we have .2145 + (−.2210) which equals −.0065. Carry these additions through the check-sum column, sum the +6 row, and check.

Step 17. Repeat step 16 with a second test, and so on as far as is necessary, always reflecting the test having the largest positive value outside of parentheses. Continue until all values in the row are either negative outside parentheses or positive inside parentheses. Carry the parentheses along from row to row to show that a test has been reflected. Parentheses mean that the sum is actually negative in sign. Sometimes after several reflections a negative sign may crop up inside parentheses. This means that the sum is actually positive again, and the test should be re-reflected. Reflections should continue until all values are negative (or positive in parentheses). The last row, at the completion of this process, is also called row B.

Step 18. Multiply the values in row B by -2 to find C for each test. All tests that had parentheses will have negative C values. Sum the C values algebraically for checking purposes. Sum them also disregarding sign for later checking purposes.

Step 19. Enter diagonal values in row D, each with a sign consistent with that of C in the same column. Each D value equals the largest residual value in its column. No matter what the sign of that residual, its new sign should be like that of the corresponding C value. Find a sum of the D's disregarding signs.

Step 20. Find E for each test, where $E = C + D$. Sum the E values disregarding signs. Check this with the sum $|C| + |D|$. $\Sigma|E| = T$.

Step 21. Compute $\sqrt{T}$ and $1/\sqrt{T}$, which equals m. Check: mT should equal $\sqrt{T}$.

Step 22. Compute the factor loadings a_2 by the product mE. The absolute sum of the loadings should equal $\sqrt{T}$.

The computation of subsequent residuals and the extraction of factors follow the same steps as those just given (see Tables 16.14 and 16.15). Table 16.15 gives the third-factor residuals with checks up to and including step 13. Had we started with actual communalities in the diagonal cells, these residuals would have vanished exactly. The nonzero residuals here show the effects of using guessed communalities.

TABLE 16.14. SECOND-FACTOR RESIDUALS AND EXTRACTION OF THE THIRD CENTROID FACTOR

a_2	Test	1	2	3	4	5	6	Check sum
	k_2	$-.156$	$-.444$	$-.230$	$-.444$	$.598$	$.665$	$-.011 = -v_2$✓
$.156$	1		$.277$	$-.335$	$-.306$	$.075$	$-.117$	$-.406$✓
$.444$	2	$.277$		$-.202$	$-.170$	$.071$	$-.015$	$-.039$✓
$.230$	3	$-.335$	$-.202$		$.266$	$-.020$	$.065$	$-.226$✓
$.444$	4	$-.306$	$-.170$	$.266$		$-.073$	$.035$	$-.248$✓
$-.598$	5	$.075$	$.071$	$-.020$	$-.073$		$.005$	$.058$✓
$-.665$	6	$-.117$	$-.015$	$.065$	$.035$	$.005$		$-.027$✓
$.011 = v_2$								$-.888$✓
	s_2	$-.429$	$-.233$	$-.277$	$-.441$	$-.307$	$-.477$	-2.164✓
	k_2v_2	$-.002$	$-.005$	$-.003$	$-.005$	$.007$	$.007$	$-.001$ $(-v_2)(v_2) = -.0001$✓
	k^2_2	$.024$	$.197$	$.053$	$.197$	$.358$	$.442$	1.271 $\Sigma a^2_2 = 1.271$✓
	$s_2 + k_2v_2 + k^2_2$	$-.407$	$-.041$	$-.227$	$-.249$	$.058$	$-.028$	$-.894$✓
	s_3	$-.406$	$-.039$	$-.226$	$-.248$	$.058$	$-.027$	$-.888$✓
	$-s_3/2 = A$	$.2030$	$.0195$	$.1130$	$.1240$	$-.0290$	$.0135$	$.4440$✓
	$+1$	$(.2030)$	$.2965$	$-.2220$	$-.1820$	$.0460$	$-.1035$	$.0380$✓
	$+2$	$(.4800)$	$(.2965)$	$-.4240$	$-.3520$	$.1170$	$-.1185$	$-.0010$✓
	$B + 5$	$(.5550)$	$(.3675)$	$-.4440$	$-.4250$	$(.1170)$	$-.1135$	$.0570$✓
	$-2B = C$	-1.110	$-.735$	$.888$	$.850$	$-.234$	$.227$	$-.114$✓ $\Sigma\lvert C\rvert = 4.044$
	D	$-.335$	$-.277$	$.335$	$.306$	$-.075$	$.117$	$\Sigma\lvert D\rvert = 1.445$
								5.489✓
	$C + D = E$	-1.445	-1.012	1.223	1.156	$-.309$	$.344$	$5.489 = T$
	$mE = a_3$	$-.617$	$-.432$	$.522$	$.493$	$-.132$	$.147$	2.343✓ $\sqrt{T} = 2.34286$
								$1/\sqrt{T} = .42683 = m$
								$mT = 2.34287$✓

The centroid-factor loadings, their squares, and the obtained communalities are shown in Table 16.16. The sums of the squared loadings show that the first factor took out about 45 per cent of the total common-factor variance, the second took out 29 per cent, and the third about 26 per cent. The

TABLE 16.15. COMPUTATION OF THE THIRD-FACTOR RESIDUALS

a_3	Test	1	2	3	4	5	6	Check sum
	k_3	.617	.432	−.522	−.493	.132	−.147	.019 = $-v_3$
−.617	1		.010	−.103	−.002	−.006	−.026	−.037✓
−.432	2	.010		.024	.043	.014	.049	.140✓
.522	3	−.013	.024		.009	.049	−.012	.057✓
.493	4	−.002	.043	.009		−.008	−.037	.005✓
−.132	5	−.006	.014	.049	−.008		.024	.073✓
.147	6	−.026	.049	−.012	−.037	.024		−.002✓
−.019 = v_3								
	s_3	−.406	−.039	−.226	−.248	.058	−.027	−.888✓
	k_3v_3	−.012	−.008	.010	.009	−.003	.003	−.001 $(-v_3)(v_3)$ = −.0004✓
	k^2_3	.381	.187	.272	.243	.017	.022	1.122 Σa^2_3 = 1.122✓
	$s_3 + k_3v_3 + k^2_3$	−.037	.140	.056	.004	.072	−.002	.233✓
	s_4	−.037	.140	.057	.005	.073	−.002	.236✓

obtained communalities turned out to be no closer to the actual ones, on the whole, than are the guessed ones. The factor loadings bear much resemblance to those that have been obtained from the same correlation matrix by using the actual communalities. Evidently it would take two or three sets of extractions with new guessed communalities each time to bring the obtained communalities close to the actual ones.

TABLE 16.16. CENTROID FACTOR MATRIX FOR PROBLEM II, WITH PROPORTIONS OF VARIANCES CONTRIBUTED BY THE CENTROID FACTORS, OBTAINED COMMUNALITIES, GUESSED COMMUNALITIES, AND ACTUAL COMMUNALITIES

Test	a_1	a_2	a_3	a^2_1	a^2_2	a^2_3	$h^2_{obt.}$	$h^2_{gues.}$	$h^2_{act.}$
1	.449	.156	−.617	.202	.024	.381	.607	.63	.81
2	.631	.444	−.432	.398	.197	.187	.782	.63	.65
3	.666	.230	.522	.444	.053	.272	.769	.72	.73
4	.528	.444	.493	.279	.197	.243	.719	.72	.81
5	.642	−.598	−.132	.412	.358	.017	.787	.72	.90
6	.493	−.665	.147	.243	.442	.022	.707	.72	.64
			Σa^2_k	1.978	1.271	1.122	4.371		
				45.2%	29.1%	25.7%	100.0%		

When to Cease Extracting Centroid Factors. In this problem we knew beforehand that there are three common factors. In research problems we ordinarily have no sure information as to how many factors to expect. When we do have, we of course make use of that information. But usually the domain in which we are making the analysis is at least partially unexplored, and we do not know how many factors are present.

We have the fact that the number of common factors equals the rank of the correlation matrix. But this is of little practical help. The reason is that we usually have a number so large that testing for the vanishing of minors becomes a prohibitive task. Along with this is the fact that there are sampling errors, and without knowing standard errors of the minors we would not know when to accept the hypothesis of zero minors.

There is no single infallible index or criterion of when we have extracted the proper number of factors. One rough criterion is in the frequency distribution of the residuals. When we think we have extracted enough from other signs (for example, the residuals look very small), we may make a frequency distribution of the residuals, both positive and negative. About all we can say, however, is that if such a distribution is bimodal by inspection, we have not extracted enough factors. When enough have been extracted, it should be unimodal and probably on the leptokurtic side. This means that we may justifiably extract one or more factors after the distribution has become unimodal. This criterion therefore tells us when we have *not* extracted a sufficient number of factors; it does not tell us for sure that we have gone far enough.

By experience, the writer, and others, have found that there is rarely any danger of extracting too many factors. The danger is in not extracting enough. If we have extracted too many, we are almost sure to find it out when we do the rotations. In that case, one or more of the factors tend to disappear; any variance they had tends to be lost to other factors. In fact, this variance is often needed to help clear up the factor structure in rotation. It is good policy, then, to extract one more factor after you feel some assurance that you have extracted enough. When any factor has one or more loadings of plus or minus .20 or higher, there is enough variance present to aid in the rotations. Even when there are two or more between .15 and .20, the factor may be useful in rotations, although it proves to be merely a "residual" factor. A residual factor is one that loses rather than gains variance in rotations, and ends up with no substantial factor loadings. "Substantial" may be defined here as greater than .25 to .30.

There are some who seem to believe that the sampling errors in the correlation matrix somehow cling to the residuals until there comes a time in the extractions when the residuals represent nothing but these errors. Although there is no proof for it, the writer believes that error variance comes out all along the way in extracting factors and that even after extraction of the last factor some portion of the residuals represents common-factor variance. This is suggested by the way in which these late-extracted factors often help in achieving a good structure in rotations.

Rotation of Reference Axes

The Importance of Rotation of Axes. On the question of rotation many psychologists differ vigorously. The opposite points of view are defended by Thurstone who does rotate and by Burt who does not. Some of those who insist that there shall be a *g* factor in every analysis point to the first centroid factor as evidence that there is such a factor. Some accept the first centroid factor as being the *g* factor. They can, and do, keep this *g* factor as representing something that all the tests have in common. In this case, however, they are then left with bipolar factors to represent the other dimensions of the system. In the realm of abilities bipolar factors are hard to justify.

There are more telling arguments against the decision not to rotate, however. One is that the centroid-factor structure is not invariant. It depends upon what tests happen to be put into the battery for analysis. Let us assume that in Prob. I we were to take out tests 4 and 5 and to substitute for them two other tests like test 2. With five vectors in the region of tests 1 and 6 and only one in the direction of test 3, the centroid would be moved drastically toward the heavy cluster. The loadings of tests 1, 2, and 6 would increase substantially on the *g* factor, and the loading of test 3 would shrink to very small size. How is it possible to assume some fixed psychological meaning attached to any centroid factor when it is subject to the whims of the investigator who designed the battery? Batteries can be changed in this manner, however, and so long as the same common factors are present, rotations generally reveal the same structure. The centroid loadings of tests may vary and the amount of rotation may vary, but the end result of rotation generally leads to reproducible structure. It is to such reproducible variables that psychological meaning can be given with justification.

Orthogonal versus Oblique Rotations. In orthogonal rotations, the axes maintain their 90-degree separations and their independence after rotation as before. In oblique rotations, each axis is rotated separately without regard to maintaining independence. Oblique rotations therefore provide greater freedom and make possible a greater number of zero factor loadings. Simple structure is easier to achieve.

There are complications, however. One must keep track of the positions of reference axes and their intercorrelations. Reference axes in oblique structures no longer exactly stand for interpretable factors. There are other considerations which will be brought out later. Here it is necessary only to have a general distinction between the two kinds of rotation and to have justification for orthogonal rotations, which will be described first. There are many factorists who prefer orthogonal rotations for other reasons than those given here.

Orthogonal Rotation in Two Dimensions. We will begin with the rotation of axes orthogonally in Prob. I. The centroid matrix is reproduced in Table 16.17. The steps are as follows:

Step 1. Plot the test configuration in the reference frame on the centroid axes (see Fig. 16.9). Label the centroid axes A_0 and B_0. After the first rotation we will have axes A_1 and B_1. Both of these sets of axes are distinct from the actual ones, A and B, except that after rotation A_1 and B_1 should come very close to A and B.

Step 2. Notice where the new axes should be located so as to produce (1) a positive manifold (when the variables are abilities) and (2) as large a number of zero loadings as possible. A good device to use in this step is a transparent draftsman's right-angle triangle, placing the apex of the right angle at the origin of the plot and turning it about the origin as a pivot until a good rotation is found. Then draw the two new axes and label them A_1 and B_1. Which axis is which is not very important. It is desirable to make A_1 nearer to A_0 and B_1 closer to B_0.

TABLE 16.17. STEPS IN THE ORTHOGONAL ROTATION OF REFERENCE AXES IN PROBLEM I

Direction Numbers (L_{01})

	A_1	B_1
A_0	1.00	.89
B_0	−.89	1.00
Σl^2	1.7921	1.7921
$\sqrt{\Sigma l^2}$	1.3387	1.3387
$1/\sqrt{\Sigma l^2} = D_{01}$	.7470	.7470

	Centroid Matrix (C) A_0	B_0		Transformation Matrix (T_{01}) (Direction Cosines) A_1	B_1	Rotated Matrix (O_1) A_1	B_1	
1	.673	−.598	A_0	.747	.665	.900	.001	1
2	.731	−.382	B_0	−.665	.747	.800	.201	2
3	.531	.598				−.001	.800	3
4	.756	.398				.300	.800	4
5	.399	.449				−.001	.601	5
6	.523	−.465				.700	.000	6
	C		×	T_{01}		=	O_1	

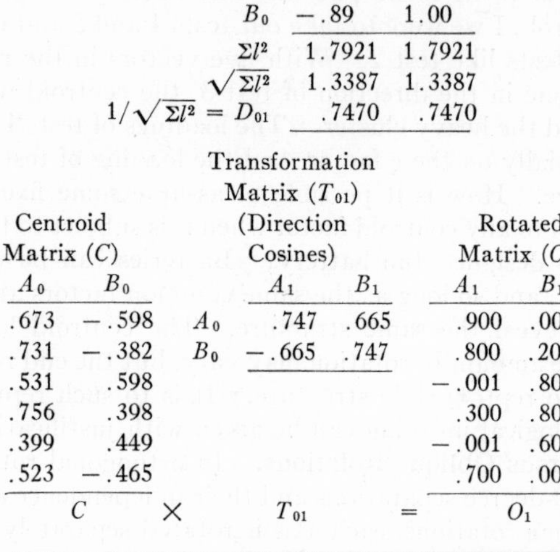

FIG. 16.9. A plot of the six test vectors of Prob. I in the reference frame of the centroid-factor axes A_0 and B_0, showing the orthogonal rotation to the new locations of reference axes at A_1 and B_1.

The Matrix of Transformation. The next steps have to do with setting up the transformation matrix T. This is the matrix by which we must multiply C, the centroid matrix, in order to arrive at O_1, the rotated matrix. With

r common factors in a problem, the transformation matrix is square, of order r. Here it will be of order 2.

Step 3. Determine the *direction numbers* of each new axis. By "direction numbers" we mean a pair of coordinates of the new axis with respect to the centroid axes. The centroid axes serve as the frame of reference at the start of the rotations. The position of axis A_1 can be described by giving a pair of coordinates of a point on that axis. Let us choose a point at a distance of 1.00 in the direction of A_0. The corresponding coordinate in the direction of B_0 is $-.89$. For axis B_1, the direction numbers are .89 and 1.00, respectively. Record the direction numbers in a matrix, L_{01}. These elements are known as l. This step and the next are the same for orthogonal and oblique rotations. Here, in an orthogonal rotation, the two pairs of direction numbers are of the same value except for a reversal in order and one reversal in sign. In the next step, then, the computational work in the two columns is identical, but it is desirable to do it twice for checking purposes. In oblique rotations the pairs of direction numbers are usually different.

Step 4. Normalize the direction numbers for each new axis. By "normalizing" we mean to find another pair of coordinates the sum of whose squares is equal to 1.0. First, we sum the squares of the direction numbers to find Σl^2. Next we find the square roots of these sums. It is this value by which the direction numbers must be divided to achieve our goal. Instead of dividing by this value we find its reciprocal, which is called D_{01}, and multiply. This is called the *stretching factor*.

Step 5. Multiply the direction numbers in matrix L_{01} by D_{01} to find the *direction cosines* for the transformation matrix T_{01}. The direction cosines for a new axis are actually the projections of that axis vector of unit length on the centroid axes. For those who know their trigonometry, it will be recognized that the direction cosines are also the sines and cosines of the angle of rotation θ. Actually, we could have measured the angle of rotation θ and could have looked up its sine and cosine in trigonometric tables. Measuring θ to the nearest degree in Fig. 16.9, we find that it is 42 degrees. The sine and cosine of an angle of 42 degrees are .743 and .669, two values not far from our direction cosines.

Step 6. Having transformation matrix T_{01}, we are ready to perform the rotation by the multiplication CT_{01}—a multiplication of the centroid matrix by the transformation matrix. The first element in rotated matrix O_1 is given by the operation $(.673)(.747) + (-.598)(-.665)$, which equals .900. The first element in the second column of O_1 is given by the operation $(.673)(.665) + (-.598)(.747)$, which equals .001.

Step 7. Check to see that the rotated matrix is reasonable in comparison with the plot, as in Fig. 16.9. For more accurate checking, a rule with divisions like those of the graph paper can be laid parallel to each new axis while checking loadings on the other axis.

Step 8. Another check after all orthogonal rotations are completed is to compute communalities. They should agree with those obtained from the centroid loadings.

Orthogonal Rotation in Three Dimensions. We will now see how the rotation process just described is extended to the case of three factors. The additional steps involved apply to rotations in any number of dimensions. We will use as our illustrative problem a centroid matrix derived from Prob. II. This centroid matrix, however, was obtained by using the known communalities in the correlation matrix and retaining diagonal-cell residuals after each extraction.

The rotation method proceeds by rotation in one plane at a time. A pair of centroid factors is selected, and their loadings are plotted on the plane made by their two axes. These axes are orthogonal to all others so that whatever happens in the way of a rotation in this plane will have no effect whatever upon the projections of the tests upon the other axes. Since the entire plane is orthogonal to all other axes, any lines within it are also orthogonal to them. If there seems to be no very obvious rotation to make in the

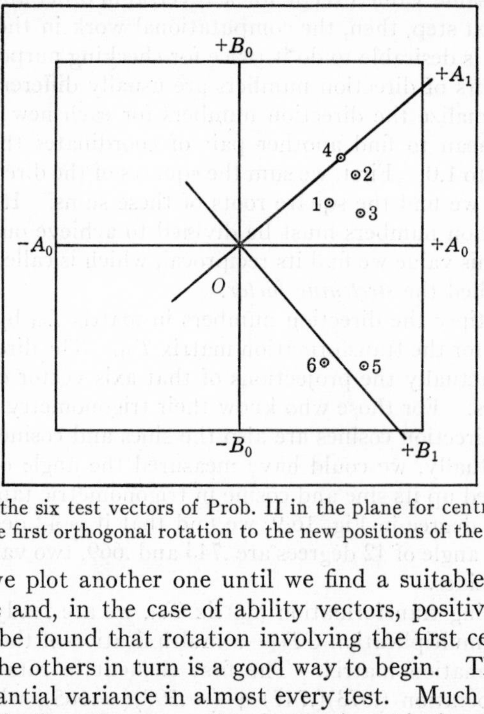

FIG. 16.10. Plot of the six test vectors of Prob. II in the plane for centroid-factor axes A_0 and B_0, showing the first orthogonal rotation to the new positions of the axes, A_1 and B_1.

plane plotted, we plot another one until we find a suitable one, aiming at simple structure and, in the case of ability vectors, positive manifold. It will sometimes be found that rotation involving the first centroid axis and one or more of the others in turn is a good way to begin. The first centroid factor has substantial variance in almost every test. Much of this variance will have to be distributed among other factors in achieving the criteria for a simple structure. But experience shows that it is not always best to rotate axis A with everything else before rotating other pairs. It is best to plot in new planes until a rather obvious rotation appears and then make it.

Our first rotation for Prob. II is in plane A_0OB_0 formed by the centroid axes A_0 and B_0. The plot is shown in Fig. 16.10, which was based upon the centroid loadings in Table 16.18, matrix C. The next operations are like steps 1 through 4 in the description of rotations in a two-dimensional problem above. This takes us up to the formation of the transformation matrix T_{01}. Here we encounter a new operation in step 5. Let us begin with step 5′ here.

Step 5′. The transformation matrix must be of order 3, since we have

TABLE 16.18. ORTHOGONAL ROTATIONS OF AXES IN PROBLEM II

Centroid Matrix (C)

	A_0	B_0	C_0
1	.493	.228	−.718
2	.626	.392	−.323
3	.658	.188	.512
4	.545	.483	.528
5	.684	−.648	−.112
6	.461	−.643	.113

Direction Numbers (L_{01})

	A_1	B_1
A_0	1.00	.87
B_0	.87	−1.00
Σl^2	1.7569	1.7569
$\sqrt{\Sigma l^2}$	1.32548	1.32548
D_{01}	.75444	.75444

First Rotated Matrix (O_1)

A_1	B_1	C_1	
.522	.152	−.718	1
.730	.115	−.323	2
.620	.290	.512	3
.728	−.007	.528	4
.091	.938	−.112	5
−.074	.788	.113	6

Direction Cosines (T_{01})

	A_1	B_1	C_1
A_0	.7544	.6564	.000
B_0	.6564	−.7544	.000
C_0	.000	.000	1.000
Σt^2	1.000	1.000	1.000

Direction Numbers (L_{12})

	A_2	C_2
A_1	1.00	.72
C_1	.72	−1.00
Σl^2	1.5184	1.5184
$\sqrt{\Sigma l^2}$	1.232235	1.232235
D_{12}	.81153	.81153

Second Rotated Matrix (O_2)

A_2	B_2	C_2	
.005	.152	.888	1
.404	.115	.689	2
.802	.290	−.054	3
.899	−.007	−.004	4
.008	.938	.144	5
.006	.788	−.135	6

Direction Cosines (T_{12})

	A_2	B_2	C_2
A_1	.812	.000	.584
B_1	.000	1.000	.000
C_1	.584	.000	−.812
Σt^2	1.000	1.000	1.000

Direction Numbers (L_{23})

	B_3	C_3
B_2	1.00	.17
C_2	−.17	1.00
Σl^2	1.0289	1.0289
$\sqrt{\Sigma l^2}$	1.014347	1.014347
D_{23}	.98586	.98586

Third Rotated Factor Matrix (O_3)

A_3	B_3	C_3	
.005	−.001	.899	1
.404	−.002	.697	2
.802	.295	−.004	3
.899	−.006	−.005	4
.008	.901	.300	5
.006	.800	.000	6

Direction Cosines (T_{23})

	A_3	B_3	C_3
A_2	1.000	.000	.000
B_2	.000	.986	.168
C_2	.000	−.168	.986
Σt^2	1.000	1.000	1.000

three factors. Notice that in matrix T_{01} (Table 16.18) the elements in the four cells involving axes A and B come from multiplying the elements of matrix L_{01} by D_{01}, consistent with previous practice. Since axis C is not being moved in this first rotation, its direction cosines are .0 on A_0 and B_0 and 1.0 on C_0. The new axes A_1 and B_1 also have projections of .0 on C_0, since they remain orthogonal to C_0, as was stated above. It is well to check the computations in this step by summing the squares of the elements in columns of matrix T_{01}. Here it was found that the check would not be satisfied unless four significant digits were used. Sometimes three decimal places will suffice.

Step 6′. Perform the matrix multiplication CT_{01} to obtain rotated matrix O_1. It will be found that the loadings for C_0 remain unchanged in O_1; therefore they can just be copied. The actual matrix multiplication involves only two columns in C and two columns and rows in T_{01}.

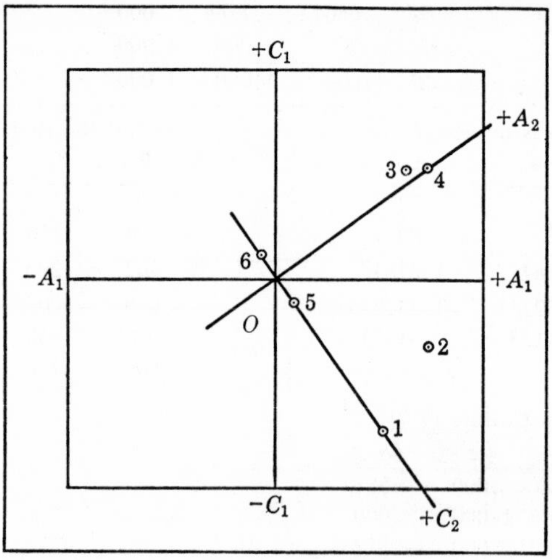

FIG. 16.11. Orthogonal rotation in the plane A_1OC_1 for Prob. II.

Step 7′. The same kind of graphic checking recommended above can be carried out here. The chief value of this checking is to catch errors in algebraic signs.

Step 8′. Plot the tests with reference to a new pair of axes based on matrix O_1. Figure 16.11 shows a plot of axes A_1 and C_1. Here it is possible to produce five zeros, or near-zeros, by a rotation. Repeat steps through 7′ to find matrix O_2. Apply the check in 7′.

Step 9′. Make a rotation in plane B_2OC_2, arriving at matrix O_3 (see Fig. 16.12 and Table 16.18).

Step 10′. Compute communalities to see whether they agree with those obtained from the centroid matrix.

Computing a Combined Matrix of Multiplication. Many investigators in reporting a factor-analysis study provide a copy of a single transformation matrix by means of which one could go directly from matrix C to matrix O_3 (or in the general case to matrix O_s, where there are s rotations). A single, combined matrix of transformation is obtained by the matrix equation:

$$U = T_{01}T_{12}T_{23} \cdots T_{(s-1)s} \qquad (16.10)$$

This equation calls for a succession of matrix multiplications in the order specified. This is illustrated for the three-dimensional problem in Table 16.19. The end result is a matrix U which is of such composition that $CU = O_3$, in Prob. II. That is, the centroid matrix multiplied by matrix U would give us the final rotated matrix.

TABLE 16.19. DERIVATION OF THE COMBINED TRANSFORMATION MATRIX FOR PROBLEM II

T_{01}

	A_1	B_1	C_1
A_0	.7544	.6564	.0
B_0	.6564	−.7544	.0
C_0	.0	.0	1.0

×

T_{12}

	A_2	B_2	C_2
A_1	.812	.0	.584
B_1	.0	1.0	.0
C_1	.584	.0	−.812

$= T_{01}T_{12}$

$T_{01}T_{12}$

	A_2	B_2	C_2
A_0	.6125728	.6564	.4405696
B_0	.5329968	−.7544	.3833376
C_0	.584	.0	−.812

×

T_{23}

	A_3	B_3	C_3
A_2	1.0	.0	.0
B_2	.0	.986	.168
C_2	.0	−.168	.986

$= T_{01}T_{12}T_{23} = U$

	A_3	B_3	C_3
A_0	.613	.573	.545
B_0	.533	−.808	.251
C_0	.584	.136	−.801

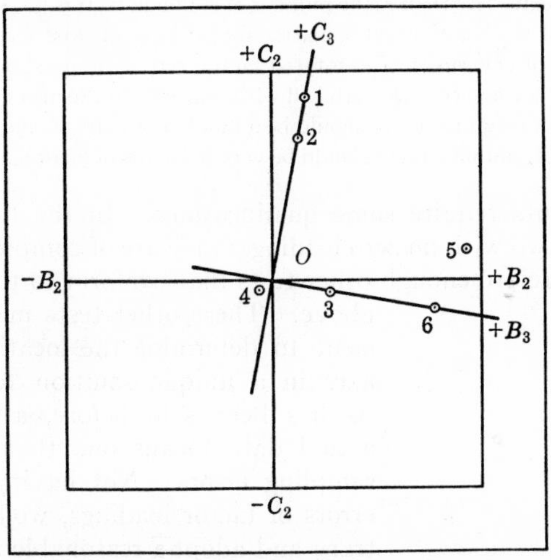

FIG. 16.12. Orthogonal rotation in the plane B_2OC_2 for Prob. II.

Correlation of the Reference Axes. Since so much computation goes into the derivation of U, it is desirable to have some check of the accuracy of the result. One check is to compute the intercorrelations of the new reference axes. In orthogonal rotations, the axes should correlate zero with one another and 1.00 with themselves. The correlation of the reference axes can be computed by the multiplication $U'U$. That is, we multiply the transpose of U by U. For the illustrative problem, the multiplication $U'U$ yields matrix M in Table 16.20. The check is satisfied. In oblique rotations this step serves a more important purpose, for then the correlations among reference axes are usually not zero. Self-correlations are 1.00, and that part still serves as a check when there are oblique rotations, but the other checking value of M is lost.

Simple Structure. Since simple structure is so important in determining where to rotate, it is time we had a more rigorous definition of the concept. Thus far, it has been implied that simple structure can be achieved by maximizing the number of zero factor loadings after rotation. This is roughly true, but it is not sufficient as a definition. Thurstone has listed a number of

TABLE 16.20. CORRELATION MATRIX OF THE ROTATED REFERENCE AXES

$U'U = M$

	A_3	B_3	C_3
A_3	1.001	.000	.000
B_3	.000	1.000	.001
C_3	.000	.001	1.000

more specific criteria of a simple structure (49, p. 335). These criteria can be more easily satisfied by oblique than by orthogonal rotations, though they apply to both.

1. Each row of the rotated factor matrix should have at least one zero. This means that each test is of complexity less than r, the number of common factors.
2. Each column of the rotated factor matrix should have at least r zeros.
3. For every pair of columns in the rotated factor matrix, there should be a number of tests having zeros in the one column matched with nonzeros in the other.
4. For every pair of columns, there should be a number of pairs of zero loadings.
5. For every pair of columns, there should be very few pairs of loadings of substantial size.

These statements require some qualifications. In the first place, there may be a test or two with no zero loadings; they are of complexity r. This is not serious if there are enough other tests that conform to the specifications above. These other tests may well be sufficient to determine the location of reference axes in a unique solution to the problem. As has been said before, a zero loading in actual data means one that is zero within sampling errors. Not having any standard errors of factor loadings, we have to be arbitrary and adopt a reasonable rule. Loadings less than .10 may well be regarded as zero for practical purposes. On some occasions even larger loadings may be tolerated as zero, particularly when the experimental sample is small. "Small" may be defined here as being less than 200.

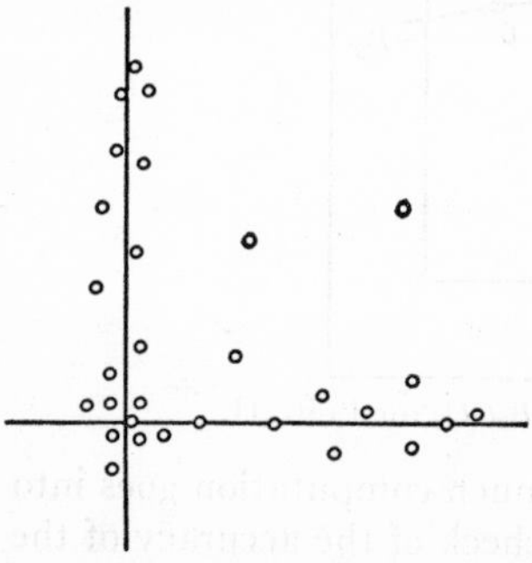

FIG. 16.13. A plot showing a somewhat idealized distribution of test vectors in a plane after rotation to simple structure.

A graphic check as to whether simple structure, or something approaching it, is achieved is often made. Plot the tests on every pair of reference axes after rotations have been completed. They should all resemble that in Fig. 16.13. Rotation to such a structure is compelling, and there is usually only one such structure possible in any problem; thus the solution is unique. Since it is unique, it must represent meaningful psychological variables.

Rotation to Psychological Meaning. There are some analyses, unfortunately, in which simple structure cannot be achieved or in which more than one solution approaches simple structure. There may have been an unfortunate combination of tests in the battery, or the complexity of tests is generally so great that there is no outstandingly compelling solution. Here one has to depend upon other criteria. If one knows that certain tests in the past have consistently been relatively pure measures of certain factors, one can rotate axes in the direction of each group of tests of a factor. This is a great convenience even when there are objective criteria of simple structure present. In an unexplored domain where factors and their relations to tests are not yet known, lacking objective criteria, one may try out one hypothesis as to meaning after another until some solution seems satisfactory. The injection of meaning, even of this hypothetical type, may lead to a final solution that also seems good objectively. Reyburn and Taylor, particularly, emphasize the importance of using meanings as guides to rotation (42). The writer's view is that we should follow the objective criteria just as far as they will take us, taking advantage of any confirmed prior knowledge of factorial structure. We should resort to the use of hypothesized meanings only after other aids fail.

TABLE 16.21. FIRST OBLIQUE ROTATION OF THE ARMY ALPHA FACTORS BY THE RADIAL METHOD

Centroid Factor Matrix (C)

	A_0	B_0	C_0
1	.465	−.293	−.271
2	.675	−.475	.434
3	.656	.000	.042
4	.720	.287	.058
5	.572	.325	.207
6	.566	−.371	−.151
7	.686	.247	−.538
8	.530	.288	.243

Rotated Oblique Factor Matrix (V_1)

$V_1 = C\Lambda_{01}$

A_1	B_1	C_1	
.484	.016	.472	1
.746	−.019	−.025	2
.324	.365	.301	3
.106	.639	.321	4
.000	.588	.117	5
.602	.007	.412	6
.124	.587	.814	7
.011	.534	.064	8

Direction Numbers (S_{01})

$S_{01} = L_{01}$

	A_1	B_1	C_1
A_0	1.00	.67	.60
B_0	−1.76	1.00	.0
C_0	.0	.0	−1.00
Σl^2	4.0976	1.4489	1.3600
$\sqrt{\Sigma l^2}$	2.0242	1.2037	1.1662
D_{01}	.49402	.83077	.85749

Intercorrelation of Reference Axes (M_1)

$M_1 = \Lambda'_{01}\Lambda_{01}$

	A_1	B_1	C_1
A_1	1.000	−.447	.254
B_1	−.447	1.000	.286
C_1	.254	.286	1.000

Direction Cosines (Λ_{01})

$\Lambda_{01} = L_{01}D_{01}$

	A_1	B_1	C_1
A_0	.4940	.5566	.5145
B_0	−.8695	.8308	.0
C_0	.0	.0	−.8575
$\Sigma\lambda^2$	1.000	1.000	1.000

Graphic Orthogonal Rotations. There are a number of alternative methods of effecting rotation of reference axes. One of the most convenient is Zimmerman's graphic method (53). There is insufficient space to describe it here. The only weakness of the method is that it does not provide us with an over-all or combined matrix of transformation. This is not missed, of course, unless one wishes to publish it. It would be possible to obtain one in conjunction with the Zimmerman method if one kept a record of each angle of rotation and multiplied successive matrices derivable from these angles.

Oblique Rotation of Reference Axes. In oblique rotations the axes are not required to maintain their 90-degree separations; each one can be rotated through its own angle. There are several methods of oblique rotations, three of which will be described here. The most generally applicable

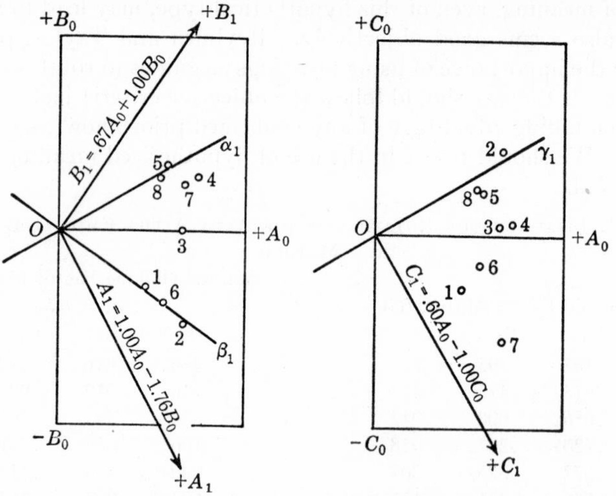

FIG. 16.14. Plots of the centroid-factor loadings for the eight Army Alpha tests preparatory to oblique rotations of the three axes by the radial method.

one is the *radial* method, which will be described first. The *extended-vectors* method is somewhat limited to problems with a small number of factors, but its description will add much to the understanding of oblique structure. One variation of the extended-vectors method—that of Harris—will be described because it leads to an interesting and useful solution. In the other two methods the reference axes no longer represent the primary traits exactly, and projections of tests on these axes are not the correlations between tests and primary traits. Harris's solution provides such correlations. The reasons for these last statements will become clearer later.

Rotation by the Radial Method. The radial method is illustrated in Tables 16.21 and 16.22, and in Figs. 16.14 and 16.15. We shall use some data from actual tests in this example, in which there is some obliqueness of structure, although the number of tests is so small that we cannot be very sure. The centroid matrix is given in Table 16.21. The tests are the eight parts of the Army Alpha Examination and the experimental sample was composed of 108 freshmen engineering students. The steps in this method are described in the next few paragraphs. You will find some of the steps very similar to those in the orthogonal rotation procedure.

Step 1. Plot the tests on several of the planes formed by pairs of centroid axes. It is necessary to plot only enough pairs to find a clear rotation for every axis.

Step 2. Locate *bounding hyperplanes* and their *normals*. Note the plot of A_0OB_0 in Fig. 16.14. The two bounding hyperplanes here are shown as the vectors α_1 and β_1. It is much clearer to see how and why β_1 is a bounding hyperplane than is α_1. Hyperplane β_1 is drawn through or near tests 1, 6, and 2. These three tests, as located in the plane A_0OB_0, present the appearance of what is called a *radial streak*. A radial streak is a group of test points forming roughly a line through the origin. When you consider more than the two dimensions pictured, these points may actually be off the plane A_0OB_0. What we see in the plane A_0OB_0 are merely projections of these points, or *traces*. A radial streak is taken to mean the trace of a hyperplane. The test points close to the hyperplane would have zero projections in the direction of a reference vector drawn perpendicular to the hyperplane.

Remember that we are looking for new reference axes on which there will be as many zero projections as possible. The trick is to put a hyperplane through a series of points and then to erect a perpendicular to the hyperplane at the origin to serve as the new reference axis. The hyperplane is also drawn at or near a boundary of the test points (that is why we call it a *bounding* hyperplane) and the perpendicular (which is called a *normal* to the hyperplane) is drawn only in the direction of the remainder of the test points. The tests farthest from the bounding hyperplane will have the largest factor loadings after rotation. The normal to hyperplane β_1 extends up and to the right in Fig. 16.14. We give the end an arrowhead to show that it is a reference vector, and we call it $+B_1$ since it is nearer to B_0 than to A_0.

The location of hyperplane α_1 is not so certain, since there is no clear radial streak. There is not always a streak so clear as that formed by tests 1, 6, and 2. But we can obtain two clearly zero projections by going between tests 5 and 8. To bring the hyperplane down nearer tests 4 and 7 would not give us a bounding plane. It would probably not do any harm to do this, since any negative projections thus created could be rotated out in a later rotation. But since we know that we are going to have a positive manifold in the end, it may pay us to work toward that condition as early as possible.

We have located new positions for axes A and B. This leaves axis C to be accounted for. In a plot in plane A_0OC_0, we locate a bounding hyperplane γ_1 through in the neighborhood of tests 2, 8, and 5. The normal which would make projections of other tests positive must extend down and to the right. We now have new positions for all the axes; therefore we proceed to rotate them. Here, unlike the orthogonal rotations, we rotate all axes at once, or all for which we can locate reasonable bounding hyperplanes. We will find that the first set of rotations does not complete the rotation task, but nearly does so in this problem.

Step 3. Obtain the direction numbers of the located normals in the following manner. Extend each normal far enough to intersect a line parallel to one of the axes, and at a distance of unity from that axis. Note the coordinates of this intersection, for they provide us with the direction numbers. Each normal can be described by stating an equation using these direction numbers (see the three equations in Fig. 16.14). The direction numbers are recorded in matrix S_{01} in Table 16.21. They are given as coordinates of the new axes, with reference to the centroid axes as the frame of reference. The zero entries in matrix S_{01} merely indicate that the new reference vector is simply still orthogonal to one of the centroid axes. It was rotated only in the plane orthogonal to that centroid axis. Were there more than three factors, we would have more zeros in each column. We have only two nonzero direction numbers in each column. We may have more than two in a row.

Step 4. In the orthogonal rotations, we had a matrix L_{01} that looked very much like S_{01} here and it was also composed of direction numbers. In the first round of oblique rotations, as here, matrix S_{01} is identical with matrix L_{01}. In later rotations it is not. The fourth step, of obtaining L from S, will be explained when we come to the next round of rotations.

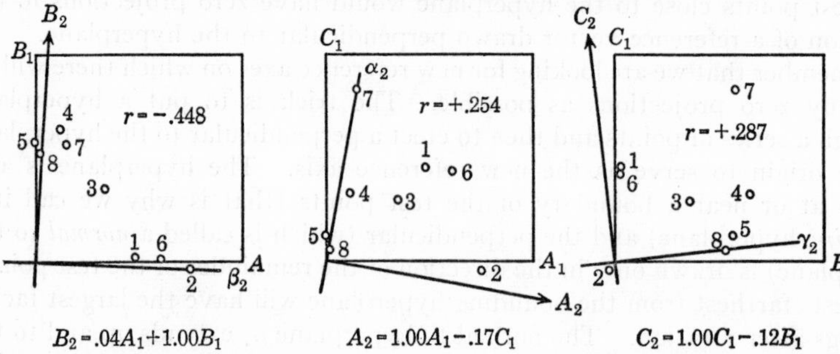

FIG. 16.15. Plot of the eight Army Alpha tests in the three planes formed by the three reference axes after rotation by the radial method. The correlation between each pair of axes is indicated. Minor rotations to improve simple structure are shown.

Step 5. Normalize the direction numbers, finding the direction cosines in Λ_{01}, the transformation matrix. The process is the same as with orthogonal rotations, and the steps are illustrated in Table 16.21.

Step 6. Check the transformation matrix Λ_{01} by summing squared direction cosines in the columns. Here we had to keep four significant digits in the elements of Λ_{01} in order to make the sums equal 1.000.

Step 7. Perform the rotation by the multiplication $C\Lambda_{01}$ to obtain the rotated oblique matrix V_1 (see Table 16.21).

Step 8. The elements of V_1 can be checked graphically by seeing that the perpendicular distances of test points from hyperplanes agree with the factor loadings. The check using communalities, which applied after orthogonal rotations, cannot be used here.

Step 9. Determine the intercorrelations of the oblique reference axes. This is done by the matrix multiplication $\Lambda'_{01}\,\Lambda_{01}$, which gives matrix M_1. The intercorrelations are not zero, indicating that the structure is oblique. Two axes, A_1 and B_1, correlate as much as $-.447$.

Step 10. Plot the test points on the new axes A_1, B_1, C_1, etc., in pairs. Although there are nonzero correlations between pairs of axes, indicating that their separations are not at 90-degree angles, we plot them at 90-degree separations just the same, making a note of the correlation between axes in each plot (see Fig. 16.15). The justification for this procedure is that in plane A_1OB_1, A_1 is thus made to do duty as the hyperplane for normal B_1, and vice versa. Hyperplane and its normal are certainly separated by 90 degrees. This is the picture we want to see. Besides, if we plotted the pairs of axes at angles indicated by their intercorrelations, we should have difficulties in accomplishing both the plotting of test points and the next rotations.

In Fig. 16.15 we see that only slight rotations are needed to effect minor improvements. There are two very slightly negative loadings that we might get rid of. There are more zeros possible by eliminating also some small positive loadings.

TABLE 16.22. SECOND OBLIQUE ROTATION OF THE ARMY ALPHA FACTORS BY THE RADIAL METHOD

Direction Numbers (S_{12})

	A_2	B_2	C_2
A_1	1.00	.04	.0
B_1	.0	1.00	−.12
C_1	−.17	.0	1.00

Direction Numbers (L_{02})

$L_{02} = \Lambda_{01}S_{12}$

	A_2	B_2	C_2
A_0	.406	.576	.488
B_0	−.870	.796	−.100
C_0	.146	.000	−.857
Σl^2	.94305	.96539	.94515
$\sqrt{\Sigma l^2}$	.97111	.98254	.97219
D_{02}	1.0297	1.0178	1.0286

Direction Cosines (Λ_{02})

$\Lambda_{02} = L_{02}D_{02}$

	A_2	B_2	C_2
A_0	.4181	.5863	.4608
B_0	−.8958	.8102	−.1029
C_0	.1503	.0000	−.8815
$\Sigma\lambda^2_{02}$	1.000	1.000	1.000

Oblique Rotated Matrix (V_2)

$V_2 = C\Lambda_{02}$

A_2	B_2	C_2	
.416	.035	.483	1
.773	.011	−.023	2
.281	.385	.265	3
.053	.655	.251	4
−.021	.599	.048	5
.546	.031	.432	6
−.015	.602	.765	7
.000	.544	.000	8

Intercorrelations of Reference Axes (M_2)

$M_2 = \Lambda'_{02}\Lambda_{02}$

	A_2	B_2	C_2
A_2	1.000	−.481	.152
B_2	−.481	1.000	.187
C_2	.152	.187	1.000

Step 11. Compute the transformation matrix Λ_{02}. There is one new operation here not required in the first rotation. It is the finding of matrix L_{02} from S_{12}. This is done by the multiplication $\Lambda_{01}S_{12}$. In other words, multiply the preceding transformation matrix by the new matrix of direction numbers. After L_{02} is found, proceed as before. But notice that the matrix of transformation is labeled Λ_{02}, the subscripts of which imply rotation from the centroid matrix to V_2, not from V_1 to V_2. It is possible to find another matrix H_{12} by which the multiplication $V_1H_{12} = V_2$, but this involves finding an additional matrix which is used for nothing else, whereas Λ_{02} is used for determining the intercorrelations of the reference axis after the second rotation. There is also probably much less chance of computation errors in

going back to the centroid matrix each time rather than putting the factor matrix through successive multiplications.

Matrix V_2 is a fairly good illustration of oblique simple structure. There are three zero loadings in two columns and four in the third (column A_2). With the exception of test 3, which has a complexity of three, there is at least one zero in every row. One test, 2, is unique for factor A in this matrix, and tests 5 and 8 are unique for factor B. These outcomes, in addition to the positive manifold, are indications that a unique solution has been achieved. Two investigators both rotating with the same procedure and the same goal would come out with minor differences in factor loadings, but the structure would be essentially the same.

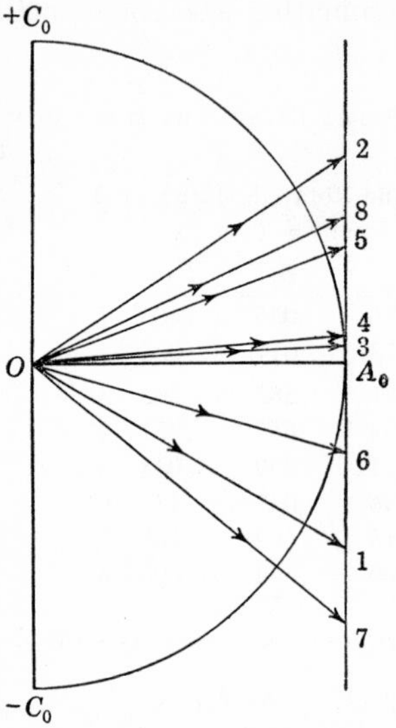

FIG. 16.16. Extended test vectors for the Army Alpha problem shown in the plane A_0OC_0. Short arrows indicate the test vectors before extension.

Oblique Rotation by the Method of Extended Vectors. In the method of extended vectors we temporarily project the test configuration outward from the origin onto a single plane that is perpendicular to centroid axis A_0 at a distance of 1.0 from the origin on that axis. This is illustrated in Fig. 16.16. In this diagram we have the eight test vectors of the Army Alpha problem illustrated. The arrowheads *within* the circle of radius 1.0 are at distance equal to h_j for each test. We see the edge of the plane tangent to the great circle at $A_0 = 1.0$. We could have used centroid axis B_0 for the vertical one just as well as C_0. The order of the ends of the extended vectors would be somewhat different, just as the order of loadings in matrix C is different in columns 2 and 3.

Suppose we turn the factor structure, the third dimension included, around to look at the plane head-on, looking down axis A_0 toward the origin. What would we see? The arrangement of points where the test vectors meet the plane would be as in Fig. 16.17, where we have plotted the points on the plane B_0OC_0 in terms of their extended coordinates. We will now see how to obtain the extended coordinates. It will be fairly obvious from Fig. 16.16 that the extended coordinates will be larger than the original ones. The successive steps for the entire extended-vector method will now be given.

Step 1. Divide each *row* of matrix C through by the first centroid factor loading a_{j1}. Better yet, find each reciprocal of a_{j1} and multiply each element of the row by it. This gives the extended vector matrix E_0 (see Table 16.23).

Step 2. Plot the test points with their extended coordinates in some of the planes, enough of them to determine a rotation for each axis. Here only one plane (B_0OC_0) is possible.

Step 3. Locate as many traces of bounding hyperplanes as are evident. These need not pass through the origin as in the radial method. In Fig. 16.17 two hyperplanes are evident. One extends through test points 2 and 8 and near 5, which gives essentially three zeros by rotation. The second extends through or near 8, 5, 4, and 7, giving four zeros. The third hyperplane is difficult to locate due to a paucity of test points. If we were to follow the rule of looking for traces, we would place a hyperplane through tests 2, 6, and 1, as we did in the radial method. If we did this, we should come out with a result similar to that obtained by the radial method.

TABLE 16.23. EXTENDING THE TEST VECTORS OF THE EIGHT ARMY ALPHA TESTS IN THE COMMON-FACTOR SPACE

	Centroid Matrix (C)				Extended-vector Matrix (E_0) $E_0 = C/a_{j1}$			
	A_0	B_0	C_0	$1/a_{j1}$	A_0	B_0	C_0	
1	.465	−.293	−.271	2.1505	1.000	−.630	−.583	1
2	.675	−.475	.434	1.4815	1.000	−.704	.643	2
3	.656	.000	.042	1.5244	1.000	.000	.064	3
4	.720	.287	.058	1.3889	1.000	.399	.081	4
5	.572	.325	.207	1.7483	1.000	.568	.362	5
6	.566	−.371	−.151	1.7668	1.000	−.655	−.267	6
7	.686	.247	−.538	1.4577	1.000	.360	−.784	7
8	.530	.288	.243	1.8868	1.000	.543	.458	8

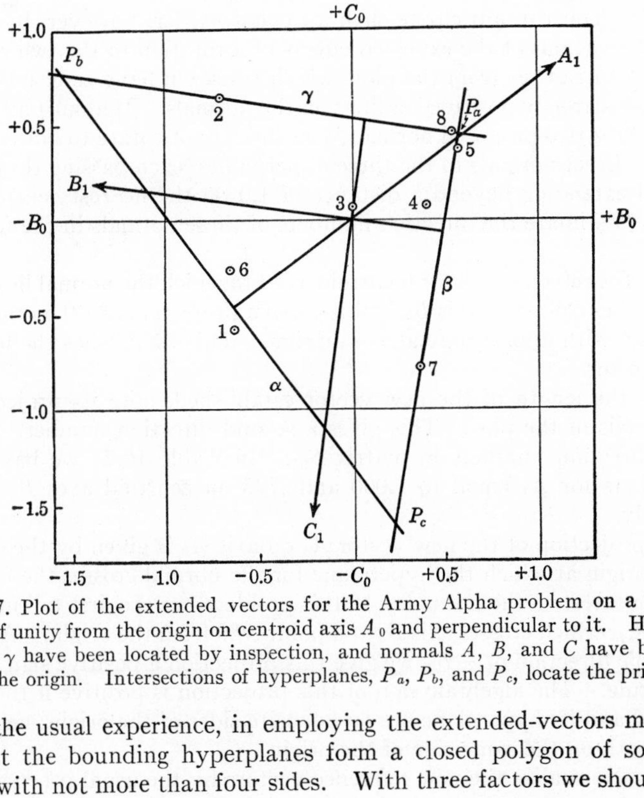

FIG. 16.17. Plot of the extended vectors for the Army Alpha problem on a plane at a distance of unity from the origin on centroid axis A_0 and perpendicular to it. Hyperplanes α, β, and γ have been located by inspection, and normals A, B, and C have been drawn through the origin. Intersections of hyperplanes, P_a, P_b, and P_c, locate the primary axes.

It is the usual experience, in employing the extended-vectors method, to find that the bounding hyperplanes form a closed polygon of some kind, usually with not more than four sides. With three factors we should expect a triangle. If the structure were clearly orthogonal, the triangle in a tridimensional problem should be equilateral. We have reason to believe that the structure in the Army Alpha problem is oblique, but only slightly so, for we shall see later that an orthogonal frame will fit the configuration of tests very well.

The location of hyperplane α in Fig. 16.17 is rather uncertain, since there are only two points, 1 and 6, to determine it, and they are close together. Plane α, therefore, has been located rather symmetrically with respect to the other two hyperplanes. The desertion of point 2 in drawing this hyperplane can be defended on the grounds of the nature of the tests. Tests 4 (Opposites), 5 (Mixed Sentences), and 8 (General Information) are decidedly of a verbal character and factor A must be the well-established verbal-comprehension factor. Test 2 is the arithmetic test, containing problems verbally presented. It is reasonable, therefore, to permit test 2 to have some verbal variance in the final solution. To put hyperplane α through point 2 would give test 2 no projection on the verbal axis. We will proceed to rotate with hyperplane α as shown in Fig. 16.17.

At this stage of the method, there is one important precaution. That is to be sure that any two hyperplanes you have selected from different plots are not actually one and the same hyperplane. You would discover this fact later, in that the two normals to such hyperplanes would be very highly correlated. You can anticipate such an event earlier, however, by making careful observations of the expected effects of a rotation to the two reference vectors. You can see from the plots which tests will have zero, moderately positive and strongly positive loadings on the normals. If almost all of these correspond for two proposed normals, you should not rotate to both of them.

Step 4. Erect normals to the three hyperplanes, each passing through the origin and extending beyond a distance of 1.0 on the nearest centroid axis.

Step 5. Estimate the direction numbers of these normals in the following manner:

a. Note the reference vector (centroid axis) to which the normal lies closest. Normal A_1 lies closest to axis B_0. It is given a projection of 1.0 on that reference vector, with appropriate algebraic sign. This establishes the length of the new vector.

b. With the length of the new vector established, note its projection on the other axis of the plot. This gives a second direction number. Record the two direction numbers in matrix S_{01}. In Table 16.24 we have direction numbers for A_1 equal to 1.000 and .725 on centroid axes B_0 and C_0, respectively.

c. The projection of the new vector A_1 on axis A_0 is given by the distance from the origin at which the hyperplane for the normal crosses the reference axis lying nearest to the normal. In this problem, we are first talking about hyperplane α which crosses axis B_0 at a point .980 from the origin. Although this is in the direction of $-B_0$, we give this projection a positive sign because of a new rule. The algebraic sign of this projection is positive if the end of the normal and its hyperplane are on opposite sides of the origin; negative if they are both on the same side of the origin.

Step 6. Normalize the new reference vectors by the usual process, determining the corresponding direction cosines. Check them by squaring and summing. We now have the matrix of transformation Λ_{01} (see Table 16.24).

Step 7. Compute the matrix of intercorrelations of reference axes M_1 by the product $\Lambda'_{01}\Lambda_{01}$ (see Table 16.24). The small r's in the Army Alpha problem show that the structure by this rotation is almost orthogonal.

TABLE 16.24. TRANSFORMATION MATRIX FOR ROTATION BY THE METHOD OF EXTENDED VECTORS, AND INTERCORRELATIONS OF NEW REFERENCE VECTORS

Direction Numbers (S_{01})
(In the first rotation, $S_{01} = L_{01}$)

	A_1	B_1	C_1
A_0	.980	.490	.537
B_0	1.000	−1.000	−.150
C_0	.725	.155	−1.000
Σl^2	2.48602	1.26412	1.31087
$\sqrt{\Sigma l^2}$	1.5767	1.1243	1.1449
D_{01}	.63423	.88941	.87342

Direction Cosines (Λ_{01})
$\Lambda_{01} = S_{01}D_{01}$

	A_1	B_1	C_1
A_0	.6215	.4358	.4690
B_0	.6342	−.8894	−.1310
C_0	.4598	.1379	−.8734

Intercorrelations of Reference Axes (M_1)
$M_1 = \Lambda'_{01}\Lambda_{01}$

	A_1	B_1	C_1
A_1	1.000	−.230	−.193
B_1	−.230	1.000	.200
C_1	−.193	.200	1.000

Step 8. Compute the oblique factor matrix E_1 by the multiplication $E_0\Lambda_{01}$ to find the projections of the *extended* test vectors on the new reference axes A_1, B_1, and C_1. If we want the projections of the *unextended* test vectors on the same axes, we could perform the multiplication of $C\Lambda_{01}$. In a three-factor problem by extended vectors only one rotation should be necessary. The product $C\Lambda_{01}$ would then save an extra step in getting back from

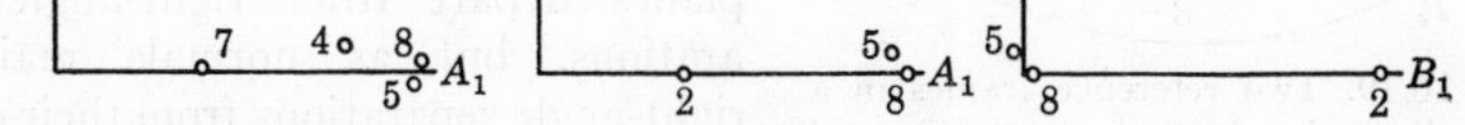

FIG. 16.18. Plots of the tests in the Army Alpha problem after oblique rotation by the method of extended vectors.

the longer test vectors to the original lengths. If more rotating is going to be needed, however, one should continue with extended vectors.

Step 9. Check to see whether any further rotations are needed by plotting the test points on all pairs of axes among $A_1, B_1, C_1, \ldots, R_1$. Show the axes as orthogonal, but write in the correlation between the pair of axes (see Fig. 16.18). No further rotations seem to be called for in this problem, unless we placed a hyperplane through points 1, 6, and 2, in the first plot. This would probably effect the same structure we could have had by placing such a hyperplane through the same three points in the first rotation. Decisions about second rotations are made, as in making the first, by drawing in bounding hyperplanes and their normals.

Step 10. Compute the rotated oblique factor matrix V_1 from the extended factor matrix E_1. This is accomplished by multiplying each row of E_1 by the same value a_{j1} that was used originally to extend the test vectors. The result of such an operation is seen in Table 16.25.

TABLE 16.25. ROTATED OBLIQUE FACTOR MATRIX, WITH EXTENDED AND UNEXTENDED TEST VECTORS

Rotated Oblique Factor Matrix with Extended Vectors (E_1)

$E_1 = E_0\Lambda_{01}$

	A_1	B_1	C_1
1	−.046	.916	1.061
2	.471	1.151	.000
3	.651	.445	.413
4	.912	.092	.346
5	1.148	−.019	.078
6	.083	.982	.788
7	.489	.008	1.107
8	1.176	.016	−.002

Rotated Oblique Factor Matrix with Unextended Vectors (V_1)

$V_1 = E_1 a_{j1} = C\Lambda_{01}$

A_1	B_1	C_1	
−.021	.426	.493	1
.318	.777	.000	2
.427	.292	.271	3
.656	.066	.249	4
.657	−.011	.045	5
.047	.556	.446	6
.335	.005	.759	7
.623	.008	−.001	8

Oblique Rotations by the Primary-axis Method. Neither of the oblique-rotation methods already described gives reference axes that represent exactly the factors that are given psychological interpretation. The vectors that should represent the underlying psychological variables that we are seeking to discover by factor analysis, in Thurstone's opinion, are the intersections of the hyperplanes, not the normals to the hyperplanes (49). In an orthogonal system the normals to hyperplanes *are* the intersections of other hyperplanes. Figure 16.8 illustrates this point. As hyperplanes depart from right-angle separations, but as normals maintain right-angle separations from their corresponding hyperplanes, the normals and intersections of hyperplanes separate. Figure 16.19 shows three hyperplanes α, β, and γ, their three normals A, B, and C, and the intersections of the hyperplanes, P_a, P_b, and P_c. It is clear that the last three vectors do depart somewhat from A, B, and C, depending upon the amount of intercorrelation of hyperplanes.

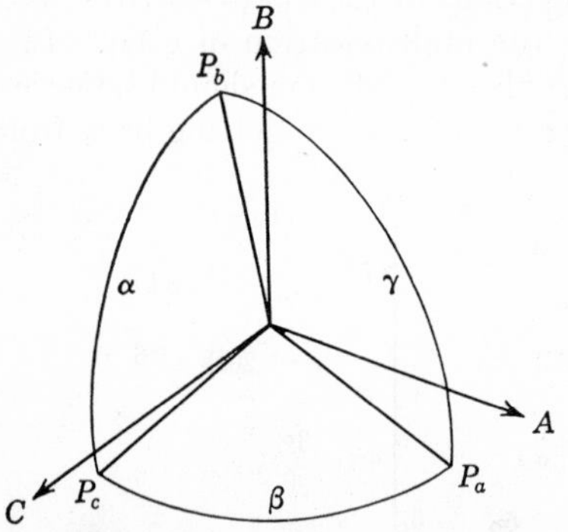

FIG. 16.19. Two reference frames in a three-dimensional system. A, B, and C are the normals to the hyperplanes α, β, and γ, respectively. P_a, P_b, and P_c are intersections of the hyperplanes lying closest to the normals A, B, and C, respectively.

Vectors P_a, P_b, and P_c are called the *primary axes* and they are taken to represent the genuine psychological factors. Since the oblique methods of rotation emphasize getting as many test points into the hyperplanes as possible, the points tend to gravitate to the intersections of hyperplanes. Tests at intersections are likely to have lower complexity than other tests. A test vector coinciding with a primary axis has a maximum complexity of $r - 2$, where r is the number of factors. A test that occurs at one primary axis only is a pure measure of a psychological factor.

The factor loadings we have been obtaining in oblique analyses, then, do not tell us how much the tests correlate with the psychological factors. Those loadings are projections of test vectors on the reference axes and not on the primary axes. The reference axes are usually so close to the primary axes that we can give the proper psychological interpretation to a factor based on the factor loadings in a matrix V. But if we want to know how much a test correlates with a psychological factor, we need to have its projection on the primary axis that stands for that psychological factor. It is possible to derive from a V matrix the correlations of tests with the psychological factors. The principles are too involved to be explained in the space available here. There is a much more direct way of achieving the same goal when the number of factors is not too large. The method was proposed by Harris (29, 30).

The Harris method follows the method of extended vectors much of the way, at least through the plotting of the hyperplanes as in Fig. 16.17. In that illustration the hyperplanes are shown as intersecting at three places, P_a, P_b, and P_c, in preparation for application of the primary-axis method. These intersections indicate the points at which the primary axes cut the plane in which we are working—the extended-vectors plane. The method calls for a rotation to the primary axes as the new reference axes. From here on, the method is parallel to the others we have seen. The steps are as follows.

Step 1. Use the coordinates of the points P_a, P_b, and P_c as the direction numbers of the new reference vectors. The coordinates on the old reference axis A_0 is 1.00 for all the points (see Table 16.26). The others are read off the scales.

If there should be any test of complexity 1 in the battery, one primary axis will extend through the point for that test in the extended-vector plane. In other words, we should look for single test points that will serve as convenient corners of the polygons that we locate in the plots. If a test does occur exactly at an intersection of two hyperplanes, the direction numbers can be obtained either from the coordinates of that point in the plot, or from the projections of that test on the corresponding centroid axes.

If there is more than one plot and if any point P_j is found on more than one plot, be sure that the coordinates used as direction numbers are consistent in the different plots. This can be accomplished by adjusting the hyperplanes until a point gives the same direction number for each reference axis.

Step 2. Normalize the new reference vectors by the usual procedure. This gives the direction cosines of the primary axes in transformation matrix K.

Step 3. Perform the matrix multiplication CK to obtain the rotated primary-axis matrix W. For the Army Alpha problem, matrix W appears in Table 16.27. Whereas matrix V, for which the reference axes are the normals to the hyperplanes, represents a factor structure, matrix W, for which the reference axes are the intersections of hyperplanes, represents what Thurstone calls a *factor pattern*. While V contains a maximal number of zero loadings, W contains very few. Matrix V_2 in Table 16.22 contains 10 zero loadings, whereas matrix W in Table 16.27 contains only 2 (when anything less than .10 is taken as zero).

TABLE 16.26. OBLIQUE ROTATION IN THE ARMY ALPHA PROBLEM BY MEANS OF THE PRIMARY-AXES METHOD

Direction Numbers (P)

	P_a	P_b	P_c
A_0	1.000	1.000	1.000
B_0	.570	−1.555	.220
C_0	.450	.770	−1.610
Σp^2	1.5274	4.0109	3.6405
$\sqrt{\Sigma p^2}$	1.2359	2.0027	1.9080
D	.80912	.49932	.52410

Direction Cosines (K)
$K = PD$

	P_a	P_b	P_c
A_0	.8091	.4993	.5241
B_0	.4612	−.7764	.1153
C_0	.3641	.3845	−.8438

Intercorrelations of Primary Axes (M)
$M = K'K$

	P_a	P_b	P_c
P_a	1.000	.185	.170
P_b	.185	1.000	−.152
P_c	.170	−.152	1.000

Step 4. Compute the matrix of intercorrelations of the primary axes, matrix M, where M, as usual, equals the transpose of a transformation matrix multiplied by that matrix. Here $M = K'K$. We see from Table 16.26 that axis P_a correlates low and positive with P_b and P_c and that the last two correlate low negative. A positive correlation means a separation of less than 90 degrees, whereas a negative correlation indicates a separation

TABLE 16.27. ROTATED FACTOR MATRIX BY THE PRIMARY-AXES METHOD FOR THE ARMY ALPHA DATA

Rotated Factor Matrix (W)
$W = CK$

Test	P_a	P_b	P_c
1	.142	.355	.439
2	.485	.873	−.067
3	.546	.344	.308
4	.736	.159	.362
5	.688	.113	.163
6	.232	.513	.381
7	.473	−.056	.842
8	.650	.134	.106

of more than 90 degrees. The correlations in M are so small as to mean that the factor pattern is almost orthogonal.

Factoring the Factors; Second-order Factors. Since M is an intercorrelation matrix, if the correlations may be taken to represent relationships between real psychological variables, the question arises as to whether we may factor the factors. If there is underlying system in the matrix and its rank is lower than its order, there is a reason for factor-analyzing it. The factors thus obtained have been called *second-order factors*. The factors found by analyzing tests are, accordingly, first-order factors.

An investigator often reports second-order factors along with his oblique rotations. Note that it is the primary-axis factors that should be analyzed, not the normals. Interpretations are usually offered for the second-order factors as representing more broad or inclusive psychological variables. Even third-order factors (from analyzing the second-order factors) have been mentioned.

The writer reserves judgment with respect to the psychological validity of factors higher than the first-order ones. The apparent intercorrelation of factors can be brought about by a number of things, such as the conditions of sampling, heterogeneity of the population, and other nonpsychological determiners. The selection of tests that one happens to have in a battery has much to do with where one locates the hyperplanes in oblique rotations. Take the Army Alpha problem, for example. Had there been in the battery other tests, such as a purely numerical-operations test and a pure test of the kind of reasoning that is involved in test 7, we would very likely have had a very good, complete trace from P_b to P_c in Fig. 16.17. Even when two radial streaks are clearly not separated by 90 degrees, but by something less, is it because they represent two correlated factors or because we were not able to construct factorially pure tests for one or both factors? When there are very few or no zero correlations in the correlation matrix R, the prognosis is not very good for finding a clear orthogonal transformation. Yet a reasonable orthogonal transformation might well be achieved. We have a real choice, then, of deciding whether to express the excess covariance in terms of tests of greater factorial complexity in an orthogonal structure or whether to express that excess covariance in terms of correlated factors and second-order factors.

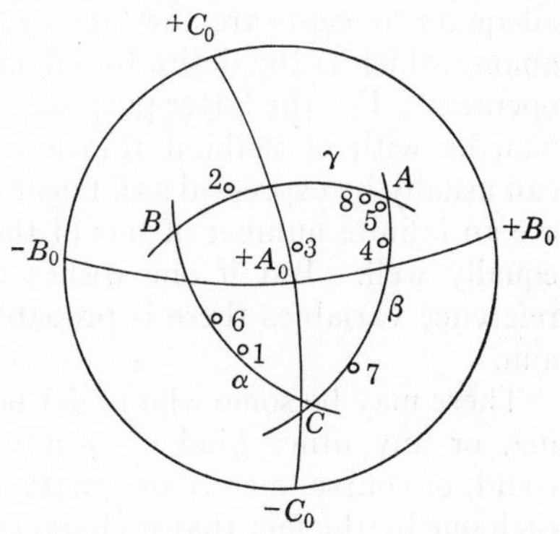

FIG. 16.20. Illustration of the configuration of the eight Army Alpha test vectors projected to the surface of a sphere. Orthogonal hyperplanes have been adjusted to the configuration.

Figure 16.20 illustrates the last few paragraphs very well. It represents the Army Alpha configuration in terms of points at which the eight test vectors cut the surface of a sphere. The plotting was done in terms of the centroid axes as the frame of reference. These are shown with great circles passing through the ends of axes B_0 and C_0. The positive end of axis A_0 is toward us through the center of gravity of the eight test vectors, as it should be. An orthogonal rotation has been effected, with three hyperplanes α, β, and γ cutting the surface so as to form a right spherical triangle, with corners at points A, B, and C. The triangle was located so as to bound as many of the points as possible and so as to place the lines of the triangle through or near a maximum number of points. We come out with a solution that is very similar to that in Fig. 16.17, where the triangle is on a plane instead of on the surface of a sphere. In fact, it was knowledge of the results in Fig. 16.20 that induced us to locate hyperplane α where it is in Fig. 16.17, rather than through points 2, 6, and 1. Had we readjusted the hyperplanes β and γ a little in Fig. 16.17, we would have been even nearer to an orthogonal rotation than we were. We could have achieved a completely orthogonal rotation by ensuring that each normal in Fig. 16.17 passed through the intersections of the other two hyperplanes and that the triangle was of proper size.

Interpretation of Factors

The most defensible reason a psychologist can have for making a factor analysis is to aim toward the clarification of useful concepts in a domain where adequate concepts are now lacking. There are, to be sure, practical reasons, among which is the desire to reduce the number of variables with which one operates. For the latter purpose only, almost any method of factor analysis will do, with or without rotations of axes. A larger number of variables can usually be expressed as a linear combination of a smaller number. There are an infinite number of sets of the smaller number that would serve about equally well. But if one wishes to attach psychological meanings to the reference variables there is probably a unique set toward which one should aim.

There may be some who prefer not to attempt to give psychological meaning, or any other kind of meaning, to factors even when rotated. One could, of course, merely designate factors by letter or by number and define each one by the fact that it characteristically shows loadings of such and such in tests such and such. One would also probably have to specify a population with certain properties. This approach to the handling of factors seems to forgo the important possibility of relating factors in a conceptual system and relating the system to other facts and principles of science. A philosophy that has resistance against naming may be commendable from some points of view. The chief fear seems to be of giving a name to something that, after all is said and done, actually does not exist. There can be no doubt of the utility of discovering unities when they do exist. Neither should there be much doubt of the utility of developing new concepts which serve us with tools with which to lay hold of events and which serve as media of communication. Especially is this true when the concepts can be supported by reference to operations by which they were derived as in factor analysis. If concepts are faulty, this will be discovered in time and changes can always be made.

The usual way of going about the interpretation of common factors is to take note of the tests, or other experimental variables, which have substantial loadings in common in each factor in contrast with other tests that have zero or low factor loadings in it. What are the common features of the first group of tests that are not shared by the second group? It may be that the main difference is that of verbal versus nonverbal, of numerical versus nonnumerical, and so on. Introspection is of some help in this. The interpreter in doing the items of tests himself can note what functions seem to characterize each test. He may ask others to report how they do the items. A list of observed properties and inferred functions may be drawn up for each test. The lists would then be compared when tests are grouped by factors.

Let us take a look at the little problem involving the eight parts of the Army Alpha Examination. Examine the factor structure as shown in matrix V_1, Table 16.25. Factor *A* has the highest loadings in tests 4 (Same—Opposites), 5 (Mixed Sentences), and 8 (General Information). It has zero loadings in tests 1 (Following Directions) and 6 (Number Series). Tests 4, 5, and 8 are verbal tests in which knowledge of words is important. Test 6 is the only completely nonverbal test in the lot. Test 1, although involving oral instructions, and hence verbal comprehension, probably requires a minimal knowledge of the meanings of the words as such. The small amount of word knowledge needed in tests 3 (Common Sense) and 7 (Mixed Relations, a verbal-analogies test) and even in 2 (Arithmetic) is consistent with the small loadings in this factor, which is evidently the well-established factor of verbal comprehension. A vocabulary test is usually the best one for this factor and usually has no other common-factor variance.

Factor *B* is evidently the well-established numerical-facility factor. The best and most unique test for it is one of numerical operations—simple additions, subtractions, etc. Tests 2 and 6 obviously depend much upon speed and accuracy of number work. Tests 4, 5, 7, and 8 have no number work involved and their loadings are zero in this factor. The appearance of test 1 with a moderate loading on this factor can be rationalized to the effect that some of its items depend upon the use of number properties or the examinees utilize number operations in their procedures.

Factor *C* is some kind of reasoning ability the precise nature of which is not clear from the limited data here. The fact that test 2, which is essentially an arithmetic reasoning test, has no relation to the factor eliminates a reasoning factor that has been called *general reasoning* (25). Its highest loadings in tests 7 and 6 suggest that factor *C* involves seeing relationships of some kind. Relationships are involved in test 1, and if the loadings near .25 in tests 3 and 4 are significant, seeing relationships must be a feature of these tests. The same-versus-opposites discrimination in test 4 provides an obvious pair of relationships, but there are only two kinds and they are present, one or the other, in every item. In tests 6 and 7 relationships vary from item to item and must be discovered by the examinee.

Note that the interpretations just given have been based upon the factor structure rather than the factor pattern. The advantage of doing so is that with more zero loadings there is more contrast apparent between tests. The word "apparent" is used advisedly here, for there is more relationship between tests with zero loadings and those with substantial loadings in an oblique structure than the loadings seem to indicate. The use of the structure is justifiable, even though the primary axes rather than the normal axes are regarded as the meaningful ones, because there is much in common between the loadings in the structure and correlations in the pattern. Projections of tests on the normal axes and on the primary axes come in almost the same rank order for the corresponding axes. The greater the correlations in matrix *M* (intercorrelations of reference axes), however, the greater the chance of some discrepancies between the two rank orders. If the discrepancies were great, it would be safer to interpret the primary axes. But in any case, the same factors would probably be named either way. The factors interpreted in an orthogonal solution would also probably be about the same as those in an oblique solution in the same problem.

Estimation of Factors in Persons

Since one of the important goals in factor analysis is to be able to assess individuals more meaningfully and economically, if we are willing to assume that interpreted factors are unities or variables, we should attempt to measure them. A limited list of factor scores would then do the work of several times as many tests and do it with greater invariance of meaning. Tests going under the same name give scores that are of fluctuating meaning and significance. Factor scores should be in the nature of a much more standard article.

There are several ways in which we can derive factor scores. We cannot obtain them directly, of course. The nearest we can come to an immediate measure, and one uncontaminated by other common-factor variances, is to find or construct a pure test for a factor. Unfortunately, there are very few known factors for which we have as yet pure scores. Among these are vocabulary tests for the verbal-comprehension or word-knowledge factor, numerical-operations tests for the numerical-facility factor, and perceptual-speed tests for the visual perceptual-speed factor. The practical methods, then, make the best of the situation and attempt to maximize in the score the variance in factors that we want to measure.

The Multiple-regression-equation Method. If we have several tests all with substantial loadings in the factor that we want to measure, a weighted combination of them is likely to correlate higher with the factor than does the best one taken alone. The procedure suggested is the least-square solution, which will yield weights that maximize the multiple correlation of the composite with the factor. For this purpose it is best not to employ the same test in more than one composite. To do so introduces some spurious correlation of composites because of identical elements over and above the common-factor variances. These additional identical elements are specific and error variances.

The multiple-regression method will be illustrated by means of the Army Alpha problem. In what follows we will use the factor loadings obtained from an orthogonal rotation of the axes. Taking the factor as the variable to be predicted from the test scores, the factor becomes the dependent variable and the test scores the independent variables. The three vectors were identified as verbal comprehension or word knowledge, numerical facility, and reasoning, which we will denote as *V*, *N*, and *R*, respectively. Let us compose three brief batteries, using no test in more than one battery. The best grouping is apparently to use tests 3, 4, 5, and 8 in the verbal battery, tests 2 and 6 in the numerical battery, and tests 1 and 7 in the reasoning battery.

For each battery we want the optimal weights to maximize the factor loadings in the composite. We know the correlations of the tests with the factor and the intercorrelations of the tests. From this information we can compute the optimal weights and the multiple correlation, which is the correlation of the composite with the factor.

In the third column of Table 16.28 are given the regression weights as determined by multiple-correlation procedures, assuming that the factor in each case has a standard deviation of 10.0. We can make this standard deviation anything we please.[1] The multiple correlations of the three composites with their corresponding factors are .854, .816, and .816. These may

TABLE 16.28. WEIGHTS FOR SELECTED TESTS IN THE ARMY ALPHA EXAMINATION FOR MEASURING FACTORS *V*, *N*, AND *R*, AND CORRELATIONS OF WEIGHTED COMPOSITES WITH THE FACTORS

Composite	Parts of Army Alpha	Optimal weights	Multiple correlations with the factors	Integral weights	Correlations of composites with factors		
					V	*N*	*R*
V	3	.517	.854	1	.853	.069	.206
	4	.687		2			
	5	.667		2			
	8	.359		1			
N	2	2.780	.816	5	.456	.815	.043
	6	.553		1			
R	1	1.005	.816	1	.400	.015	.816
	7	.831		1			

be compared with the largest correlations between single tests and the same factors: .715 for test 4, .801 for test 2, and .803 for test 7. In the one instance, at least, it appears to pay to make a combination to measure a factor. In the other two cases apparently it does not, though it is possible that combinations will reduce correlations with factors that we do not want to measure with a score.

Since weights to three decimal places, like those in Table 16.28, are impractical to work with, we can choose very simple integral weights that are roughly—even *very* roughly—proportional to them. In the fifth column of Table 16.28 are given the simplest of such integral weights. By means of the formula for correlation of weighted sums with a single variable, the correlations of each weighted composite with each of the three factors are

[1] If the standard deviation for a factor is chosen as 10.0, the standard deviation of the composite scores will equal 10 times the multiple *R*. If we want the standard deviation of the composite to be 10, therefore, we should choose a standard deviation for the factor equal to $10/R$ in determining the regression weights.

found (22). In no case is the correlation with the leading factor more than .001 lower than that for the optimal weights. The verbal composite has gratifyingly low correlations with factors *N* and *R*. The other two composites have too much correlation with factor *V* for satisfactory discrimination. Using as factor loadings the correlations of composites with factors, we can estimate the intercorrelations of the composites in so far as these factors determine them. These are minimum correlations. They are $r_{VN} = .436$, $r_{VR} = .522$, and $r_{NR} = .091$.

The Suppression Method. Guilford and Michael (26) have proposed another general principle for the measure of factors, a method that emphasizes the suppression of variances that we do not want in a composite. In the preceding illustration, we found that when we weight the tests in composites for the measurement of both the *N* factor and the *R* factor, we have considerable verbal variance involved. We could reduce that undesired variance considerably by bringing into the combination a test of the verbal factor and giving it a negative weight.

The procedure recommended is to select the one best test to measure each factor. If this test has involved in its scores too much variance in a secondary common factor or possibly in two secondary common factors, find suitable measures of those secondary factors and develop a scoring formula that will reduce those unwanted variances. The use of a suppression test may result in enhancing the variance in the factor that we want to measure as well as in reducing that in the factors we do not want to measure. The assigned weights that reduce the unwanted variance may also reduce the desired variance, however. The problems of weighting the suppression variable are too involved to be discussed in the space available here. The interested reader is referred to the article by Guilford and Michael for further details. The reader is warned here, however, that it takes large samples to establish dependable suppression weights.

Some Special Problems in Factor Analysis

Some Determiners of Factor Structures. The factors found in a particular analysis and their loadings in the tests depend somewhat upon the circumstances surrounding the source of the data on which the analysis was based. This is merely a special instance of a more general principle recognized by scientists in general. Some of the determining conditions have to do with the nature of the tests and the combinations of tests used in the analysis. Other conditions have to do with the population selected, the kind of sampling, and the conditions of testing that prevailed. We will consider these conditions very briefly in turn.

Properties of the Tests and Scores. If we are dealing with tests of abilities, there should be some concern regarding difficulty level. Difficulty is relative to the population tested, of course. The optimal level is one of moderate difficulty so that distributions of scores are symmetrical, not skewed, and complete, not truncated. If it turns out that a test is either too difficult or too easy and gives a skewed distribution, there are two feasible solutions. If the sample is rather large (say 300 or more) and especially if the score scale is a coarse one, the distribution can be dichotomized. The division should be as near the median as possible. If all distributions are dichotomized, the appropriate correlation coefficient to use is the tetrachoric r, as an estimate of the Pearson product-moment r. If some distributions are dichotomized and some not, between the two kinds of distribution a biserial r, also an estimate of the Pearson r, is the appropriate one. There is no objection to mixing different types of coefficients in a correlation matrix so long as all are estimates of the same kind of r. If the skewed distribution is on a finely graded scale, and especially if N is not large, the scores should be converted into a normalized distribution, on a T-score scale or a C-score scale.

Another aspect of the difficulty problem is that the tests should be of very similar difficulty levels. Correlations of tests differing widely in difficulty tend to be smaller than those of tests of equal difficulty. If we have succeeded in making all tests of median difficulty, we have also equated them for difficulty. It would be possible to equate them at some level lower or higher than median difficulty, however. If there are several difficulty levels represented by different tests, dichotomizing distributions near the medians will help, but probably will not entirely correct for the effects involved (7, 16, 19).

It should go without saying that score variables that are intercorrelated by means of the Pearson r should satisfy the ordinary requirements for computing that coefficient. Marked skewing of a distribution, as mentioned above, is an indication that those requirements are probably not satisfied. Other irregularities of distributions should also call for caution and for corrective measures. Some distributions are truncated at one end. The remedy may be to dichotomize the distribution. Some distributions may be bimodal or otherwise multimodal. This may suggest a combination of two or more populations, each with its own mode, or it may be an artifact of the scoring procedure. The question of heterogeneous populations will be dealt with later. A seriously saw-toothed distribution not due to heterogeneity of population may be dichotomized, provided one can see no good reasons against it.

Some thought should be given to the scoring formula that is applied to a test. A change in the scoring formula may change the factorial picture of the test materially (15, 25). The number of right responses, the number of wrong responses, the number right minus some weighted number of wrong responses are the most common types of scoring formulas. Sometimes it is desirable to make separate analyses of the right-responses score and the wrong-responses score. It is often assumed that they are almost interchangeable scores (in reverse direction, of course). But the correlation between these two scores is often low and even zero, which means that their common factors differ considerably. By knowing their relations to factors when used separately, one can predict what the factor composition of any weighted combination of the two will be.

Variables analyzed in the same matrix should be experimentally independent. There should be no reason for relationship except the existence of common factors. Spurious correlations arise when correlated variables are not experimentally independent. Dependence may arise in a large number of ways. One of the more common ways is the derivation of two or more scores from the same responses. A test that is scored in two ways is likely to yield spuriously interrelated variables. Sometimes one such score includes the other, as in the case of a standing-height score and a sitting-height score. In the scoring of interest inventories and personality inventories, many items are often weighted similarly in several different scores. The correlations between such scores are spurious because of the identical elements of specific and error variance in addition to that of common-factor variance. The intercorrelations of ratings are spurious to the extent that the raters are influenced by the halo effect and other sources of constant errors.

The ordinary factor analysis by what is known as the *R* technique calls for normative measurements. It would be wrong to use *ipsative* measurements in the intercorrelation of experimental variables. Ipsative measurements for each individual are distributed about the mean of that individual, not about the population mean. Individual differences in ipsative measurements have little meaning because there is not a single scale for all individuals. Ipsative scores arise when traits for an individual are ranked for that individual, directly or by some other procedure such as pair comparisons. The forced-choice type of item, in which we have something approaching pair comparisons, often gives scores with strong ipsative properties. They should not be used for correlations of variables over a population of individuals. Ipsative scores are the appropriate ones to use when we intercorrelate persons. Such intercorrelations are appropriate for application of the *Q* technique in factor analysis, to be described later.

The time limit of tests is another important thing to consider. The same test given as a speed test and again as a power test may have radically changed factor loadings (12). In planning a test to be used in a factor analysis, we should give serious consideration to the time allowed. Preliminary experiments with the test should help to determine whether the desired amount of speeding has been achieved.

Nature of the Population. The question of population sampling for a factor analysis is essentially the same as for any experimental investigation. There are certain controls that one arbitrarily imposes so as to facilitate bringing out a factor structure as clearly as one can. In general, one tries to achieve a homogeneous population with respect to variables that he does not want to intrude as common factors and yet a population in which individual differences in the factorial variables in which he is interested do have substantial variances.

It is good practice to control on the very common variables of age, sex, and educational level. The main reason is that if two or more of the factors are appreciably correlated with these variables, they will appear to be correlated with one another when actually they are not. That is, the correlation of factors in a particular investigation is probably often due to these external linkages rather than to intrinsic ones. If we were to sample a population varying all the way from idiots to geniuses in the analysis of abilities, we should undoubtedly find strong correlations among all factors. Second-order factors, then, may well represent merely population features and not personal, psychological features.

In this connection the reader should be cautioned about combining data from two or more samples in order to achieve a large N in making a factor analysis. Before combining samples one should test for significant differences in means on the experimental variables to be analyzed. Where there are significant and material differences in means, some adjustments should be made before combining the data for obtaining intercorrelations. Scaling the sample distributions to one with a common mean and a common standard deviation for each test would be one procedure. Dichotomizing each sample distribution at its own median before setting up a combined tetrachoric table would be another. Still another solution would be to obtain a correlation matrix for each sample separately, then to average corresponding coefficients to obtain a single matrix. If the two or more populations are very different, however, the correlations from pairs of tests should be examined for significant differences.

The motivation of the individuals while taking the tests is another important consideration. For tests of ability, ideally we would want a high, even level of motivation throughout all tests. Examinees who are competing for coveted assignments would provide one of the best situations for achieving this condition. With tests of interests and of temperament traits, of the questionnaire type, however, we have to be concerned about too much motivation of some kinds. In these connections we do *not* want the atmosphere of competition for coveted positions. Rather, we want a mental set for cooperation and honesty.

For more detailed discussions of problems of selection of samples, the reader is referred to Thurstone (49) and Thomson (45).

The Q Technique of Factor Analysis. We can regard a table of scores as a matrix in which there are as many columns as tests and as many rows as persons. The correlations in the R technique are between columns. In the Q technique the correlations are, in principle, between rows, that is to say, between persons.

The Q technique is one of practical appeal when the number of experimental variables is very large and the number of individuals is very small. For example, if we have measures of 20 persons on 200 tests it would be ridiculous to intercorrelate the 200 tests with an N of 20. Instead, we can intercorrelate the 20 persons with an N of 200.

The question arises, however, whether the factors obtained by the Q technique are identical with the factors obtained by the R technique. Writers do not agree on the answer to this question. The best conclusion seems to be that what the Q technique brings out is personality types or syndromes. Persons having outstanding combinations of traits in common will show these as factors in the Q technique. Only when a syndrome is dominated by a single common factor would a Q-technique factor coincide with an R-technique factor.

There is much interest, of course, in types and syndromes in clinical psychology. It is there that the Q technique promises most utility. It is there that we are likely to have a multitude of information about a small number of persons rather than a limited amount of information about a multitude of persons.

There are one or two precautions to be observed in undertaking a *Q* analysis. The scores for such an analysis should be ipsative measures. The scores should be distributed about the mean of an individual for each individual, not about the mean of the population for each test. This leads to the requirement that the means for all individuals be equated. When the "scores" correlated person to person are responses to single items, the mean for a person is the proportion that he answered in the specified manner, for example "Yes." This proportion will vary from person to person. The means must somehow be equated. There are two procedures for doing this.

One of these procedures is known as the *Q*-sort method. Suppose a patient is to react to a list of statements by saying which ones apply to him, or a therapist is to do it for him. In a *Q* sort, instead of responding "Yes" or "No" to each item, the rater sorts the statements into a number of piles, for example, nine, each pile having in it a specified number of items as required to form a normal distribution. The piles are in rank order, the highest containing those items that are most descriptive of the person and the lowest containing those that are least descriptive.

The other procedure, proposed by Holley,[1] deals with responses of "Yes" and "No." The correlation of two persons would be in the form of a tetrachoric *r*, where scores are either 1 or 0. Suppose two persons gave two-category responses that yielded the first tetrachoric table shown in Table 16.29. Their means are .4 and .7, respectively. The tetrachoric *r* based

TABLE 16.29. CORRELATION BETWEEN TWO PERSONS BASED UPON TWO-CATEGORY SCORES

Original Table

		Person 1		
		Yes	No	Both
Person 2	Yes	140	20	160
	No	140	100	240
	Both	280	120	400

Revised Table

		Person 1		
		Yes	No	Both
Person 2	Yes	120	80	200
	No	80	120	200
	Both	200	200	400

upon the table is .52. But the effect of the difference in means is to produce an asymmetrical distribution in the four cells, with a very small proportional cell frequency of .05. This fact artificially raises the correlation. If that small frequency had been .00, the correlation would have been 1.00. The scatter of the four frequencies suggests a nonlinear regression, in which case the tetrachoric *r* does not apply. One remedy is to take the like-signed frequencies (140 and 100) and average them, also the unlike-signed frequencies (140 and 20). The average in either case is used in both cells from which it came. The table thus looks like the second one in Table 16.29. Now the means of both individuals are alike, namely, .50. The table is symmetrical throughout, and we have the same total frequencies of like-signed and unlike-signed cases as before. The tetrachoric *r* is now .31—smaller, as we should expect.

[1] J. W. Holley, in a personal communication.

This coefficient is essentially the same as the correlation known as the unlike-signs coefficient. The formula is

$$r_u = \cos \pi \frac{U}{U + L} \tag{16.11}$$

where U = number of cases with unlike signs
L = number of cases with like signs
π = 180 degrees

Applied to the data in Table 16.29, we have $r_u = \cos 72° = .309$.

Analysis by the *P* Technique. The *P* technique brings into the picture the variations of a single person over a population of occasions. The occasions might be daily, weekly, or monthly samplings of behavior. By the application of correlation to such measurements the covariations of observable qualities in time are used to determine the underlying sources of covariation. One could intercorrelate tests, in which case one would need a very large sample of occasions. The analysis would be analogous to that of the *R* technique. One could also correlate occasions, in which case one would need a very large number of tests. The analysis would be analogous to the *Q* technique. Only one or two analyses that have employed the *P* technique have been reported (5, 10).

Cattell (8) gives an extended, systematic discussion of all the possible combinations of the variations of persons, tests, and occasions that are potentially sources of data for factor analysis. It remains to be seen how much the unusual combinations have to offer in the way of fruitful approaches. Thus far, the *R* technique, with correlations of tests in populations of persons, has been the prevailing one.

The Design of Factor-analysis Investigations. We have already seen some of the precautions that should be taken in connection with a factor analysis. There are other considerations that must be faced if one is to do a successful analysis and do it efficiently. Many a study has fallen short of what it could have accomplished had greater pains been taken. So much labor goes into the computations in an analysis that it pays to ensure that the outcome is worth what it cost. Judicious planning and thoughtful preparation will be rewarding. The following suggestions will help.

1. Select an appropriate domain for investigation. In some investigations, everything seems to be thrown in that is convenient. It is unwise to attempt to analyze just any correlation matrix that comes along. This approach often leads to disappointments. It is also unwise to throw together just any list of tests that happens to be available. Many tests, even successful ones on the market, are wholly unsuitable for factor-analysis purposes. This is especially true of interest and personality inventories (23). The selection of tests should follow a good deal of theorizing about the domain of investigation. The theorizing should determine what kinds of tests will be needed. The chances are that very few existent tests will serve the purpose exactly and many will have to be tailor-made for the investigation.

The domain selected might be as broad as that of "human-interest factors" or as narrow as that of "perceptual-closure abilities." The broader the domain, the larger the number of factors to be expected, if coverage is comprehensive in the tests used. It is well to select a domain in which one expects not more than 15 factors and in which therefore not more than 50 tests will be involved. It is very important to have at least three times as many tests as factors. This is to ensure that the rotations shall be overdetermined. The domain selected should not be too limited in scope. For example, a study concentrated on deductive-reasoning abilities might involve tests of such similar properties that specific variances come out as common factors.

2. Develop hypotheses concerning the factors in the domain. This is probably the most important step in a factorial investigation. It is too commonly overlooked. One should attempt to decide beforehand how many factors there will be in the domain and what kind of trait each one is. The latter task involves several alternative hypotheses concerning the nature of each factor expected.

3. Suitable tests should be selected or constructed. The preceding step is a crucial one for determining what kinds of tests will be needed. The hypothesis that there is a certain kind of factor, with certain specified qualities, calls for two or more tests meeting those particular specifications. After the tests that seem to be required are assembled or written, it is likely that we find that certain ones involve already known factors—for example, verbal, numerical, or perceptual factors. If one of these factors is likely to be present to some degree in two or more of the tests, we should add to the battery at least one test known to be good for bringing out the factor. This segregates the variances in known factors, leaving the picture clearer with respect to the new factors. Tests designed for either known or unknown factors should be made as univocal as possible. That is, we should aim at one-factor tests.

The tests should be of high internal consistency, but the time required in administration is also an important consideration. There must often be compromises. A large battery runs into much examinee time and often there are absolute limits for the total testing time. Short tests are therefore desirable, as short as they can be and yet give sufficient reliability. A lower limit of .60 might be given as a standard for reliability. Certainly, there must be sufficient true variance to give a test vector enough length to help determine where rotations shall go. It should be seen from factor theory that reliability limits communality and communality limits test-vector length. Low reliability does not, presumably, alter the direction of a test vector and thus alter the factor structure. There are methods of estimating from a short, less reliable test what the factor loadings would be in a test of the same kinds of items of greater length (27).

4. Select a suitable population. This should be done before the tests are assembled so that the tests will also be suitable for the population in which the study is to be made. The problems of difficulty level of tests were mentioned before, and so were the problems of homogeneity of the population. Those discussions need not be repeated here.

5. Obtain a sample of adequate size. Although there are no known ways

of estimating sampling fluctuation in rotated factor loadings, it is obvious that we should be concerned with the reliability of the correlation coefficients with which we start an analysis. Errors in correlation coefficients will be reflected in errors in factor loadings.

Experience seems to show that when Pearson r's are used, a minimum N of 200 is good policy. Verifiable results have been obtained in important studies in which there have been less than 200 examinees (25). Factor loadings from samples near 200 have been fairly consistent with loadings in the same factors and tests from samples above 1,000. When tetrachoric correlations are used, a minimum number of 300 is recommended. The upper limits will depend upon the compulsion of the investigator and the circumstances of testing arrangements.

6. Extract the factors with communalities in the diagonal cells of the correlation matrix; then rotate reference axes. The reasons for these operations and the steps for carrying them out have been given in some detail.

7. Interpret the rotated factors. Here, as in the forming of hypotheses preceding the analysis, the psychologist has the opportunity and the responsibility to exert all the intuitive powers he can muster. The interpretation of a factor is actually the revision of an old hypothesis or the forming of a new one. One should be in much better position to form adequate hypotheses concerning the nature of factors after the analysis than he was before. Modifications in a hypothesis lead to a better study of a factor in the next analysis. Eventually it is expected that the hypotheses concerning a factor will converge and its properties will become accepted as "established."

Some Applications of Factor Analysis

It is the limited objective of this closing section merely to point out a few of the varied problems to which factor analysis has been applied, its places of greatest usefulness, and some of the implications of its use in connection with important but difficult psychological problems.

Types of Domains in Which Factorial Studies Are Made. Although originally designed to explore the underlying variables in human abilities, with the finding of what Thurstone has called primary abilities, factor analysis has seen even more use in the search for primary interests, attitudes, and temperament traits. Wolfle summarized the factorial studies up to the year 1940 (52). By 1946, Cattell wrote a volume on personality in which factor theory and results are basic and in which scores of studies are mentioned. The data that were analyzed came from three main sources—ratings, questionnaires (both single items and total scores have been intercorrelated), and performance tests. These kinds of material do not by any means exhaust the possibilities. By 1947, the U.S. Army Air Force had reported some four years of wartime research on test development in which factor analysis played a key role (25). In 1951, French summarized results and collated factors derived from aptitude and achievement tests (14).

Analyses have also been made in some rather unusual domains not always obviously analogous to the situation of tests and individual differences.

Two or three studies have been made in the attempt to discover or verify phenomenal properties of sensory responses (34, 35). Several studies have attempted to discover aesthetic variables (13, 24, 31). One or two studies have attacked the problem of humor from this approach (1). Some attempts to arrive at basic variables in human physique have been promising (38, 41, 48). Voting behavior of limited populations such as legislative bodies has been an interesting application (6, 28). A notable application outside of psychology has been the analysis of allergy reactions to various substances (2).

Fields Most Likely to Gain by Factorial Methods. As yet, the field most directly susceptible to the findings of factor analysis is that of vocational psychology. This is true for the operations of select'on, of classification, and of guidance. The practical advantages of the factorial approach have been pointed out by the writer elsewhere (21, 25). There is not space to elaborate upon those advantages here. In general terms the benefits to vocational psychology are as follows.

In selection of personnel for certain assignments we obtain the greatest efficiency of selection if the test or test battery we use measures all the significant common factors involved in success on the job. There will come a time when job assignments will be specified in terms of weighted combinations of the factors. When these combinations are known, we can write the prescriptions for successful tests to use in selecting personnel. When tests prove valid for a certain selection purpose, the explanation is in terms of the common factors that are related both to the tests and to success on the job. A battery of factorial tests achieves great economy of testing effort. There need be a maximum of only one test per common factor involved. Many present batteries, composed of many tests, may be wasteful in that they measure over and over again the same factors, limited in number.

In the classification of personnel, univocal factor tests definitely come into their own. In selection, we can tolerate two or more common factors per test, provided all are also related to the job criterion and all are weighted to advantage. In classification, we sort persons among jobs so that differential prediction becomes very important. If we are to say that person *A* should be assigned to job *X* in preference to *Y* or *Z*, or if we are to say that of two persons, *A* and *B*, the assignments should be to jobs *X* and *Z*, respectively, and not the reverse, we must be able to discriminate as much as possible the *patterns* of abilities of *A* and *B*. We are concerned with *differences* in job patterns and in individual patterns of traits rather than in amounts of ability in each factor as such. We cannot establish patterns and differences in relatively unique variables without having separate measures of the factors.

In vocational guidance much emphasis is placed upon personality profiles. The latter term here is sufficiently broad to include abilities as well as interests and temperament traits. A profile is difficult to interpret unless the nature of the scores that go into it is known. The best way of knowing the nature of a score is to have it factor analyzed. A profile is of little use if the scores on which it is based intercorrelate very highly. This calls for relatively unique score variables, which would mean that each measures a factor rather univocally.

Clinical psychology generally would find the concepts developed by factor analysis very useful. Where they have been tried, and this is unfortunately on very rare occasion, they have proved to be understandable, communicable, and dependable. There is little more that one could ask of a concept. What is more, the factor concept has referents, a fact which passes the hurdles of semantic and operational standards! As Cattell has pointed out, the most important step in mastering problems of personality is to have a good list of descriptive terms (8).

Experimental psychology has more problems involving unknown variables than it realizes. A superficial justification of this remark is the fact that most of its measurements are of the nature of test scores. Studies of learning, memory, motivation, and thinking commonly utilize measurements that belong in the category of test scores. These scores are as likely to be factorially complex as those of vocational psychology. Their underlying psychological variables are usually assumed but actually are usually unknown. There is much that one can do with experimental variables in the way of framing laws on that same level. In terms of more fundamental theory and systematic ramifications, however, it is likely that much is missed.

The Factorial Approach to Some Important Problems. Not all the criticisms leveled at the mental-test movement by the supposedly uninformed layman are without point or significance. Many generalizations about age differences, sex differences, and racial differences are as conflicting as they are unjust because it is not known just what abilities the tests are sampling. There can no longer be any excuse for basing conclusions about mental growth and decline upon test of "general intelligence" and upon one battery of tests in one population and upon another battery in another population. There may be a different curve of growth and decline for every one of the primary abilities, and no one will be justified hereafter in presenting growth curves without specifying the function or functions of which he speaks. The problem is further complicated by the question of how the abilities are organized at different ages, in the two sexes, in different races, and in tests of different levels of difficulty.

In the same class is the great question of the extent to which ability can be improved by training. This much-debated problem breaks up when we apply factor thinking. It is then a question of which primary abilities can be improved and to what extent. The many conflicting answers we have had to this question in the past may readily find reconciliation when the problem of nature versus nurture is recast in this form. Let us attempt to answer these more fundamental questions before we launch into the more complicated but more socially vital problems. Our answers will gain far more respect and lead to far greater social consequences and our efforts in human engineering will be placed upon a firm scientific basis.

Problems

1. Using Data 16*A*, extract four centroid factors, using the highest coefficient of correlation in each column as the estimated communality. What is the evidence as to the number of factors that should be extracted?

DATA 16A. INTERCORRELATIONS OF NINE AIR FORCE TESTS, THEIR MEANS AND STANDARD DEVIATIONS*

Test	1	2	3	4	5	6	7	8	9
1		.38	.55	.06	−.04	.05	.07	.05	.08
2	.38		.36	.40	.28	.40	.11	.15	.13
3	.55	.36		.10	.01	.18	.13	.12	.10
4	.06	.40	.10		.32	.60	.04	.06	.13
5	−.04	.28	.01	.32		.35	.08	.13	.11
6	.05	.40	.18	.60	.35		.01	.06	.07
7	.07	.11	.13	.04	.08	.01		.45	.32
8	.05	.15	.12	.06	.13	.06	.45		.32
9	.08	.13	.10	.13	.11	.07	.32	.32	
M	48.1	18.5	19.3	7.3	27.2	14.5	27.8	31.3	15.5
σ	19.9	7.0	11.9	3.7	6.7	8.3	5.6	7.5	5.1

* The statistics given in this table did not arise from a single administration of the tests to the same sample. They are selected as being typical, however, from a number of different sources (25). The population was composed of aviation students as they took classification tests during World War II. The N's varied from about 400 to about 8,000 for the intercorrelations.

Nature of the tests:

1. AAF Vocabulary—a multiple-choice synonym test.
2. Technical Vocabulary (Pilot)—composed of terms such as an aircraft pilot learns.
3. Reading Comprehension—based on short paragraphs such as a pilot has to read in technical manuals.
4. Tool Functions—on knowledge of the uses of common tools.
5. Biographical Data Blank (Pilot)—containing items about past experiences.
6. Mechanical Information—mostly about knowledge of automotive equipment and repairs.
7. Spatial Orientation I—requires rapid matching of aerial photographs.
8. Speed of Identification—requires rapid matching of pictures of airplanes.
9. Pattern Assembly—a paper-formboard type of test.

For more details concerning these tests, see Guilford and Lacey (25).

2. Rotate the axes orthogonally by one or more of the methods described in the chapter, aiming at simple structure and positive manifold.
3. Rotate the axes to oblique simple structure, using the radial method. Determine the correlations between the reference axes.
4. Compute an extended-vector matrix. Rotate axes in two ways: one in which the normals to hyperplanes are the new reference axes and the other in which the primary axes are the reference axes.
5. Give your interpretation of the factors after rotations.
6. Set up a small battery to measure each factor. Determine the weights to be used in combining the test scores and the factor loadings of the composite. Limit the computation of factor loadings to the main factor and any likely secondary ones.

REFERENCES

1. ANDREWS, T. G. A factorial analysis of responses to the comic as a study of personality. *J. gen. Psychol.*, 1943, **28**, 209–224.

2. ———. Statistical studies of allergy. *J. Allergy*, 1943, **14,** 322–328; 1948, **19,** 43–46.
3. Burt, C. *The Factors of the Mind.* New York: Macmillan, 1941.
4. ——— and Stephenson, W. Alternate views of correlations between persons. *Psychometrika*, 1939, **4,** 269–281.
5. ——— and Watson, H. Factor analysis of assessments for a single person. *Brit. J. Psychol., Statist. Sec.*, 1951, **4,** 179–191.
6. Carlson, H. B., and Harrell, W. Voting groups among leading Congressmen obtained by means of the inverted factor technique. *J. soc. Psychol.*, 1942, **16,** 51–61.
7. Carroll, J. B. The effect of difficulty and chance success on correlations between items or between tests. *Psychometrika*, 1945, **10,** 1–19.
8. Cattell, R. B. *Description and Measurement of Personality.* Yonkers, N.Y.: World, 1946.
9. ———. *Factor Analysis.* New York: Harper, 1952.
10. ———, Cattell, A. K. S., and Rhymer, R. M. P-technique demonstrated in determining psycho-physiological source traits in a normal individual. *Psychometrika*, 1947, **12,** 267–288.
11. ——— and Luborsky, L. B. P-technique demonstrated as a new clinical method for determining personality and symptom structure. *J. gen. Psychol.*, 1950, **42,** 3–24.
12. Davidson, W. M., and Carroll, J. B. Speed and level components in time-limit scores: A factor analysis. *Educ. psychol. Measmt.*, 1945, **5,** 411–427.
13. Eysenck, H. J. The general factor in aesthetic judgments. *Brit. J. Psychol., Gen. Sec.*, 1940, **31,** 94–102.
14. French, J. W. The description of aptitude and achievement tests in terms of rotated factors. *Psychometr. Monogr.*, No. 5, 1951.
15. Fruchter, B. Factorial content of right-response and wrong-response scores in a battery of experimental aptitude tests. Ph.D. dissertation, University of Southern California Library, 1948.
16. Gourlay, N. Difficulty factors arising from the use of tetrachoric correlations in factor analysis. *Brit. J. Psychol., Statist. Sec.*, 1951, **4,** 65–76.
17. Green, R. F., Guilford, J. P., Christensen, P. R., and Comrey, A. L. A factor-analytic study of reasoning. *Psychometrika*, 1953, **18,** 135–160.
18. Guilford, J. P. Unitary traits of personality and factor theory. *Amer. J. Psychol.*, 1936, **48,** 673–680.
19. ———. The difficulty of a test and its factor composition. *Psychometrika*, 1941, **6,** 67–78.
20. ———. A note on the discovery of a G factor by means of the centroid method of analysis. *Psychometrika*, 1941, **6,** 205–208.
21. ———. Factor analysis in a test-development program. *Psychol. Rev.*, 1948, **55,** 79–94.
22. ———. *Fundamental Statistics in Psychology and Education.* 2d ed. New York: McGraw-Hill, 1950.
23. ———. When not to factor analyze. *Psychol. Bull.*, 1952, **49,** 26–37.
24. ——— and Holley, J. W. A factorial approach to the analysis of variances in esthetic judgments. *J. exp. Psychol.*, 1949, **39,** 208–218.
25. ——— and Lacey, J. I. (eds.). *Printed Classification Tests. Army Air Force Aviation Psychology Research Program Reports, Report* 5. Washington, D.C.: U.S. Government Printing Office, 1947.
26. ——— and Michael, W. B. Approaches to univocal factor scores. *Psychometrika*, 1948, **13,** 1–22.
27. ——— and ———. Changes in common-factor loadings as tests are altered homogeneously in length. *Psychometrika*, 1950, **15,** 237–249.
28. Harris, C. W. A factor analysis of selected senate roll calls, 80th Congress. *Educ. psychol. Measmt.*, 1948, **8,** 583–591.

29. ———. Direct rotation to primary structure. *J. educ. Psychol.*, 1948, **39**, 449–468.
30. ———. Projections of three types of factor pattern. *J. exp. Educ.*, 1949, **17**, 335–345.
31. HARSH, C. M., BEEBE-CENTER, J. G., and BEEBE-CENTER, R. Further evidence regarding preferential judgments of polygonal forms. *J. Psychol.*, 1939, **7**, 343–350.
32. HOLZINGER, K. J., and HARMAN, H. H. *Factor Analysis: A Synthesis of Factorial Methods.* Chicago: University of Chicage Press, 1941.
33. HOTELLING, H. Analysis of a complex of statistical variables into principal components. *J. educ. Psychol.*, 1933, **24**, 417–441.
34. JONES, F. N. A factor analysis of visibility data. *Amer. J. Psychol.*, 1948, **61**, 361–369.
35. KARLIN, J. E. A factorial study of auditory function. *Psychometrika*, 1942, **7**, 251–279.
36. KELLEY, T. L. *Crossroads in the Mind of Man.* Stanford: Stanford University Press, 1928.
37. ———. *Essential Traits of Mental Life.* Cambridge, Mass.: Harvard University Press, 1935.
38. MOORE, T. V., and HSÜ, E. H. Factorial analysis of anthropological measurements in psychotic patients. *Hum. Biol.*, 1946, **18**, 133–157.
39. ———, STAFFORD, J. W., and HSÜ, E. H. Obverse analysis of personality. *J. Personality*, 1947, **16**, 11–48.
40. PEEL, E. A. A new method of analyzing aesthetic preferences. *Psychometrika*, 1946, **11**, 129–137.
41. REES, W. L., and EYSENCK, H. J. A factorial study of human constitution. *J. ment. Sci.*, 1945, **91**, 8–21.
42. REYBURN, H. A., and TAYLOR, J. G. On the interpretation of common factors. *Psychometrika*, 1943, **8**, 53–64.
43. SPEARMAN, C. "General intelligence," objectively determined and measured. *Amer. J. Psychol.*, 1904, **15**, 201–293.
44. ———. *Abilities of Man.* New York: Macmillan, 1927.
45. THOMSON, G. H. *The Factorial Analysis of Human Ability.* 3d ed. Boston: Houghton Mifflin, 1948.
46. THURSTONE, L. L. *Vectors of Mind.* Chicago: University of Chicago Press, 1935.
47. ———. A factorial study of perception. *Psychometr. Monogr.*, No. 4, 1944.
48. ———. Factor analysis of body types. *Psychometrika*, 1946, **11**, 15–21.
49. ———. *Multiple Factor Analysis.* Chicago: University of Chicago Press, 1947.
50. VAN STEENBERG, N. J. F. Factors in the learning behavior of the albino rat. *Psychometrika*, 1939, **4**, 179–200.
51. WHIPPLE, G. M. *Manual of Mental and Physical Tests.* Baltimore: Warwick and York, 1914.
52. WOLFLE, D. Factor analysis to 1940. *Psychometr. Monogr.*, No. 3, 1940.
53. ZIMMERMAN, W. S. A simple graphical method for orthogonal rotation of axes. *Psychometrika*, 1946, **11**, 51–56.

APPENDIX

Table A. Squares and Square Roots of Numbers from 1 to 1,000*

Number	Square	Square root	Number	Square	Square root
1	1	1.0000	41	16 81	6.4031
2	4	1.4142	42	17 64	6.4807
3	9	1.7321	43	18 49	6.5574
4	16	2.0000	44	19 36	6.6332
5	25	2.2361	45	20 25	6.7082
6	36	2.4495	46	21 16	6.7823
7	49	2.6458	47	22 09	6.8557
8	64	2.8284	48	23 04	6.9282
9	81	3.0000	49	24 01	7.0000
10	1 00	3.1623	50	25 00	7.0711
11	1 21	3.3166	51	26 01	7.1414
12	1 44	3.4641	52	27 04	7.2111
13	1 69	3.6056	53	28 09	7.2801
14	1 96	3.7417	54	29 16	7.3485
15	2 25	3.8730	55	30 25	7.4162
16	2 56	4.0000	56	31 36	7.4833
17	2 89	4.1231	57	32 49	7.5498
18	3 24	4.2426	58	33 64	7.6158
19	3 61	4.3589	59	34 81	7.6811
20	4 00	4.4721	60	36 00	7.7460
21	4 41	4.5826	61	37 21	7.8102
22	4 84	4.6904	62	38 44	7.8740
23	5 29	4.7958	63	39 69	7.9373
24	5 76	4.8990	64	40 96	8.0000
25	6 25	5.0000	65	42 25	8.0623
26	6 76	5.0990	66	43 56	8.1240
27	7 29	5.1962	67	44 89	8.1854
28	7 84	5.2915	68	46 24	8.2462
29	8 41	5.3852	69	47 61	8.3066
30	9 00	5.4772	70	49 00	8.3666
31	9 61	5.5678	71	50 41	8.4261
32	10 24	5.6569	72	51 84	8.4853
33	10 89	5.7446	73	53 29	8.5440
34	11 56	5.8310	74	54 76	8.6023
35	12 25	5.9161	75	56 25	8.6603
36	12 96	6.0000	76	57 76	8.7178
37	13 69	6.0828	77	59 29	8.7750
38	14 44	6.1644	78	60 84	8.8318
39	15 21	6.2450	79	62 41	8.8882
40	16 00	6.3246	80	64 00	8.9443

* From Sorenson. Statistics for students of psychology and education.

TABLE A. SQUARES AND SQUARE ROOTS OF NUMBERS FROM 1 TO 1,000.* (*Continued*)

Number	Square	Square root	Number	Square	Square root
81	65 61	9.0000	121	1 46 41	11.0000
82	67 24	9.0554	122	1 48 84	11.0454
83	68 89	9.1104	123	1 51 29	11.0905
84	70 56	9.1652	124	1 53 76	11.1355
85	72 25	9.2195	125	1 56 25	11.1803
86	73 96	9.2736	126	1 58 76	11.2250
87	75 69	9.3274	127	1 61 29	11.2694
88	77 44	9.3808	128	1 63 84	11.3137
89	79 21	9.4340	129	1 66 41	11.3578
90	81 00	9.4868	130	1 69 00	11.4018
91	82 81	9.5394	131	1 71 61	11.4455
92	84 64	9.5917	132	1 74 24	11.4891
93	86 49	9.6437	133	1 76 89	11.5326
94	88 36	9.6954	134	1 79 56	11.5758
95	90 25	9.7468	135	1 82 25	11.6190
96	92 16	9.7980	136	1 84 96	11.6619
97	94 09	9.8489	137	1 87 69	11.7047
98	96 04	9.8995	138	1 90 44	11.7473
99	98 01	9.9499	139	1 93 21	11.7898
100	1 00 00	10.0000	140	1 96 00	11.8322
101	1 02 01	10.0499	141	1 98 81	11.8743
102	1 04 04	10.0995	142	2 01 64	11.9164
103	1 06 09	10.1489	143	2 04 49	11.9583
104	1 08 16	10.1980	144	2 07 36	12.0000
105	1 10 25	10.2470	145	2 10 25	12.0416
106	1 12 36	10.2956	146	2 13 16	12.0830
107	1 14 49	10.3441	147	2 16 09	12.1244
108	1 16 64	10.3923	148	2 19 04	12.1655
109	1 18 81	10.4403	149	2 22 01	12.2066
110	1 21 00	10.4881	150	2 25 00	12.2474
111	1 23 21	10.5357	151	2 28 01	12.2882
112	1 25 44	10.5830	152	2 31 04	12.3288
113	1 27 69	10.6301	153	2 34 09	12.3693
114	1 29 96	10.6771	154	2 37 16	12.4097
115	1 32 25	10.7238	155	2 40 25	12.4499
116	1 34 56	10.7703	156	2 43 36	12.4900
117	1 36 89	10.8167	157	2 46 49	12.5300
118	1 39 24	10.8628	158	2 49 64	12.5698
119	1 41 61	10.9087	159	2 52 81	12.6095
120	1 44 00	10.9545	160	2 56 00	12.6491

* From Sorenson. Statistics for students of psychology and education.

TABLE A. SQUARES AND SQUARE ROOTS OF NUMBERS FROM 1 TO 1,000.* (*Continued*)

Number	Square	Square root	Number	Square	Square root
161	2 59 21	12.6886	201	4 04 01	14.1774
162	2 62 44	12.7279	202	4 08 04	14.2127
163	2 65 69	12.7671	203	4 12 09	14.2478
164	2 68 96	12.8062	204	4 16 16	14.2829
165	2 72 25	12.8452	205	4 20 25	14.3178
166	2 75 56	12.8841	206	4 24 36	14.3527
167	2 78 89	12.9228	207	4 28 49	14.3875
168	2 82 24	12.9615	208	4 32 64	14.4222
169	2 85 61	13.0000	209	4 36 81	14.4568
170	2 89 00	13.0384	210	4 41 00	14.4914
171	2 92 41	13.0767	211	4 45 21	14.5258
172	2 95 84	13.1149	212	4 49 44	14.5602
173	2 99 29	13.1529	213	4 53 69	14.5945
174	3 02 76	13.1909	214	4 57 96	14.6287
175	3 06 25	13.2288	215	4 62 25	14.6629
176	3 09 76	13.2665	216	4 66 56	14.6969
177	3 13 29	13.3041	217	4 70 89	14.7309
178	3 16 84	13.3417	218	4 75 24	14.7648
179	3 20 41	13.3791	219	4 79 61	14.7986
180	3 24 00	13.4164	220	4 84 00	14.8324
181	3 27 61	13.4536	221	4 88 41	14.8661
182	3 31 24	13.4907	222	4 92 84	14.8997
183	3 34 89	13.5277	223	4 97 29	14.9332
184	3 38 56	13.5647	224	5 01 76	14.9666
185	3 42 25	13.6015	225	5 06 25	15.0000
186	3 45 96	13.6382	226	5 10 76	15.0333
187	3 49 69	13.6748	227	5 15 29	15.0665
188	3 53 44	13.7113	228	5 19 84	15.0997
189	3 57 21	13.7477	229	5 24 41	15.1327
190	3 61 00	13.7840	230	5 29 00	15.1658
191	3 64 81	13.8203	231	5 33 61	15.1987
192	3 68 64	13.8564	232	5 38 24	15.2315
193	3 72 49	13.8924	233	5 42 89	15.2643
194	3 76 36	13.9284	234	5 47 56	15.2971
195	3 80 25	13.9642	235	5 52 25	15.3297
196	3 84 16	14.0000	236	5 56 96	15.3623
197	3 88 09	14.0357	237	5 61 69	15.3948
198	3 92 04	14.0712	238	5 66 44	15.4272
199	3 96 01	14.1067	239	5 71 21	15.4596
200	4 00 00	14.1421	240	5 76 00	15.4919

* From Sorenson. Statistics for students of psychology and education.

TABLE A. SQUARES AND SQUARE ROOTS OF NUMBERS FROM 1 TO 1,000.* (*Continued*)

Number	Square	Square root	Number	Square	Square root
241	5 80 81	15.5242	281	7 89 61	16.7631
242	5 85 64	15.5563	282	7 95 24	16.7929
243	5 90 49	15.5885	283	8 00 89	16.8226
244	5 95 36	15.6205	284	8 06 56	16.8523
245	6 00 25	15.6525	285	8 12 25	16.8819
246	6 05 16	15.6844	286	8 17 96	16.9115
247	6 10 09	15.7162	287	8 23 69	16.9411
248	6 15 04	15.7480	288	8 29 44	16.9706
249	6 20 01	15.7797	289	8 35 21	17.0000
250	6 25 00	15.8114	290	8 41 00	17.0294
251	6 30 01	15.8430	291	8 46 81	17.0587
252	6 35 04	15.8745	292	8 52 64	17.0880
253	6 40 09	15.9060	293	8 58 49	17.1172
254	6 45 16	15.9374	294	8 64 36	17.1464
255	6 50 25	15.9687	295	8 70 25	17.1756
256	6 55 36	16.0000	296	8 76 16	17.2047
257	6 60 49	16.0312	297	8 82 09	17.2337
258	6 65 64	16.0624	298	8 88 04	17.2627
259	6 70 81	16.0935	299	8 94 01	17.2916
260	6 76 00	16.1245	300	9 00 00	17.3205
261	6 81 21	16.1555	301	9 06 01	17.3494
262	6 86 44	16.1864	302	9 12 04	17.3781
263	6 91 69	16.2173	303	9 18 09	17.4069
264	6 96 96	16.2481	304	9 24 16	17.4356
265	7 02 25	16.2788	305	9 30 25	17.4642
266	7 07 56	16.3095	306	9 36 36	17.4929
267	7 12 89	16.3401	307	9 42 49	17.5214
268	7 18 24	16.3707	308	9 48 64	17.5499
269	7 23 61	16.4012	309	9 54 81	17.5784
270	7 29 00	16.4317	310	9 61 00	17.6068
271	7 34 41	16.4621	311	9 67 21	17.6352
272	7 39 84	16.4924	312	9 73 44	17.6635
273	7 45 29	16.5227	313	9 79 69	17.6918
274	7 50 76	16.5529	314	9 85 96	17.7200
275	7 56 25	16.5831	315	9 92 25	17.7482
276	7 61 76	16.6132	316	9 98 56	17.7764
277	7 67 29	16.6433	317	10 04 89	17.8045
278	7 72 84	16.6733	318	10 11 24	17.8326
279	7 78 41	16.7033	319	10 17 61	17.8606
280	7 84 00	16.7332	320	10 24 00	17.8885

* From Sorenson. Statistics for students of psychology and education.

TABLE A. SQUARES AND SQUARE ROOTS OF NUMBERS FROM 1 TO 1,000.* (*Continued*)

Number	Square	Square root	Number	Square	Square root
321	10 30 41	17.9165	361	13 03 21	19.0000
322	10 36 84	17.9444	362	13 10 44	19.0263
323	10 43 29	17.9722	363	13 17 69	19.0526
324	10 49 76	18.0000	364	13 24 96	19.0788
325	10 56 25	18.0278	365	13 32 25	19.1050
326	10 62 76	18.0555	366	13 39 56	19.1311
327	10 69 29	18.0831	367	13 46 89	19.1572
328	10 75 84	18.1108	368	13 54 24	19.1833
329	10 82 41	18.1384	369	13 61 61	19.2094
330	10 89 00	18.1659	370	13 69 00	19.2354
331	10 95 61	18.1934	371	13 76 41	19.2614
332	11 02 24	18.2209	372	13 83 84	19.2873
333	11 08 89	18.2483	373	13 91 29	19.3132
334	11 15 56	18.2757	374	13 98 76	19.3391
335	11 22 25	18.3030	375	14 06 25	19.3649
336	11 28 96	18.3303	376	14 13 76	19.3907
337	11 35 69	18.3576	377	14 21 29	19.4165
338	11 42 44	18.3848	378	14 28 84	19.4422
339	11 49 21	18.4120	379	14 36 41	19.4679
340	11 56 00	18.4391	380	14 44 00	19.4936
341	11 62 81	18.4662	381	14 51 61	19.5192
342	11 69 64	18.4932	382	14 59 24	19.5448
343	11 76 49	18.5203	383	14 66 89	19.5704
344	11 83 36	18.5472	384	14 74 56	19.5959
345	11 90 25	18.5742	385	14 82 25	19.6214
346	11 97 16	18.6011	386	14 89 96	19.6469
347	12 04 09	18.6279	387	14 97 69	19.6723
348	12 11 04	18.6548	388	15 05 44	19.6977
349	12 18 01	18.6815	389	15 13 21	19.7231
350	12 25 00	18.7083	390	15 21 00	19.7484
351	12 32 01	18.7350	391	15 28 81	19.7737
352	12 39 04	18.7617	392	15 36 64	19.7990
353	12 46 09	18.7883	393	15 44 49	19.8242
354	12 53 16	18.8149	394	15 52 36	19.8494
355	12 60 25	18.8414	395	15 60 25	19.8746
356	12 67 36	18.8680	396	15 68 16	19.8997
357	12 74 49	18.8944	397	15 76 09	19.9249
358	12 81 64	18.9209	398	15 84 04	19.9499
359	12 88 81	18.9473	399	15 92 01	19.9750
360	12 96 00	18.9737	400	16 00 00	20.0000

* From Sorenson. Statistics for students of psychology and education.

TABLE A. SQUARES AND SQUARE ROOTS OF NUMBERS FROM 1 TO 1,000.* (*Continued*)

Number	Square	Square root	Number	Square	Square root
401	16 08 01	20.0250	441	19 44 81	21.0000
402	16 16 04	20.0499	442	19 53 64	21.0238
403	16 24 09	20.0749	443	19 62 49	21.0476
404	16 32 16	20.0998	444	19 71 36	21.0713
405	16 40 25	20.1246	445	19 80 25	21.0950
406	16 48 36	20.1494	446	19 89 16	21.1187
407	16 56 49	20.1742	447	19 98 09	21.1424
408	16 64 64	20.1990	448	20 07 04	21.1660
409	16 72 81	20.2237	449	20 16 01	21.1896
410	16 81 00	20.2485	450	20 25 00	21.2132
411	16 89 21	20.2731	451	20 34 01	21.2368
412	16 97 44	20.2978	452	20 43 04	21.2603
413	17 05 69	20.3224	453	20 52 09	21.2838
414	17 13 96	20.3470	454	20 61 16	21.3073
415	17 22 25	20.3715	455	20 70 25	21.3307
416	17 30 56	20.3961	456	20 79 36	21.3542
417	17 38 89	20.4206	457	20 88 49	21.3776
418	17 47 24	20.4450	458	20 97 64	21.4009
419	17 55 61	20.4695	459	21 06 81	21.4243
420	17 64 00	20.4939	460	21 16 00	21.4476
421	17 72 41	20.5183	461	21 25 21	21.4709
422	17 80 84	20.5426	462	21 34 44	21.4942
423	17 89 29	20.5670	463	21 43 69	21.5174
424	17 97 76	20.5913	464	21 52 96	21.5407
425	18 06 25	20.6155	465	21 62 25	21.5639
426	18 14 76	20.6398	466	21 71 56	21.5870
427	18 23 29	20.6640	467	21 80 89	21.6102
428	18 31 84	20.6882	468	21 90 24	21.6333
429	18 40 41	20.7123	469	21 99 61	21.6564
430	18 49 00	20.7364	470	22 09 00	21.6795
431	18 57 61	20.7605	471	22 18 41	21.7025
432	18 66 24	20.7846	472	22 27 84	21.7256
433	18 74 89	20.8087	473	22 37 29	21.7486
434	18 83 56	20.8327	474	22 46 76	21.7715
435	18 92 25	20.8567	475	22 56 25	21.7945
436	19 00 96	20.8806	476	22 65 76	21.8174
437	19 09 69	20.9045	477	22 75 29	21.8403
438	19 18 44	20.9284	478	22 84 84	21.8632
439	19 27 21	20.9523	479	22 94 41	21.8861
440	19 36 00	20.9762	480	23 04 00	21.9089

* From Sorenson. Statistics for students of psychology and education.

TABLE A. SQUARES AND SQUARE ROOTS OF NUMBERS FROM 1 TO 1,000.* (*Continued*)

Number	Square	Square root	Number	Square	Square root
481	23 13 61	21.9317	521	27 14 41	22.8254
482	23 23 24	21.9545	522	27 24 84	22.8473
483	23 32 89	21.9773	523	27 35 29	22.8692
484	23 42 56	22.0000	524	27 45 76	22.8910
485	23 52 25	22.0227	525	27 56 25	22.9129
486	23 61 96	22.0454	526	27 66 76	22.9347
487	23 71 69	22.0681	527	27 77 29	22.9565
488	23 81 44	22.0907	528	27 87 84	22.9783
489	23 91 21	22.1133	529	27 98 41	23.0000
490	24 01 00	22.1359	530	28 09 00	23.0217
491	24 10 81	22.1585	531	28 19 61	23.0434
492	24 20 64	22.1811	532	28 30 24	23.0651
493	24 30 49	22.2036	533	28 40 89	23.0868
494	24 40 36	22.2261	534	28 51 56	23.1084
495	24 50 25	22.2486	535	28 62 25	23.1301
496	24 60 16	22.2711	536	28 72 96	23.1517
497	24 70 09	22.2935	537	28 83 69	23.1733
498	24 80 04	22.3159	538	28 94 44	23.1948
499	24 90 01	22.3383	539	29 05 21	23.2164
500	25 00 00	22.3607	540	29 16 00	23.2379
501	25 10 01	22.3830	541	29 26 81	23.2594
502	25 20 04	22.4054	542	29 37 64	23.2809
503	25 30 09	22.4277	543	29 48 49	23.3024
504	25 40 16	22.4499	544	29 59 36	23.3238
505	25 50 25	22.4722	545	29 70 25	23.3452
506	25 60 36	22.4944	546	29 81 16	23.3666
507	25 70 49	22.5167	547	29 92 09	23.3880
508	25 80 64	22.5389	548	30 03 04	23.4094
509	25 90 81	22.5610	549	30 14 01	23.4307
510	26 01 00	22.5832	550	30 25 00	23.4521
511	26 11 21	22.6053	551	30 36 01	23.4734
512	26 21 44	22.6274	552	30 47 04	23.4947
513	26 31 69	22.6495	553	30 58 09	23.5160
514	26 41 96	22.6716	554	30 69 16	23.5372
515	26 52 25	22.6936	555	30 80 25	23.5584
516	26 62 56	22.7156	556	30 91 36	23.5797
517	26 72 89	22.7376	557	31 02 49	23.6008
518	26 83 24	22.7596	558	31 13 64	23.6220
519	26 93 61	22.7816	559	31 24 81	23.6432
520	27 04 00	22.8035	560	31 36 00	23.6643

* From Sorenson. Statistics for students of psychology and education.

TABLE A. SQUARES AND SQUARE ROOTS OF NUMBERS FROM 1 TO 1,000.* (*Continued*)

Number	Square	Square root	Number	Square	Square root
561	31 47 21	23.6854	601	36 12 01	24.5153
562	31 58 44	23.7065	602	36 24 04	24.5357
563	31 69 69	23.7276	603	36 36 09	24.5561
564	31 80 96	23.7487	604	36 48 16	24.5764
565	31 92 25	23.7697	605	36 60 25	24.5967
566	32 03 56	23.7908	606	36 72 36	24.6171
567	32 14 89	23.8118	607	36 84 49	24.6374
568	32 26 24	23.8328	608	36 96 64	24.6577
569	32 37 61	23.8537	609	37 08 81	24.6779
570	32 49 00	23.8747	610	37 21 00	24.6982
571	32 60 41	23.8956	611	37 33 21	24.7184
572	32 71 84	23.9165	612	37 45 44	24.7385
573	32 83 29	23.9374	613	37 57 69	24.7588
574	32 94 76	23.9583	614	37 69 96	24.7790
575	33 06 25	23.9792	615	37 82 25	24.7992
576	33 17 76	24.0000	616	37 94 56	24.8193
577	33 29 29	24.0208	617	38 06 89	24.8395
578	33 40 84	24.0416	618	38 19 24	24.8596
579	33 52 41	24.0624	619	38 31 61	24.8797
580	33 64 00	24.0832	620	38 44 00	24.8998
581	33 75 61	24.1039	621	38 56 41	24.9199
582	33 87 24	24.1247	622	38 68 84	24.9399
583	33 98 89	24.1454	623	38 81 29	24.9600
584	34 10 56	24.1661	624	38 93 76	24.9800
585	34 22 25	24.1868	625	39 06 25	25.0000
586	34 33 96	24.2074	626	39 18 76	25.0200
587	34 45 69	24.2281	627	39 31 29	25.0400
588	34 57 44	24.2487	628	39 43 84	25.0599
589	34 69 21	24.2693	629	39 56 41	25.0799
590	34 81 00	24.2899	630	39 69 00	25.0998
591	34 92 81	24.3105	631	39 81 61	25.1197
592	35 04 64	24.3311	632	39 94 24	25.1396
593	35 16 49	24.3516	633	40 06 89	25.1595
594	35 28 36	24.3721	634	40 19 56	25.1794
595	35 40 25	24.3926	635	40 32 25	25.1992
596	35 52 16	24.4131	636	40 44 96	25.2190
597	35 64 09	24.4336	637	40 57 69	25.2389
598	35 76 04	24.4540	638	40 70 44	25.2587
599	35 88 01	24.4745	639	40 83 21	25.2784
600	36 00 00	24.4949	640	40 96 00	25.2982

* From Sorenson. Statistics for students of psychology and education.

TABLE A. SQUARES AND SQUARE ROOTS OF NUMBERS FROM 1 TO 1,000.* (*Continued*)

Number	Square	Square root	Number	Square	Square root
641	41 08 81	25.3180	681	46 37 61	26.0960
642	41 21 64	25.3377	682	46 51 24	26.1151
643	41 34 49	25.3574	683	46 64 89	26.1343
644	41 47 36	25.3772	684	46 78 56	26.1534
645	41 60 25	25.3969	685	46 92 25	26.1725
646	41 73 16	25.4165	686	47 05 96	26.1916
647	41 86 09	25.4362	687	47 19 69	26.2107
648	41 99 04	25.4558	688	47 33 44	26.2298
649	42 12 01	25.4755	689	47 47 21	26.2488
650	42 25 00	25.4951	690	47 61 00	26.2679
651	42 38 01	25.5147	691	47 74 81	26.2869
652	42 51 04	25.5343	692	47 88 64	26.3059
653	42 64 09	25.5539	693	48 02 49	26.3249
654	42 77 16	25.5734	694	48 16 36	26.3439
655	42 90 25	25.5930	695	48 30 25	26.3629
656	43 03 36	25.6125	696	48 44 16	26.3818
657	43 16 49	25.6320	697	48 58 09	26.4008
658	43 29 64	25.6515	698	48 72 04	26.4197
659	43 42 81	25.6710	699	48 86 01	26.4386
660	43 56 00	25.6905	700	49 00 00	26.4575
661	43 69 21	25.7099	701	49 14 01	26.4764
662	43 82 44	25.7294	702	49 28 04	26.4953
663	43 95 69	25.7488	703	49 42 09	26.5141
664	44 08 96	25.7682	704	49 56 16	26.5330
665	44 22 25	25.7876	705	49 70 25	26.5518
666	44 35 56	25.8070	706	49 84 36	26.5707
667	44 48 89	25.8263	707	49 98 49	26.5895
668	44 62 24	25.8457	708	50 12 64	26.6083
669	44 75 61	25.8650	709	50 26 81	26.6271
670	44 89 00	25.8844	710	50 41 00	26.6458
671	45 02 41	25.9037	711	50 55 21	26.6646
672	45 15 84	25.9230	712	50 69 44	26.6833
673	45 29 29	25.9422	713	50 83 69	26.7021
674	45 42 76	25.9615	714	50 97 96	26.7208
675	45 56 25	25.9808	715	51 12 25	26.7395
676	45 69 76	26.0000	716	51 26 56	26.7582
677	45 83 29	26.0192	717	51 40 89	26.7769
678	45 96 84	26.0384	718	51 55 24	26.7955
679	46 10 41	26.0576	719	51 69 61	26.8142
680	46 24 00	26.0768	720	51 84 00	26.8328

* From Sorenson. Statistics for students of psychology and education.

TABLE A. SQUARES AND SQUARE ROOTS OF NUMBERS FROM 1 TO 1,000.* (*Continued*)

Number	Square	Square root	Number	Square	Square root
721	51 98 41	26.8514	761	57 91 21	27.5862
722	52 12 84	26.8701	762	58 06 44	27.6043
723	52 27 29	26.8887	763	58 21 69	27.6225
724	52 41 76	26.9072	764	58 36 96	27.6405
725	52 56 25	26.9258	765	58 52 25	27.6586
726	52 70 76	26.9444	766	58 67 56	27.6767
727	52 85 29	26.9629	767	58 82 89	27.6948
728	52 99 84	26.9815	768	58 98 24	27.7128
729	53 14 41	27.0000	769	59 13 61	27.7308
730	53 29 00	27.0185	770	59 29 00	27.7489
731	53 43 61	27.0370	771	59 44 41	27.7669
732	53 58 24	27.0555	772	59 59 84	27.7849
733	53 72 89	27.0740	773	59 75 29	27.8029
734	53 87 56	27.0924	774	59 90 76	27.8209
735	54 02 25	27.1109	775	60 06 25	27.8388
736	54 16 96	27.1293	776	60 21 76	27.8568
737	54 31 69	27.1477	777	60 37 29	27.8747
738	54 46 44	27.1662	778	60 52 84	27.8927
739	54 61 27	27.1846	779	60 68 41	27.9106
740	54 76 00	27.2029	780	60 84 00	27.9285
741	54 90 81	27.2213	781	60 99 61	27.9464
742	55 05 64	27.2397	782	61 15 24	27.9643
743	55 20 49	27.2580	783	61 30 89	27.9821
744	55 35 36	27.2764	784	61 46 56	28.0000
745	55 50 25	27.2947	785	61 62 25	28.0179
746	55 65 16	27.3130	786	61 77 96	28.0357
747	55 80 09	27.3313	787	61 93 69	28.0535
748	55 95 04	27.3496	788	62 09 44	28.0713
749	56 10 01	27.3679	789	62 25 21	28.0891
750	56 25 00	27.3861	790	62 41 00	28.1069
751	56 40 01	27.4044	791	62 56 81	28.1247
752	56 55 04	27.4226	792	62 72 64	28.1425
753	56 70 09	27.4408	793	62 88 49	28.1603
754	56 85 16	27.4591	794	63 04 36	28.1780
755	57 00 25	27.4773	795	63 20 25	28.1957
756	57 15 36	27.4955	796	63 36 16	28.2135
757	57 30 49	27.5136	797	63 52 09	28.2312
758	57 45 64	27.5318	798	63 68 04	28.2489
759	57 60 81	27.5500	799	63 84 01	28.2666
760	57 76 00	27.5681	800	64 00 00	28.2843

* From Sorenson. Statistics for students of psychology and education.

TABLE A. SQUARES AND SQUARE ROOTS OF NUMBERS FROM 1 TO 1,000.* (*Continued*)

Number	Square	Square root	Number	Square	Square root
801	64 16 01	28.3019	841	70 72 81	29.0000
802	64 32 04	28.3196	842	70 89 64	29.0172
803	64 48 09	28.3373	843	71 06 49	29.0345
804	64 64 16	28.3049	844	71 23 36	29.0517
805	64 80 25	28.3725	845	71 40 25	29.0689
806	64 96 36	28.3901	846	71 57 16	29.0861
807	65 12 49	28.4077	847	71 74 09	29.1033
808	65 28 64	28.4253	848	71 91 04	29.1204
809	65 44 81	28.4429	849	72 08 01	29.1376
810	65 61 00	28.4605	850	72 25 00	29.1548
811	65 77 21	28.4781	851	72 42 01	29.1719
812	65 93 44	28.4956	852	72 59 04	29.1890
813	66 09 69	28.5132	853	72 76 09	29.2062
814	66 25 96	28.5307	854	72 93 16	29.2233
815	66 42 25	28.5482	855	73 10 25	29.2404
816	66 58 56	28.5657	856	73 27 36	29.2575
817	66 74 89	28.5832	857	73 44 49	29.2746
818	66 91 24	28.6007	858	73 61 64	29.2916
819	67 07 61	28.6082	859	73 78 81	29.3087
820	67 24 00	28.6356	860	73 96 00	29.3258
821	67 40 41	28.6531	861	74 13 21	29.3428
822	67 56 84	28.6705	862	74 30 44	29.3598
823	67 73 29	28.6880	863	74 47 69	29.3769
824	67 89 76	28.7054	864	74 64 96	29.3939
825	68 06 25	28.7228	865	74 82 25	29.4109
826	68 22 76	28.7402	866	74 99 56	29.4279
827	68 39 29	28.7576	867	75 16 89	29.4449
828	68 55 84	28.7750	868	75 34 24	29.4618
829	68 72 41	28.7924	869	75 51 61	29.4788
830	68 89 00	28.8097	870	75 69 00	29.4958
831	69 05 61	28.8271	871	75 86 41	29.5127
832	69 22 24	28.8444	872	76 03 84	29.5296
833	69 38 89	28.8617	873	76 21 29	29.5466
834	69 55 56	28.8791	874	76 38 76	29.5635
835	69 72 25	28.8964	875	76 56 25	29.5804
836	69 88 96	28.9137	876	76 73 76	29.5973
837	70 05 69	28.9310	877	76 91 29	29.6142
838	70 22 44	28.9482	878	77 08 84	29.6311
839	70 39 21	28.9655	879	77 26 41	29.6479
840	70 56 00	28.9828	880	77 44 00	29.6648

* From Sorenson. Statistics for students of psychology and education.

TABLE A. SQUARES AND SQUARE ROOTS OF NUMBERS FROM 1 TO 1,000.* (*Continued*)

Number	Square	Square root	Number	Square	Square root
881	77 61 61	29.6816	921	84 82 41	30.3480
882	77 79 24	29.6985	922	85 00 84	30.3645
883	77 96 89	29.7153	923	85 19 29	30.3809
884	78 14 56	29.7321	924	85 37 76	30.3974
885	78 32 25	29.7489	925	85 56 25	30.4138
886	78 49 96	29.7658	926	85 74 76	30.4302
887	78 67 69	29.7825	927	85 93 29	30.4467
888	78 85 44	29.7993	928	86 11 84	30.4631
889	79 03 21	29.8161	929	86 30 41	30.4795
890	79 21 00	29.8329	930	86 49 00	30.4959
891	79 38 81	29.8496	931	86 67 61	30.5123
892	79 56 64	29.8664	932	86 86 24	30.5287
893	79 74 49	29.8831	933	87 04 89	30.5450
894	79 92 36	29.8998	934	87 23 56	30.5614
895	80 10 25	29.9166	935	87 42 25	30.5778
896	80 28 16	29.9333	936	87 60 96	30.5941
897	80 46 09	29.9500	937	87 79 69	30.6105
898	80 64 04	29.9666	938	87 98 44	30.6268
899	80 82 01	29.9833	939	88 17 21	30.6431
900	81 00 00	30.0000	940	88 36 00	30.6594
901	81 18 01	30.0167	941	88 54 81	30.6757
902	81 36 04	30.0333	942	88 73 64	30.6920
903	81 54 09	30.0500	943	88 92 49	30.7083
904	81 72 16	30.0666	944	89 11 36	30.7246
905	81 90 25	30.0832	945	89 30 25	30.7409
906	82 08 36	30.0998	946	89 49 16	30.7571
907	82 26 49	30.1164	947	89 68 09	30.7734
908	82 44 64	30.1330	948	89 87 04	30.7896
909	82 62 81	30.1496	949	90 06 01	30.8058
910	82 81 00	30.1662	950	90 25 00	30.8221
911	82 99 21	30.1828	951	90 44 01	30.8383
912	83 17 44	30.1993	952	90 63 04	30.8545
913	83 35 69	30.2159	953	90 82 09	30.8707
914	83 53 96	30.2324	954	91 01 16	30.8869
915	83 72 25	30.2490	955	91 20 25	30.9031
916	83 90 56	30.2655	956	91 39 36	30.9192
917	84 08 89	30.2820	957	91 58 49	30.9354
918	84 27 24	30.2985	958	91 77 64	30.9516
919	84 45 61	30.3150	959	91 96 81	30.9677
920	84 64 00	30.3315	960	92 16 00	30.9839

* From Sorenson. Statistics for students of psychology and education.

TABLE A. SQUARES AND SQUARE ROOTS OF NUMBERS FROM 1 TO 1,000.* (*Continued*)

Number	Square	Square root	Number	Square	Square root
961	92 35 21	31.0000	981	96 23 61	31.3209
962	92 54 44	31.0161	982	96 43 24	31.3369
963	92 73 69	31.0322	983	96 62 89	31.3528
964	92 92 96	31.0483	984	96 82 56	31.3688
965	93 12 25	31.0644	985	97 02 25	31.3847
966	93 31 56	31.0805	986	97 21 96	31.4006
967	93 50 89	31.0966	987	97 41 69	31.4166
968	93 70 24	31.1127	988	97 61 44	31.4325
969	93 89 61	31.1288	989	97 81 21	31.4484
970	94 09 00	31.1448	990	98 01 00	31.4643
971	94 28 41	31.1609	991	98 20 81	31.4802
972	94 47 84	31.1769	992	98 40 64	31.4960
973	94 67 29	31.1929	993	98 60 49	31.5119
974	94 86 76	31.2090	994	98 80 36	31.5278
975	95 06 25	31.2250	995	99 00 25	31.5436
976	95 25 76	31.2410	996	99 20 16	31.5595
977	95 45 29	31.2570	997	99 40 09	31.5753
978	95 64 84	31.2730	998	99 60 04	31.5911
979	95 84 41	31.2890	999	99 80 01	31.6070
980	96 04 00	31.3050	1000	100 00 00	31.6228

* From Sorenson, H. Statistics for students of psychology and education. New York: McGraw-Hill, 1936.

TABLE B. AREA AND ORDINATE OF THE NORMAL CURVE RELATED TO z.[1]

z (x/σ)	Area	Ordinate (y)	z	Area	Ordinate (y)
.00	.0000000	.3989423	46	.1772419	.3588903
.01	.0039894	.3989223	.47	.1808225	.3572253
.02	.0079783	.3988625	.48	.1843863	.3555325
.03	.0119665	.3987628	.49	.1879331	.3538124
.04	.0159534	.3986233	.50	.1914625	.3520653
.05	.0199388	.3984439			
.06	.0239222	.3982248	.51	.1949743	.3502919
.07	.0279032	.3979661	.52	.1984682	.3484925
.08	.0318814	.3976677	.53	.2019440	.3466677
.09	.0358564	.3973298	.54	.2054015	.3448180
.10	.0398278	.3969525	.55	.2088403	.3429439
.11	.0437953	.3965360	.56	.2122603	.3410458
.12	.0477584	.3960802	.57	.2156612	.3391243
.13	.0517168	.3955854	.58	.2190427	.3371799
.14	.0556700	.3950517	.59	.2224047	.3352132
.15	.0596177	.3944793	.60	.2257469	.3332246
.16	.0635595	.3938684	.61	.2290691	.3312147
.17	.0674949	.3932190	.62	.2323711	.3291840
.18	.0714237	.3925315	.63	.2356527	.3271330
.19	.0753454	.3918060	.64	.2389137	.3250623
.20	.0792597	.3910427	.65	.2421539	.3229724
.21	.0831662	.3902419	.66	.2453731	.3208638
.22	.0870644	.3894038	.67	.2485711	.3187371
.23	.0909541	.3885286	.68	.2517478	.3165929
.24	.0948349	.3876166	.69	.2549029	.3144317
.25	.0987063	.3866681	.70	.2580363	.3122539
.26	.1025681	.3856834	.71	.2611479	.3100603
.27	.1064199	.3846627	.72	.2642375	.3078513
.28	.1102612	.3836063	.73	.2673049	.3056274
.29	.1140919	.3825146	.74	.2703500	.3033893
.30	.1179114	.3813878	.75	.2733726	.3011374
.31	.1217195	.3802264	.76	.2763727	.2988724
.32	.1255158	.3790305	.77	.2793501	.2965948
.33	.1293000	.3778007	.78	.2823046	.2943050
.34	.1330717	.3765372	.79	.2852361	.2920038
.35	.1368307	.3752403	.80	.2881446	.2896916
.36	.1405764	.3739106	.81	.2910299	.2873689
.37	.1443088	.3725483	.82	.2938919	.2850364
.38	.1480273	.3711539	.83	.2967306	.2826945
.39	.1517317	.3697277	.84	.2995458	.2803438
.40	.1555417	.3682707	.85	.3023375	.2779849
.41	.1590970	.3667817	.86	.3051055	.2756182
.42	.1627573	.3652627	.87	.3078498	.2732444
.43	.1664022	.3637136	.88	.2105703	.2708640
.44	.1700314	.3621349	.89	.3132671	.2684774
.45	.1736448	.3605270	.90	.3159399	.2660852

[1] From Kent, "The Elements of Statistics."

TABLE B. AREA AND ORDINATE OF THE NORMAL CURVE RELATED TO z.[1]
(*Continued*)

z	Area	Ordinate (y)	z	Area	Ordinate (y)
.91	.3185887	.2636880	1.36	.4130850	.1582248
.92	.3212136	.2612863	1.37	.4146565	.1560797
.93	.3238145	.2588805	1.38	.4162067	.1539483
.94	.3263912	.2564713	1.39	.4177356	.1518308
.95	.3289439	.2540591	1.40	.4192433	.1497275
.96	.3314724	.2516443	1.41	.4207302	.1476385
.97	.3339768	.2492277	1.42	.4221962	.1455641
.98	.3364569	.2468095	1.43	.4236415	.1435046
.99	.3389129	.2443904	1.44	.4250663	.1414600
1.00	.3413447	.2419707	1.45	.4264707	.1394306
1.01	.3437524	.2395511	1.46	.4278550	.1374165
1.02	.3461358	.2371320	1.47	.4292191	.1354181
1.03	.3484950	.2347138	1.48	.4305634	.1334353
1.04	.3508300	.2322970	1.49	.4318879	.1314684
1.05	.3531409	.2298821	1.50	.4331928	.1295176
1.06	.3554277	.2274696	1.51	.4344783	.1275830
1.07	.3576903	.2250599	1.52	.4357445	.1256646
1.08	.3599289	.2226535	1.53	.4369916	.1237628
1.09	.3621434	.2202508	1.54	.4382198	.1218775
1.10	.3643339	.2178522	1.55	.4394292	.1200090
1.11	.3665005	.2154582	1.56	.4406201	.1181573
1.12	.3686431	.2130691	1.57	.4417924	.1163225
1.13	.3707619	.2106856	1.58	.4429466	.1145048
1.14	.3728568	.2083078	1.59	.4440826	.1127042
1.15	.3749281	.2059363	1.60	.4452007	.1109208
1.16	.3769756	.2035714	1.61	.4463011	.1091548
1.17	.3789995	.2012135	1.62	.4473839	.1074061
1.18	.3809999	.1988631	1.63	.4484493	.1056748
1.19	.3829768	.1965205	1.64	.4494974	.1039611
1.20	.3849303	.1941861	1.65	.4505285	.1022649
1.21	.3868606	.1918602	1.66	.4515428	.1005864
1.22	.3887676	.1895432	1.67	.4525403	.0989255
1.23	.3906514	.1872354	1.68	.4535213	.0972823
1.24	.3925123	.1849373	1.69	.4544860	.0956568
1.25	.3943502	.1826491	1.70	.4554345	.0940491
1.26	.3961653	.1803712	1.71	.4563671	.0924591
1.27	.3979577	.1781038	1.72	.4572838	.0908870
1.28	.3997274	.1758474	1.73	.4581849	.0893326
1.29	.4014747	.1736022	1.74	.4590705	.0877961
1.30	.4031995	.1713686	1.75	.4599408	.0862773
1.31	.4049021	.1691468	1.76	.4607961	.0847764
1.32	.4065825	.1669370	1.77	.4616364	.0832932
1.33	.4082409	.1647397	1.78	.4624620	.0818278
1.34	.4098773	.1625551	1.79	.4632730	.0803801
1.35	.4114920	.1603833	1.80	.4640697	.0789502

[1] From Kent. "The Elements of Statistics."

TABLE B. AREA AND ORDINATE OF THE NORMAL CURVE RELATED TO z.[1] (*Continued*)

z	Area	Ordinate (y)	z	Area	Ordinate (y)
1.81	.4648521	.0775379	2.26	.4880894	.0310319
1.82	.4656205	.0761433	2.27	.4883962	.0303370
1.83	.4663750	.0747663	2.28	.4886962	.0296546
1.84	.4671159	.0734068	2.29	.4889893	.0289847
1.85	.4678432	.0720649	2.30	.4892759	.0283270
1.86	.4685572	.0707404	2.31	.4895559	.0276816
1.87	.4692581	.0694333	2.32	.4898296	.0270481
1.88	.4699460	.0681436	2.33	.4900969	.0264265
1.89	.4706210	.0668711	2.34	.4903581	.0258166
1.90	.4712834	.0656158	2.35	.4906133	.0252182
1.91	.4719334	.0643777	2.36	.4908625	.0246313
1.92	.4725711	.0631566	2.37	.4911060	.0240556
1.93	.4731966	.0619524	2.38	.4913437	.0234910
1.94	.4738102	.0607652	2.39	.4915758	.0229374
1.95	.4744119	.0595947	2.40	.4918025	.0223945
1.96	.4750021	.0584409	2.41	.4920237	.0218624
1.97	.4755808	.0573038	2.42	.4922397	.0213407
1.98	.4761482	.0561831	2.43	.4924506	.0208294
1.99	.4767045	.0550789	2.44	.4926564	.0203284
2.00	.4772499	.0539910	2.45	.4928572	.0198374
2.01	.4777844	.0529192	2.46	.4930531	.0193563
2.02	.4783083	.0518636	2.47	.4932443	.0188850
2.03	.4788217	.0508239	2.48	.4934309	.0184233
2.04	.4793248	.0498001	2.49	.4936128	.0179711
2.05	.4798178	.0487920	2.50	.4937903	.0175283
2.06	.4803007	.0477996	2.51	.4939634	.0170947
2.07	.4807738	.0468226	2.52	.4941323	.0166701
2.08	.4812372	.0458611	2.53	.4943001	.0162452
2.09	.4816911	.0449148	2.54	.4944574	.0158476
2.10	.4821356	.0439836	2.55	.4946139	.0154493
2.11	.4825708	.0430674	2.56	.4947664	.0150596
2.12	.4829970	.0421661	2.57	.4949151	.0146782
2.13	.4834142	.0412795	2.58	.4950600	.0143051
2.14	.4838226	.0404076	2.59	.4952012	.0139401
2.15	.4842224	.0395500	2.60	.4953388	.0135830
2.16	.4846137	.0387069	2.61	.4954729	.0132337
2.17	.4849966	.0378779	2.62	.4956035	.0128921
2.18	.4853713	.0370629	2.63	.4957308	.0125581
2.19	.4857379	.0362619	2.64	.4958547	.0122315
2.20	.4860966	.0354746	2.65	.4959754	.0119122
2.21	.4864474	.0347009	2.66	.4960930	.0116001
2.22	.4867906	.0339408	2.67	.4962074	.0112951
2.23	.4871263	.0331939	2.68	.4963189	.0109969
2.24	.4874545	.0324603	2.69	.4964274	.0107056
2.25	.4877755	.0317397	2.70	.4965330	.0104209

[1] From Kent, "The Elements of Statistics."

TABLE B. AREA AND ORDINATE OF THE NORMAL CURVE RELATED TO z.[1] (*Continued*)

z	Area	Ordinate (y)	z	Area	Ordinate (y)
2.71	.4966358	.0101428	3.16	.4992112	.0027075
2.72	.4967359	.0098712	3.17	.4992378	.0026231
2.73	.4968333	.0096058	3.18	.4992636	.0025412
2.74	.4969280	.0093466	3.19	.4992886	.0024615
2.75	.4970202	.0090936	3.20	.4993129	.0023841
2.76	.4971099	.0088465	3.21	.4993363	.0023089
2.77	.4971972	.0086052	3.22	.4993590	.0022358
2.78	.4972821	.0083697	3.23	.4993810	.0021649
2.79	.4973646	.0081398	3.24	.4994024	.0020960
2.80	.4974449	.0079155	3.25	.4994230	.0020290
2.81	.4975229	.0076965	3.26	.4994429	.0019641
2.82	.4975988	.0074829	3.27	.4994623	.0019010
2.83	.4976726	.0072744	3.28	.4994810	.0018397
2.84	.4977443	.0070711	3.29	.4994991	.0017803
2.85	.4978140	.0068728	3.30	.4995166	.0017226
2.86	.4978818	.0066793	3.31	.4995335	.0016666
2.87	.4979476	.0064907	3.32	.4995499	.0016122
2.88	.4980116	.0063067	3.33	.4995658	.0015595
2.89	.4980738	.0061274	3.34	.4995811	.0015084
2.90	.4981342	.0059525	3.35	.4995959	.0014587
2.91	.4981929	.0057821	3.36	.4996103	.0014106
2.92	.4982498	.0056160	3.37	.4996242	.0013639
2.93	.4983052	.0054541	3.38	.4996376	.0013187
2.94	.4983589	.0052963	3.39	.4996505	.0012748
2.95	.4984111	.0051426	3.40	.4996631	.0012322
2.96	.4984618	.0049929	3.41	.4996752	.0011910
2.97	.4985110	.0048470	3.42	.4996869	.0011510
2.98	.4985588	.0047050	3.43	.4996982	.0011122
2.99	.4986051	.0045666	3.44	.4997091	.0010747
3.00	.4986501	.0044318	3.45	.4997197	.0010383
3.01	.4986938	.0043007	3.46	.4997299	.0010030
3.02	.4987361	.0041729	3.47	.4997398	.0009689
3.03	.4987772	.0040486	3.48	.4997493	.0009358
3.04	.4988171	.0039276	3.49	.4997585	.0009037
3.05	.4988558	.0038098	3.50	.4997674	.0008727
3.06	.4988933	.0036951	3.51	.4997759	.0008426
3.07	.4989297	.0035836	3.52	.4997842	.0008135
3.08	.4989650	.0034751	3.53	.4997922	.0007853
3.09	.4989992	.0033695	3.54	.4997999	.0007581
3.10	.4990324	.0032668	3.55	.4998074	.0007317
3.11	.4990646	.0031669	3.56	.4998146	.0007061
3.12	.4990957	.0030698	3.57	.4998215	.0006814
3.13	.4991260	.0029754	3.58	.4998282	.0006575
3.14	.4991553	.0028835	3.59	.4998347	.0006343
3.15	.4991836	.0027943	3.60	.4998409	.0006119

[1] From Kent, "The Elements of Statistics."

TABLE B. AREA AND ORDINATE OF THE NORMAL CURVE RELATED TO *z*.[1]
(*Continued*)

z	Area	Ordinate (*y*)	*z*	Area	Ordinate (*y*)
3.61	.4998469	.0005902	4.06	.4999755	.0001051
3.62	.4998527	.0005693	4.07	.4999765	.0001009
3.63	.4998583	.0005490	4.08	.4999775	.0000969
3.64	.4998637	.0005294	4.09	.4999784	.0000930
3.65	.4998689	.0005105	4.10	.4999793	.0000893
3.66	.4998739	.0004921	4.11	.4999802	.0000857
3.67	.4998787	.0004744	4.12	.4999811	.0000822
3.68	.4998834	.0004573	4.13	.4999819	.0000789
3.69	.4998879	.0004408	4.14	.4999826	.0000757
3.70	.4998922	.0004248	4.15	.4999834	.0000726
3.71	.4998964	.0004093	4.16	.4999841	.0000697
3.72	.4999004	.0003800	4.17	.4999848	.0000668
3.73	.4999043	.0003661	4.18	.4999854	.0000641
3.74	.4999080	.0003526	4.19	.4999861	.0000615
3.75	.4999116	.0003386	4.20	.4999867	.0000589
3.76	.4999150	.0003396	4.21	.4999872	.0000565
3.77	.4999184	.0003271	4.22	.4999878	.0000542
3.78	.4999216	.0003149	4.23	.4999883	.0000519
3.79	.4999247	.0003032	4.24	.4999888	.0000498
3.80	.4999277	.0002919	4.25	.4999893	.0000477
3.81	.4999305	.0002810	4.26	.4999898	.0000457
3.82	.4999333	.0002705	4.27	.4999902	.0000438
3.83	.4999359	.0002604	4.28	.4999907	.0000420
3.84	.4999385	.0002506	4.29	.4999911	.0000402
3.85	.4999409	.0002411	4.30	.4999915	.0000385
3.86	.4999433	.0002320	4.31	.4999918	.0000369
3.87	.4999456	.0002232	4.32	.4999922	.0000354
3.88	.4999478	.0002147	4.33	.4999925	.0000339
3.89	.4999499	.0002065	4.34	.4999929	.0000324
3.90	.4999519	.0001987	4.35	.4999932	.0000310
3.91	.4999539	.0001910	4.36	.4999935	.0000297
3.92	.4999557	.0001837	4.37	.4999938	.0000284
3.93	.4999575	.0001766	4.38	.4999941	.0000272
3.94	.4999593	.0001698	4.39	.4999943	.0000261
3.95	.4999609	.0001633	4.40	.4999946	.0000249
3.96	.4999625	.0001569	4.41	.4999948	.0000239
3.97	.4999641	.0001508	4.42	.4999951	.0000228
3.98	.4999655	.0001449	4.43	.4999953	.0000218
3.99	.4999670	.0001393	4.44	.4999955	.0000209
4.00	.4999683	.0001338	4.45	.4999957	.0000200
4.01	.4999696	.0001286	4.46	.4999959	.0000191
4.02	.4999709	.0001235	4.47	.4999961	.0000183
4.03	.4999721	.0001186	4.48	.4999963	.0000175
4.04	.4999733	.0001140	4.49	.4999964	.0000167
4.05	.4999744	.0001094	4.50	.4999966	.0000160

[1] From Kent, "The Elements of Statistics."

TABLE C. DEVIATES AND ORDINATES FOR AREAS UNDER THE NORMAL CURVE[1]

Area from z = 0	z	Ordinate at z	Area from z = 0	z	Ordinate at z	Area from z = 0	z	Ordinate at z
.000	0.0000	.3989	**.040**	0.1004	.3969	**.080**	0.2019	.3909
.001	0.0025	.3989	**.041**	0.1030	.3968	**.081**	0.2045	.3907
.002	0.0050	.3989	**.042**	0.1055	.3967	**.082**	0.2070	.3905
.003	0.0075	.3989	**.043**	0.1080	.3966	**.083**	0.2096	.3903
.004	0.0100	.3989	**.044**	0.1105	.3965	**.084**	0.2121	.3901
.005	0.0125	.3989	**.045**	0.1130	.3964	**.085**	0.2147	.3899
.006	0.0150	.3989	**.046**	0.1156	.3963	**.086**	0.2173	.3896
.007	0.0175	.3989	**.047**	0.1181	.3962	**.087**	0.2198	.3894
.008	0.0201	.3989	**.048**	0.1206	.3961	**.088**	0.2224	.3892
.009	0.0226	.3988	**.049**	0.1231	.3959	**.089**	0.2250	.3890
.010	0.0251	.3988	**.050**	0.1257	.3958	**.090**	0.2275	.3887
.011	0.0276	.3988	**.051**	0.1282	.3957	**.091**	0.2301	.3885
.012	0.0301	.3988	**.052**	0.1307	.3955	**.092**	0.2327	.3883
.013	0.0326	.3987	**.053**	0.1332	.3954	**.093**	0.2353	.3881
.014	0.0351	.3987	**.054**	0.1358	.3953	**.094**	0.2378	.3878
.015	0.0376	.3987	**.055**	0.1383	.3951	**.095**	0.2404	.3876
.016	0.0401	.3986	**.056**	0.1408	.3950	**.096**	0.2430	.3873
.017	0.0426	.3986	**.057**	0.1434	.3949	**.097**	0.2456	.3871
.018	0.0451	.3985	**.058**	0.1459	.3947	**.098**	0.2482	.3868
.019	0.0476	.3985	**.059**	0.1484	.3946	**.099**	0.2508	.3866
.020	0.0502	.3984	**.060**	0.1510	.3944	**.100**	0.2533	.3863
.021	0.0527	.3984	**.061**	0.1535	.3943	**.101**	0.2559	.3861
.022	0.0552	.3983	**.062**	0.1560	.3941	**.102**	0.2585	.3858
.023	0.0577	.3983	**.063**	0.1586	.3940	**.103**	0.2611	.3856
.024	0.0602	.3982	**.064**	0.1611	.3938	**.104**	0.2637	.3853
.025	0.0627	.3982	**.065**	0.1637	.3936	**.105**	0.2663	.3850
.026	0.0652	.3981	**.066**	0.1662	.3935	**.106**	0.2689	.3848
.027	0.0677	.3980	**.067**	0.1687	.3933	**.107**	0.2715	.3845
.028	0.0702	.3980	**.068**	0.1713	.3931	**.108**	0.2741	.3842
.029	0.0728	.3979	**.069**	0.1738	.3930	**.109**	0.2767	.3840
.030	0.0753	.3978	**.070**	0.1764	.3928	**.110**	0.2793	.3837
.031	0.0778	.3977	**.071**	0.1789	.3926	**.111**	0.2819	.3834
.032	0.0803	.3977	**.072**	0.1815	.3924	**.112**	0.2845	.3831
.033	0.0828	.3976	**.073**	0.1840	.3922	**.113**	0.2871	.3828
.034	0.0853	.3975	**.074**	0.1866	.3921	**.114**	0.2898	.3825
.035	0.0878	.3974	**.075**	0.1891	.3919	**.115**	0.2924	.3823
.036	0.0904	.3973	**.076**	0.1917	.3917	**.116**	0.2950	.3820
.037	0.0929	.3972	**.077**	0.1942	.3915	**.117**	0.2976	.3817
.038	0.0954	.3971	**.078**	0.1968	.3913	**.118**	0.3002	.3814
.039	0.0979	.3970	**.079**	0.1993	.3911	**.119**	0.3029	.3811

[1] Adapted from K. J. Holzinger, "Statistical Tables for Students in Education and Psychology," 1925, through the courtesy of the University of Chicago Press.

TABLE C. DEVIATES AND ORDINATES FOR AREAS UNDER THE NORMAL CURVE. (*Continued*)

Area from z = 0	z	Ordinate at z	Area from z = 0	z	Ordinate at z	Area from z = 0	z	Ordinate at z
.120	0.3055	.3808	**.165**	0.4261	.3643	**.210**	0.5534	.3423
.121	0.3081	.3804	**.166**	0.4289	.3639	**.211**	0.5563	.3417
.122	0.3107	.3801	**.167**	0.4316	.3635	**.212**	0.5592	.3412
.123	0.3134	.3798	**.168**	0.4344	.3630	**.213**	0.5622	.3406
.124	0.3160	.3795	**.169**	0.4372	.3626	**.214**	0.5651	.3401
.125	0.3186	.3792	**.170**	0.4399	.3621	**.215**	0.5681	.3395
.126	0.3213	.3789	**.171**	0.4427	.3617	**.216**	0.5710	.3389
.127	0.3239	.3786	**.172**	0.4454	.3613	**.217**	0.5740	.3384
.128	0.3266	.3782	**.173**	0.4482	.3608	**.218**	0.5769	.3378
.129	0.3292	.3779	**.174**	0.4510	.3604	**.219**	0.5799	.3372
.130	0.3319	.3776	**.175**	0.4538	.3599	**.220**	0.5828	.3366
.131	0.3345	.3772	**.176**	0.4565	.3595	**.221**	0.5858	.3360
.132	0.3372	.3769	**.177**	0.4593	.3590	**.222**	0.5888	.3354
.133	0.3398	.3766	**.178**	0.4621	.3585	**.223**	0.5918	.3349
.134	0.3425	.3762	**.179**	0.4649	.3581	**.224**	0.5948	.3343
.135	0.3451	.3759	**.180**	0.4677	.3576	**.225**	0.5978	.3337
.136	0.3478	.3755	**.181**	0.4705	.3571	**.226**	0.6008	.3331
.137	0.3505	.3752	**.182**	0.4733	.3567	**.227**	0.6038	.3325
.138	0.3531	.3748	**.183**	0.4761	.3562	**.228**	0.6068	.3319
.139	0.3558	.3745	**.184**	0.4789	.3557	**.229**	0.6098	.3313
.140	0.3585	.3741	**.185**	0.4817	.3552	**.230**	0.6128	.3306
.141	0.3611	.3738	**.186**	0.4845	.3548	**.231**	0.6158	.3300
.142	0.3638	.3734	**.187**	0.4874	.3543	**.232**	0.6189	.3294
.143	0.3665	.3730	**.188**	0.4902	.3538	**.233**	0.6219	.3288
.144	0.3692	.3727	**.189**	0.4930	.3533	**.234**	0.6250	.3282
.145	0.3719	.3723	**.190**	0.4959	.3528	**.235**	0.6280	.3275
.146	0.3745	.3719	**.191**	0.4987	.3523	**.236**	0.6311	.3269
.147	0.3772	.3715	**.192**	0.5015	.3518	**.237**	0.6341	.3263
.148	0.3799	.3712	**.193**	0.5044	.3513	**.238**	0.6372	.3256
.149	0.3826	.3708	**.194**	0.5072	.3508	**.239**	0.6403	.3250
.150	0.3853	.3704	**.195**	0.5101	.3503	**.240**	0.6433	.3244
.151	0.3880	.3700	**.196**	0.5129	.3498	**.241**	0.6464	.3237
.152	0.3907	.3696	**.197**	0.5158	.3493	**.242**	0.6495	.3231
.153	0.3934	.3692	**.198**	0.5187	.3487	**.243**	0.6526	.3224
.154	0.3961	.3688	**.199**	0.5215	.3482	**.244**	0.6557	.3218
.155	0.3989	.3684	**.200**	0.5244	.3477	**.245**	0.6588	.3211
.156	0.4016	.3680	**.201**	0.5273	.3472	**.246**	0.6620	.3204
.157	0.4043	.3676	**.202**	0.5302	.3466	**.247**	0.6651	.3198
.158	0.4070	.3672	**.203**	0.5330	.3461	**.248**	0.6682	.3191
.159	0.4097	.3668	**.204**	0.5359	.3456	**.249**	0.6713	.3184
.160	0.4125	.3664	**.205**	0.5388	.3450	**.250**	0.6745	.3178
.161	0.4152	.3660	**.206**	0.5417	.3445	**.251**	0.6776	.3171
.162	0.4179	.3656	**.207**	0.5446	.3440	**.252**	0.6808	.3164
.163	0.4207	.3652	**.208**	0.5476	.3434	**.253**	0.6840	.3157
.164	0.4234	.3647	**.209**	0.5505	.3429	**.254**	0.6871	.3151

TABLE C. DEVIATES AND ORDINATES FOR AREAS UNDER THE NORMAL CURVE. (*Continued*)

Area from $z = 0$	z	Ordinate at z	Area from $z = 0$	z	Ordinate at z	Area from $z = 0$	z	Ordinate at z
.255	0.6903	.3144	**.300**	0.8416	.2800	**.345**	1.0152	.2383
.256	0.6935	.3137	**.301**	0.8452	.2791	**.346**	1.0194	.2373
.257	0.6967	.3130	**.302**	0.8488	.2783	**.347**	1.0237	.2362
.258	0.6999	.3123	**.303**	0.8524	.2774	**.348**	1.0279	.2352
.259	0.7031	.3116	**.304**	0.8560	.2766	**.349**	1.0322	.2342
.260	0.7063	.3109	**.305**	0.8596	.2757	**.350**	1.0364	.2332
.261	0.7095	.3102	**.306**	0.8633	.2748	**.351**	1.0407	.2321
.262	0.7128	.3095	**.307**	0.8669	.2740	**.352**	1.0450	.2311
.263	0.7160	.3087	**.308**	0.8705	.2731	**.353**	1.0494	.2300
.264	0.7192	.3080	**.309**	0.8742	.2722	**.354**	1.0537	.2290
.265	0.7225	.3073	**.310**	0.8779	.2714	**.355**	1.0581	.2279
.266	0.7257	.3066	**.311**	0.8816	.2705	**.356**	1.0625	.2269
.267	0.7290	.3058	**.312**	0.8853	.2696	**.357**	1.0669	.2258
.268	0.7323	.3051	**.313**	0.8890	.2687	**.358**	1.0714	.2247
.269	0.7356	.3044	**.314**	0.8927	.2678	**.359**	1.0758	.2237
.270	0.7388	.3036	**.315**	0.8965	.2669	**.360**	1.0803	.2226
.271	0.7421	.3029	**.316**	0.9002	.2660	**.361**	1.0848	.2215
.272	0.7454	.3022	**.317**	0.9040	.2651	**.362**	1.0893	.2204
.273	0.7488	.3014	**.318**	0.9078	.2642	**.363**	1.0939	.2193
.274	0.7521	.3007	**.319**	0.9116	.2633	**.364**	1.0985	.2182
.275	0.7554	.2999	**.320**	0.9154	.2624	**.365**	1.1031	.2171
.276	0.7588	.2992	**.321**	0.9192	.2615	**.366**	1.1077	.2160
.277	0.7621	.2984	**.322**	0.9230	.2606	**.367**	1.1123	.2149
.278	0.7655	.2976	**.323**	0.9269	.2596	**.368**	1.1170	.2138
.279	0.7688	.2969	**.324**	0.9307	.2587	**.369**	1.1217	.2127
.280	0.7722	.2961	**.325**	0.9346	.2578	**.370**	1.1264	.2115
.281	0.7756	.2953	**.326**	0.9385	.2568	**.371**	1.1311	.2104
.282	0.7790	.2945	**.327**	0.9424	.2559	**.372**	1.1359	.2093
.283	0.7824	.2938	**.328**	0.9463	.2550	**.373**	1.1407	.2081
.284	0.7858	.2930	**.329**	0.9502	.2540	**.374**	1.1455	.2070
.285	0.7892	.2922	**.330**	0.9542	.2531	**.375**	1.1503	.2059
.286	0.7926	.2914	**.331**	0.9581	.2521	**.376**	1.1552	.2047
.287	0.7961	.2906	**.332**	0.9621	.2511	**.377**	1.1601	.2035
.288	0.7995	.2898	**.333**	0.9661	.2502	**.378**	1.1650	.2024
.289	0.8030	.2890	**.334**	0.9701	.2492	**.379**	1.1700	.2012
.290	0.8064	.2882	**.335**	0.9741	.2482	**.380**	1.1750	.2000
.291	0.8099	.2874	**.336**	0.9782	.2473	**.381**	1.1800	.1989
.292	0.8134	.2866	**.337**	0.9822	.2463	**.382**	1.1850	.1977
.293	0.8169	.2858	**.338**	0.9863	.2453	**.383**	1.1901	.1965
.294	0.8204	.2849	**.339**	0.9904	.2443	**.384**	1.1952	.1953
.295	0.8239	.2841	**.340**	0.9945	.2433	**.385**	1.2004	.1941
.296	0.8274	.2833	**.341**	0.9986	.2423	**.386**	1.2055	.1929
.297	0.8310	.2825	**.342**	1.0027	.2413	**.387**	1.2107	.1917
.298	0.8345	.2816	**.343**	1.0069	.2403	**.388**	1.2160	.1905
.299	0.8381	.2808	**.344**	1.0110	.2393	**.389**	1.2212	.1893

TABLE C. DEVIATES AND ORDINATES FOR AREAS UNDER THE NORMAL CURVE. (*Continued*)

Area from z = 0	z	Ordinate at z	Area from z = 0	z	Ordinate at z	Area from z = 0	z	Ordinate at z
.390	1.2265	.1880	**.430**	1.4758	.1343	**.470**	1.8808	.0680
.391	1.2319	.1868	**.431**	1.4833	.1328	**.471**	1.8957	.0662
.392	1.2372	.1856	**.432**	1.4909	.1313	**.472**	1.9110	.0643
.393	1.2426	.1843	**.433**	1.4985	.1298	**.473**	1.9268	.0623
.394	1.2481	.1831	**.434**	1.5063	.1283	**.474**	1.9431	.0604
.395	1.2536	.1818	**.435**	1.5141	.1268	**.475**	1.9600	.0585
.396	1.2591	.1806	**.436**	1.5220	.1253	**.476**	1.9774	.0565
.397	1.2646	.1793	**.437**	1.5301	.1237	**.477**	1.9954	.0545
.398	1.2702	.1780	**.438**	1.5382	.1222	**.478**	2.0141	.0525
.399	1.2759	.1768	**.439**	1.5464	.1207	**.479**	2.0335	.0505
.400	1.2816	.1755	**.440**	1.5548	.1191	**.480**	2.0537	.0484
.401	1.2873	.1742	**.441**	1.5632	.1176	**.481**	2.0749	.0464
.402	1.2930	.1729	**.442**	1.5718	.1160	**.482**	2.0969	.0443
.403	1.2988	.1716	**.443**	1.5805	.1144	**.483**	2.1201	.0422
.404	1.3047	.1703	**.444**	1.5893	.1128	**.484**	2.1444	.0400
.405	1.3106	.1690	**.445**	1.5982	.1112	**.485**	2.1701	.0379
.406	1.3165	.1677	**.446**	1.6072	.1096	**.486**	2.1973	.0357
.407	1.3225	.1664	**.447**	1.6164	.1080	**.487**	2.2262	.0335
.408	1.3285	.1651	**.448**	1.6258	.1064	**.488**	2.2571	.0312
.409	1.3346	.1637	**.449**	1.6352	.1048	**.489**	2.2904	.0290
.410	1.3408	.1624	**.450**	1.6449	.1031	**.490**	2.3263	.0267
.411	1.3469	.1610	**.451**	1.6546	.1015	**.491**	2.3656	.0243
.412	1.3532	.1597	**452**	1.6646	.0998	**.492**	2.4089	.0219
.413	1.3595	.1583	**.453**	1.6747	.0982	**.493**	2.4573	.0195
.414	1.3658	.1570	**.454**	1.6849	.0965	**.494**	2.5121	.0170
.415	1.3722	.1556	**.455**	1.6954	.0948	**.495**	2.5758	.0145
.416	1.3787	.1542	**.456**	1.7060	.0931	**.496**	2.6521	.0118
.417	1.3852	.1529	**.457**	1.7169	.0914	**.497**	2.7478	.00915
.418	1.3917	.1515	**.458**	1.7279	.0897	**.498**	2.8782	.00634
.419	1.3984	.1501	**.459**	1.7392	.0879	**.499**	3.0902	.00336
.420	1.4051	.1487	**.460**	1.7507	.0862	**.4995**	3.2905	.00178
.421	1.4118	.1473	**.461**	1.7624	.0844	**.4999**	3.7190	.00040
.422	1.4187	.1458	**.462**	1.7744	.0826	**.49995**	3.8906	.00021
.423	1.4255	.1444	**.463**	1.7866	.0809	**.49999**	4.2649	.00004
.424	1.4325	.1430	**.464**	1.7991	.0791			
.425	1.4395	.1416	**.465**	1.8119	.0773			
.426	1.4466	.1401	**.466**	1.8250	.0755			
.427	1.4538	.1387	**.467**	1.8384	.0736			
.428	1.4611	.1372	**.468**	1.8522	.0718			
.429	1.4684	.1357	**.469**	1.8663	.0699			

TABLE D. SIGNIFICANT VALUES OF r, R AND t*

Degrees of freedom	Number of variables									t
	2	3	4	5	6	7	9	13	25	
1	.997	.999	.999	.999	1.000	1.000	1.000	1.000	1.000	12.706
	1.000	**1.000**	**1.000**	**1.000**	**1.000**	**1.000**	**1.000**	**1.000**	**1.000**	**63.657**
2	.950	.975	.983	.987	.990	.992	.994	.996	.998	4.303
	.990	**.995**	**.997**	**.998**	**.998**	**.998**	**.999**	**.999**	**1.000**	**9.925**
3	.878	.930	.950	.961	.968	.973	.979	.986	.993	3.182
	.959	**.976**	**.983**	**.987**	**.990**	**.991**	**.993**	**.995**	**.998**	**5.841**
4	.811	.881	.912	.930	.942	.950	.961	.973	.986	2.776
	.917	**.949**	**.962**	**.970**	**.975**	**.979**	**.984**	**.989**	**.994**	**4.604**
5	.754	.836	.874	.898	.914	.925	.941	.958	.978	2.571
	.874	**.917**	**.937**	**.949**	**.957**	**.963**	**.971**	**.980**	**.989**	**4.032**
6	.707	.795	.839	.867	.886	.900	.920	.943	.969	2.447
	.834	**.886**	**.911**	**.927**	**.938**	**.946**	**.957**	**.969**	**.983**	**3.707**
7	.666	.758	.807	.838	.860	.876	.900	.927	.960	2.365
	.798	**.855**	**.885**	**.904**	**.918**	**.928**	**.942**	**.958**	**.977**	**3.499**
8	.632	.726	.777	.811	.835	.854	.880	.912	.950	2.306
	.765	**.827**	**.860**	**.882**	**.898**	**.909**	**.926**	**.946**	**.970**	**3.355**
9	.602	.697	.750	.786	.812	.832	.861	.897	.941	2.262
	.735	**.800**	**.836**	**.861**	**.878**	**.891**	**.911**	**.934**	**.963**	**3.250**
10	.576	.671	.726	.763	.790	.812	.843	.882	.932	2.228
	.708	**.776**	**.814**	**.840**	**.859**	**.874**	**.895**	**.922**	**.955**	**3.169**
11	.553	.648	.703	.741	.770	.792	.826	.868	.922	2.201
	.684	**.753**	**.793**	**.821**	**.841**	**.857**	**.880**	**.910**	**.948**	**3.106**
12	.532	.627	.683	.722	.751	.774	.809	.854	.913	2.179
	.661	**.732**	**.773**	**.802**	**.824**	**.841**	**.866**	**.898**	**.940**	**3.055**
13	.514	.608	.664	.703	.733	.757	.794	.840	.904	2.160
	.641	**.712**	**.755**	**.785**	**.807**	**.825**	**.852**	**.886**	**.932**	**3.012**
14	.497	.590	.646	.686	.717	.741	.779	.828	.895	2.145
	.623	**.694**	**.737**	**.768**	**.792**	**.810**	**.838**	**.875**	**.924**	**2.977**
15	.482	.574	.630	.670	.701	.726	.765	.815	.886	2.131
	.606	**.677**	**.721**	**.752**	**.776**	**.796**	**.825**	**.864**	**.917**	**2.947**
16	.468	.559	.615	.655	.686	.712	.751	.803	.878	2.120
	.590	**.662**	**.706**	**.738**	**.762**	**.782**	**.813**	**.853**	**.909**	**2.921**
17	.456	.545	.601	.641	.673	.698	.738	.792	.869	2.110
	.575	**.647**	**.691**	**.724**	**.749**	**.769**	**.800**	**.842**	**.902**	**2.898**
18	.444	.532	.587	.628	.660	.686	.726	.781	.861	2.101
	.561	**.633**	**.678**	**.710**	**.736**	**.756**	**.789**	**.832**	**.894**	**2.878**
19	.433	.520	.575	.615	.647	.674	.714	.770	.853	2.093
	.549	**.620**	**.665**	**.698**	**.723**	**.744**	**.778**	**.822**	**.887**	**2.861**
20	.423	.509	.563	.604	.636	.662	.703	.760	.845	2.086
	.537	**.608**	**.652**	**.685**	**.712**	**.733**	**.767**	**.812**	**.880**	**2.845**
21	.413	.498	.552	.592	.624	.651	.693	.750	.837	2.080
	.526	**.596**	**.641**	**.674**	**.700**	**.722**	**.756**	**.803**	**.873**	**2.831**
22	.404	.488	.542	.582	.614	.640	.682	.740	.830	2.074
	.515	**.585**	**.630**	**.663**	**.690**	**.712**	**.746**	**.794**	**.866**	**2.819**
23	.396	.479	.532	.572	.604	.630	.673	.731	.823	2.069
	.505	**.574**	**.619**	**.652**	**.679**	**.701**	**.736**	**.785**	**.859**	**2.807**

* Adapted from H. A. Wallace and G. W. Snedecor, "Correlation and Machine Calculation," 1931, by courtesy of the authors.

TABLE D. SIGNIFICANT VALUES OF r, R AND t[1]. (*Continued*)

Degrees of freedom	Number of variables									t
	2	3	4	5	6	7	9	13	25	
24	.388	.470	.523	.562	.594	.621	.663	.722	.815	2.064
	.496	**.565**	**.609**	**.642**	**.669**	**.692**	**.727**	**.776**	**.852**	**2.797**
25	.381	.462	.514	.553	.585	.612	.654	.714	.808	2.060
	.487	**.555**	**.600**	**.633**	**.660**	**.682**	**.718**	**.768**	**.846**	**2.787**
26	.374	.454	.506	.545	.576	.603	.645	.706	.802	2.056
	.478	**.546**	**.590**	**.624**	**.651**	**.673**	**.709**	**.760**	**.839**	**2.779**
27	.367	.446	.498	.536	.568	.594	.637	.698	.795	2.052
	.470	**.538**	**.582**	**.615**	**.642**	**.664**	**.701**	**.752**	**.833**	**2.771**
28	.361	.439	.490	.529	.560	.586	.629	.690	.788	2.048
	.463	**.530**	**.573**	**.606**	**.634**	**.656**	**.692**	**.744**	**.827**	**2.763**
29	.355	.432	.482	.521	.552	.579	.621	.682	.782	2.045
	.456	**.522**	**.565**	**.598**	**.625**	**.648**	**.685**	**.737**	**.821**	**2.756**
30	.349	.426	.476	.514	.545	.571	.614	.675	.776	2.042
	.449	**.514**	**.558**	**.591**	**.618**	**.640**	**.677**	**.729**	**.815**	**2.750**
35	.325	.397	.445	.482	.512	.538	.580	.642	.746	2.030
	.418	**.481**	**.523**	**.556**	**.582**	**.605**	**.642**	**.696**	**.786**	**2.724**
40	.304	.373	.419	.455	.484	.509	.551	.613	.720	2.021
	.393	**.454**	**.494**	**.526**	**.552**	**.575**	**.612**	**.667**	**.761**	**2.704**
45	.288	.353	.397	.432	.460	.485	.526	.587	.696	2.014
	.372	**.430**	**.470**	**.501**	**.527**	**.549**	**.586**	**.640**	**.737**	**2.690**
50	.273	.336	.379	.412	.440	.464	.504	.565	.674	2.008
	.354	**.410**	**.449**	**.479**	**.504**	**.526**	**.562**	**.617**	**.715**	**2.678**
60	.250	.308	.348	.380	.406	.429	.467	.526	.636	2.000
	.325	**.377**	**.414**	**.442**	**.466**	**.488**	**.523**	**.577**	**.677**	**2.660**
70	.233	.286	.324	.354	.379	.401	.438	.495	.604	1.994
	.302	**.351**	**.386**	**.413**	**.436**	**.456**	**.491**	**.544**	**.644**	**2.648**
80	.217	.269	.304	.332	.356	.377	.413	.469	.576	1.990
	.283	**.330**	**.362**	**.389**	**.411**	**.431**	**.464**	**.516**	**.615**	**2.638**
90	.205	.254	.288	.315	.338	.358	.392	.446	.552	1.987
	.267	**.312**	**.343**	**.368**	**.390**	**.409**	**.441**	**.492**	**.590**	**2.632**
100	.195	.241	.274	.300	.322	.341	.374	.426	.530	1.984
	.254	**.297**	**.327**	**.351**	**.372**	**.390**	**.421**	**.470**	**.568**	**2.626**
125	.174	.216	.246	.269	.290	.307	.338	.387	.485	1.979
	.228	**.266**	**.294**	**.316**	**.335**	**.352**	**.381**	**.428**	**.521**	**2.616**
150	.159	.198	.225	.247	.266	.282	.310	.356	.450	1.976
	.208	**.244**	**.270**	**.290**	**.308**	**.324**	**.351**	**.395**	**.484**	**2.609**
200	.138	.172	.196	.215	.231	.246	.271	.312	.398	1.972
	.181	**.212**	**.234**	**.253**	**.269**	**.283**	**.307**	**.347**	**.430**	**2.601**
300	.113	.141	.160	.176	.190	.202	.223	.258	.332	1.968
	.148	**.174**	**.192**	**.208**	**.221**	**.233**	**.253**	**.287**	**.359**	**2.592**
400	.098	.122	.139	.153	.165	.176	.194	.225	.291	1.966
	.128	**.151**	**.167**	**.180**	**.192**	**.202**	**.220**	**.250**	**.315**	**2.588**
500	.088	.109	.124	.137	.148	.157	.174	.202	.262	1.965
	.115	**.135**	**.150**	**.162**	**.172**	**.182**	**.198**	**.225**	**.284**	**2.586**
1000	.062	.077	.088	.097	.105	.112	.124	.144	.188	1.962
	.081	**.096**	**.106**	**.115**	**.122**	**.129**	**.141**	**.160**	**.204**	**2.581**
∞										1.960
										2.576

TABLE E. TABLE OF χ^2*

n	P = .99	.98	.95	.90	.80	.70	.50	.30	.20	.10	.05	.02	.01
1	.000157	.000628	.00393	.0158	.0642	.148	.455	1.074	1.642	2.706	3.841	5.412	6.635
2	.0201	.0404	.103	.211	.446	.713	1.386	2.408	3.219	4.605	5.991	7.824	9.210
3	.115	.185	.352	.584	1.005	1.424	2.366	3.665	4.642	6.251	7.815	9.837	11.341
4	.297	.429	.711	1.064	1.649	2.195	3.357	4.878	5.989	7.779	9.488	11.668	13.277
5	.554	.752	1.145	1.610	2.343	3.000	4.351	6.064	7.289	9.236	11.070	13.388	15.086
6	.872	1.134	1.635	2.204	3.070	3.828	5.348	7.231	8.558	10.645	12.592	15.033	16.812
7	1.239	1.564	2.167	2.833	3.822	4.671	6.346	8.383	9.803	12.017	14.067	16.622	18.475
8	1.646	2.032	2.733	3.490	4.594	5.527	7.344	9.524	11.030	13.362	15.507	18.168	20.090
9	2.088	2.532	3.325	4.168	5.380	6.393	8.343	10.656	12.242	14.684	16.919	19.679	21.666
10	2.558	3.059	3.940	4.865	6.179	7.267	9.342	11.781	13.442	15.987	18.307	21.161	23.209
11	3.053	3.609	4.575	5.578	6.989	8.148	10.341	12.899	14.631	17.275	19.675	22.618	24.725
12	3.571	4.178	5.226	6.304	7.807	9.034	11.340	14.011	15.812	18.549	21.026	24.054	26.217
13	4.107	4.765	5.892	7.042	8.634	9.926	12.340	15.119	16.985	19.812	22.362	25.472	27.688
14	4.660	5.368	6.571	7.790	9.467	10.821	13.339	16.222	18.151	21.064	23.685	26.873	29.141
15	5.229	5.985	7.261	8.547	10.307	11.721	14.339	17.322	19.311	22.307	24.996	28.259	30.578
16	5.812	6.614	7.962	9.312	11.152	12.624	15.338	18.418	20.465	23.542	26.296	29.633	32.000
17	6.408	7.255	8.672	10.085	12.002	13.531	16.338	19.511	21.615	24.769	27.587	30.995	33.409
18	7.015	7.906	9.390	10.865	12.857	14.440	17.338	20.601	22.760	25.989	28.869	32.346	34.805
19	7.633	8.567	10.117	11.651	13.716	15.352	18.338	21.689	23.900	27.204	30.144	33.687	36.191
20	8.260	9.237	10.851	12.443	14.578	16.266	19.337	22.775	25.038	28.412	31.410	35.020	37.566
21	8.897	9.915	11.591	13.240	15.445	17.182	20.337	23.858	26.171	29.615	32.671	36.343	38.932
22	9.542	10.600	12.338	14.041	16.314	18.101	21.337	24.939	27.301	30.813	33.924	37.659	40.289
23	10.196	11.293	13.091	14.848	17.187	19.021	22.337	26.018	28.429	32.007	35.172	38.968	41.638
24	10.856	11.992	13.848	15.659	18.062	19.943	23.337	27.096	29.553	33.196	36.415	40.270	42.980
25	11.524	12.697	14.611	16.473	18.940	20.867	24.337	28.172	30.675	34.382	37.652	41.566	44.314
26	12.198	13.409	15.379	17.292	19.820	21.792	25.336	29.246	31.795	35.563	38.885	42.856	45 642
27	12.879	14.125	16.151	18.114	20.703	22.719	26.336	30.319	32.912	36.741	40.113	44.140	46.963
28	13.565	14.847	16.928	18.939	21.588	23.647	27.336	31.391	34.027	37.916	41.337	45.419	48.278
29	14.256	15.574	17.708	19.768	22.475	24.577	28.336	32.461	35.139	39.087	42.557	46.693	49.588
30	14.953	16.306	18.493	20.599	23.364	25.508	29.336	33.530	36.250	40.256	43.773	47.962	50.892

* Adapted from R. A. Fisher, "Statistical Methods for Research Workers," 4th ed., pp. 104 *f*; 1932, by courtesy of Oliver and Boyd, Ltd. For larger values of n, the expression $\sqrt{2\chi^2} - \sqrt{2n - 1}$ may be interpreted as a t ratio.

TABLE F.* 5 PER CENT (ROMAN TYPE) AND 1 PER CENT (BOLD-FACED TYPE) POINTS FOR THE DISTRIBUTION OF F

n_2	n_1 degrees of freedom (for greater variance)																							n_2
	1	2	3	4	5	6	7	8	9	10	11	12	14	16	20	24	30	40	50	75	100	200	500	∞	
1	161 **4,052**	200 **4,999**	216 **5,403**	225 **5,625**	230 **5,764**	234 **5,859**	237 **5,928**	239 **5,981**	241 **6,022**	242 **6,056**	243 **6,082**	244 **6,106**	245 **6,142**	246 **6,169**	248 **6,208**	249 **6,234**	250 **6,258**	251 **6,286**	252 **6,302**	253 **6,323**	253 **6,334**	254 **6,352**	254 **6,361**	254 **6,366**	1
2	18.51 **98.49**	19.00 **99.01**	19.16 **99.17**	19.25 **99.25**	19.30 **99.30**	19.33 **99.33**	19.36 **99.34**	19.37 **99.36**	19.38 **99.38**	19.39 **99.40**	19.40 **99.41**	19.41 **99.42**	19.42 **99.43**	19.43 **99.44**	19.44 **99.45**	19.45 **99.46**	19.46 **99.47**	19.47 **99.48**	19.47 **99.48**	19.48 **99.49**	19.49 **99.49**	19.49 **99.49**	19.50 **99.50**	19.50 **99.50**	2
3	10.13 **34.12**	9.55 **30.81**	9.28 **29.46**	9.12 **28.71**	9.01 **28.24**	8.94 **27.91**	8.88 **27.67**	8.84 **27.49**	8.81 **27.34**	8.78 **27.23**	8.76 **27.13**	8.74 **27.05**	8.71 **26.92**	8.69 **26.83**	8.66 **26.69**	8.64 **26.60**	8.62 **26.50**	8.60 **26.41**	8.58 **26.35**	8.57 **26.27**	8.56 **26.23**	8.54 **26.18**	8.54 **26.14**	8.53 **26.12**	3
4	7.71 **21.20**	6.94 **18.00**	6.59 **16.69**	6.39 **15.98**	6.26 **15.52**	6.16 **15.21**	6.09 **14.98**	6.04 **14.80**	6.00 **14.66**	5.96 **14.54**	5.93 **14.45**	5.91 **14.37**	5.87 **14.24**	5.84 **14.15**	5.80 **14.02**	5.77 **13.93**	5.74 **13.83**	5.71 **13.74**	5.70 **13.69**	5.68 **13.61**	5.66 **13.57**	5.65 **13.52**	5.64 **13.48**	5.63 **13.46**	4
5	6.61 **16.26**	5.79 **13.27**	5.41 **12.06**	5.19 **11.39**	5.05 **10.97**	4.95 **10.67**	4.88 **10.45**	4.82 **10.27**	4.78 **10.15**	4.74 **10.05**	4.70 **9.96**	4.68 **9.89**	4.64 **9.77**	4.60 **9.68**	4.56 **9.55**	4.53 **9.47**	4.50 **9.38**	4.46 **9.29**	4.44 **9.24**	4.42 **9.17**	4.40 **9.13**	4.38 **9.07**	4.37 **9.04**	3.46 **9.02**	5
6	5.99 **13.74**	5.14 **10.92**	4.76 **9.78**	4.53 **9.15**	4.39 **8.75**	4.28 **8.47**	4.21 **8.26**	4.15 **8.10**	4.10 **7.98**	4.06 **7.87**	4.03 **7.79**	4.00 **7.72**	3.96 **7.60**	3.92 **7.52**	3.87 **7.39**	3.84 **7.31**	3.81 **7.23**	3.77 **7.14**	3.75 **7.09**	3.72 **7.02**	3.71 **6.99**	3.69 **6.94**	3.68 **6.90**	3.67 **6.88**	6
7	5.59 **12.25**	4.74 **9.55**	4.35 **8.45**	4.12 **7.85**	3.97 **7.46**	3.87 **7.19**	3.79 **7.00**	3.73 **6.84**	3.68 **6.71**	3.63 **6.62**	3.60 **6.54**	3.57 **6.47**	3.52 **6.35**	3.49 **6.27**	3.44 **6.15**	3.41 **6.07**	3.38 **5.98**	3.34 **5.90**	3.32 **5.85**	3.29 **5.78**	3.28 **5.75**	3.25 **5.70**	3.24 **5.67**	3.23 **5.65**	7
8	5.32 **11.26**	4.46 **8.65**	4.07 **7.59**	3.84 **7.01**	3.69 **6.63**	3.58 **6.37**	3.50 **6.19**	3.44 **6.03**	3.39 **5.91**	3.34 **5.82**	3.31 **5.74**	3.28 **5.67**	3.23 **5.56**	3.20 **5.48**	3.15 **5.36**	3.12 **5.28**	3.08 **5.20**	3.05 **5.11**	3.03 **5.06**	3.00 **5.00**	2.98 **4.96**	2.96 **4.91**	2.94 **4.88**	2.93 **4.86**	8
9	5.12 **10.56**	4.26 **8.02**	3.86 **6.99**	3.63 **6.42**	3.48 **6.06**	3.37 **5.80**	3.29 **5.62**	3.23 **5.47**	3.18 **5.35**	3.13 **5.26**	3.10 **5.18**	3.07 **5.11**	3.02 **5.00**	2.98 **4.92**	2.93 **4.80**	2.90 **4.73**	2.86 **4.64**	2.82 **4.56**	2.80 **4.51**	2.77 **4.45**	2.76 **4.41**	2.73 **4.36**	2.72 **4.33**	2.71 **4.31**	9
10	4.96 **10.04**	4.10 **7.56**	3.71 **6.55**	3.48 **5.99**	3.33 **5.64**	3.22 **5.39**	3.14 **5.21**	3.07 **5.06**	3.02 **4.95**	2.97 **4.85**	2.94 **4.78**	2.91 **4.71**	2.86 **4.60**	2.82 **4.52**	2.77 **4.41**	2.74 **4.33**	2.70 **4.25**	2.67 **4.17**	2.64 **4.12**	2.61 **4.05**	2.59 **4.01**	2.56 **3.96**	2.55 **3.93**	2.54 **3.91**	10
11	4.84 **9.65**	3.98 **7.20**	3.59 **6.22**	3.36 **5.67**	3.20 **5.32**	3.09 **5.07**	3.01 **4.88**	2.95 **4.74**	2.90 **4.63**	2.86 **4.54**	2.82 **4.46**	2.79 **4.40**	2.74 **4.29**	2.70 **4.21**	2.65 **4.10**	2.61 **4.02**	2.57 **3.94**	2.53 **3.86**	2.50 **3.80**	2.47 **3.74**	2.45 **3.70**	2.42 **3.66**	2.41 **3.62**	2.40 **3.60**	11
12	4.75 **9.33**	3.88 **6.93**	3.49 **5.95**	3.26 **5.41**	3.11 **5.06**	3.00 **4.82**	2.92 **4.65**	2.85 **4.50**	2.80 **4.39**	2.76 **4.30**	2.72 **4.22**	2.69 **4.16**	2.64 **4.05**	2.60 **3.98**	2.54 **3.86**	2.50 **3.78**	2.46 **3.70**	2.42 **3.61**	2.40 **3.56**	2.36 **3.49**	2.35 **3.46**	2.32 **3.41**	2.31 **3.38**	2.30 **3.36**	12
14	4.60 **8.86**	3.74 **6.51**	3.34 **5.56**	3.11 **5.03**	2.96 **4.69**	2.85 **4.46**	2.77 **4.28**	2.70 **4.14**	2.65 **4.03**	2.60 **3.94**	2.56 **3.86**	2.53 **3.80**	2.48 **3.70**	2.44 **3.62**	2.39 **3.51**	2.35 **3.43**	2.31 **3.34**	2.27 **3.26**	2.24 **3.21**	2.21 **3.14**	2.19 **3.11**	2.16 **3.06**	2.14 **3.02**	2.13 **3.00**	14

TABLE F.* 5 PER CENT (ROMAN TYPE) AND 1 PER CENT (BOLD-FACED TYPE) POINTS FOR THE DISTRIBUTION OF F. (*Continued*)

n_2	n_1 degrees of freedom (for greater variance)																								n_2
	1	2	3	4	5	6	7	8	9	10	11	12	14	16	20	24	30	40	50	75	100	200	500	∞	
17	4.45 **8.40**	3.59 **6.11**	3.20 **5.18**	2.96 **4.67**	2.81 **4.34**	2.70 **4.10**	2.62 **3.93**	2.55 **3.79**	2.50 **3.63**	2.45 **3.59**	2.41 **3.52**	2.38 **3.45**	2.33 **3.35**	2.29 **3.27**	2.23 **3.16**	2.19 **3.08**	2.15 **3.00**	2.11 **2.92**	2.08 **2.86**	2.04 **2.79**	2.02 **2.76**	1.99 **2.70**	1.97 **2.67**	1.96 **2.65**	**17**
20	4.35 **8.10**	3.49 **5.85**	3.10 **4.94**	2.87 **4.43**	2.71 **4.10**	2.60 **3.87**	2.52 **3.71**	2.45 **3.56**	2.40 **3.45**	2.35 **3.37**	2.31 **3.30**	2.28 **3.23**	2.23 **3.13**	2.18 **3.05**	2.12 **2.94**	2.08 **2.86**	2.04 **2.77**	1.99 **2.69**	1.96 **2.63**	1.92 **2.56**	1.90 **2.53**	1.87 **2.47**	1.85 **2.44**	1.84 **2.42**	20
24	4.26 **7.82**	3.40 **5.61**	3.01 **4.72**	2.78 **4.22**	2.62 **3.90**	2.51 **3.67**	2.43 **3.50**	2.36 **3.36**	2.30 **3.25**	2.26 **3.17**	2.22 **3.09**	2.18 **3.03**	2.13 **2.93**	2.09 **2.85**	2.02 **2.74**	1.98 **2.66**	1.94 **2.58**	1.89 **2.49**	1.86 **2.44**	1.82 **2.36**	1.80 **2.33**	1.76 **2.27**	1.74 **2.23**	1.73 **2.21**	24
30	4.17 **7.56**	3.32 **5.39**	2.92 **4.51**	2.69 **4.02**	2.53 **3.70**	2.42 **3.47**	2.34 **3.30**	2.27 **3.17**	2.21 **3.06**	2.16 **2.98**	2.12 **2.90**	2.09 **2.84**	2.04 **2.74**	1.99 **2.66**	1.93 **2.55**	1.89 **2.47**	1.84 **2.38**	1.79 **2.29**	1.76 **2.24**	1.72 **2.16**	1.69 **2.13**	1.66 **2.07**	1.64 **2.03**	1.62 **2.01**	30
40	4.08 **7.31**	3.23 **5.18**	2.84 **4.31**	2.61 **3.83**	2.45 **3.51**	2.34 **3.29**	2.25 **3.12**	2.18 **2.99**	2.12 **2.88**	2.07 **2.80**	2.04 **2.73**	2.00 **2.66**	1.95 **2.56**	1.90 **2.49**	1.84 **2.37**	1.79 **2.29**	1.74 **2.20**	1.69 **2.11**	1.66 **2.05**	1.61 **1.97**	1.59 **1.94**	1.55 **1.88**	1.53 **1.84**	1.51 **1.81**	40
50	4.03 **7.17**	3.18 **5.06**	2.79 **4.20**	2.56 **3.72**	2.40 **3.41**	2.29 **3.18**	2.20 **3.02**	2.13 **2.88**	2.07 **2.78**	2.02 **2.70**	1.98 **2.62**	1.95 **2.56**	1.90 **2.46**	1.85 **2.39**	1.78 **2.26**	1.74 **2.18**	1.69 **2.10**	1.63 **2.00**	1.60 **1.94**	1.55 **1.86**	1.52 **1.82**	1.48 **1.76**	1.46 **1.71**	1.44 **1.68**	50
70	3.98 **7.01**	3.13 **4.92**	2.74 **4.08**	2.50 **3.60**	2.35 **3.29**	2.23 **3.07**	2.14 **2.91**	2.07 **2.77**	2.01 **2.67**	1.97 **2.59**	1.93 **2.51**	1.89 **2.45**	1.84 **2.35**	1.79 **2.28**	1.72 **2.15**	1.67 **2.07**	1.62 **1.98**	1.56 **1.88**	1.53 **1.82**	1.47 **1.74**	1.45 **1.69**	1.40 **1.62**	1.37 **1.56**	1.35 **1.53**	70
100	3.94 **6.90**	3.09 **4.82**	2.70 **3.98**	2.46 **3.51**	2.30 **3.20**	2.19 **2.99**	2.10 **2.82**	2.03 **2.69**	1.97 **2.59**	1.92 **2.51**	1.88 **2.43**	1.85 **2.36**	1.79 **2.26**	1.75 **2.19**	1.68 **2.06**	1.63 **1.98**	1.57 **1.89**	1.51 **1.79**	1.48 **1.73**	1.42 **1.64**	1.39 **1.59**	1.34 **1.51**	1.30 **1.46**	1.28 **1.43**	100
150	3.91 **6.81**	3.06 **4.75**	2.67 **3.91**	2.43 **3.44**	2.27 **3.14**	2.16 **2.92**	2.07 **2.76**	2.00 **2.62**	1.94 **2.53**	1.89 **2.44**	1.85 **2.37**	1.82 **2.30**	1.76 **2.20**	1.71 **2.12**	1.64 **2.00**	1.59 **1.91**	1.54 **1.83**	1.47 **1.72**	1.44 **1.66**	1.37 **1.56**	1.34 **1.51**	1.29 **1.43**	1.25 **1.37**	1.22 **1.33**	150
200	3.89 **6.76**	3.04 **4.71**	2.65 **3.88**	2.41 **3.41**	2.26 **3.11**	2.14 **2.90**	2.05 **2.73**	1.98 **2.60**	1.92 **2.50**	1.87 **2.41**	1.83 **2.34**	1.80 **2.28**	1.74 **2.17**	1.69 **2.09**	1.62 **1.97**	1.57 **1.88**	1.52 **1.79**	1.45 **1.69**	1.42 **1.62**	1.35 **1.53**	1.32 **1.48**	1.26 **1.39**	1.22 **1.33**	1.19 **1.28**	200
400	3.86 **6.70**	3.02 **4.66**	2.62 **3.83**	2.39 **3.36**	2.23 **3.06**	2.12 **2.85**	2.03 **2.69**	1.96 **2.55**	1.90 **2.46**	1.85 **2.37**	1.81 **2.29**	1.78 **2.23**	1.72 **2.12**	1.67 **2.04**	1.60 **1.92**	1.54 **1.84**	1.49 **1.74**	1.42 **1.64**	1.38 **1.57**	1.32 **1.47**	1.28 **1.42**	1.22 **1.32**	1.16 **1.24**	1.13 **1.19**	400
1,000	3.85 **6.66**	3.00 **4.62**	2.61 **3.80**	2.38 **3.34**	2.22 **3.04**	2.10 **2.82**	2.02 **2.66**	1.95 **2.53**	1.89 **2.43**	1.84 **2.34**	1.80 **2.26**	1.76 **2.20**	1.70 **2.09**	1.65 **2.01**	1.58 **1.89**	1.53 **1.81**	1.47 **1.71**	1.41 **1.61**	1.36 **1.54**	1.30 **1.44**	1.26 **1.38**	1.19 **1.28**	1.13 **1.19**	1.08 **1.11**	1,000
∞	3.84 **6.64**	2.99 **4.60**	2.60 **3.78**	2.37 **3.32**	2.21 **3.02**	2.09 **2.80**	2.01 **2.64**	1.94 **2.51**	1.88 **2.41**	1.83 **2.32**	1.79 **2.24**	1.75 **2.18**	1.69 **2.07**	1.64 **1.99**	1.57 **1.87**	1.52 **1.79**	1.46 **1.69**	1.40 **1.59**	1.35 **1.52**	1.28 **1.41**	1.24 **1.36**	1.17 **1.25**	1.11 **1.15**	1.00 **1.00**	∞

* Reproduced from Snedecor, G. W. Statistical methods. Ames, Iowa: Collegiate, 1937. Pp. 174–177. By permission of the author.

TABLE G. FUNCTIONS OF p, q, z, AND y, WHERE p AND q ARE PROPORTIONS ($p + q = 1.00$) AND z AND y ARE CONSTANTS OF THE UNIT NORMAL DISTRIBUTION CURVE*

p (or q)	A pq	B $\sqrt{pq}$	C pq/y	D $\sqrt{pq}/y$	E p/y	F y/p	G zy/p	H y	I zy/q	J y/q	K q/y	L $\sqrt{p/q}$	M $\sqrt{q/p}$	q (or p)
.99	.0099	.0995−	.3715	3.733	37.15−	.02692	−.06262	.02665	6.2002	2.665	.3752	9.950	.1005	.01
.98	.0196	.1400	.4048	2.892	20.24	.04941	−.1015	.04842	4.9719	2.421	.4131	7.000	.1429	.02
.97	.0291	.1706	.4277	2.507	14.26	.07015	−.1319	.06804	4.2657	2.268	.4409	5.686	.1759	.03
.96	.0384	.1960	.4456	2.274	11.14	.08976	−.1571	.08617	3.7717	2.154	.4642	4.899	.2041	.04
.95	.0475	.2179	.4605	2.113	9.211	.1086	−.1786	.1031	3.3928	2.063	.4848	4.359	.2294	.05
.94	.0564	.2375−	.4735	1.994	7.891	.1267	−.1970	.1191	3.0868	1.985	.5037	3.958	.2526	.06
.93	.0651	.2551	.4848	1.900	6.926	.1444	−.2131	.1343	2.8307	1.918	.5213	3.645	.2743	.07
.92	.0736	.2713	.4951	1.825	6.188	.1616	−.2271	.1487	2.6110	1.858	.5381	3.391	.2949	.08
.91	.0819	.2862	.5043	1.762	5.604	.1785	−.2393	.1624	2.4191	1.804	.5542	3.180	.3145	.09
.90	.0900	.3000	.5128	1.709	5.128	.1950	−.2499	.1755	2.2491	1.755	.5698	3.000	.3333	.10
.89	.0979	.3129	.5206	1.664	4.733	.2113	−.2591	.1880	2.0966	1.709	.5850	2.844	.3516	.11
.88	.1056	.3250	.5279	1.625	4.399	.2273	−.2671	.2000	1.9587	1.667	.5999	2.708	.3693	.12
.87	.1131	.3363	.5346	1.590	4.112	.2432	−.2739	.2115	1.8330	1.627	.6145	2.587	.3865	.13
.86	.1204	.3470	.5409	1.559	3.864	.2588	−.2796	.2226	1.7175	1.590	.6290	2.478	.4035	.14
.85	.1275	.3571	.5468	1.532	3.646	.2743	−.2843	.2332	1.6110	1.554	.6433	2.380	.4201	.15
.84	.1344	.3666	.5524	1.507	3.452	.2896	−.2880	.2433	1.5123	1.521	.6576	2.291	.4365	.16
.83	.1411	.3756	.5576	1.484	3.280	.3049	−.2909	.2531	1.4203	1.489	.6718	2.210	.4525	.17
.82	.1476	.3842	.5625	1.464	3.125	.3200	−.2929	.2624	1.3344	1.458	.6860	2.134	.4685	.18
.81	.1539	.3923	.5671	1.446	2.985	.3350	−.2941	.2714	1.2538	1.428	.7002	2.065	.4844	.19
.80	.1600	.4000	.5715	1.429	2.858	.3500	−.2946	.2800	1.1781	1.400	.7144	2.000	.5000	.20
.79	.1659	.4073	.5756	1.413	2.741	.3648	−.2942	.2882	1.1067	1.372	.7287	1.940	.5156	.21
.78	.1716	.4142	.5796	1.399	2.634	.3796	−.2931	.2961	1.0393	1.346	.7430	1.883	.5311	.22
.77	.1771	.4208	.5832	1.386	2.536	.3943	−.2913	.3036	.9754	1.320	.7575	1.830	.5465	.23
.76	.1824	.4271	.5867	1.374	2.445	.4090	−.2889	.3109	.9149	1.295	.7720	1.780	.5620	.24
.75	.1875	.4330	.5900	1.363	2.360	.4237	−.2858	.3178	.8573	1.271	.7867	1.732	.5774	.25

* When p is less than .50, interchange p and q, as the headings of the first and last columns indicate.

TABLE G. FUNCTIONS OF p, q, z, AND y, WHERE p AND q ARE PROPORTIONS ($p + q = 1.00$) AND z AND y ARE CONSTANTS OF THE UNIT NORMAL DISTRIBUTION CURVE.* (*Continued*)

p (or q)	A pq	B $\sqrt{pq}$	C pq/y	D $\sqrt{pq}/y$	E p/y	F y/p	G zy/p	H y	I zy/q	J y/q	K q/y	L $\sqrt{p/q}$	M $\sqrt{q/p}$	q (or p)
.74	.1924	.4386	.5931	1.352	2.281	.4384	—.2820	.3244	.8026	1.248	.8016	1.687	.5928	.26
.73	.1971	.4440	.5961	1.343	2.208	.4529	—.2775	.3306	.7504	1.225	.8166	1.644	.6082	.27
.72	.2016	.4490	.5989	1.334	2.139	.4675	—.2725	.3366	.7006	1.202	.8318	1.604	.6236	.28
.71	.2059	.4538	.6015	1.326	2.074	.4822	—.2668	.3423	.6532	1.180	.8472	1.565	.6391	.29
.70	.2100	.4583	.6040	1.318	2.013	.4967	—.2605	.3477	.6078	1.159	.8628	1.528	.6547	.30
.69	.2139	.4625—	.6063	1.311	1.956	.5113	—.2535	.3528	.5643	1.138	.8787	1.492	.6703	.31
.68	.2176	.4665—	.6085	1.304	1.902	.5259	—.2460	.3576	.5227	1.118	.8949	1.458	.6860	.32
.67	.2211	.4702	.6106	1.298	1.850	.5405	—.2378	.3621	.4828	1.097	.9112	1.425	.7018	.33
.66	.2244	.4737	.6124	1.293	1.801	.5552	—.2290	.3664	.4445	1.078	.9279	1.393	.7178	.34
.65	.2275	.4770	.6142	1.288	1.755	.5698	—.2196	.3704	.4078	1.058	.9449	1.363	.7338	.35
.64	.2304	.4800	.6158	1.283	1.711	.5845	—.2095	.3741	.3725	1.039	.9623	1.333	.7500	.36
.63	.2331	.4828	.6174	1.279	1.669	.5993	—.1989	.3776	.3387	1.020	.9800	1.305	.7663	.37
.62	.2356	.4854	.6188	1.275	1.628	.6141	—.1876	.3808	.3061	1.002	.9980	1.277	.7829	.38
.61	.2379	.4877	.6200	1.271	1.590	.6290	—.1757	.3837	.2748	.9938	1.016	1.251	.7996	.39
.60	.2400	.4899	.6212	1.268	1.553	.6439	—.1631	.3863	.2447	.9659	1.035	1.225	.8165	.40
.59	.2419	.4918	.6223	1.265	1.518	.6589	—.1499	.3888	.2158	.9482	1.055	1.200	.8336	.41
.58	.2436	.4936	.6232	1.263	1.484	.6739	—.1361	.3909	.1879	.9307	1.074	1.175	.8510	.42
.57	.2451	.4951	.6240	1.260	1.451	.6891	—.1215	.3928	.1611	.9134	1.095	1.151	.8686	.43
.56	.2464	.4964	.6247	1.259	1.420	.7043	—.1063	.3944	.1353	.8964	1.116	1.128	.8864	.44
.55	.2475	.4975—	.6253	1.257	1.390	.7196	—.09043	.3958	.1105	.8796	1.137	1.106	.9045	.45
.54	.2484	.4984	.6258	1.256	1.360	.7351	—.07382	.3969	.0867	.8629	1.159	1.083	.9229	.46
.53	.2491	.4991	.6262	1.255	1.332	.7506	—.05650	.3978	.0637	.8464	1.181	1.062	.9417	.47
.52	.2496	.4996	.6264	1.254	1.305	.7662	—.03843	.3984	.0416	.8301	1.205	1.041	.9608	.48
.51	.2499	.4999	.6266	1.253	1.279	.7820	—.01960	.3988	.0204	.8139	1.229	1.020	.9802	.49
.50	.2500	.5000	.6267	1.253	1.253	.7979	—.00000	.3989	.0000	.7979	1.253	1.000	1.0000	.50

TABLE H. MÜLLER-URBAN WEIGHTS AND PRODUCTS WITH s' AND z*

p		$s' = 1$		$s' = 2$			$s' = 3$			$s' = 4$		
		w	wz	ws'	ws'^2	$ws'z$	ws'	ws'^2	$ws'z$	ws'	ws'^2	$ws'z$
.01	.99	.1127	.2622	.2254	.4508	.5243	.3381	1.0142	.7865	.4508	1.8030	1.0486
.02	.98	.1881	.3864	.3762	.7525	.7727	.5644	1.6931	1.1591	.7525	3.0099	1.5454
.03	.97	.2499	.4700	.4998	.9996	.9400	.7497	2.2491	1.4100	.9996	3.9984	1.8800
.04	.96	.3036	.5316	.6073	1.2146	1.0632	.9109	2.7328	1.5947	1.2146	4.8582	2.1263
.05	.95	.3519	.5788	.7038	1.4076	1.1576	1.0557	3.1671	1.7365	1.4076	5.6304	2.3153
.06	.94	.3954	.6147	.7907	1.5814	1.2294	1.1861	3.5582	1.8441	1.5814	6.3258	2.4587
.07	.93	.4351	.6421	.8702	1.7403	1.2842	1.3052	3.9157	1.9263	1.7403	6.9613	2.5683
.08	.92	.4718	.6629	.9435	1.8871	1.3257	1.4153	4.4259	1.9886	1.8871	7.5483	2.6515
.09	.91	.5059	.6783	1.0118	2.0236	1.3566	1.5177	4.5531	2.0349	2.0236	8.0944	2.7132
.10	.90	.5376	.6889	1.0751	2.1502	1.3778	1.6127	4.8380	2.0667	2.1502	8.6008	2.7556
.11	.89	.5673	.6958	1.1346	2.2692	1.3916	1.7019	5.1056	2.0874	2.2692	9.0766	2.7832
.12	.88	.5953	.6995	1.1907	2.3813	1.3990	1.7860	5.3580	2.0985	2.3813	9.5253	2.7980
.13	.87	.6215	.7001	1.2430	2.4860	1.4001	1.8645	5.5935	2.1002	2.4860	9.9440	2.8002
.14	.86	.6463	.6982	1.2927	2.5853	1.3965	1.9390	5.8170	2.0947	2.5853	10.3413	2.7930
.15	.85	.6697	.6941	1.3394	2.6788	1.3882	2.0091	6.0273	2.0823	2.6788	10.7152	2.7764
.16	.84	.6921	.6882	1.3842	2.7683	1.3765	2.0762	6.2287	2.0647	2.7683	11.0733	2.7530
.17	.83	.7129	.6802	1.4257	2.8515	1.3604	2.1386	6.4158	2.0406	2.8515	11.4059	2.7208
.18	.82	.7327	.6707	1.4653	2.9307	1.3413	2.1980	6.5940	2.0120	2.9307	11.7227	2.6826
.19	.81	.7515	.6598	1.5031	3.0061	1.3195	2.2546	6.7638	1.9793	3.0061	12.0245	2.6391
.20	.80	.7695	.6476	1.5390	3.0780	1.2953	2.3085	6.9255	1.9429	3.0780	12.3120	2.5905
.21	.79	.7865	.6342	1.5729	3.1459	1.2685	2.3594	7.0782	1.9027	3.1459	12.5835	2.5369
.22	.78	.8025	.6197	1.6051	3.2102	1.2394	2.4076	7.2229	1.8591	3.2102	12.8406	2.4789
.23	.77	.8179	.6043	1.6357	3.2714	1.2085	2.4536	7.3607	1.8128	3.2714	13.0858	2.4171
.24	.76	.8323	.5879	1.6646	3.3293	1.1757	2.4970	7.4909	1.7636	3.3293	13.3171	2.3515
.25	.75	.8460	.5706	1.6921	3.3842	1.1413	2.5381	7.6144	1.7119	3.3842	13.5366	2.2826
.26	.74	.8590	.5526	1.7180	3.4360	1.1053	2.5770	7.7310	1.6579	3.4360	13.7440	2.2105
.27	.73	.8713	.5339	1.7426	3.4852	1.0679	2.6139	7.8417	1.6018	3.4852	13.9408	2.1358
.28	.72	.8830	.5146	1.7659	3.5318	1.0293	2.6489	7.9466	1.5439	3.5318	14.1274	2.0585
.29	.71	.8939	.4947	1.7878	3.5755	.9893	2.6816	8.0449	1.4840	3.5755	14.3021	1.9786
.30	.70	.9043	.4742	1.8085	3.6170	.9484	2.7128	8.1383	1.4226	3.6170	14.4682	1.8968
.31	.69	.9140	.4532	1.8280	3.6561	.9064	2.7421	8.2262	1.3597	3.6561	14.6243	1.8129
.32	.68	.9232	.4318	1.8464	3.6929	.8636	2.7697	8.3090	1.2954	3.6929	14.7715	1.7272
.33	.67	.9317	.4099	1.8634	3.7268	.8197	2.7951	8.3853	1.2296	3.7268	14.9072	1.6395
.34	.66	.9398	.3876	1.8797	3.7594	.7753	2.8196	8.4586	1.1630	3.7594	15.0376	1.5506
.35	.65	.9473	.3650	1.8945	3.7890	.7300	2.8418	8.5253	1.0950	3.7890	15.1562	1.4600
.36	.64	.9542	.3420	1.9084	3.8168	.6841	2.8626	8.5878	1.0261	3.8168	15.2672	1.3682
.37	.63	.9607	.3188	1.9214	3.8429	.6376	2.8822	8.6465	.9565	3.8429	15.3715	1.2753
.38	.62	.9666	.2953	1.9332	3.8663	.5906	2.8997	8.6992	.8858	3.8663	15.4653	1.1811
.39	.61	.9720	.2715	1.9440	3.8881	.5430	2.9161	8.7482	.8145	3.8881	15.5523	1.0860
.40	.60	.9768	.2475	1.9537	3.9074	.4950	2.9306	8.7916	.7425	3.9074	15.6296	.9899
.41	.59	.9814	.2233	1.9627	3.9254	.4466	2.9441	8.8322	.6699	3.9254	15.7018	.8932
.42	.58	.9853	.1989	1.9706	3.9413	.3978	2.9560	8.8679	.5968	3.9413	15.7651	.7957
.43	.57	.9888	.1744	1.9776	3.9551	.3488	2.9663	8.8990	.5232	3.9551	15.8205	.6976
.44	.56	.9918	.1497	1.9836	3.9671	.2995	2.9753	8.9260	.4492	3.9671	15.8685	.5989
.45	.55	.9943	.1249	1.9886	3.9772	.2499	2.9829	8.9487	.3748	3.9772	15.9088	.4998
.46	.54	.9964	.1001	1.9928	3.9855	.2001	2.9891	8.9674	.3002	3.9855	15.9421	.4003
.47	.53	.9980	.0751	1.9959	3.9918	.1502	2.9938	8.9816	.2253	3.9918	15.9672	.3005
.48	.52	.9991	.0501	1.9982	3.9963	.1002	2.9972	8.9917	.1503	3.9963	15.9853	.2004
.49	.51	.9998	.0251	1.9996	3.9991	.0501	2.9993	8.9980	.0752	3.9991	15.9965	.1003
.50		1.0000	0	2.0000	4.0000	0	3.0000	9.0000	0	4.0000	16.0000	0

* Adapted by permission from R. S. Woodworth, *Experimental Psychology*. New York: Holt, 1938.

TABLE J. TRIGONOMETRIC FUNCTIONS [1]

ANGLE	SIN	COS	TAN	ANGLE	SIN	COS	TAN
0°	.000	1.000	.000	**45°**	.707	.707	1.000
1°	.018	.999	.018	**46°**	.719	.695	1.036
2°	.035	.999	.035	**47°**	.731	.682	1.072
3°	.052	.998	.052	**48°**	.743	.669	1.111
4°	.070	.997	.070	**49°**	.755	.656	1.150
5°	.087	.996	.087	**50°**	.766	.643	1.192
6°	.105	.994	.105	**51°**	.777	.629	1.235
7°	.122	.992	.123	**52°**	.788	.616	1.280
8°	.139	.990	.141	**53°**	.799	.602	1.327
9°	.156	.988	.158	**54°**	.809	.588	1.376
10°	.174	.985	.176	**55°**	.819	.574	1.428
11°	.191	.982	.194	**56°**	.829	.559	1.483
12°	.208	.978	.213	**57°**	.839	.545	1.540
13°	.225	.974	.231	**58°**	.848	.530	1.600
14°	.242	.970	.249	**59°**	.857	.515	1.664
15°	.259	.966	.268	**60°**	.866	.500	1.732
16°	.276	.961	.287	**61°**	.875	.485	1.804
17°	.292	.956	.306	**62°**	.883	.469	1.881
18°	.309	.951	.325	**63°**	.891	.454	1.963
19°	.326	.946	.344	**64°**	.899	.438	2.050
20°	.342	.940	.364	**65°**	.906	.423	2.144
21°	.358	.934	.384	**66°**	.914	.407	2.246
22°	.375	.927	.404	**67°**	.921	.391	2.356
23°	.391	.921	.424	**68°**	.927	.375	2.475
24°	.407	.914	.445	**69°**	.934	.358	2.605
25°	.423	.906	.466	**70°**	.940	.342	2.747
26°	.438	.899	.488	**71°**	.946	.326	2.904
27°	.454	.891	.510	**72°**	.951	.309	3.078
28°	.469	.883	.532	**73°**	.956	.292	3.271
29°	.485	.875	.554	**74°**	.961	.276	3.487
30°	.500	.866	.577	**75°**	.966	.259	3.732
31°	.515	.857	.601	**76°**	.970	.242	4.011
32°	.530	.848	.625	**77°**	.974	.225	4.331
33°	.545	.839	.649	**78°**	.978	.208	4.705
34°	.559	.829	.675	**79°**	.982	.191	5.145
35°	.574	.819	.700	**80°**	.985	.174	5.671
36°	.588	.809	.727	**81°**	.988	.156	6.314
37°	.602	.799	.754	**82°**	.990	.139	7.115
38°	.616	.788	.781	**83°**	.992	.122	8.144
39°	.629	.777	.810	**84°**	.994	.105	9.514
40°	.643	.766	.839	**85°**	.996	.087	11.430
41°	.656	.755	.869	**86°**	.997	.070	14.300
42°	.669	.743	.900	**87°**	.998	.052	19.081
43°	.682	.731	.933	**88°**	.999	.035	28.636
44°	.695	.719	.966	**89°**	.999	.018	57.290

[1] From Smail, "College Algebra."

TABLE K. FOUR-PLACE LOGARITHMS OF NUMBERS[1]

N.	0	1	2	3	4	5	6	7	8	9
0	—	0000	3010	4771	6021	6990	7782	8451	9031	9542
1	0000	0414	0792	1139	1461	1761	2041	2304	2553	2788
2	3010	3222	3424	3617	3802	3979	4150	4314	4472	4624
3	4771	4914	5051	5185	5315	5441	5563	5682	5798	5911
4	6021	6128	6232	6335	6435	6532	6628	6721	6812	6902
5	6990	7076	7160	7243	7324	7404	7482	7559	7634	7709
6	7782	7853	7924	7993	8062	8129	8195	8261	8325	8388
7	8451	8513	8573	8633	8692	8751	8808	8865	8921	8976
8	9031	9085	9138	9191	9243	9294	9345	9395	9445	9494
9	9542	9590	9638	9685	9731	9777	9823	9868	9912	9956
10	0000	0043	0086	0128	0170	0212	0253	0294	0334	0374
11	0414	0453	0492	0531	0569	0607	0645	0682	0719	0755
12	0792	0828	0864	0899	0934	0969	1004	1038	1072	1106
13	1139	1173	1206	1239	1271	1303	1335	1367	1399	1430
14	1461	1492	1523	1553	1584	1614	1644	1673	1703	1732
15	1761	1790	1818	1847	1875	1903	1931	1959	1987	2014
16	2041	2068	2095	2122	2148	2175	2201	2227	2253	2279
17	2304	2330	2355	2380	2405	2430	2455	2480	2504	2529
18	2553	2577	2601	2625	2648	2672	2695	2718	2742	2765
19	2788	2810	2833	2856	2878	2900	2934	2945	2967	2989
20	3010	3032	3054	3075	3096	3118	3139	3160	3181	3201
21	3222	3243	3263	3284	3304	3324	3345	3365	3385	3404
22	3424	3444	3464	3483	3502	3522	3541	3560	3579	3598
23	3617	3636	3655	3674	3692	3711	3729	3747	3766	3784
24	3802	3820	3838	3856	3874	3892	3909	3927	3945	3962
25	3979	3997	4014	4031	4048	4065	4082	4099	4116	4133
26	4150	4166	4183	4200	4216	4232	4249	4265	4281	4298
27	4314	4330	4346	4362	4378	4393	4409	4425	4440	4456
28	4472	4487	4502	4518	4533	4548	4564	4579	4594	4609
29	4624	4639	4654	4669	4683	4698	4713	4728	4742	4757
30	4771	4786	4800	4814	4829	4843	4857	4871	4886	4900
31	4914	4928	4942	4955	4969	4983	4997	5011	5024	5038
32	5051	5065	5079	5092	5105	5119	5132	5145	5159	5172
33	5185	5198	5211	5224	5237	5250	5263	5276	5289	5302
34	5315	5328	5340	5353	5366	5378	5391	5403	5416	5428
35	5441	5453	5465	5478	5490	5502	5514	5527	5539	5551
36	5563	5575	5587	5599	5611	5623	5635	5647	5658	5670
37	5682	5694	5705	5717	5729	5740	5752	5763	5775	5786
38	5798	5809	5821	5832	5843	5855	5866	5877	5888	5899
39	5911	5922	5933	5944	5955	5966	5977	5988	5999	6010
40	6021	6031	6042	6053	6064	6075	6085	6096	6107	6117
41	6128	6138	6149	6160	6170	6180	6191	6201	6212	6222
42	6232	6243	6253	6263	6274	6284	6294	6304	6314	6325
43	6335	6345	6355	6365	6375	6385	6395	6405	6415	6425
44	6435	6444	6454	6464	6474	6484	6493	6503	6513	6522
45	6532	6542	6551	6561	6571	6580	6590	6599	6609	6618
46	6628	6637	6646	6656	6665	6675	6684	6693	6702	6712
47	6721	6730	6739	6749	6758	6767	6776	6785	6794	6803
48	6812	6821	6830	6839	6848	6857	6866	6875	6884	6893
49	6902	6911	6920	6928	6937	6946	6955	6964	6972	6981
50	6990	6998	7007	7016	7024	7033	7042	7050	7059	7067
N.	0	1	2	3	4	5	6	7	8	9

Prop. Parts

	22	21	20	19	18	17	16	15	14	13	12	11	9	8
1	2.2	2.1	2.0	1.9	1.8	1.7	1.6	1.5	1.4	1.3	1.2	1.1	0.9	0.8
2	4.4	4.2	4.0	3.8	3.6	3.4	3.2	3.0	2.8	2.6	2.4	2.2	1.8	1.6
3	6.6	6.3	6.0	5.7	5.4	5.1	4.8	4.5	4.2	3.9	3.6	3.3	2.7	2.4
4	8.8	8.4	8.0	7.6	7.2	6.8	6.4	6.0	5.6	5.2	4.8	4.4	3.6	3.2
5	11.0	10.5	10.0	9.5	9.0	8.5	8.0	7.5	7.0	6.5	6.0	5.5	4.5	4.0
6	13.2	12.6	12.0	11.4	10.8	10.2	9.6	9.0	8.4	7.8	7.2	6.6	5.4	4.8
7	15.4	14.7	14.0	13.3	12.6	11.9	11.2	10.5	9.8	9.1	8.4	7.7	6.3	5.6
8	17.6	16.8	16.0	15.2	14.4	13.6	12.8	12.0	11.2	10.4	9.6	8.8	7.2	6.4
9	19.8	18.9	18.0	17.1	16.2	15.3	14.4	13.5	12.6	11.7	10.8	9.9	8.1	7.2

[1] From Smail, "College Algebra."

TABLE K. FOUR-PLACE LOGARITHMS OF NUMBERS.[1] (*Continued*)

N.	0	1	2	3	4	5	6	7	8	9
50	6990	6998	7007	7016	7024	7033	7042	7050	7059	7067
51	7076	7084	7093	7101	7110	7118	7126	7135	7143	7152
52	7160	7168	7177	7185	7193	7202	7210	7218	7226	7235
53	7243	7251	7259	7267	7275	7284	7292	7300	7308	7316
54	7324	7332	7340	7348	7356	7364	7372	7380	7388	7396
55	7404	7412	7419	7427	7435	7443	7451	7459	7466	7474
56	7482	7490	7497	7505	7513	7520	7528	7536	7543	7551
57	7559	7566	7574	7582	7589	7597	7604	7612	7619	7627
58	7634	7642	7649	7657	7664	7672	7679	7686	7694	7701
59	7709	7716	7723	7731	7738	7745	7752	7760	7767	7774
60	7782	7789	7796	7803	7810	7818	7825	7832	7839	7846
61	7853	7860	7868	7875	7882	7889	7896	7903	7910	7917
62	7924	7931	7938	7945	7952	7959	7966	7973	7980	7987
63	7993	8000	8007	8014	8021	8028	8035	8041	8048	8055
64	8062	8069	8075	8082	8089	8096	8102	8109	8116	8122
65	8129	8136	8142	8149	8156	8162	8169	8176	8182	8189
66	8195	8202	8209	8215	8222	8228	8235	8241	8248	8254
67	8261	8267	8274	8280	8287	8293	8299	8306	8312	8319
68	8325	8331	8338	8344	8351	8357	8363	8370	8376	8382
69	8388	8395	8401	8407	8414	8420	8426	8432	8439	8445
70	8451	8457	8463	8470	8476	8482	8488	8494	8500	8506
71	8513	8519	8525	8531	8537	8543	8549	8555	8561	8567
72	8573	8579	8585	8591	8597	8603	8609	8615	8621	8627
73	8633	8639	8645	8651	8657	8663	8669	8675	8681	8686
74	8692	8698	8704	8710	8716	8722	8727	8733	8739	8745
75	8751	8756	8762	8768	8774	8779	8785	8791	8797	8802
76	8808	8814	8820	8825	8831	8837	8842	8848	8854	8859
77	8865	8871	8876	8882	8887	8893	8899	8904	8910	8915
78	8921	8927	8932	8938	8943	8949	8954	8960	8965	8971
79	8976	8982	8987	8993	8998	9004	9009	9015	9020	9025
80	9031	9036	9042	9047	9053	9058	9063	9069	9074	9079
81	9085	9090	9096	9101	9106	9112	9117	9122	9128	9133
82	9138	9143	9149	9154	9159	9165	9170	9175	9180	9186
83	9191	9196	9201	9206	9212	9217	9222	9227	9232	9238
84	9243	9248	9253	9258	9263	9269	9274	9279	9284	9289
85	9294	9299	9304	9309	9315	9320	9325	9330	9335	9340
86	9345	9350	9355	9360	9365	9370	9375	9380	9385	9390
87	9395	9400	9405	9410	9415	9420	9425	9430	9435	9440
88	9445	9450	9455	9460	9465	9469	9474	9479	9484	9489
89	9494	9499	9504	9509	9513	9518	9523	9528	9533	9538
90	9542	9547	9552	9557	9562	9566	9571	9576	9581	9586
91	9590	9595	9600	9605	9609	9614	9619	9624	9628	9633
92	9638	9643	9647	9652	9657	9661	9666	9671	9675	9680
93	9685	9689	9694	9699	9703	9708	9713	9717	9722	9727
94	9731	9736	9741	9745	9750	9754	9759	9763	9768	9773
95	9777	9782	9786	9791	9795	9800	9805	9809	9814	9818
96	9823	9827	9832	9836	9841	9845	9850	9854	9859	9863
97	9868	9872	9877	9881	9886	9890	9894	9899	9903	9908
98	9912	9917	9921	9926	9930	9934	9939	9943	9948	9952
99	9956	9961	9965	9969	9974	9978	9983	9987	9991	9996
100	0000	0004	0009	0013	0017	0022	0026	0030	0035	0039
N.	0	1	2	3	4	5	6	7	8	9

Prop. Parts

	9	**8**	**7**	**6**	**5**	**4**
1	0.9	0.8	0.7	0.6	0.5	0.4
2	1.8	1.6	1.4	1.2	1.0	0.8
3	2.7	2.4	2.1	1.8	1.5	1.2
4	3.6	3.2	2.8	2.4	2.0	1.6
5	4.5	4.0	3.5	3.0	2.5	2.0
6	5.4	4.8	4.2	3.6	3.0	2.4
7	6.3	5.6	4.9	4.2	3.5	2.8
8	7.2	6.4	5.6	4.8	4.0	3.2
9	8.1	7.2	6.3	5.4	4.5	3.6

[1] From Smail, "College Algebra."

TABLE L. ANGLES, IN DEGREES, CORRESPONDING TO PERCENTAGES, WHERE THE ANGLE EQUALS ARCSIN $\sqrt{P/100}$, WHERE P IS A PERCENTAGE*

P	0	1	2	3	4	5	6	7	8	9
0.0	0	0.57	0.81	0.99	1.15	1.28	1.40	1.52	1.62	1.72
0.1	1.81	1.90	1.99	2.07	2.14	2.22	2.29	2.36	2.43	2.50
0.2	2.56	2.63	2.69	2.75	2.81	2.87	2.92	2.98	3.03	3.09
0.3	3.14	3.19	3.24	3.29	3.34	3.39	3.44	3.49	3.53	3.58
0.4	3.63	3.67	3.72	3.76	3.80	3.85	3.89	3.93	3.97	4.01
0.5	4.05	4.09	4.13	4.17	4.21	4.25	4.29	4.33	4.37	4.40
0.6	4.44	4.48	4.52	4.55	4.59	4.62	4.66	4.69	4.73	4.76
0.7	4.80	4.83	4.87	4.90	4.93	4.97	5.00	5.03	5.07	5.10
0.8	5.13	5.16	5.20	5.23	5.26	5.29	5.32	5.35	5.38	5.41
0.9	5.44	5.47	5.50	5.53	5.56	5.59	5.62	5.65	5.68	5.71
1	5.74	6.02	6.29	6.55	6.80	7.04	7.27	7.49	7.71	7.92
2	8.13	8.33	8.53	8.72	8.91	9.10	9.28	9.46	9.63	9.81
3	9.98	10.14	10.31	10.47	10.63	10.78	10.94	11.09	11.24	11.39
4	11.54	11.68	11.83	11.97	12.11	12.25	12.39	12.52	12.66	12.79
5	12.92	13.05	13.18	13.31	13.44	13.56	13.69	13.81	13.94	14.06
6	14.18	14.30	14.42	14.54	14.65	14.77	14.89	15.00	15.12	15.23
7	15.34	15.45	15.56	15.68	15.79	15.89	16.00	16.11	16.22	16.32
8	16.43	16.54	16.64	16.74	16.85	16.95	17.05	17.16	17.26	17.36
9	17.46	17.56	17.66	17.76	17.85	17.95	18.05	18.15	18.24	18.34
10	18.44	18.53	18.63	18.72	18.81	18.91	19.00	19.09	19.19	19.28
11	19.37	19.46	19.55	19.64	19.73	19.82	19.91	20.00	20.09	20.18
12	20.27	20.36	20.44	20.53	20.62	20.70	20.79	20.88	20.96	21.05
13	21.13	21.22	21.30	21.39	21.47	21.56	21.64	21.72	21.81	21.89
14	21.97	22.06	22.14	22.22	22.30	22.38	22.46	22.55	22.63	22.71
15	22.79	22.87	22.95	23.03	23.11	23.19	23.26	23.34	23.42	23.50
16	23.58	23.66	23.73	23.81	23.89	23.97	24.04	24.12	24.20	24.27
17	24.35	24.43	24.50	24.58	24.65	24.73	24.80	24.88	24.95	25.03
18	25.10	25.18	25.25	25.33	25.40	25.48	25.55	25.62	25.70	25.77
19	25.84	25.92	25.99	26.06	26.13	26.21	26.28	26.35	26.42	26.49
20	26.56	26.64	26.71	26.78	26.85	26.92	26.99	27.06	27.13	27.20
21	27.28	27.35	27.42	27.49	27.56	27.63	27.69	27.76	27.83	27.90
22	27.97	28.04	28.11	28.18	28.25	28.32	28.38	28.45	28.52	28.59
23	28.66	28.73	28.79	28.86	28.93	29.00	29.06	29.13	29.20	29.27
24	29.33	29.40	29.47	29.53	29.60	29.67	29.73	29.80	29.87	29.93
25	30.00	30.07	30.13	30.20	30.26	30.33	30.40	30.46	30.53	30.59
26	30.66	30.72	30.79	30.85	30.92	30.98	31.05	31.11	31.18	31.24
27	31.31	31.37	31.44	31.50	31.56	31.63	31.69	31.76	31.82	31.88
28	31.95	32.01	32.08	32.14	32.20	32.27	32.33	32.39	32.46	32.52
29	32.58	32.65	32.71	32.77	32.83	32.90	32.96	33.02	33.09	33.15
30	33.21	33.27	33.34	33.40	33.46	33.52	33.58	33.65	33.71	33.77

* Reproduced from a table given by Snedecor, G. W., *Statistical Methods*, 4th ed., Ames, Iowa: Iowa State College Press, by permission.

TABLE L. ANGLES, IN DEGREES, CORRESPONDING TO PERCENTAGES, WHERE THE ANGLE EQUALS ARCSIN $\sqrt{P/100}$, WHERE P IS A PERCENTAGE. (*Continued*)

P	0	1	2	3	4	5	6	7	8	9
31	33.83	33.89	33.96	34.02	34.08	34.14	34.20	34.27	34.33	34.39
32	34.45	34.51	34.57	34.63	34.70	34.76	34.82	34.88	34.94	35.00
33	35.06	35.12	35.18	35.24	35.30	35.37	35.43	35.49	35.55	35.61
34	35.67	35.73	35.79	35.85	35.91	35.97	36.03	36.09	36.15	36.21
35	36.27	36.33	36.39	36.45	36.51	36.57	36.63	36.69	36.75	36.81
36	36.87	36.93	36.99	37.05	37.11	37.17	37.23	37.29	37.35	37.41
37	37.47	37.52	37.58	37.64	37.70	37.76	37.82	37.88	37.94	38.00
38	38.06	38.12	38.17	38.23	38.29	38.35	38.41	38.47	38.53	38.59
39	38.65	38.70	38.76	38.82	38.88	38.94	39.00	39.06	39.11	39.17
40	39.23	39.29	39.35	39.41	39.47	39.52	39.58	39.64	39.70	39.76
41	39.82	39.87	39.93	39.99	40.05	40.11	40.16	40.22	40.28	40.34
42	40.40	40.46	40.51	40.57	40.63	40.69	40.74	40.80	40.86	40.92
43	40.98	41.03	41.09	41.15	41.21	41.27	41.32	41.38	41.44	41.50
44	41.55	41.61	41.67	41.73	41.78	41.84	41.90	41.96	42.02	42.07
45	42.13	42.19	42.25	42.30	42.36	42.42	42.48	42.53	42.59	42.65
46	42.71	42.76	42.82	42.88	42.94	42.99	43.05	43.11	43.17	43.22
47	43.28	43.34	43.39	43.45	43.51	43.57	43.62	43.68	43.74	43.80
48	43.85	43.91	43.97	44.03	44.08	44.14	44.20	44.25	44.31	44.37
49	44.43	44.48	44.54	44.60	44.66	44.71	44.77	44.83	44.89	44.94
50	45.00	45.06	45.11	45.17	45.23	45.29	45.34	45.40	45.46	45.52
51	45.57	45.63	45.59	45.75	45.80	45.86	45.92	45.97	46.03	46.09
52	46.15	46.20	46.26	46.32	46.38	46.43	46.49	46.55	46.61	46.66
53	46.72	46.78	46.83	46.89	46.95	47.01	47.06	47.12	47.18	47.24
54	47.29	47.35	47.41	47.47	47.52	47.58	47.64	47.70	47.75	47.81
55	47.87	47.93	47.98	48.04	48.10	48.16	48.22	48.27	48.33	48.39
56	48.45	48.50	48.56	48.62	48.68	48.73	48.79	48.85	48.91	48.97
57	49.02	49.08	49.14	49.20	49.26	49.31	49.37	49.43	49.49	49.54
58	49.60	49.66	49.72	49.78	49.84	49.89	49.95	50.01	50.07	50.13
59	50.18	50.24	50.30	50.36	50.42	50.48	50.53	50.59	50.65	50.71
60	50.77	50.83	50.89	50.94	51.00	51.06	51.12	51.18	51.24	51.30
61	51.35	51.41	51.47	51.53	51.59	51.65	51.71	51.77	51.83	51.88
62	51.94	52.00	52.06	52.12	52.18	52.24	52.30	52.36	52.42	52.48
63	52.53	52.59	52.65	52.71	52.77	52.83	52.89	52.95	53.01	53.07
64	53.13	53.19	53.25	53.31	53.37	53.43	53.49	53.55	53.61	53.67
65	53.73	53.79	53.85	53.91	53.97	54.03	54.09	54.15	54.21	54.27
66	54.33	54.39	54.45	54.51	54.57	54.63	54.70	54.76	54.82	54.88
67	54.94	55.00	55.06	55.12	55.18	55.24	55.30	55.37	55.43	55.49
68	55.55	55.61	55.67	55.73	55.80	55.86	55.92	55.98	56.04	56.11
69	56.17	56.23	56.29	56.35	56.42	56.48	56.54	56.60	56.66	56.73
70	56.79	56.85	56.91	56.98	57.04	57.10	57.17	57.23	57.29	57.35

TABLE L. ANGLES, IN DEGREES, CORRESPONDING TO PERCENTAGES, WHERE THE ANGLE EQUALS ARCSIN $\sqrt{P/100}$, WHERE P IS A PERCENTAGE. (*Continued*)

P	0	1	2	3	4	5	6	7	8	9
71	57.42	57.48	57.54	57.61	57.67	57.73	57.80	57.89	57.92	57.99
72	58.05	58.12	58.18	58.24	58.31	58.37	58.44	58.50	58.56	58.63
73	58.69	58.76	58:82	58.89	58.95	59.02	59.08	59.15	59.21	59.28
74	59.34	59.41	59.47	59.54	59.60	59.67	59.74	59.80	59.87	59.93
75	60.00	60.07	60.13	60.20	60.27	60.33	60.40	60.47	60.53	60.60
76	60.67	60.73	60.80	60.87	60.94	61.00	61.07	61.14	61.21	61.27
77	61.34	61.41	61.48	61.55	61.62	61.68	61.75	61.82	61.89	61.96
78	62.03	62.10	62.17	62.24	62.31	62.37	62.44	62.51	62.58	62.65
79	62.72	62.80	62.87	62.94	63.01	63.08	63.15	63.22	63.29	63.36
80	63.44	63.51	63.58	63.65	63.72	63.79	63.87	63.94	64.01	64.08
81	64.16	64.23	64.30	64.38	64.45	64.52	64.60	64.67	64.75	64.82
82	64.90	64.97	65.05	65.12	65.20	65.27	65.35	65.42	65.50	65.57
83	65.65	65.73	65.80	65.88	65.96	66.03	66.11	66.19	66.27	66.34
84	66.42	66.50	66.58	66.66	66.74	66.81	66.89	66.97	67.05	67.13
85	67.21	67.29	67.37	67.45	67.54	67.62	67.70	67.78	67.86	67.94
86	68.03	68.11	68.19	68.28	68.36	68.44	68.53	68.61	68.70	68.78
87	68.87	68.95	69.04	69.12	69.21	69.30	69.38	69.47	69.56	69.64
88	69.73	69.82	69.91	70.00	70.09	70.18	70.27	70.36	70.45	70.54
89	70.63	70.72	70.81	70.91	71.00	71.09	71.19	71.28	71.37	71.47
90	71.56	71.66	71.76	71.85	71.95	72.05	72.15	72.24	72.34	72.44
91	72.54	72.64	72.74	72.84	72.95	73.05	73.15	73.26	73.36	73.46
92	73.57	73.68	73.78	73.89	74.00	74.11	74.21	74.32	74.44	74.55
93	74.66	74.77	74.88	75.00	75.11	75.23	75.35	75.46	75.58	75.70
94	75.82	75.94	76.06	76.19	76.31	76.44	76.56	76.69	76.82	76.95
95	77.08	77.21	77.34	77.48	77.61	77.75	77.89	78.03	78.17	78.32
96	78.46	78.61	78.76	78.91	79.06	79.22	79.37	79.53	79.69	79.86
97	80.02	80.19	80.37	80.54	80.72	80.90	81.09	81.28	81.47	81.67
98	81.87	82.08	82.29	82.51	82.73	82.96	83.20	83.45	83.71	83.98
99.0	84.26	84.29	84.32	84.35	84.38	84.41	84.44	84.47	84.50	84.53
99.1	84.56	84.59	84.62	84.65	84.68	84.71	84.74	84.77	84.80	84.84
99.2	84.87	84.90	84.93	84.97	85.00	85.03	85.07	85.10	85.13	85.17
99.3	85.20	85.24	85.27	85.31	85.34	85.38	85.41	85.45	85.48	85.52
99.4	85.56	85.60	85.63	85.67	85.71	85.75	85.79	85.93	85.87	85.91
99.5	85.95	85.99	86.03	86.07	86.11	86.15	86.20	86.24	86.28	86.33
99.6	86.37	86.42	86.47	86.51	86.56	86.61	86.66	86.71	86.76	86.81
99.7	86.86	86.91	86.97	87.02	87.08	87.13	87.19	87.25	87.31	87.37
99.8	87.44	87.50	87.57	87.64	87.71	87.78	87.86	87.93	88.01	88.10
99.9	88.19	88.28	88.38	88.48	88.60	88.72	88.85	89.01	88.19	89.43
100.0	90.00									

TABLE M. RANKS CORRESPONDING TO *C*-SCALE VALUES FOR DIFFERENT NUMBERS OF THINGS RANKED

Number ranked	*C*-scale values								
	1	2	3	4	5	6	7	8	9
10	..	10	9	7–8	5–6	3–4	2	1	
11	..	11	9–10	8	5–7	4	2–3	1	
12	..	12	10–11	8–9	6–7	4–5	2–3	1	
13	13	.....	11–12	9–10	6–8	4–5	2–3	...	1
14	14	.....	12–13	9–11	7–8	4–6	2–3	...	1
15	15	14	13	10–12	7–9	4–6	3	2	1
16	16	15	13–14	11–12	7–10	5–6	3–4	2	1
17	17	16	14–15	11–13	8–10	5–7	3–4	2	1
18	18	17	15–16	12–14	8–11	5–7	3–4	2	1
19	19	18	16–17	12–15	9–11	5–8	3–4	2	1
20	20	19	16–18	13–15	9–12	6–8	3–5	2	1
21	21	20	17–19	14–16	9–13	6–8	3–5	2	1
22	22	21	18–20	14–17	10–13	6–9	3–5	2	1
23	23	22	19–21	15–18	10–14	6–9	3–5	2	1
24	24	22–23	20–21	15–19	11–14	6–10	4–5	2–3	1
25	25	23–24	20–22	16–19	11–15	7–10	4–6	2–3	1
26	26	24–25	21–23	17–20	11–16	7–10	4–6	2–3	1
27	27	25–26	22–24	17–21	12–16	7–11	4–6	2–3	1
28	28	26–27	23–25	18–22	12–17	7–11	4–6	2–3	1
29	29	27–28	23–26	18–22	13–17	8–12	4–7	2–3	1
30	30	28–29	24–27	19–23	13–18	8–12	4–7	2–3	1

INDEX

Page numbers in **boldface** type indicate bibliographical references